125 NATURE HOT SPOTS IN BRITISH COLUMBIA

The Best Parks, Conservation Areas and Wild Places

Lyndsay Fraser and Christina Smyth

FIREFLY BOOKS

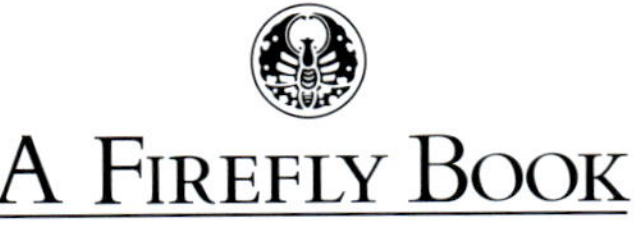

A Firefly Book

Published by Firefly Books Ltd. 2023
Copyright © 2023 Firefly Books Ltd.
Text copyright © 2018, 2023 Lyndsay Fraser and Christina Smyth
Photographs © as listed below and on page 272

First printing

Library of Congress Control Number: 2022946636

Library and Archives Canada Cataloguing in Publication
Title: 125 nature hot spots in British Columbia : the best parks,
   conservation areas and wild places / Lyndsay Fraser and Christina Smyth.
Other titles: 100 nature hot spots in British Columbia |
   One hundred twenty-five nature hot spots in British Columbia
Names: Fraser, Lyndsay, 1986- author. | Smyth, Christina, 1989- author.
Description: Includes index. | Previous edition published under title:
   100 nature hot spots in British Columbia.
Identifiers: Canadiana 2022043872 | ISBN 9780228104124 (softcover)
Subjects: LCSH: Natural areas—British Columbia—Guidebooks. |
   LCSH: Parks—British Columbia—Guidebooks. |
   LCSH: Protected areas—British Columbia—Guidebooks. |
   LCSH: Wilderness areas—British Columbia—Guidebooks. |
   LCSH: British Columbia—Description and travel. |
   LCSH: British Columbia—Guidebooks. | LCGFT: Guidebooks.
Classification: LCC FC3807 .F73 2023 | DDC 917.1104—dc23

Published in the United States by
Firefly Books (U.S.) Inc.
P.O. Box 1338, Ellicott Station
Buffalo, New York 14205

Published in Canada by
Firefly Books Ltd.
50 Staples Avenue, Unit 1
Richmond Hill, Ontario L4B 0A7

Cover design: Stacey Cho
Interior design: Kimberley Young and Stacey Cho
Maps: George Walker

Cover photo credits:
Front cover: Shutterstock/Tomas Nevesely
Back cover (top to bottom): Shutterstock/Tom Reichner;
   Shutterstock/Alf Damp; Doug Fraser

Printed in China

Canada 🍁 We acknowledge the financial support of the Government of Canada.

Dedication

To Dina, whose kindness and compassion make the world a brighter place.
   —C.S.

To my incredible and beloved Grannie, whose adventurous, playful and generous spirit will continue to inspire me for the rest of my life.
   —L.F.

Acknowledgements

We would like to acknowledge the First Nations who have lived on and cared for this land for thousands of years. It is through their sustainable practices, now combined with the efforts of the parks and other conservation and protection agencies, that these beautiful spaces continue to thrive.

While writing *125 Nature Hot Spots in British Columbia* we worked with and were supported by a number of people. A big thank you to our team at Firefly: Julie Takasaki for her enthusiasm and collaborative editing; Kimberley Young for the initial design; Stacey Cho for this edition's design updates; George Walker for his maps; and Michael Worek and Lionel Koffler for their ongoing support. We would also like to thank *125 Nature Hot Spots in Ontario* author Chris Earley for putting us in touch with our dedicated team at Firefly.

We reached out to a number of photographers and would like to thank all those credited on page 272 for sharing their talents. A special thank you goes out to Doug Fraser, who contributed numerous photographs and enthusiastically joined in on many adventures to explore new hot spots.

For their input and expertise during the writing process we would like to thank the following organizations: Parks Canada; BC Parks; Recreation Sites and Trails BC; the Burgess Shale Geoscience Foundation; Gwaii Haanas National Park Reserve, National Marine Conservation Area Reserve and Haida Heritage Site; Creston Wildlife Management Area; Dan Strickland; UBC Okanagan; the Cumberland Community Forest Society; the Ktunaxa Nation Council; and the Bulkley Valley Museum.

And, finally, to the friends and family who supported us during our writing: Bryan Sexauer; Annalyn MacWhirter; Marlyn, Lew and Tom Smyth; Chris Earley; Doug, Susan and Kevin Fraser; Lyndsay's lifelong besties — Erin Beaupre, Missy Loach and Kara Huard; and her "farm fam" — Michael-Anthony, Michelle Fillion, Corey Sheiding and Carolyn Mark; our dogs, Myra and Jade, for getting us out on even the rainy days; our cats, Flicker and Phoebe, for lap-warming duties during long days at the computer; and so many more. Thank you all for your support!

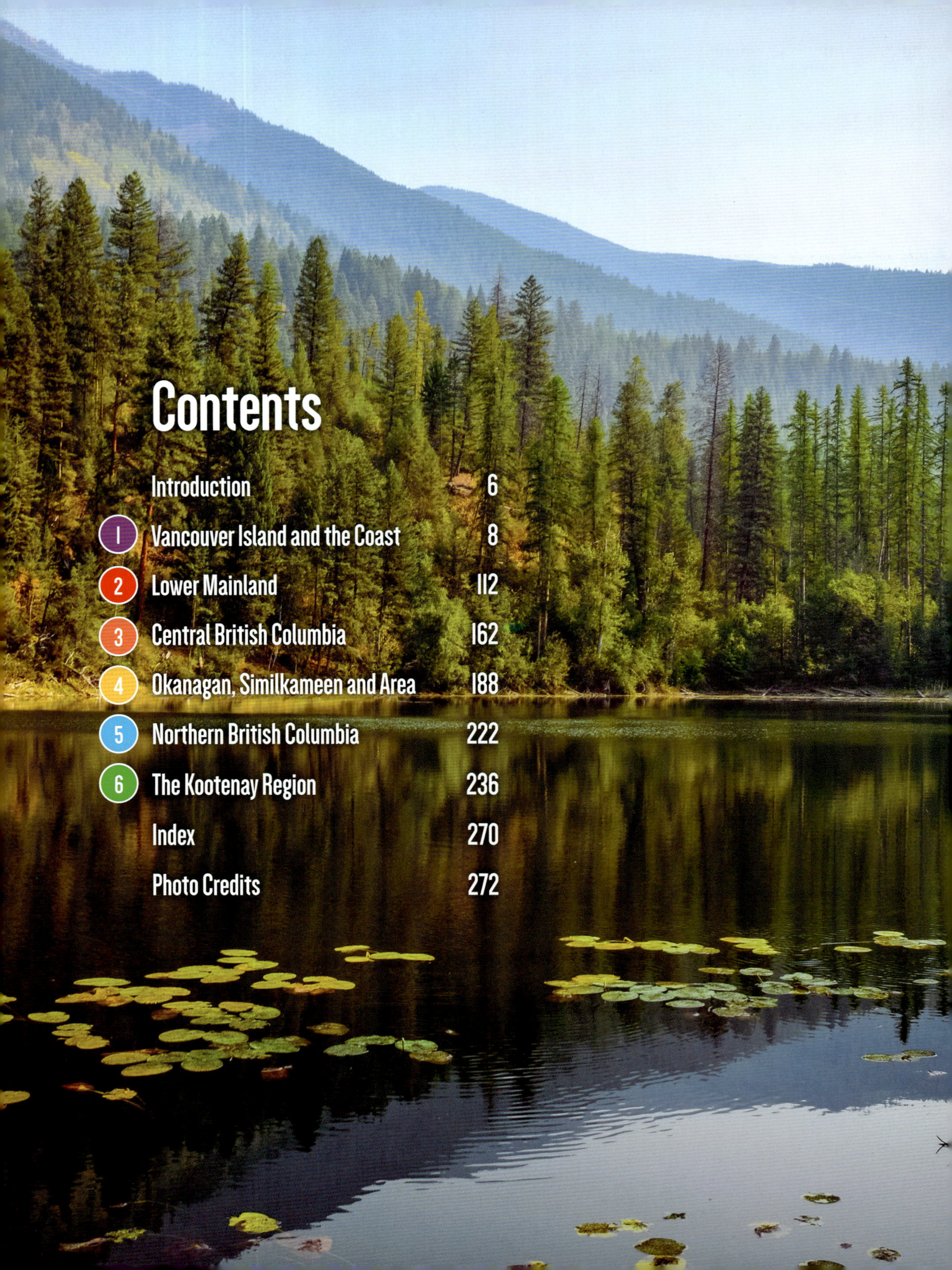

Contents

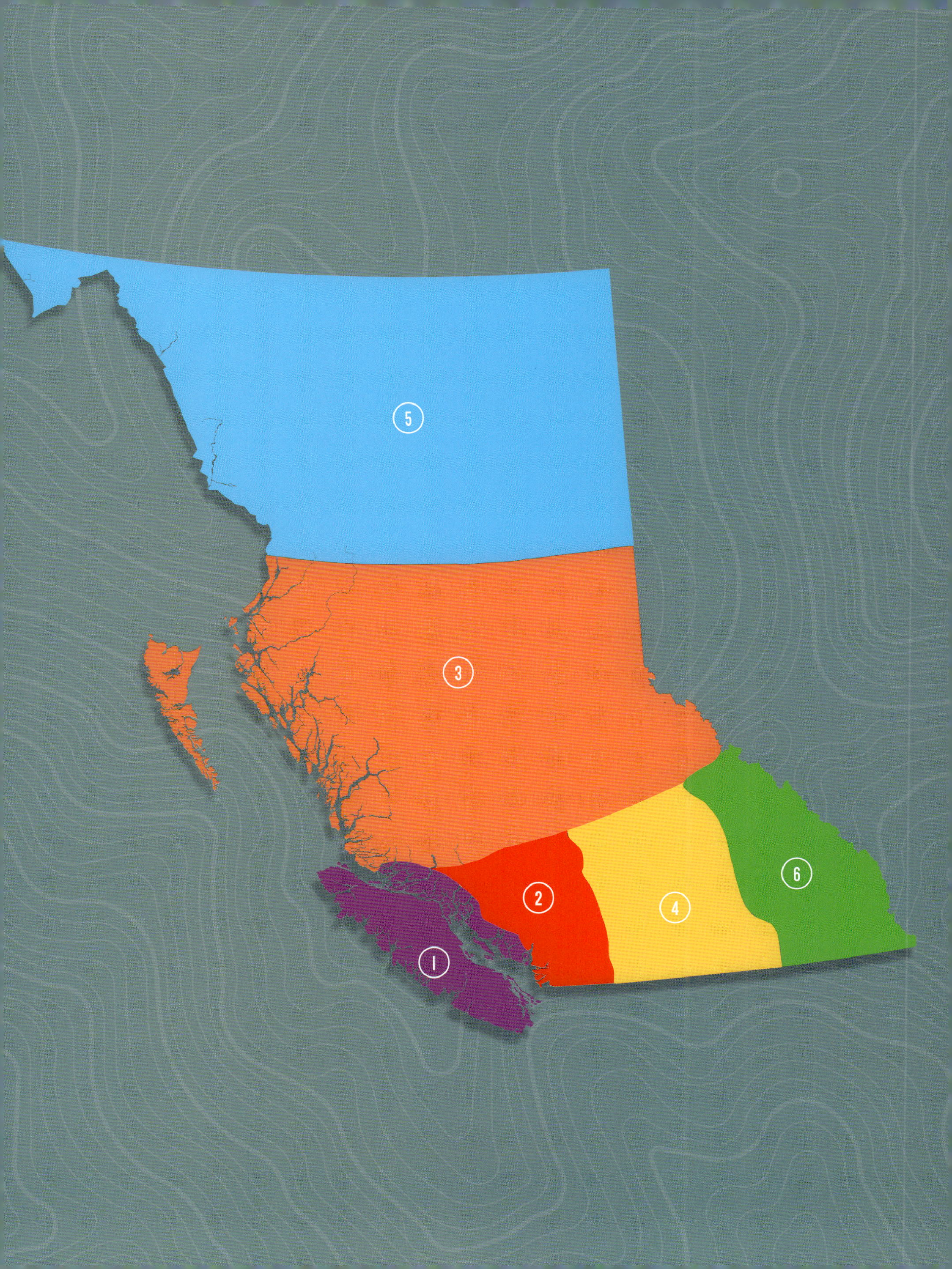

1
2
3
4
5
6

Introduction

Dominated by towering mountains and craggy coastlines, Canada's westernmost province is so geologically diverse that the nature hot spots found here are nothing less than abundant and varied. As such it brings us great pleasure to share 25 new, and many updated, nature hot spots since *100 Nature Hot Spots in British Columbia* was published in 2018.

British Columbia is one of the best places in the world for viewing large mammals — massive grizzly bears gathering at rivers and streams for salmon feasts, humpback whales clownishly leaping and breaching in deep waters along the coast and bighorn sheep clashing their horns together in a valiant battle for breeding rights on mountain sides. That said, there is much more to the rich natural history here than large mammals. Of the country's 15,000 species of fungi, 10,000 are in BC. Over 500 species of birds have been recorded in the province, and nearly half of the country's reptilian and amphibian species can be found here as well. Many species of plants and animals, such as the Vancouver Island marmot and the hotwater physa, are endemic to BC, meaning they're found nowhere else in the world.

All of this translates to a province so naturally rich that there is something for everyone to enjoy, whether you're keen on wildflowers, lichens, mosses, fossils or other natural wonders. To protect it all, British Columbia has established the most extensive park system in the country, encompassing seven national parks, over 1,000 provincially protected spaces — which include parks, conservancies and ecological reserves — and countless regional parks and protected areas managed by local conservancies, land trusts, landowners and volunteer organizations. This stunning province also covers the traditional territories of over 200 diverse First Nations each carrying different ecological knowledge and cultural traditions. Throughout the province, visitors may encounter over 30 languages and tour many important historical sites, some of which date back over 10,000 years. Wherever possible we have shared First Nations' territory information and history as well as the original names for the places. First Nations languages are traditionally oral, so names have been written and recorded in collaboration with speakers of the language. Some symbols may look unfamiliar as the languages differ phonetically from English, but there are many resources, such as firstvoices.com, where you can learn greetings and how to pronounce the names of places and Nations across British Columbia.

We've organized this book by region to give you snapshots of some exceptional places to explore in different corners of the province. Some hot spots are a quick turn off a main road, while others are a little more challenging to reach. Whether it's a long drive down a logging road or a nautical journey on a ferry, we assure you all are worth the effort to get there! A number of hot spots are easily accessible to nature lovers of any ability, but some may require greater physical prowess and more extensive trip planning. Be aware of your own abilities and limitations and plan accordingly. We hope this book provides inspiration and insight as you design your own adventures, but we highly recommend you check park websites, weather forecasts, trail conditions and tide times ahead of your trip, and take other relevant precautions for the site you're visiting. There are many fantastic websites and guidebooks with detailed descriptions of what to expect on hikes of all difficulty levels throughout BC. Note that many sites do not have Wi-Fi or cellular network service, so if you're using your phone it's important that you plan in advance and download maps and information.

Nature Hot Spots and Dogs

As dog lovers who take our own furry companions on many outdoor adventures, we strongly recommend that you leave your pets at home while exploring many of these destinations, given their delicate nature. Even the most well-behaved dogs are capable of disrupting a sensitive ecosystem, and their presence and excrement may attract dangerous wildlife or scare animals away, which could affect your wildlife-watching experience. If you wish to bring your dog, please contact the destination in advance to learn about limitations and any precautions you must take. Please obey all signs, dispose of your pet's excrement appropriately and take additional care when meeting other people and pets.

While we ourselves are passionate explorers of this beautiful province, and hope you are too, we are also well aware of the environmental risks that come with increased human traffic to these areas. Shrinking wild spaces, increased pollution, a changing climate, human-caused forest fires and an ever-growing human population all play a part in impacting these sensitive ecosystems. We urge those who visit to be respectful of the amazing places we all have the privilege of exploring. In addition to getting out there and admiring these natural wonders, please support the terrific conservation programs run by your regional, provincial and national parks, not-for-profit organizations and other protection agencies. Their tireless efforts help ensure there are nature hot spots to cherish for generations to come.

Along with keeping these spaces safe from human impact, we want readers to stay safe themselves. Weather in the mountains can change quickly, tides can rise suddenly and trails may not always be obvious. Be sure to carry these 10 essentials whenever you are hiking: water, food, extra clothing, fire-starting materials, a light source, first-aid supplies, a communication device, a map of the area, sun protection and an emergency shelter, such as a tarp. Always carry bear spray in bear country, and learn how to stay safe during wildlife encounters with Wild Safe BC (wildsafebc.com).

Happy exploring!

These icons appear throughout to give you an idea of the available activities and features at each hot spot:

- Hiking
- Wildlife viewing
- Cycling
- Kayaking, canoeing or rafting
- Swimming
- Scuba diving or snorkelling
- Surfing
- Skiing
- Snowshoeing
- Rock climbing
- Camping
- Caving
- Accessible

Information regarding universal access has been taken from available data provided by each location. Please note that this data may refer to specific trails, parking or toilets at the hot spot, and visitors with accessibility needs may be unable to experience fully the highlights we profile. Please confirm the availability of accessible facilities and trails prior to departure.

To find specific accessibility information for many BC Parks, including photographs and detailed descriptions of the facilities available, visit bcparks.ca/accessibility. Spinal Cord Injury BC (accessiblebc.ca) also provides detailed information on a wide range of outdoor spaces, from municipal, provincial and federal parks to recreation sites and visitors' centres.

QR Codes

This edition introduces QR codes in place of URLs for the website listed for each hot spot. To scan a QR code, open the camera app on your phone or a QR code reader, focus the camera on the QR code and when a link appears, tap on the link.

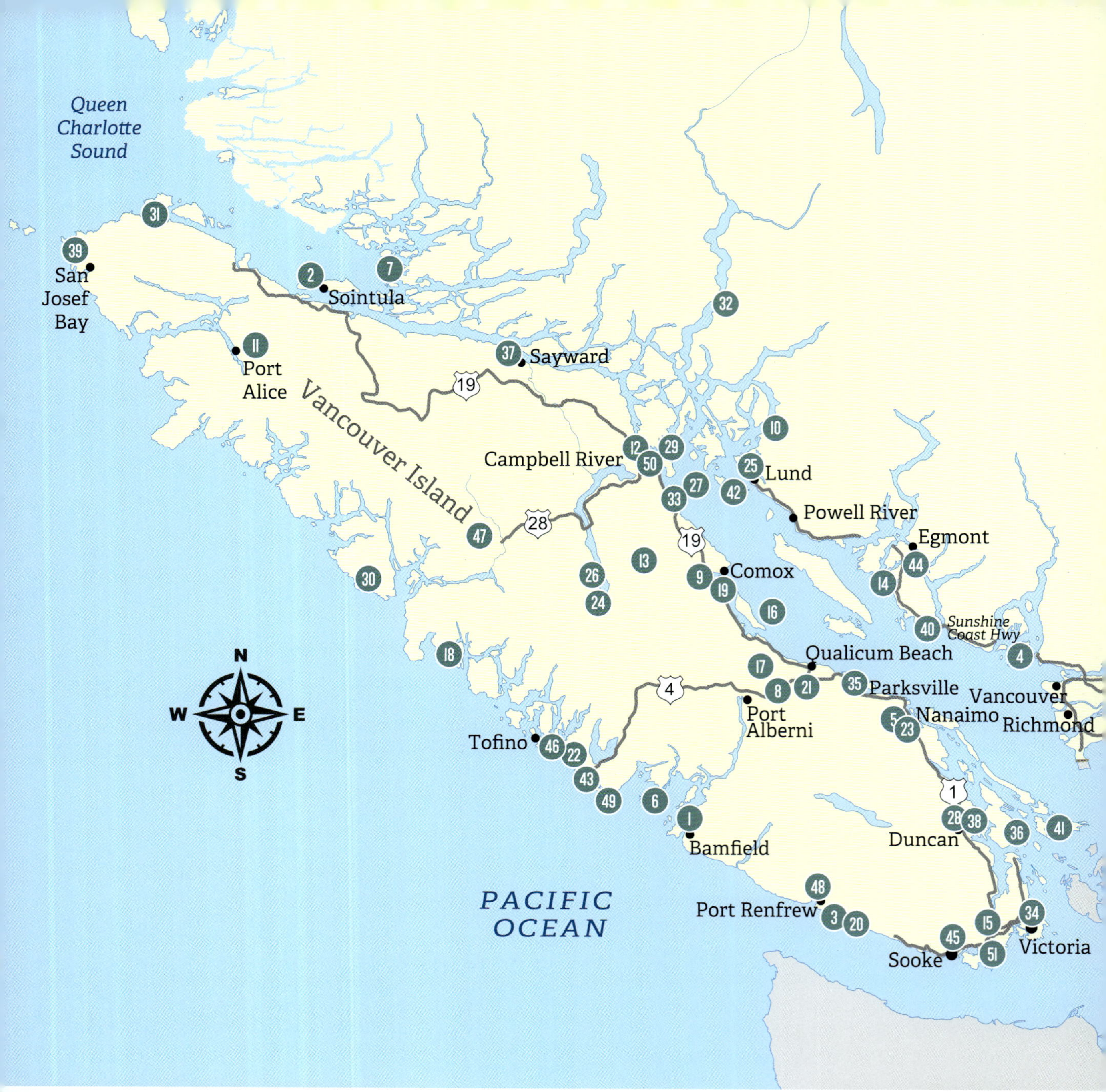

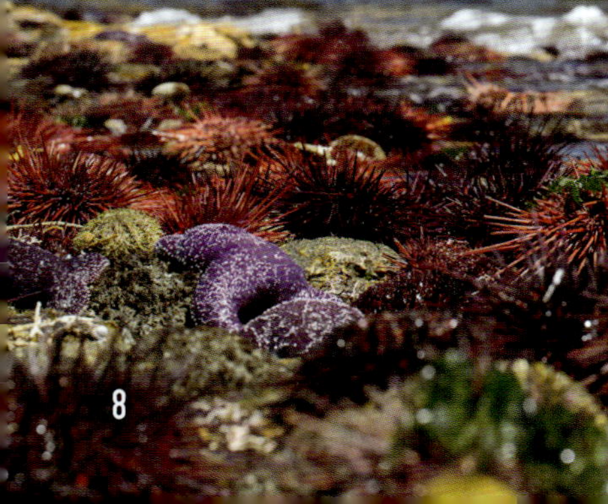

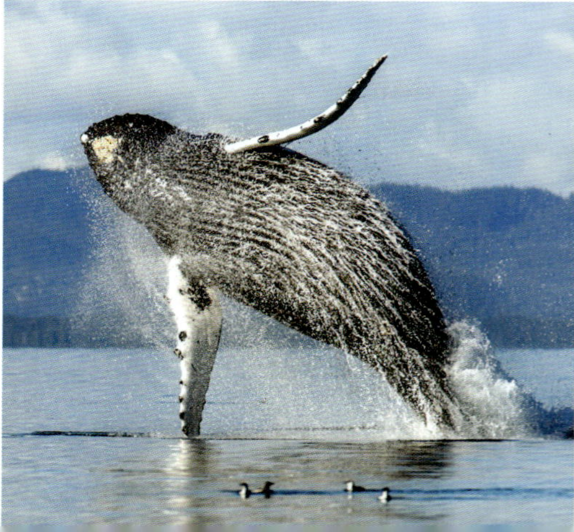

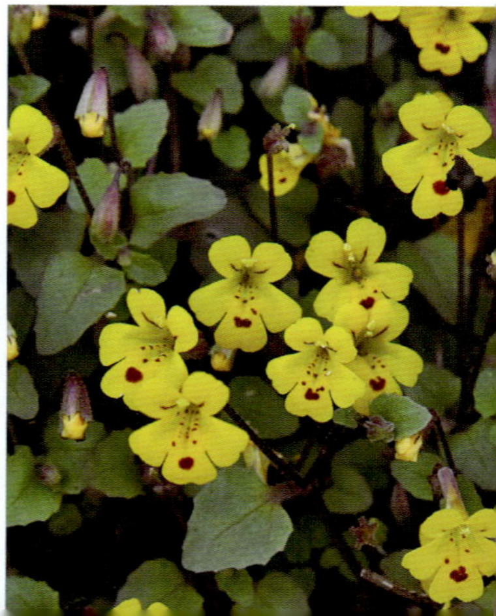

Queen
Charlotte
Sound
San
Josef
Bay
Sointula
Port
Alice
Vancouver Island
Sayward
19
Campbell River
28
Lund
Powell River
Egmont
Comox
19
Sunshine
Coast Hwy
Qualicum Beach
Parksville
Vancouver
Port
Alberni
Nanaimo
Richmond
4
Tofino
1
Duncan
Bamfield
PACIFIC
OCEAN
Port Renfrew
Victoria
Sooke
N
W E
S

Vancouver Island and the Coast

Bamfield

A sanctuary for marine life on the west coast of Vancouver Island

What Makes This Hot Spot Hot?

- Visitors can explore one of the most biodiverse marine habitats in Canada.
- Short hikes lead to views of migratory paths for thousands of whales.
- A world-renowned marine research station provides more information on the natural history of the area.

Address: Bamfield, BC
Tel.: N/A
Website:

Bamfield Marine
Sciences Centre

GPS Coordinates
Latitude: 48.82788
Longitude: −125.13427

Open year-round

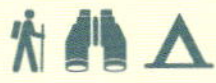

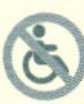

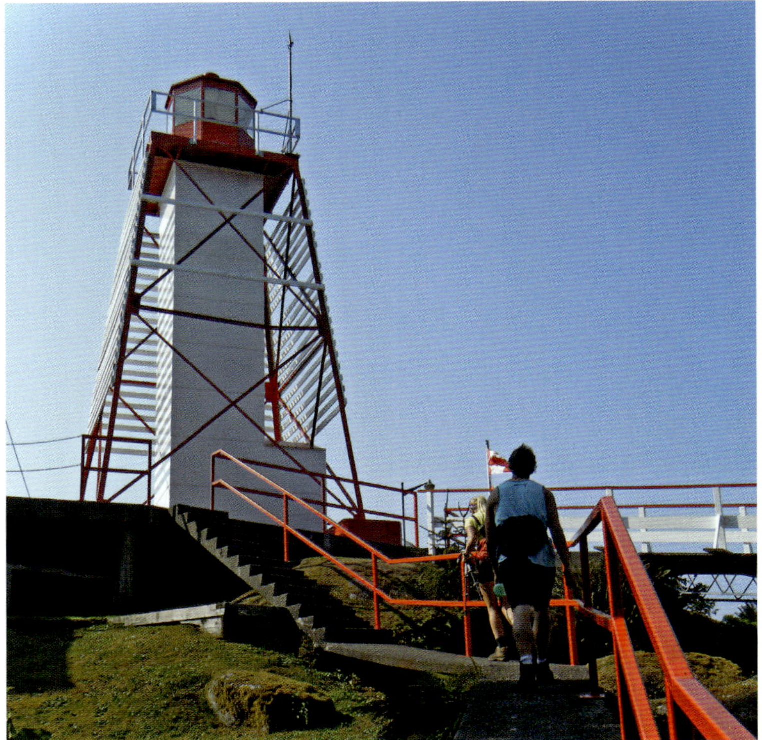

↗ **The Cape Beale Lighthouse is the first lighthouse on Vancouver Island.**

Visit nearby tidepools one day then camp on a remote sandy beach and visit a historic lighthouse the next, all while soaking in the beauty of a small ocean town. The most accessible beaches are a short boat ride across the Bamfield Inlet. A walk along an easy trail will lead you to Brady's Beach and Eagle Bay, where the shoreline hosts towering sea stacks surrounded by sand and rocky beaches. Explore tidepools filled with a variety of sea stars, anemones and other marine invertebrates. Look carefully in these pools and you may see small, beautifully coloured sea slugs, such as opalescent nudibranchs, crawling upside-down on the water's surface.

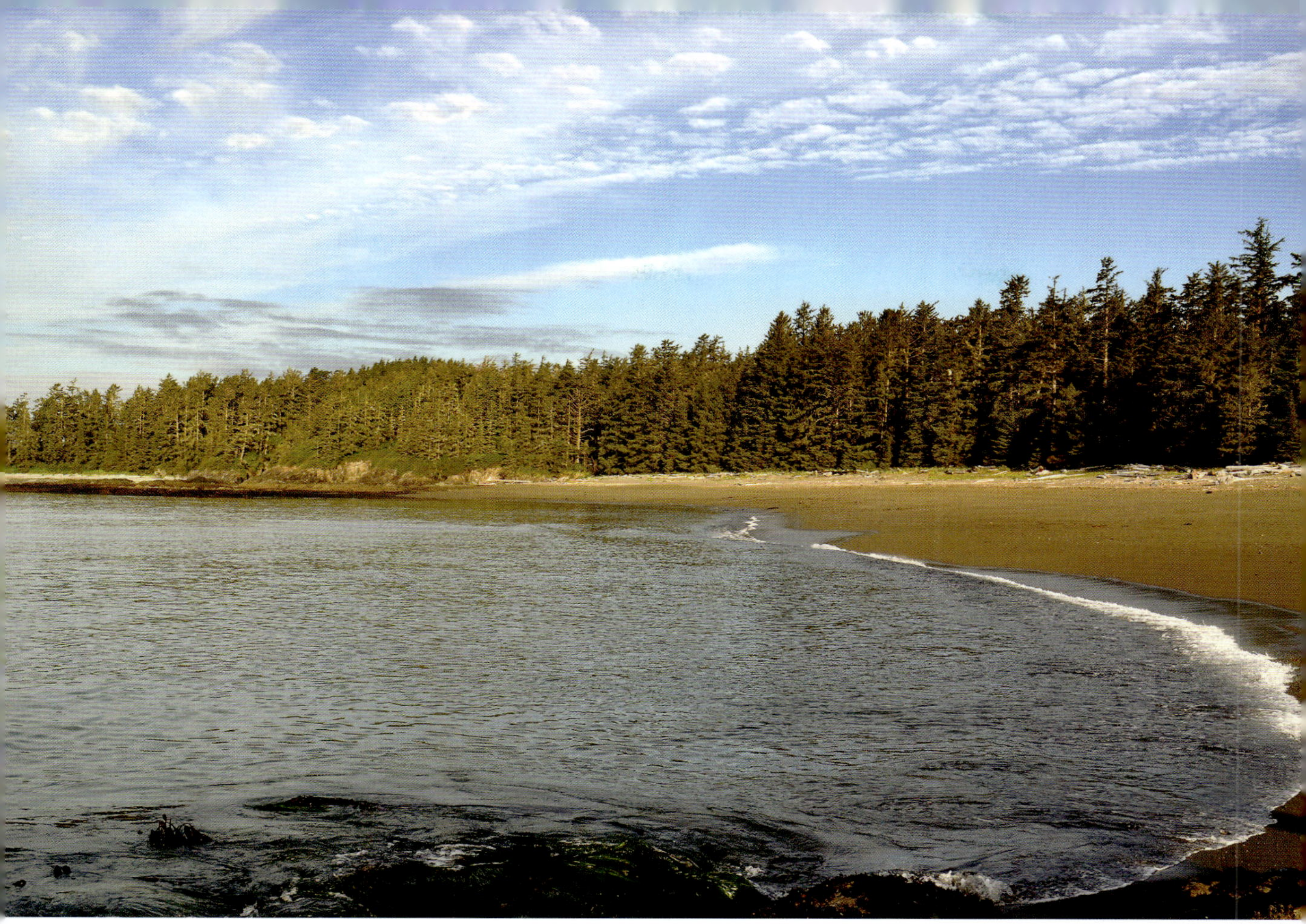

For the more ambitious hiker, a moderate trail leads through old-growth temperate rainforest to Cape Beale. After venturing through a forest of lush ferns, mosses and towering cedars, make your way to Tapaltos or Keeha Beach. These expansive sandy beaches feature an abundance of rocky tidepools, sea stacks and arching rock formations. Most people take day hikes to these beaches as the trek is approximately a 7-kilometre round trip. Others may choose to camp at Tapaltos then continue on to the Cape Beale Lighthouse, another 4.5 kilometres, the next day. Along this trail the forest slowly morphs into bogs, sandflats and windblown meadows with small, hardy trees. The rocky point upon which the historic Cape Beale Lighthouse is perched looks out onto the open ocean. Past the crashing waves grey whales are a frequent sight, particularly during the summer months.

Book a tour to visit the National Historic Site of Kiix̣in with a First Nation's guide. You will learn about huu-ay-aht history and visit the village of Kiix̣in, the only complete traditional First Nations village currently known of on BC's southern coast.

Keeha Beach makes a beautiful campsite, with rocky tidepools along a sandy beach.

Tidepools are home to a wide variety of sea life, including the giant green anemone.

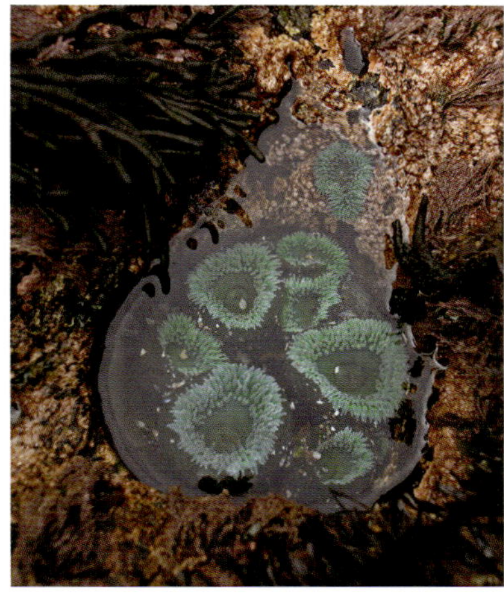

Bere Point Regional Park

Old-growth Sitkas, cedars dripping with lichens and a smooth pebble beach that just might provide a chance to witness a unique orca behaviour

What Makes This Hot Spot Hot?

- Northern resident orcas are the only BC orcas to display beach-rubbing behaviour.
- Giant old-growth Sitka spruce can be viewed along a beautiful trail.
- Once your hike is finished, the nearby community of Sointula has much to explore and a rich history to share.

Address: Sointula, Malcolm Island, BC
Tel.: (250) 973-2001
Website:

Regional District of Mount Waddington

GPS Coordinates
Latitude: 50.66618
Longitude: –127.05373

Open year-round

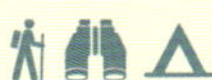

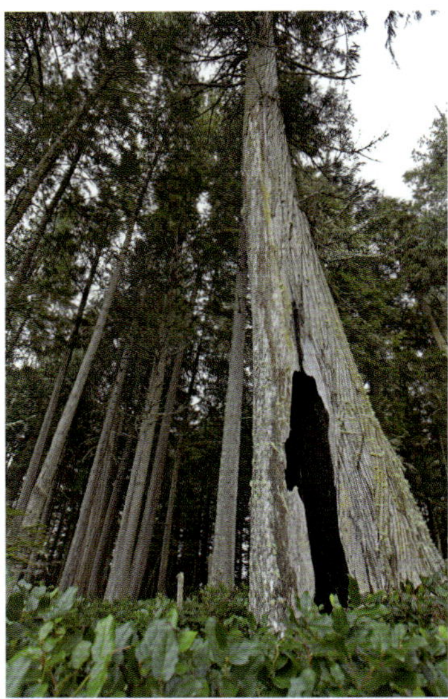

↗ **Skirted by dense salal, a redcedar nearly completely hollow from fire damage lives on.**

The aptly named Beautiful Bay Trail on Malcolm Island, just a short ferry ride from Port McNeill, offers stunning views of the Queen Charlotte Strait and ample opportunities for a nature adventure. The 5-kilometre trail first meanders through dense salal undergrowth so tall it gives the impression of a hedge lining the path. Beautiful sun- and wind-weathered Western hemlock and redcedars loom large, their trunks and branches dusted and dripping with various lichens. Farther down the trail the forest canopy thickens and the undergrowth opens up, as light reaching the forest floor becomes scarce. The path winds through a spectacular forest, offering glimpses of the sparkling bay. This pristine environment is home to a number of ancient Sitka spruce, which tower over their neighbours, the largest reaching heights of more than 60 metres.

Although a rare sight for the occasional visitor, one population of orca whales, the Northeast Pacific northern resident orca, is known to display a distinctive behaviour along this park's pebbly beach that is not performed by any other orca populations sharing BC coastal waters. Swimming right up to the shallow waters of the beach, these whales roll and writhe as they rub their bodies across the smooth stones.

The puzzling habit appears to offer no biological advantage; otherwise other local orca populations would be expected to share this trait. It is therefore believed to be

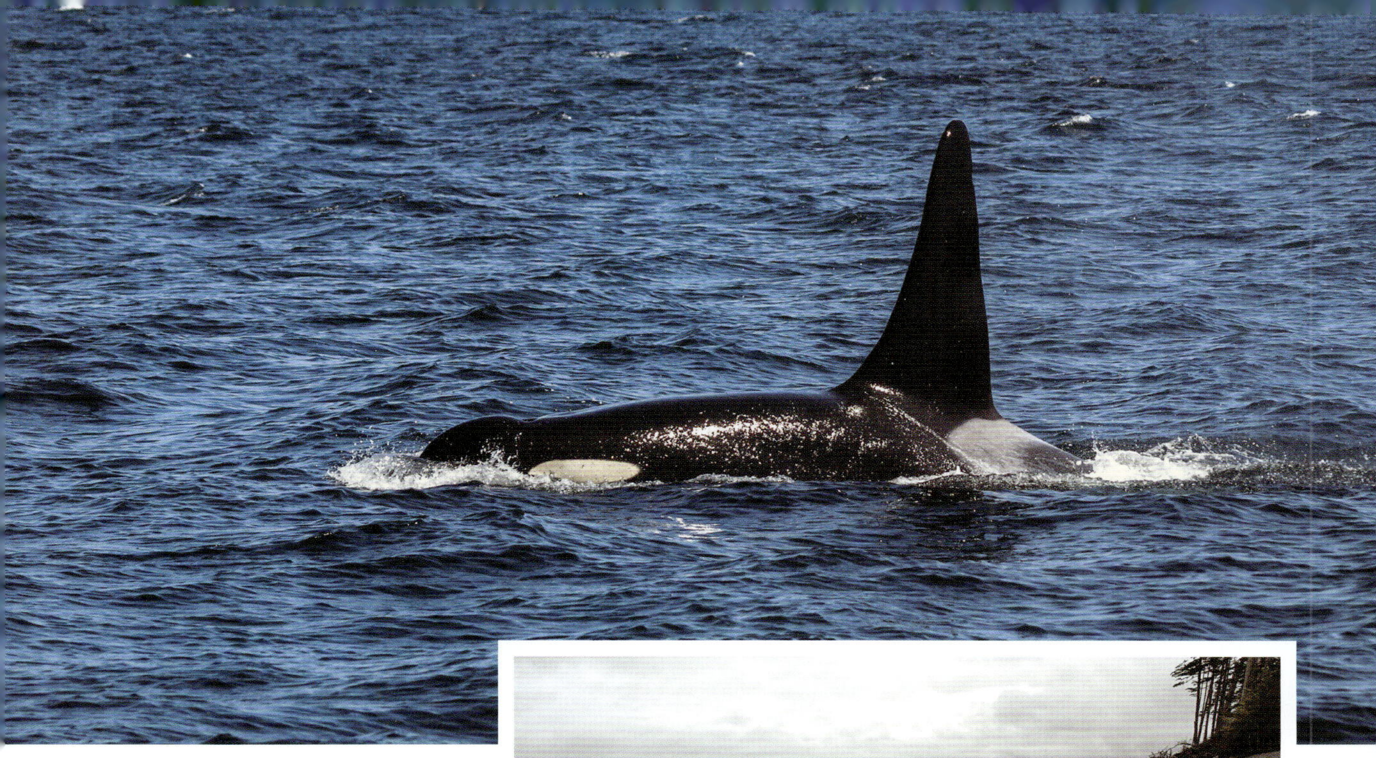

a cultural custom, unique to these whales. From the looks of it, it probably feels pretty good too. Although rare to see, you may choose to linger within view of the beach for some time just in case. To avoid disturbing these magnificent animals during their curious display, be mindful to watch for whales from the whale-watching platform along the trail and not directly from the beach.

Although a day spent at Beautiful Bay is worth the trip alone, plan to explore the rest of the island as well — the entire 24-kilometre length of it. Malcolm Island is part of the unceded territories of the Kwakwakw'akw peoples, including the 'Naṃgis, Mamalilikala and Kwakuitl Nations, but it was once populated as a Finnish utopian socialist community. The island's co-op store is still used, over 100 years since it first opened, and be sure you pop into the resource centre when you first arrive for advice on how to make the most of your visit to this wonderful community. Be careful, Malcolm Island's wilderness and its friendly human inhabitants may steal your heart, making it difficult to board the ferry and say farewell.

↑ **Round stones make for the perfect rubbing beach for the northern resident orcas.**

↖ **Orca whales frequent the waters around Bere Point.**

JUAN DE FUCA PROVINCIAL PARK

Botanical Beach

This shoreline's remarkably diverse intertidal life provides an opportunity to witness some of BC's most fascinating marine fauna first-hand

What Makes This Hot Spot Hot?

- Tidepools are home to extremely diverse varieties of species.
- To reach the beaches visitors can walk a beautiful temperate rainforest trail loop, which also connects to the Juan de Fuca Trail.
- There are opportunities to see marine mammals, such as orcas, grey whales, seals, sea lions and otters.

Address: Juan de Fuca Provincial Park, off West Coast Road (Hwy 14) near Port Renfrew, BC
Tel.: (250) 474-1336
Website:

BC Parks

GPS Coordinates
Latitude: 48.53407
Longitude: −124.44342

Open year-round

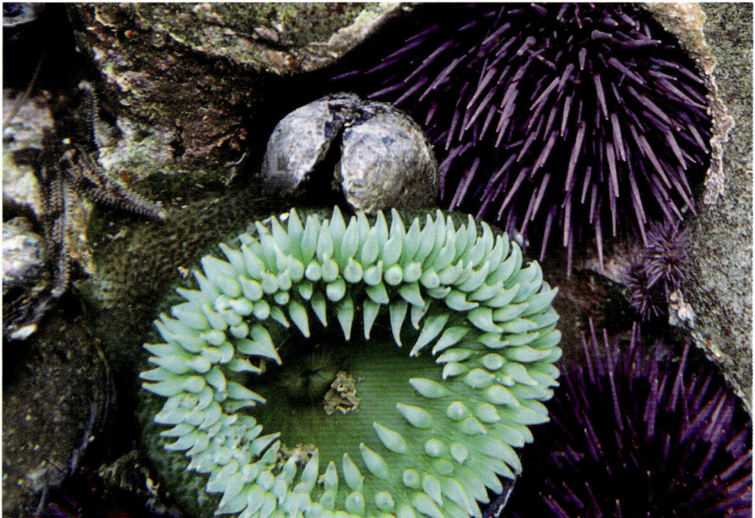

A short walk through coastal temperate rainforest, a beautiful experience in itself, will bring you to the perfect spot to experience the diverse marine life of the Pacific Northwest. Protected within the boundaries of Juan de Fuca Provincial Park, Botanical Beach is the ideal spot for exploring the rich intertidal zone, the area that lies between the highest and lowest tides.

Botanical Beach is home to an abundance of life, so expect to see multiple species of crabs, snails, sea anemones, limpets, barnacles, sea urchins, mussels, chitons, sea stars and brittle stars, as well as the occasional nudibranch or sea cucumber. The crystal-clear tidepools allow for perfect viewing, but take the time to carefully examine each one — you will be surprised at what comes to life. An unassuming snail shell may be home to one of several species of hermit crab, and giant green anemones may be seen using their stinging tentacles to catch a meal.

The marine life is fragile and the rocks can be very slippery,

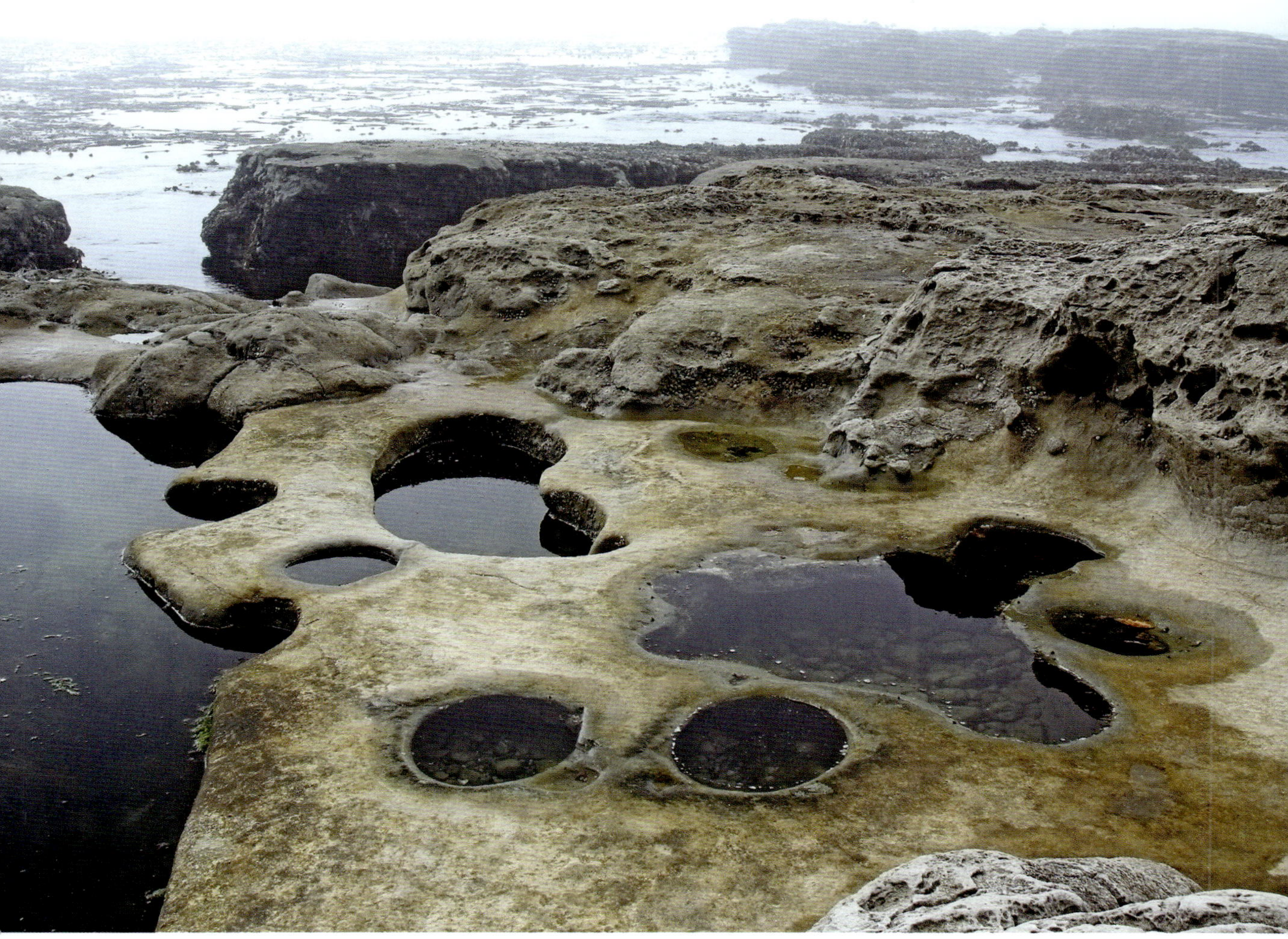

so step thoughtfully — delicate snails, limpets, barnacles and other amazing creatures inhabit most surfaces, carefully enclosed in their shells to avoid desiccating while waiting for the tide to return. Plan your trip with the tides in mind, arriving at least an hour before low tide for time to explore the entire stretch of this family-friendly shoreline. The parking lot of this popular spot fills up quickly, so arriving early in the morning is best.

Botany Bay, an adjacent beach accessible from the same trail loop, is also worth a visit for beautiful views of rugged cliffs and the black basalt shoreline. While the intertidal life is well worth the trip on all but the coldest days of the year, the area also offers opportunities for large marine mammal sightings — California and northern sea lions can be seen during the summer months, and harbour seals and river otters are also frequently spotted in the area. It is not uncommon for these shores to be visited by orcas or even grey whales as they migrate north up the coast between March and April.

↑ The fascinating geology of this park has created unique viewing opportunities, as the sandstone has been carved away by wave-tossed rocks and boulders that have ground uniquely smooth and deep pools into the shoreline.

↖ Purple sea urchins use their sharp spines to grind out shallow cavities into the sandstone for a place to reside at low tide.

Bowen Island

Life thrives in and around this small island community

What Makes This Hot Spot Hot?

- Visitors can get from seaside to lakeshore with a quick walk through the forest.
- The waters of Howe Sound are perfect to kayak or canoe around the island.
- A hike to a high point offers views of Vancouver and Howe Sound from a new perspective.

Address: Bowen Island, BC
Tel.: (604) 224-5739
Website:

Tourism Bowen Island

GPS Coordinates
Latitude: 49.37676
Longitude: –123.37015

Open year-round

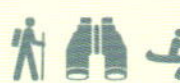

↗ **Pileated woodpeckers can be spotted around the trails near Killarney Lake.**

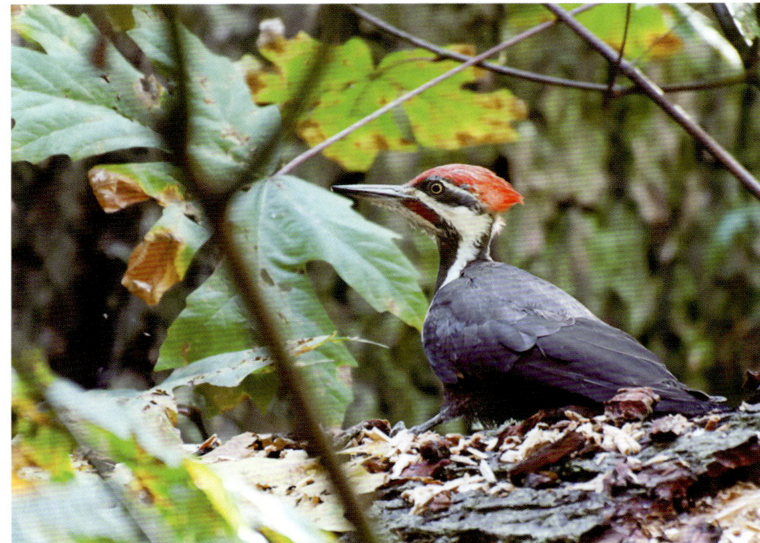

A short ferry ride from Horseshoe Bay or a water taxi from downtown Vancouver will take you to this beautiful island situated at the mouth of Howe Sound. At just over 52 square kilometres, Bowen Island has both inland and ocean hot spots to tour. Steep shores make kayaking a good alternative for the ocean explorer, and kayak tours and rentals are available on the island. From the water you can view picturesque rocky shores and watch for the marine mammals that frequent these waters, from orcas and porpoises to sea lions and otters. (Of course, remember to keep a safe distance from these creatures.) Great blue herons and bald eagles are a common sight from land and water on Snug Cove and Deep Bay, just to the north.

For an inland hiking adventure, travel along the main road and follow signs for Killarney Lake on the Crippen Regional Park trails. A hike over rolling hills through cedar and hemlock forests leads to Killarney Lake, and the trails around the lake offer boardwalks and scenic viewpoints. At the north end of the lake is a marshy area full of lily pads, algae and the stumps of old cedar trees. This environment is perfect for dragonflies and other insects, which attract insectivorous birds, making it an excellent area for birdwatchers. Pileated woodpeckers, red-breasted sapsuckers, pied-billed grebes and a host of other tree- and water-loving birds have been sighted in this area.

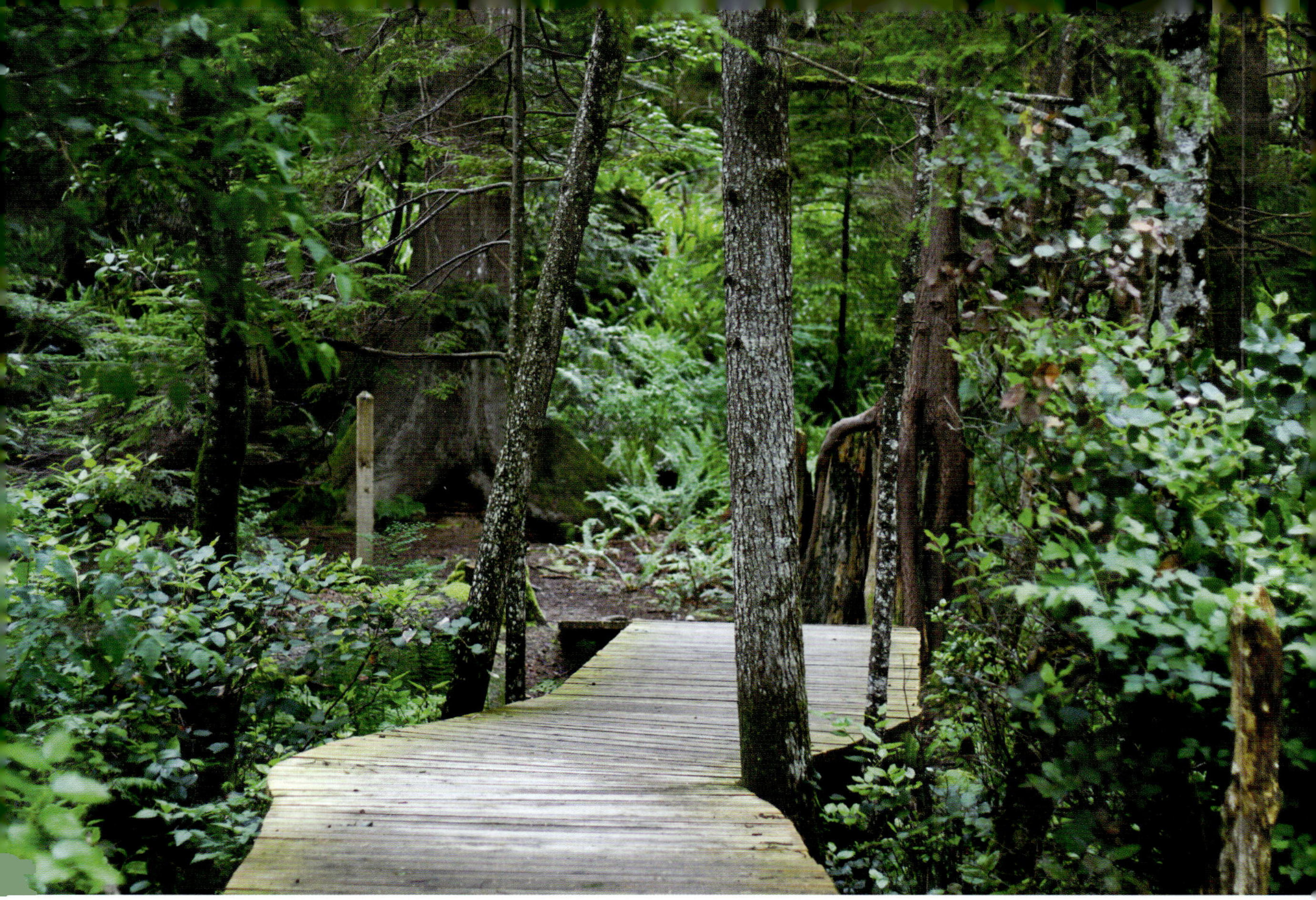

For a hike with a view head south after exiting the ferry and walk along the sandy beach of Snug Cove. A short but steep hike leads you through the forest to a lookout point. On a clear day you may see Howe Sound, Vancouver and the rocky shores of Bowen Island from a higher vantage point. No camping is permitted on this island, so be mindful of the ferry times, which change throughout the year.

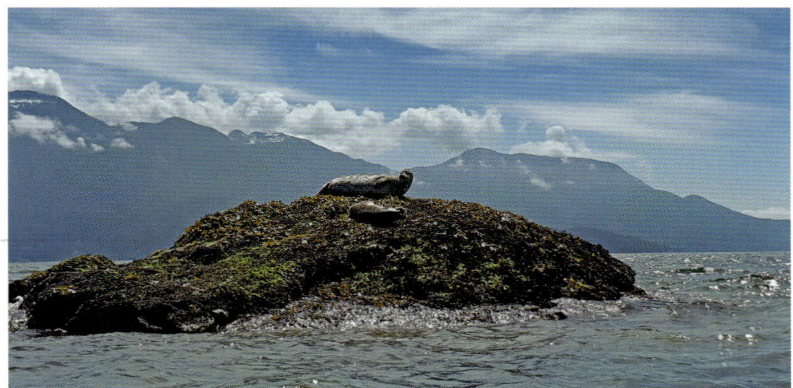

↑ Seals enjoy the sunshine on a nearby rock at low tide.

↖ A boardwalk leads hikers through enchanting forests.

Bowen Park

A nature escape that brings coho salmon to the heart of a city

What Makes This Hot Spot Hot?

- This site provides wildlife viewing opportunities in central Nanaimo.
- Coho salmon now spawn in the Millstone River thanks to a human-made side channel.
- Interpretive trails allow for birding opportunities year-round.

Address: 500 Bowen Road, Nanaimo, BC
Tel.: (250) 756-5200
Website:

City of Nanaimo

GPS Coordinates
Latitude: 49.173432
Longitude: −123.960510

Open year-round

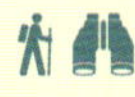

♿ **(Check ahead)**

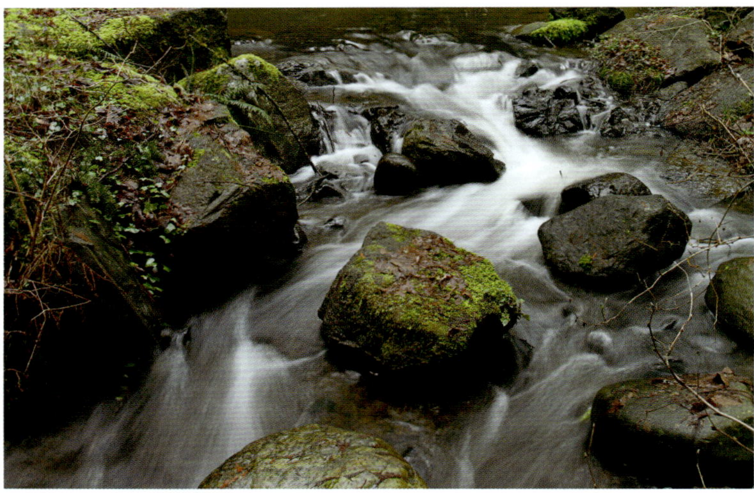

Even in the heart of a city natural treasures can be found, and a short walk into a forest can leave you shrouded in wilderness. The 36-hectare Bowen Park in the city of Nanaimo is home to beautiful waterfalls that become quite dramatic in late winter and early spring as the water levels rise. Watch for common mergansers diving into the rushing waters, and listen for the dramatic song of the Pacific wren — a tune so lengthy and complex, it is hard to believe it is coming from such a tiny, secretive bird, barely larger than a hummingbird.

Although the park is home to a playground, curling club, picnic area and recreation centre, do not let the bustling east end of this city park fool you, as there is lots of nature to be seen. For the best access to the trails and to avoid the busy facilities, use the park entrance off Wakesiah Avenue.

The interpretive trails of Bowen Park pass through the forest and trace the meandering Millstone River, where you can find a human-made side channel created to support the critically declining coho salmon, allowing them passage into the river. Stepping pools, fishways and an alternative path around Bowen Park's rushing falls allow the salmon to continue upstream to spawn. Although it was a significant undertaking in the park, the development of this channel paid off almost immediately — the very day water was released into the newly developed side channel in 2007, coho began to use it. Now hundreds of salmon use this route, and local students raise and release salmon fry into the channel each year. The channel was so well designed that within a few years it looked as though it was a natural stream that had always been a part of this ecosystem.

A family of barred owls has been nesting in the park for years, and if you are lucky, you might get a chance to watch young owls learning important skills from their parents. The owlets can sometimes be seen at the river's edge being taught how to hunt for crayfish in the shallow water. After the owl family has split at the end of the summer, young owls may still be found in the area, demonstrating what they have learned from their parents earlier in the season.

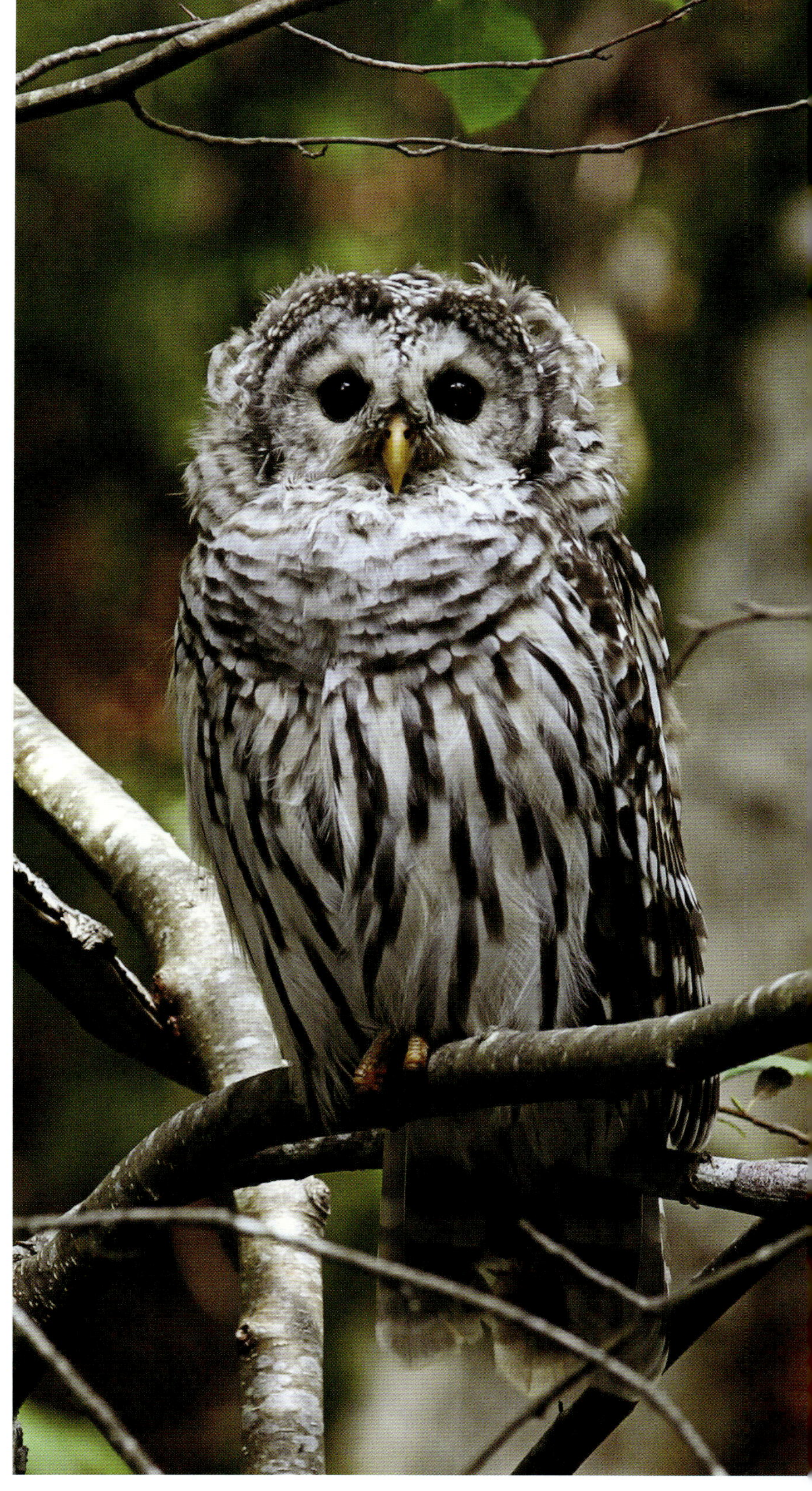

PACIFIC RIM NATIONAL PARK RESERVE

Broken Group Islands

An archipelago within a national park protects an ocean paradise

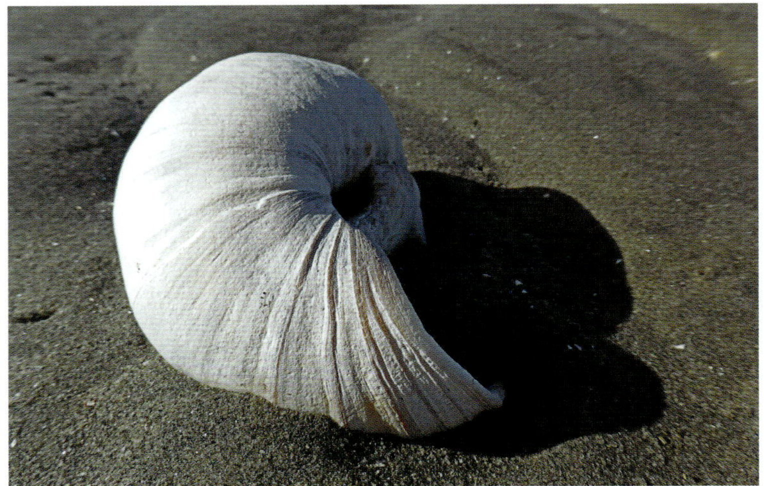

↗ **The shell of a moon snail.**

The Broken Group Islands are an archipelago of over 100 islands with white sand beaches, rocky shores, a rich Indigenous history and many opportunities for wildlife viewing. Visitors frequently spot seals, sea lions, grey whales and a variety of other ocean mammals. However, the biodiversity of these islands is most notably demonstrated in the intertidal zone, by the marine invertebrates that inhabit these waters.

On Wouwer Island you will find the Great Tide Pool, which is large enough to swim in and filled with many ocean animals, including sea cucumbers, sea stars and moon snails. Visit at low tide for the best opportunity to get up close and personal with these creatures. If you are feeling ambitious and wish to take a dip, bring a wetsuit and a snorkel as the water is cold year-round.

The summer months bring an abundance of bioluminescent micro-organisms called diatoms. When disturbed these diatoms emit a burst of blue-white light. After the sun sets, run your hand through the water and watch it glow behind you. If you are lucky you may see a school of fish creating a moving ball of light beneath the ocean surface.

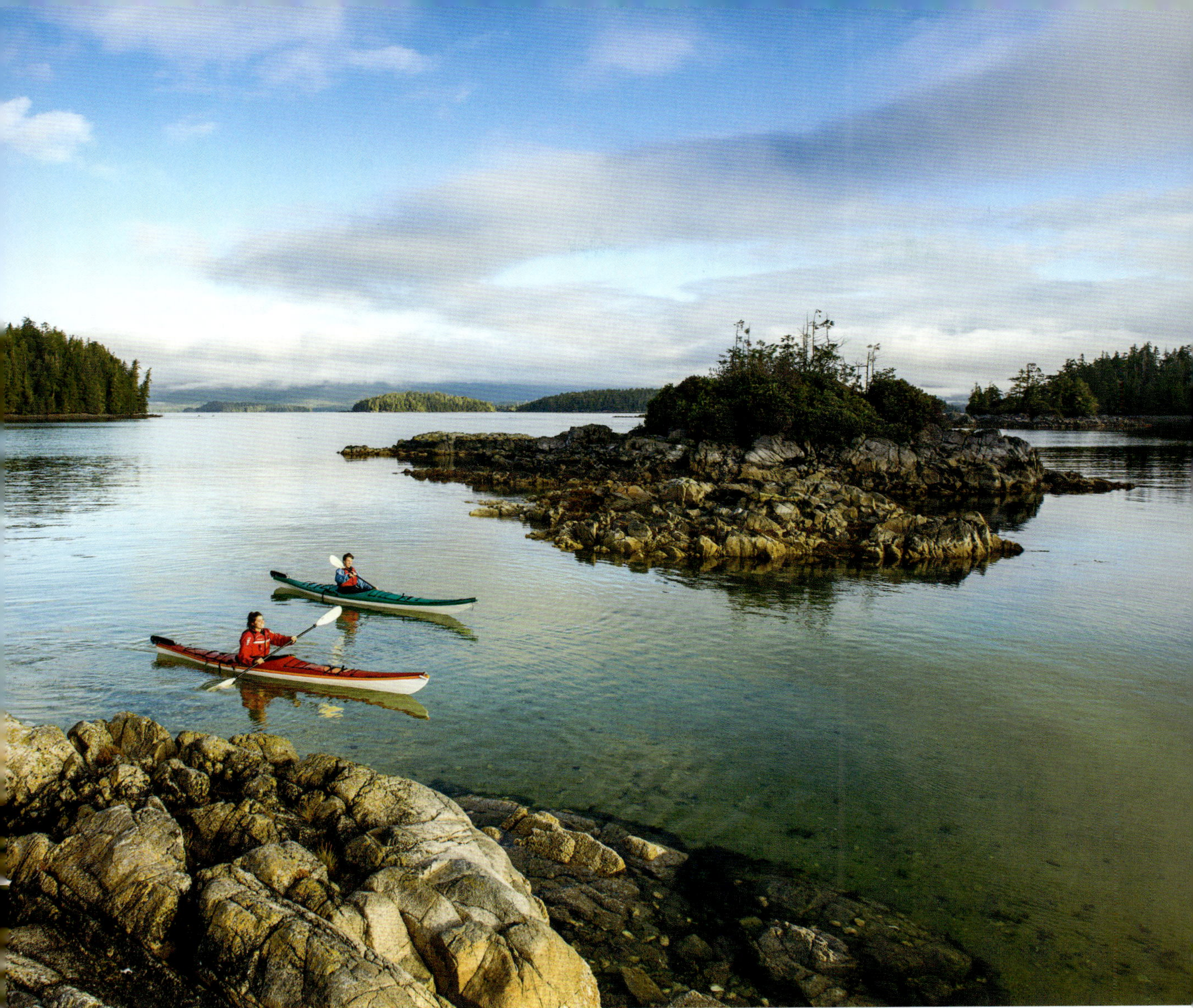

Plan your visit in mid-August for the best chance of experiencing this natural wonder.

The Broken Group Islands are situated within the Pacific Rim National Park Reserve. Beach keepers maintain the area and have a wealth of information to share with visitors. They may be able to point you towards culturally significant areas of the Tseshaht First Nation, to whom this archipelago is of great importance. Benson Island, the birthplace of the Tseshaht, has an interpretive display featuring a traditionally carved house post. A guided kayak tour from Ucluelet is the easiest way to access these islands. For experienced kayakers, another option is to rent a water taxi to carry kayaks to the islands and then explore the archipelago on your own.

Broughton Archipelago Marine Provincial Park

Explore BC's largest marine park for a chance to see whales and sea otters in the wild

What Makes This Hot Spot Hot?

- Dozens of undeveloped islands provide habitat for coastal wildlife.
- This is the largest marine park in British Columbia, best explored by boat or kayak.
- Orcas, humpbacks, minke whales and sea otters frequent these waters.

Address: 30 km east of Port McNeill, BC (accessible by boat only)
Tel.: (1-800) 689-9025
Website:

BC Parks

GPS Coordinates
Latitude: 50.68424
Longitude: −126.69372

Open year-round

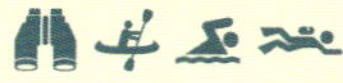

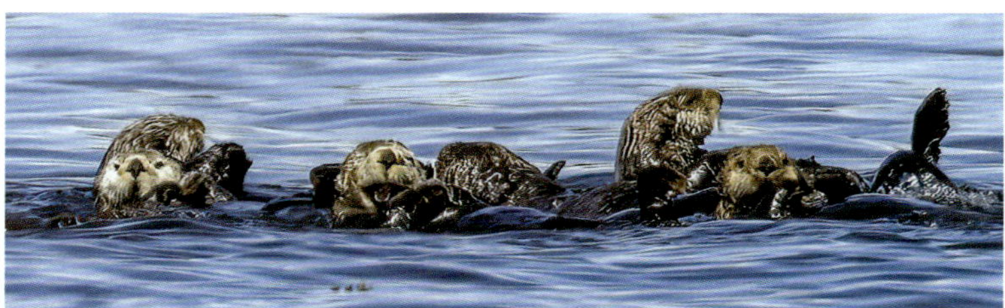

Located near the mouth of Knight Inlet off northern Vancouver Island, Broughton Archipelago Provincial Park is BC's largest marine park. The sheltered waters and dozens of undeveloped islands and islets protected within its boundary create the perfect setting for wildlife viewing by boat or kayak.

While there is reason to be enthusiastic about all creatures great and small, we often reserve a special level of excitement for seeing large mammals in the wild. Broughton Archipelago is one of the best places in all BC to observe some of the biggest animals that inhabit the waters and shorelines of our coasts, from black bears to sea lions to porpoises.

Though definitely not the largest, sea otters are arguably one of the cutest residents of the area. Once completely decimated from the coast of BC because of the fur trade, sea otter populations have been steadily climbing since their reintroduction to northwest Vancouver Island beginning in the late 1960s. With their return, kelp forests are also recovering, as otters feast on the sea urchins that can overwhelm this key ocean habitat.

Humpback whales have also made an incredible comeback after being nearly erased by whalers, and they are now a common but nonetheless momentous sighting. With their humped dorsal fin, these large baleen, or toothless, whales are hard to miss, especially if they're in the mood for showing off. Known as the "clowns of the sea," humpbacks can often be seen waving their flippers, slapping their tails and leaping nearly clear out of the water.

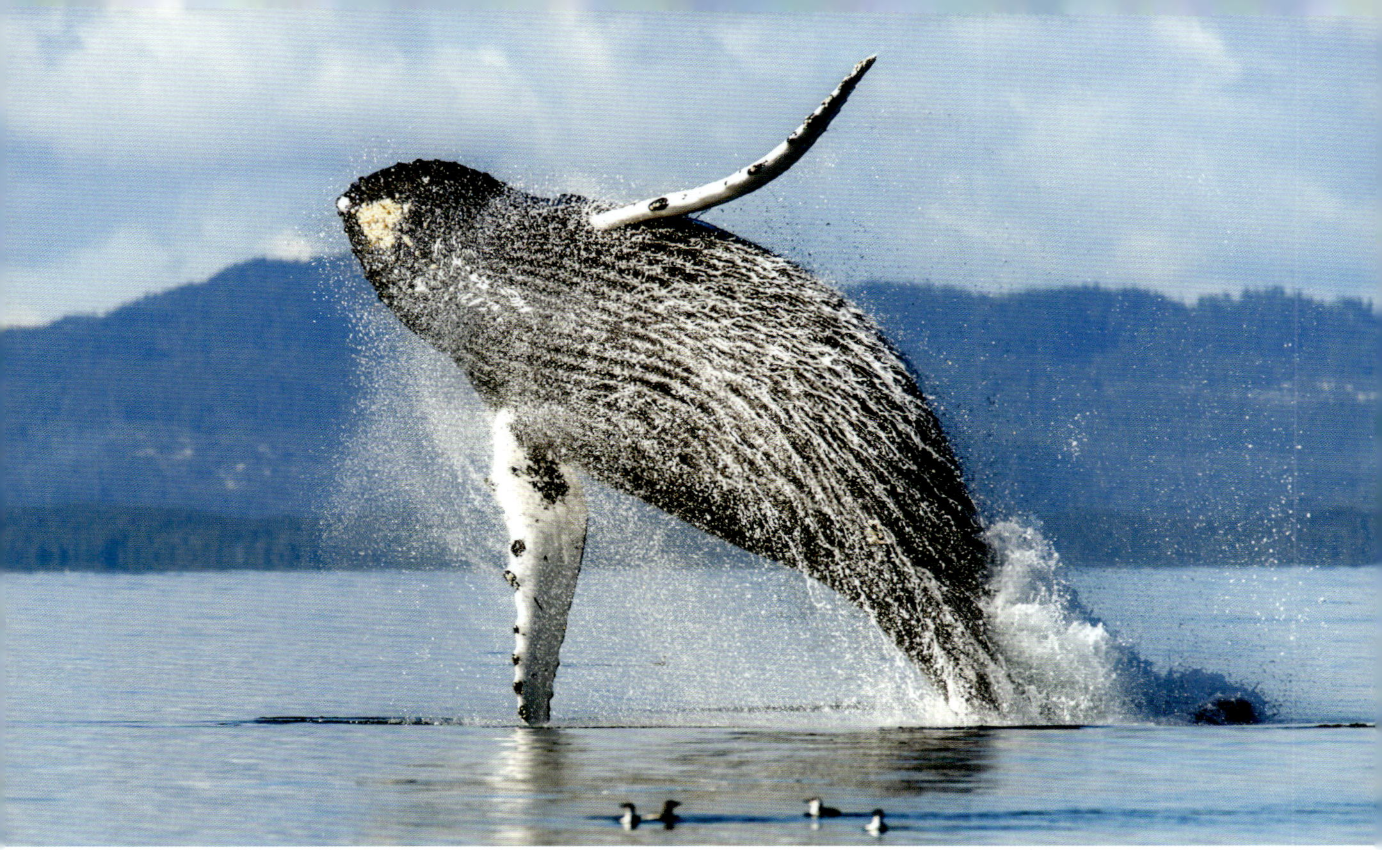

Minke whales are the smallest baleen whale off the BC coast and are built for speed. Their elusive behaviour and long dives make them tricky to spot, but you might catch a glimpse of one before it disappears from sight. For a chance to see pods of orcas, explore the western boundaries of the park in late summer and early fall.

The communities of Port McNeill and Telegraph Cove are popular jumping-off points for exploring this area — each with ample opportunities for guided boat tours or multiday kayaking expeditions. It's vital that you or any tour company hired adhere to the required minimal distances from marine animals to ensure their comfort and safety, as well as yours. For more information visit seeablowgoslow.org.

In Port McNeill, be sure to visit the Marine Education and Research Society office to learn about the important work this dedicated team of scientists is conducting in the area. If starting your adventure from Telegraph Cove, pop into the Whale Interpretive Centre to admire their amazing display of marine mammal skeletons.

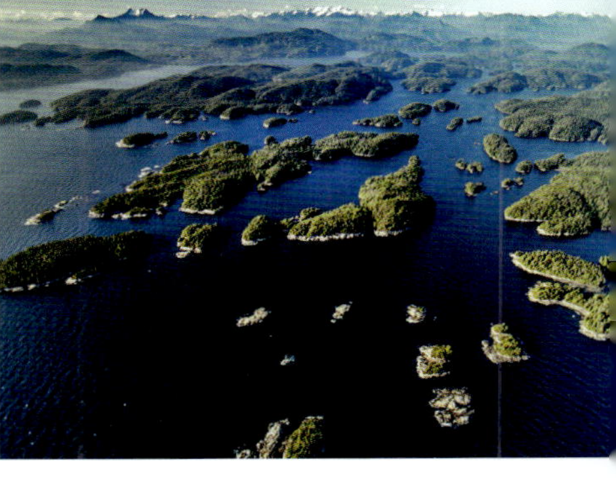

↑ This marine provincial park includes dozens of islands along the mouth of Knight Inlet.

↖ Humpback whales are known for putting on a show, sometimes leaping nearly clear out of the water.

← Sea otters often raft up together in this marine park, sometimes in numbers of 70 or more.

MacMILLIAN PROVINCIAL PARK

Cathedral Grove

While some trees remain standing, other fallen giants provide food and shelter for the diverse flora and fauna of Cathedral Grove

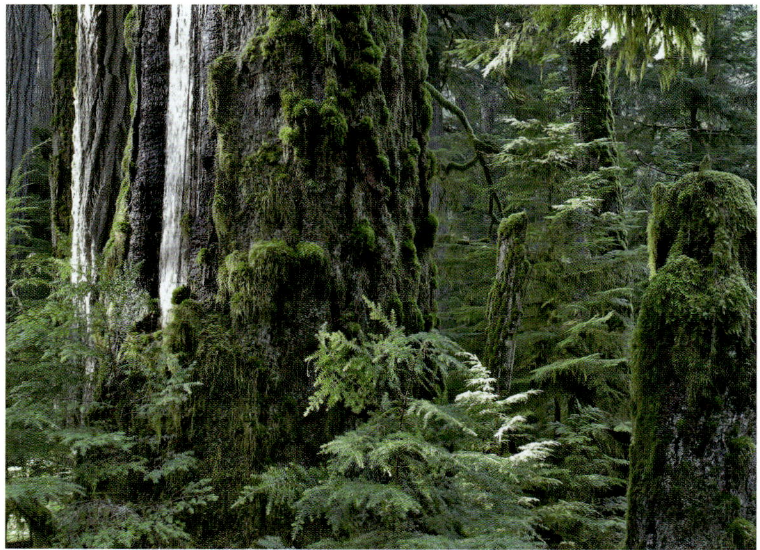

What Makes This Hot Spot Hot?

- Easily accessed trails wind through groves of giant trees.
- The park contains imposing 800-year-old Douglas-firs and western redcedars.
- Nurse logs provide nutrients and habitats for countless organisms.

Address: MacMillan Provincial Park, Alberni Hwy (Hwy 4), Port Alberni, BC
Tel.: (250) 474-1336
Website:

BC Parks

GPS Coordinates
Latitude: 49.2876
Longitude: −124.66648

Open year-round

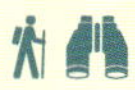

 (Check ahead)

↗ **An entire community of mosses and lichens inhabits the trunks of these massive trees.**

Cathedral Grove, found in MacMillan Provincial Park, may be the most famous old-growth forest in British Columbia, and for good reason. Douglas-firs and western redcedars, some over 800 years old, tower over their awestruck admirers. Most of the province's biggest stands of Douglas-fir of this maturity are difficult to access or, sadly, still being logged for timber, but this stand is thankfully very easy to reach. Despite its large number of annual visitors, this forest remains a treasure trove of natural wonders worth visiting.

In 1997 a severe windstorm swept through the park, and hundreds of these ancient trees fell. Although this storm severly damaged the trail system (some of the trails were never reopened), the ecosystem itself continues to thrive. The massive fallen trees maintain a vital role, even in their death. Sunlight, able to reach the forest floor once again, stimulates new growth in an understory that had been largely deprived of

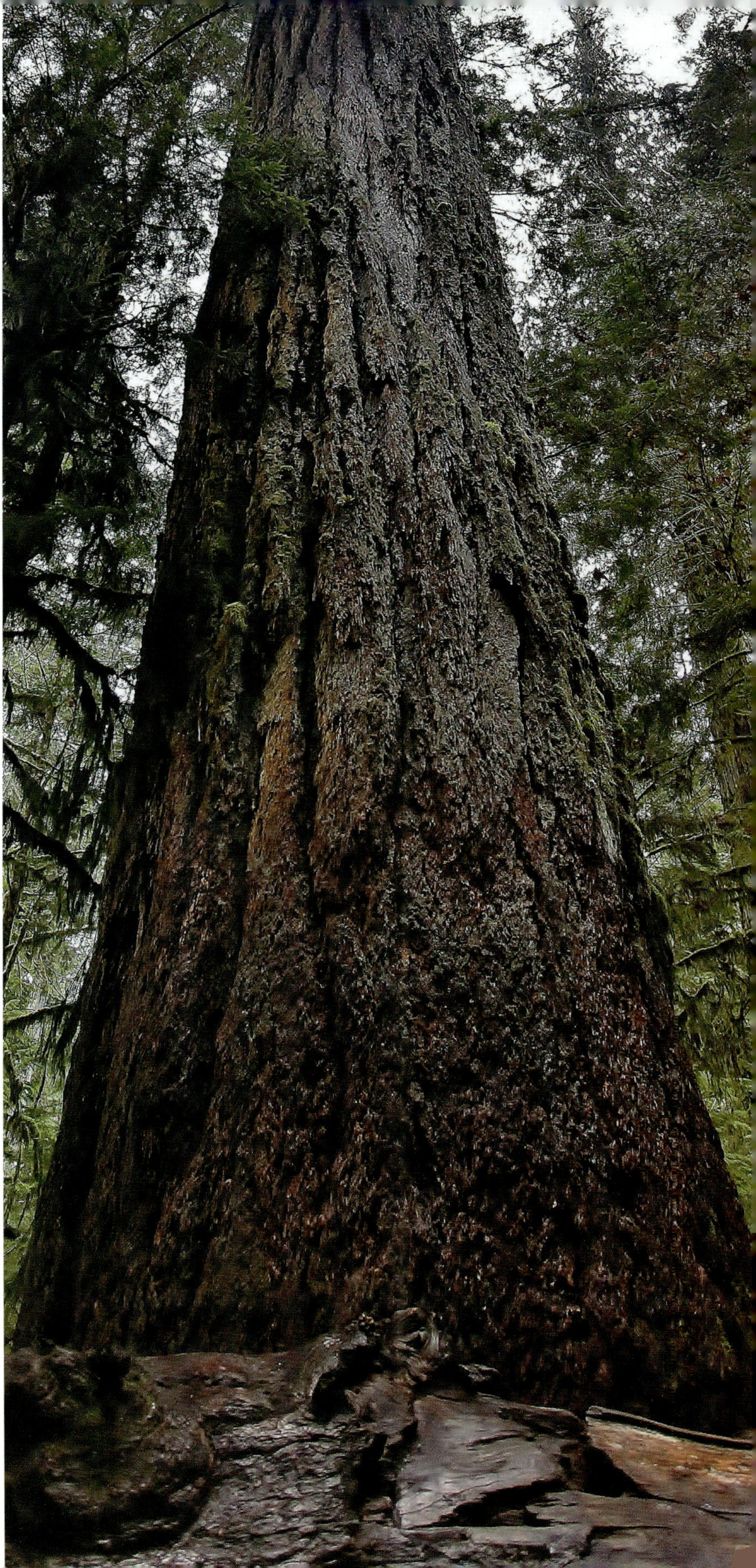

the sun's rays for hundreds of years. The stumps and logs of these fallen trees act as a nursery for new growth, providing nutrients and ideal conditions for the next generation of plants, which sprout and take root on their decaying bodies. Nurse logs have become home to a diverse assortment of fungi, mosses, insects and other flora and fauna, as the nutrients once locked in their massive trunks are freed up for other organisms to thrive on for decades to come.

Since the storm, the network of trails through the 301 hectares of ancient trees has been limited, but there is still much to see. On the south side of Alberni Highway, be sure to pay your respects to the largest Douglas-fir in the grove, which is an astounding 9 metres in circumference. On the north side of the highway you can explore a large tract of western redcedars near Cameron Lake. Do not forget your phone or camera, as you will most certainly want to document your time spent among such noble giants.

Cumberland Community Forest Park

Witness an incredible amphibian migration in this protected forest

What Makes This Hot Spot Hot?

- Community-led efforts have saved large portions of this incredible forest from ongoing logging activity.
- It's a perfect destination for mushroom enthusiasts, as fungi are found in abundance in the fall.
- Western toadlets make an incredible annual migration from Allen Lake into the surrounding forest.

Address: Cumberland, BC
Tel.: N/A
Website:

Cumberland Community Forest Society

GPS Coordinates
Latitude: 49.61618
Longitude: –125.03465

Open year-round

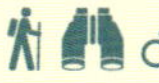

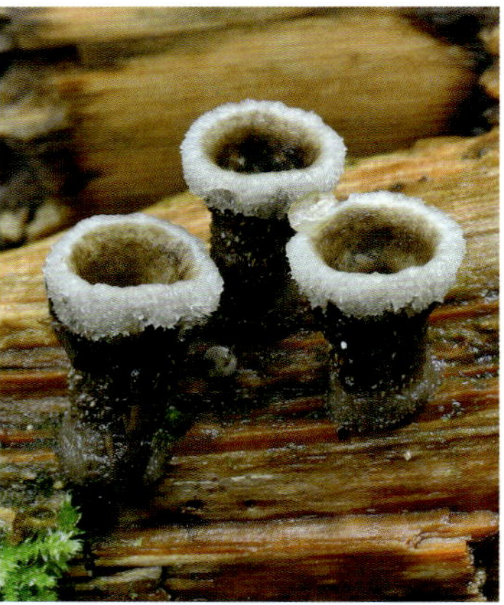

Just a stone's throw from the historic streets of the village of Cumberland, you'll find the Cumberland Community Forest Park. This protected park exists thanks to the efforts of local volunteers who have been working tirelessly to preserve large tracts of this forest for over 20 years. The Cumberland Community Forest Society has purchased over 200 hectares of forest, now protected within a conservation covenant.

The trail network is multiuse, so expect to share space with mountain bikers, runners, hikers and other outdoor enthusiasts. Pay attention to signage that alerts you of each trail's recommended use. The often-packed parking lot illustrates an increased demand for nature experiences from a growing population, and it also serves as an important reminder to tread carefully through these precious wild spaces. For those tempted to wander off-trail for a dip, know that the creeks and lakes within the forest are fragile and feed local drinking water sources, so please do not swim in them.

In the fall you'll find an abundance of fruiting fungi in the forest, from lobster mushrooms to coral fungi. Accurate identification can be challenging for many species, but their descriptive common names can help guide you, as is the case for jellied bird's nest fungus.

This forest is also host to an incredible amphibian migration each year, usually spread over two to three weeks in

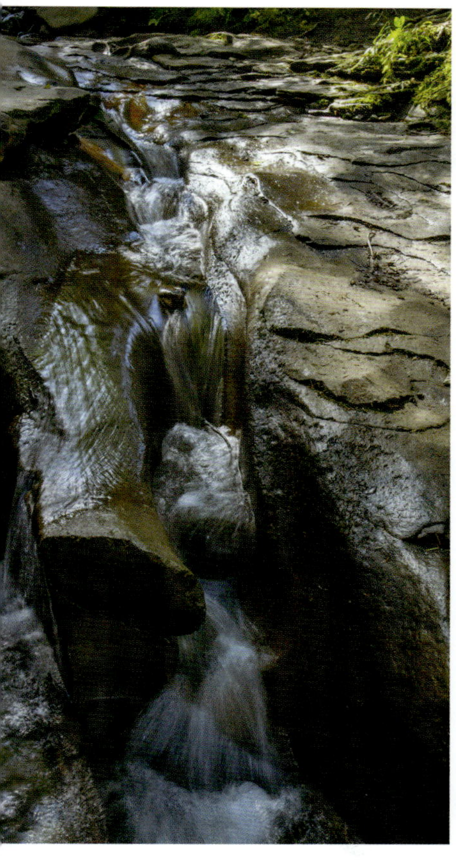

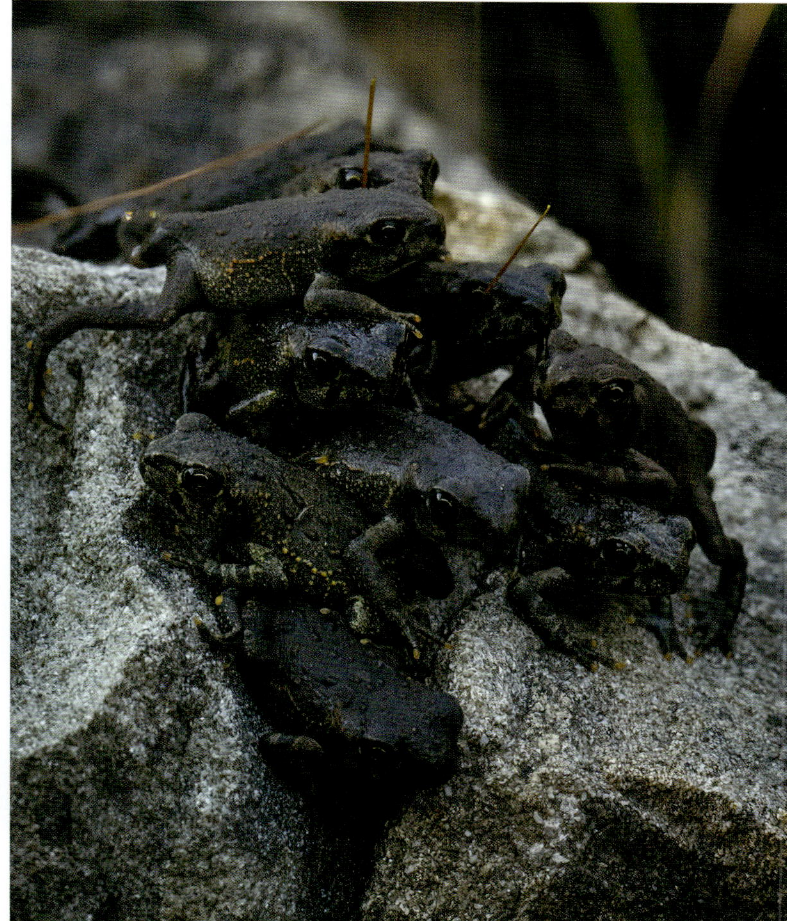

July and August. Tens of thousands of tiny western toadlets emerge from Allen Lake and surrounding waters, travelling as far as 5 kilometres into the forests, where they'll continue to grow and eventually hibernate for the winter.

At only 10 millimetres in length, even large throngs of these tiny travellers can be difficult to see before it's too late. Thankfully, volunteers take to the trails to track toadlet movements, install signage, close routes and engage hundreds of trail users to ensure these tiny amphibians have their best shot at survival.

The annual migration of these bumpy, clumsy treasures is a reminder that this forest is a true nature hot spot, and one that needs to be enjoyed with the utmost care. Unfortunately, much of the connected forest outside of the community park boundaries is still owned by timber companies and slated for logging in the future. Visit cumberlandforest.com to support the ongoing efforts to return more of this forest back to the commons.

↑ **Tiny western toadlets pile on top of each other, soaking in the sun on their last few days by the lake's edge before beginning their epic journey into the surrounding forests.**

↖ **As tempting as it looks, taking a dip in Perseverance Creek puts this delicate ecosystem at risk, so enjoy the views from the land.**

← **A raindrop hitting the cup of a jellied bird's nest fungus is enough to launch its "eggs" out of the nest — in other words, spread its spores.**

Desolation Sound Marine Provincial Park

Stunning shorelines to explore, where the mountains meet the ocean

What Makes This Hot Spot Hot?

- The area has some of the warmest ocean waters north of Mexico.
- Many inlets and islands create the perfect setting for exploring this park by water.
- Fjords create a dramatic backdrop against the calm protected waters of this sound.

Address: 32 km north of Powell River, BC
Tel.: (250) 286-9992
Website:

BC Parks

GPS Coordinates
Latitude: 50.11232
Longitude: −124.68836

Open March to October

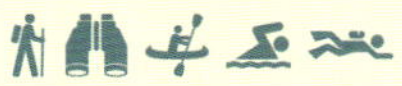

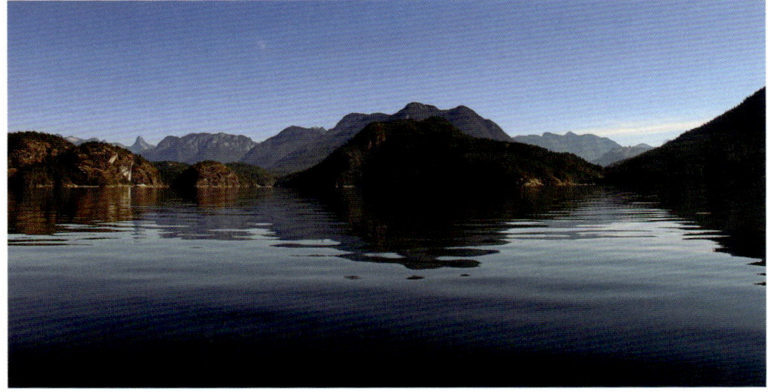

When Captain George Vancouver visited these waters in 1792, he deemed the shoreline so remote and inhospitable that he gave it the name Desolation Sound. While he clearly failed to recognize the area's natural beauty and ecological importance, its incredible natural value was not lost on the Klahoose, Tla'amin and Xwémalhkwu (Homalco) First Nations who had been visiting and inhabiting this sound for thousands of years prior to colonization. The dramatic shorelines are inaccessible by car even today, but the warm protected waters and dramatic scenery of this 8,449-hectare marine park make it the perfect paradise for nature lovers to explore by water.

Desolation Sound Marine Provincial Park makes up the northern boundary of the Sunshine Coast, past the village of Lund, where the Sunshine Coast Highway ends. Long ago the huge valleys were slowly carved by ancient glaciers before becoming submerged by the rising sea. The resulting steep forested fjords of this marine haven are breathtaking. These coastal mountains ascend from the shore almost

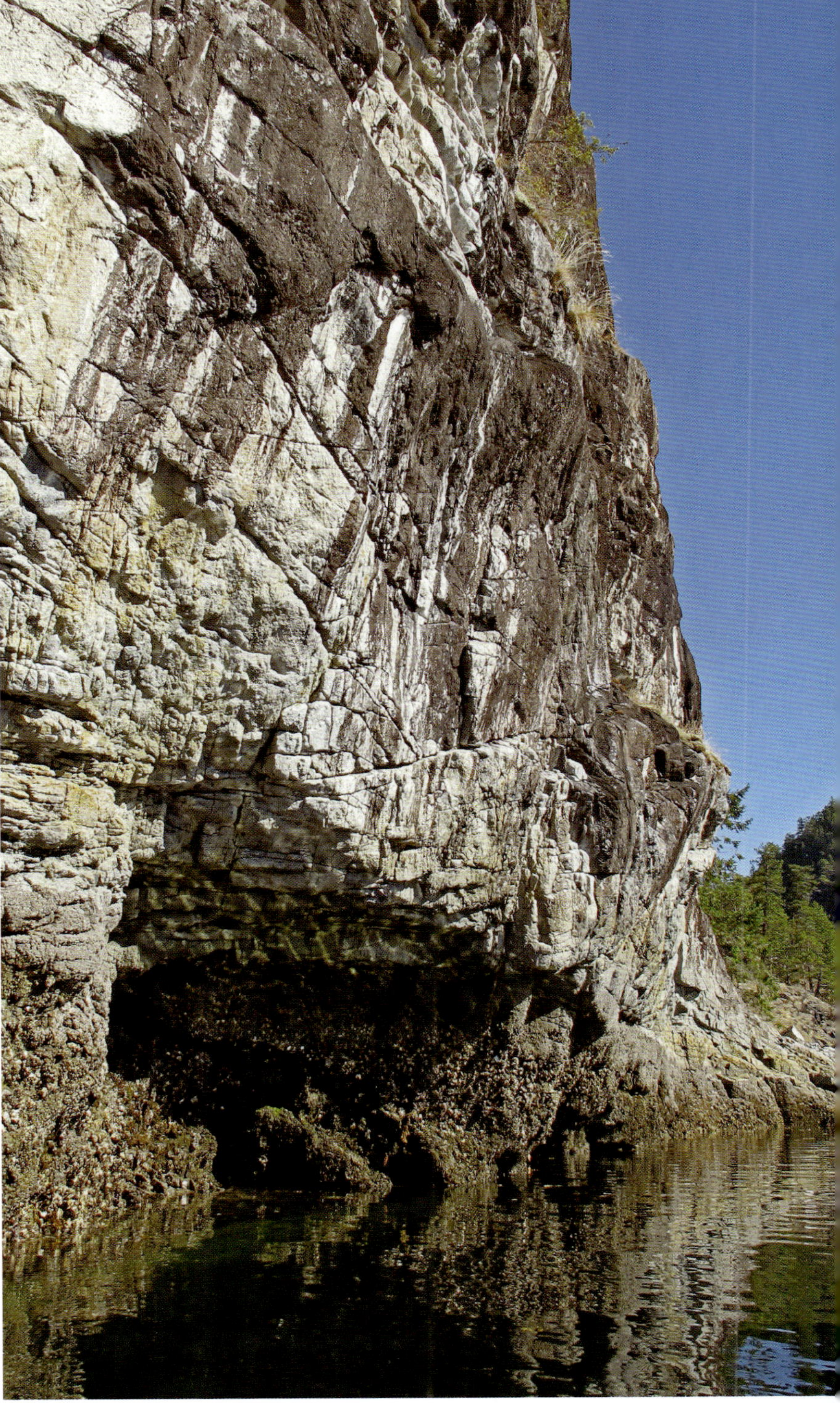

perpendicular to the sea, to heights of over 2,000 metres in some areas. The many inlets and islands create a seemingly endless coastline to discover at your leisure.

The narrows straits and passages of the area slow the tidal waves coming into the sound. As opposite tidal waves meet coming from the north and south, they create disordered and complex tidal patterns and weaken the tidal currents. This is what allows the surface water to stay extremely calm and the temperature to be comfortable in the summer, making the park a perfect place for exploring nature in the water, whether you are swimming, snorkelling, scuba diving, boating or kayaking.

Make sure you get in close to the shoreline as you explore the dramatic scenery. Giant sunflower stars, spiny rockfish, sea cucumbers, oysters and much more make up just some of the diverse intertidal life here. Purple sea stars can be seen clinging vertically from the rock faces as the tide recedes, while harbour seals sun themselves on the more gently sloped rocky shores.

ALICE LAKE LOOP

Devil's Bath and Eternal Fountain

Karst landforms surrounding Alice Lake have created Canada's largest cenote and a disappearing waterfall

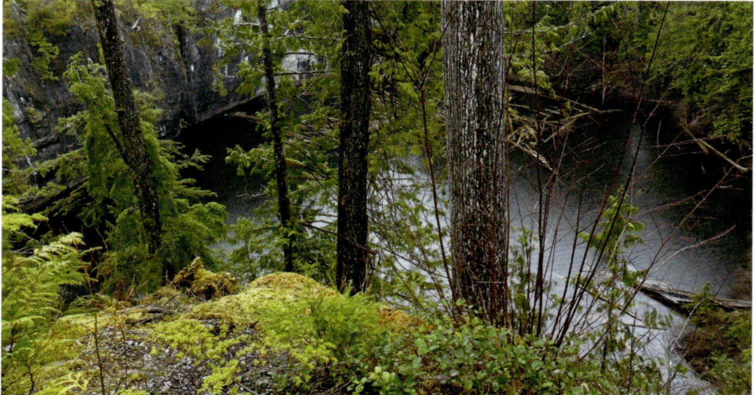

What Makes This Hot Spot Hot?

- Visitors have access to views of one of Canada's largest cenotes.
- Trails lead to the dramatic Eternal Fountain, which disappears into caves below.
- Karst windows provide views into the rushing water hidden in underground caves.

Address: Alice Lake Road, Mount Waddington, BC
Tel.: (250) 956-3301
Website:

Vancouver Island North

GPS Coordinates
Latitude: 50.39533
Longitude: −127.30425

Open year-round

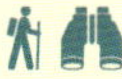

Although the Alice Lake Loop is a rough, active logging road that should not be conquered without a truck, it is worth the rutted and potholed drive to witness impressive examples of the power of dramatically surging freshwater as it shapes the landscape.

With a circumference of 359 metres and reaching a depth of 44 metres, Devil's Bath is one of Canada's largest cenotes, a sinkhole fed by groundwater. Photos do not do this colossal geologic rarity justice, so you will have to go see it yourself. Cenotes are often created when sections of cave roofs collapse, revealing a previously hidden cavernous system below. Cenotes and underground caves are typical features of karst landforms. This unique terrain commonly forms when limestone bedrock dissolves below the water table. Devil's Bath connects to the Benson River Cave through a submerged tunnel. At the surface trees cling desperately to the edges of the vertical cliff that drops down to the water far below, and in the calm waters of the sinkhole float giant logs of trees that lost their hold in days past.

Another stop along the Alice Lake Loop not to be missed is Eternal Fountain. This waterfall gives the impression of a fountain on a continuous loop: a powerful surge of water gushes from the rock face, falls nearly 5 metres into a moss-covered rocky opening in the forest floor and then disappears from sight. This type of waterfall is known as a resurgence, when an underground stream returns to the surface. The swallet, where the stream disappears back into the ground, flows through concealed caves below. Stay on the trails to avoid the risk of falling — with so many underground caves, there are hidden openings and unstable ground. Additional karst windows into this underwater course can be viewed just a short distance from Eternal Fountain, all nestled within a beautiful temperate forest backdrop.

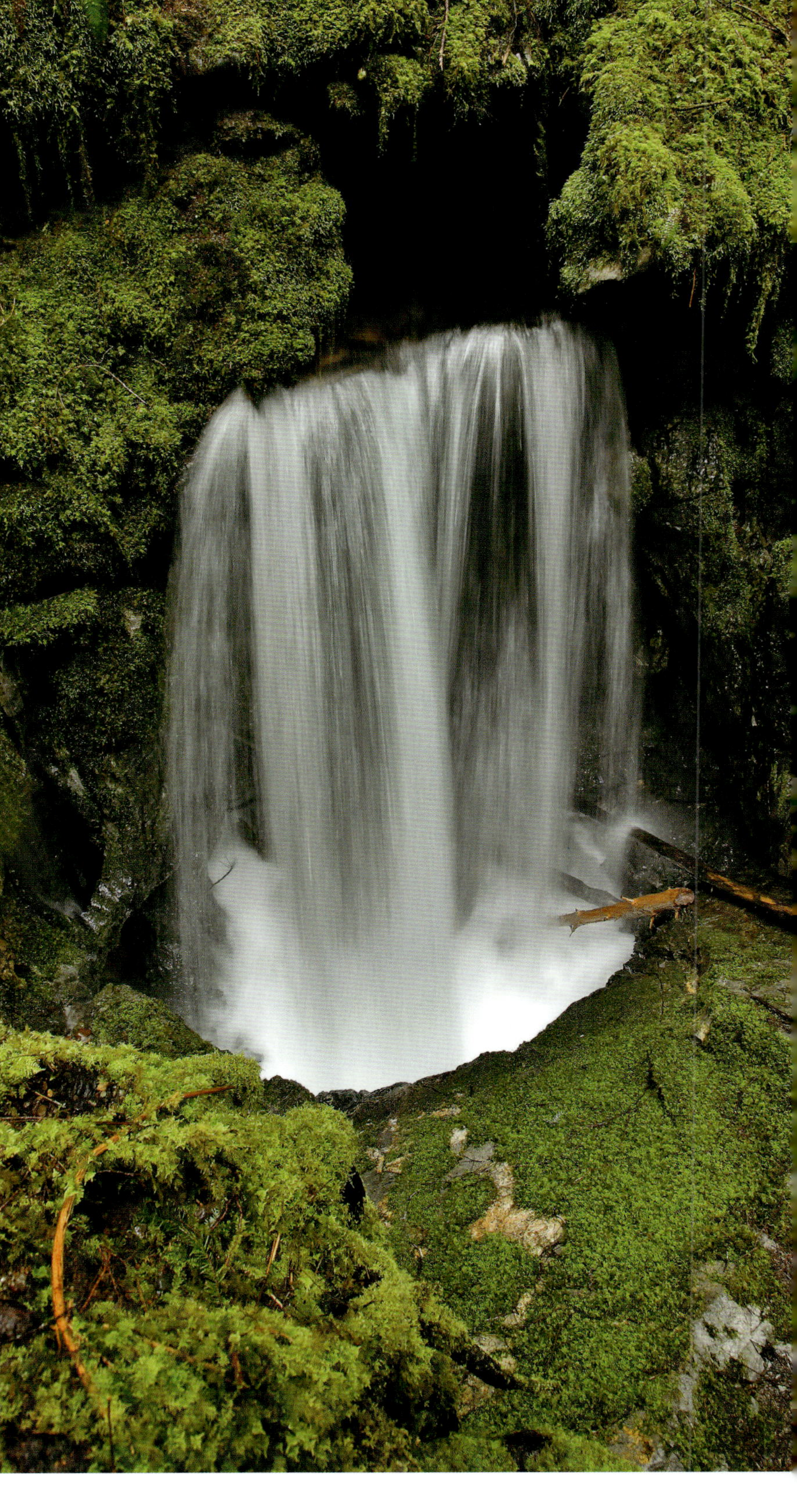

Elk Falls Provincial Park

The Campbell River crashes down into a steep canyon enveloped by tranquil forest

What Makes This Hot Spot Hot?

- Elk Falls is an impressive 25-metre plunge into a large canyon.
- A suspension bridge makes for better views of the falls.
- Five species of salmon spawn in the channels.

Address: Gold River Hwy (Hwy 28), Campbell River, BC
Tel.: (250) 474-1336
Website:

BC Parks

GPS Coordinates
Latitude: 50.04094
Longitude: −125.31999

Open year-round

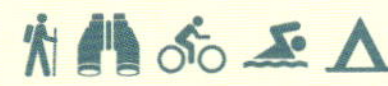
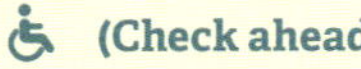

♿ **(Check ahead)**

↗ **Viewing platforms and a suspension bridge let you experience the monumental rush of water from above the falls.**

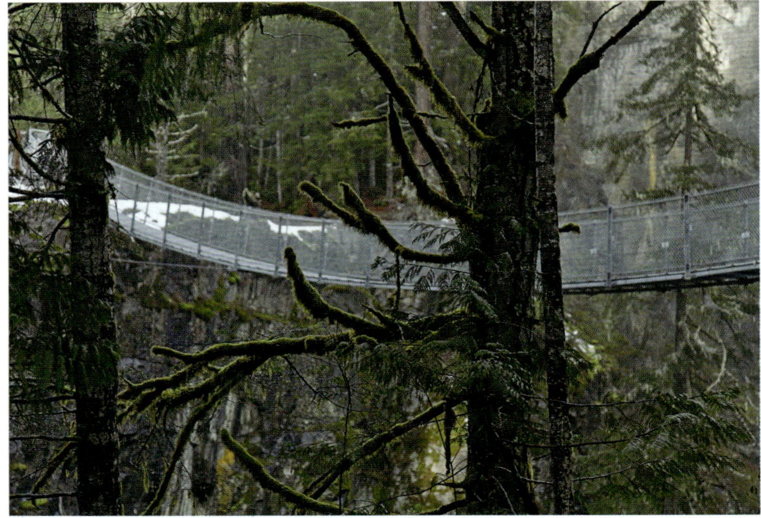

As notable and distinguished as its namesake, the sight of Elk Falls' 25-metre drop is certainly worth the trip just a few kilometres outside of the city of Campbell River. The falls are most dramatic in the winter, when the river becomes swollen from the fall and winter rains and plunges over the rock face into a steep canyon. The suspension bridge and viewing platforms make for a perfect photo opportunity of Elk Falls from multiple angles.

A year-round attraction, the 1,074-hectare Elk Falls Provincial Park has a lot to explore in addition to the falls. Although much of the forest is secondary growth, it is also home to the only significant stand of old-growth Douglas-fir north of MacMillan Provincial Park. The Millennium Trail, which connects the Elk Falls Trail to the Canyon View Trail, brings you through some of the oldest trees in the park. Near the midway point, a large gully of devil's club is worth stopping to admire, but stay on the trail and do not touch the large maple

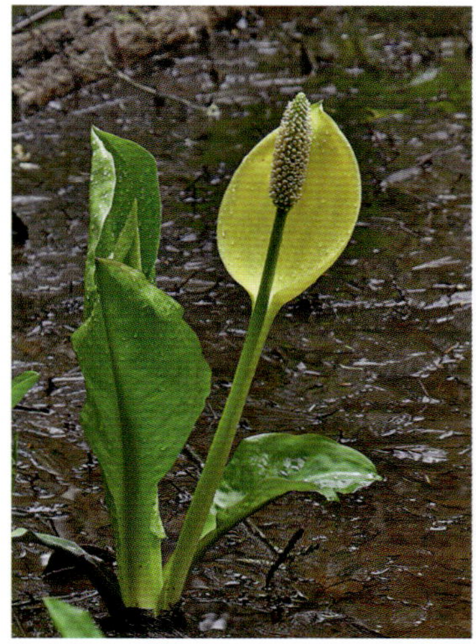

leaf-shaped leaves, unless you want to learn first-hand how this plant got its name. Accidentally brushing the brittle spines that cover the plant is extremely unpleasant.

In the fall five species of salmon spawn in the park's waters. In the early spring, give yourself ample time to explore the Canyon View Trail on the hunt for wildflowers and birding opportunities. You may be lucky to find chocolate lilies, western trilliums and Pacific bleeding hearts, or the appropriately named western skunk cabbage. This water-loving plant will provide a familiar pungent olfactory clue as to its whereabouts. The skunk cabbage uses its distinct odour to attract beetles, flies and other insects, tricking them into pollinating its flower by fooling them into expecting a rotten meal. A beautiful, yellow bract, or modified leaf, surrounds a thick spike covered in a cluster of tiny flowers. Perhaps after taking some time to adjust to the smell, you will feel inclined to call these plants by their friendlier nickname — swamp lantern.

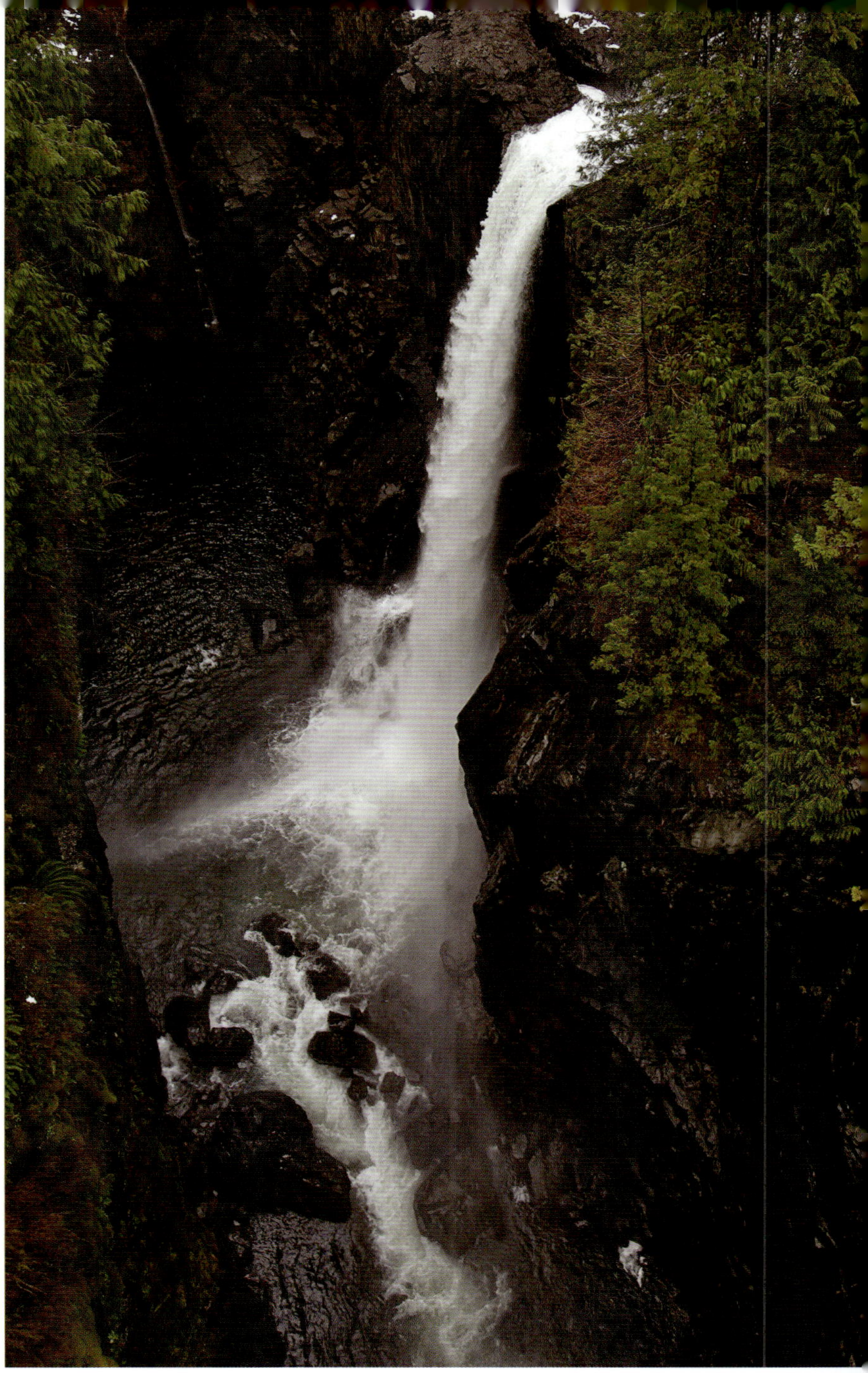

↑ **The Campbell River plunges down Elk Falls into the chasm below.**

↖ **The western skunk cabbage is mostly known for its smell, despite its impressive beauty.**

STRATHCONA PROVINCIAL PARK

Forbidden Plateau

The easternmost section of British Columbia's oldest provincial park is a must-do on Vancouver Island regardless of the season

What Makes This Hot Spot Hot?

- Unique plant and animal life dominates the landscape, thriving in both the wetlands and the difficult conditions of the alpine meadows.
- The Canada jays in Paradise Meadows are not shy, and visitors will find themselves surrounded by this bird during snack breaks on the trail.
- Views of Vancouver Island's mountains are stunning from Mount Albert Edward, one of the highest peaks on the island.

Address: Strathcona Provincial Park, Nordic Drive, Comox-Strathcona, BC
Tel.: (1-844) 435-9453
Website:

BC Parks

GPS Coordinates
Latitude: 49.74525
Longitude: –125.31923

Open year-round

♿ **(Check ahead)**

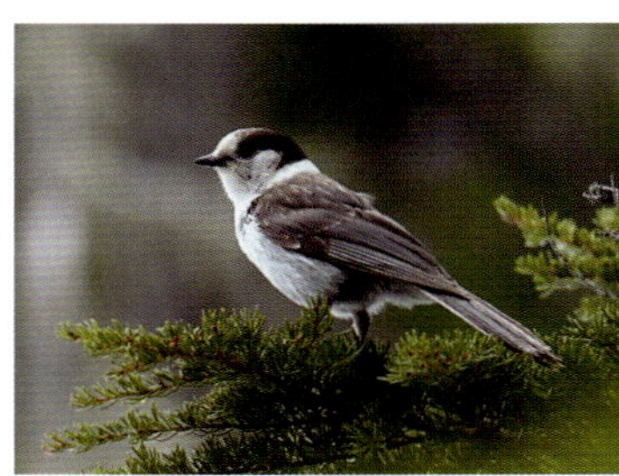

In the heart of Vancouver Island lies the oldest provincial park in British Columbia. Established in 1911, Strathcona Provincial Park boasts over 250,000 hectares of dense forests, alpine peaks, glaciers and waterfalls. It can be difficult to know where to begin! Forbidden Plateau is one of the more easily reachable areas and hosts some of the most spectacular alpine landscapes in the park. Starting in the subalpine hemlock forest near Mount Washington's ski area, visitors can stroll along the Paradise Meadows Trail, where gentle boardwalks move through wetlands abuzz with dragonflies in the warmer months. Many unique and beautiful flowers bloom in the meadows. Violets, monkeyflowers and mountain heather thrive in the fields alongside the trails.

Hikers will find themselves surrounded by Canada jays during snack stops and lunch breaks. These friendly and sleek black, grey and white birds are Canada's unofficial national bird. Canada jays may seem to have an insatiable appetite, and to the observer it may seem like they are gathering more than they can eat. The observer may be correct; Canada jays will store food in lichens and under flakes of tree bark to retrieve later in the winter. Like any true Canadian, these birds do not let the snow stop them from going about their business. In March, while Forbidden Plateau is still a winter wonderland, the jays are busy at work on the trunks of coniferous trees building their nests. They gather twigs, bark strips and lichen to form a cup then line it with soft insulating materials, such as animal fur and feathers. The female incubates the eggs and covers the nestlings to keep them warm while the male does most of the work of bringing food to his growing family. Young jays leave their nests in

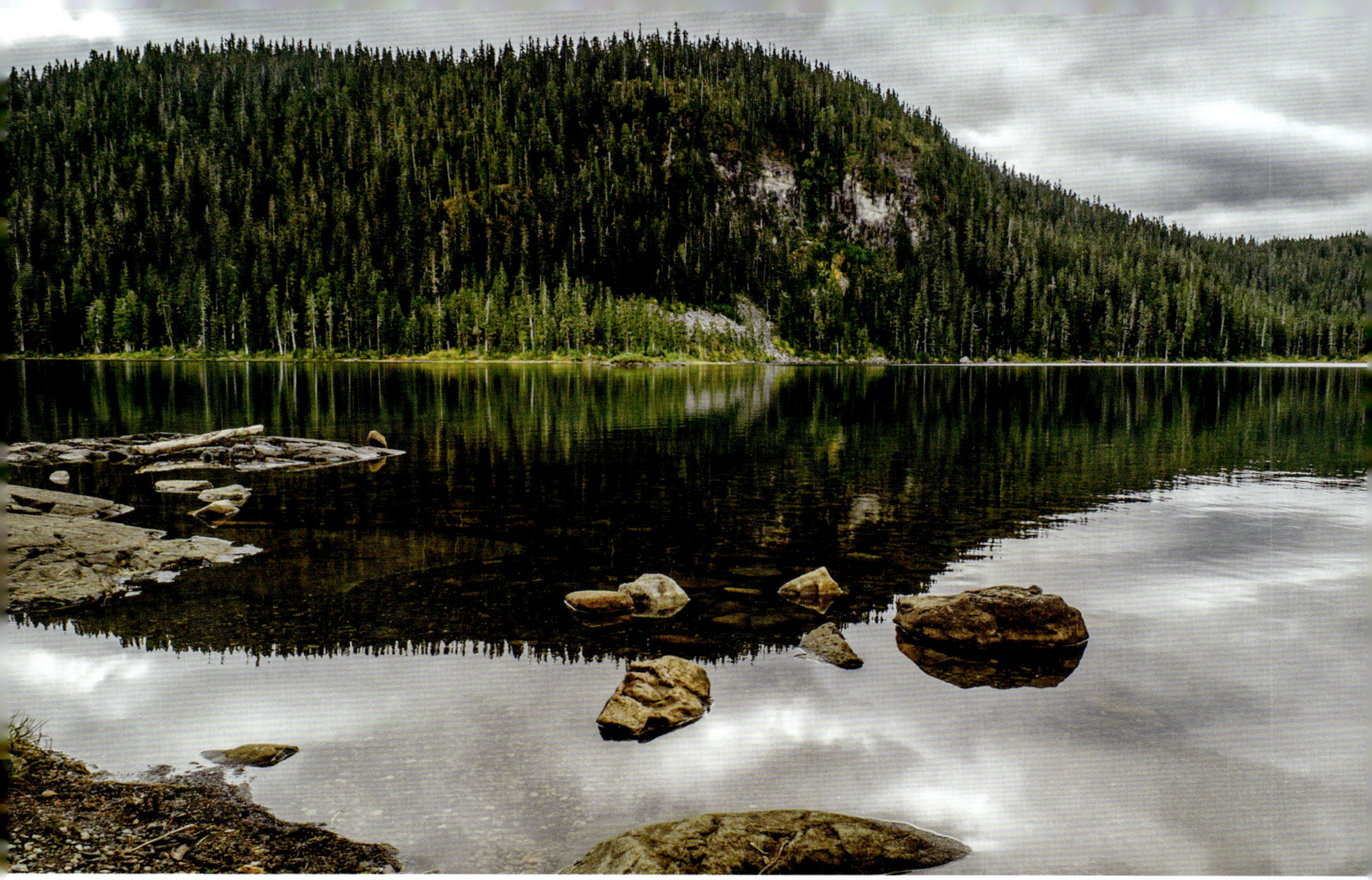

May, while much of the thick blanket of snow remains on the ground. Researchers are interested in studying the western race of Canada jays found in Paradise Meadows because its appearance and behaviour are notably different from the races that live in the boreal forests and the Rocky Mountains. The Canada jays of Paradise Meadows/Forbidden Plateau typically live in large social groups of five to 10 birds. More observations will be necessary to answer questions regarding the genetics and behaviour of these birds, but it is possible the western race constitutes a species that is separate from the Canada jays of northern and eastern Canada.

Both Lake Helen Mackenzie and Circlet Lake are fantastic backcountry camping sites. Lake Helen Mackenzie is an easy overnight destination and a relatively level hike from Paradise Meadows. Circlet Lake, which sits in a natural basin and is surrounded by small trees, rests at the foot of a steep incline in the trail along which hikers can continue to Mount Albert Edward, the sixth-highest peak on Vancouver Island. At the peak, hikers are treated to captivating views of the surrounding mountains. Forbidden Plateau is a small but rich slice of paradise that is an excellent gateway to the rest of the park, where there is even more to explore.

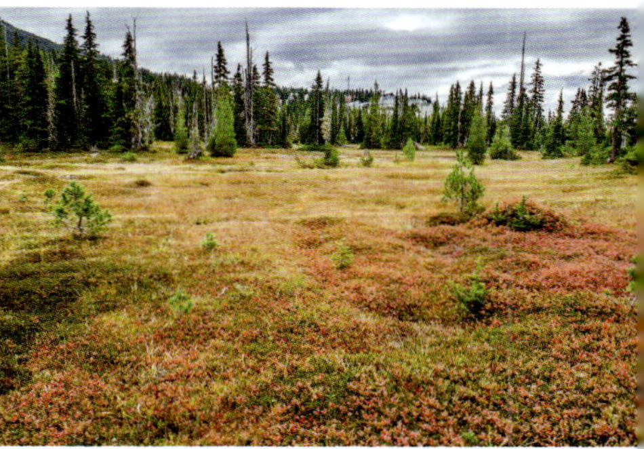

↑ A series of trails and boardwalks meanders through meadows and wetlands surrounded by hemlock forests.

↖ Lake Helen Mackenzie features backcountry campsites.

← Canada jays are abundant in these hemlock forests.

Francis Point Provincial Park

Fragile reindeer lichen blankets the steep banks of this Sunshine Coast hot spot

What Makes This Hot Spot Hot?

- A healthy population of reindeer lichen thrives along the rocky bluffs.
- There are amazing views of the Salish Sea, with ample opportunities for birding from the shore.
- The bluffs are home to rare species of plants and a high diversity of encrusting lichens, mosses and liverworts.

Address: Merrill Road, Madeira Park, BC
Tel.: N/A
Website:

Sunshine Coast Trails

GPS Coordinates
Latitude: 49.61296
Longitude: −124.05919

Open year-round

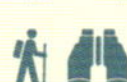

→ **Giant arbutus trees thrive along these coastal bluffs.**

Francis Point Provincial Park protects a unique and fascinating ecosystem. The dry, low-elevation forest type found here occurs only on the eastern side of Vancouver Island and in limited locations along the Sunshine Coast, making this rare, protected hot spot a must-see. The park's main trail splits into two: the trail forking to the right provides a short walk up some stairs to views of the Salish Sea, while the trail to the left provides an hour's worth of hiking along the gorgeous bluffs.

If you continue on the left trail past the small lighthouse, you will reach a grove of giant arbutus trees. Their divided trunks sprawl out across the rocky edge and grow nearly horizontal to the ground before eventually turning towards the sky. The rocky bluffs are carpeted in a wonderful collection of grasses, wildflowers, mosses and lichens. The blue-listed dune bentgrass and a rare native subspecies of red fescue are present in this rich community.

The most prominent feature of the rocks, reindeer lichen covers large sections of the dry, wind-battered cliffs, adorning the landscape in a beautiful pale-green hue.

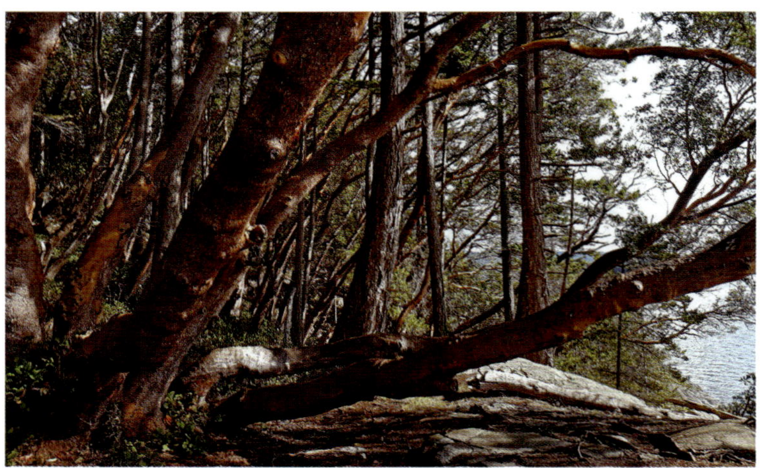

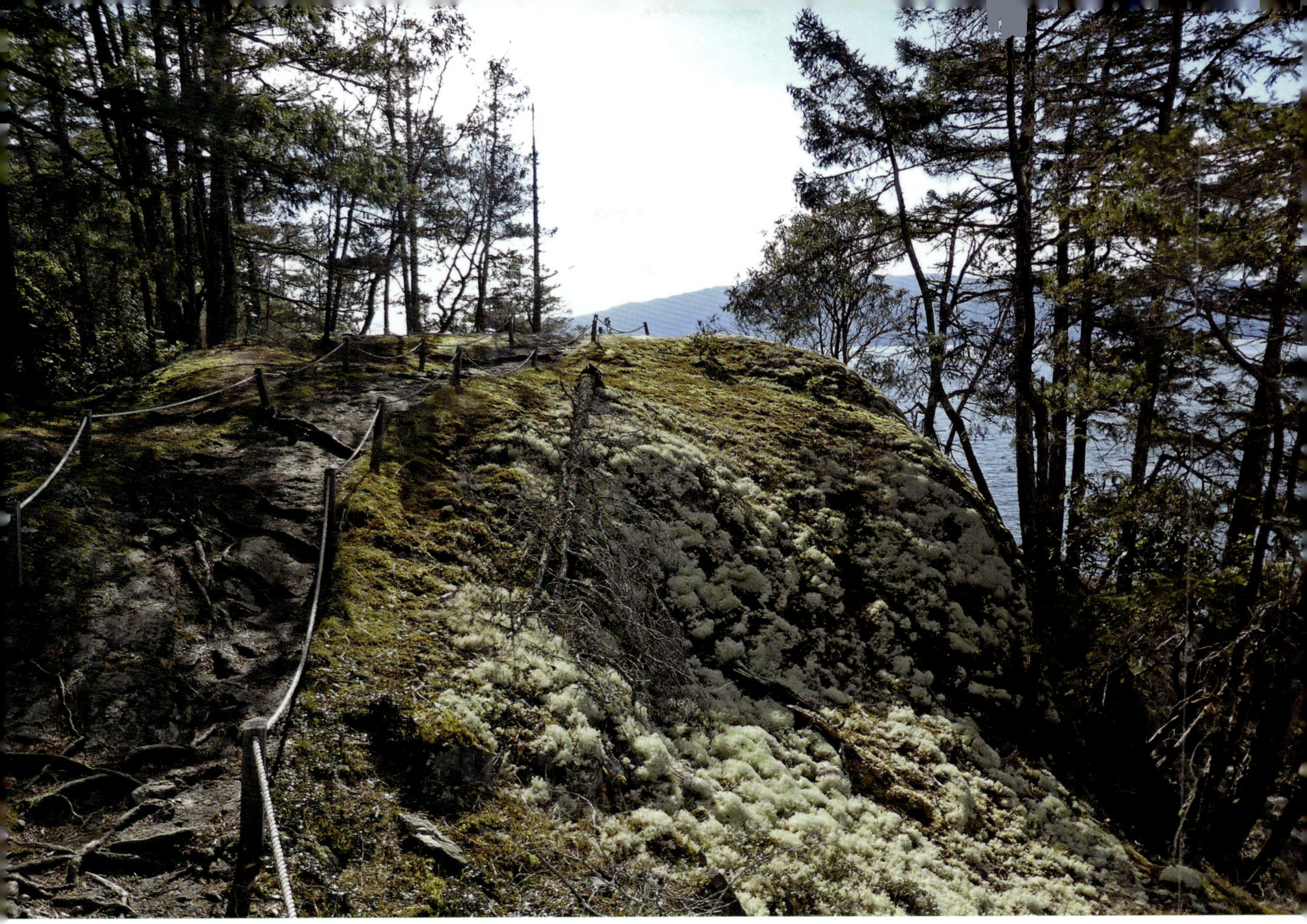

Lichens may be plant-like in some ways, but they are not plants. They are, in fact, made up of two or three organisms that are fused together in a symbiotic relationship: a multicellular fungus as well as an algae or a photosynthesizing bacteria, and at times a yeast, working together to create their own food. This pale, blanketing lichen only grows several millimetres a year and is sensitive to disturbance. It can take decades to grow and re-establish, so stay on the trail to keep this rare ecosystem intact. Adjacent to the provincial parkland there is an additional 17 hectares of protected shoreline as part of an ecological reserve. This area is not open to the public to fully protect its delicate ecological system, which has some of the densest concentrations of reindeer lichen.

Although the park is accessed through a residential area and can be tricky to find because of poor wayfinding, it is well worth the journey. The park is perfect for captivating ocean views adjacent to unique and biodiverse coastal communities and is an especially fascinating hot spot for those with a penchant for looking at lichens.

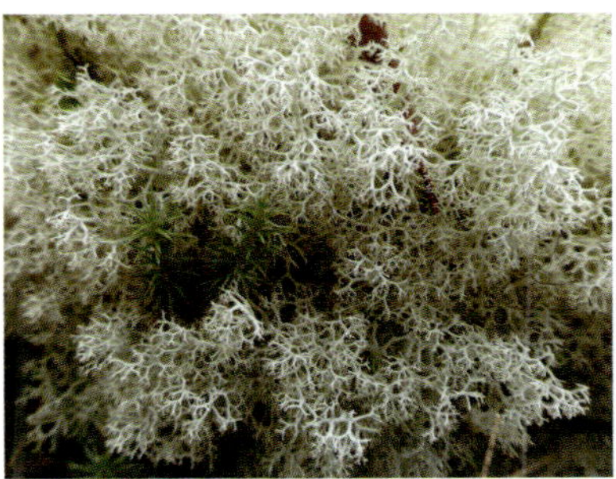

↑ The delicate branching of reindeer lichen, although extremely fragile on contact, can withstand the harsh conditions of these rocky bluffs.

↖ Careful footing and good boots are required as the trail can be steep, with both smooth, slippery rocks and sections laden with roots. But the effort pays off in abundance.

Goldstream Provincial Park

An old-growth forest within easy reach of Victoria

↗ **Bigleaf maple line the trails through this old-growth forest.**

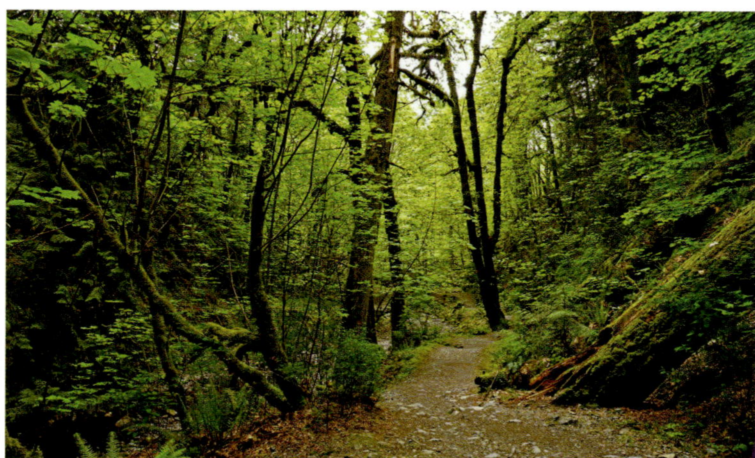

Towering 600-year-old giants in the form of Douglas-fir and western redcedar create dramatic scenes throughout Goldstream Provincial Park. Upon arrival, you are almost at once engulfed in a diverse and ancient forest, home to Western hemlock, bigleaf maple, black cottonwood and more.

Just a short, 16-kilometre trip from Victoria, this gorgeous park is one of the most reachable old-growth parks in British Columbia, making it one of the few places to experience an ancient old-growth temperate forest so close to an urban centre.

Goldstream is also home to a large chum salmon run, which numbers in the thousands each year. Observation platforms make it one of the most popular places for viewing this annual spectacle. For the adult salmon, this spawn is their last journey, and the dying fish draw in numerous other species that descend onto the river to take advantage of the easy meals. Hundreds of bald eagles visit the park in late fall and early winter to feast on the spent salmon carcasses along the shore, making this one of the highest concentrations of these remarkable raptors in the entire country.

Unlike most other species of Pacific salmon, chum are poor

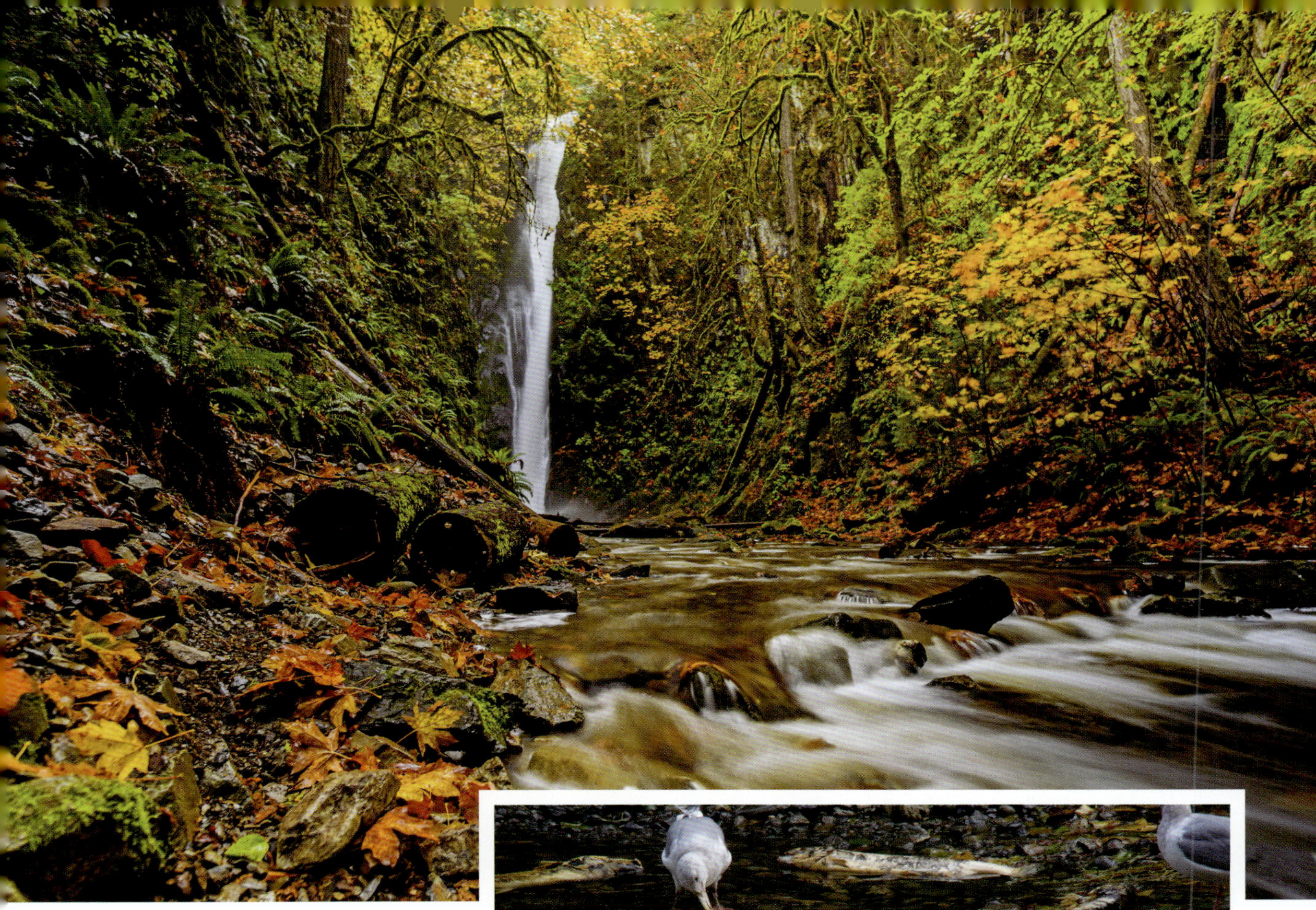

jumpers and are therefore relegated to spawning in streams and rivers not impeded by waterfalls or human-made barriers. As a result, chum are more affected by habitat damage than are other salmon species, favouring streams hugging the coastal waters. Chum are the most widely distributed of the coastal salmon. They can be identified by the dark vertical bars, called watermarks, which develop along their sides when they reach maturity and prior to migrating from the ocean to streams and rivers for spawning. Sometimes referred to as dog salmon, the mature males develop canine-like teeth, used to battle for access to females. The best spawning sites are in cool, shallow waters, and the best time for viewing the spawning in Goldstream is from late October to the end of November, as chum are the last salmon species to spawn on the West Coast.

↑ The salmon are dying as they swim upstream to perform their final task, drawing a range of opportunistic predators ready for an easy meal.

↖ Goldstream Provincial Park is lovely in the late fall, which is also the best time to view the salmon spawning.

Helliwell Provincial Park

A beautiful nature escape on a lovely island, well worth the two ferry trips

What Makes This Hot Spot Hot?

- Dramatic, rounded bluffs punctuate the beautiful coastline.
- Old-growth Garry oak meadows are filled with wildflowers in the spring.
- Scuba divers may have a chance encounter with the elusive sixgill shark.

Address: Helliwell Road, Hornby Island, BC
Tel.: (250) 308-4479
Website:

BC Parks

GPS Coordinates
Latitude: 49.51935
Longitude: –124.59811

Open year-round

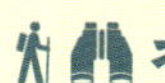

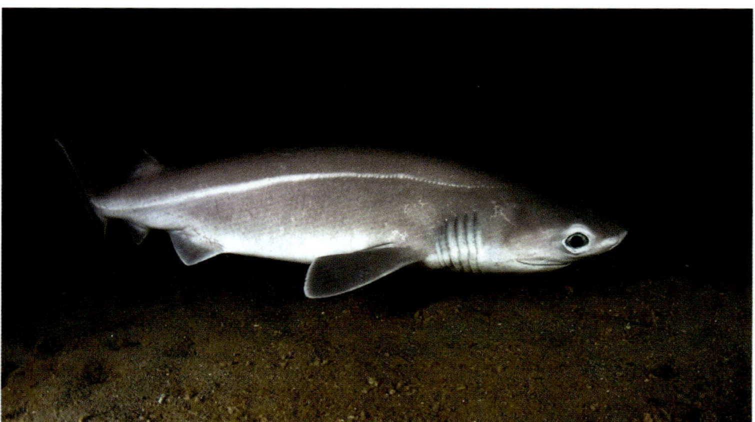

➤ **This sixgill shark pup is a rare but remarkable sight.**

Two short ferry rides from Vancouver Island will get you to the shores of Hornby Island, a 29-square-kilometre island that includes an impressive expanse of protected wilderness. In the far northeast corner of the island you will find the ecologically diverse Helliwell Provincial Park. The park's impressive bluffs are distinct from most of the Gulf Islands, carved by glaciers that covered the island as recently as 14,000 years ago. As they receded, they left behind high, rounded bluffs and stranded angular boulders, or erratics, carried from distant locations.

The 7 kilometres of trails in the park weave through forests of old-growth Douglas-fir, Garry oak and arbutus trees, and out to meadows atop the dramatic bluffs. In the spring the shoreline meadows are covered with vibrant wildflowers, including the miniscule but charming poverty clover, a blue-listed species.

Lookouts of the rocky coastline give ample opportunity to watch for humpback whales, orcas, seals and winter congregations of sea-loving birds, like long-tailed ducks, white-winged scoters and common mergansers. Look out for black oystercatchers searching for mussels and limpets at low tide, and bald eagles roosting in standing dead trees as they watch over the meadows.

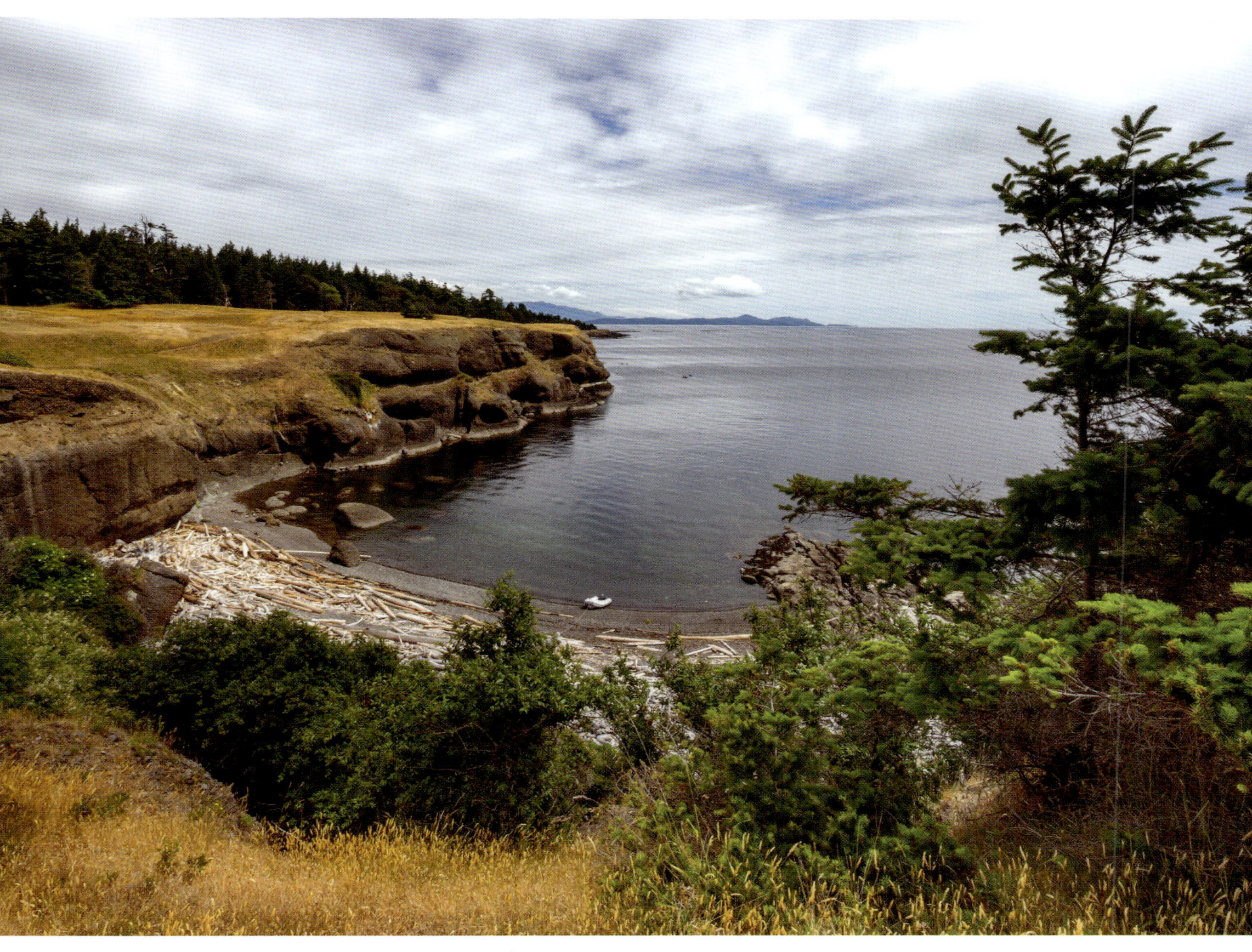

Of the 2,872 hectares of protected area, only 69 are land, while the rest includes the surrounding marine environment. Flora Islet, off the end of St. John's Point, was added to the protection of the park in part because of its unusual deep-sea visitors. Normally found up to 1,000 metres deep in the ocean, the rarely seen bluntnose sixgill shark has chosen this park as one of the few locations in the world where it visits shallower waters, attracting shark enthusiasts from all over the map. Most sharks have five gills, and there are only a few surviving members of this otherwise ancient family — some of the sixgill's closest relatives date back 200 million years. A sighting of these sharks is certainly not guaranteed, but for those lucky enough to see one, it will surely be a once in a lifetime experience.

↑ **Receding glaciers shaped the steep but rounded bluffs of Helliwell Park thousands of years ago.**

Horne Lake Caves Provincial Park

An underground journey through geological history

What Makes This Hot Spot Hot?

- Water from melting glaciers dissolved thick layers of limestone, carving out the chambers and tunnels of these caves.
- Stalactites and other cave formations have been growing underground for thousands of years.
- Visitors can experience "absolute darkness." A true cave has at least one area where no light penetrates.

Address: 3905 Horne Lake Caves Road, Qualicum Beach, BC
Tel.: (250) 248-7829
Website:

BC Parks

GPS Coordinates
Latitude: 49.34581
Longitude: −124.75095

Open year-round

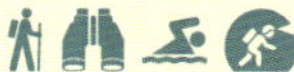

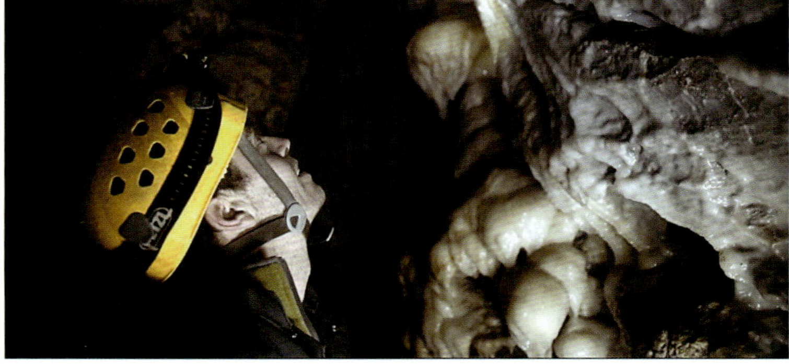

Step into geological history beneath the surface of Vancouver Island. Over 1,000 caves make up a network of tunnels through polished limestone, giving the island the highest density of caves in North America. From Horne Lake follow signs through the forest on well-marked trails to two stunning examples of karst caves formed by glacial water dissolving the porous limestone. This limestone layer was formed during the Permian period and comprises millions of invertebrates that have been compressed into a rock layer.

The two self-guided caves are beautiful and well worth the trip on their own. Cave in groups of three to six, and be sure you have the necessary equipment, including two light sources per person, warm clothing and helmets. However, hiring a guide will provide a much more informative experience and give you access to some of the most spectacular caves in North America. Tight squeezes open into cavernous rooms, an underground waterfall seven storeys high cascades into even deeper passages, and in an area called the China Shop, large cave formations adorn the walls and

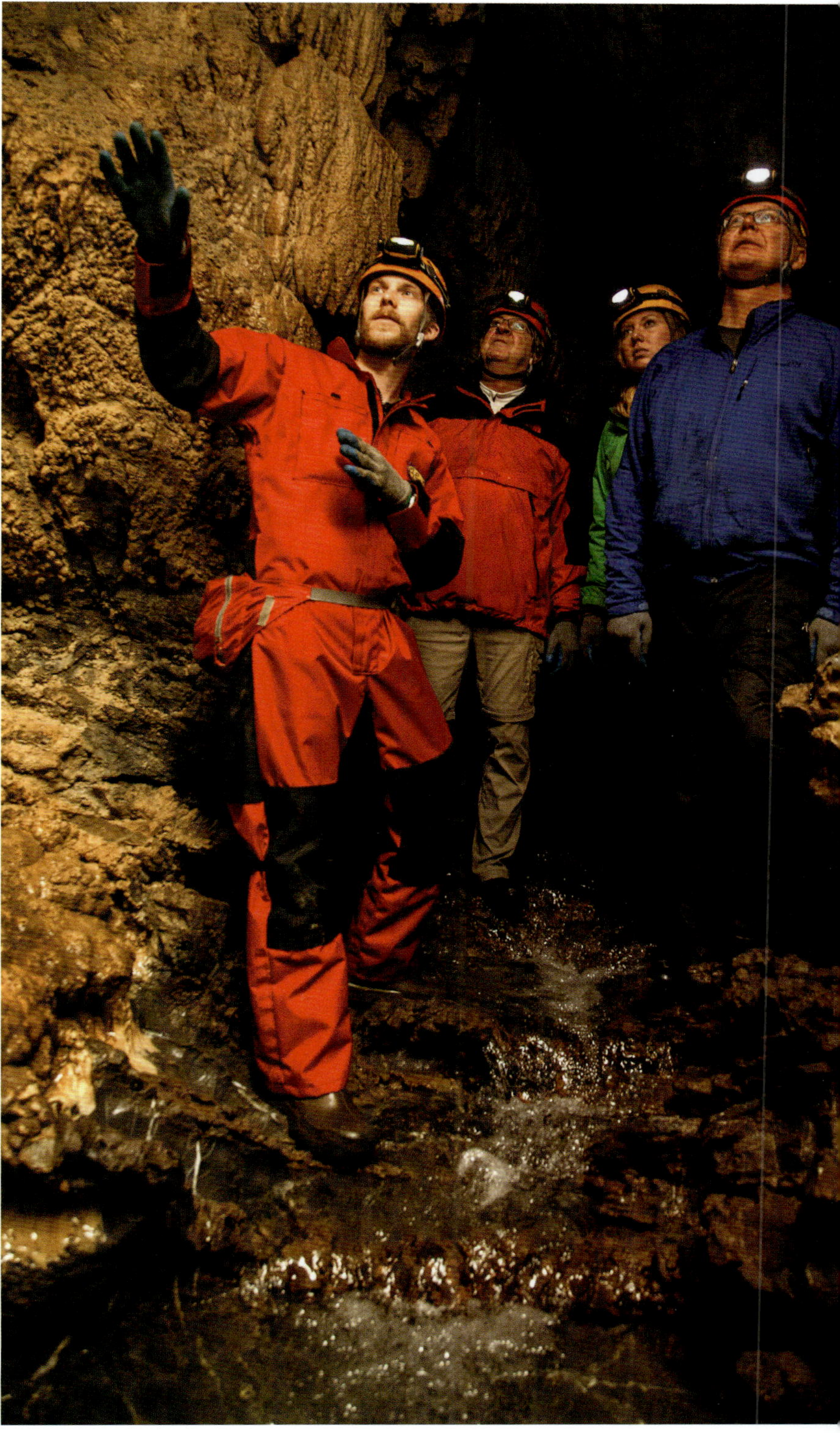

→ A guide points out some of the interesting geological features in a cave.

↙ Visitors often stand in awe of the limestone cave formations.

cling to the roof. Throughout the caves, among large stalactites, thin hollow tubes known as soda straws hang from the roof, taking upwards of 100 years to grow 1 centimetre.

Absolute darkness that results in a lack of plant life and a consistently cool year-round temperature make caves a hostile environment for life. The small number of animals that do live in caves tend to winter in them, or live near the entrances where they may leave to hunt. Keep an eye open for harvestmen, square-legged camel crickets and the long-toed salamander. Although bats are not normally seen in the caves of Horne Lake, they are present on Vancouver Island and sometimes winter in the island's caves. Wash your clothing between visiting any caving area to prevent potentially spreading the deadly white-nose fungus. While it is not harmful to humans it is quick to spread in bats and results in devastating population crashes.

MAQUINNA MARINE PROVINCIAL PARK

Hot Springs Cove

Geothermal hot springs meet the frigid waters of the Pacific Ocean in a coastal forest

What Makes This Hot Spot Hot?

- Hot springs cascade through rocky pools into the cool waters of the Pacific, making this natural paradise a literal hot spot.
- Local wildlife, a boardwalk through a cedar forest and oceanside pools offer a variety of sceneries and viewing opportunities all in one location.
- Visitors are given a unique view of British Columbia's rugged coast as they travel to and from the cove via float plane or boat.

Address: Maquinna Marine Provincial Park, Alberni-Clayoquot, BC
Tel.: (250) 474-1336
Website:

BC Parks

GPS Coordinates
Latitude: 49.36689
Longitude: –126.27222

Open year-round

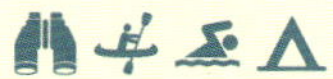

Remote, rugged and beautiful, Hot Springs Cove in Maquinna Marine Provincial Park is on many island-bound travellers' wish lists. From Tofino these natural hot springs are accessible exclusively by boat or float plane. Each offers its own unique and scenic tour of the wild west coast. Wildlife you may spot en route includes eagles, seals, bears and whales. The best chances of spotting grey and humpback whales is between March and October as they make their way north to feed in the cold waters of the Pacific Northwest.

Upon arrival an easy stroll along a boardwalk through a cedar forest leads visitors to a series of rocky pools into which hot water spills, gradually cooling before entering the ocean. Stand beneath a steaming waterfall before relaxing in one of the pools. The ebb and flow of the tide varies the temperature of the pools throughout the day, with the lowest-level pools being the coolest. After feeling the cold ocean water it may be difficult to believe that the Pacific Ocean is actually the source of the hot springs. Water from the Pacific moves through cracks in the ocean floor where it is heated before being pushed back to the surface. After completing a 5-kilometre journey underground, the water near the surface has a temperature of approximately 50 degrees Celsius. It cools quickly upon reaching the surface, but can be unbearably hot in some of the highest pools.

The springs are lovely year-round, and although spring and winter can be quite stormy, if you happen to be in the area on a nice day the off-season offers a more intimate experience.

Be sure to bring food, water and good shoes for the walk in, as well as shoes that can get wet while moving between the hot pools in the rocky intertidal zone.

➚ **A steaming waterfall between the pools.**

➙ **Water flows between a series of pools into the ocean.**

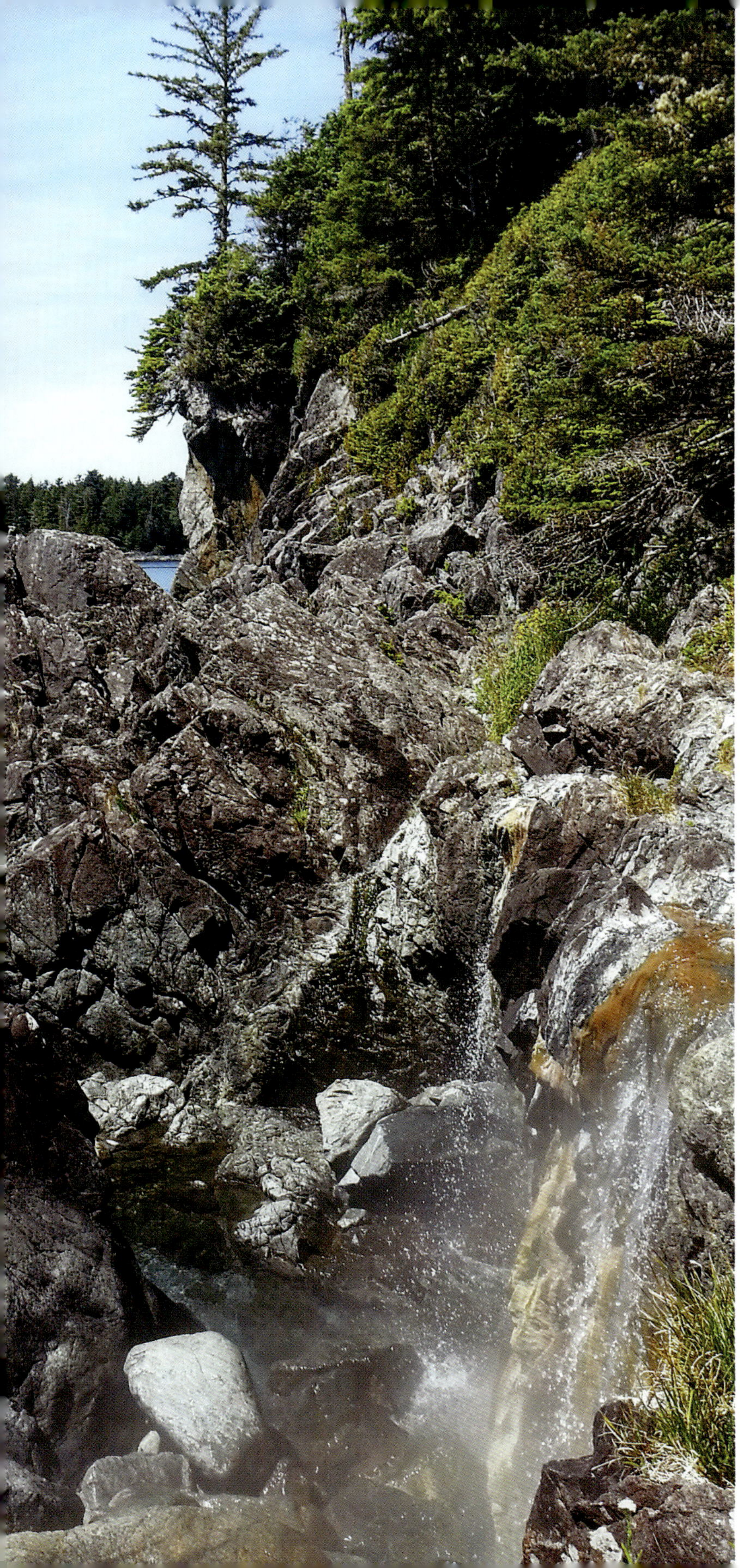

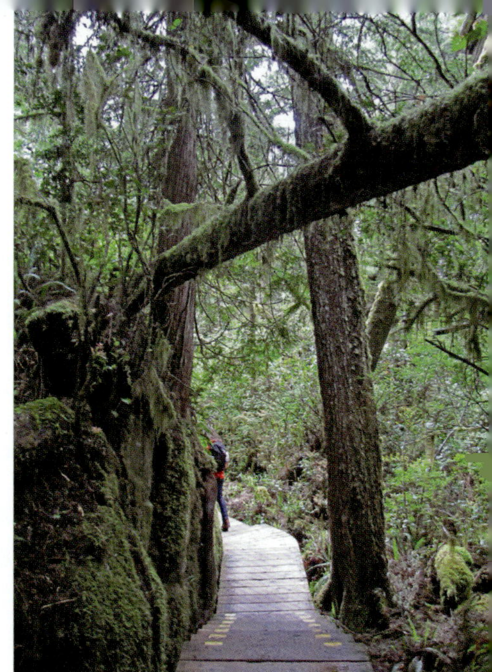

↑ **The boardwalk through the coastal rainforest is a great way to stretch your legs before relaxing in the springs.**

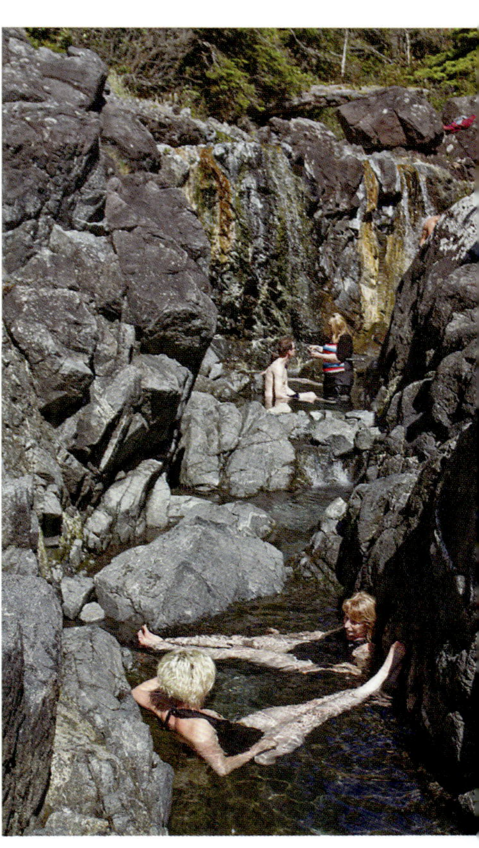

Jáji7em and Kw'ulh Marine Park

Wildflowers blanket the delicate sand dunes of these small protected islands, which are only accessible at low tide

What Makes This Hot Spot Hot?

- This cluster of small islands becomes a wildflower haven in the spring.
- The walk out to the island provides perfect conditions for exploring the exposed intertidal life.
- The rare sand-verbena moth is found in the park thanks to the presence of its only host plant.

Address: Best accessed via a trail through Morning Beach Park, 7600 Denman Road, Denman Island, BC
Tel.: N/A
Website:

BC Parks

GPS Coordinates
Latitude: 49.61899
Longitude: −124.85222

Open year-round

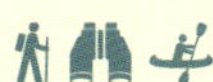

Jáji7em and Kw'ulh Marine Park includes a number of small islands called the Seal Islets. Sandy Island is the largest of the islands, with a stand of Douglas-fir at its centre that is surrounded by white sand beaches. This small, forested area is home to a bald eagle nest, and a number of other notable bird species make their way to this green patch, including Pacific slope flycatchers and Audubon's warblers.

These islands are accessible only by water or walking out at a low tide, so plan accordingly, including your return, otherwise it is a long wait for the waters to recede again! Low tide exposes a plethora of sand life: the seemingly limitless invertebrate specimens, both dead and alive, include moon snails, the introduced mudflat snails, clams, mussels, sand dollars, kelp and shore crabs, calcareous tube worms, limpets and more.

There are also fantastic

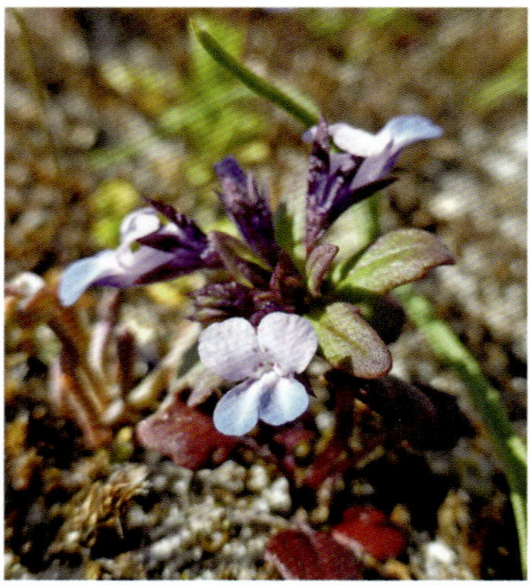

shorebird viewing opportunities along your low-tide walk, especially if you time your visit with the herring spawn in the early spring, when millions of washed-up eggs attract waves of wildlife to the area. Caspian terns and brant geese can be seen during their migration, and large numbers of dunlin and western sandpipers visit the area. Killdeer nest on the ground across the island, and you might be lucky enough to witness a protective parent feigning injury to draw you away from the nest. Tread carefully, as their nests are nearly impossible to spot because of their impeccable camouflage.

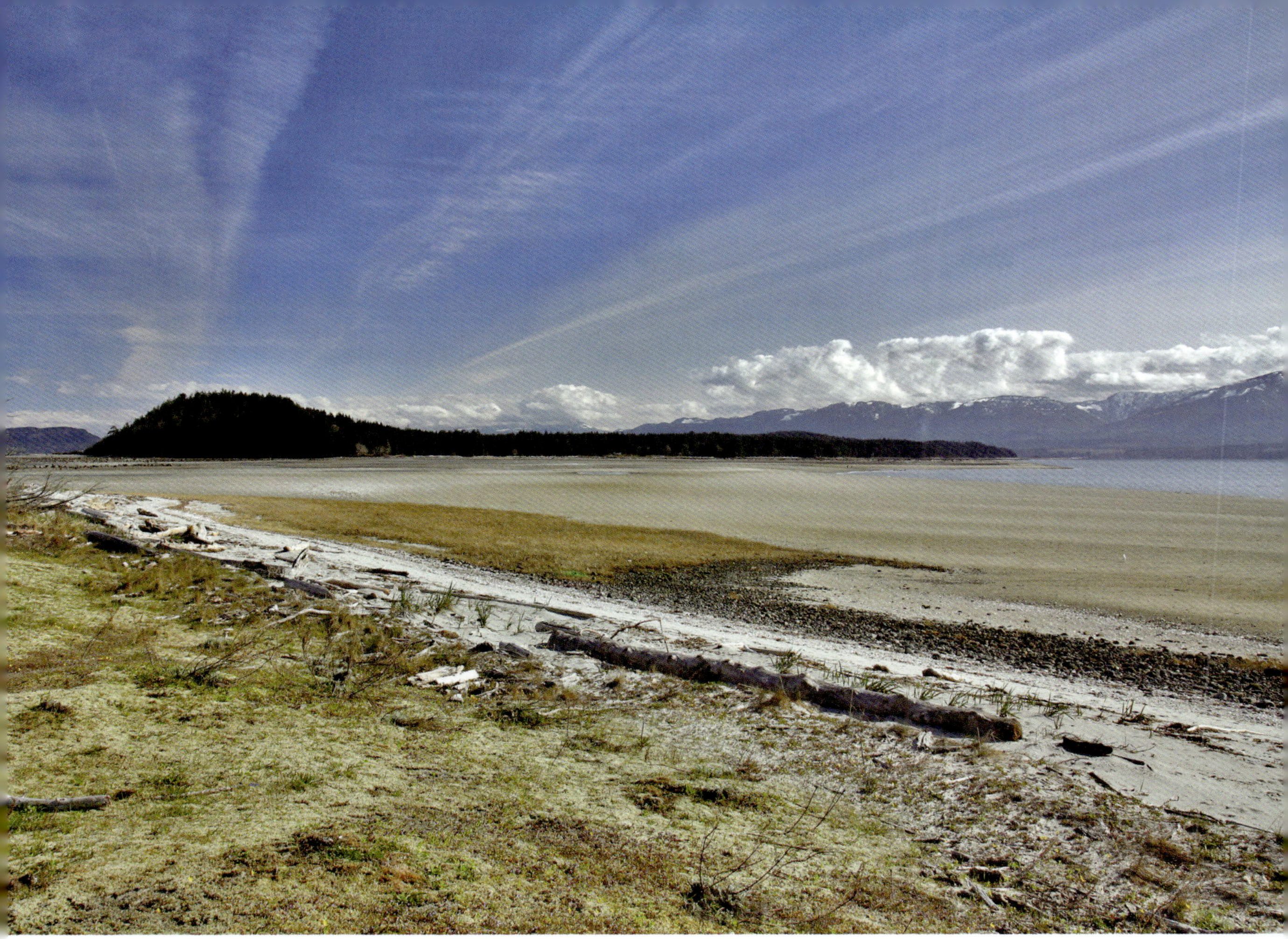

Spring wildflowers are one of the main attractions of the marine park, and the park requires careful use of the trails, as this ecosystem is extremely fragile. The sandy dunes become covered in sheets of vibrant colours as the spring progresses — early flowers include goldstar, woodland star, blue-eyed Mary and red-flowering currant. As the weeks progress, clumps of sea blush, larkspur and chickweed begin to bloom.

This spectacular wildflower haven attracts some noteworthy insect life as well. The striking anise swallowtail visits the islands, and one special visitor has been spotted in this unique ecosystem. The rare sand-verbena moth is found in only four locations in all of British Columbia. Yellow sand-verbena, one of the 140 species of wildflower found in the park, is the only host plant for this rare moth, which depends on the plant for nearly all its life stages. Eggs are laid in the flowers, larvae feed on the leaves and the adult moths feed on the nectar.

↑ **The land area of the park expands dramatically at low tide, exposing a whole new level of diversity in this hot spot.**

← **Blue-eyed Mary is a tiny but gorgeous flower found along the sandy edges in April.**

↓ **Goldstar is one of the earlier spring flowers to bloom on the sandy dunes of this marine park.**

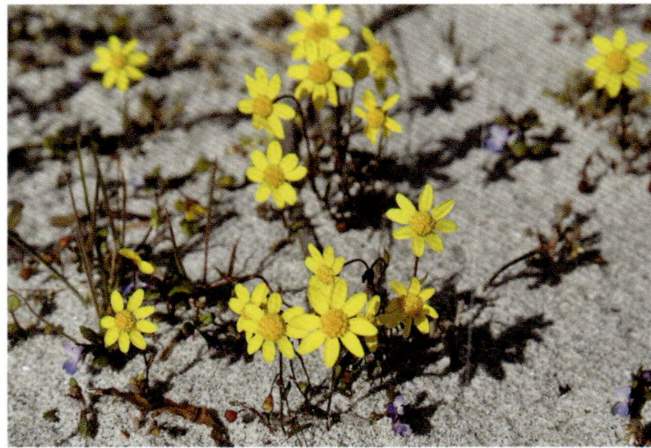

Juan de Fuca Marine Trail

Wind in and out of lush forests onto beautiful beaches along this incredible stretch of western shoreline

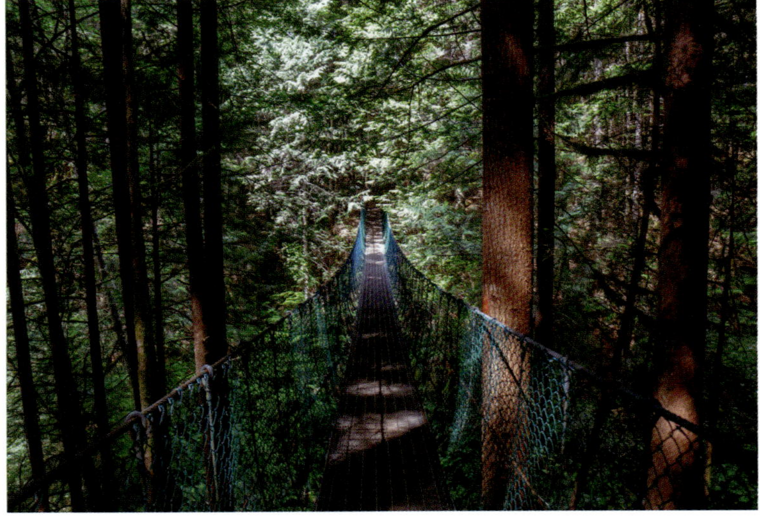

What Makes This Hot Spot Hot?

- Enjoy ample marine wildlife viewing opportunities along this rugged coast.
- Experience the full 47-kilometre wilderness trek or choose to explore sections from one of several access points.
- Dazzling waterfalls spill out onto the beaches at several points throughout the park.

Address: Juan de Fuca Provincial Park, BC
Tel.: (1-800) 689-9025
Website:

BC Parks

GPS Coordinates
Latitude: 48.43795
Longitude: −124.09291

Open year-round

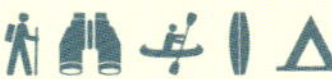

If you're considering hiking the West Coast Trail or the even more challenging North Coast Trail but are hesitant to make the jump, the Juan de Fuca Marine Trail is a great way to test your backpacking prowess on a shorter, more manageable marine trail adventure.

That isn't to say it's an easy through-hike by any means, and it still requires significant careful planning to ensure a safe and successful journey. Expect quite difficult sections on this 47-kilometre route, which takes you on a foggy, muddy, rooty and, of course, breathtaking adventure along the western shoreline of southern Vancouver Island. The entire trail is usually hiked in three to five days and can be travelled in either direction. In 2022, new trail facilities were added to the park, including bridges, boardwalks, stairs and ladders.

The trail can be explored in smaller segments as well, as there are four trailheads that allow easier in-and-out access: China Beach, Sombrio Beach, Parkinson Creek and Botanical Beach. Keep in mind that

◄ **Well-constructed suspension bridges help make this challenging trail more manageable.**

although Sombrio is a spectacular and expansive beach, its ease of access, combined with great surfing opportunities, means that it can be extremely busy. If you're looking for a quiet place to recuperate after a long day of hiking, this may not be the place to set up camp, especially on weekends during the summer months. Sombrio is still well worth a thorough exploration though: driftwood provides places to stop and rest, and waterfalls break through the forest, their waters snaking their way across the cobble beach to meet the ocean.

Plan your trip around tide times and weather to ensure easy access along the beach sections of the trail, as some areas become cut off during high tides and storms. Orange balls indicate safe exits from the beach back to the trail. Regularly scan the ocean as there are chances to see humpbacks, orcas and grey whales along the way. Watch for bears browsing along the shoreline, where seals and sea lions might also make an appearance. Regardless of

which direction you hike in, plan ahead and leave time to explore the phenomenal tidepools at Botanical Beach, at the northwest end of the trail.

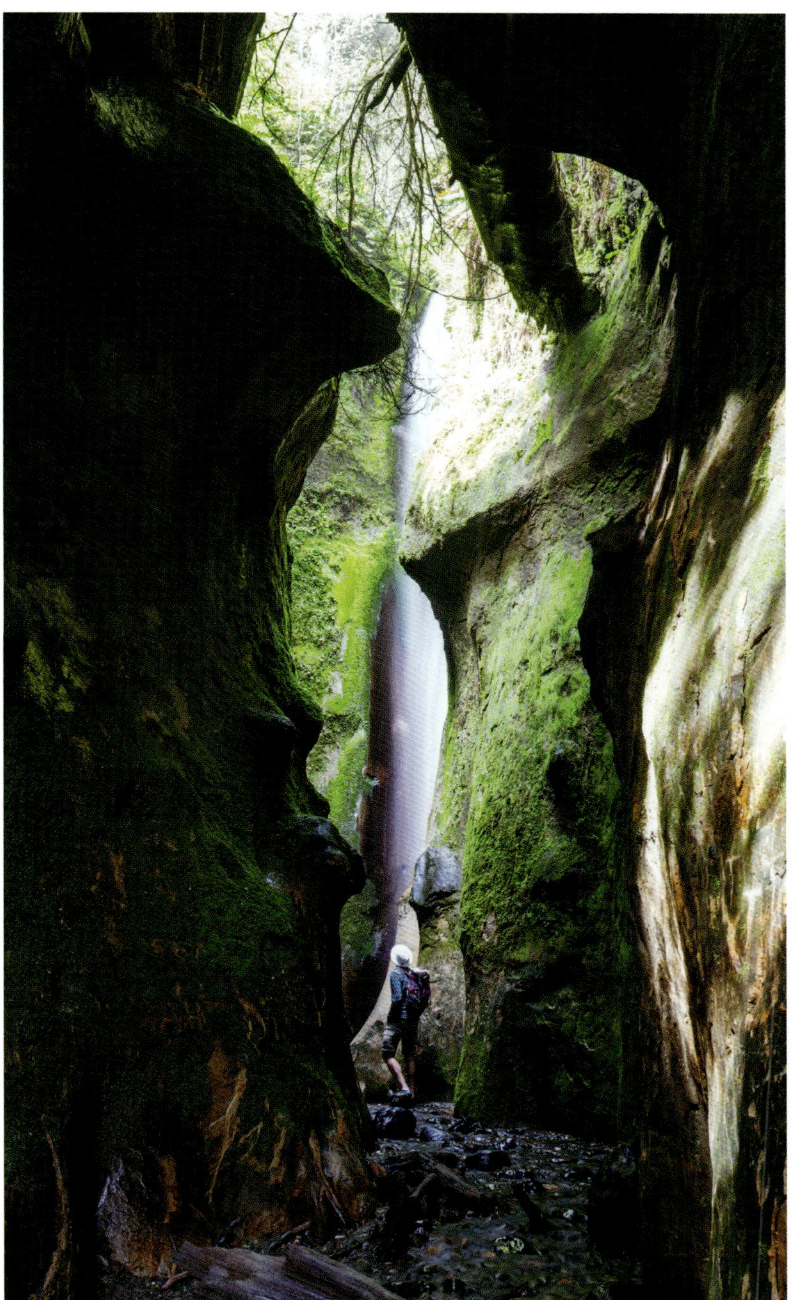

↑ **The very popular Hidden Waterfall can be found deep in a narrow slot canyon along Sombrio Beach.**

Little Qualicum Falls Provincial Park

Rugged rocks and a raging river are the main attractions of this beautiful provincial park

What Makes This Hot Spot Hot?

- This is an easily accessed park on central Vancouver Island, just off the highway.
- The upper and lower falls are viewable from trails and lookouts.
- Orchids can be found blooming in the spring.

Address: 4001 Alberni Hwy (Hwy 4), Qualicum Beach, BC
Tel.: (250) 474-1336
Website:

BC Parks

GPS Coordinates
Latitude: 49.3083
Longitude: −124.54241

Open year-round for day use but only May to September for camping

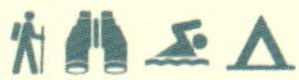

♿ (Check ahead)

Brilliant turquoise water rushes through the narrow canyons of Little Qualicum Falls Provincial Park, which is found off the Alberni Highway (Highway 4). Many of the cliffs are straight drops down to the water. Although strained and twisted trees grasp at the cliff rocks and soil to stop from toppling into the water, many have found their way into the torrents below, as evidenced by the large logs lying across the narrow gorges throughout the park.

The upper falls of the park have cut through rock, creating a tandem drop before the waters continue to spiral down the river in a hurried descent to the ocean, though not before crashing through another set of impressive falls. Bridges traverse the water to allow for views on either side of the river.

Keep your eyes out for the American dipper, a uniquely aquatic songbird that does not seem to mind the roar of the water as it bobs in and out of the torrents. These birds, with their nearly uniform grey plumage accented by their blinking white eye-lids, walk along the river bottom searching for aquatic insects to eat. Dippers use the dramatic cliff faces for their nest sites, raising their broods high up on the rocks to escape predators and floods.

Winter and spring are the best times to view the falls because of the greater flow of water along the river. Planning your trip in the spring will also give you the added bonus of orchid blooms. There are many types of orchids along the forest trails surrounding the falls for those looking carefully. The calypso orchid, a single pale-purple flower with a delicate spotted lip, is rare across the province but locally common in this part of Vancouver Island. The western coralroot, another orchid, can develop up to

40 flowers on a single stalk shooting up from coral-like rhizomes. With no green photosynthesizing leaves, it instead saps its energy from fungi. In a complex and secretive underground waltz, fungi receive minerals and carbon symbiotically from tree roots and are themselves parasitized by the orchid.

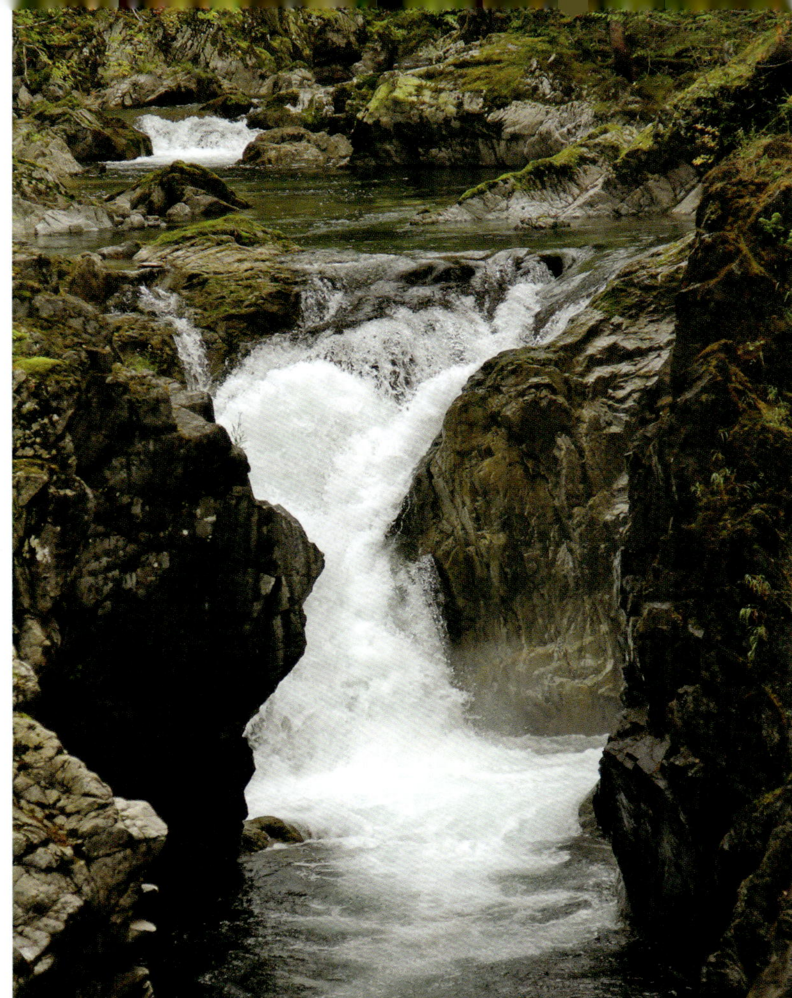

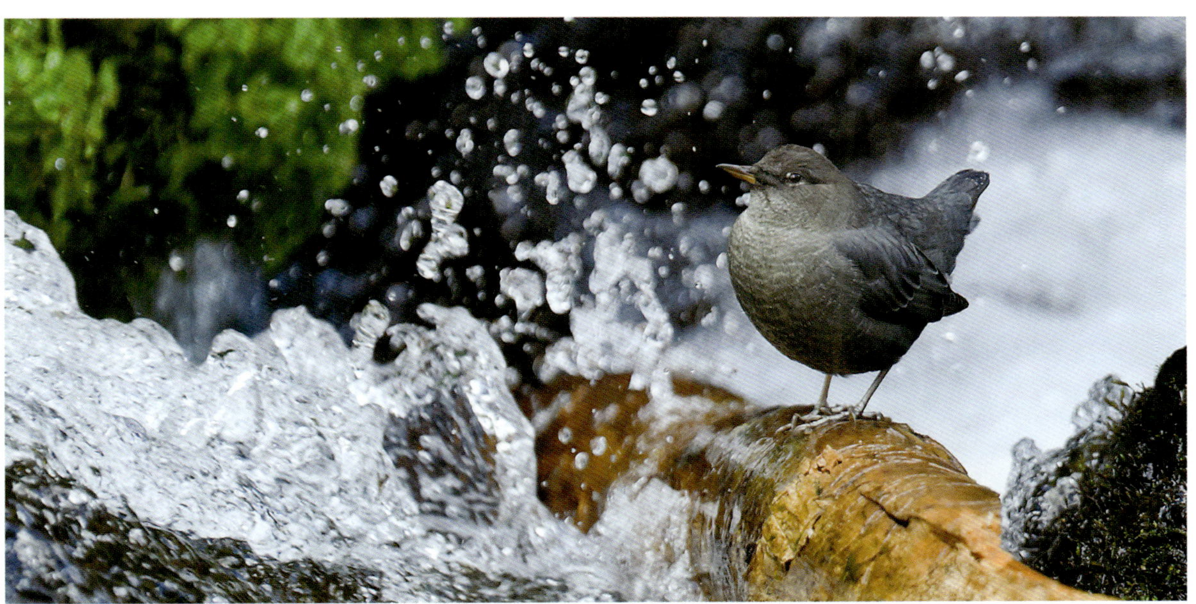

Long Beach

This long, sandy beach may have you exploring the seashore for days

What Makes This Hot Spot Hot?

- Peering into tidepools reveals sea stars, anemones and other interesting intertidal organisms.
- Migrating grey whales are frequently sighted in the spring on their way north from Mexico.
- Trails through the forest behind the beach offer interpretive signs and glimpses of the ocean between large trees.

Address: Pacific Rim National Park Reserve, 485 Wick Road, Ucluelet, BC
Tel.: (250) 726-3500
Website:

Parks Canada

GPS Coordinates
Latitude: 49.06758
Longitude: –125.74935

Open year-round

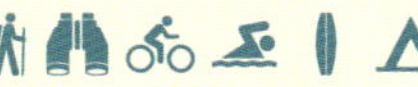

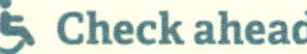

♿ Check ahead

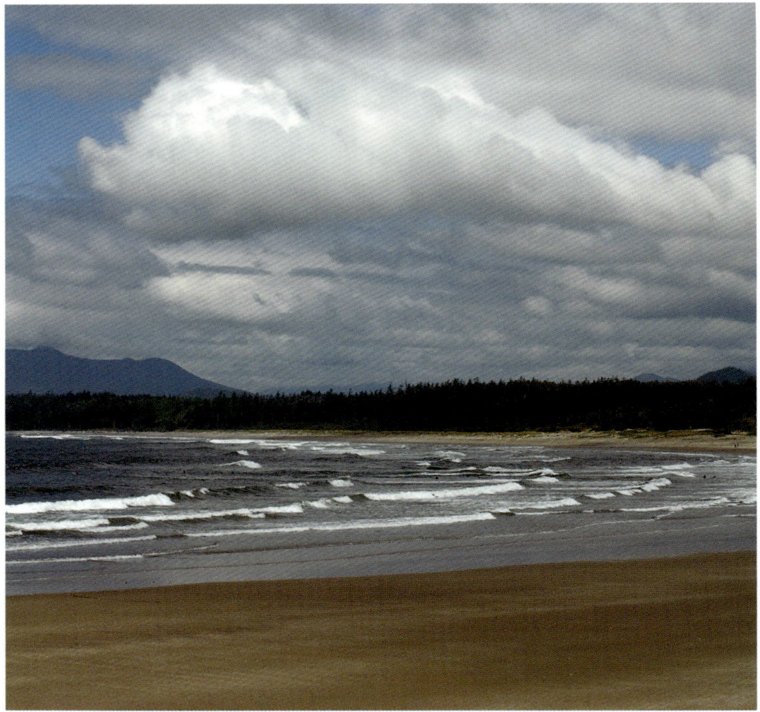

Surfers are a common sight amid the waves at Long Beach.

This long, sandy beach, spanning 16 kilometres along the west coast of Vancouver Island, is one of the earliest recorded surfing beaches in British Columbia. It is divided into three areas: Wikaninnish, Combers and Incinerator Rock. The seashore and surrounding forests offer many opportunities for exploration by naturalists.

From Combers Beach you can view Sea Lion Rock, a nesting haven for seabirds and a popular area for sea lions to hang out. If you are particularly interested in birds, loiter in the estuary at Combers Beach, where the river leaves the forest and enters the ocean. A mixture of salt and fresh water creates a nutrient-rich habitat, attracting birds. Trumpeter swans are known to frequent this area.

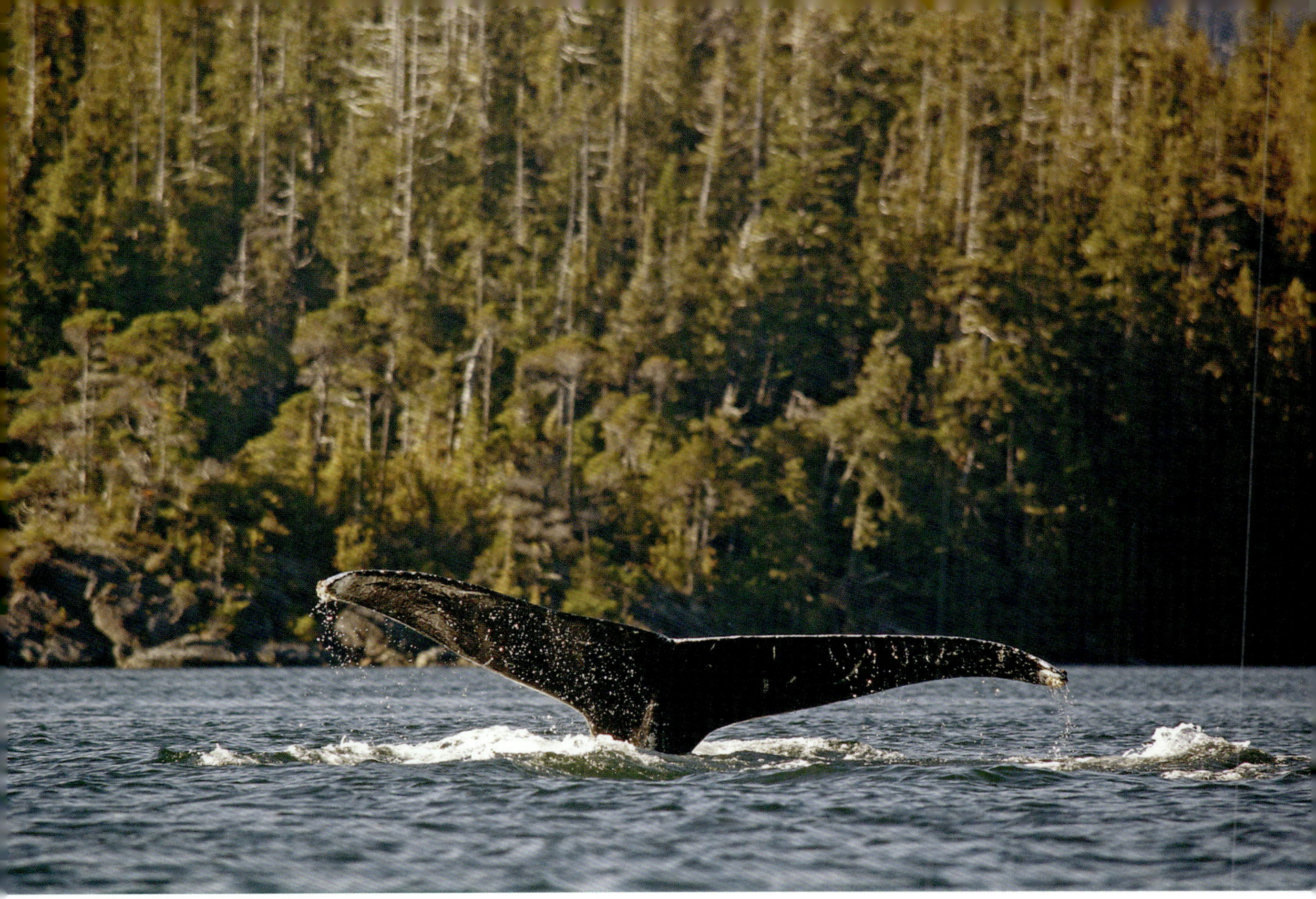

Migrating grey whales return from Mexico to the Pacific Northwest in the spring; stroll the beach in March for the best chance to see one. Other cetaceans you may spot include humpback whales, orcas and a variety of porpoises.

Hollows in rocky outcroppings create sanctuaries at low tide for sea stars, anemones and the occasional small fish. Safe from marine predators, these critters are trapped in these small tidepools until the ocean rises again to cover them. Organisms that have adapted to live in tidepools are unique and hardy. They must be able to survive a wide range of temperatures and adjust to lowered oxygen levels as the sun heats the water and animals in the pools produce waste.

On Wick Road, at the southern end of the beach, you will find the Kwisitis Visitor Centre. Interpretive displays provide information about the natural history of the area and the Nuu-chah-nulth First Nations. From here, access trails through the forest, which can provide a welcome respite from a hot day on the beach. You may see signs warning of dangerous riptides in the area, so swimming is not recommended in many places along this beach.

↑ Humpback whales are frequently sighted from shore and sea.

↓ Sea stars, like this ochre sea star, feed on barnacles and mussels.

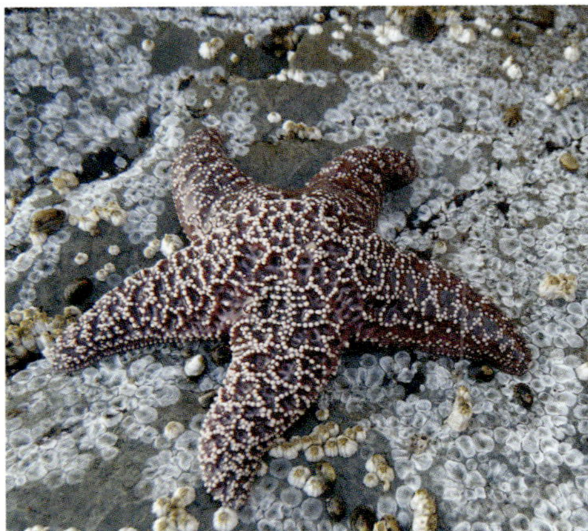

Lotus Pinnatus Park

This urban park is home to one of BC's rarest wildflowers

What Makes This Hot Spot Hot?

- Wildflowers completely blanket the open areas of this park in the spring.
- Trails take you into the forest where even more wildflowers can be found poking through the understory.
- This park is one of only a handful of sites where meadow bird's-foot trefoil can be found in the province.

Address: 100 Lotus Pinnatus Drive, Nanaimo, BC (cut off from vehicle access, park at Harewood Mines Road)
Tel.: (250) 756-5200
Website:

City of Nanaimo

GPS Coordinates
Latitude: 49.13934
Longitude: −123.96043

Open year-round; April to June for wildflowers

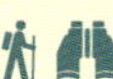

A destination to visit throughout the spring and early summer, Lotus Pinnatus Park displays wave after wave of wildflower blooms. Common camas, shortspur sea blush and seep monkeyflower blanket the sunny open meadows of the park, but the forested paths prove to be fruitful for botanizing as well.

The park is named after an extremely rare wildflower in the pea family, meadow bird's-foot trefoil, which was formerly named *Lotus pinnatus*. The plant has since been renamed *Hosackia pinnata* and is no longer considered to be in the genus *Lotus*. This red-listed species is found in only a few locations in BC, all of which are in and around Nanaimo. Look for its beautiful yellow and white flowers in moist depressions at clearing edges from May to June.

One-flowered broomrape emerges from the soil with a single delicate flower at the end of each stalk but produces no leaves whatsoever. This parasitic specialist has no need for photosynthesizing, instead feeding on the root systems

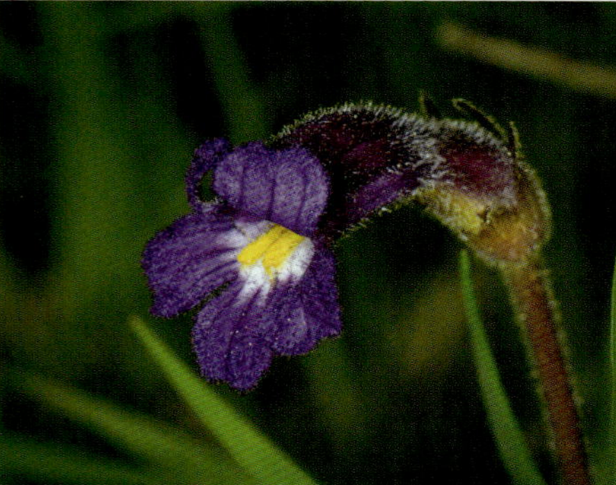

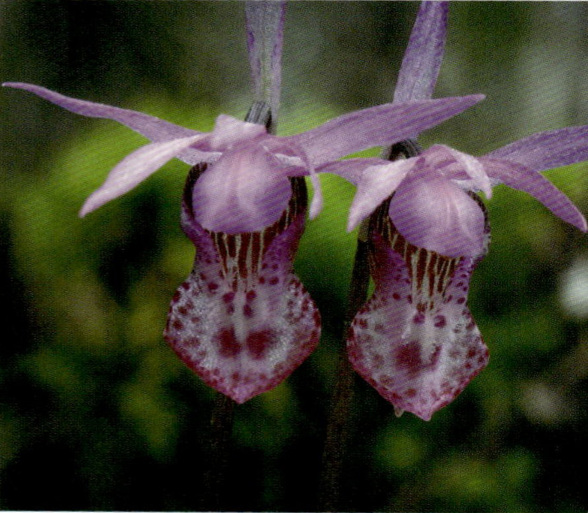

of nearby plants. Spotted coralroot orchid is another parasitic species found in Lotus Pinnatus Park, sapping energy from the mycelia of nearby fungi instead of plants.

Once in the forest, keep an eye out for large numbers of western fairy-slippers blooming in the understory. Also known as calypso orchids,

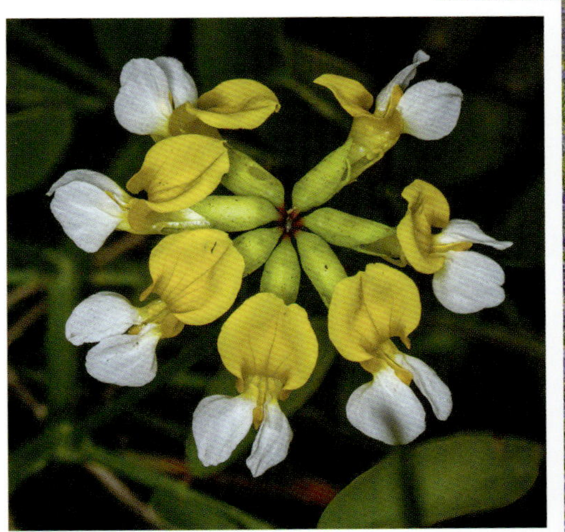

this plant tricks bees into a visit that provides them with little gain. Drawn in by false advertising, the bumble bee does the work of pollinating without any sweet reward, as the flower doesn't produce nectar. Their blooms are timed in the early spring to lure in new juvenile queen bees that haven't yet figured out these flowers aren't worth their time.

These and many other plants in the park are incredibly delicate and their root systems are easily damaged, so stay on the trail at all times. Without their showy flowers, many practically vanish from sight for the rest of the year, so time your visit in the spring to catch them during their short but exceptional flowering spectacle.

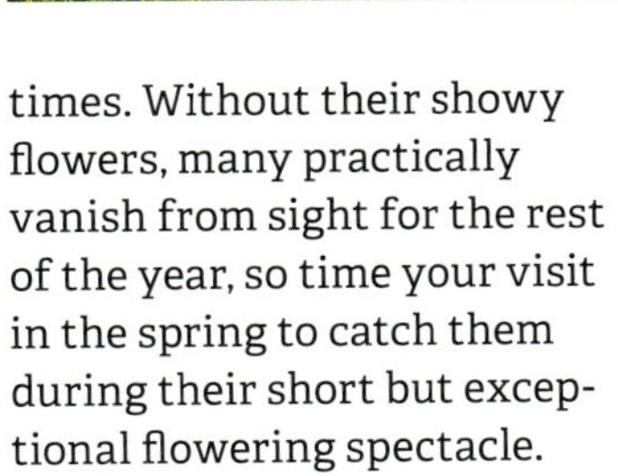

↑ Visit in the spring to experience the incredible wildflower blooms that blanket the open meadows of this park.

Lower and Upper Myra Falls

Beautiful falls within an unusual provincial park that contains a working mine

What Makes This Hot Spot Hot?

- Have a picnic beside the turquoise pools and impressive tiers of Lower Myra Falls.
- Hike through sections of old-growth forest to reach Upper Myra Falls.
- The juxtaposition of wilderness adventure and resource extraction serves as a reminder of our collective impact on the surrounding environment.

Address: Westmin Road, Strathcona-Westmin Provincial Park, BC
Tel.: (1-800) 689-9025
Website:

BC Parks

GPS Coordinates
Latitude: 49.57712
Longitude: −125.56534

Open year-round

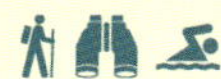

Lower and Upper Myra Falls are often referred to as being within Strathcona Provincial Park, but these trails actually fall within the dramatically distinctive Strathcona-Westmin Provincial Park. This portion was separated from the rest of Strathcona Park in the 1960s in order to create a Class-B park, which has significantly looser guidelines on what development and non-recreational activities are permitted.

The trail to the Lower Myra Falls, which is found near the south end of Buttle Lake is an easy 1-kilometre stroll. Bring a picnic and lounge on the basalt and limestone rocks as the clear waters of this tiered waterfall swirl by through turquoise pools before quickly emptying into Buttle Lake far below. The forest surrounding Buttle Lake was cut and the lake flooded when the Strathcona Dam was built on nearby Upper Campbell Lake in the 1950s. Giant weathered and waterlogged stumps rise up from mudflats along the shorelines of the lake when the water level is low, a reminder of the ecosystem that once existed there.

The stark difference in park classification is glaring once you attempt to access the Upper Myra Falls trailhead, as it requires you to drive through the middle of a large active mine. This mine produces over a million tonnes of ore annually, which contains zinc, copper, gold and silver. Alarmingly vibrant settlement ponds are visible alongside the main road that cuts through the mine, giving you a glimpse of the by-products of the industrial processes at work. Drive slowly and obey all signage for safe access through the site.

The Upper Myra Falls trail takes you past large moss- and fern-covered boulders settled within an old-growth forest, which is dominated by redcedar, Douglas-fir, Western hemlock and grand fir. After about 3 kilometres of moderately difficult hiking, you'll be rewarded with a view of these steep falls nestled in a densely forested canyon.

This juxtaposition of backcountry access and serene

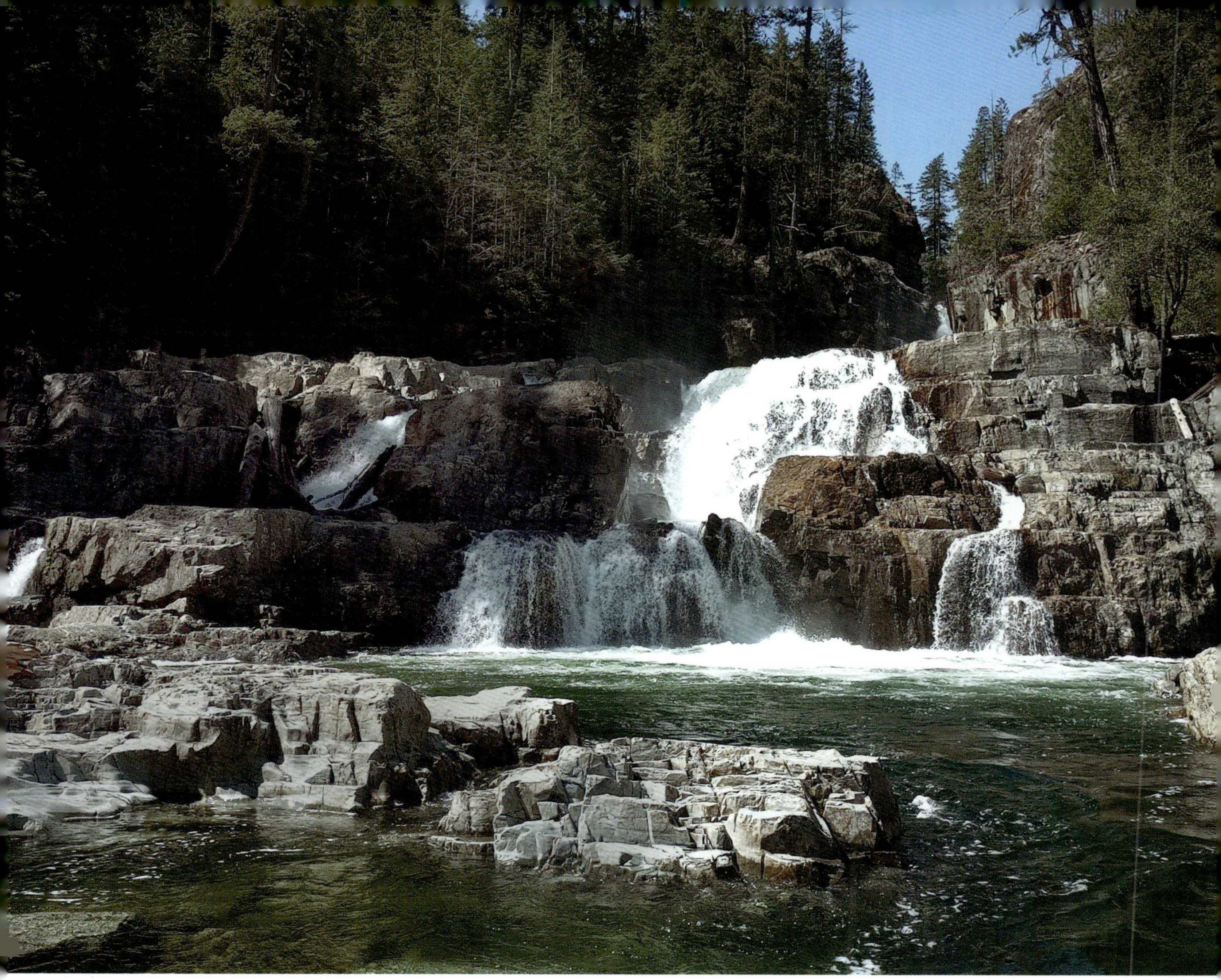

↑ **Lower Myra Falls cascade down many tiers into colourful and remarkably clear pools before continuing to flow into Buttle Lake far below.**

→ **The Upper Myra Falls trail brings you across beautiful streams through lush forest before reaching the final view of the falls.**

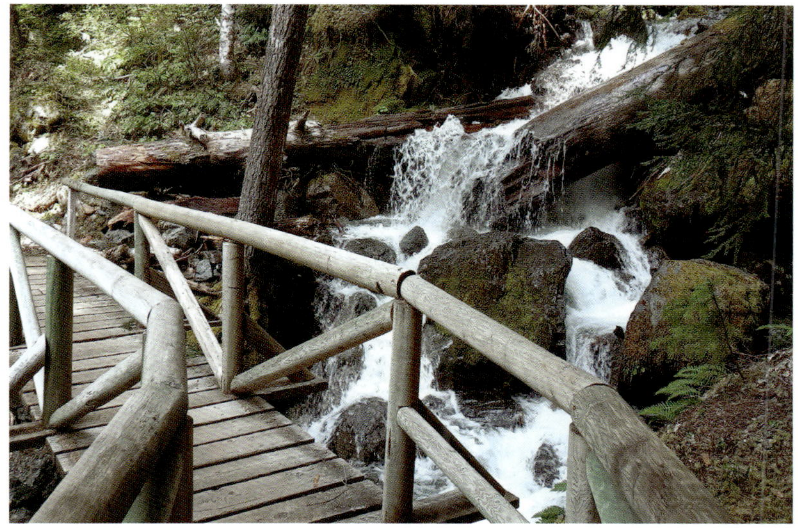

waterfalls against large-scale resource extraction should serve as a dramatic reminder of the often-invisible impact our daily lives have on the environment, both locally and around the globe.

Manzanita Bluffs

Enjoy this nature hot spot as part of a rewarding day hike or as just one stop on an incredible 180-kilometre trek across the upper Sunshine Coast

What Makes This Hot Spot Hot?

- The bluffs offer incredible views of Savary Island, Vancouver Island and the Salish Sea.
- Songbirds flit around between the flaking, twisted branches of manzanita and arbutus.
- Experience this trail as a day hike or just one of many stops along the Sunshine Coast Trail.

Address: Malaspina Road access point, Powell River, BC
Tel.: N/A
Website:

Sunshine Coast Trail

GPS Coordinates
Latitude: 49.97329
Longitude: −124.70973

Open year-round

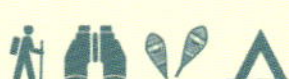

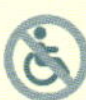

↗ **The flowers of the appropriately named sugarstick poke up through the forest floor early and mid-summer.**

The Sunshine Coast Trail exists thanks to an amazing team of outdoor enthusiasts who banded together to link some of the most beautiful nature areas across the Sunshine Coast. They formed the non-profit Powell River Parks and Wilderness Society, and their efforts resulted in a 180-kilometre long hiking trail. It travels through the traditional territory of the Tla'amin and shíshálh Nations, spanning the entire upper portion of the Sunshine Coast, from the mouth of Desolation Sound to Saltery Bay.

The full length of the immaculately maintained trail system can be conquered over a 10-to-14-day journey by experienced backpackers. There are also great day trip opportunities, with access points throughout the trail system that allow these beautiful nature areas to be visited in bite-sized chunks instead.

If accessing the Manzanita Bluffs as a day trip, the Malaspina Road access is a great starting point, as is the Sarah Point Road entrance

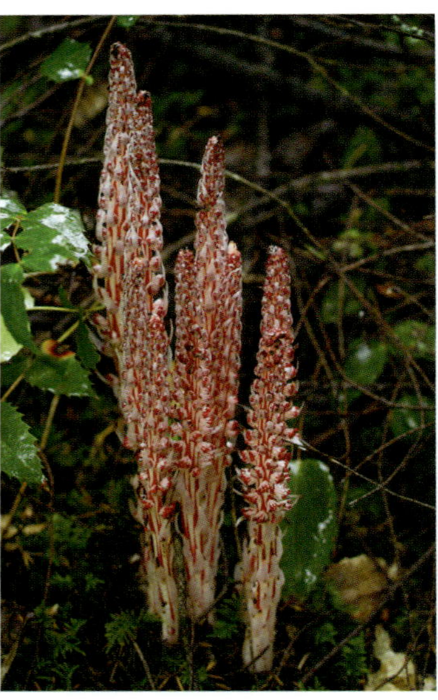

for a slightly shorter journey. Along this stretch you'll move through several distinct ecosystems. About a third of the way, a bench invites you to take a break and enjoy the view over Okeover Inlet before continuing to gain elevation in your hike. Mosses and lichens blanket the exposed rocky hillsides along this section. Be on the lookout for the many beautiful but fleeting flowers that briefly bloom along the trail, including sugarstick, western starflower and Pacific coralroot.

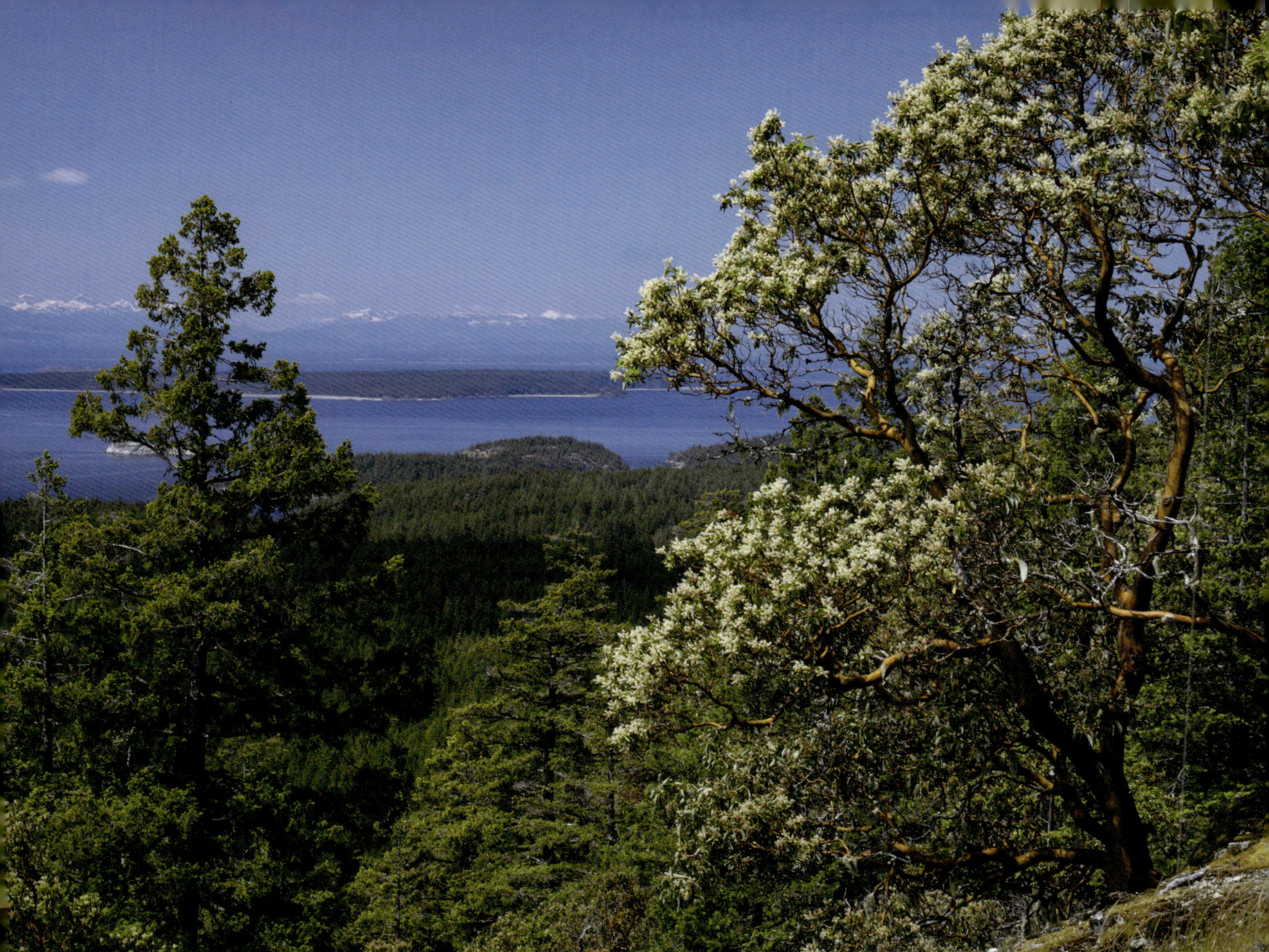

The Manzanita Bluffs look out over the Salish Sea with perfect views of Savary Island and the Copeland Islands, so sit and take in this incredible scenery from another perfectly placed bench. The namesake of this bluff, Columbia manzanita, is abundant at this elevation. This twisted evergreen shrub is a relative of the arbutus tree, evident in its smooth bark that flakes and peels over time. There's ample bird activity to keep you entertained, as western tanagers and other songbirds flit about the large arbutus and old-growth Douglas-fir that also grow along the bluffs.

For those planning to camp along the Sunshine Coast Trail, the first-come, first-served Manzanita Hut, one of many along the route, provides ample room for overnight stays and even preparing meals. It's highly recommended that you purchase a copy of the *Sunshine Coast Trail Guidebook* by R.E. Walz to gain access to a great depth of information about the trail and to support the amazing team that keeps this trail in incredible condition.

STRATHCONA PROVINCIAL PARK

Marble Meadows

Walk on an ancient ocean floor high in the mountains while searching for fossilized marine life beneath your feet

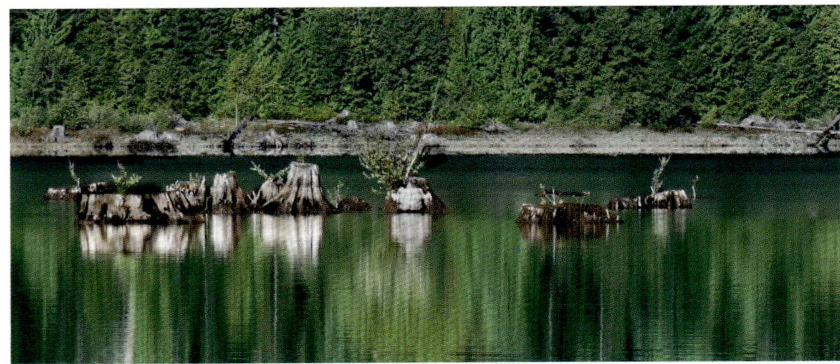

What Makes This Hot Spot Hot?

- The landscape is an ancient ocean floor of limestone embedded with fossils of crinoids and brachiopods.
- This alpine ecosystem has a diverse population of flowers and birds and panoramic views of Strathcona Provincial Park.
- Water has carved beautiful blue lakes and rolling hills into the karst landscape.

Address: 20 km south of Strathcona Park Lodge on Westmin Road, Comox-Strathcona, BC
Tel.: (1-844) 435-9453
Website:

BC Parks

GPS Coordinates
Latitude: 49.69407
Longitude: –125.63052

Open year-round

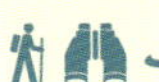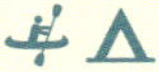

↗ **The waters of Buttle Lake cover stumps of cedar and Douglas-fir.**

The journey to Marble Meadows is a part of its magic. Paddling across Buttle Lake to access the Marble Meadows Trail, boaters float atop an old forest. The lake rose 30 metres in the mid-1950s when the Strathcona dam was built. The forest around the lake was logged prior to the damming, and the clear water covers giant stumps of cedar and Douglas-fir. When the water is lower the stumps line the shores. Marble Meadows is 1,300 meters above Buttle Lake, and the landscape between the two moves through old-growth forest, subalpine meadows, and is capped by water-carved limestone.

The limestone landscape of the meadows is dotted with a number of beautiful lakes. Next to Wheaton Lake sits the Wheaton Hut where visitors may camp. Stunted trees and plants grow in shallow soil. On the western edge of the meadows, a blocky ridge connects two prominent peaks: Mount McBride and Morrison Spire. This ridge offers panoramic views of Strathcona Provincial Park, including the tallest mountain on Vancouver Island, the Golden Hinde. On the ridge, the yellow of cinquefoil, the white of matte saxifrage and the purple of western sweet vetch pop out in bunches amid blocky limestone.

Below the stunning scenery and between the alpine plants lie an abundance of 280-million-year-old fossils.

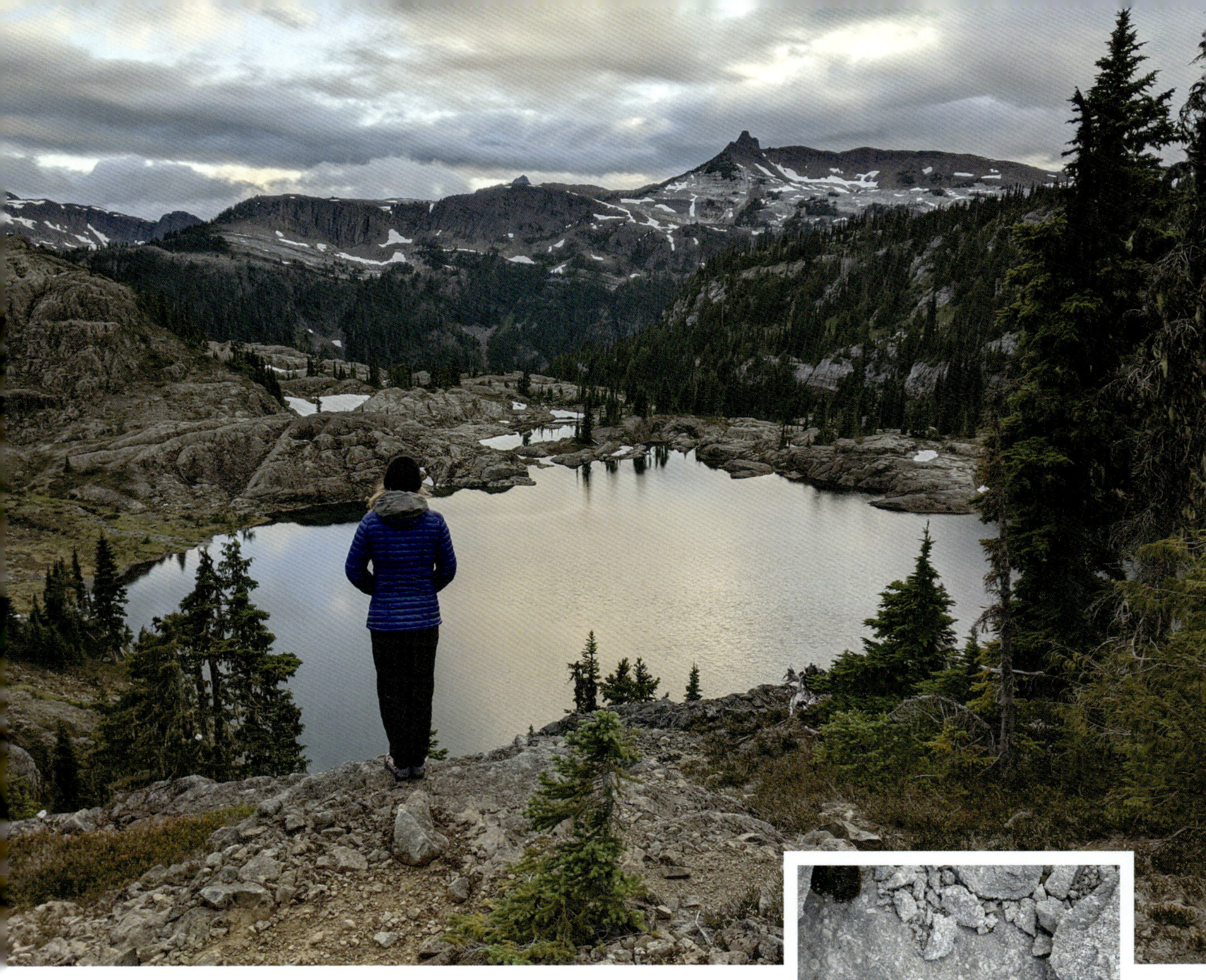

Following the strenuous hike up, it may be hard to believe that this was once an ocean floor but for the embedded crinoids, brachiopods and other marine creatures. Crinoids are by far the most abundant fossil found here and are a type of marine invertebrate in the same phylum as sea stars. They have stalk-like bodies that anchor onto rocks, with a holdfast and beautiful feather-like arms extending into the water, giving them their nickname "sea-lily."

Strathcona Provincial Park is home to many animals, including elk, cougars and a variety of birds, such as the white-tailed ptarmigan. Experienced hikers can continue on through more challenging terrain to other trails in the park or experience the meadows as an in-and-out hike.

From ancient ocean fossils to modern-day plants, birds and mammals, a visit to Marble Meadows is like a trip through time.

↑ **Crinoids and brachiopods from an ancient ocean are preserved as fossils in the limestone.**

↖ **Morrison Spire, as seen from Wheaton Lake.**

Mitlenatch Island Nature Provincial Park

A tiny island with an impressive breeding bird population in the Strait of Georgia

What Makes This Hot Spot Hot?

- Thousands of glaucous-winged gulls nest inside the boundaries of this 155-hectare park.
- Other seabirds, including pigeon guillemots, pelagic cormorants and black oyster-catchers, nest on the island.
- Harbour seals and California and Steller's sea lions haul up on the rocky shores.

Address: Mitlenatch Island, Strait of Georgia, BC
Tel.: N/A
Website:

BC Parks

GPS Coordinates
Latitude: 49.95075
Longitude: −125.00210

Open year-round

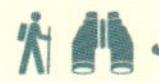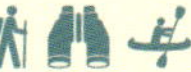

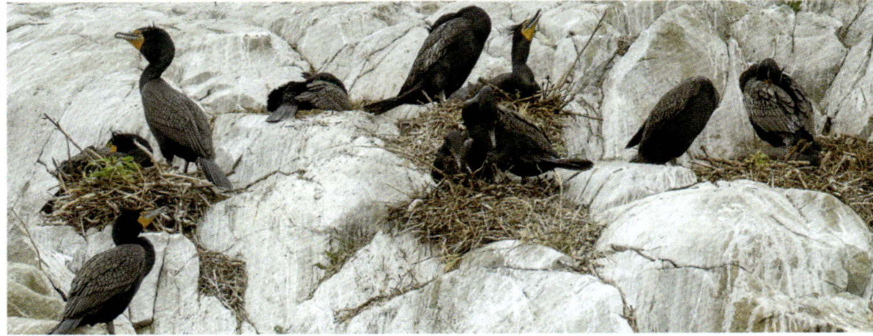

Accessible only by water, Mitlenatch Island Nature Provincial Park, home to the second-largest seabird-nesting colony in the entire Strait of Georgia, protects a very sensitive eco-system. The trip to the island requires careful planning — several groups offer chartered tours to visit the colonies — but the effort to experience this extraordinary island first-hand is well worth it.

Although most of the island is closed to the public to protect the sensitive nature of the place, you will not have trouble finding superb birding opportunities here. The park is seemingly overflowing with life, as massive breeding bird colonies return year after year. Thousands of pairs of glaucous-winged gulls nest on Mitlenatch Island. A bird blind provides a great opportunity for watching chicks inter-acting with their parents in June after they have hatched.

Pigeon guillemots breed on the island, their nests no more than a few chips of rocks or shells placed in crevices or under boulders or large pieces of driftwood. Seeing them come ashore is a special treat because it gives you an opportunity to admire their vibrant red feet.

Large numbers of cormo-rants nest right on the rocky

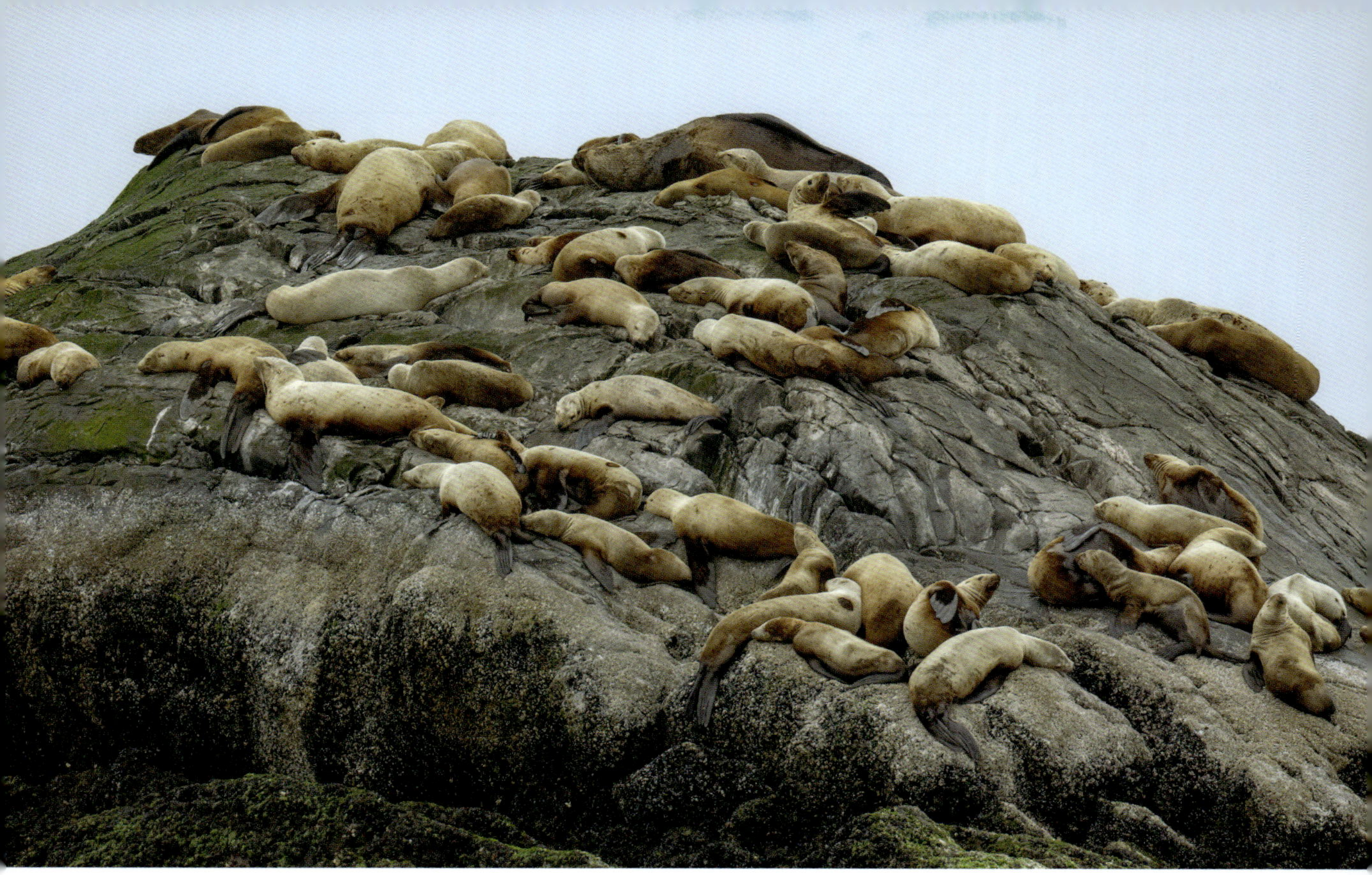

cliffs of the island, which become stained white with their guano over time. While double-crested cormorants take up the most real estate building their large, messy stick nests out on the rocks, the smaller pelagic cormorants choose to nest on the narrower, steeper ledges below. It is not exclusively marine bird species that nest on the island, though. Songbirds, northwestern crows and even a common raven pair have been seen nesting here.

In late April blooming wildflowers begin to blanket the island, including sea blush, chocolate lilies, common camas and even pricklypear cacti, which flower later in the summer. Garter snakes are often seen along the path that traverses the island. Watch for harbour seals, as well as both species of sea lion, California and Steller's, that like to drag themselves up on the rocky shores of the park. This area also becomes an important moulting site for harlequin ducks before moving on to their summer territories for breeding.

It is important that every visitor stays on the trail and respects the birds' comfort and space requirements so as not to disturb this island colony. Some species, like pelagic cormorants, are particularly sensitive to disturbance. Boaters and kayakers are asked to watch from a reasonable distance.

↑ **Steller's sea lions sun themselves up on the rocky shoreline.**

← **Double-crested cormorants build big messy nests in close quarters along the rocky cliffs of the island.**

↓ **A pigeon guillemot shows off its vibrant mouth while calling.**

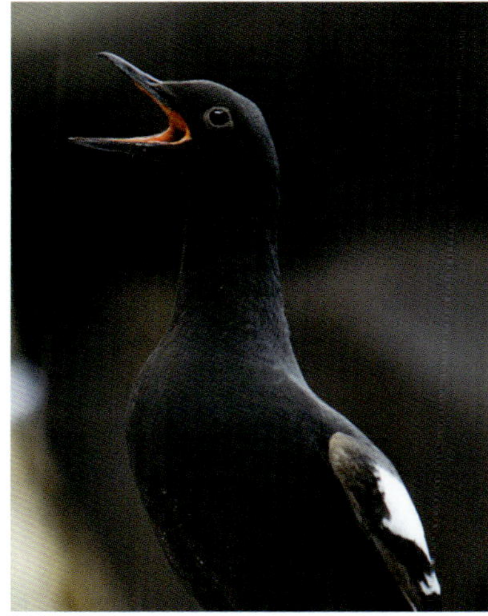

Mount Tzouhalem Ecological Reserve

Tread carefully when visiting one of the best examples of Garry oak meadows in BC

What Makes This Hot Spot Hot?

- An incredible variety of wildflowers paint the open meadow each spring.
- Gnarled Garry oak trees stand out against the backdrop of North Cowichan.
- This is one of the few places in BC where deltoid balsamroot grows.

Address: Mount Tzouhalem, North Cowichan, BC (note that Mount Tzouhalem was formalized as the preferred spelling by Cowichan Tribes)
Tel.: (1-800) 689-9025
Website:

BC Parks

GPS Coordinates
Latitude: 48.78877
Longitude: −123.63811

Open year-round, watch signage for trail closures

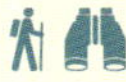

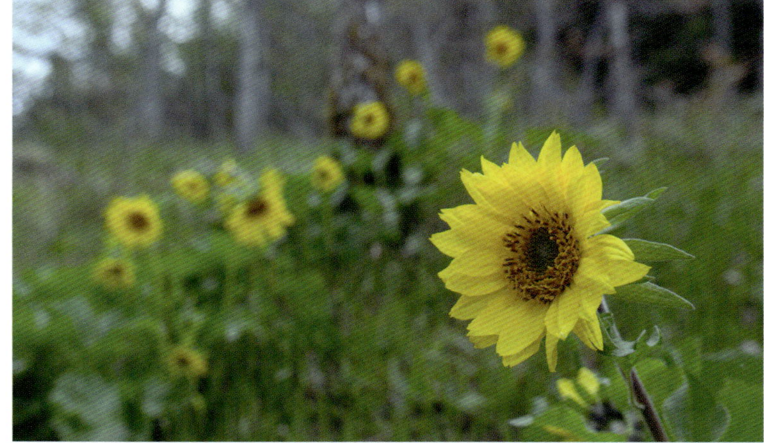

Mount Tzouhalem is a popular destination for hikers and mountain bikers who take advantage of the complex trail system and rocky plateau with views of Cowichan Bay and the Coast Mountains. But for those more interested in wildflower viewing than strenuous outdoor activity, the endangered Garry oak meadow protected within the nearby Mount Tzouhalem Ecological Reserve is an incredible place to visit.

Less than five per cent of the Garry oak ecosystems in Canada remain in a near-natural state, most having been largely cleared for human development or dramatically altered by invasive species. Protected areas like this reserve are exceedingly important as over 100 species at risk have been identified in these ecosystems.

Garry oak meadows such as this were once carefully managed and at times purposely burned by First Nations to maintain their incredible value as a source of food production, in particular to cultivate and harvest camas bulbs. Colonization caused a major rupture in this important relationship, and the meadows are now often left to grow into mixed transitional forests.

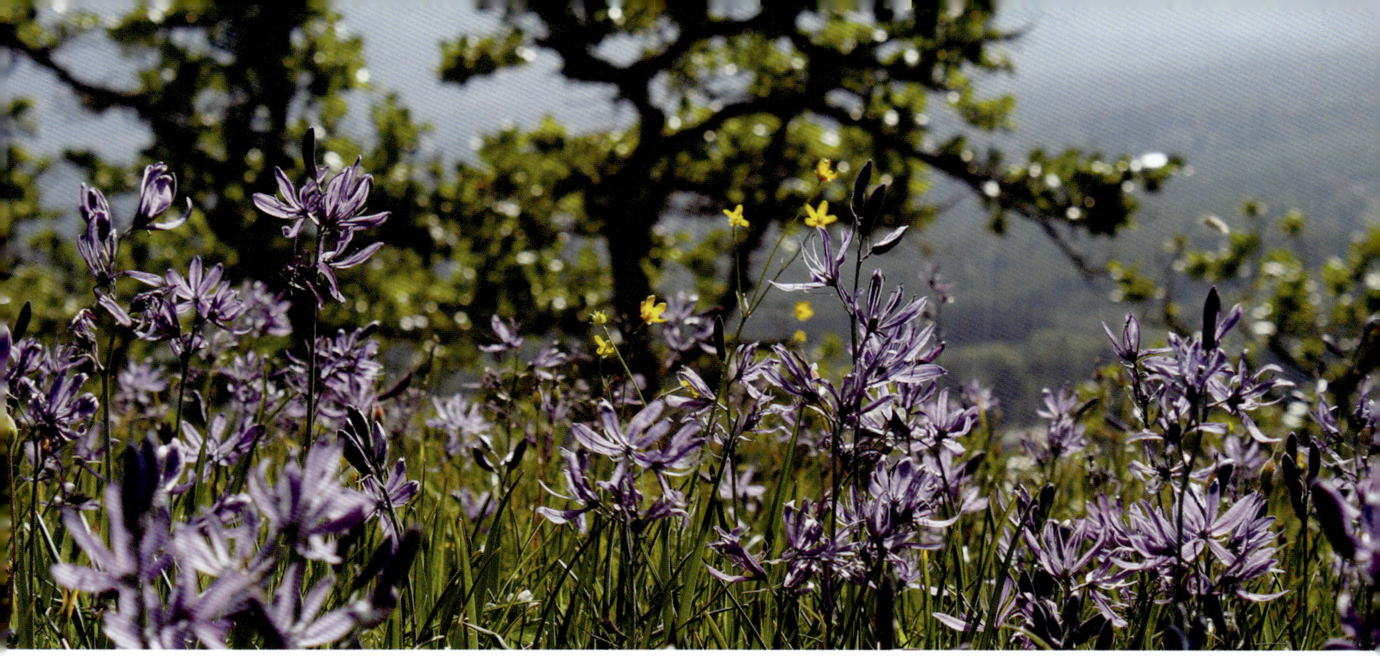

Between scattered oaks, this open meadow displays an incredible wildflower bloom each spring. Common camas, western buttercup and shortspur sea blush blanket the hillsides in blue-violet and pink hues. There are many other wildflowers to be on the lookout for, including spring gold, Henderson's shooting star and pockets of chocolate lilies. Meadow death camas grow throughout and, as the name suggests, are highly toxic to humans. Without the distinct flowers to separate them, the death camas bulbs are incredibly difficult to discern from the edible common camas — just another reason not to illegally harvest plants from this incredible ecosystem.

The park is also home to a rare wild sunflower that is only found at a handful of sites in Canada, all of which are on Vancouver Island. Visit on a sunny day in May to see the gorgeous oversized blooms of the red-listed deltoid balsamroot in full show. One cluster is conveniently located right beside the trail to stave off the temptation to trample through the meadow for a closer look.

Compared to a provincial park, the ecological reserve designation translates to a higher degree of protection. While Mount Tzouhalem Ecological Reserve remains open to the public for limited nature-viewing opportunities, keep in mind the existing trail may be relocated or closed at times to better protect this sensitive site. Pay attention to any subtle signage posted and ensure you only travel on clearly marked trails.

↑ Gnarled Garry oak trees become completely surrounded by vibrant blooms each spring.

← This ecological reserve is one of the few places in all of Canada to witness the big, showy flowers of deltoid balsamroot.

↓ Chocolate lilies grow in small clusters throughout the meadow, using their beautiful but foul smelling flowers to attract flies for pollination.

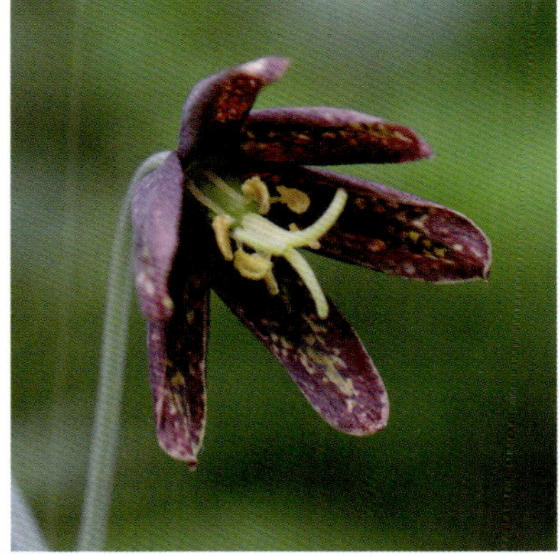

SMALL INLET MARINE PROVINCIAL PARK

Newton Lake Trail

Take a dip in one of Quadra Island's many gorgeous lakes at the end of a rewarding hike through Western hemlock forest

What Makes This Hot Spot Hot?

- The trail leads to a great swimming spot on the beautiful, blue Newton Lake.
- This area has a wonderful representative Western hemlock forest.
- A wide range of bird and mammal species can be seen on the trail and around the lake's edge.

Address: Small Inlet Marine Provincial Park, Granite Bay Road, Quadra Island, BC
Tel.: N/A
Website:

Quadra Island Trails

GPS Coordinates
Latitude: 50.23685
Longitude: –125.29042

Open year-round

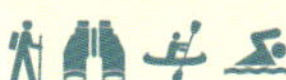

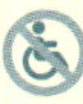

↗ **The clear blue waters of Newton Lake are picturesque.**

The Discovery Islands are a group of rugged, forested islands lodged between Vancouver Island and the Mainland, of which Quadra Island is one. Easily accessed by a 10-minute ferry ride from Campbell River, Quadra is home to some of the best lakes on the islands. Naturally, Quadra Island attracts many watersport enthusiasts, but there are abundant nature exploration opportunities by foot. The Newton Lake Trail is a great route for accessing these pleasant lakes without putting a paddle in the water.

Located on the northwest side of Quadra Island, the 878-hectare Small Inlet Marine Provincial Park is frequently used as an anchorage for long-distance boaters travelling along the coast to Alaska, but the park is also enjoyable when accessed from the land via a hiking trail from Granite Bay Road. Those looking for an even longer hike can continue past Newton Lake to eventually reach Small Inlet.

Although the start requires some surefootedness on jagged and uneven rocks, the trail eventually transitions to more manageable dirt and roots. Before arriving at Newton Lake, the trail passes a small marshy lake and through coastal Western hemlock forest. Western hemlock is one of the most shade tolerant trees of the Pacific coast. It also creates the densest canopy of all trees on the west coast, so understory growth is quite limited in these forests. As you travel along the gradually climbing trail, watch for Pacific banana slugs as they plod across the path looking for fallen leaves and other debris to eat. As the second-largest slug in the world, they should be hard to miss.

It is understandable why the cool, fresh waters of Newton Lake make for a popular swimming destination, especially after hiking a few kilometres on a sunny day. The lake reflects a deep green-blue hue, juxtaposed against lush green plant life that grows right to the water's edge. This swimming spot is a great place to look for red-breasted sapsuckers drilling holes in the bark of nearby trees. Sapsuckers have a specialized tongue that enables them to soak up the sap as it flows from the holes it creates. Several species of hummingbirds take advantage of sapsucker feeding holes; for example, the rufous hummingbird has been seen following sapsuckers around during the day.

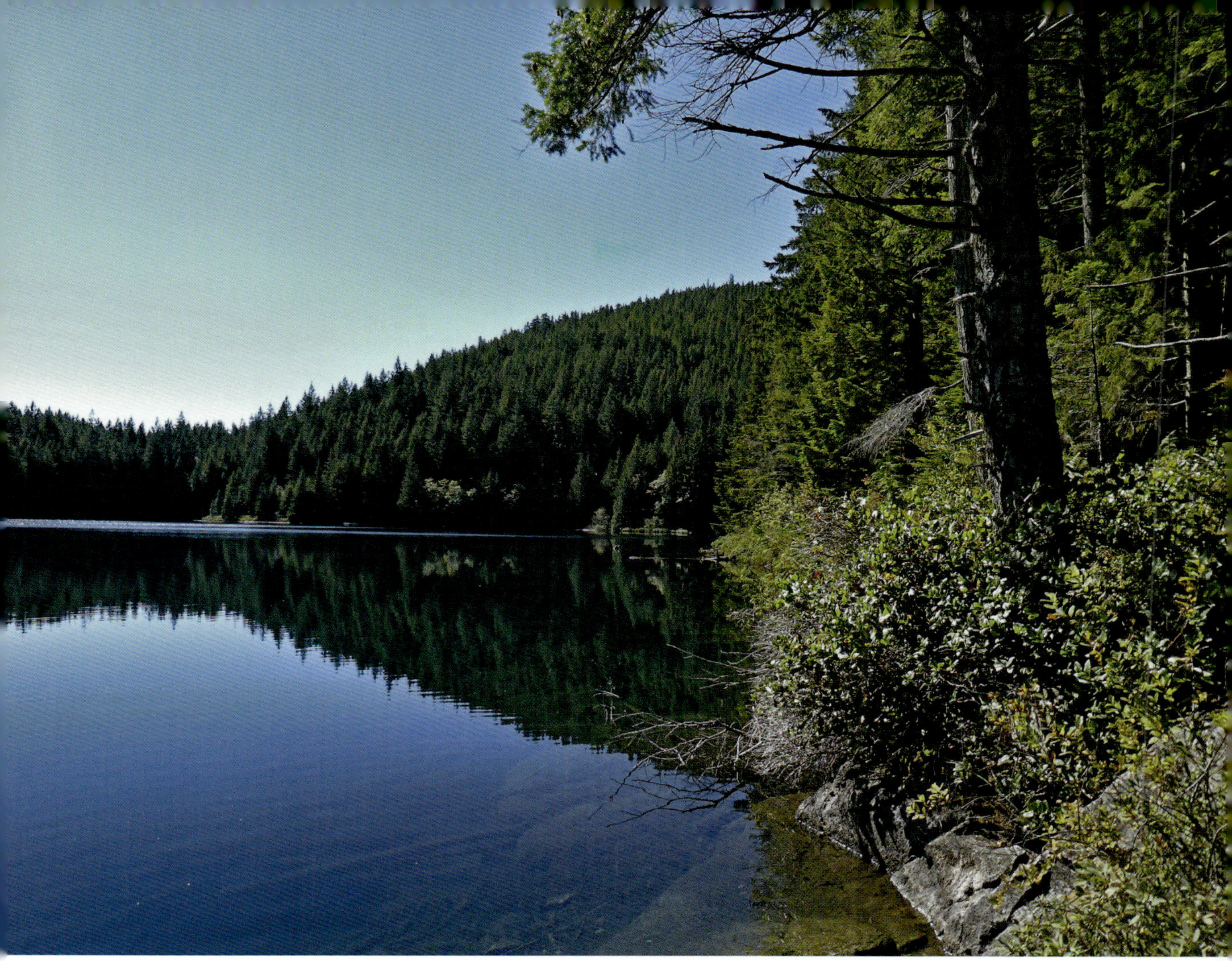

The best way to plan your hiking trip around Quadra Island is to pick up the detailed trail map published by the Quadra Island Trails Committee. This guide is available for purchase at various locations on Quadra, and proceeds from it support upkeep of Quadra's trails by local volunteers.

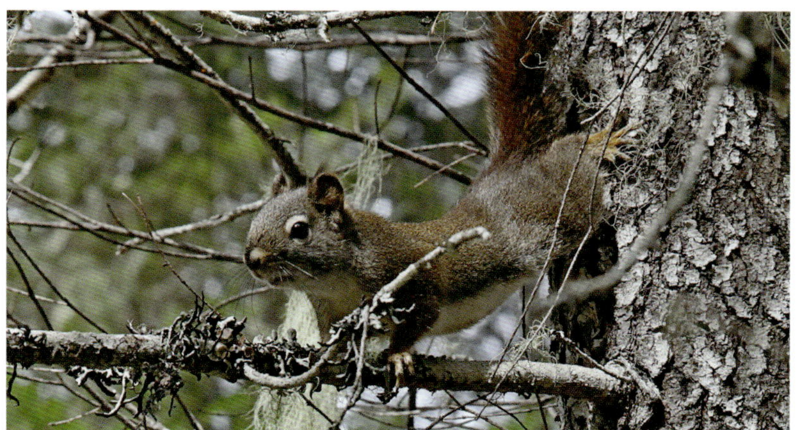

↑ **Spirited red squirrels scold forest intruders.**

Nootka Island

Where ocean and forest meet to form a stunning coastal landscape with a rich history

What Makes This Hot Spot Hot?

- Coastal wolves dig for clams in the intertidal zone, bridging marine and terrestrial ecosystems.
- A variety of migratory whales and porpoises surface off shore, and sea lions bask on rocks in the sunshine.
- Archaeological sites have been found showcasing thousands of years of Mowachaht history, including carvings and village sites.

Address: Nootka Island, BC
Tel.: N/A
Website:

MB Guiding

GPS Coordinates
Latitude: 49.59145
Longitude: −126.64810

Open year-round; usually hiked from June to September

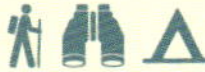

 ♿ **(Check ahead; some boat tours may have accessible options)**

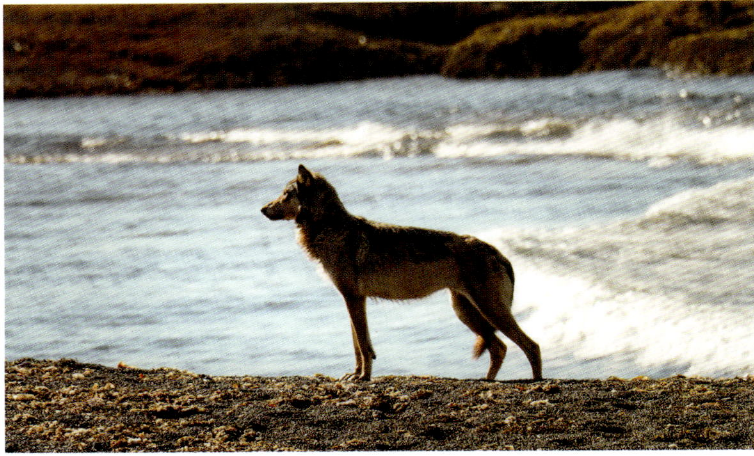

Humpback whales blow sprays of water against the horizon, colourful nudibranchs live in tidepools on the rocky shores, and coastal wolves roam the sandy beaches. Remote Nootka Island has one of the most beautiful coastal landscapes BC has to offer. It is often experienced by hiking the 34-kilometre Nootka Trail, which is rich in both natural and First Nations history.

The small village of Yuquot at the southern end of the island has been occupied by the Mowachaht people for over 4,300 years. Here, a church contains interpretive signs and carvings where visitors can learn about the history of the island. Farther west, at Bajo Point, are the remains of the seasonal fishing village E'as. This site has long been reclaimed by the forest, however amid the undergrowth, beneath Sitka spruce, sit three prominent depressions where buildings once stood. Fishing villages such as this are likely where coastal First Nations began whaling, and the whales in these waters are abundant.

During spring and summer the sprays of humpbacks, grey whales, orcas and porpoises project from the ocean surface as these marine mammals

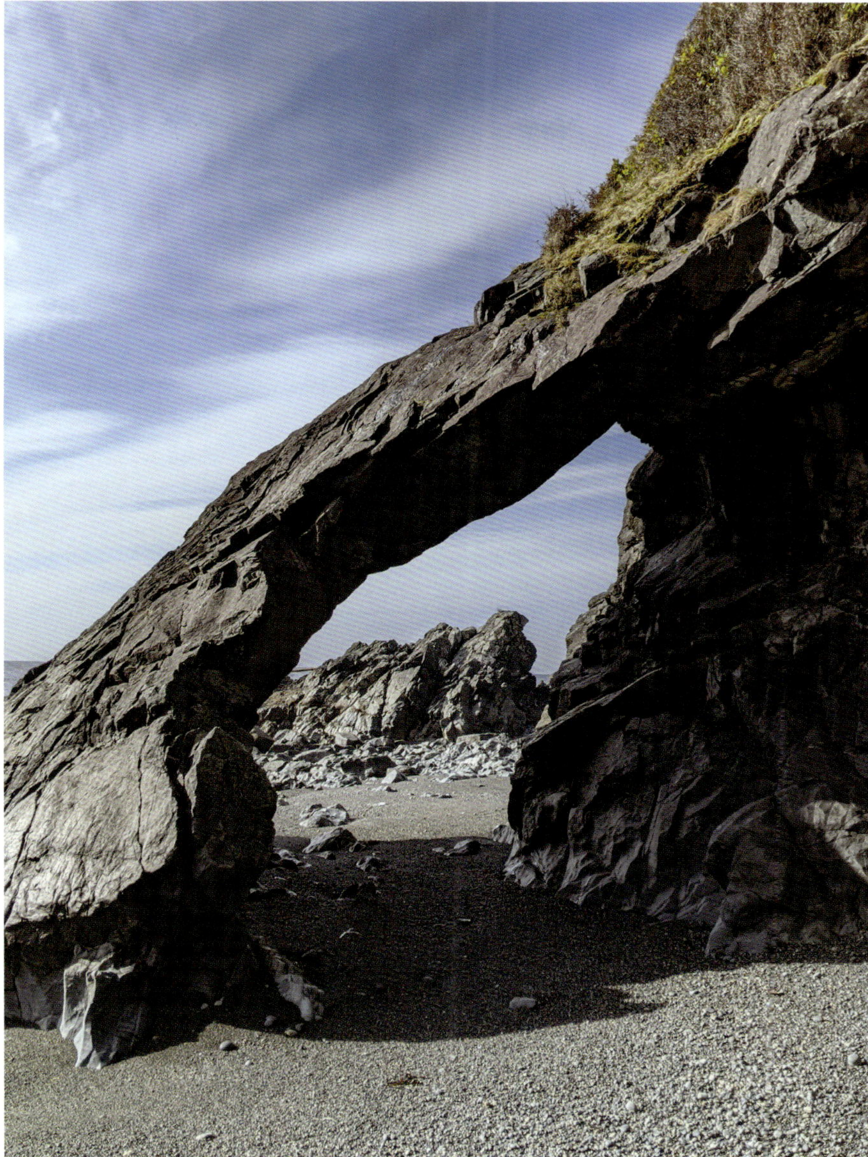

Unique rock formations can be found along the coastline.

Coastal wolves roam the beaches, leaving their footprints in the sand.

surface for a breath. Seals and sea lions are often visible sunning themselves on rocky points and swimming closer to shore. Binoculars are a recommended item on the Nootka Trail and are also helpful for spotting bald eagles soaring overhead and perching high in the trees.

There are also many terrestrial mammals around, including bears, cougars and coastal wolves. Wolf tracks are a common sight on the sandy beaches of Nootka Island, and lucky hikers may even see a wolf digging for clams or relaxing in the sun. Coastal wolves are genetically distinct from their inland relatives and bridge marine and terrestrial ecosystems by consuming salmon, barnacles and other sea creatures. About 85 per cent of the diet of a coastal wolf comes from the ocean.

Between the worlds of the whales and the wolves, another magical space exists. Tidepools and channels in the rocky shelves offer a delightful insight into the biodiversity of the Pacific. Limpets, crabs, chitons, anemones, sea stars and others make their homes in the area between the lowest low tide and highest high tide.

On Nootka Island it is easy to see that the forest and ocean are deeply intertwined and why it is critical that we protect both ecosystems in our changing world.

North Coast Trail

This coastal hiking trail wraps around the northern tip of Vancouver Island, transporting hikers through bogs and forests and along the ocean

What Makes This Hot Spot Hot?

- Inland, the trail travels through forests and bogs.
- Wildlife along the trail includes wolves and bears, which roam the beaches and leave tracks in the sand.
- Long portions of the trail are on beaches, making for potential whale sightings.

Address: Cape Scott Provincial Park, Cape Scott Park Road, 64 km west of Port Hardy, BC
Tel.: (1-844) 435-9453
Website:

BC Parks

GPS coordinates (west end of trail):
Latitude: 50.68438
Longitude: −128.26260

Open year-round

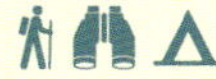

→ **The forests are home to many creatures, such as this fledgling northern saw-whet owl.**

In 1995 a strip of land running along the northern coast of Vancouver Island was added to Cape Scott Provincial Park. With this addition came a vision: a trail traversing the rugged coast along the tip of Vancouver Island. The North Coast Trail has hikers balancing on logs in bogs, whale watching from pebble beaches and searching for wolf tracks in the sand. Most hikers access Shushartie Bay by boat and hike the 60-kilometre trail east to west.

On the east, boardwalks traverse bogs — wetlands filled with peat moss. Look closely for the carnivorous sundew, which traps insects with a sticky secretion on red spikes. Labrador shrubs grow elongated green leaves with an orange fuzzy underside. The leaves can be made into a tea and the white flowers have been used medicinally by coastal First Nations. However, be wary: Labrador can be confused for a poisonous bog laurel growing nearby with more waxy green leaves.

Ducking in and out of the coastal rainforest, visitors have a unique chance to experience both the forest and the ocean on one trail. In the forest hikers scramble over the roots of magnificent redwood

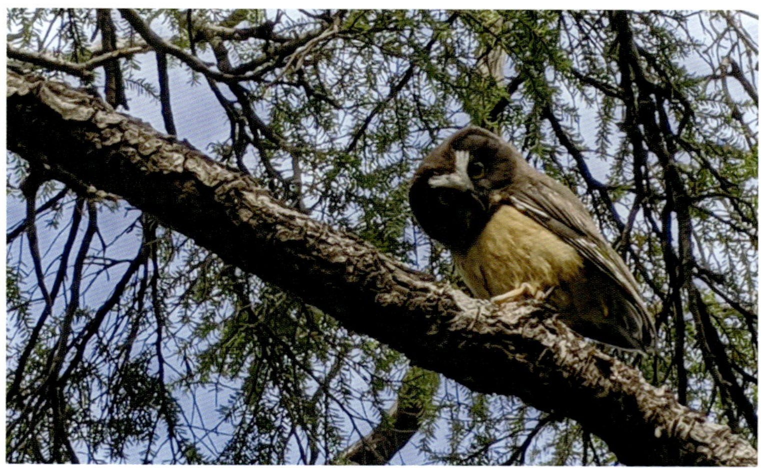

cedars and Sitka spruce. Cable cars whizz over river mouths, and out of the forest the open beaches make for excellent whale watching. Orcas and humpbacks are often sighted in this area. On the sandy beaches, tracks of bears and coastal wolves may be found. Bears meander the beaches flipping logs and searching piles of seaweed for crabs and insects to eat. Coastal wolves, genetically different from their relatives inland, dig for clams in the sand.

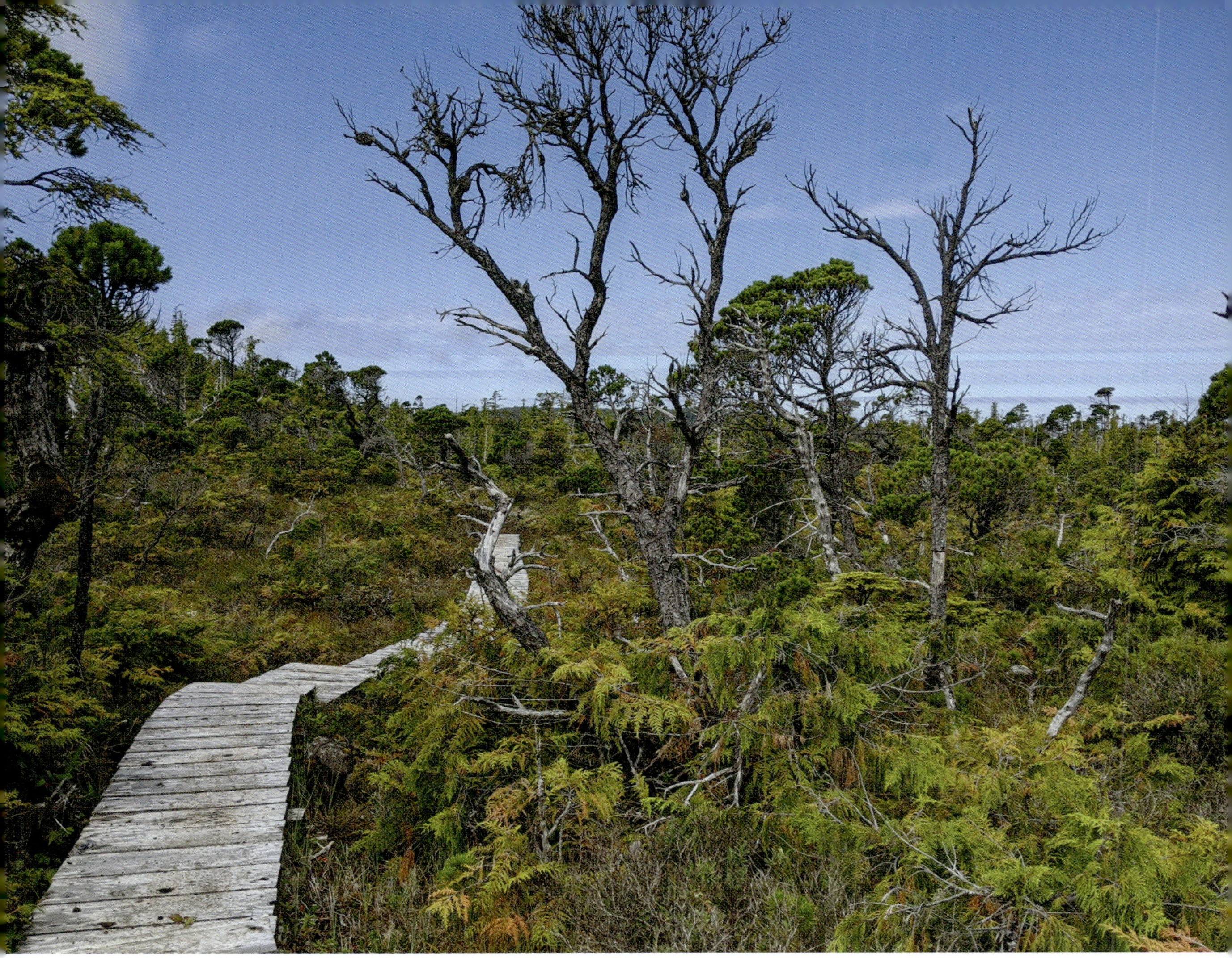

The brilliant blue water on some of the sandy beaches lends the landscape an almost tropical feel. A balanced and beautiful tour of the north island, this trail is a must-do for coastal hikers. An additional 10-kilometre detour to the Cape Scott Lighthouse takes hikers to the westernmost point on Vancouver Island and has two campsites nearby. For those wanting a taste of this trail without the 60-plus-kilometre commitment, San Josef Bay shares the same western trailhead in Cape Scott Provincial Park.

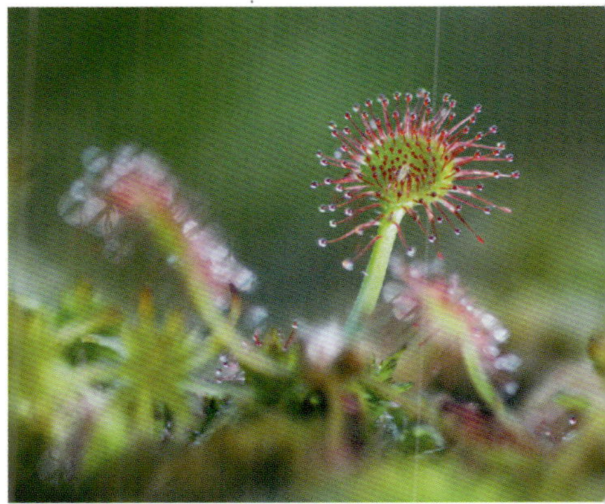

↑ **Sundew in the bogs lures and traps insects in its sticky secretions.**

↖ **Bogs along the trail host unique plants, such as labrador and bog laurel.**

Orford River in Bute Inlet

Watch grizzly bears feast on salmon while learning directly from the incredible stewards of this land

What Makes This Hot Spot Hot?

- Chum and coho salmon spawn in the Orford River, attracting a great diversity of wildlife.
- Grizzly bears journey annually to these waters to feed on the salmon and their eggs.
- Indigenous guides bring you to their traditional territory for an incredible wildlife and cultural immersion.

Address: Bute Inlet, BC (main access via Campbell River)
Tel.: (250) 923-0602
Website:

Homalco Tours

GPS coordinates
Latitude: 50.59528
Longitude: –124.86412

Open year-round; August to October for grizzly watching

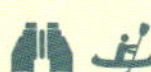

↗ **During the spawn, chum salmon develop a dark stripe that runs through calico streaking.**

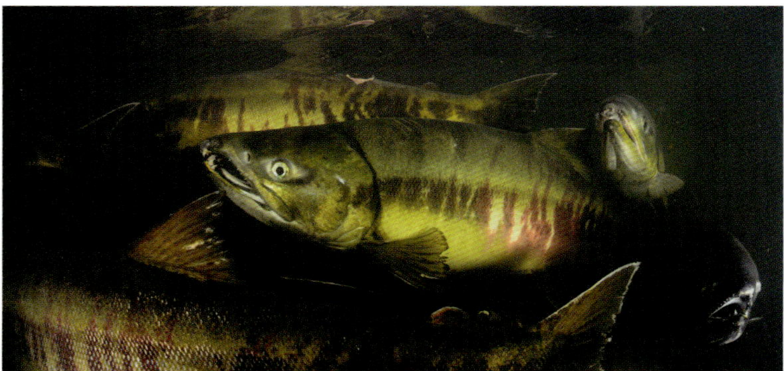

Beautiful Bute Inlet is an 80-kilometre-long fjord along British Columbia's coast, typically accessed from Campbell River on Vancouver Island. Mountains rise up from the inlet a towering 2,700 metres above sea level, making for a dramatic and breathtaking setting for phenomenal nature-viewing opportunities. The cold, glacier-fed waters of the Orford River drain into the inlet, creating a magnificent turquoise hue.

The land you will visit is the traditional territory of the Xwémalhkwu or Homalco First Nation, who have been the stewards of this land since time immemorial. To this day, their efforts to enhance the populations of salmon, bear and other wildlife through low-impact practices is a vital part of this incredible nature haven.

Before grizzly bears return to the mountains for winter hibernation, they need to bulk up on rich foods in the coastal valleys. In the fall, chum and coho salmon swim into Bute Inlet to seek out spawning beds and lay their eggs.

This spawn draws grizzly bears as well as a great diversity of other wildlife to the riverbanks. Black bears may be seen taking advantage of an easy salmon meal along the shoreline, typically dragging their meal farther into the forest, away from their much larger relatives. The mess they leave

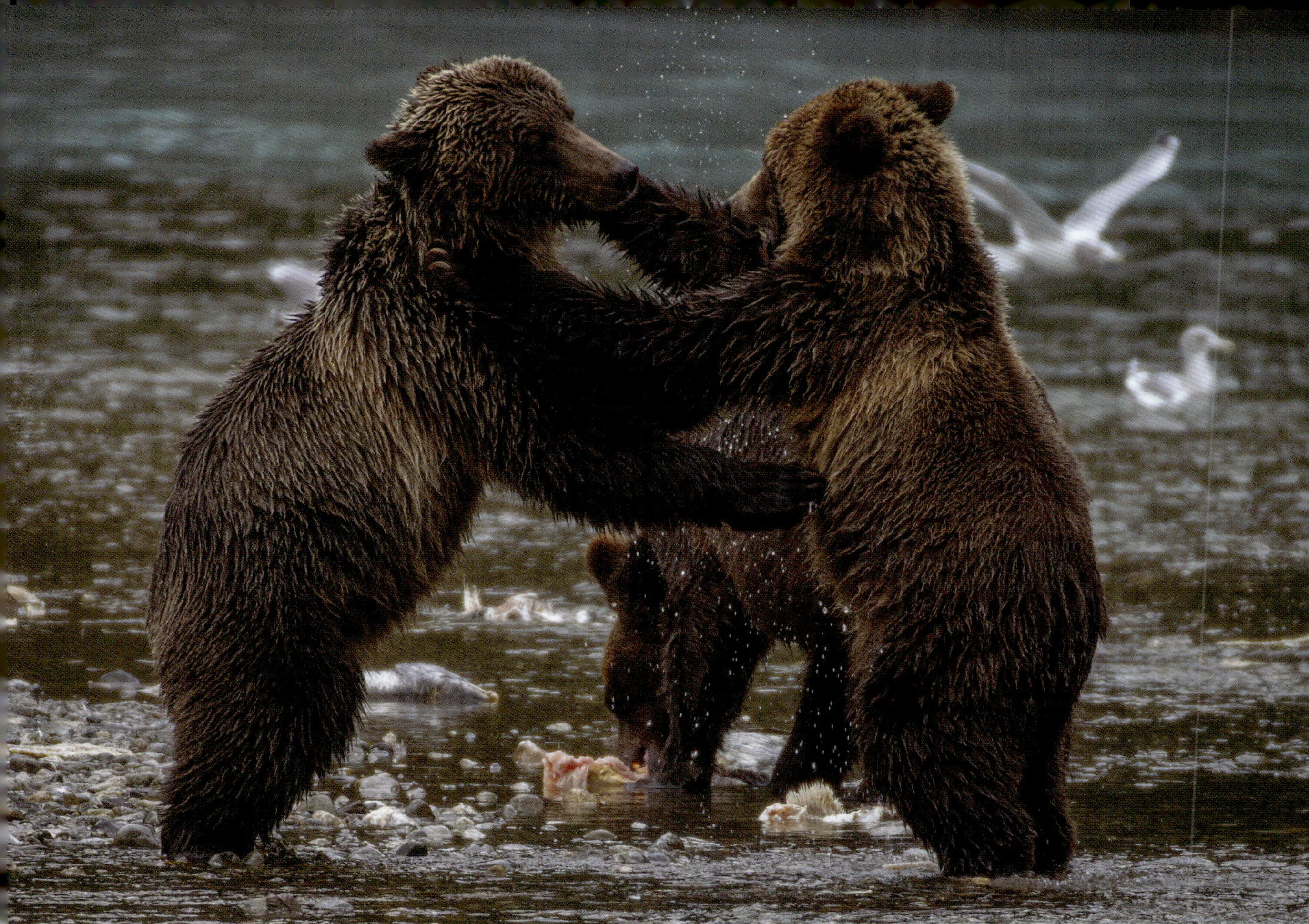

↑ **Spawning salmon make for easy pickings, so grizzly bears have time to playfully exchange blows between mouthfuls.**

behind on the forest floor in turn feeds the soil. Trees on the banks of salmon spawns grow three times faster than those growing along rivers without these incredibly important fish. The best time to visit to watch the salmon spawn is late August to mid-October, before the grizzlies return to their wintering grounds.

There are multiple ways to explore this beautiful area, including several boat and kayaking tour opportunities, but it's highly recommended that you participate in the Homalco Wildlife & Cultural Tours that begin with a comfortable boat ride from Campbell River. Once in Orford Bay, blinds and viewing areas are set up in popular grizzly feeding locations, giving you a safe place to watch them feed without causing stress or disturbance.

These incredible tours offer much more than bear sightings, however. They will provide you with a richer understanding of the wildlife in Bute Inlet and Xwémalhkwu culture and history. This fully Indigenous-owned tour company offers a truly once-in-a-lifetime experience that's memorable from the moment you leave Campbell River until your return.

Oyster Bay Shoreline Regional Park

The mudflats of this small but lively park provide great opportunities for birding year-round

What Makes This Hot Spot Hot?

- Marine mudflats make this an ideal spot for shorebirds.
- Purple martins nest in boxes over the water.
- Large rafts of ducks overwinter in the protected waters.

Address: 1.4 km east of Iron River Road on South Island Hwy (Hwy 19A), Campbell River, BC
Tel.: N/A
Website:

Strathcona Regional District

GPS Coordinates
Latitude: 49.89521
Longitude: –125.14768

Open year-round

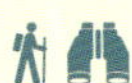

Despite its location right on the South Island Highway (Highway 19A), halfway between Courtenay and Campbell River, Oyster Bay Shoreline Regional Park is so small that if you are not looking carefully, you just might miss it. Even so, do not discount this birding hot spot, as the 4-hectare park features extensive mudflats that attract a mob of overwintering and migratory birds.

This area was originally created as a human-made causeway to protect floating timber that had been harvested from

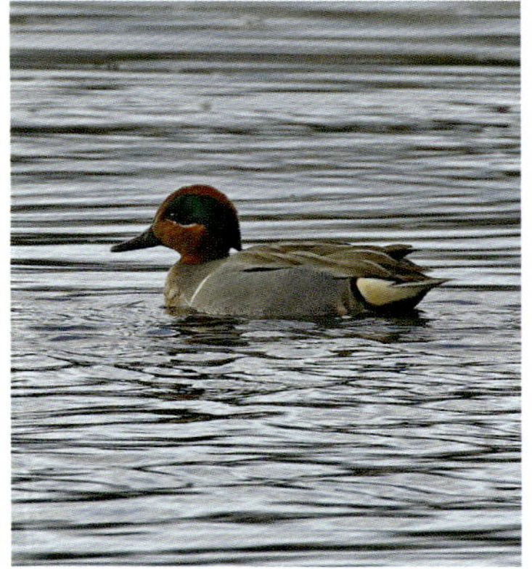

nearby forests, but natural materials accumulated along the shore after the log boom was no longer in use. The protected waters eventually developed extensive mudflats, now bursting with life. The smorgasbord of marine invertebrates present in the muck draws congregations of dunlins and black-bellied plovers in the winter. A little higher up the beach, among the stones and woody debris, you may see black turnstones poking around for a meal. Least and western sandpipers make stops here during their migrations to and from their winter homes to the south.

The nest boxes overlooking the flats become home to purple martins each spring, when you can watch their aerial dance above the water as they catch meals on the wing. The mudflats are not safe to walk on, but there is a rocky beach and raised dyke for observing the action along the shore. It helps to

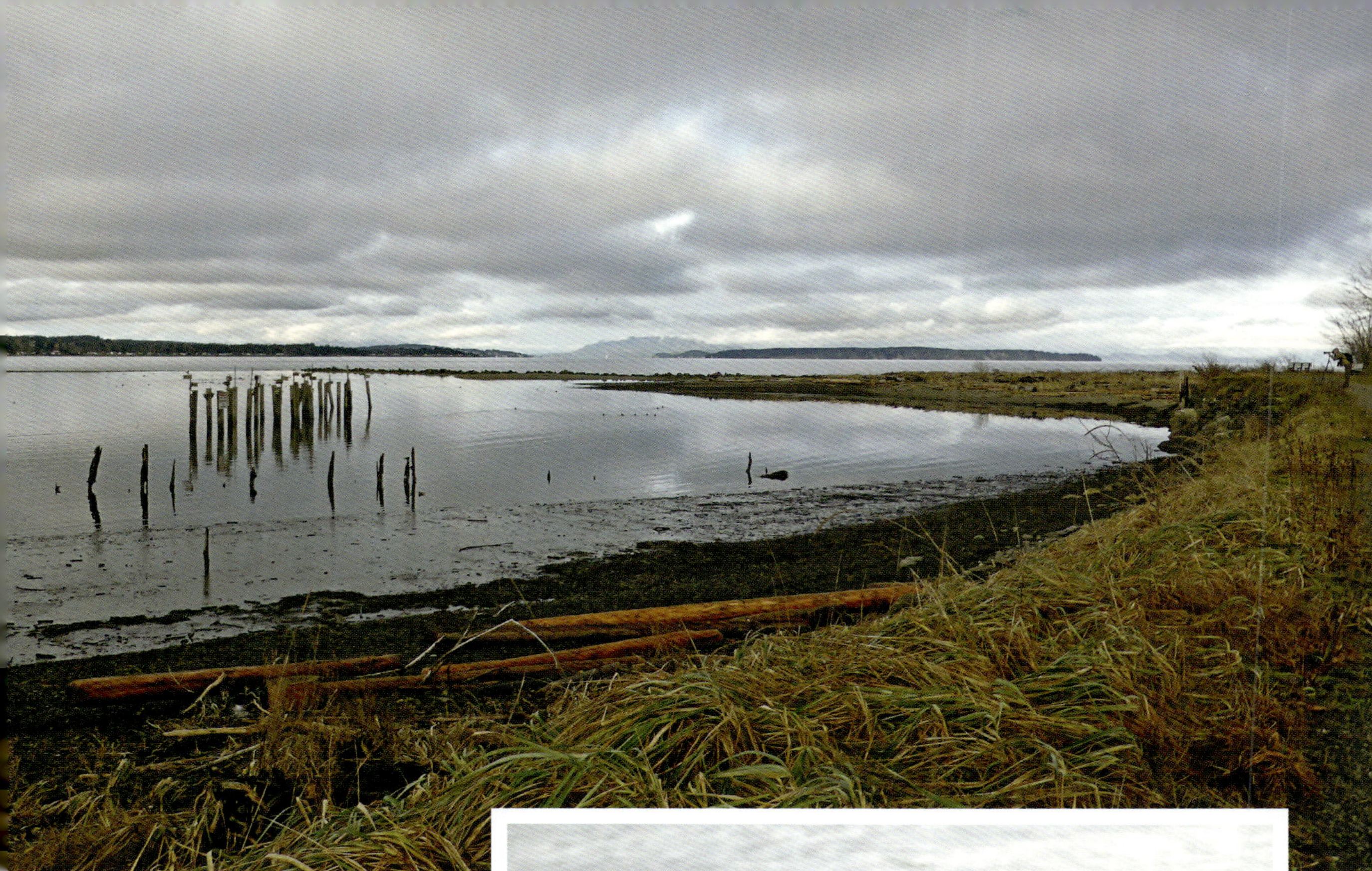

visit the park outside of low tide so that the birds are forced in a bit closer to solid ground by the high waters.

The land barrier that once provided floating logs with protection from the rougher waters now attracts a large number of waterfowl for the same reason. At first glance, a large raft of ducks may look exclusively made up of mallards and American wigeons, but look closely and you may find green-winged teals, northern pintails and Eurasian wigeons. These dabbling ducks can be seen feeding almost continually by skimming the surface or tipping underwater to grab a meal in the shallow waters, spending a substantial portion of their time bottom-up. Although it may only take 15 minutes to walk the entire park, you may find yourself lingering a long while at Oyster Bay, as the furious feeding activity of the assembled birds provides endless entertainment.

↑ **Dunlins barely take the time to look up from their constant feasting on invertebrates in the mud.**

↖ **A retired log boom in Oyster Bay has become a hot spot for bird activity.**

← **Green-winged teals are among the many species of duck that take refuge in the calm waters.**

PKOLS

Four distinct habitat zones provide year-round nature viewing opportunities in this scenic lookout over Greater Victoria

What Makes This Hot Spot Hot?

- Early spring wildflowers add colour and even more intrigue to the rock outcroppings near the summit of PKOLS.
- The park offers impressive views of Victoria and the surrounding land and ocean.
- Four distinct habitat zones make this an important, biologically diverse urban park.

Address: Churchill Drive, Saanich, BC
Tel.: (250) 475-1775
Website:

Victoria Trails

GPS Coordinates
Latitude: 48.49237
Longitude: −123.34543

Open year-round

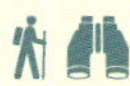

 **(Check ahead)**

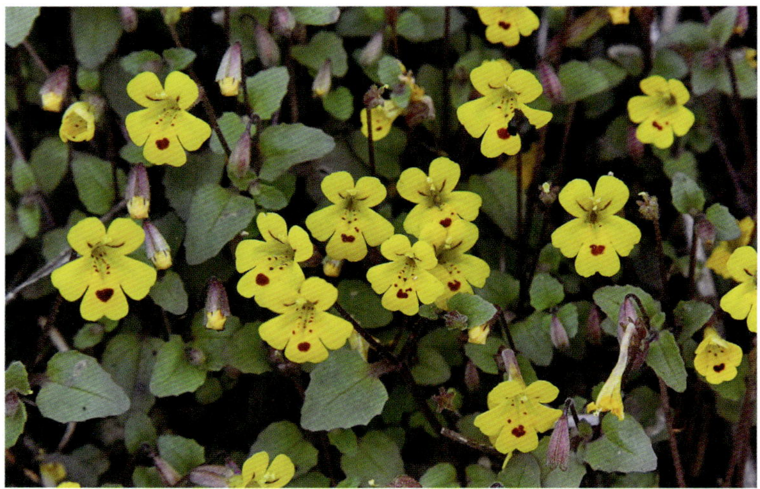

↗ **A cluster of chickweed monkeyflower provides a vibrant splash of yellow on the rocky slopes of PKOLS.**

With four distinct habitat zones, the great diversity of flora and fauna found within the 188 hectares of PKOLS provides endless opportunities for exploration and discovery.

Although still known to many by its colonial name, Mount Douglas, this biologically and culturally important landmark has been reclaimed as PKOLS, in recognition of its status as an important meeting place for many First Nations. Nation-to-Nation negotiations took place on the land, and this name change is a step in supporting ongoing efforts of Indigenous and settler populations to restore balanced relationships to the lands they call home.

The park boundary includes a rich coastal zone, where a diversity of intertidal life is supported by the eelgrass and kelp. The lower forests are home to an array of tree species, as well as a restored salmon spawning channel in Douglas Creek. Although trails are accessed from the base of PKOLS and range from easy to difficult, a road also leads to the peak so that the rock outcropping can be reached more easily.

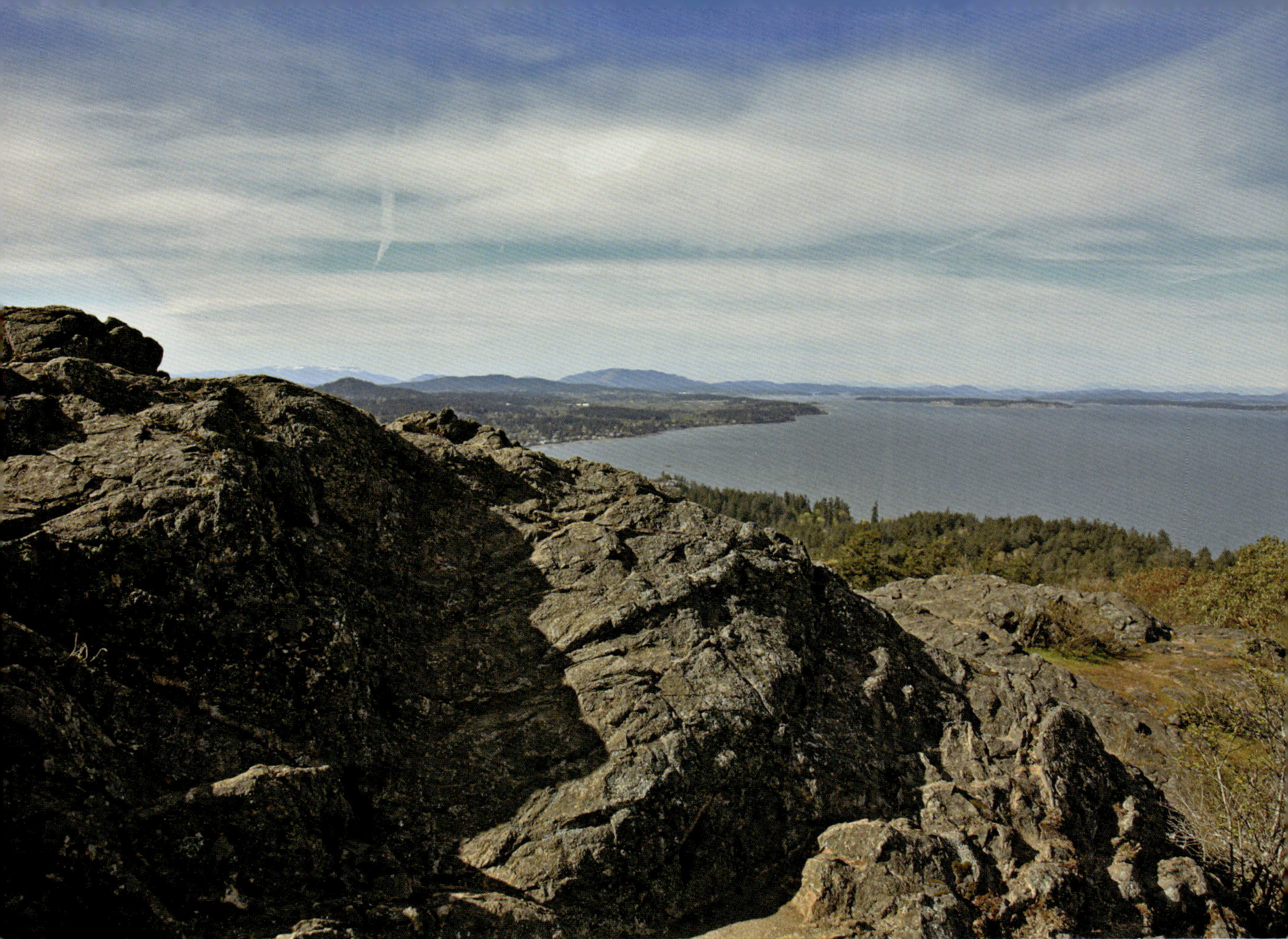

The dry and exposed Garry oak upper zone of the park is the perfect area for botanizing, as wildflowers such as shooting stars, stonecrop and fawn lilies can be found flowering in the spring and tucked into crevasses among the gnarled Garry oak trees. One particularly spectacular early spring flower spread throughout this zone is chickweed monkeyflower. Named for the comical grinning face displayed on each brilliant yellow flower, this wildflower can be found in dense patches in shady cracks of the rocky slopes on PKOLS.

Large numbers of white fawn lilies also pop up seemingly out of nowhere in the early spring, blanketing the forest floor at lower elevations.

The trails within the park range from easy to strenuous, and you can spend hours traversing through the different habitats on the 25-kilometre trail system. With spectacular views of Victoria, as well as the surrounding land and ocean, PKOLS is a must-see nature hot spot of lower Vancouver Island. Pack for a picnic and plan to spend the day exploring the largest urban forest of the Saanich Peninsula.

↑ **Visitors can enjoy the sprawling view of land and ocean from the top of PKOLS.**

Rathtrevor Beach Provincial Park

A vital stopover for brant geese en route to their high arctic breeding grounds

What Makes This Hot Spot Hot?

- Low tide exposes intertidal life nearly a kilometre from shore.
- Brant geese arrive in droves and stay to feast on fish eggs during the herring spawn.
- Sand dollars appear in large numbers at low tide.

Address: 1240 Rath Road, Parksville, BC
Tel.: (250) 474-1336
Website:

BC Parks

GPS Coordinates
Latitude: 49.31863
Longitude: −124.27083

Open year-round

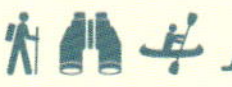

♿ (Check ahead)

→ **Sand dollar tests can be found across the exposed sands at low tide.**

Parksville's Rathtrevor Beach Provincial Park has 5 kilometres of hiking trails through old-growth forest tracing the shoreline and facing stunning views of the Salish Sea. That is reason enough to visit. However, visiting this park at low tide when the ocean recedes nearly a kilometre from the shoreline is the main attraction of this environment, for both people and wildlife.

Nestled against the smooth stones, soft sand and occasional colonies of barnacles embedded onto rocks, sand dollars are abundant at low tide. Finding a living sand dollar is rare, since most of the visible ones are dead and range in colour from pale beige to a light-tan leather shade. Living sand dollars are blackish-purple in colour and almost velvety to the touch — they are covered in tiny spines that they use to pass food particles to the specialized hairs that carry the food the rest of the way to the mouth. Once dead, the spines fall off their naked, rigid skeletons, known as tests, revealing a five-petal flower pattern on the upper side, which signals where the tube feet would have been on the living animal.

The only sand dollar species found on the BC coast is the eccentric sand dollar, which can occur in dense populations and ranges from sandy bays to more open coastal waters. These animals are quite fragile, so living specimens should be left alone and the shells of dead sand dollars should be left for future visitors to enjoy. Collecting specimens in provincial

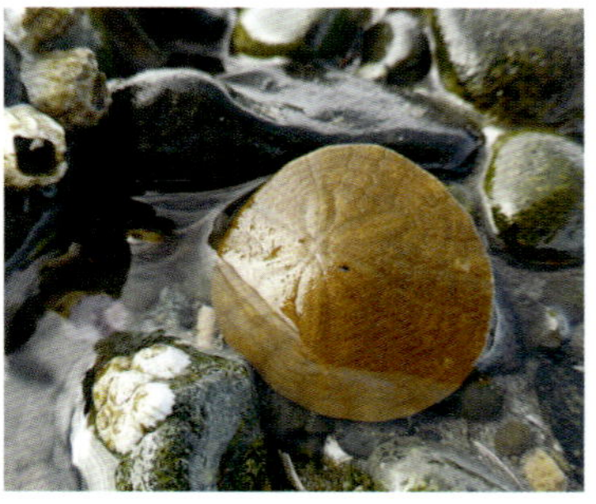

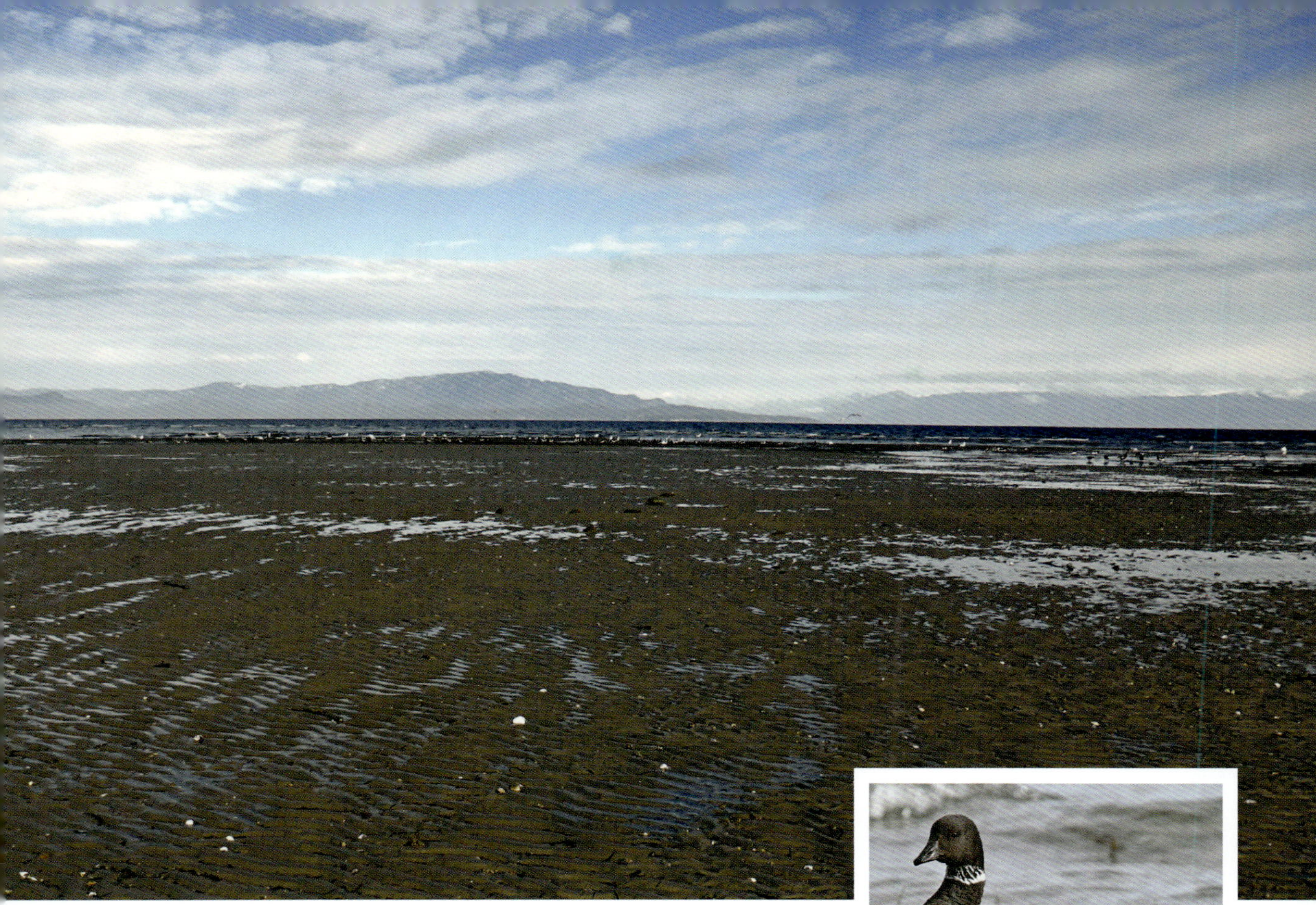

parks is illegal, and shells will one day become a part of the soft sand that makes this beach so spectacular.

February through April is the ideal time to plan a trip to Rathtrevor to see the migrating brant geese. These geese make the journey from Baja California, working their way up the coast and stopping in bays and estuaries during their migration. Brants can be seen by the thousands during the Pacific herring spawn when they, as well as countless other species, feast on the herring eggs that are washed close to the shore. By May the geese continue their journey to their breeding grounds in the high arctic — no other geese nest as far north as the brants. While stopped over in Rathtrevor, the brants are particularly vulnerable because they need to rest and feed to complete the remainder of their migration north. During the brant season, pets are not allowed on the beach. This migration garners such attention and even has a festival named after it — for over 30 years, the annual Brant Wildlife Festival has been celebrating geese and all things natural in the area. Events are held over multiple weeks attracting nature nuts of all ages to celebrate and share in this natural wonder.

↑ The brant geese of the Pacific Coast have much darker bellies than the Atlantic populations.

↖ The expansive shoreline of Rathtrevor Beach at low tide attracts many birds to feast on the exposed marine life.

Ruckle Provincial Park

A unique park built on a legacy of farming

What Makes This Hot Spot Hot?

- Visitors are given a rare chance to learn about wildlife and farm-life in the same location.
- Extensive trails weave through diverse ecological communities.
- Opportunities abound for marine mammal watching.

Address: Beaver Point Road, Salt Spring Island, BC
Tel.: (250) 539-2115
Website:

BC Parks

GPS Coordinates
Latitude: 48.78061
Longitude: −123.38593

Open year-round

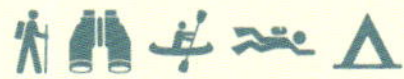

One of the Gulf Islands' largest provincial parks emerged from a legacy of family farming on Salt Spring Island, which dates back to 1872. Today visitors can still experience parts of the rich farming history on their visit to Ruckle Provincial Park while exploring the extensive trail system that brings nature enthusiasts through Garry oak meadows, coastal forests and rocky shorelines. The park is open for exploration year-round, although it is best to wait to camp when full service is offered in the park from the spring through to the fall.

For more than a century, descendants of the Ruckle family have farmed on the island property, making it the oldest continually operating farm in the province. Although a portion of the land remains a private working farm, BC Parks now manages the 529 hectares that were donated by the Ruckle Family in the 1970s. Although some of the original farm structures are still standing, including the farmhouse, keep in mind that the farmland is private property and should be viewed from the designated trails and roads.

The juxtaposition of ecological communities and human development serves as an important reminder of the

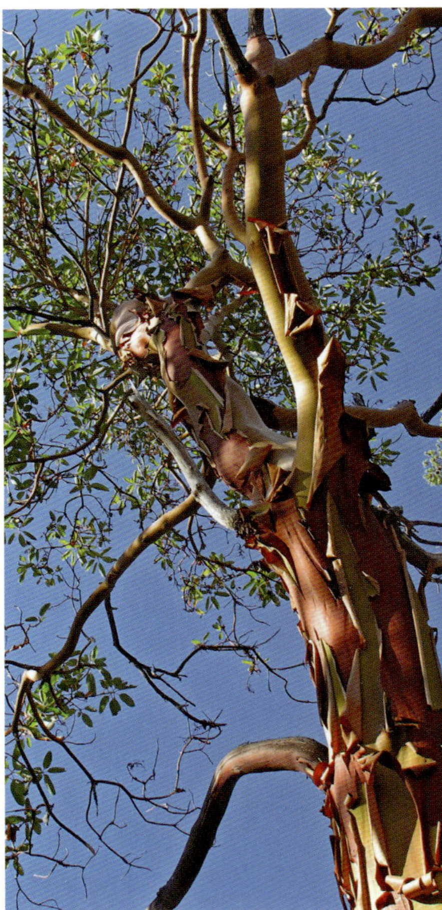

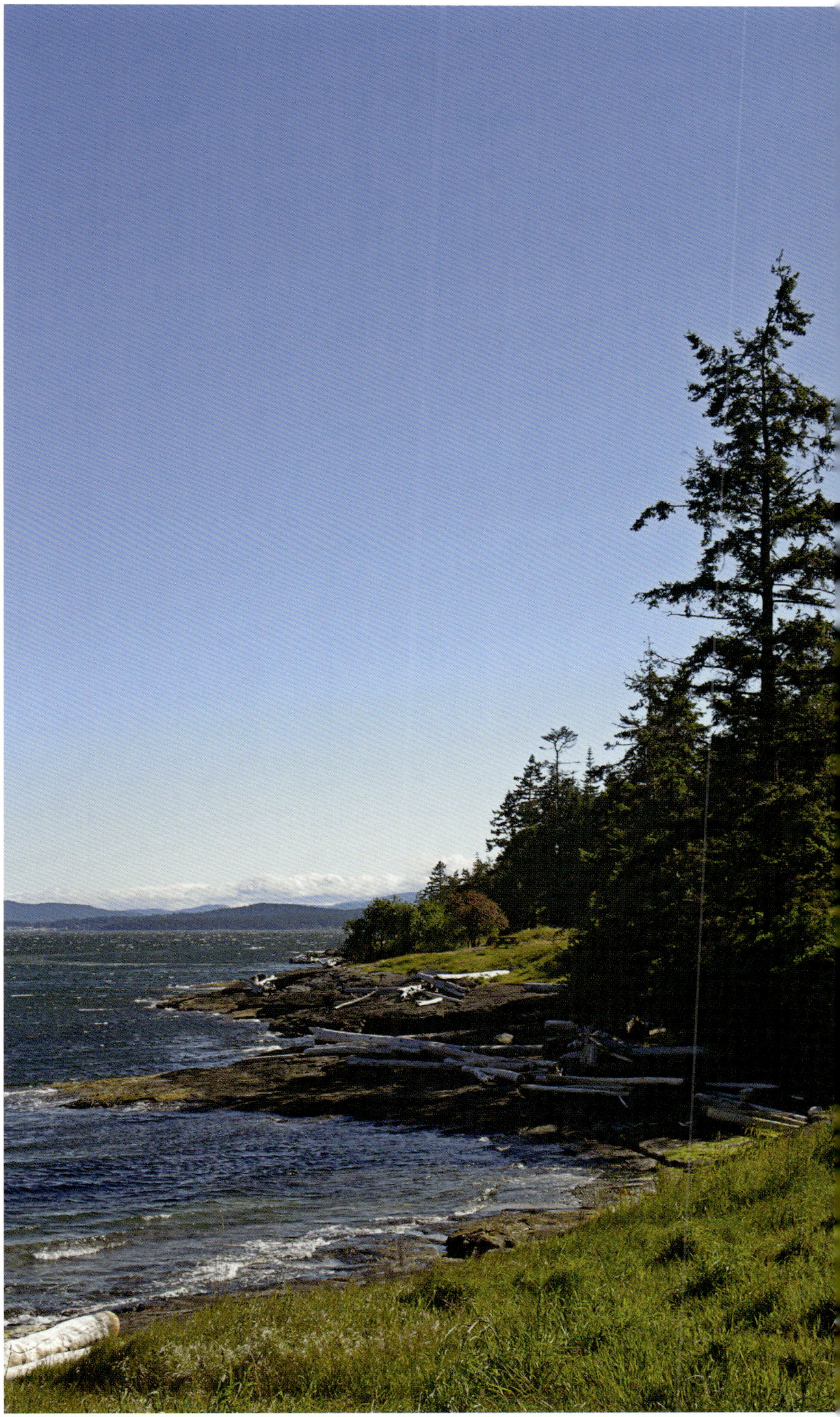

→ **There are many stunning views from the shoreline.**

↙ **The park is home to the uniquely beautiful arbutus, Canada's only native broadleaf evergreen tree.**

impact humans can have on the Gulf Islands. Livestock on the farm and heavy visitor use of some areas have contributed to the spread of invasive species such as carpet burweed and Scotch broom. Park staff and volunteers are working hard to limit the spread of some of these damaging species. A mixture of sensitive, undisturbed areas starkly contrast with those places that have been greatly transformed by human activity. An interesting mix of Douglas-fir and arbutus trees creates a unique setting before the forest gives way to the twisted Garry oaks that inhabit the thin shoreline meadows.

A rich kelp forest offshore attracts many interesting visitors to watch out for along the 7 kilometres of park shoreline. A variety of birds, including double-crested cormorants and bald eagles, can be seen looking for a meal in this important fish-feeding area. River otters, seals and sea lions are often observed rolling through the waves, and orca whales frequent the Swanson Channel between Salt Spring and North Pender Island.

Salmon River Estuary Conservation Area

A north island estuary that is home to a large population of Roosevelt elk

What Makes This Hot Spot Hot?

- Large populations of Roosevelt elk frequent the area.
- All species of Pacific salmon are found here: sockeye, chinook, coho, pink, chum, steelhead trout and cutthroat trout.
- As part of the Pacific Flyway, this area is an important stopover for migratory birds.

Address: Salmon River Main Line, Sayward, BC
Tel.: (604) 924-9771
Website:

Village of Sayward

GPS Coordinates
Latitude: 50.36999
Longitude: −125.94135

Open year-round

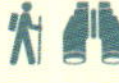

Although estuaries only occupy a small fraction of coastal land area, a huge number of species depend on them for parts of their life cycles. Along an otherwise fairly rough and rugged northern coastline, the Salmon River Estuary Conservation Area provides a nutrient-rich feeding ground and much-needed habitat for a wide range of species, making this a noteworthy estuary on Vancouver Island.

Aptly named, this particular estuary provides important habitat to all species of Pacific salmon, but it is a critical habitat too for the northern pygmy owl, the northern goshawk and the marbled murrelet. The estuary is also part of the Pacific Flyway, an important migratory route for many bird species.

In addition to providing vital fish and bird habitat, the conservation area provides essential grazing space for Roosevelt elk. These elk migrate locally and can be seen most often during the winter months when large numbers of them move down to lower elevations to graze.

There are about 3,200 Roosevelt elk in British Columbia, with over 3,000 residing on Vancouver Island. Their population on the Mainland has dwindled because of human development and activity, but the island remains a stronghold for this species. Populations reach their highest density north of Campbell River, but without extensive protected areas, these animals are forced to graze dangerously close to roads and human settlements. The largest of the elk family, Roosevelt elk play a valuable role in the ecosystem because they promote new growth by clearing underbrush through grazing. They are also an important food source of the rare Vancouver Island wolf.

While birding and botanizing along Kelly's Trail, also

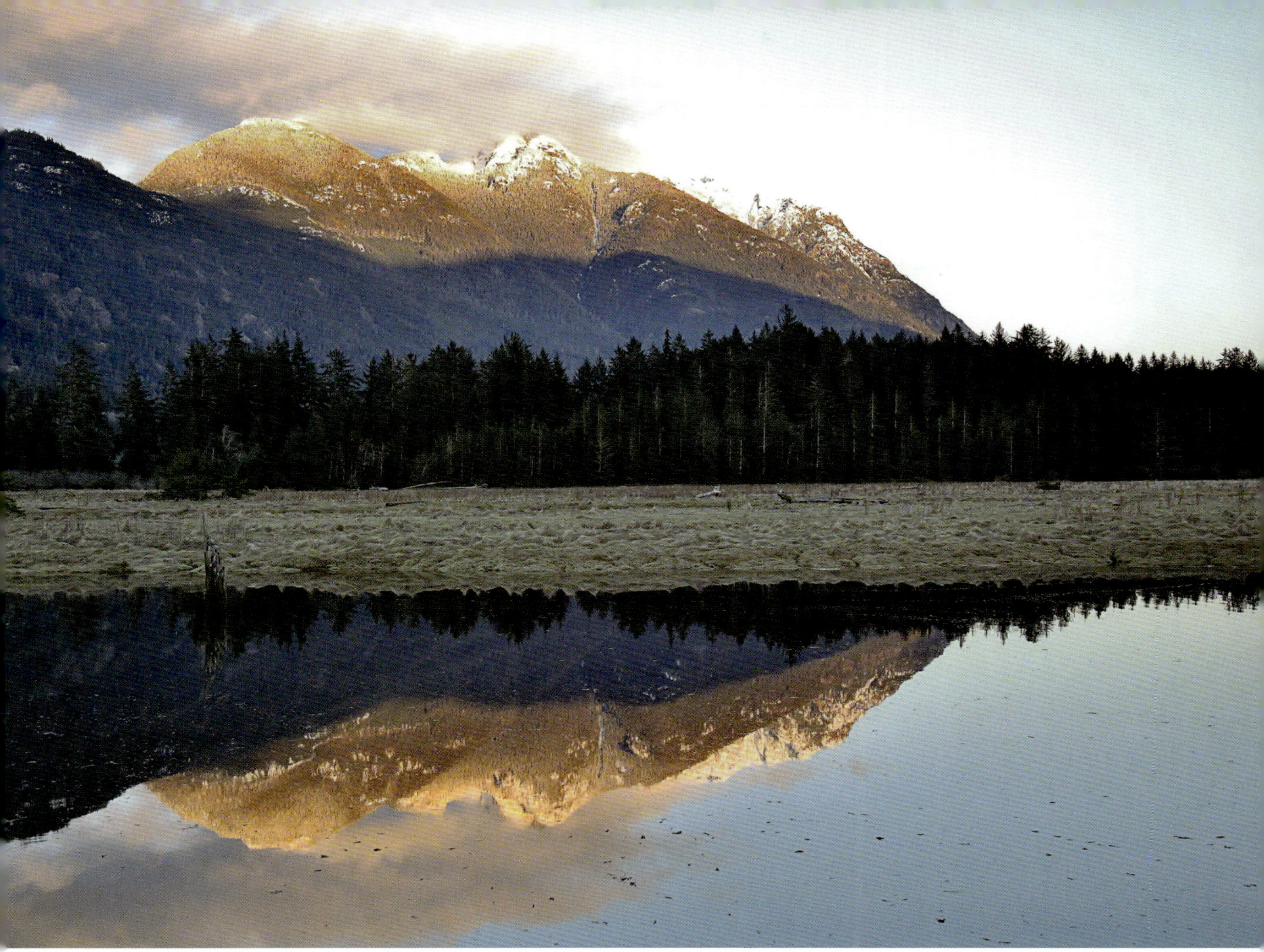

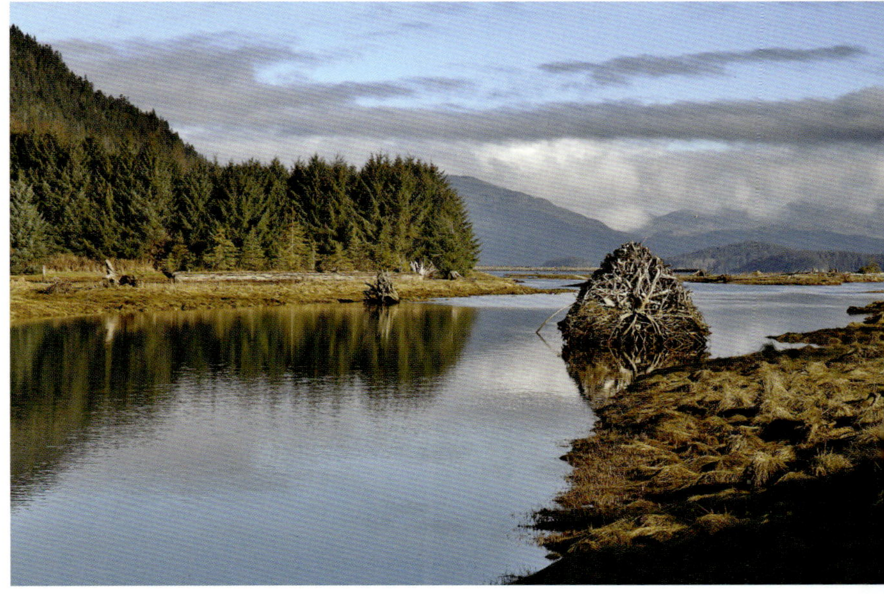

look for places elk have left their mark in the forest — you might spot signs of antlers being rubbed on trees during the fall rut. Along the Estuary Trail, be sure to check out the bird blind that was installed for viewing the congregations of birds that feed within the estuary.

S'amunu (Somenos) Conservation Area

This urban wetland attracts some very large winter birds

What Makes This Hot Spot Hot?

- About 1,000 trumpeter swans call this wetland their winter home.
- An annual WildWings Festival celebrates the beauty and diversity of the area.
- S'amunu Xatsa' (Somenos Lake) and Garry oak woods attract an even greater array of wildlife.

Address: Off of Island Hwy (Hwy 1), Duncan, BC
Tel.: (250) 732-0462
Website:

Somenos Marsh Wildlife Society

GPS Coordinates
Latitude: 48.79179
Longitude: −123.70846

Open year-round

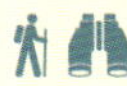

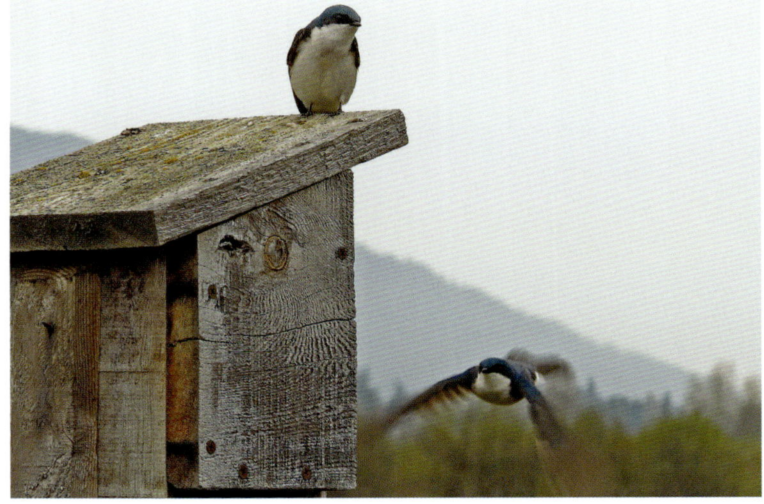

Prior to colonization, the wetlands and surrounding lands of the S'amunu watershed were village sites and an important travel corridor of the Quw'utsun Mustimuhw/Cowichan Tribes. Over time colonial land-use practices have degraded this ecologically rich area, so in order to protect the great diversity of wildlife found in these sensitive ecosystems, a conservation area was eventually established. Now it is deemed a globally significant Important Bird Area by Bird Life International, the S'amunu (Somenos) Conservation Area supports over 200 species of bird and is a worthy hot spot to visit any time of the year. Flood levels can rise over 2 metres in winter, turning fields into wetland. This is when you will see the most celebrated inhabitants of the marsh, the trumpeter swans. This marsh, situated along the Island Highway (Highway 1)

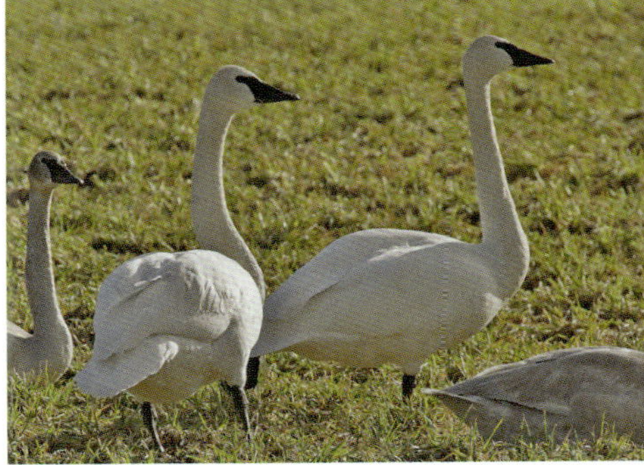

just outside the city of Duncan, is remarkably the second-largest overwintering spot on Vancouver Island for these beautiful birds. About 1,000 swans may be seen in the marsh, representing 5 per cent of the world's population of this species. As the largest native flying bird in Canada, they are a striking size, even for swans. With males weighing more than 11 kilograms, they need a lot of space for takeoff, which makes the fields of S'amunu an ideal spot for the winter months before heading back north to breed.

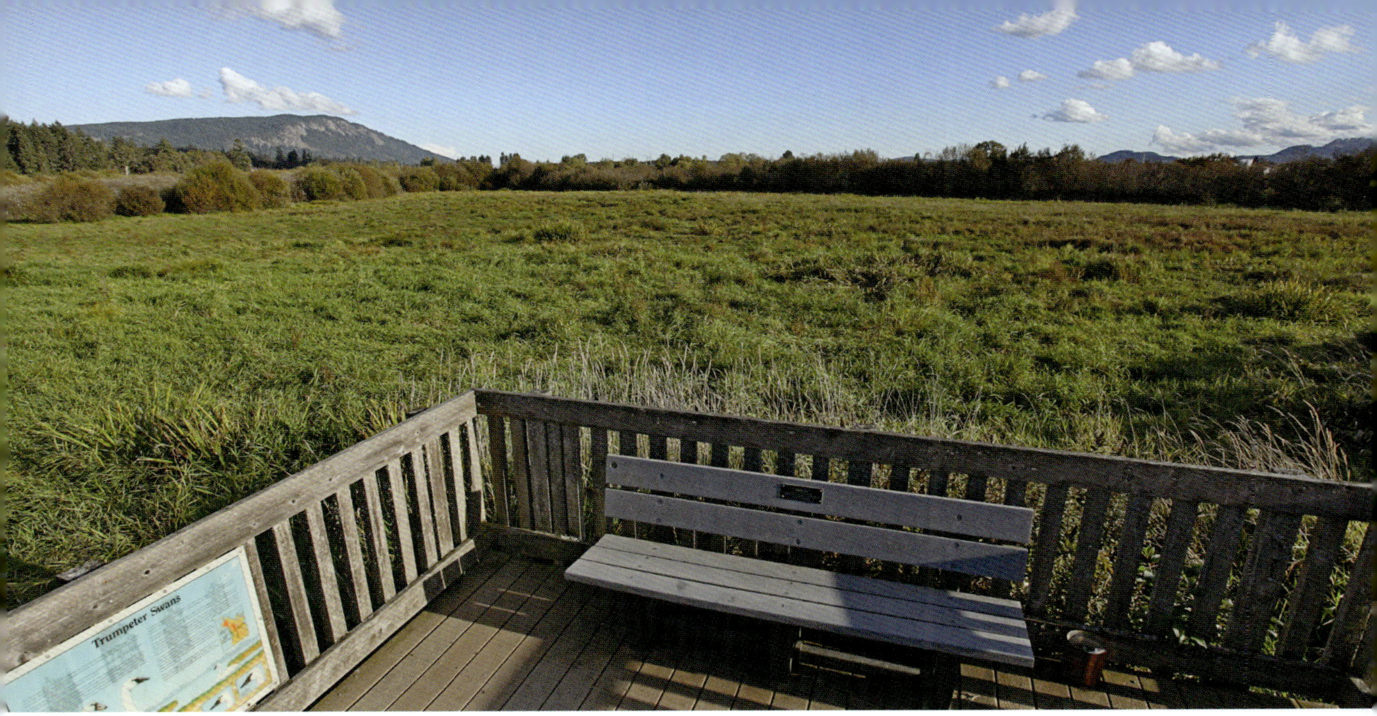

A little farther down the road, Drinkwater Dock overlooks S'amunu Xatsa', or Somenos Lake, home to waterfowl, songbirds and mammals year-round, including beavers and muskrats. The best winter viewing is along Watt's Walk when the fields are visited by many ducks, with green-winged teals and wood ducks in good numbers. Two pairs of barn owls are known to nest in the area as well. On the east side of the marsh is a Garry oak protected area.

Although tree swallows get their name from their habit of nesting in tree cavities, they happily raise their young in nest boxes. By the early spring these metallic-blue aerial acrobats will have already returned to stake their claim to the boxes around the marsh long before most other migrators arrive.

The Somenos Marsh Wildlife Society hosts an annual Wild-Wings Nature and Arts Festival every fall to celebrate local biodiversity through guided walks, talks, movie screenings and more. This family-friendly event is spread over multiple days, and participating in some of the festivities is a great way to meet local wildlife experts and fellow nature enthusiasts.

↑ Summer in S'amunu Marsh, before the fields surrounding the boardwalk become flooded with fall rains.

← Pairs of tree swallows return each year to breed in the nest boxes placed around the marsh.

↑ Trumpeter swans become local celebrities during their winter stopover.

CAPE SCOTT PROVINCIAL PARK

San Josef Bay

The sea stacks of San Josef Bay are a must-see along the northern shores of Vancouver Island

What Makes This Hot Spot Hot?

- Sea stacks, weathered away by wave action, are an iconic image of the North Coast.
- The intertidal life is teeming with activity at low tide.
- Several beaches, including some with caves, are open for exploration during low tide.

Address: Cape Scott Provincial Park, Cape Scott Park Road, 64 km west of Port Hardy, BC
Tel.: (1-844) 435-9453
Website:

BC Parks

GPS Coordinates
Latitude: 50.68498
Longitude: –128.26271

Open year-round

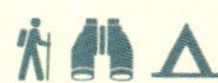
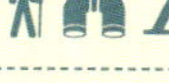

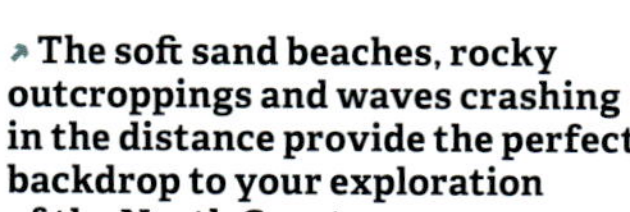

The soft sand beaches, rocky outcroppings and waves crashing in the distance provide the perfect backdrop to your exploration of the North Coast.

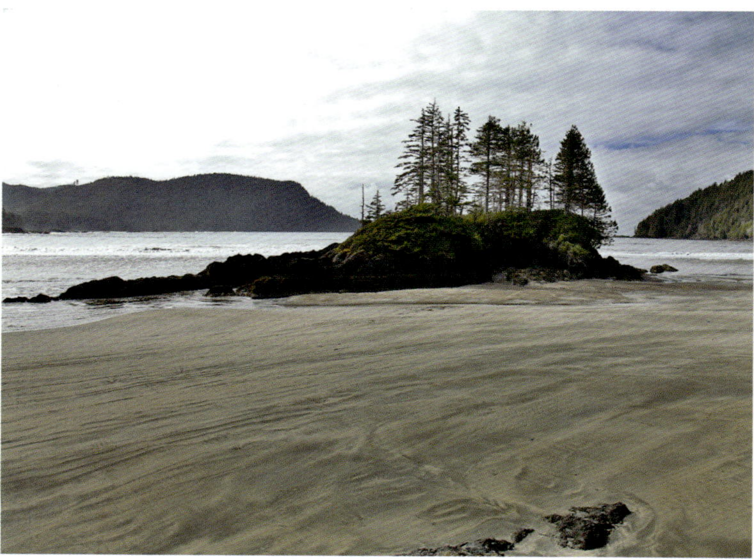

Cape Scott Provincial Park is famously home to the North Coast Trail, a rugged and challenging weeklong backpacking trail. However, within the park there are also multiple day-use trails that allow visitors to experience this incredible park, on the most northern tip of Vancouver Island, without the challenges and commitment of a multiday journey.

The San Josef Bay Trail is an easy but rewarding hike within the park. After a 45-minute flat walk through gorgeous old-growth coastal temperate rainforest, the trail opens up to a set of spectacular fine sand beaches along BC's most western coastland. Plan your trip to arrive at the beach at low tide to explore the exposed tidepools, which are packed with chitons, anemones, huge snail colonies, sea stars, sand dollars and more.

At low tide, with dramatic, crashing open-ocean waves as the backdrop, the most famous and unique scenes of this park are revealed — sea stacks, which are towering volcanic rock structures formed as the rough oceans wore away the rock, create one of the most picturesque scenes anywhere on the island. The stacks are topped with twisted and wind-battered bonsai-like trees. As you explore the beaches, there are opportunities to dip into sea caves and to view wildlife. Eagles, ospreys, scoters, otters and whales may be visible along the shore, and occasionally wolves visit these beaches.

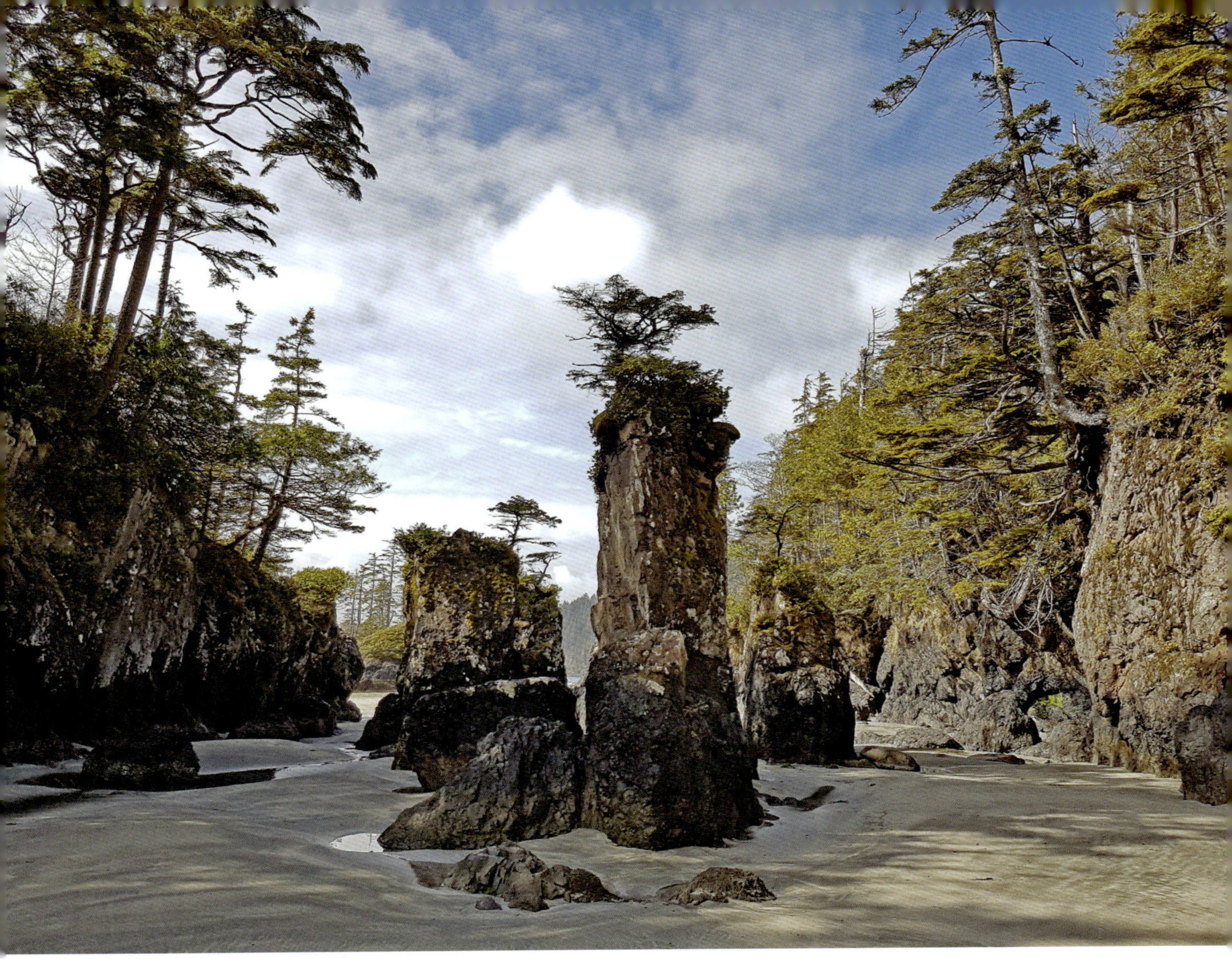

This trip requires careful planning, as the logging roads to the park are heavily used and very rough — a truck is highly recommended. The weather can be unpredictable on the coast, and tide table knowledge is essential to make the most of this hot spot. That said, the planning effort is well worth it to visit one of the most beautiful locations in the province.

↑ Sea stacks at low tide.

→ **A breeding congregation of wrinkled dogwinkle can be found at low tide, with a chiton thrown in for good measure.**

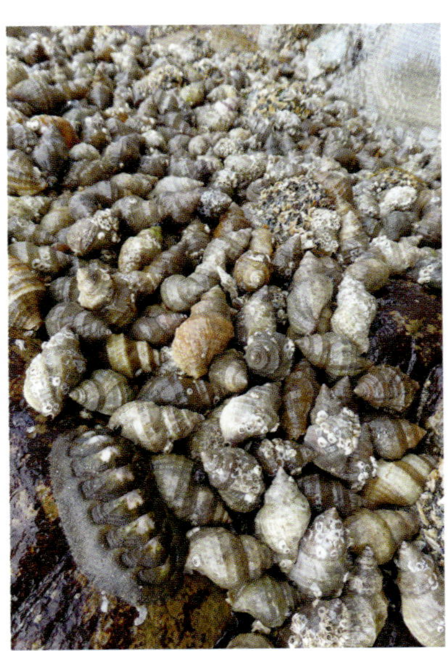

Sargeant Bay Provincial Park

Shorelines, wetlands and a salmon creek to explore, as well as views of a rare peat bog at the end of a fabulous forest hike

↗ **The cheekily named fairy barf lichen can be found in Sargeant Bay Provincial Park.**

Although Sargeant Bay Provincial Park is only 142 hectares, within its boundaries there are many significant and varied habitats for nature lovers to see and enjoy. A pristine peat bog in a lush forest, beach access along the terminus of a salmon-bearing creek, a beaver lodge and a wetland separated from the beach by a raised bank are all ready to explore through a diverse trail system.

The 2.5-kilometre Triangle Lake Trail provides scenic views of old-growth forest mixed with largely coniferous second-growth forest and arbutus trees standing along rocky ridges, before arriving at Triangle Lake and looping back down to Colvin Creek. Upon arrival, you may notice this lake is not a lake at all, but a vital peat bog wetland.

Peat is an accumulation of dead organic matter, largely made up of sphagnum mosses. Requiring a narrow range of conditions to form, peat bogs cover only a small percentage of the world's land surface and yet perform necessary water filtration services for large

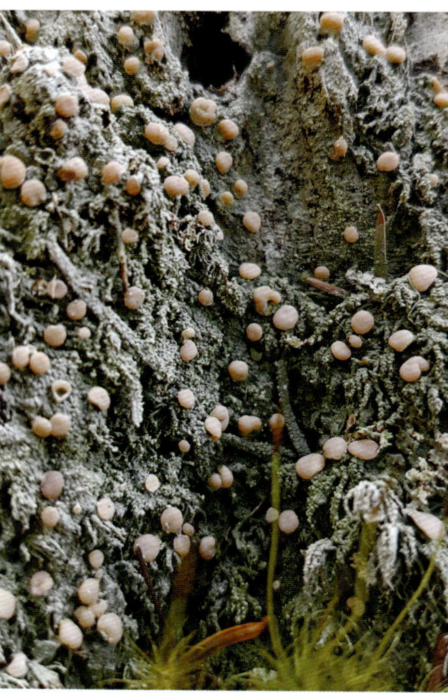

bodies of fresh water. Unfortunately, peat bogs are becoming rare because of environmental degradation. A select community of plants are commonly found in bog systems, including sphagnum moss, bog cranberry and carnivorous plants, like the round-leaved sundew. The trail provides views of the bog, but the sensitive environment itself is inaccessible, since it is almost entirely surrounded by rocky ridges. In the spring and summer you may be lucky enough to hear the calls or spot some activity of olive-sided flycatchers and common yellowthroats, two bird species that visit the bog in the warmer seasons.

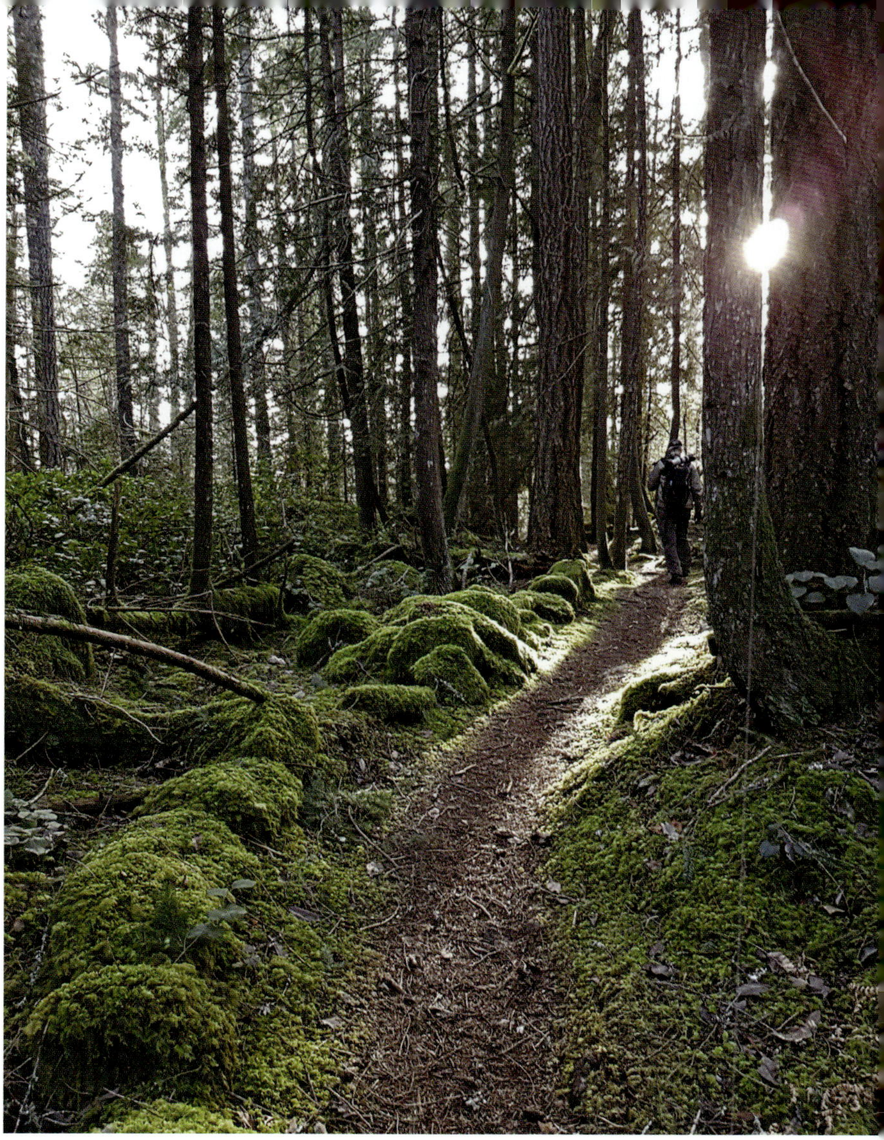

The shoreline marsh provides great birding opportunities, whose residents include Virginia rails, great blue herons and many species of woodpecker and owl. Spring and summer mark the return of many migrant species, including western tanagers, back-headed grosbeaks and a wide range of warblers and flycatchers. A fish ladder was installed to allow chum and coho salmon passage to Colvin Creek from the ocean. Although industrious beavers have dammed up the waterway in front of this structure, a small channel, wide enough to allow the salmon through, remains open.

↗ **The moss-covered forest floor along the Triangle Lake Trail.**

→ **Views of the peat bog from high above.**

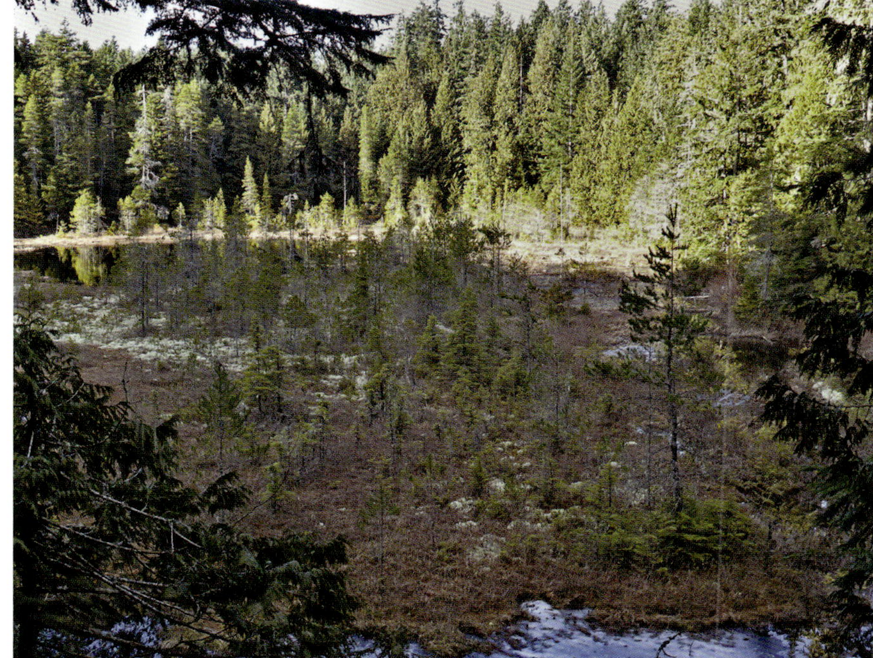

GULF ISLANDS NATIONAL PARK RESERVE

Saturna Island

Saturna Island provides exquisite whale-watching opportunities — from the shore!

What Makes This Hot Spot Hot?

- Resident and transient orcas frequent the beautiful coastline of East Point.
- Unique oceanside rock formations provide additional explorations while soaking in the views.
- Harbour seals breed along the shores, and pups can be seen patiently waiting for their mothers to return.

Address: Narvaez Bay Road, Saturna, BC
Tel.: (250) 654-4000
Website:

Parks Canada

GPS Coordinates
Latitude: 48.80668
Longitude: –123.16513

Open year-round

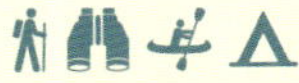

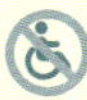

↗ **This large hollowed out rock is a great example of the Geoffrey formation rocks that overlook the shoreline.**

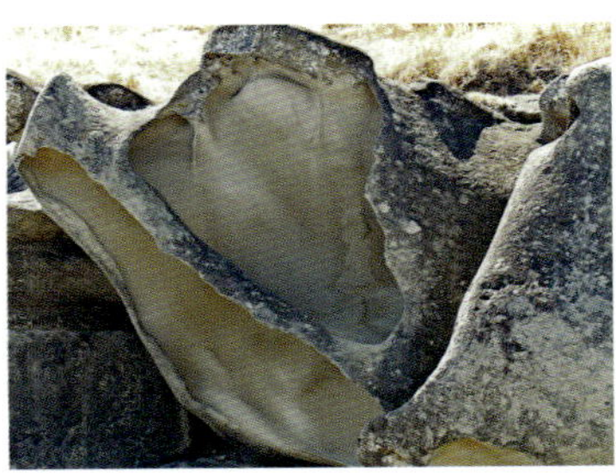

Easily accessible yet one of the least crowded of the Gulf Islands, Saturna is an optimal place for wildlife viewing. Nearly half of the island is protected as parkland, most of which is designated as part of the Gulf Islands National Park Reserve. This park covers 36 square kilometres spread over 15 islands, as well as numerous islets and marine zones. Within the boundaries of the park on Saturna, Echo Bay along the Narvaez Bay Trail provides beautiful views of Boundary Pass, the strait that runs along the boundary between Washington State and British Columbia, and looks out towards the San Juan Islands across the border.

The Gulf Islands National Park Reserve offers a great opportunity for exploring remarkable rock formations, best viewed along East Point where Geoffrey formation rocks dominate the landscape. The sandstone beds of the shoreline erode in a pattern known as taphoni, or honeycomb weathering — one of the most distinctive features of this landscape. This type of weathering occurs when salt from the ocean crystalizes within the pores of the sandstone beds, prying apart the mineral grains and opening the rock up to other forms of weathering.

East Point is also one of the best lookouts in the province for whale watching from the land, as endangered southern resident orca whales are regular visitors to the area from May until late autumn. It is not uncommon to see passing whales nearly hug the shoreline, and if you are really lucky, you may witness fascinating orca behaviours as they socialize offshore: breaching, leaping or perhaps even spy-hopping, which is when they hold their heads above the waterline, becoming not only the watched but the watcher too. Transient orcas, which prefer to eat mammals, unlike the almost exclusively fish-eating residents, also pass through the area, likely interested in the number of harbour seals, as well as the Steller sea lions that visit the area in the fall and winter.

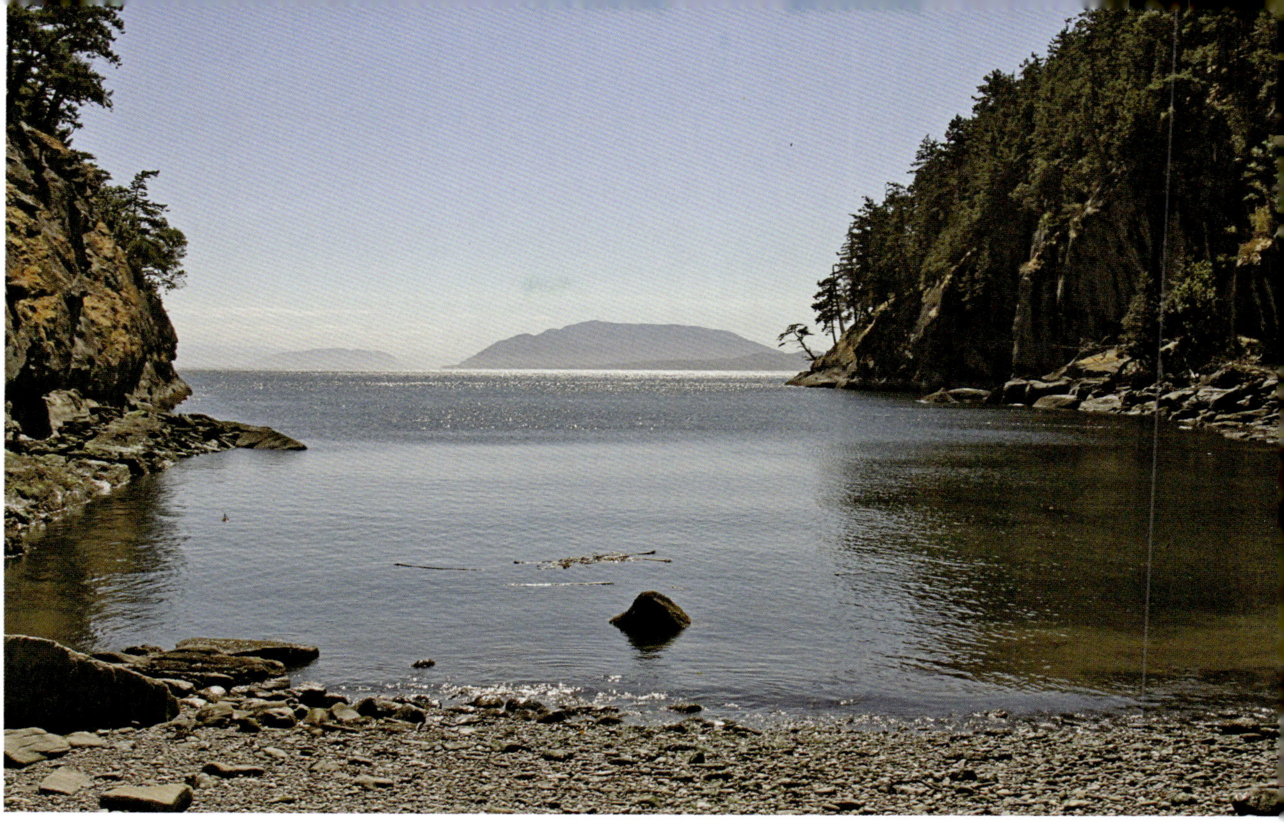

In the summer East Point becomes a special area for viewing harbour seals. Seal pups patiently wait on the shore for their mothers to return after feeding at sea. On average a pup weighs 11 kilograms at birth and quickly doubles its weight in the first month, feeding on its mother's rich milk. It is a delight to watch the young pups not only plod across the rocks in a caterpillar-like motion but also explore the surrounding water and become comfortable with the ocean they will call home. All visitors should keep a significant distance from any seals and pups while enjoying their playful antics.

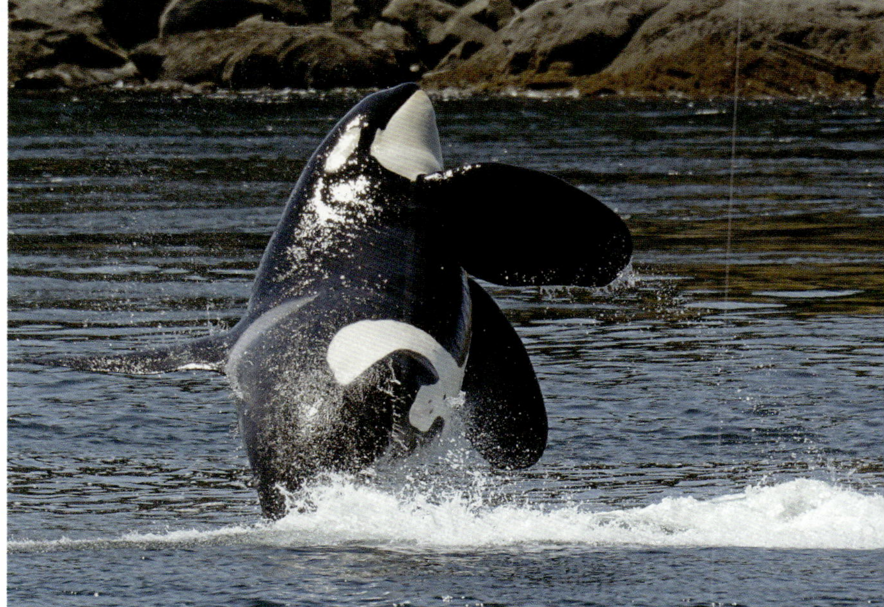

↑ **East Point is one of the best places in the province to watch orca whales from the shore.**

↖ **Echo Bay looks out across the marine border between Canada and the United States.**

Savary Island

This narrow island is one of the few places in all of Canada to hike through ancient forested sand dunes

What Makes This Hot Spot Hot?

- Savary's forested sand dunes represent the best example of this rare ecosystem in Canada.
- Some of the largest arbutus trees in all of BC are found on the island.
- The beautiful sand cliffs are nesting sites for swallows and kingfishers.

Address: Savary Island Land Trust, Savary Island, BC
Tel.: (604) 483-4743
Website:

Savary Island Land Trust

GPS Coordinates
Latitude: 49.94155
Longitude: −124.81946

Open year-round

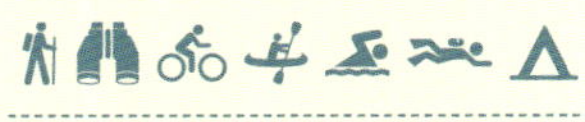

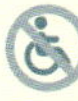

Incredible sandy beaches and rare ecosystems can be found a short boat ride from the village of Lund, just off of BC's Sunshine Coast. The small island of Savary is famous for its white sand beaches, but in reality the sand doesn't end there. In fact, aside from a granite outcropping on one end of the island, all of Savary is essentially a large sandbar.

Many of the beaches feature beautiful and extremely fragile sand cliffs which are already rapidly eroding, so please do not climb, walk on, carve into or touch the cliffs.

Northern rough-winged swallows catch small flying insects on the wing over the beach and water before returning to the steep sandy banks to feed their young. Unlike bank swallows, this aerial insectivore doesn't dig its own burrow. The burrows may have been created previously by kingfishers, which can also be found frequenting these beaches.

This sandy island is extremely fragile, with the south side eroding at a shocking 0.41 metres per year. The winds and waters do their fair share of eroding this fragile island, but human activity

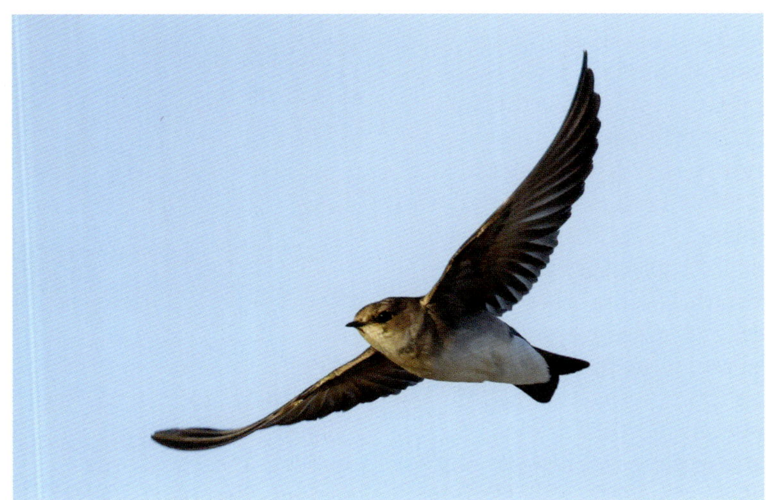

→ **Northern rough-winged swallows can be found flying low over the beach, snatching insects on the wing before returning to their burrows built into the sandy cliffs.**

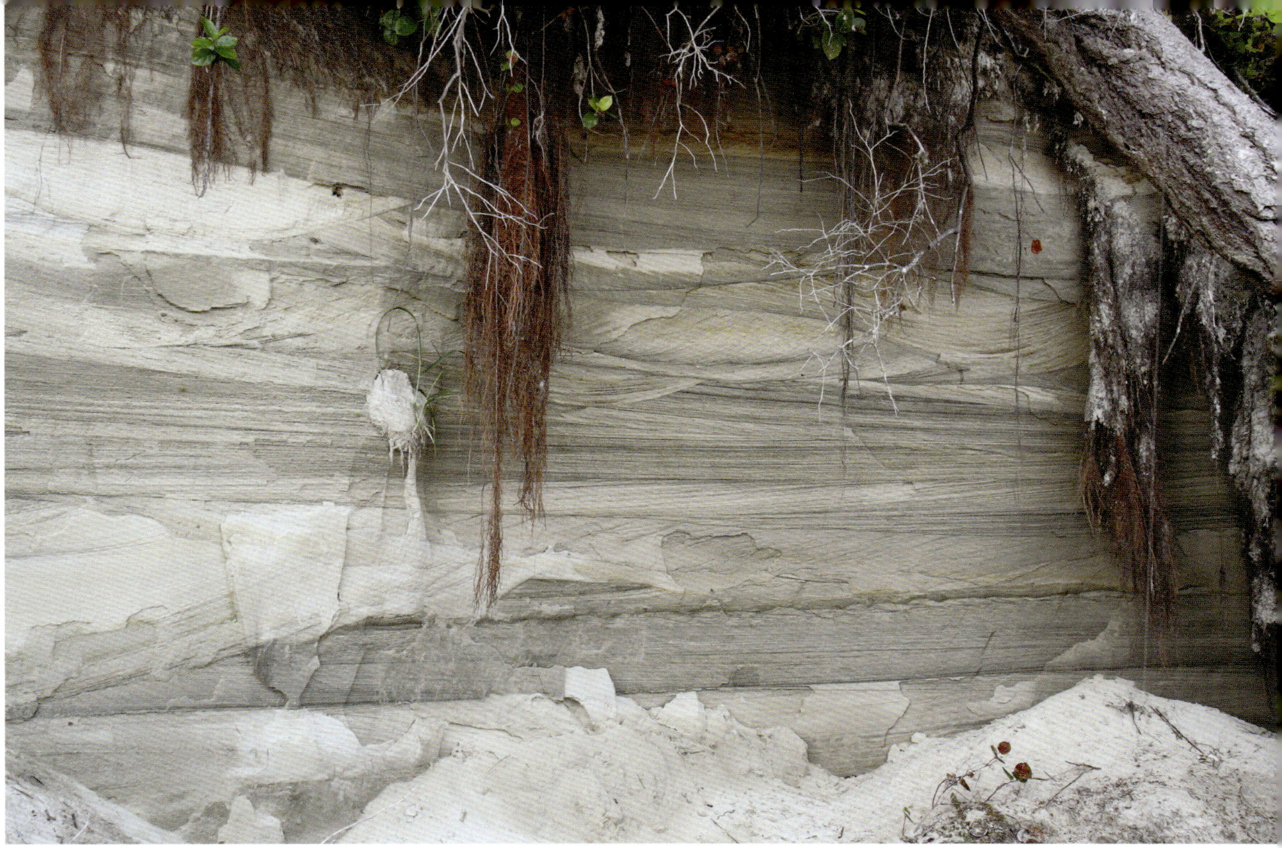

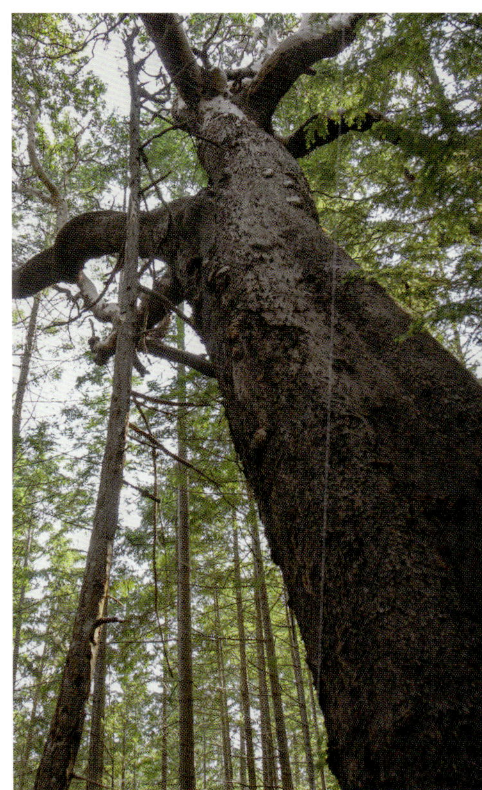

can greatly contribute to its decline. Savary has only a hundred or so off-grid permanent residents, but the population booms during the summer, making it the most densely subdivided island in BC. As a result of the delicate sand substrate and high population density, the trails and remaining undeveloped areas are in urgent need of protection.

Thankfully the Savary Island Land Trust and the Nature Trust of BC together protect a 350-acre parcel of land that makes up the entire central section of the island, spanning across to both shorelines. Known locally as the "Heart of Savary," this forest grows atop an ancient dune topography, making it especially fragile. This protected land is home to some of the largest arbutus trees in BC, as well as an old-growth cedar grove.

Savary Island is only 7.5 kilometres long and in most sections under a kilometre wide, so it's best to leave your car behind and explore by bicycle and foot. That said, please beware that hiking trails are to be explored by foot only, as wheeled vehicles greatly contribute to surface disturbance and erosion.

↑ **The beautiful and fragile cliffs reveal layer upon layer of delicate sand, providing a glimpse into the foundation of this extremely unique and constantly eroding island.**

→ **Gigantic arbutus trees grow in the ancient dune forests of this island, their massive branches reaching out in all directions.**

Shorepine Bog Trail

A nutrient-depleted ecosystem home to carnivorous herbs and twisted trees

What Makes This Hot Spot Hot?

- Visitors can discover fascinating acid-thriving bog plants.
- Stunted trees create a dreamy, bizarre landscape.
- A boardwalk loop keeps feet dry and protects delicate plants.

Address: Pacific Rim National Park Reserve, Wick Road, Ucluelet, BC
Tel.: (250) 726-3500
Website:

Parks Canada

GPS Coordinates
Latitude: 49.01354
Longitude: −125.65518

Open year-round

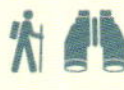

♿ (Check ahead)

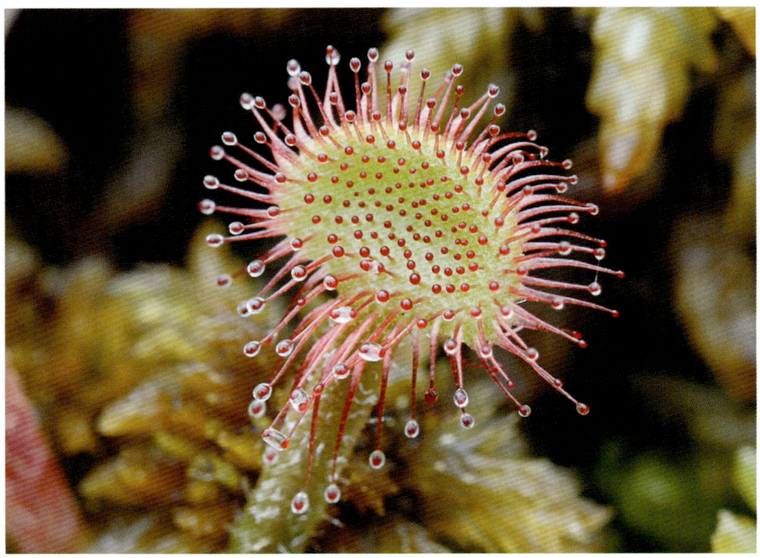

↗ **A close-up of the sticky secretions of the round-leaved sundew, a fabulous carnivorous bog plant.**

Surrounded almost entirely by temperate rainforest, oddly gnarled trees help the Shorepine Bog Trail stand out as a unique nature hot spot in the Pacific Rim National Park Reserve. The shore pine, or lodgepole pine, found in this bog are stunted and mangled because of harsh growing conditions created by the acidic soils of the bog. Bogs are characterized by poor drainage and the presence of a thick carpet of sphagnum moss. The sphagnum acidifies the bog, resulting in slow rates of decay and extremely low nutrient availability. The effects on plant life are evident in the twisted and stunted appearance of the shore pines.

Plants have also evolved amazing strategies to thrive in these nutrient-poor environments. While some species found along the trail, like Labrador tea, bog blueberry, bog-laurel, goldthread and bog cranberry, depend on their roots to extract scarce but necessary nutrients, others have found a different means of obtaining what they need — not through their roots, but their leaves. Round-leaved sundews are carnivorous plants with specialized leaves covered in tiny hairs, tipped with sticky fluid. This sweet-smelling fluid attracts and then ensnares any insects that make the mistake of landing. The leaves secrete enzymes to digest their prey, and essential nitrogen and other nutrients are absorbed to support the plant's growth. Although hawks, snakes and the occasional bear may visit the bog, the tiny sundew is a likely candidate for the most abundant carnivore in the area.

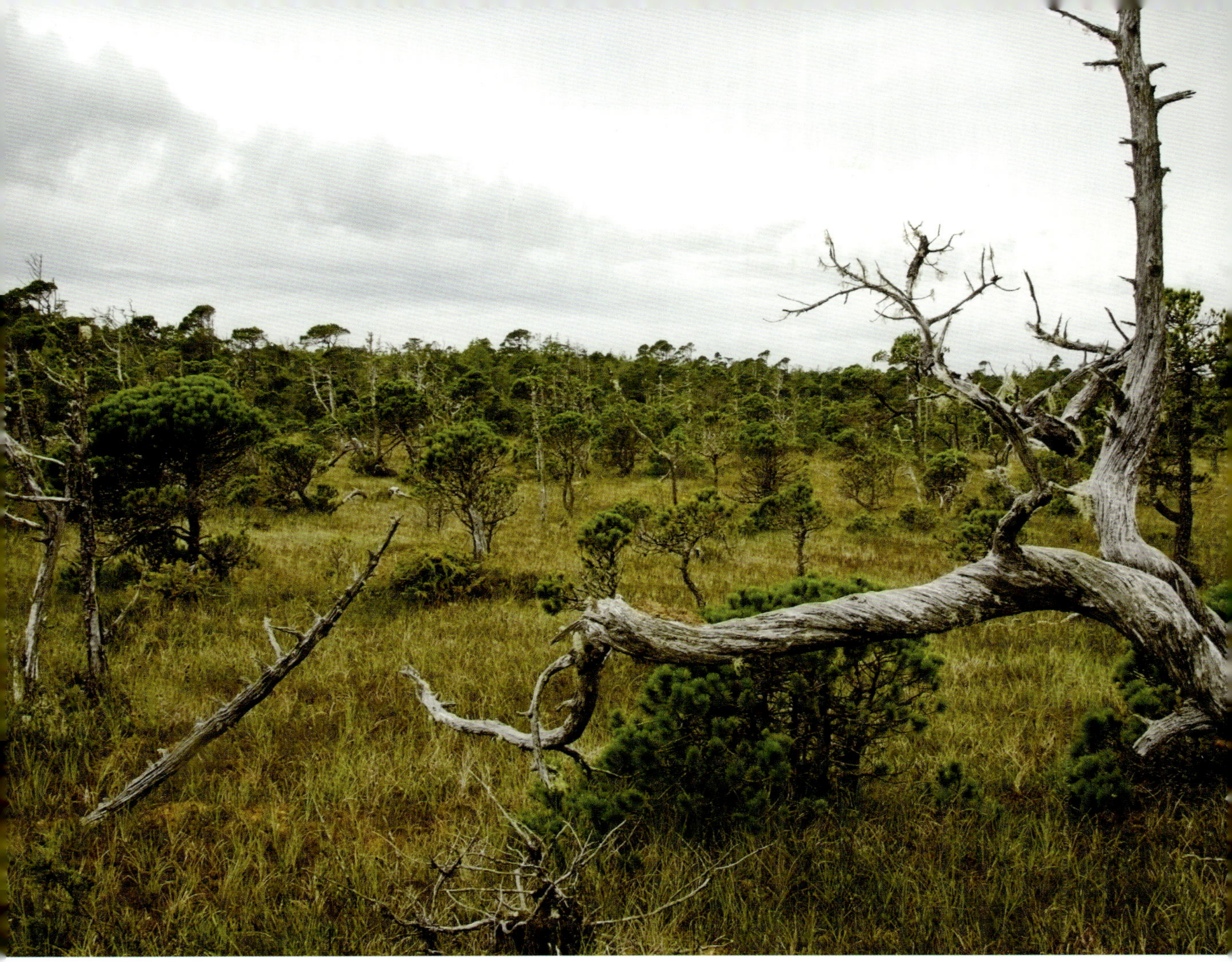

This 800-metre loop is mostly boardwalk to protect the delicate bog ecosystem, so please stay on the trail. The sphagnum moss in this area may be over a metre thick and hundreds of years old. There are plenty of opportunities for botanizing in this beautiful and unique pocket that should not be passed up as you adventure through the rainforests and beaches of the Pacific Rim National Park Reserve.

↑ Gnarled shore pine trees grow up out of the carpet of moss.

↓ A thick layer of sphagnum moss acidifies the water and creates unique growing conditions for other plants.

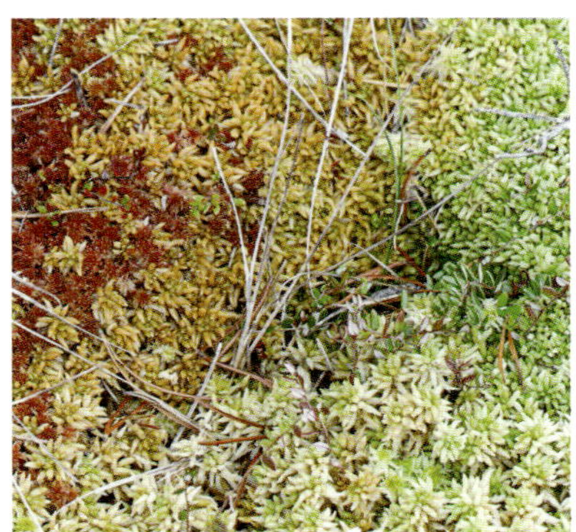

Skookumchuck Narrows Provincial Park

Nearly 800 billion litres of water crash and whirl through the narrows on a 3-metre tide

What Makes This Hot Spot Hot?

- The park has some of the world's largest tidal rapids, famous for their spectacular whirlpools.
- There is great tidal life viewing along the mudflats and rocky shoreline at low tide.
- Wildlife is abundant in the cold, nutrient-rich waters of the narrows.

Address: Egmont Road, Egmont, BC
Tel.: (604) 885-3714
Website:

BC Parks

GPS Coordinates
Latitude: 49.73997
Longitude: –123.90915

Open year-round

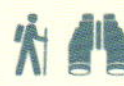

Home to one of the world's fastest and largest tidal rapids, Skookumchuck Narrows Provincial Park provides an opportunity to witness an impressive force of nature, as well as enjoy some unique wildlife viewing opportunities in the same trip. As the dramatic turbulence of the rapids is completely dependent on the tides, be sure to plan your visit accordingly and aim to arrive for high tide to witness the peak power of the water.

Nearly 800 billion litres of water can be seen rushing through the narrows that connect the Sechelt and Jervis Inlets on a 3-metre tide, reaching speeds of up to 30 kilometres per hour. Turbulent rapids and whirlpools are created as tidal streams flowing from one end are restricted by the narrow channel, causing the tide to rise much more quickly on one side. This difference in tide depth creates river-like currents raging through the area with each rise of the tides.

Watch for harbour seals and sea lions feeding and frolicking in the strong currents. Kayakers may also be seen flipping and rolling in the rapids, but please be aware of the fierce danger of these waters, as only extremely experienced whitewater kayakers should venture into the water as the tides surge. The dramatic flood tide can best be viewed from Roland Point, about 3.5 kilometres down the 4-kilometre trail. The North Point, just another 500 metres away, offers plenty of opportunities for viewing whirlpool activity in addition to wildlife watching.

Plan to give yourself enough time to also experience ebb tide in the park as the sea level falls, revealing rich intertidal life. Accessible rocky tidepools are home to a wide variety of urchins, sea stars, crabs, anemones, chitons and more. The 123-hectare park is also home to many types

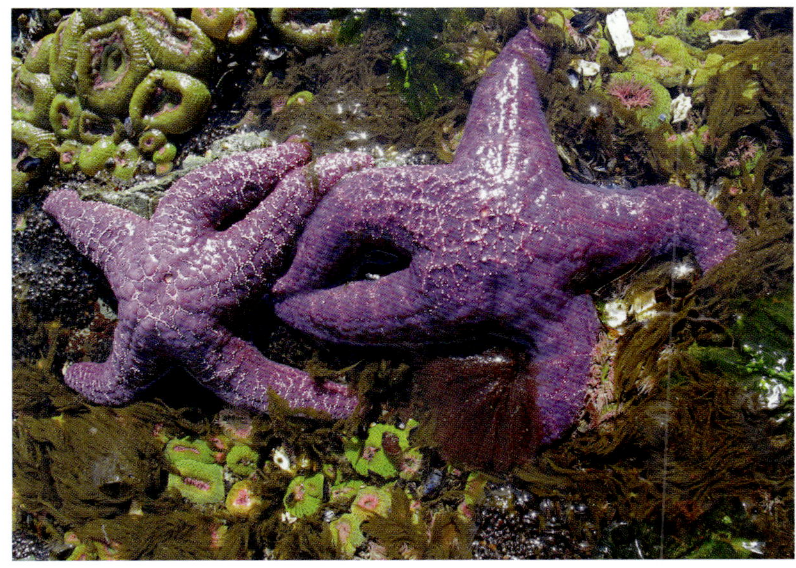

of waterfowl thanks to its cold, nutrient-rich waters. Overwintering grebes, loons, cormorants and other sea-faring avian species arrive in the hundreds, including large numbers of the provincially threatened marbled murrelets. Bonaparte's gulls can sometimes be seen in the thousands.

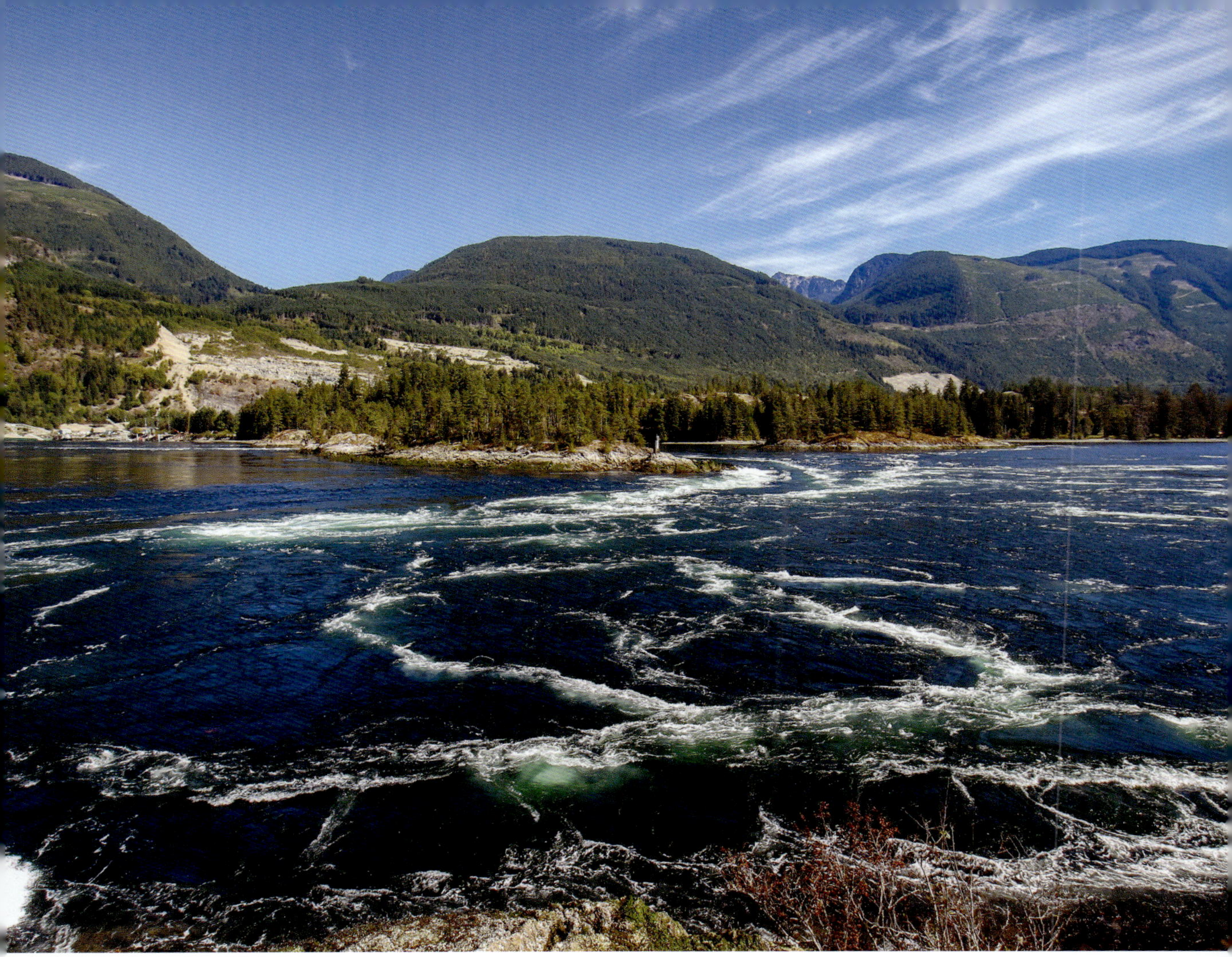

↑ **The rushing water creates whirlpools and whitewater across the inlet.**

→ **You may find purple sea stars at rest next to pink-tipped anemones in tidepools.**

Sooke Potholes

Popular swimming holes transport you back in time to a period when glaciers dramatically shaped the land

What Makes This Hot Spot Hot?

- Salmon spawning occurs in the Sooke River.
- Glacial movement and meltwater carved the bedrock 15,000 years ago, creating dramatic potholes.
- Spring wildflowers bloom along the hiking trails that lead in and out of viewpoints along the river.

Address: Sooke River Road, Sooke, BC
Tel.: (250) 474-1336
Website:

Capital Regional District

GPS Coordinates
Latitude: 48.42843
Longitude: −123.71239

Open year-round

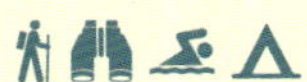

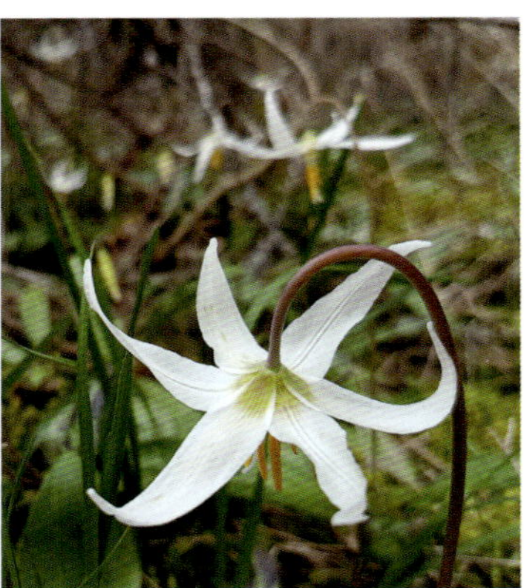

↗ **The nodding flowers of the white fawn lilies, one of the beautiful wildflowers blooming alongside the Sooke Potholes.**

The Sooke Potholes take you on a journey through time when these unique rock formations were initially formed, about 15,000 years ago. Envision the entire area covered in expansive ice packs, the massive glaciers scraping away at the surface of the land below. Huge boulders were carried great distances by these glaciers and deposited in new locations along the way. Beneath the glacial ice, meltwater surged, carving deep pathways through the rock below as it forced its way between ice and rock. The boulders left behind by the glaciers created additional weathering action as their motion and friction further carved the bedrock.

Today you can experience the spectacular results of an ice age long gone. Deep pools formed in river rock and the clear freshwater pools, reflecting green against the dramatic rock formations, not only are of geological interest but also make for great swimming holes. Note that in the early spring the high water runoff and surging Sooke River are too powerful for safe swimming, so wait for water levels to settle later in the year before taking a dip.

The deep canyons and the smooth, polished and sometimes very deep pools create a beautiful backdrop for nature viewing, as the area is also significant for its wildlife. Larger species, including black bears and Roosevelt elk, use this river as a corridor connecting larger spans of wild land. The river supports both chinook and coho salmon runs as well, providing additional wildlife viewing opportunities. This stretch of the Sooke River is protected within both a provincial and regional park, and the Spring Salmon Place, or KWL-UCHUN Campground, is operated by the T'Sou-ke Nation. As this area is sacred land with an important and culturally significant salmon habitat, T'Sou-ke community members are helping to ensure the area and its wildlife are properly protected and respected.

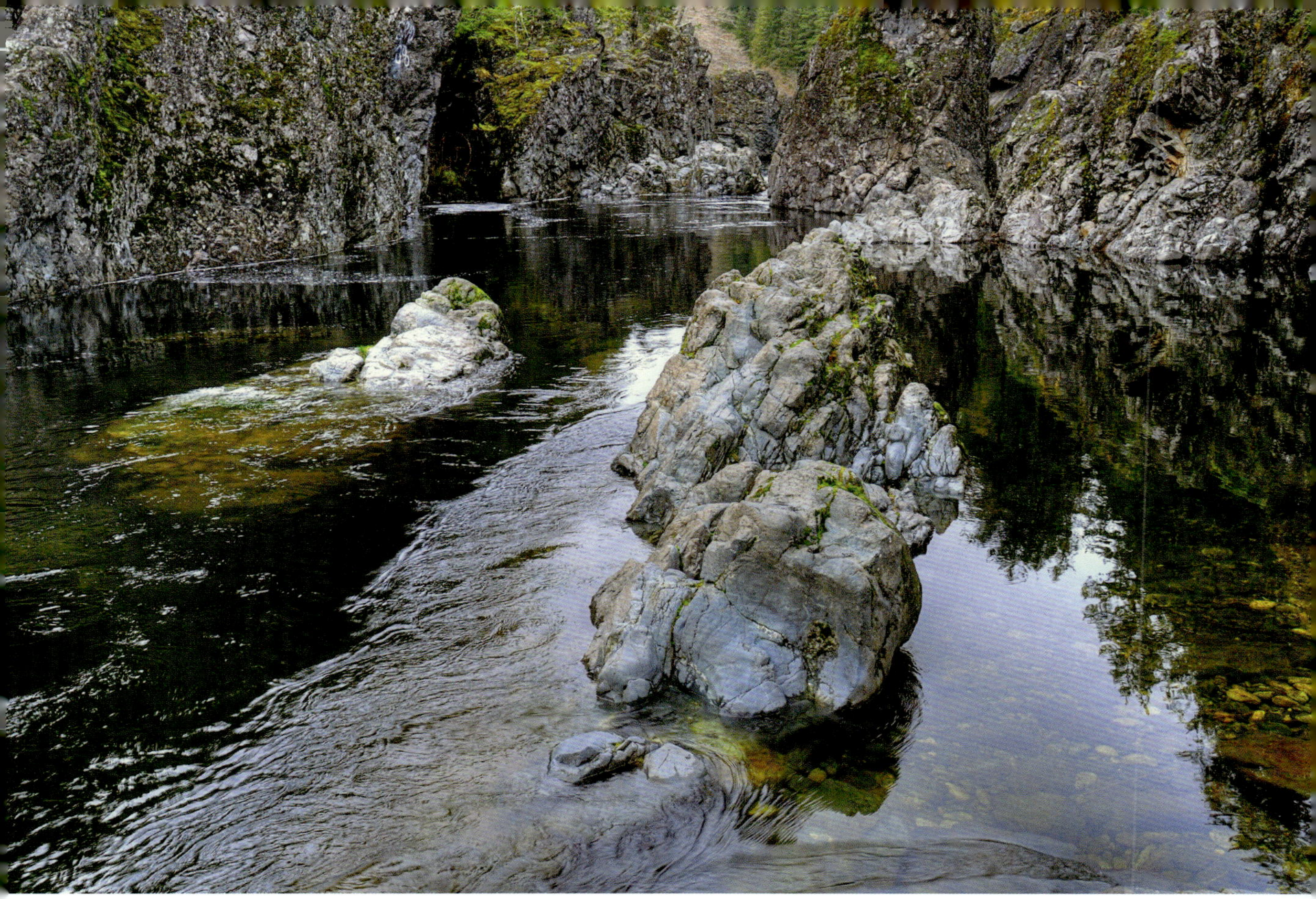

You can see diverse types of wildflowers along the hiking trails that follow the river system. One of BC's most exquisite flowers, the white fawn lily is found in abundance in the early spring. These early blooming flowers are not to be missed, with their delicate nodding heads and the gorgeous chestnut-brown mottling on their leaves that hint at the flowers' association with a spotted deer fawn that is shrouded in the dappled light of the forest. These alluring plants live just a little inland from the riverside, preferring slightly drier and more open habitat to other understory flowers. The red-listed Sierra wood fern is also found in the park.

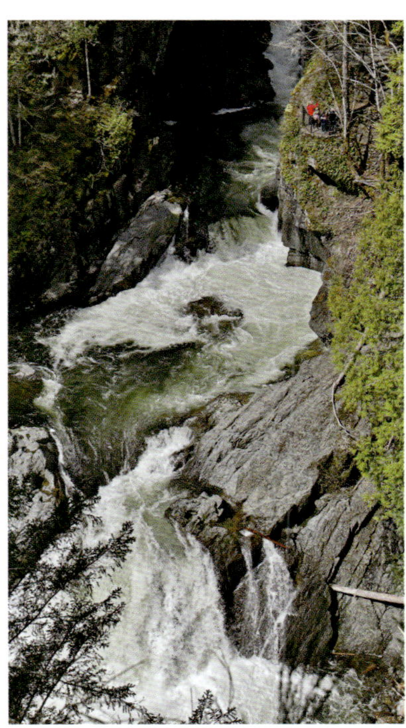

Tofino Mudflats Wildlife Management Area

One of the most important wetland areas for migrating waterfowl and shorebirds in the province

What Makes This Hot Spot Hot?

- The eelgrass beds support a diverse aquatic community.
- Tens of thousands of ducks and geese overwinter in the sheltered waters.
- More than 100,000 western sandpipers visit the mudflats in the summer and fall.

Address: Main access via Sharp Road, 6 km north of the Pacific Rim National Park boundary, along the Pacific Rim Hwy (Hwy 4), Tofino, BC
Tel.: N/A
Website:

Raincoast Education Society

GPS Coordinates
Latitude: 49.1023
Longitude: −125.85536

Open year-round

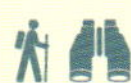

In addition to 338 hectares of forested land, this wildlife haven contains a staggering 1,770 hectares of tidal flats, eelgrass meadows, salt marshes and estuaries. As an integral part of the Clayoquot Sound UNESCO Biosphere Reserve, the Tofino Mudflats Wildlife Management Area is known as one of the most important habitats along the Pacific Flyway.

Where salty ocean waves meet fresh water from the surrounding land, nutrient-rich organic sediments are deposited, creating a muddy sludge that feeds a bountiful community of crabs, clams, ghost shrimp and ribbon worms. This in turn creates a nourishing banquet for travel-weary migrating shorebirds to feast upon. The mud can be nearly 2 metres deep!

The mudflats are also home to Vancouver Island's largest beds of eelgrass, a marine plant species that acts not only as a source of food for visiting avian species but also as a nursery for fish. These beds provide habitat for crustaceans and molluscs as well, which help feed the migratory bird populations.

The mudflats are teeming with birdlife, and not just during spring migration periods. Tens of thousands of ducks and geese overwinter here, and over 100,000 western sandpipers visit the mudflats throughout the summer and fall. In a single day, surveys have counted as many as 19,000. On top of the staggering number of western sandpipers, over 40 species of shorebird frequent the area, including dunlins, sanderlings, short- and long-billed dowitchers, black-bellied plover and least sandpipers. Throughout the year the area is a perfect location to watch for loons, herons, grebes, waterfowl and cormorants. The mudflats are also one of the 10 most critical habitats for overwintering waterfowl,

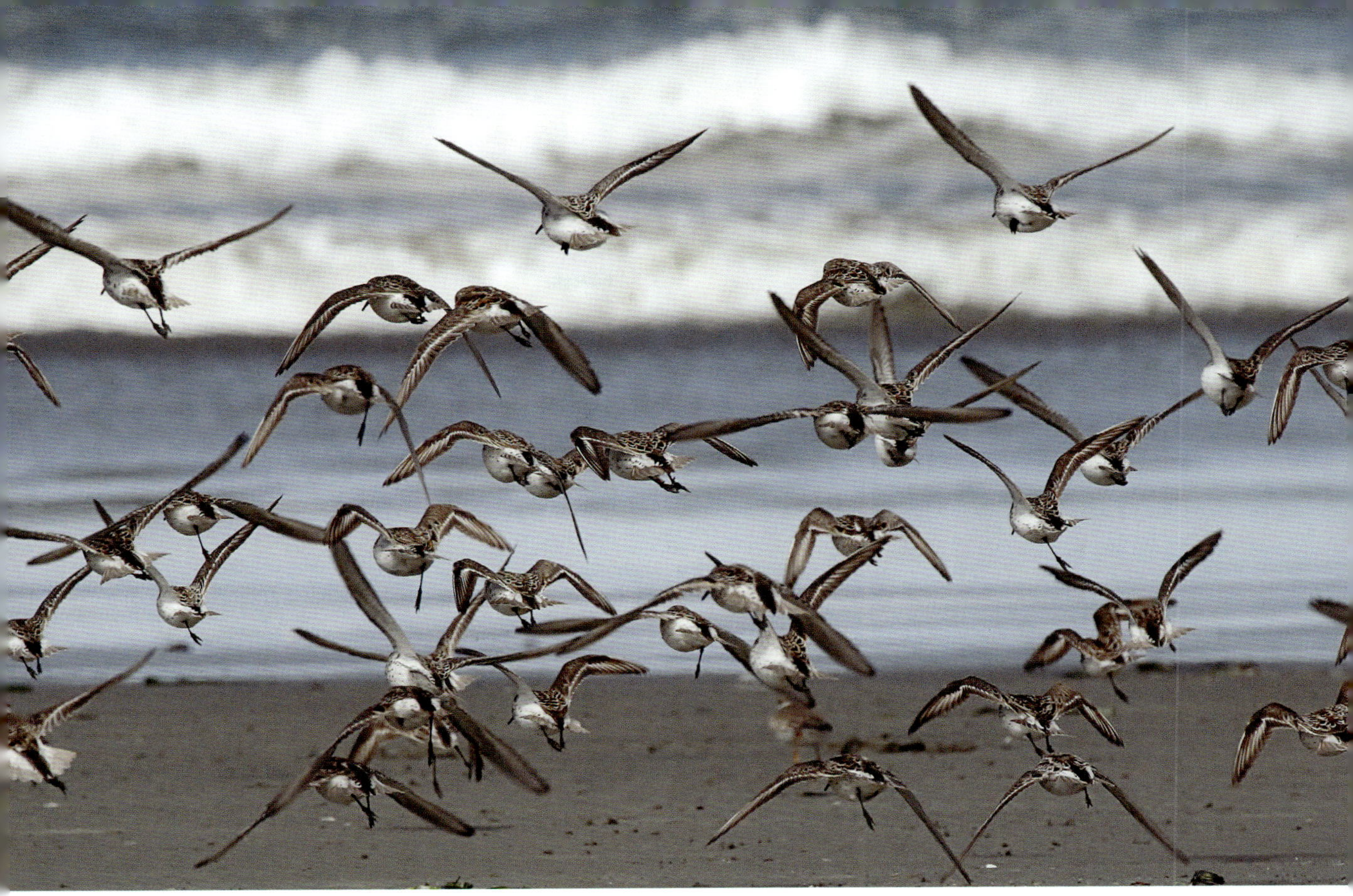

↑ **A fling of western sandpipers takes off along the mudflats.**

including green-winged teal, common mergansers, northern pintails, surf scoters, buffleheads and mallards. The area draws in some of the highest densities of these birds in the whole province, which makes it a year-round birding destination.

The terrestrial lands protected within the area also host a great diversity of avian species, ranging from birds of prey to hummingbirds, that either pass through during migration or breed in the lands adjacent to the mudflats. Woodpeckers take advantage of the standing dead trees near the shoreline, and peregrine falcons are sometimes seen hunting along the mudflats during shorebird migration.

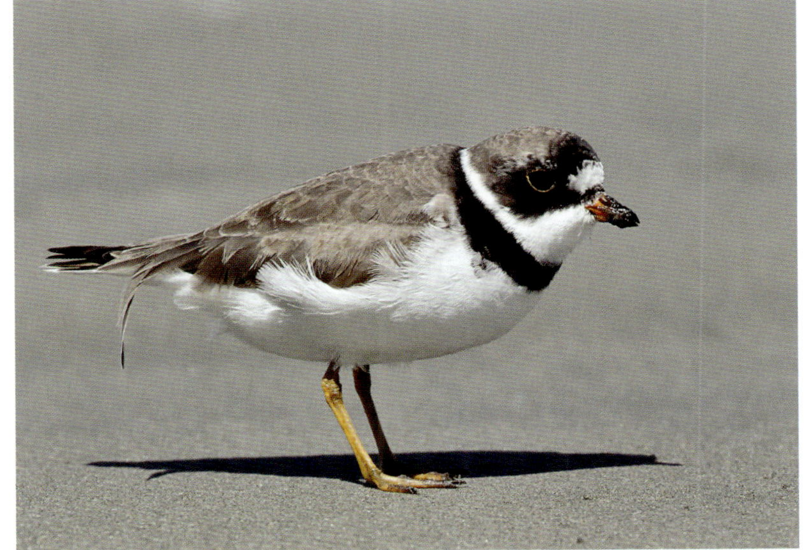

↑ **Semipalmated plovers follow a distinct behavioural pattern while feeding along the flats: run, stop, stare and snatch.**

Upana Caves

This self-guided recreation site provides even novice cave enthusiasts a unique opportunity for exploration

What Makes This Hot Spot Hot?

- The Upana River weaves in and out of the caves, having carved out a passage through the rock thousands of years ago.
- These are some of the most accessible caves on Vancouver Island, where inexperienced cavers can comfortably explore without a guide.
- Wildflowers line the stretches of trail between cave openings.

Address: Head Bay Road, between Gold River and Tahsis, BC
Tel.: N/A
Website: N/A

GPS Coordinates
Latitude: 49.81855
Longitude: −126.24529

Open year-round

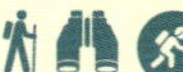 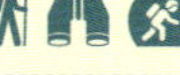

→ **Square-legged camel crickets can be found hiding in the cracks and crevices of these caves.**

Travel the long and winding Highway 28 west of Campbell River to immerse yourself in a remote wilderness setting with many nature-exploring opportunities within reach. Just west of Gold River you'll find Upana Caves, a self-guided day-use site with amazing caves for enthusiasts of any experience level.

The distinctive karst features of these caves are thanks to soluble bedrock that was, and continues to be, transformed by acidic water seeping through the forest floor. The result is an underground drainage system with many interconnected passages waiting to be explored.

Not much thrives where little light reaches, but the caves aren't completely devoid of life. Harvestmen, a type of arachnid often mistaken for a spider, are sometimes found inside the cave, as are square-legged camel crickets, named for their humped back. Without wings, these crickets cannot create the typical chirp this family is famous for, but their extra-long legs and antennae allow them to move about in low light. While one site is named Insect Cave

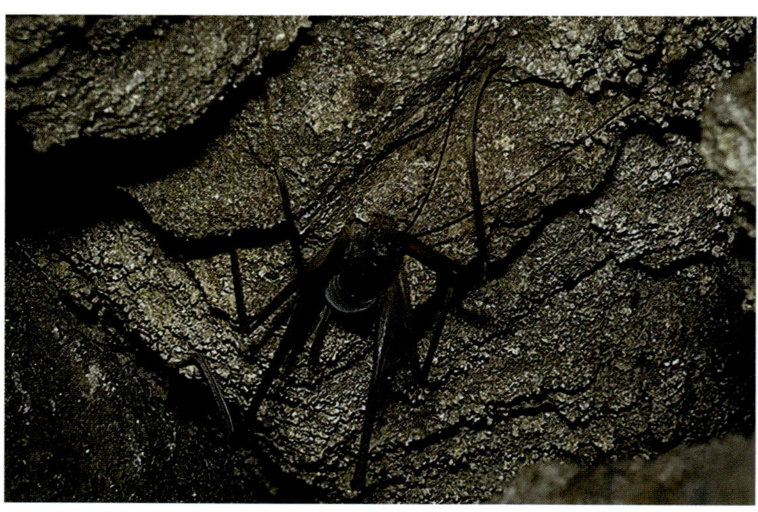

for a reason, there's a chance of seeing arachnids and insects in any of the caves.

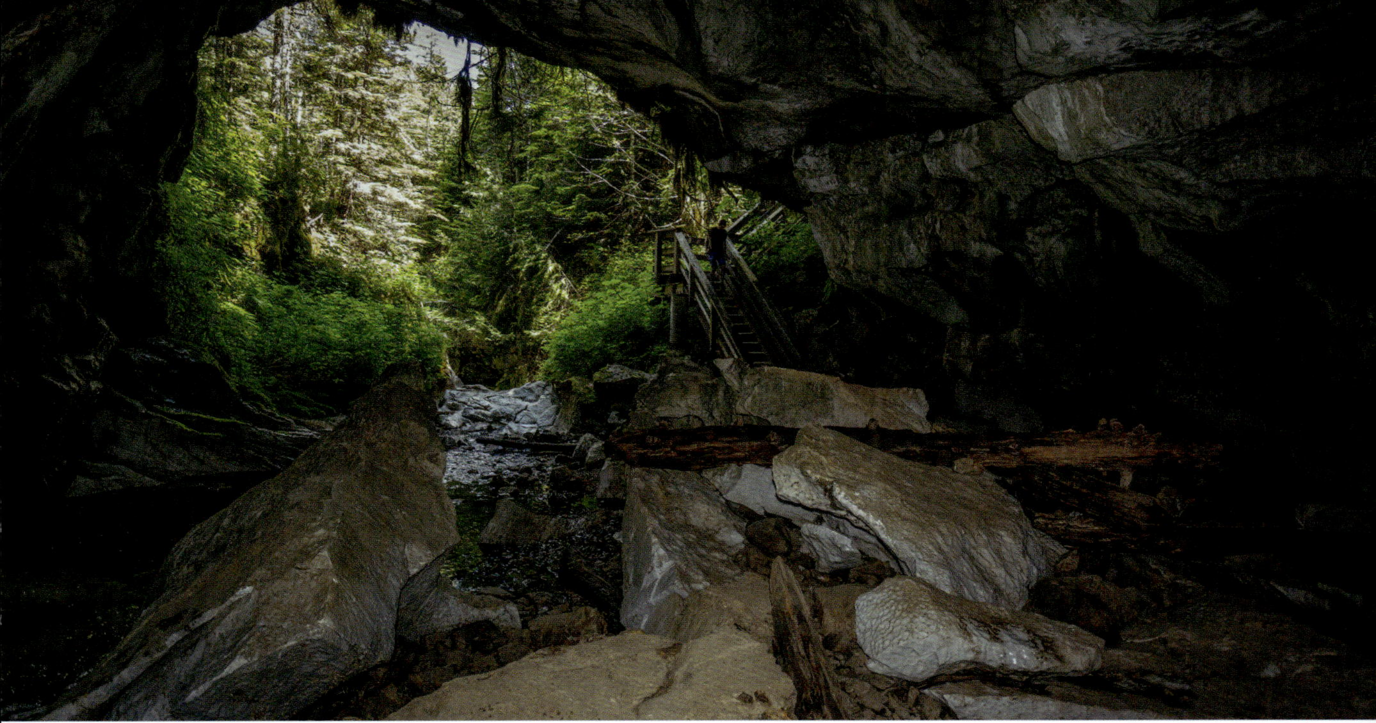

All the caves here provide a great introduction to caving for those with little experience, but Corner-Slither Cave can be explored more extensively by those confident in their abilities. Here, multiple passages and entrances can be accessed through a few tight squeezes.

Resurgence Cave was formed in large part by the Upana River, which still flows through it. A well-built staircase leads you down to its main entrance. Smooth, scalloped walls of white marble stand out throughout this cave — these rocks were once limestone, transformed under great heat and pressure.

Western maidenhair ferns hang along the rocky ledges outside of the caves, and the surrounding forest is great for botanizing. Blankets of bunchberry line the trail, interspersed with rose twisted-stalk, green false hellebore and queen's cup. Look for the bright red flowers of western columbine along the riverbank.

Even if only exploring the shallowest caves, ensure you're prepared for your visit. Wear a helmet to protect yourself from any accidental bumps, and don't forget multiple light sources and warm waterproof layers. These caves stay cool even on the hottest summer days. Stay on designated trails as there may be deep openings hidden in the forest floor.

↑ A stairway brings you down into Resurgence Cave, where you'll find smooth scalloped marble alongside the limestone.

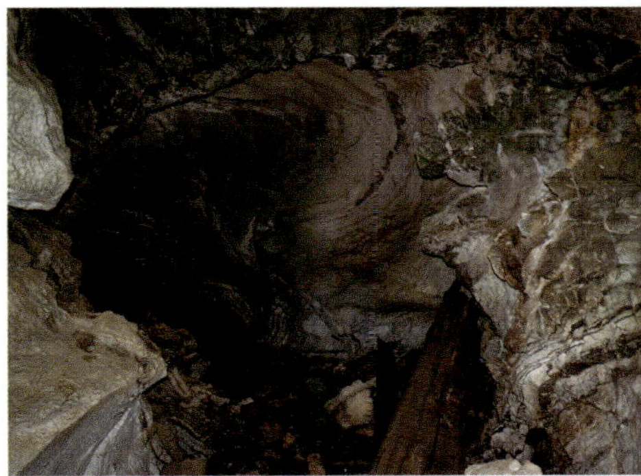

↑ Be prepared with the proper gear, including the right footwear to ensure steady footing in wet and slippery areas of the caves.

PACIFIC RIM NATIONAL PARK RESERVE

West Coast Trail

A marine trail that is the ultimate adventure for lovers of the ocean and coastal forests

What Makes This Hot Spot Hot?

- Rich with history, this lifesaving trail travels through the traditional territories of three Nuu-chah-nulth First Nations.
- Visitors can hike through coastal rainforests and bogs and along seashores with tidepools, all over the course of three to seven days.
- Whales and other marine mammals are frequently sighted from shore.

Address: Pacific Rim National Park Reserve, between Port Renfrew and Bamfield, BC
Tel.: (250) 762-4212
Website:

Parks Canada

GPS Coordinates
Latitude: 48.57706
Longitude: −124.41772

Open from May to September

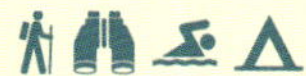

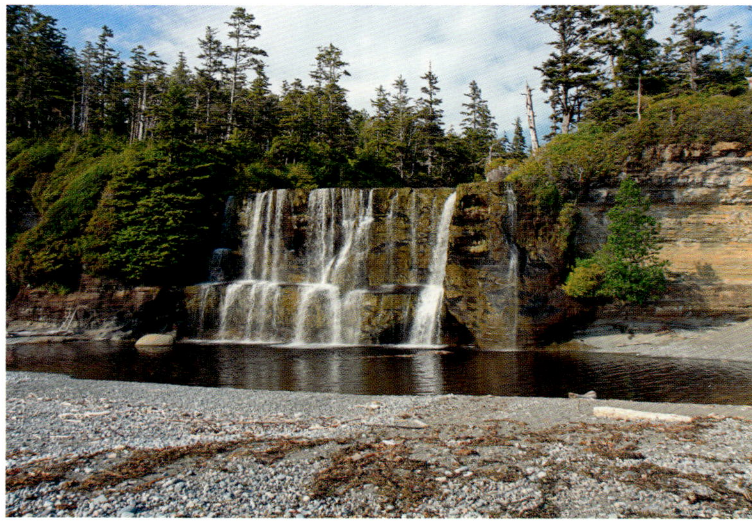

The West Coast Trail, 75 kilometres of breathtaking scenery, draws hikers from across North America. This nature hot spot is worth the preparation it takes to hike and camp for about five nights. The trail meanders in and out of old-growth forest, spending some time among towering cedars, and then moves to the rocky and sandy beaches.

As hikers pass by the old-growth cedar trees they may notice some have strips of bark missing. These trees are culturally modified, meaning the bark was stripped for cultural purposes, often strips would have been used by local First Nations for many types of weaving. Some of these large cedar trees were also cut and hollowed to create dugout canoes.

Having a tide table handy is necessary both for safety while hiking and so hikers can visit the beaches at low tide. On sandy or rocky beaches there is an abundance of intertidal treasures. It is no wonder low tide was referred to by various First Nations as "the table being set." Gooseneck barnacles and mussels cling to rocks, and crabs scuttle about the sand. Search for tidepools where anemones, bright purple sea urchins and a wide variety of sea stars and algae make their homes.

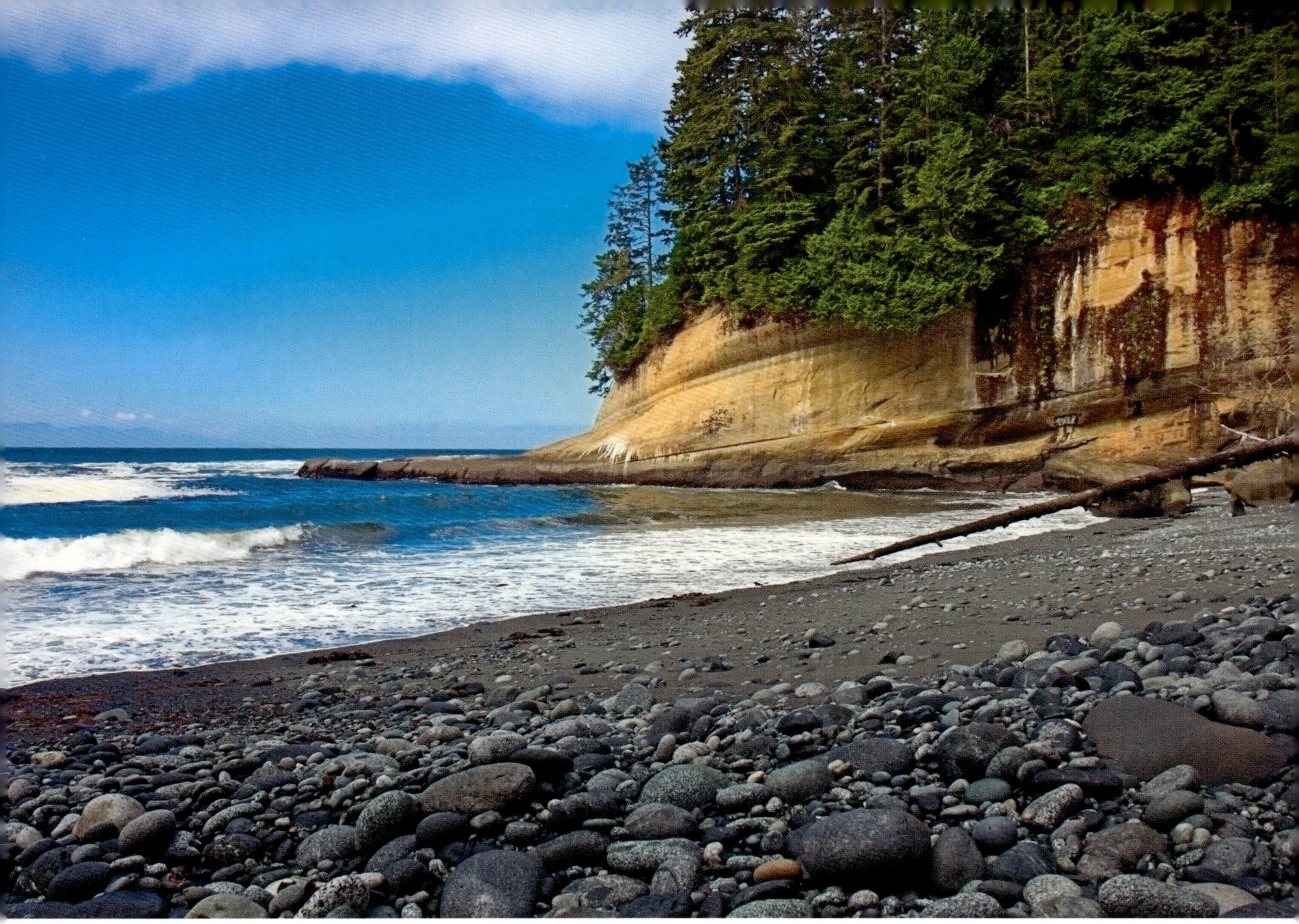

The views along the trail do not disappoint. One of the most picturesque campsites along the hike is near the stunning Tsusiat Falls, where fresh water cascades out of the forest and onto a beach. In addition to being beautiful, the West Coast Trail is rich in history. It runs through the traditional territories of three Nuu-chah-nulth Nations: Huu-ay-aht, Ditidaht and Pacheedaht. The rocky coastline was responsible for many shipwrecks in the 19th and 20th centuries, and so eventually lighthouses, telegraph wires and shelters for shipwreck victims were established along this trail, which at the time was named the Dominion Life Saving Trail.

The West Coast Trail is a through-hike going from Port Renfrew to Bamfield and does have a shuttle linking the two locations. It is well maintained by Parks Canada and requires a fee from hikers. Ladders, bridges and campsites are all in amazing condition.

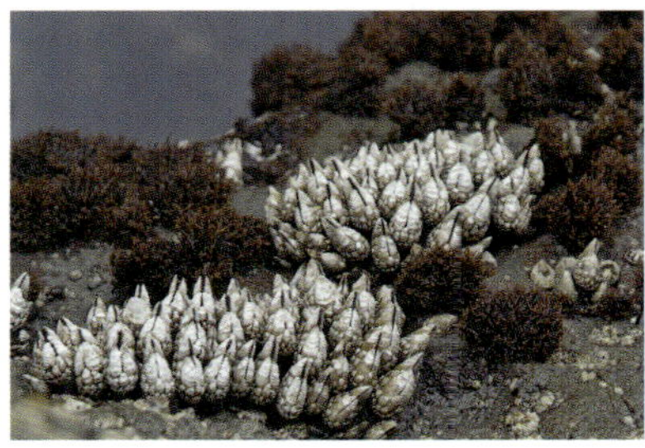

↑ **Gooseneck barnacles cling to the rocks in the intertidal zone.**

↖ **The hike is often along scenic rocky and sandy beaches.**

← **Tsusiat Falls is just one of the gorgeous beaches along the trail.**

Wild Pacific Trail

The vision of a man named Oyster Jim was put into action to create this series of free trails

What Makes This Hot Spot Hot?

- Hikers can explore the Ancient Cedars Trail to view towering redcedars up to 800 years old.
- There are opportunities for whale watching at the Amphitrite Lighthouse.
- Storm watchers frequent the Lighthouse Loop to watch powerful waves collide with the rocky shores.

Address: Ucluelet, BC
Tel.: N/A
Website:

Wild Pacific Trail

GPS Coordinates
Latitude: 48.93858
Longitude: −125.56079

Open year-round

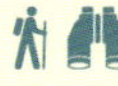

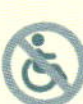

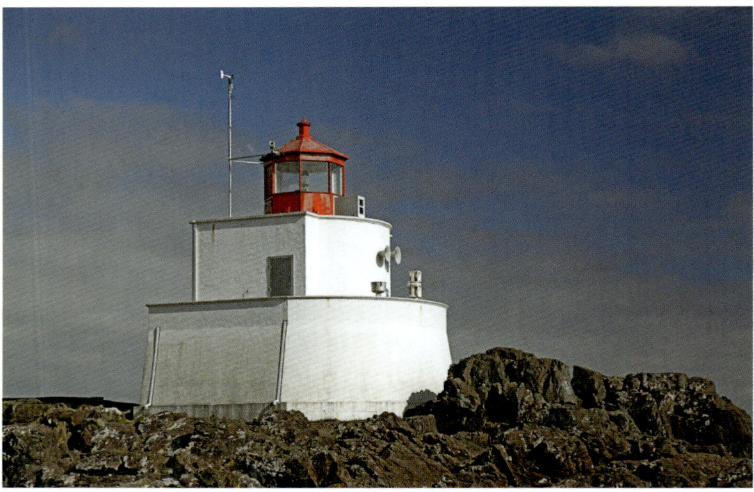

The Amphitrite Lighthouse was built in response to a shipwreck that occurred in 1906.

The Wild Pacific Trail is composed of two main sections of trails that showcase the diversity of the West Coast. Along the trails, you can gaze out on the open ocean as waves crash onto the rocky shores and then admire an old-growth rainforest of cedars, some of which are hundreds of years old, towering over the shiny-leaved bushes of salal.

On the Lighthouse Loop, visitors can tour rocky shorelines en route to the Amphitrite Lighthouse. This well-kept trail with little elevation gain offers access to all. Built over 100 years ago, the lighthouse is situated at the northern mouth of Barkley Sound. From here you can spot the Broken Group Islands and watch the sunset over the open ocean. On windy days, the waves wildly crash on the rocks, showcasing the power of the Pacific Ocean and making this a popular place for storm watchers. Search the horizon for waterspouts shooting out of the ocean or grey whales, humpbacks and orcas that could be swimming just below the surface.

The second section of the Wild Pacific Trail is a more

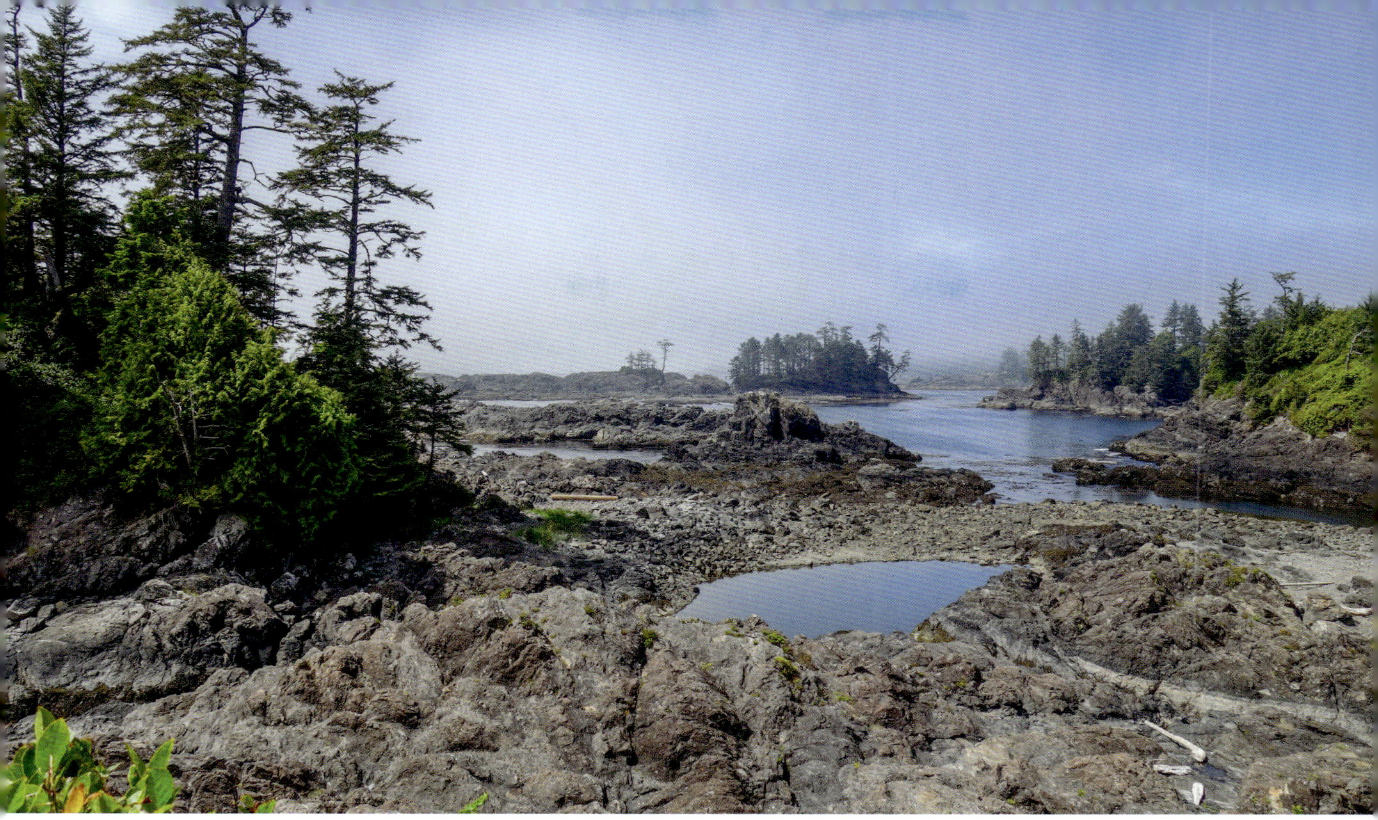

sheltered experience with a wider variety of trail options. Hiking the Ancient Cedars and Rocky Bluffs trails is a humbling experience. Giant redcedar, two of which are over 800 years old, tower above the trail alongside old-growth Sitka spruce and Western hemlock. Redcedars are sometimes referred to as the tree of life because they have so many uses to coastal First Nations. Dugout canoes were carved from these trees, and redcedar bark was carefully stripped and woven into clothing and baskets. The Ancient Cedars Trail can be done as an independent loop or it can be connected to the Rocky Bluffs Trail, which follows along the seashore and provides visitors with views of beautiful rock formations and open ocean.

Seals and sea lions are often sighted just offshore in a protected area known informally as the "sea lion pool."

In 1979 Oyster Jim Martin moved to Ucluelet to farm oysters. Inspired by his stunning surroundings, he soon thought up the idea of creating a hiking trail along Ucluelet's coastline. Eventually his dream was put into action. In 1999 the Wild Pacific Trail Society, which is responsible for the development and maintenance of the trail, was established, ensuring this incredible area would be preserved and freely accessible to visitors.

↑ Powerful waves and winds make it difficult for plants to survive on the rocky shores of the Lighthouse Loop.

→ Cedar and fir trees tower over the trails, including the Lighthouse Loop.

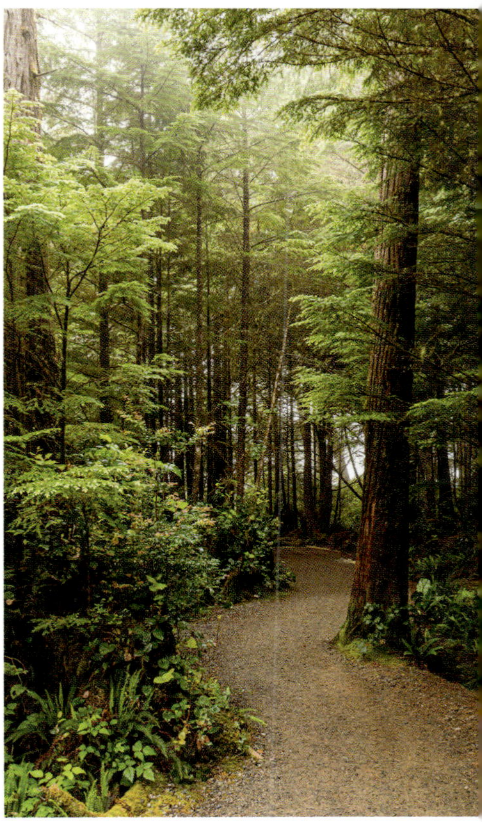

Willow Point Reef

Low tide exposes an incredible diversity of life directly off the Campbell River's shore

What Makes This Hot Spot Hot?

- At low tide, crevices and pools are teeming with sea stars, urchins and much more.
- Large boulders create great sheltered hideouts to investigate.
- This reef is one of the most easily accessed hot spots for intertidal exploration on all Vancouver Island.

Address: South Island Hwy, Campbell River, BC
Tel.: N/A
Website: N/A

GPS Coordinates
Latitude: 49.97061
Longitude: –125.20624

Open year-round

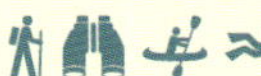

↗ **Red urchins can be found in abundance at the farthest point of the reef, but they are only exposed in numbers at the lowest of tides.**

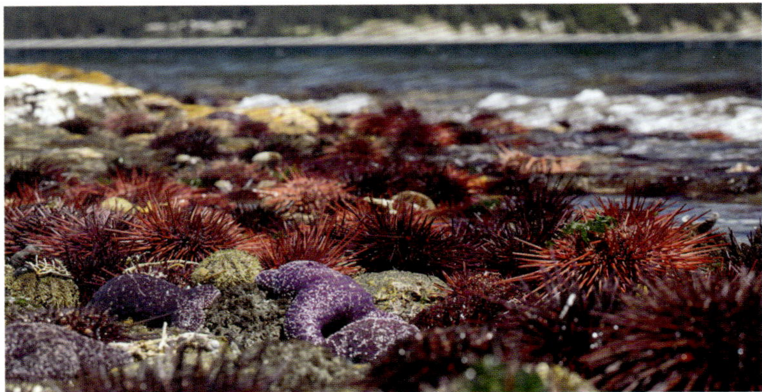

It may be surprising to learn that one of the best hot spots for viewing intertidal life on all Vancouver Island is found just off the highway that cuts through Campbell River. Willow Point Reef doesn't have the deep, round tidepools you might expect. Instead, crevices and shallow pools in the long stretches of flat rock create temporary saltwater refuges. As the sea recedes, the exposed reef forms a distinct point — with so much to see, begin your exploration about an hour before peak low tide to make the most of it.

Willow Point Reef hosts an incredible diversity of life, from fish to crabs to sea cucumbers to chitons and even the occasional abalone or nudibranch. Tread very carefully as the seaweed-covered rocks are not only incredibly slippery, but also teaming with life. Large boulders dot the intertidal landscape, so come prepared to crouch and kneel in order to get a better vantage point for peeking underneath. Soft bodies of sea anemones hang slackly from under these rocks, their long columns drooping heavily without the aid of the water's buoyancy.

Green sea urchins are abundant, and huge numbers of bright red urchins also become visible on particularly low tides. Ochre sea stars fill nearly every crevice with brilliant purple, pink and orange hues, and leather stars cling to the undersides of rocks or rest in shallow pools. Other stars may make an appearance too, including Pacific blood stars, giant pink stars and, if you're really lucky, the many-legged sunflower stars.

Daisy brittle stars, found in a wide array of colours and patterns, hide out under flat rocks along the tip of the reef. As their name implies, these distant relatives of sea stars are extremely fragile, so look but don't touch. This hands-off rule applies for all life found along the reef to minimize disturbance to these wondrous creatures.

Willow Point Reef is not a formal marine park and lacks any wayfinding signage, but luckily it isn't too difficult to find. Jaycee Park provides the closest access, with concrete steps that bring you down to the beach. There is additional parking available at the Ken Forde Boat Ramp if you're up for a bit more walking along the slippery, seaweed-covered shoreline.

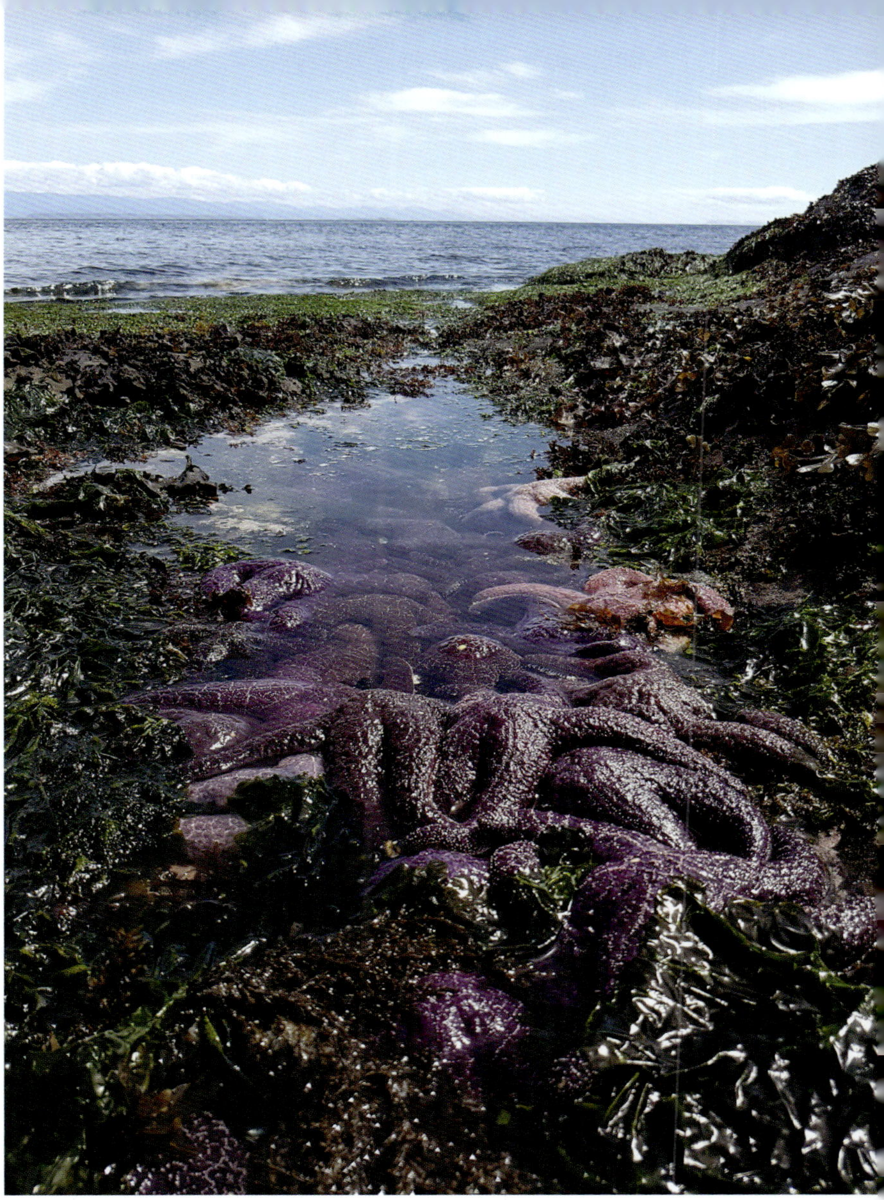

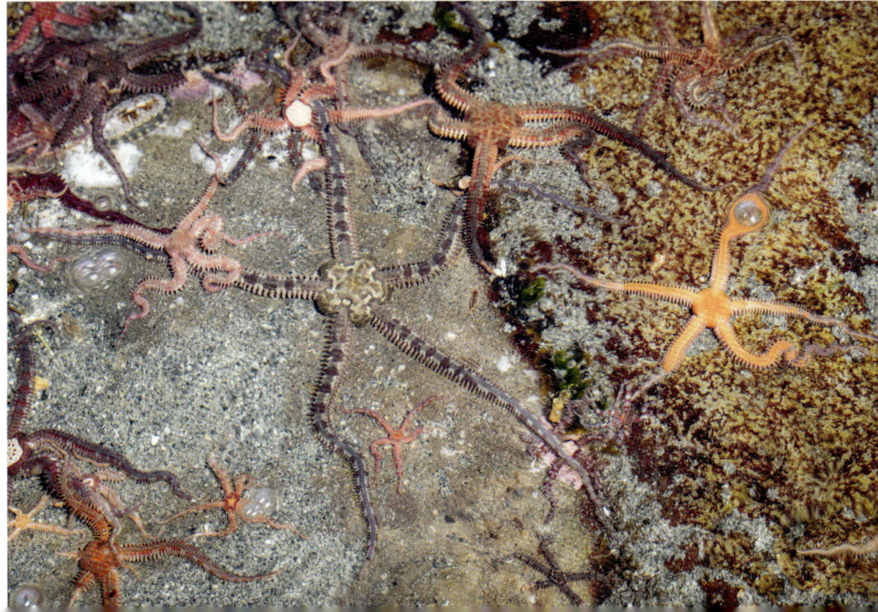

Witty's Lagoon Regional Park

One of the most ecologically diverse parks in the region is worth planning a full day around

What Makes This Hot Spot Hot?

- Diverse habitats attract a wide range of species that thrive within the forest, marsh, lagoon and shorelines of this park.
- The picturesque Sitting Lady Falls is just a short hike from the parking lot.
- The park's forest is home to many bigleaf maples, whose giant vibrant green leaves provide a beautiful contrast against the conifers.

Address: 4115 Metchosin Road, Victoria, BC
Tel.: (250) 360-3000
Websites:

Capital Regional District

GPS Coordinates
Latitude: 48.38907
Longitude: −123.52461

Open year-round

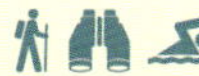

→ **Flowering bigleaf maples along the forest trail.**

Although celebrated for its namesake body of water, Witty's Lagoon Regional Park also encompasses coniferous and mixed forests, sandy beaches, rugged shores and salt marshes, in addition to its brackish lagoon, all found within its 22.6-hectare area.

You will find many bigleaf maple trees amid the towering Douglas-fir along the park's trail, which splits and provides multiple angles to enjoy stunning views of Bilston Creek spilling over Sitting Lady Falls to feed fresh water into Witty's Lagoon. A dramatic cascade in the winter and early spring, the falls slow nearly to a trickle in the peak of summer. Although replenished with fresh water at this head, the lagoon is brackish thanks to the salt water at its mouth. The shallow and warm waters of the lagoon attract a variety of salt-tolerant animals that come to feed on the plentiful microscopic aquatic organisms. Migrating birds enjoy the brackish waters of the lagoon as part of their stopover in the spring and fall.

During the highest tides of the winter, the salt water floods over the spit into the

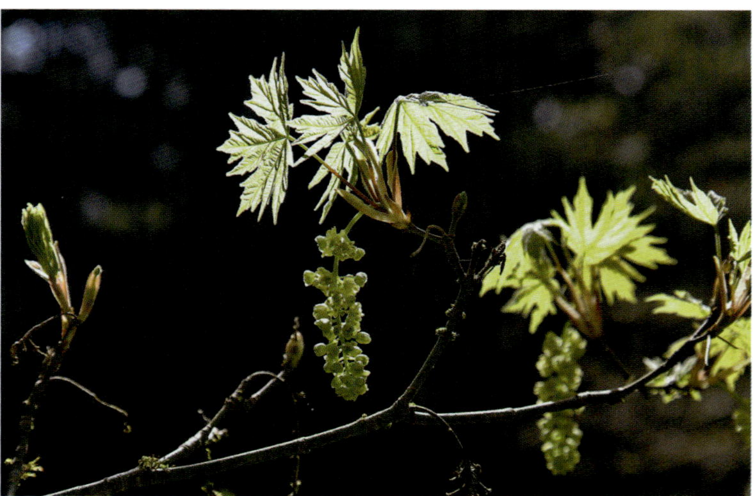

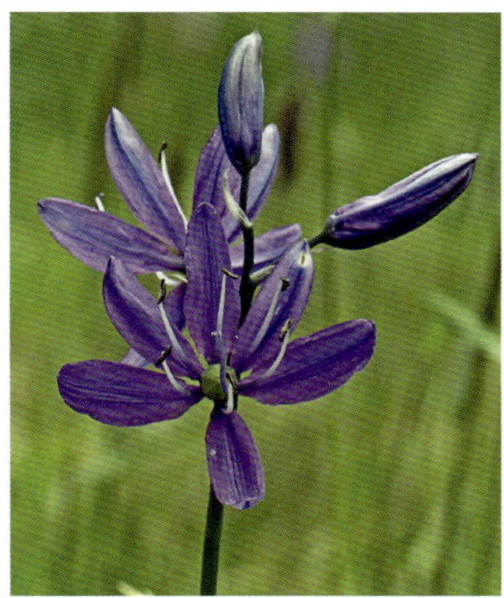

land beyond. Here the salty wetland conditions are home to a distinctive sampling of plants, since few species tolerate the salty conditions and seasonal flooding. The parasitic salt marsh dodders cling to the dense mats of glassworts in this unique site and are among the salt-tolerant plants that are a critical food source for visiting birds.

Time your visit right and you are in for a brilliant spring wildflower display throughout the understory of the forest. In Tower Point's open, grassy meadows you will find impressive numbers of vivid purple and blue Menzie's larkspur and common camas lilies.

The wide beach is often busy with visitors enjoying the sunshine, ocean waves and beautiful views, but despite being a popular area for human activity, there is still much other life to see along the vast expanse of shoreline. Hermit crabs scurry along in their hijacked snail shells, and shield limpets cling to their spot on the rocky outcroppings. River otters and harbour seals make the most of the rolling waves and kelp beds offshore.

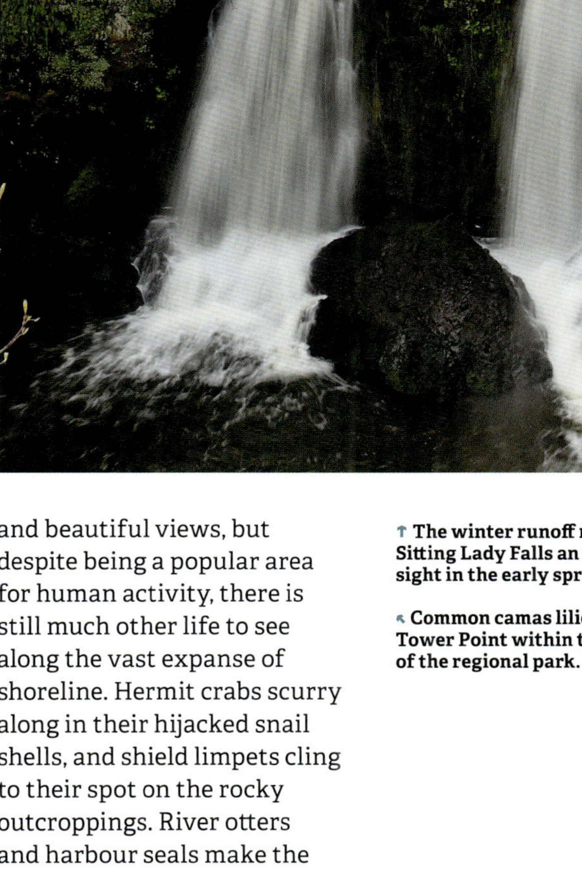

↑ The winter runoff makes Sitting Lady Falls an impressive sight in the early spring.

↖ Common camas lilies bloom at Tower Point within the boundaries of the regional park.

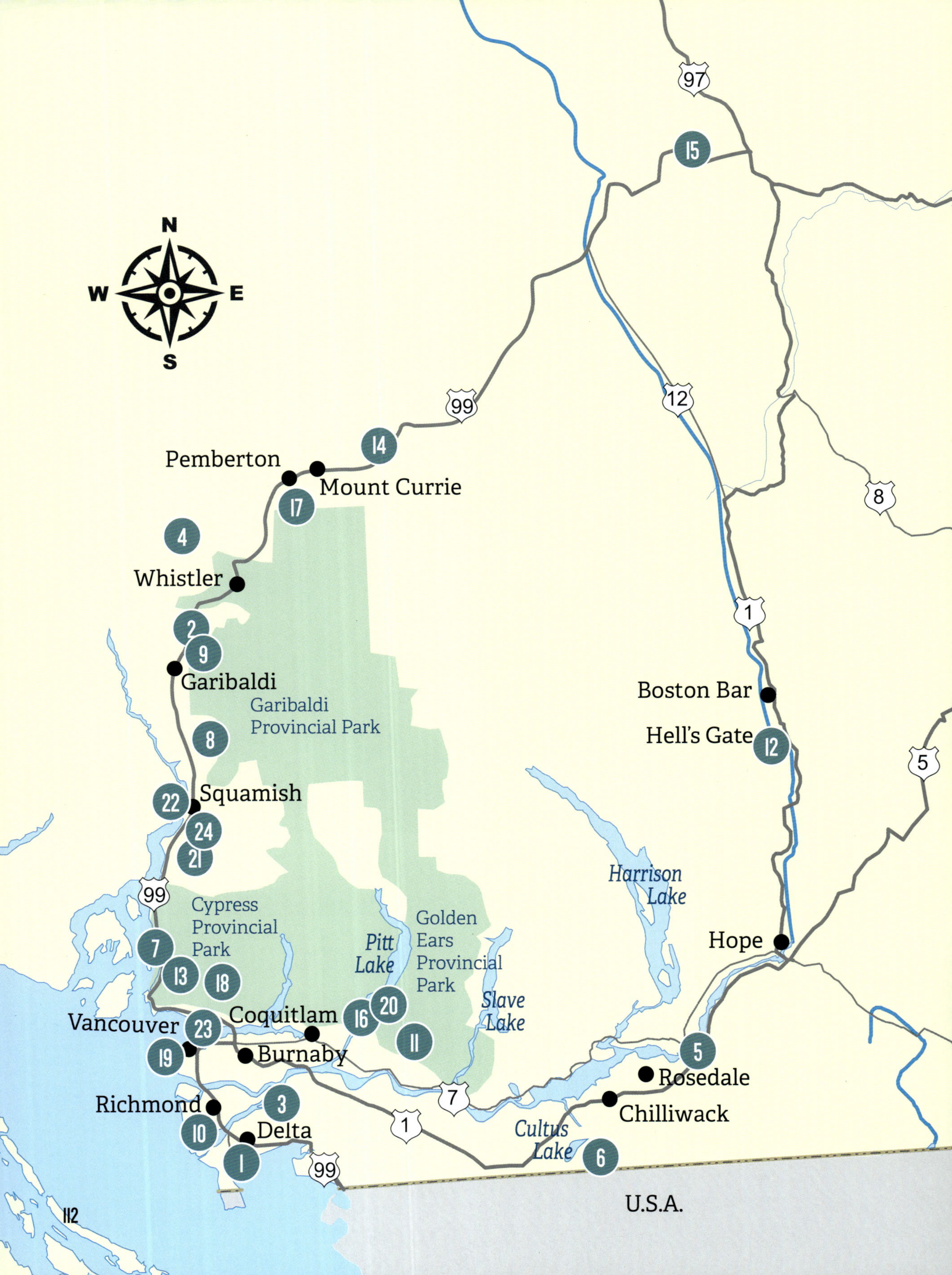

N
W E
S
97
15
99
12
14
Pemberton
Mount Currie
17
4
8
Whistler
2
9
Garibaldi
Garibaldi Provincial Park
Boston Bar
8
Hell's Gate
12
5
22
Squamish
24
21
Harrison Lake
99
Cypress Provincial Park
Golden Ears Provincial Park
Pitt Lake
Slave Lake
7
13
18
Hope
16
20
Vancouver
23
11
19
Burnaby
Coquitlam
5
Rosedale
Richmond
3
Chilliwack
10
Delta
1
7
1
Cultus Lake
6
99
U.S.A.

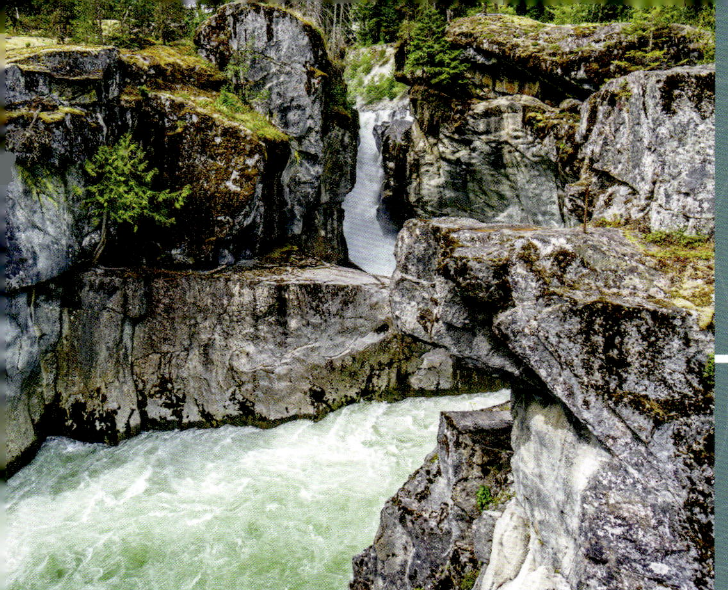

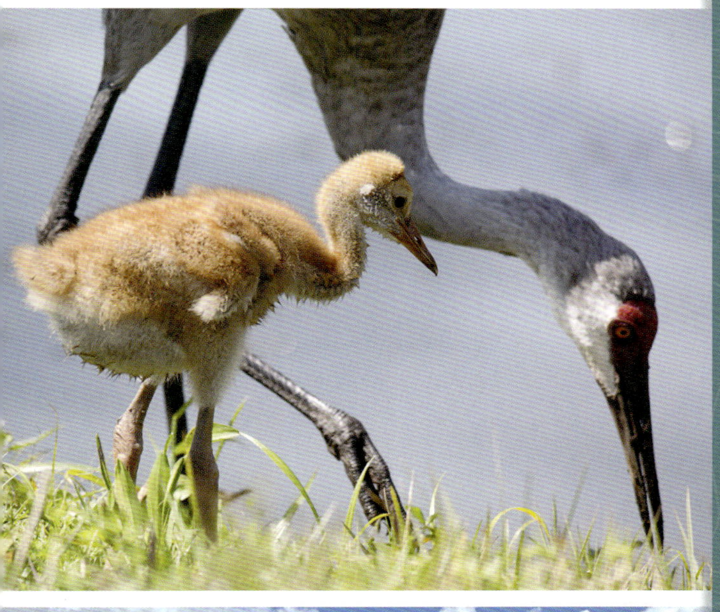

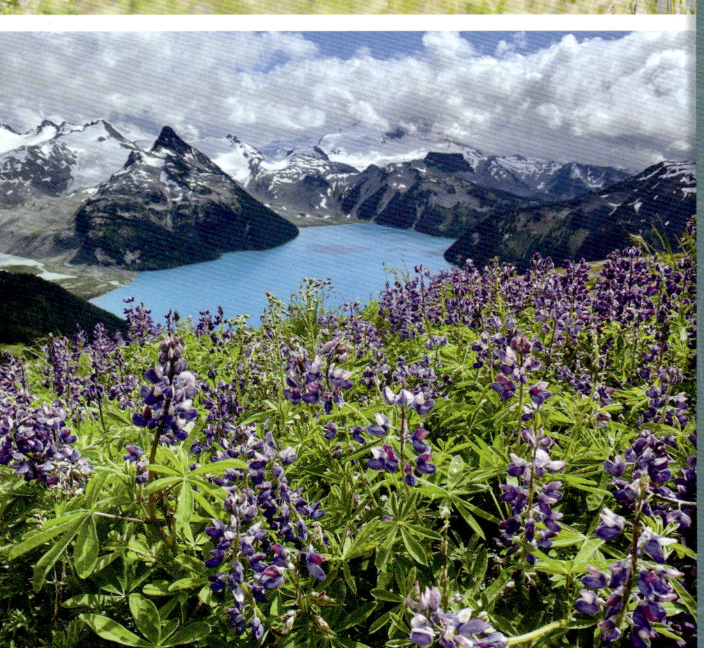

Lower Mainland

Boundary Bay Regional Park

This peninsula is vital to migratory birds and is an internationally recognized Important Bird Area

What Makes This Hot Spot Hot?

- Fresh water meets ocean mudflats, creating naturalist opportunities for plant lovers and birders.
- Thousands of birds rest and refuel here during their migration.
- Birders can visit any time of year as birds of prey overwinter here.

Address: Boundary Bay Road, Delta, BC
Tel.: (604) 224-5739
Website:

Metro Vancouver

GPS Coordinates
Latitude: 49.01844
Longitude: −123.04974

Open year-round

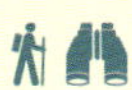

(Check ahead)

➜ **The mudflats are a perfect habitat for marine invertebrates and attract many water birds.**

Boundary Bay is truly a birder's paradise. Be sure to bring your binoculars, as this park is an internationally recognized Important Bird Area. Thousands of birds stop here to rest and refuel on their migratory journey along the Pacific Flyway between Alaska and South America.

Over the course of a day on the beach you might spot a great horned owl perched near a trail, watch sandpipers feed in the mudflats, observe many different species of ducks and spy songbirds in the shrubs. These beach trails are set up for people who like to take their time and soak in their surroundings. The branching trail system has multiple viewing platforms with interpretive signs. Trails loop along the windswept shores, through forested and grassy areas and between salty marshes.

As the park sits within the boundaries of the Fraser River Estuary, fresh water flows into the ocean here, creating an environment in the mudflats that is perfect for marine invertebrates. This makes the park the ultimate feasting ground for hungry migratory birds. This varied landscape is also home to small rodents, which makes Boundary Bay an important place for birds of prey as well. The opportunity to view snowy owls and other birds overwintering here attracts birders during the winter months when the shores are less crowded. However, there is never a bad time to visit this park. May and June are particularly good times to view migratory birds.

The variety of ecosystems that supports all of this life also supports unique plants such as saltbush and salicornia, also known as sea asparagus, which grows exclusively in salt marshes and along beaches. Salicornia is a succulent plant that changes from green to red seasonally. If you look closely you may see moth caterpillars feeding on the plant.

As this is an important area for tired and hungry birds it is crucial that dogs remain on leashes and people stick to the designated paths in the park to allow the birds to refuel in peace.

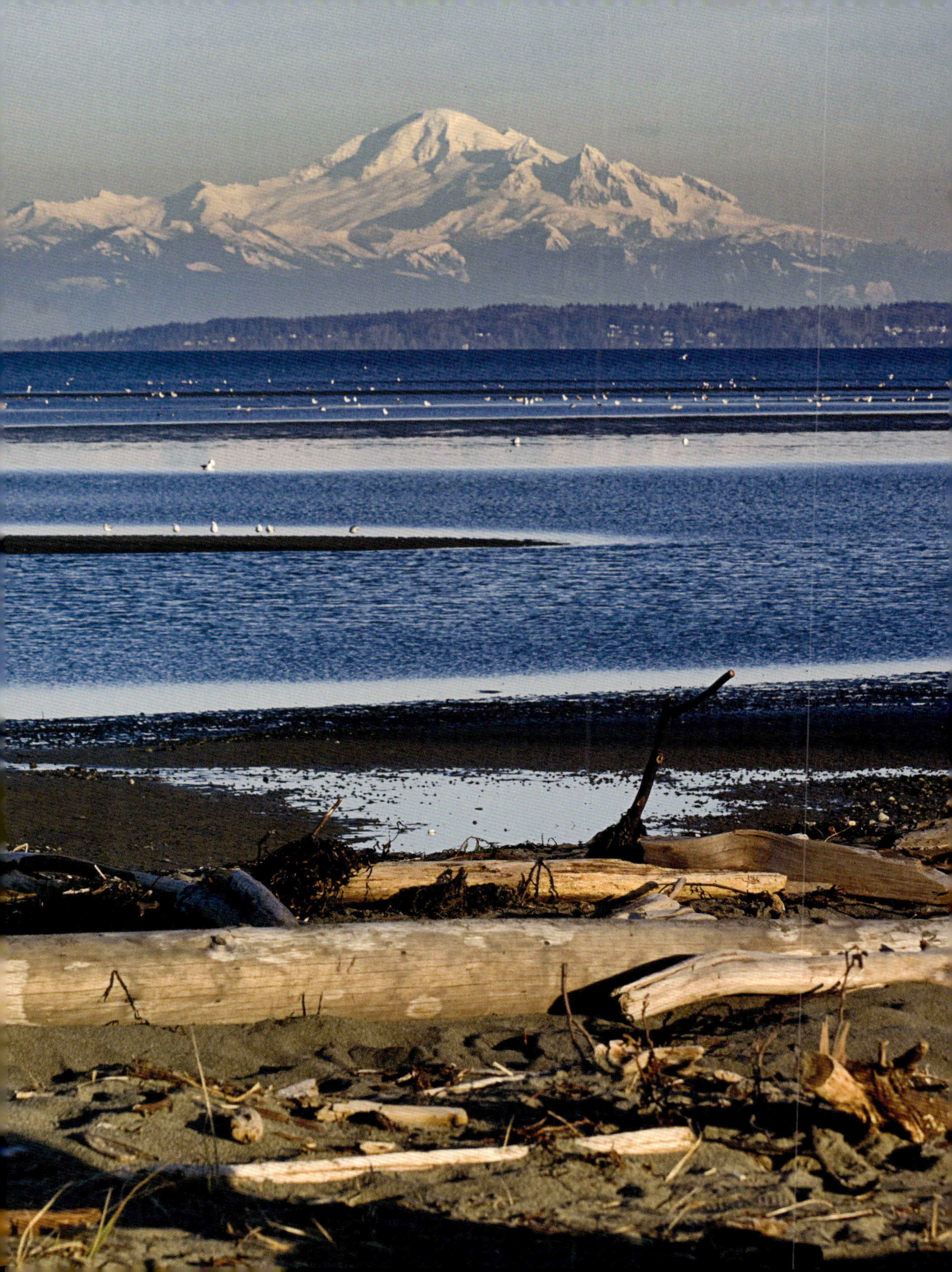

BRANDYWINE FALLS PROVINCIAL PARK

Brandywine Falls

Rushing water flows from the forest into a cavernous basin surrounded by steep rock walls

What Makes This Hot Spot Hot?

- The forest is a protected area for red-legged frogs, a blue-listed species.
- Visitors get multiple viewpoints of the 70-metre waterfall carving its way through volcanic basalt rock.
- Dense pine forests, rare for coastal British Columbia, allow you to view a unique environment normally associated with the Interior.

Address: Brandywine Falls Provincial Park, Whistler, BC
Tel.: (604) 986-9371
Website:

BC Parks

GPS Coordinates
Latitude: 50.03599
Longitude: −123.11950

Open year-round

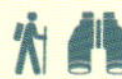 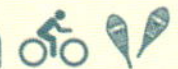

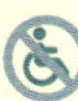

↗ **The northern red-legged frog may be seen in the wetlands around the falls.**

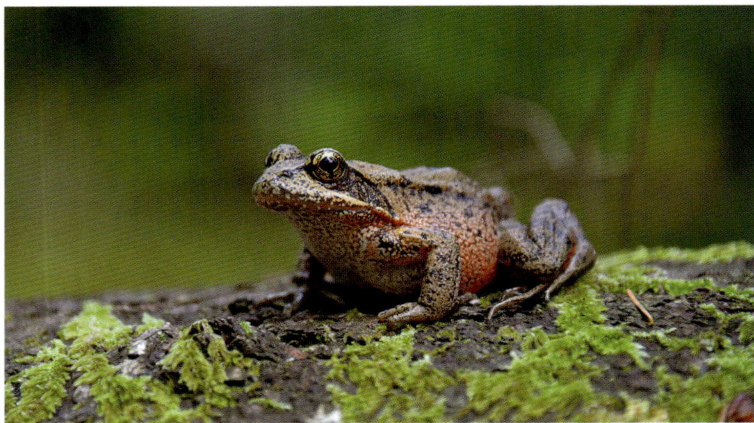

Whistler is known primarily as a skiing destination, but it is surrounded by natural beauty. Brandywine Falls Provincial Park is just south of Whistler and makes for a beautiful day trip. The falls can be reached on relatively easy trails that are a short distance from the parking lot. The Brandywine Creek exits the pine forest abruptly and cascades 70 metres into a large basin surrounded by steep, rocky cliffs. The surrounding lodgepole pine forest is rare for coastal British Columbia, an area that generally boasts moist cedar forests. You may feel like you are travelling through an Interior forest, without the road trip. Glaciers shaped this landscape, wearing down the volcanic rock that the river and surrounding water bodies now occupy. With multiple viewing platforms a short distance from the trailhead, this waterfall is a stunning example of the beauty of British Columbia. Brandywine Falls is a spectacular sight in both summer and winter.

Snowshoers frequent the area during the winter months. Although the parking lot gate is not open during winter, a parking area alongside the road remains plowed. In the winter the basin is filled with snow and splash-back

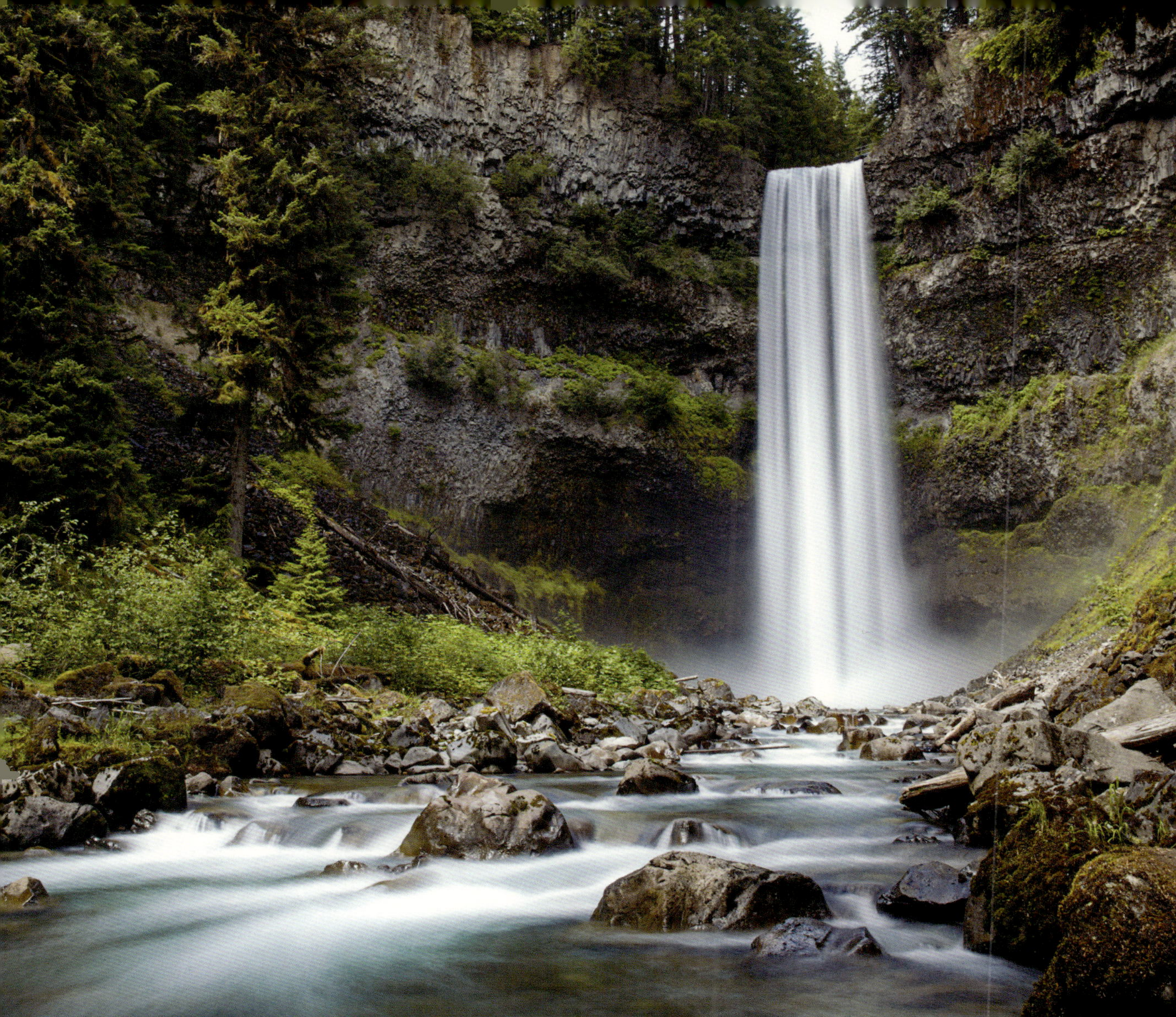

from the waterfall freezes on the surrounding rock faces, leaving icicles hanging from rocky outcrops.

More trails in the park lead to lakes, streams and marshy areas. Combined with the forest this area creates a perfect habitat for the northern red-legged frog. A medium-sized frog named for its red underbelly and hind legs, the red-legged frog is a blue-listed species in British Columbia. Found only along the southern coast of the Mainland and throughout Vancouver Island, these frogs prefer damp forests with slow moving water. Keep an eye out for them on the meandering trails as they spend most of their adult lives hiding under forest debris, only returning to water to hunt and breed.

↑ Brandywine Falls continues to carve the rocky landscape with a steady stream of flowing water.

Burns Bog Delta Nature Reserve

The largest raised peat bog on North America's west coast

What Makes This Hot Spot Hot?

- The area is a key nesting habitat for the greater sandhill crane.
- It is home to regionally rare species, including Pacific water shrews, southern red-backed voles and painted turtles.
- Extensive peat bogs like this one act as carbon sinks, absorbing and storing large amounts of carbon.

Address: Nordel Court, Delta, BC
Tel.: (604) 572-0373
Website:

Burns Bog
Conservation Society

GPS Coordinates
Latitude: 49.14354
Longitude: –122.92940

Open year-round

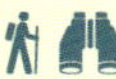

Burns Bog is the largest undeveloped urban landmass in North America. At 3,000 hectares, its area is eight times that of Stanley Park, and it is a vital habitat in the Lower Mainland. Over 2,000 hectares are inaccessible to the public, protected as the Burns Bog Ecological Conservancy Area, but nature enthusiasts can still explore this special bog habitat by visiting the Delta Nature Reserve on the eastern perimeter of the bog. Raised boardwalks allow for great views of the bog and forest, but the area often floods, so come prepared for wet weather and a flooded walking path.

A vital stopover for migrating birds, the bog is an especially fabulous birding destination in the spring, but there are significant birding opportunities year-round. Burns Bog provides habitat for locally rare birds — blue-listed species found around the bog include purple martin, green herons, and barn and short-eared owls.

Keep your ears tuned for the bugling cry of the greater sandhill crane, which can be heard over 4 kilometres away. Most of the cranes pass through the area during migration, but the bog is also one of only a few nesting sites these graceful birds use in the Lower Mainland. Known for their dancing skills, sandhill cranes court each other using a fantastic display of leaping, bowing and flapping their outstretched wings while hopping and spinning.

The red-listed southern red-backed vole was once believed to be extirpated from Canada until a population was discovered in Burns Bog in 1999. The Pacific water shrew, one of the world's smallest diving mammals, is found nowhere else in Canada but southwestern British Columbia, and although in decline, this red-listed species calls Burns Bog home. BC's southwestern population of painted turtles is also red-listed, so

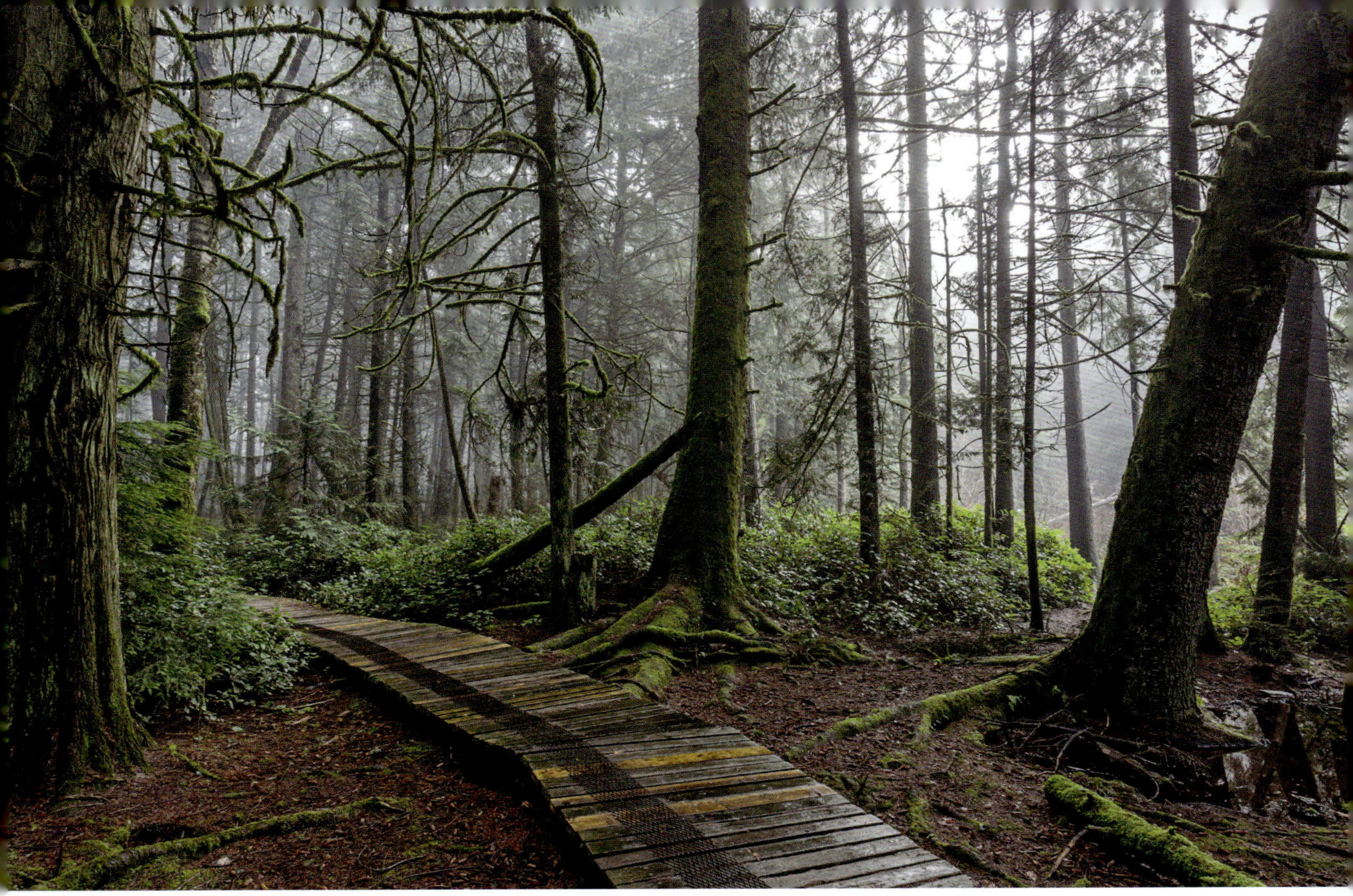

Burns Bog provides a critical habitat for the province's only native freshwater turtle.

This area is a wonderful spot for dragonfly enthusiasts, as it is home to species that are often difficult to find elsewhere in the Lower Mainland. Zigzag and subarctic darners are typically found in northern peatland habitat but can be spotted at Burns Bog, along with chalk-fronted corporals and yellow-legged meadowhawks.

The sphagnum moss in the bog began accumulating thousands of years ago. In some areas of the bog the peat deposits are over 20 metres deep. This is where the classification of raised peat bog comes from, as the peat is raised above the groundwater table. Peatland is an incredibly important carbon sink, storing vast quantities of biomass that might otherwise be converted into carbon dioxide and methane — both greenhouse gases. Peat is often used for agriculture, or extracted for fuel or horticultural use, so protecting peatland like Burns Bog is not only vital to the biodiversity it supports but also as a critical carbon repository on a warming planet.

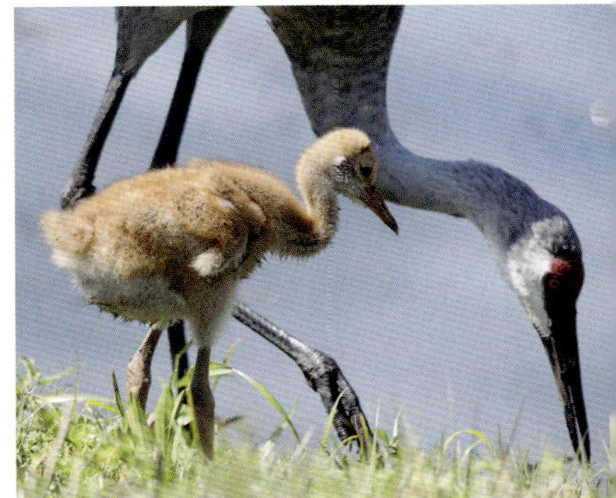

↑ Raised boardwalks run through the nature reserve, allowing views of the bog and forest.

→ A greater sandhill crane chick is a special sight at Burns Bog.

Callaghan Valley

Abundant with natural beauty year-round, this area is a destination for winter sports enthusiasts and summer hikers

What Makes This Hot Spot Hot?

- Visitors can snowshoe or ski through alpine forests and meadows while enjoying breathtaking views of the coastal mountains.
- In the summer hikers enjoy a different experience as they stroll through the same meadows and past streams and wetlands.
- The oldest cedar trees in the Sea-to-Sky Corridor line some of the trails.

Address: 5 Callaghan Road, Whistler, BC
Tel.: (604) 964-0060
Website:

Ski Callaghan

GPS Coordinates
Latitude: 50.13948
Longitude: −123.11361

Open seasonally, weather permitting. Check the website for hours and conditions

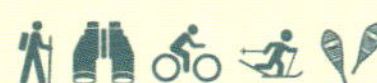

♿ **(Check ahead)**

Within the Callaghan Valley are two nordic ski areas and a number of backcountry trails. Whistler Olympic Park, in the Madeley Creek basin, was home to the Nordic events at the 2010 Olympic Winter Games. With a combined 120 kilometres of groomed trails, Whistler Olympic Park and the nearby Callaghan Country are both spectacular places for nordic skiing and snowshoeing.

Against the backdrop of surrounding mountains, the cross-country ski and snowshoe trails wind through forests, marshes and meadows. The snowshoe trails cover both old- and second-growth forests, and the oldest cedar trees in the Sea-to-Sky Corridor line the route along the Real Life Snowshoe Trail. Expect to see the branches of hemlock and fir trees collecting snow, which muffles noise and creates the feeling of a winter wonderland.

Stop in one of the many viewpoints to behold stunning vistas of the surrounding

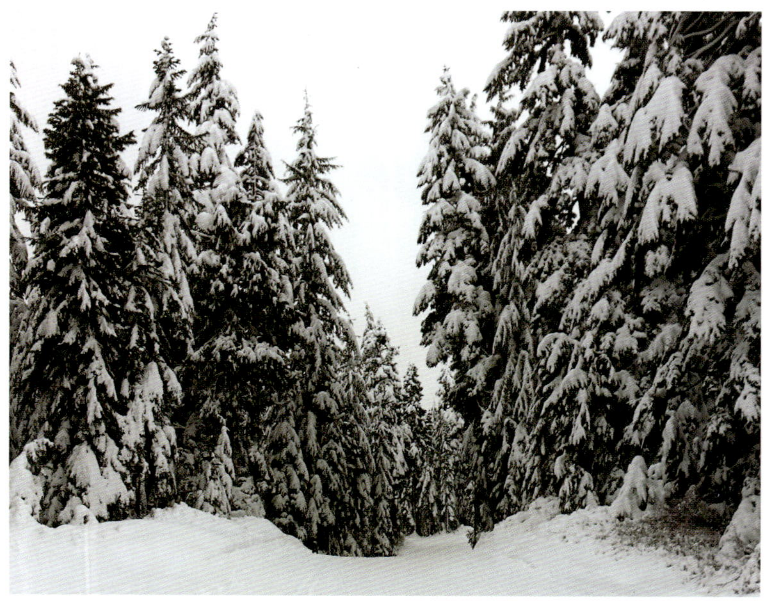

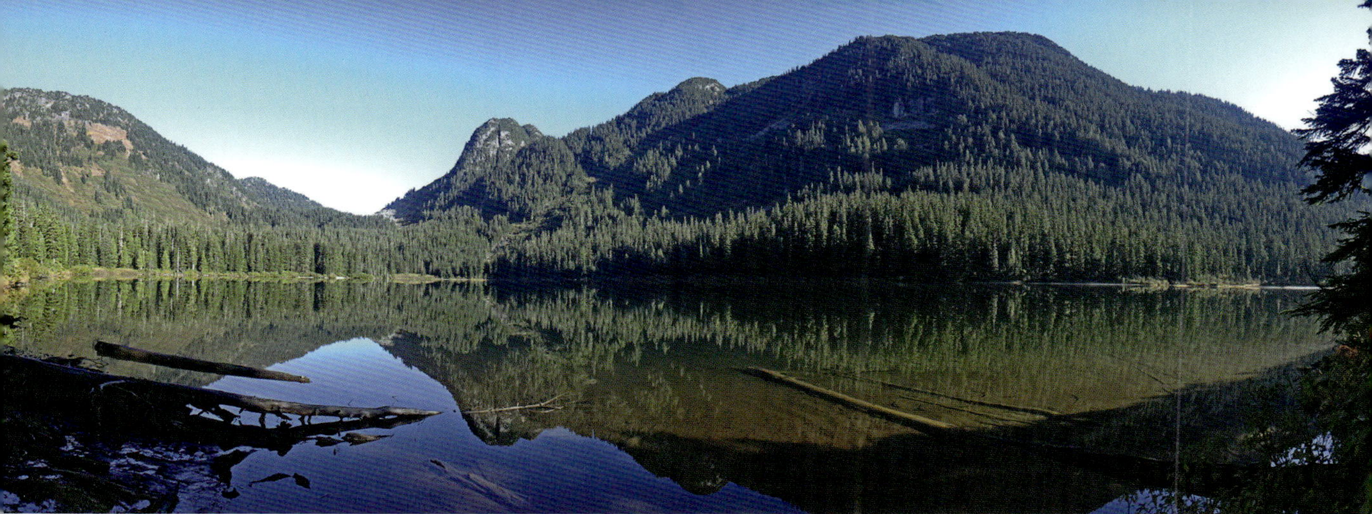

mountains, such as the distinctive Black Tusk, which sits in nearby Garibaldi Provincial Park. One of the most spectacular snowshoe routes is the Alexander Falls Trail, which takes hikers to the base of a 17-metre waterfall. Depending on the time of year, the falls may be a tower of frozen ice.

A number of trails through the forests, meadows and wetlands can be enjoyed in the summer, including hikes to beautiful alpine lakes like Hanging Lake and Rainbow Lake. The diverse ecosystem of the valley supports many birds and mammals, such as weasels, bobcats and moose. During the summer months bears are occasionally sighted, and American dippers and other birds frequent the streams and wetlands of the area.

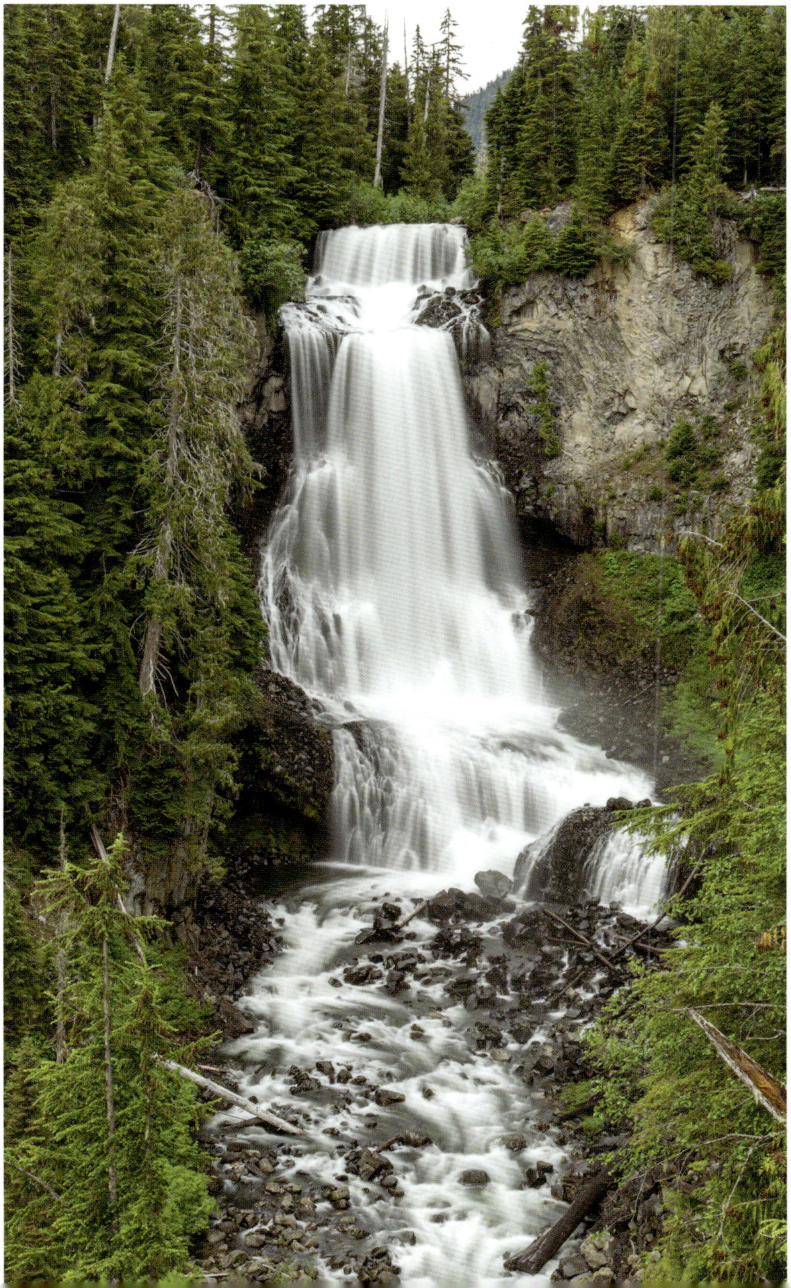

↑ Lakes and mountain views throughout the park reward hikers and cross-country skiers.

→ Alexander Falls is beautiful in both summer and winter.

← The variety of cross-country ski trails will delight both beginner and expert skiers.

Cheam Lake Wetlands Regional Park

A restored lake and wetland habitat that was once drained for mining

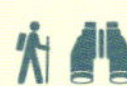

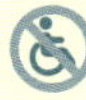

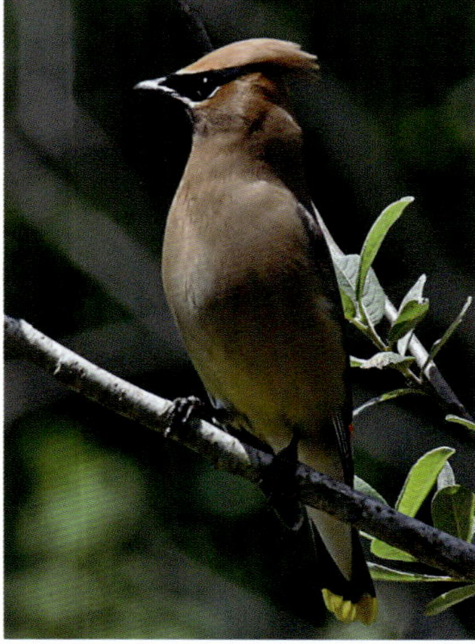

▸ **Cedar waxwings make their
presence known with high trills as
they descend on trees in the park.**

Despite undergoing over 100 years of active mining and logging, today Cheam Lake Wetlands Regional Park is a vibrant wetland habitat replete with diverse flora and fauna. Over 185 species of birds have been documented visiting the parkland, just outside of Chilliwack, making it a wonderful destination for birding. Before becoming the park present today, marl limestone was extracted from the lake bottom for use as a fertilizer from 1944 until 1988. Two years later the park was created to restore the natural wetland habitat.

Many species breed here as well, including marsh wrens, western wood-pewees, tree swallows, Bullock's orioles, yellow warblers, common yellowthroats and cedar waxwings. Keep your eyes peeled for redheads, grey catbirds and American redstarts in the area, who typically reside farther inland but visit the park.

Cedar waxwings are often heard before they are seen — not because they are particularly inconspicuous, but simply because they are constantly chattering! Waxwings call often as they fly from tree to tree in search of food, their high trills and whistles carrying through the air. Cedar waxwings look like they have been painted in watercolour, their feathers smoothly transitioning between grey, soft rusty brown and pale yellow, and intensely highlighted with lemon yellow, red and black.

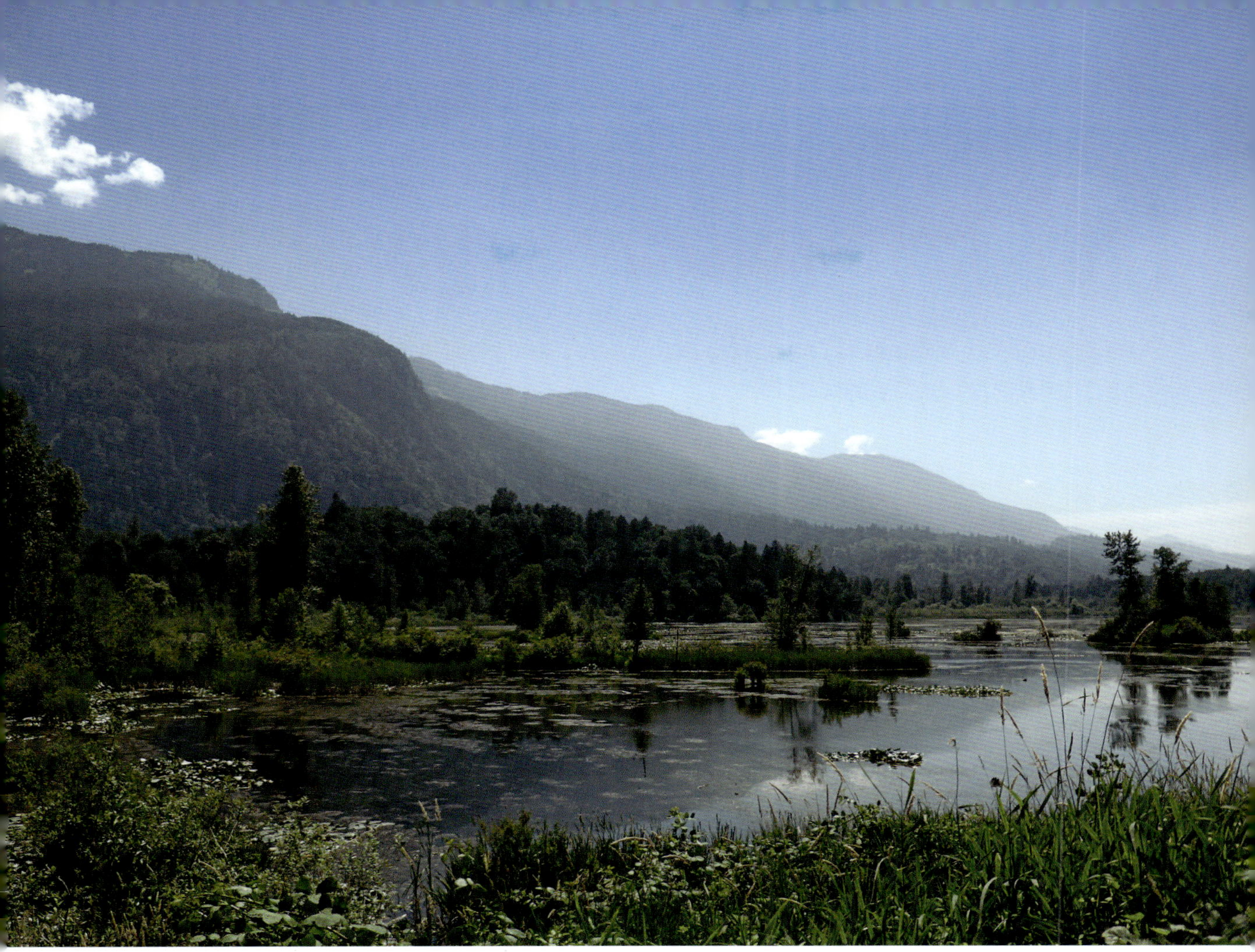

Look for flocks of these elegant birds as they search for berries to gorge on or dragonflies and mayflies to grab on the wing as they flit across the water.

Birds are not the only animals to make a triumphant comeback in the area after years of disturbance. Notable mammal representation in the park includes North American beavers, muskrats and river otters. Even bobcats make a rare appearance.

Cheam Lake Wetlands Regional Park supports 10 species of dragonfly and damselfly, including the small but easily distinguishable and aptly named dot-tailed whiteface. Look for them at the edge of the boardwalk that takes you to an elevated platform for great views over the lake. They may briefly perch among the yellow pond-lilies at the lake's edge. The massive floating flowers of this aquatic perennial are bright yellow and impossible to miss. What you are actually seeing are the giant exaggerated sepals, not the petals at all — the true petals are hidden from view inside the thick, waxy yellow cup.

↑ **The park is nestled in the beautiful rolling hills of the Fraser Valley.**

↓ **The thick, waxy floating flowers of the yellow pond-lily are widespread in the wetland.**

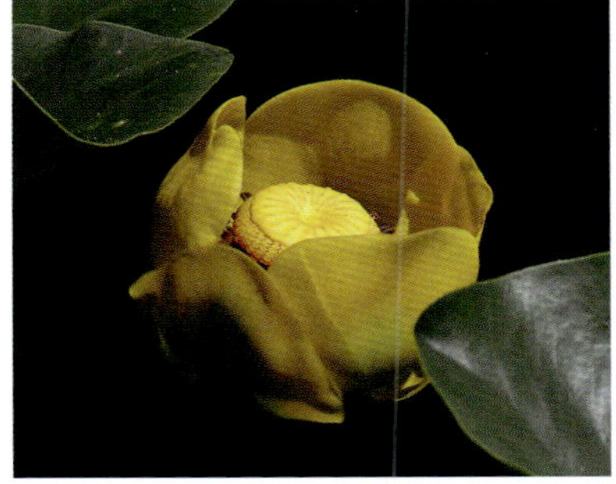

CULTUS LAKE PROVINCIAL PARK

Cultus Lake

This beautiful lake and transitional forest are perfect for a family-friendly vacation

What Makes This Hot Spot Hot?

- In the transition zone between two forest types lies a large, warm lake surrounded by tree-covered mountains.
- Colourful dragonflies and damselflies swoop in and out of the forest and along the lakeshore.
- Birds and other wildlife call this forest home, and with trails and viewpoints it is a lovely space for hiking and wildlife watching.

Address: Cultus Lake Provincial Park, 4165 Columbia Valley Road, Cultus Lake, BC
Tel.: (604) 858-3334
Website:

BC Parks

GPS Coordinates
Latitude: 49.03729
Longitude: −121.99199

Open year-round

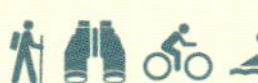

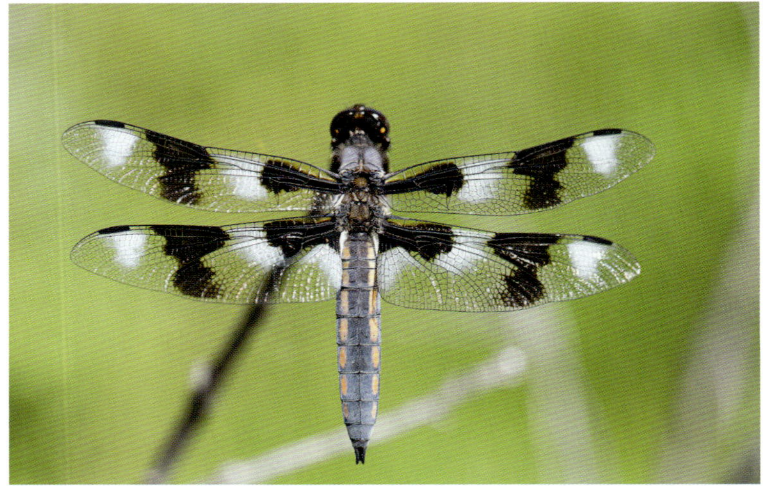

Tucked in the foothills of the Cascade Mountains, Cultus Lake is surrounded by lush, forested hills. The trails and campsites are well maintained, and the provincial park is family friendly. The lake itself is perfect for swimming, and plenty of wildlife can be seen and heard on the lakeshore and in the surrounding forest. There are deer, coyotes and some of the park's 100 species of birds to see as well as a number of fish species, including the endangered Cultus Lake sockeye salmon. Cultus Lake is encircled by natural spaces through which wildlife travels. The surrounding forest, too, is a transitional area where the coastal Douglas-fir zone meets coastal Western hemlock. These two forests combine to create a unique niche for wildlife.

Near the lake you will find dragonflies and damselflies darting between the trees and along the lakeshore. Requiring oxygen-rich water with plenty of plant life, dragonflies indicate that an ecosystem is thriving. Look out for the male white-faced meadowhawk and the eight-spotted skimmer. If you have the opportunity to

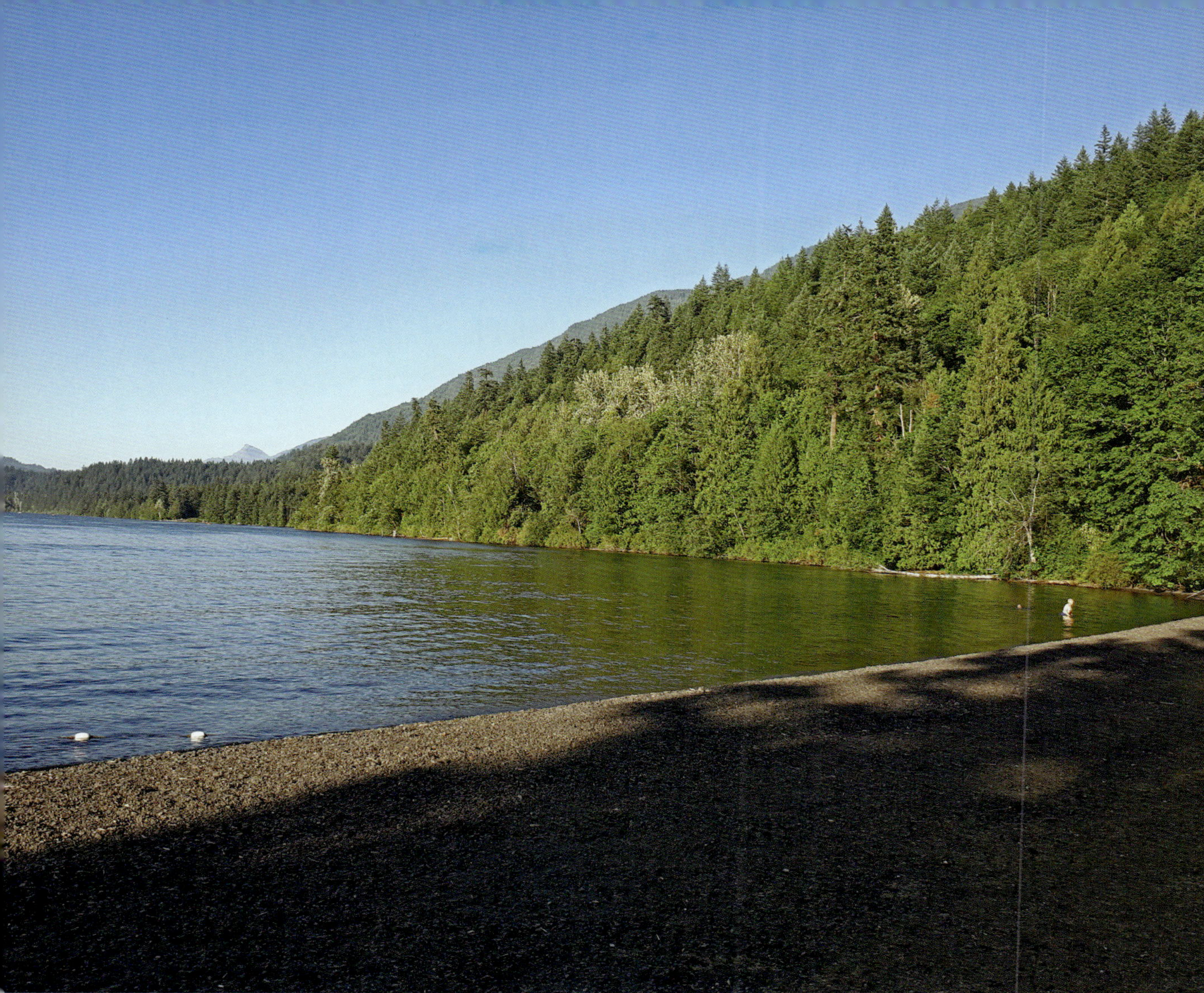

see one of these fliers land, get up close and have a look at the spectacular colours and patterns on its body and wings. The meadowhawk has a white face contrasted with a brilliant red body, while the skimmer has stunning black and white bands along its wings.

Explore the forest on the Giant Douglas-fir Trail. As the name implies, the trail leads to a huge 800-year-old tree — truly an imposing sight. On the forest floor you will find the leaves of the broadleaf maple alongside cones of Douglas-fir and hemlock. Another must-do trail is Teapot Hill, which travels through a shaded, mossy forest alongside a stream and opens to a spectacular view of the lake. The lake was once a large basin, but was dammed by a landslide. According to oral histories of the Stó:lō First Nation, the basin had underground rivers that led to the ocean.

↑ **The lake is a very inviting swim spot.**

← **The eight-spotted skimmer is one of many dragonfly species you may see around the lake.**

Cypress Provincial Park

Escape to a winter wonderland for an afternoon and be home in time for dinner

What Makes This Hot Spot Hot?

- A wintertime paradise less than an hour's drive from downtown Vancouver offers snowshoeing and cross-country and downhill skiing.
- Named for the cypress tree this old-growth forest shapes the subalpine landscape.
- Forests and meadows support a variety of wildlife, including the snowshoe hare and pileated woodpecker.

Address: Greater Vancouver, BC
Tel.: (604) 926-5612
Website:

BC Parks

GPS Coordinates
Latitude: 49.40574
Longitude: −123.21762

Open year-round

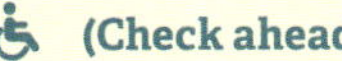

♿ **(Check ahead)**

Vancouverites are spoiled by the many green spaces within their city, so it is common for them to forget they are also surrounded by rugged wilderness. Cypress Provincial Park provides easy access to the Coast Mountains and is just a short drive from downtown.

From mid-November through March a thick blanket of snow covers the mountains. You can snowshoe up the Hollyburn Peak Trail, which takes you through an old-growth forest to an alpine peak with spectacular views of Vancouver and the surrounding mountains. This trail starts at the Nordic Area of Cypress Mountain Resort, where snowshoes can be rented at a reasonable rate. The forest itself is composed of mountain hemlock, white pine, amabilis fir and cypress trees that are up to 1,000 years old. Mountain hemlock create small sanctuaries for winter animals as their flexible branches bow to the ground under the weight of the snow. Around these trees there may be tracks of squirrels, pine martens and snowshoe hares, which are named for their large feet that allow them to sit atop the snow. Snowshoe hares are difficult to see during the winter because they change colour seasonally from a greyish brown in the warmer months to white to match the snow. While the hare may be difficult to spot, you will see obvious tracks where it has hopped between tree wells. Canada jays are frequently sighted in the park and are not shy of humans.

In the spring, marshes, lakes and fields of berries emerge from under the snow. The Yew Lake Trail is a short interpretive walk through marshland, while the Four Lakes Loop offers a longer hike through a variety of ecosystems. Look for the pileated woodpecker drilling small holes in tree trunks in search of insects. For experienced hikers the Howe Sound Crest Trail, usually done as a two-night backpacking trip, traces an alpine ridge along rugged terrain and offers magnificent views of Howe Sound.

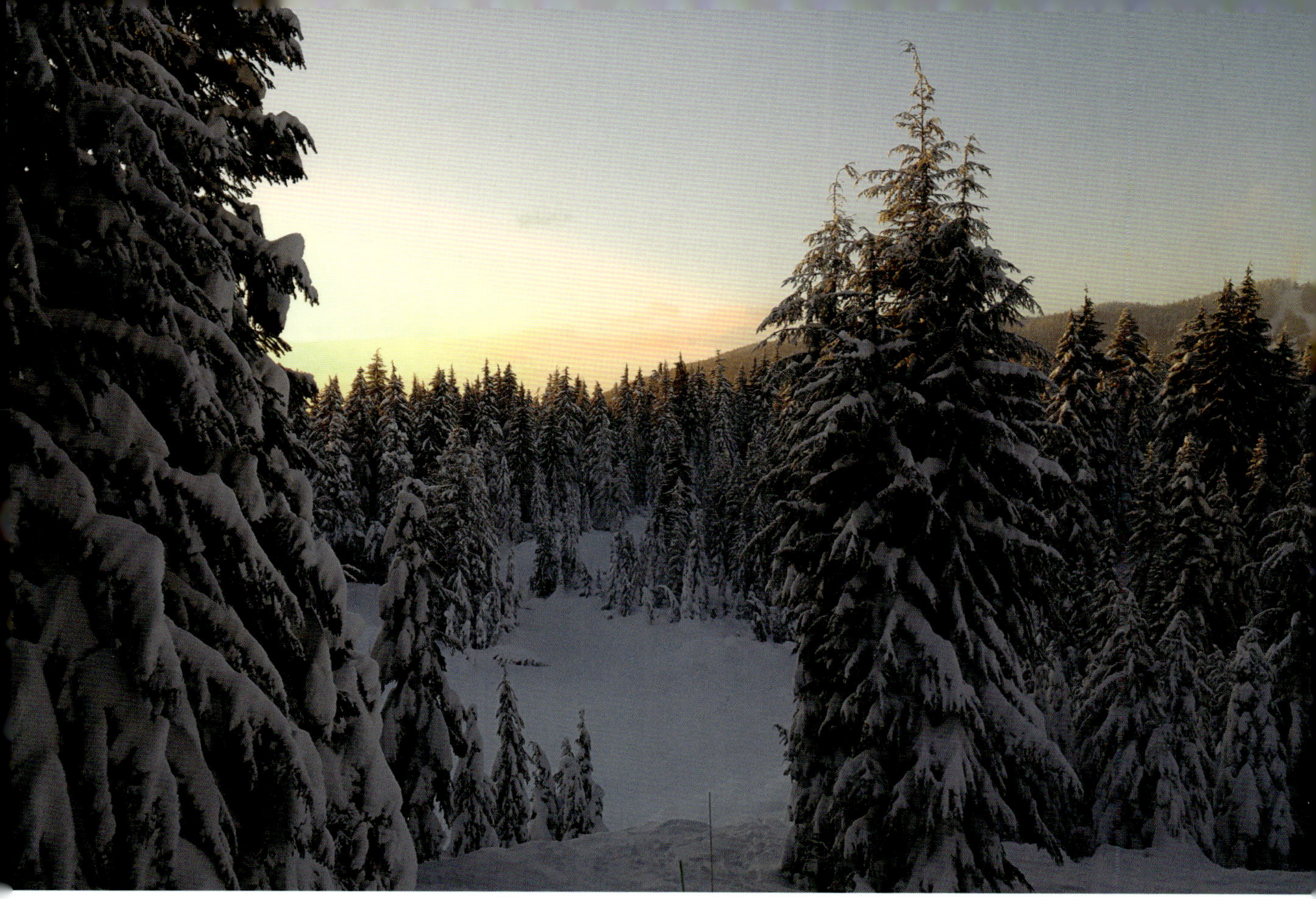

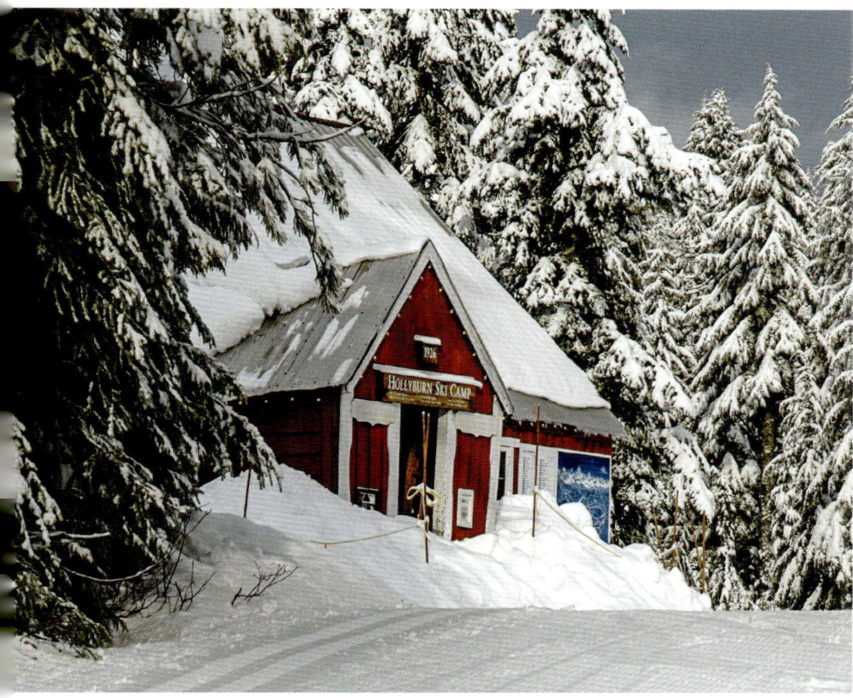

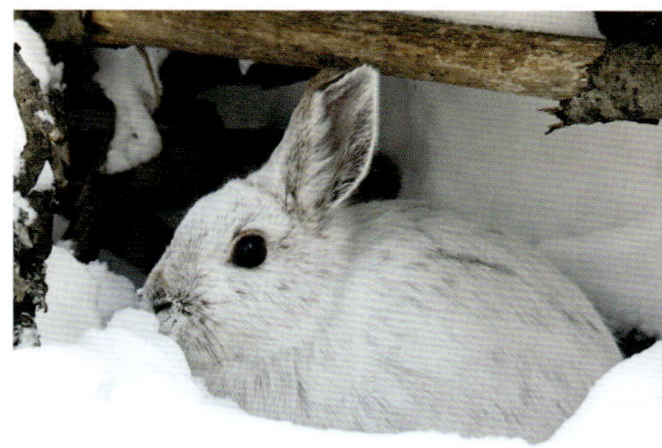

↑ Covered in snow the trees in Cypress Provincial Park give the feeling of a winter wonderland.

↓ Snowshoe hares are often seen hopping between trees.

← In winter the historic Hollyburn Lodge restaurant opens its doors and can be accessed only by cross-country skiing or snowshoeing.

GARIBALDI PROVINCIAL PARK

Elfin Lakes Trail

Alpine lakes act as mirrors for the coastal mountains in this tranquil environment that is perfect for wildlife watching

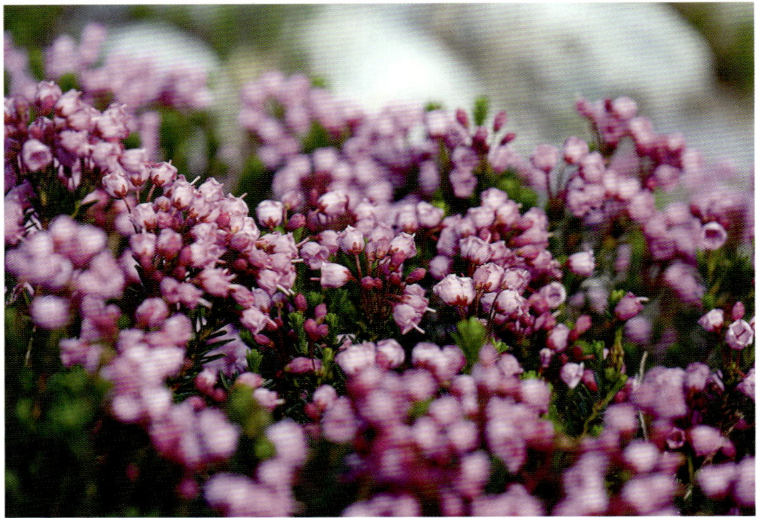

What Makes This Hot Spot Hot?

- Black bears forage in fields of berries and alpine flowers.
- The area has unique panoramic views of the coastal mountains.
- Ideal for wildlife and plant enthusiasts the Elfin Lakes Trail meanders through a variety of ecosystems, from coastal forests to an alpine ridge.

Address: Garibaldi Provincial Park, Garibaldi Park Road, Squamish, BC
Tel.: (1-800) 689-9025
Website:

BC Parks

GPS Coordinates
Latitude: 49.7884
Longitude: –122.98844

Open year-round

↗ **Delicate pink mountain-heather grows along the trails.**

Elfin Lakes Trail in Garibaldi Provincial Park is well known by Vancouverites and Squamish locals for its rugged beauty. As the trail approaches the treeline of the dense coastal forest, visitors will find the Red Heather warming hut, used by backcountry skiers in the winter. In the summer months the hut is surrounded by fields of rolling hills filled with flowers and shrubs in front of a stunning backdrop of coastal mountains. A lucky hiker may spot a black bear feeding on berries in the meadows. In the spring, bears live at lower elevations. As the snow melts, however, they move up the mountains into fields that are rich with berries and filled with insects they can eat off the bottoms of overturned logs. It is in the fall that hikers are most likely to see these bears gorging themselves on berries. During this time of year black bears spend up to 20 hours a day eating in preparation for hibernation.

Beyond the Red Heather hut the trail continues to gain elevation and the vegetation becomes typical of an alpine ecosystem with delicate flowers and plants, such as the heather for which the area is named. The final stretch of the trail meanders along a ridge, with sensational views of the surrounding mountains, including the Garibaldi massif, on either side of the ridge. At the end of the trail two serene alpine lakes with a panoramic view make the journey worth every step. On a still day these alpine lakes act as mirrors to the surrounding peaks and glaciers. Hikers can cool off with a swim in the upper lake; the lower lake is reserved for water collection by campers. To hike to the Elfin Lakes and back is 21 kilometres, and although many do this trail as a full-day trip, there are also backcountry camping opportunities.

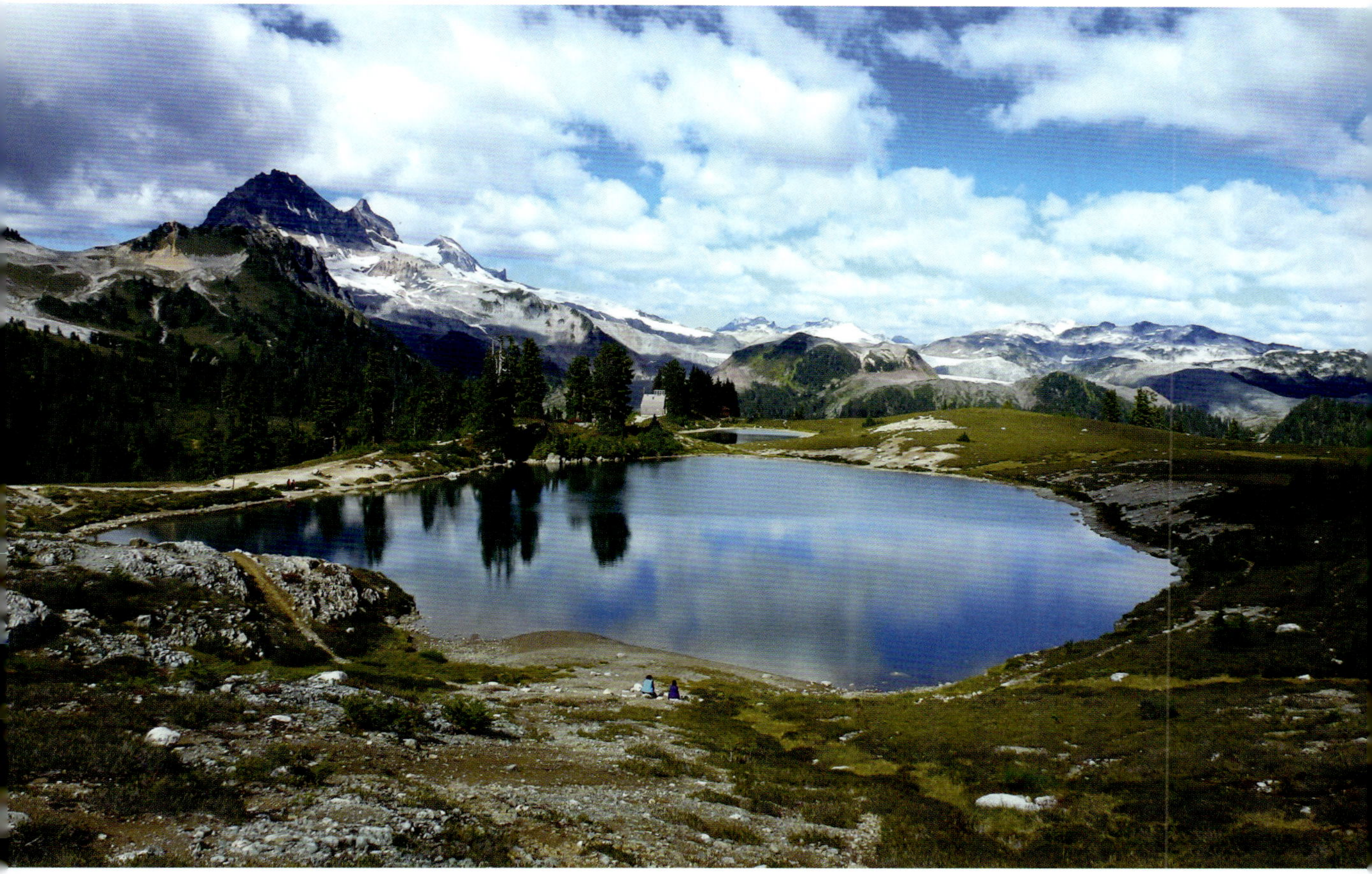

↑ **The stunning alpine lakes reflect the surrounding peaks on a calm day.**

↙ **Bears make their way up the mountains to graze in the surrounding fields.**

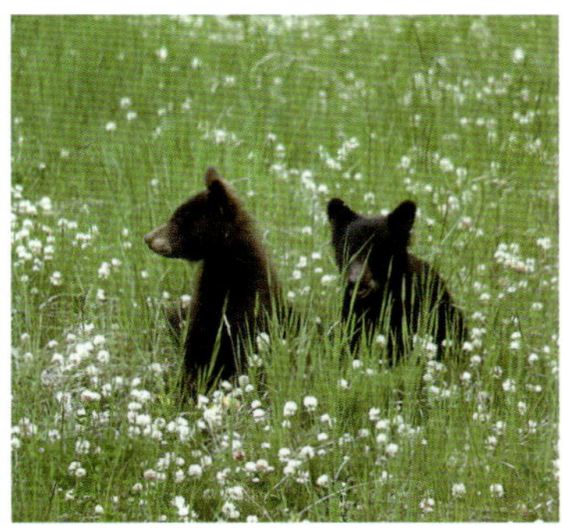

Garibaldi Lake and the Black Tusk

This alpine landscape was shaped by volcanic activity and contains a beautiful blue lake and awe-inspiring views

What Makes This Hot Spot Hot?

- Visitors can hike to the top of an extinct volcano and gaze out at the landscape it helped shape.
- Meadows of colourful alpine flowers frame mountain views.
- A brilliant blue glacier-fed lake is held in place by a barrier of hardened lava.

Address: Garibaldi Provincial Park, Garibaldi Park Road, Squamish, BC
Tel.: (1-800) 689-9025
Website:

BC Parks

GPS coordinates (Rubble Creek entrance):
Latitude: 49.95727
Longitude: −123.12023

Open year-round

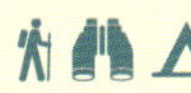

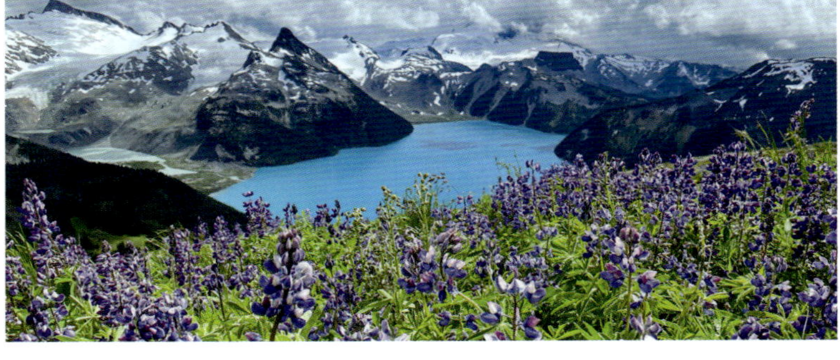

Between Squamish and Whistler, a jagged fin pierces the eastern skyline. This peak is the plug of an extinct volcano known as the Black Tusk. Called the "Landing Place of the Thunderbird" by the S̲k̲w̲x̲wú7mesh and the "Place Where the Thunderbird Rests" by the Lílʼwat, the peak holds importance to both nations. Many drive by and see the Black Tusk from a distance, but up close an extraordinary landscape surrounds the volcano.

Hikers may access this area of Garibaldi Provincial Park via the Helm Creek Trail or Rubble Creek Trail.

At lower elevations, closer to the trailheads, expect to hike through coastal old-growth forests of western redcedar and Douglas-fir. Higher up, the forest opens into meadows and stands of tall, thin mountain hemlock. In the summer the meadows are abundant with colourful flowers, such as glacier lily, lupine and red paintbrush. Mountains covered in glaciers dominate the horizon, encircling the large, turquoise Garibaldi Lake. This whole landscape was shaped by volcanic activity. Garibaldi lake itself is held in place by a barrier over 300 meters high that formed when a river of lava met the wall of a glacier. The barrier can be seen from the highway, but hikers can get a unique perspective of it at a viewpoint on the Rubble Creek Trail.

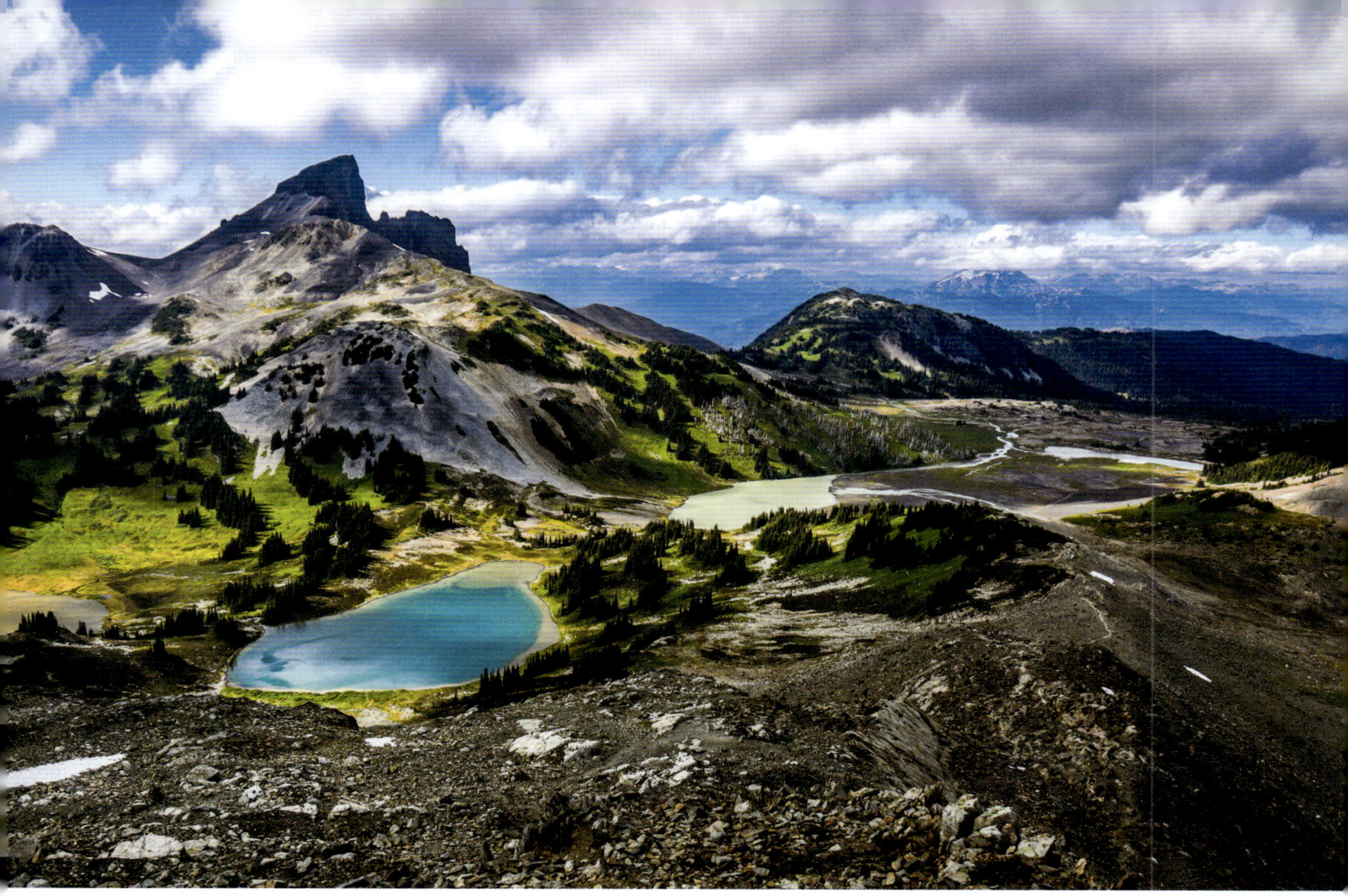

About 1.1 to 1.3 million years ago, the Black Tusk was one of many active volcanoes in this area. It was a cone-shaped stratovolcano, built up of many layers. In a more recent period of volcanic activity 170,000 years ago, an eruption created a plug of hardened lava in the volcano. Over time the surrounding cone was worn away exposing the jagged volcanic plug we see today. The Black Tusk Trail goes up to the base of the lava plug itself, but note that going to the very top is an exposed scramble and a helmet should be worn. East of the Black Tusk is the Cinder Cone, another extinct volcano, and between the two are the Cinder Flats. Walking along the Helm Creek Trail through the flats feels almost apocalyptic as there is little plant life in the dark volcanic earth.

For a full view of Garibaldi Lake, the Black Tusk, the meadows and beyond, many hikers visit Panorama Ridge. From this ridge the mountains stretch out in all directions across Garibaldi Provincial Park. Hike the Elfin Lakes Trail to explore another stunning section of this vast and diverse park.

↑ **The fin-shaped Black Tusk towers over the volcanic landscape.**

← **Fields of lupin bloom in the alpine.**

↓ **The barrier holding Garibaldi Lake was formed when lava met the edge of a glacier.**

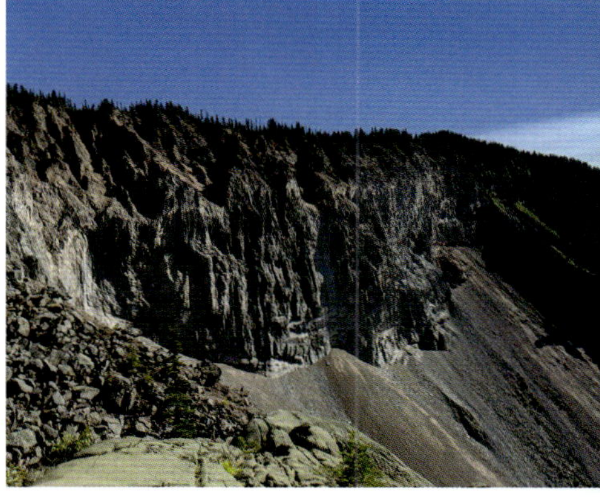

George C. Reifel Bird Sanctuary

Each year lesser snow geese arrive at their winter home and blanket the sanctuary

What Makes This Hot Spot Hot?

- Tens of thousands of lesser snow geese spend the winter here.
- Northern saw-whet owls roost along the trails during the day.
- Migratory birds stop over in huge numbers every spring and fall.

Address: 5191 Robertson Road, Delta, BC
Tel.: (604) 946-6980
Website:

George C. Reifel Migratory Bird Sanctuary

GPS Coordinates
Latitude: 49.09845
Longitude: −123.17847

Open year-round, reservations required

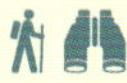

Each spring and fall, during migration, thousands of shorebirds take refuge in the 300 hectares of the George C. Reifel Bird Sanctuary. The marshes, fields and sloughs of the protected area are a year-round attraction for birders, and the sanctuary is considered one of the top 10 birding destinations in Canada. To manage the number of visitors in the park at any one time, reservations are now required, so remember to plan your trip ahead. The blinds located at multiple spots around the marsh make for great viewing opportunities, and the raised dykes provide the perfect setting for an early morning stroll.

Although the spring and fall are assumed to be the most exciting times to visit the sanctuary, its most famous visitors appear in the winter, marking their own arrival with enthusiastic and sometimes deafening honks as they lay claim to the surrounding fields and wetlands. Tens of thousands of lesser snow geese descend on the sanctuary in the late fall after completing their lengthy journey from Russia's Wrangel Island high in the Arctic. Despite arriving by the thousands, these giant gangs of geese may sometimes be difficult to spot because they do not stay in one place for the entire winter. If you cannot find them while walking the trails through the sanctuary, check the fields and estuaries that surround the marsh, since early morning disturbances can shift the birds to new locations. Look out for groupings of geese that include several greyer individuals — this is likely a family unit who made the journey together. The grey birds are part of the summer's brood yet to fully transition into their snowy white plumage.

Roosting during the daylight hours after a night of hunting, one of the smallest members of the owl family is frequently found in the sanctuary in

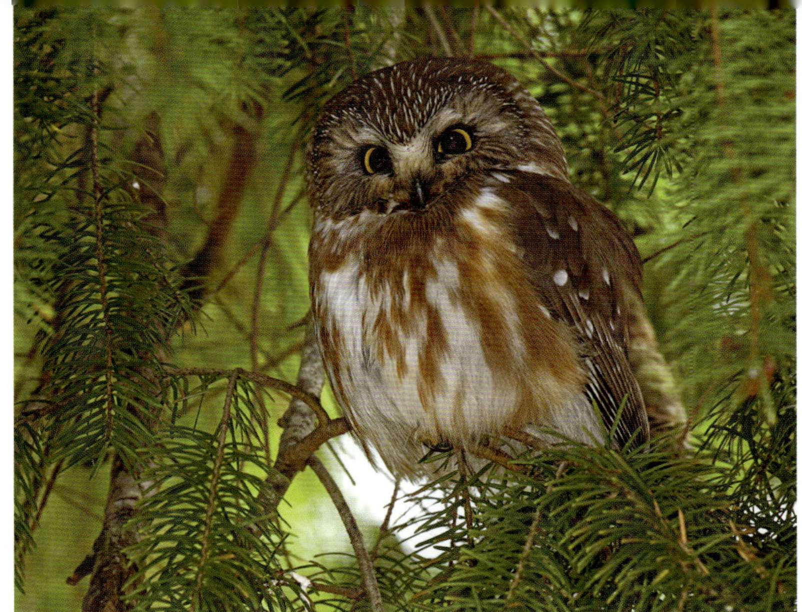

winter. The northern saw-whet owl is an absolute delight to see, and thankfully it does visitors a favour by roosting close to eye-level along the sanctuary trails. This small, bark-coloured bird with its dramatic white angled brow and cat-like eyes may be found on lower branches of western redcedar and Douglas-fir, or well hidden in holly.

Be very careful not to disturb the owls, even though they may be roosting close to the trail — they are trying to avoid larger predators and conserve energy until the night. By pointing out their roosts, you might accidently bring their presence to the attention of nearby passerines who will be sure to harass them until they leave the area. These enchanting owls are seldom seen despite their extensive range, and saw-whets are not often found here in the fall, so visit from December to March for your best chance to see one of Canada's most endearing owls.

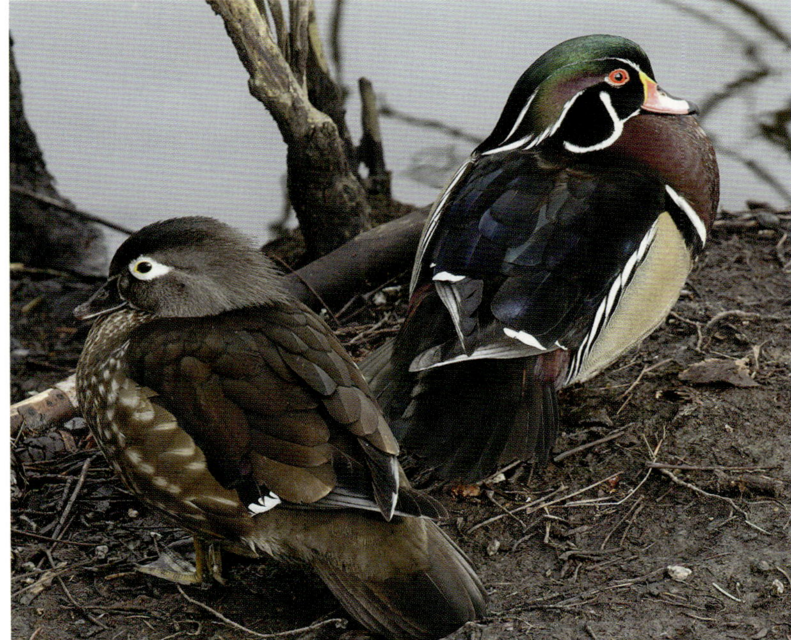

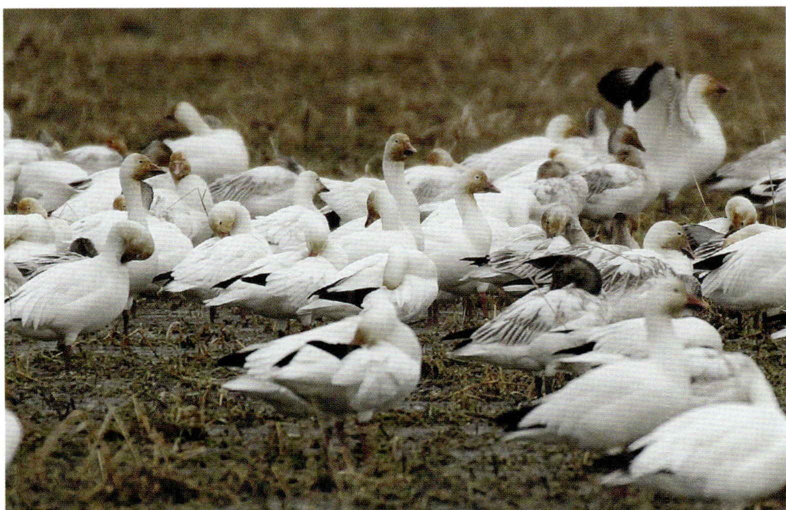

Golden Ears Provincial Park

This gigantic park blends outdoor recreation with wilderness preservation

What Makes This Hot Spot Hot?

- One of the largest provincial parks in British Columbia, it is part of a much larger green corridor and is home to a diverse population of wildlife.
- This area was the traditional hunting ground for the Coast Salish and Interior Salish First Nations.
- Marshes and forests in valleys and along mountain slopes ring with the songs of the many birds found throughout the park.

Address: Golden Ears Parkway, Maple Ridge, BC
Tel.: (604) 466-8325
Website:

BC Parks

GPS Coordinates
Latitude: 49.2501
Longitude: −122.53807

Open year-round

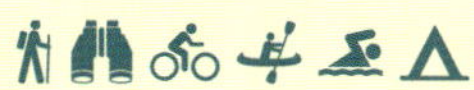

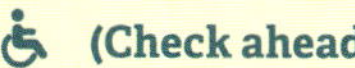 **(Check ahead)**

➤ **Named for its distinctive colouring, the chestnut-backed chickadee is a common sight all year long.**

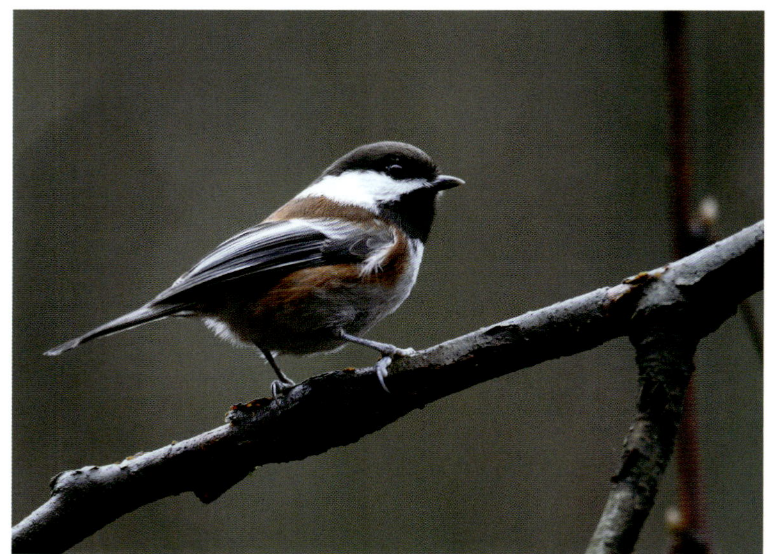

Just outside the town of Maple Ridge and an easy day trip from Vancouver, Golden Ears is one of the largest provincial parks in British Columbia. Initially part of Garibaldi Provincial Park, north of Squamish, it was separated in 1927. Named for two distinct peaks known as the Golden Ears, the park's 62,540 hectares provide outstanding recreational opportunities in addition to protecting beautiful natural spaces.

Alouette Lake is an excellent camping and swimming spot that attracts locals and visitors from around British Columbia. With numerous beaches and access to many hiking trails, it is easy to see why this lake is so popular. Before becoming a recreational area, the Alouette Valley hosted one of the largest logging operations in the province. A fire in 1931 raged through the valley, and much of the area is now second-growth forest. Nearly 90 years after the fire, it is interesting to hike between the new- and old-growth areas.

After years of logging, the forest in the Alouette Valley

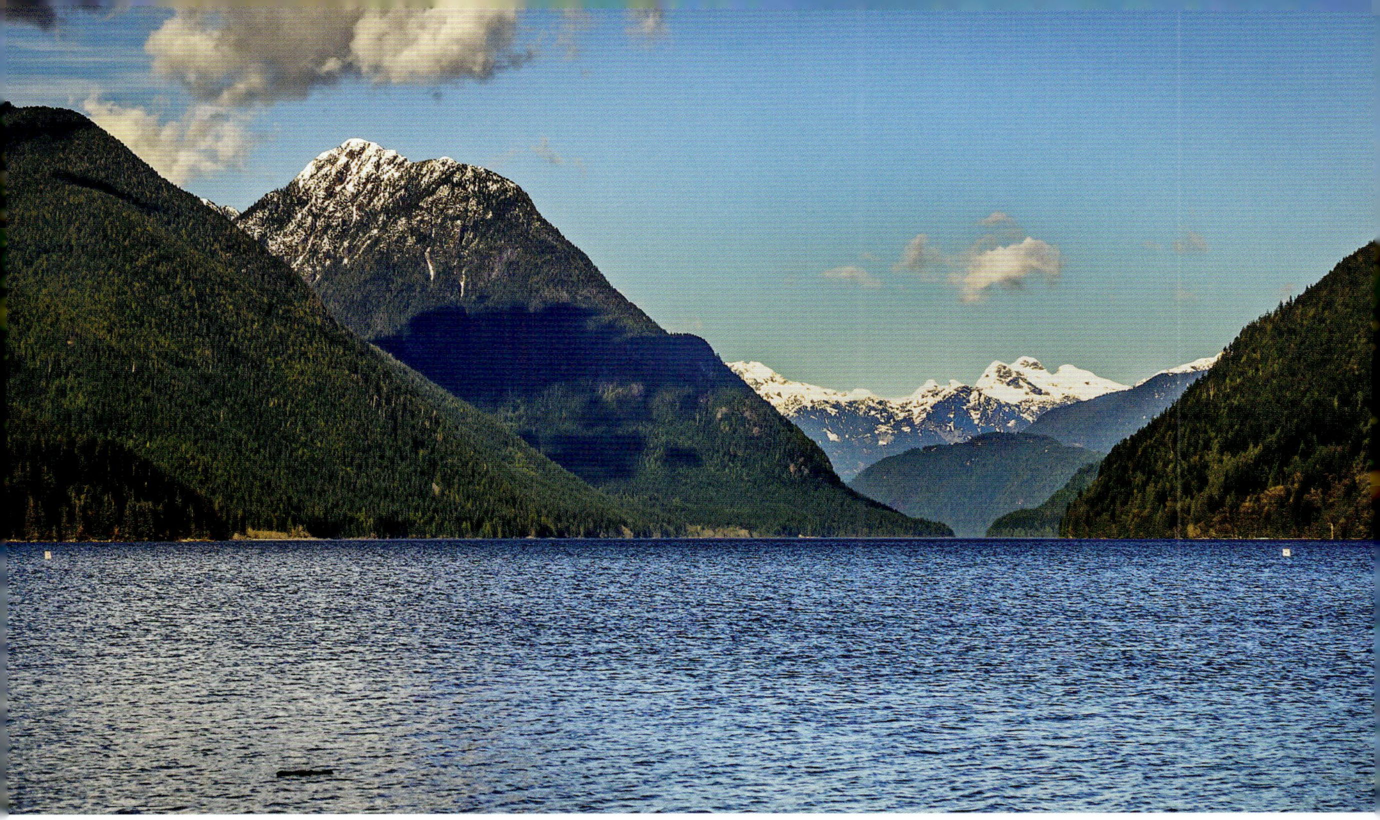

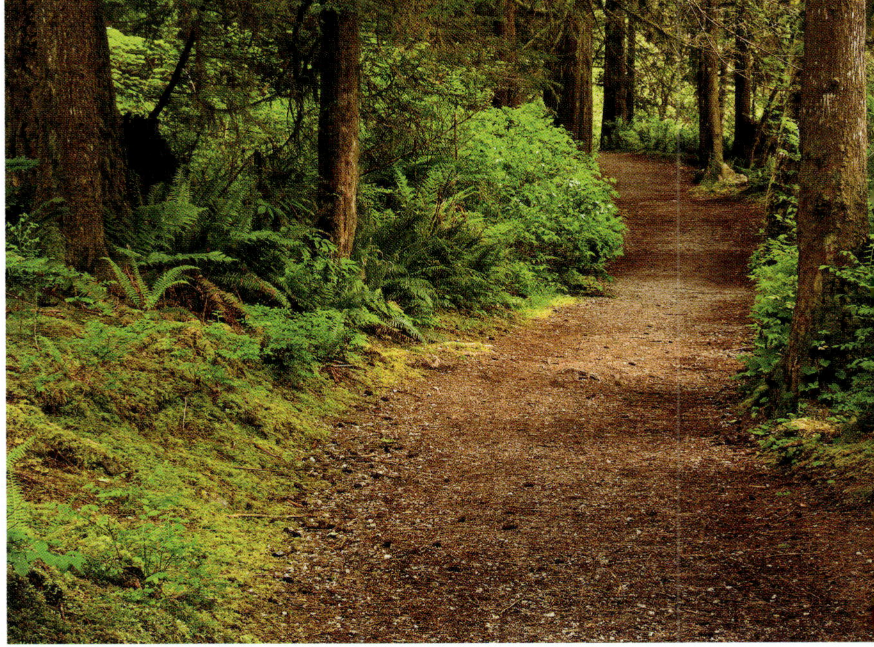

has reclaimed the land for an abundance of flora and fauna. The wildlife is difficult to miss. Pine siskins and chestnut-backed chickadees sing along the trails, and belted kingfishers perch alongside bodies of water. Goats scale rocky cliffs along the alpine mountain, and beavers are known to have dams in the many waterways throughout the park. Northern flying squirrels live in the trees, though they are nocturnal and not easy to see.

The hiking trails are well maintained and offer views of picturesque waterfalls and gorgeous mountains, strolls through both the new- and old-growth forests and access to alpine peaks. The terrain in this park is quite mountainous, so be prepared for some real hiking.

↑ **Strolls through lush forests lead to waterfalls and other beautiful sights.**

↖ **Alouette Lake is a popular destination for day trips and camping.**

Hell's Gate

A bird's-eye view of one of the largest natural obstacles faced by salmon that spawn up the Fraser River

What Makes This Hot Spot Hot?

- A sudden narrowing of the Fraser River results in the deep and rapid waters of Hell's Gate.
- A rockslide in the gorge caused a plummet in fish populations, but with innovative engineering the number of fish travelling through has been increasing dramatically.
- An aerial tram offers a sweeping view of the spectacular gorge.

Address: 43111 Trans-Canada Hwy (Hwy 1), Boston Bar, BC
Tel.: (604) 867-9277
Website:

Hell's Gate Airtram

GPS Coordinates
Latitude: 49.78327
Longitude: −121.44733

Open in the summer

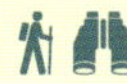

 **(Check ahead)**

Hell's Gate is a popular place for tourists to take an adrenaline-inducing aerial tram over the Fraser River to a quaint area with a suspension bridge, fisheries exhibit and restaurant. But this area boasts much more than just a thrilling tram ride. The sudden narrowing of the Fraser River below forces a huge volume of water between granite cliffs only 35 metres apart. As the spring melt brings more water to the Fraser, the water levels increase. They have been recorded as high as 30 metres — about the height of a 10-storey building! The water here is so treacherous that, after visiting the canyon, explorer Simon Fraser described the gorge as "a place where no human should venture, for surely these are the gates of Hell."

While the geology itself is amazing, the most impressive feature of this place is below the muddy waters. From July through October thousands of salmon battle against the river's powerful flow to reach their spawning grounds — an incredible undertaking for even the strongest fish. Historically exhausted salmon would rest where the water was less powerful, along the shore or in small eddies, which are slow-moving whirlpools created by geological features. The ease of catching the tired fish made Hell's Gate an ideal seasonal fishing ground for the Nlaka'pamux First Nations.

Millions of salmon used to pass through Hell's Gate annually to their upriver spawning grounds. A large rockslide in 1913 during the construction of the Canadian Pacific Railway created nearly impossible conditions for the salmon to navigate. Fishing was restricted, and a variety of attempts were made to restore the salmon's migration pathway. Today you can see fishways on both sides of the river that create a gradual rise through slower-moving water for the salmon to use. These engineering efforts have seen a significant increase in the number of fish returning to their spawning grounds.

→ **The Hell's Gate aerial tram gives visitors a bird's-eye view of the Fraser River.**

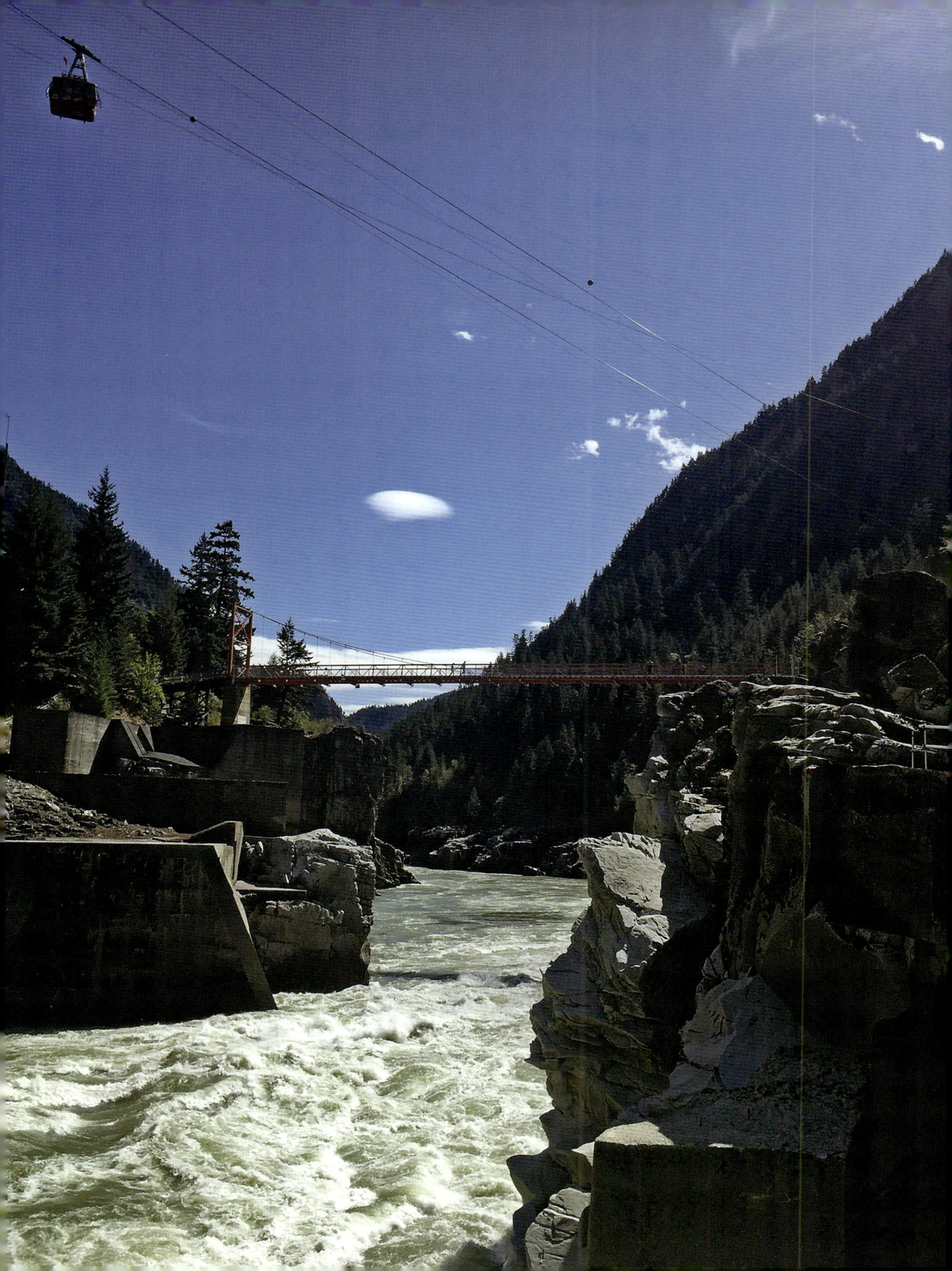

Howe Sound Crest Trail

A trail along a ridge that parallels the shore of Howe Sound, with stunning views of surrounding islands and peaks and a diversity of wildlife

What Makes This Hot Spot Hot?

- A panoramic view of the Howe Sound in all its glory, including Bowen Island and the Sunshine Coast.
- Blueberry bushes and other beautiful plants line the trails along subalpine lakes.
- A variety of wildlife including butterflies and birds enjoy this nature hot spot.

Address: Cypress Bowl Road, West Vancouver, BC
Tel.: (604) 926-5612
Website:

BC Parks

GPS Coordinates
Latitude: 49.39724
Longitude: −123.20568

Open year-round

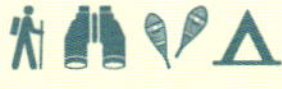

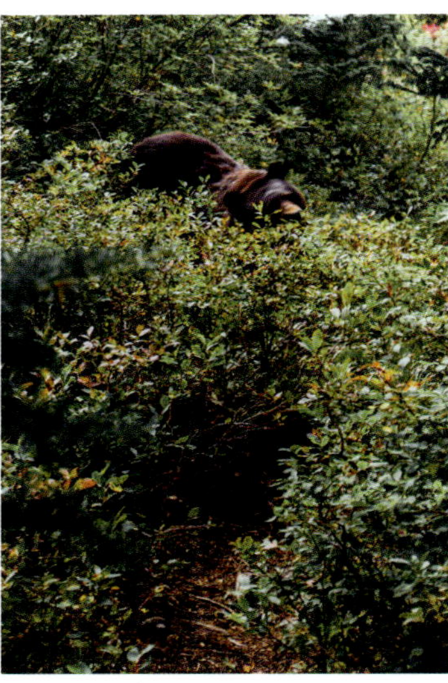

↗ **A black bear eats blueberries from bushes that line sections of the trail in the summer months.**

A skyline ridge parallels Howe Sound that navigates several prominent peaks and offers views of the ocean and islands below. This strip of green was added to Cypress Provincial Park in 1982 to protect 30 kilometres of ridges, lakes and forest home to many plants and wildlife.

Perhaps the most prominent features of the trail, visible from the city of Vancouver, are the Sisters, also referred to as the Lions. These well-known peaks are about midway along the trail. The Sisters are said to have brought peace to the Skwxwú7mesh Nation by marrying twin brothers of the Haida Nation, with whom the Skwxwú7mesh were at war.

Birders may visit hoping for a glimpse of a three-toed woodpecker, for which the trail has developed a reputation. It is almost a guarantee to see grouse and Canada jays scavenging for bits of granola bar along the trail. A diverse insect population inhabits the trail, including many butterflies. Species of fritillary, arnica checkerspot and hoary comma have all been spotted on the ridge. The scalloped wings of the hoary comma camouflage it against the grey rock when its wings are closed, but when they open they are a beautiful orange. Butterflies are quite particular as to where they lay their eggs; the hoary comma chooses currants and gooseberries, where its caterpillars will feast before forming their chrysalises.

Plenty of plants, lichens and fungi can be found both below the treeline by lakes and waterfalls and higher up along in the meadows and alpine.

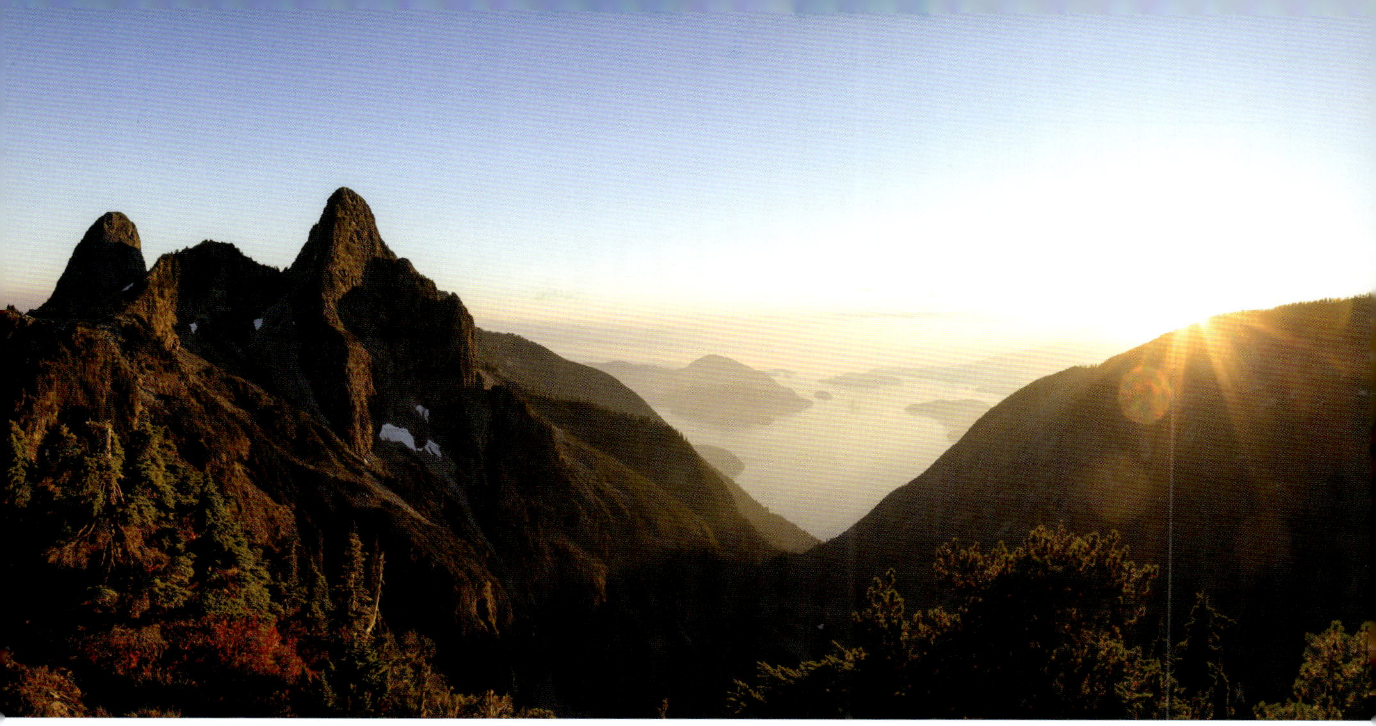

Keep an eye out for lipstick powderhorn lichen, with bright red bulbs terminating its green stalks. Roots and small shrubby plants poke out of the shallow soil over rock. Hardy blueberry bushes line sections of the trail, providing an important food source for black bears in the area.

The Howe Sound Crest Trail is truly multiple nature hot spots rolled into one. Visitors can hike the full trail as an overnight backpacking trip or day hike a number of trails to waterfalls, lakes and summits.

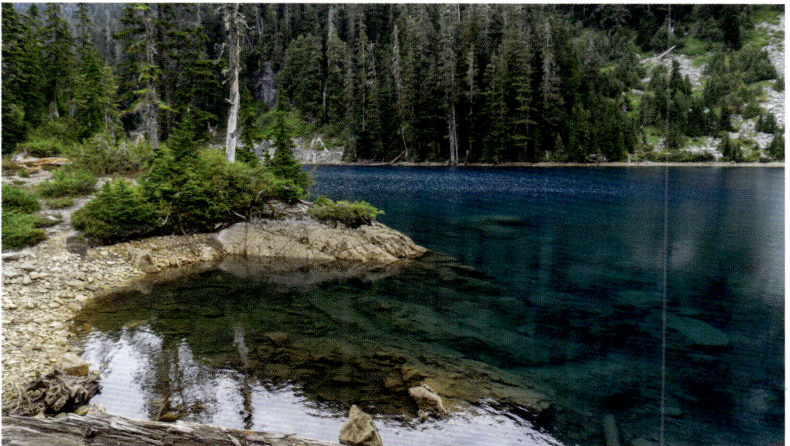

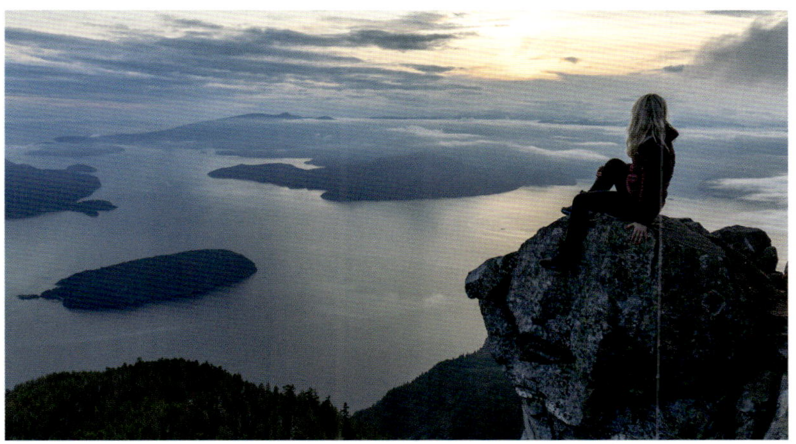

Joffre Lakes Provincial Park

Alpine lakes are fed by a glacier that continues to shape the landscape

What Makes This Hot Spot Hot?

- Travelling through glacier-carved terrain reveals how the receding Matier Glacier continues to carve the landscape.
- Mountain birds, including the three-toed woodpecker, live in the forest surrounding the lakes.
- Visitors can stroll through picturesque forests of tall, thin trees that are characteristic of alpine regions.

Address: Duffey Lake Road, Mount Currie, BC
Tel.: (1-800) 689-9025
Website:

BC Parks

GPS Coordinates
Latitude: 50.354
Longitude: –122.48923

Open year-round

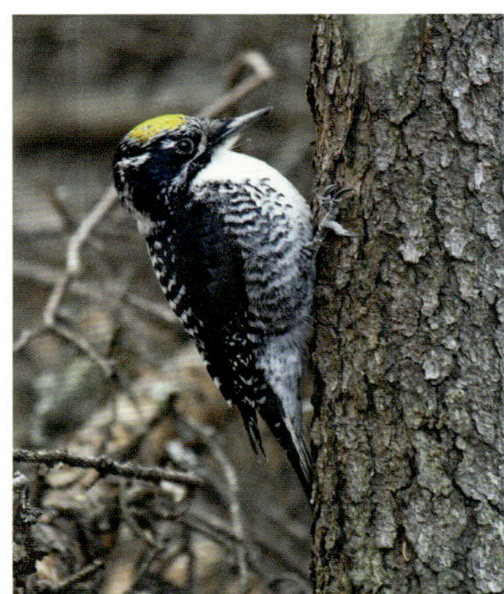

A recent addition to British Columbia's provincial parks, the Joffre Lakes have been known as a recreation site for decades by mountaineers, but only obtained park status in 1996. The first people recorded to reach the top of the iconic Matier and Joffre peaks did so in 1957. Since then the area has became a popular hiking area to view the jagged peaks and mountain wildlife. A naturalist with a keen eye will spot many mountain birds, including the Canada jay and American three-toed woodpecker, around the lakes.

The Matier Glacier melts and feeds silt-filled water into three alpine lakes, turning them a stunning turquoise. Lower Joffre Lake is an easy five-minute walk from the trailhead and has spectacular views of the surrounding mountains through a subalpine forest of tall, thin trees. In the winter, snow blankets the trees, weighing down their branches. A combination of wind, cold temperatures and heavy snow causes the trees to grow slowly and have shortened branches, giving them their "thin" appearance.

The trail gains elevation as it approaches Middle Joffre Lake, where the view gets even better. The trees become shorter, and thin soil gives way to talus slopes characteristic of a landscape carved by glaciers. The trail becomes even more rugged towards Upper Joffre Lake, passing by waterfalls with small creek crossings. The chirp of an American pika or a rock shifting beneath the hooves of a mountain goat may grab your attention as you move into the alpine zone. The tranquil wilderness surrounding Upper Joffre Lake, situated in a bowl below rugged mountains, is worth the effort of the hike.

The three-toed woodpecker, with its distinctive yellow cap, may be seen on trees around the lakes.

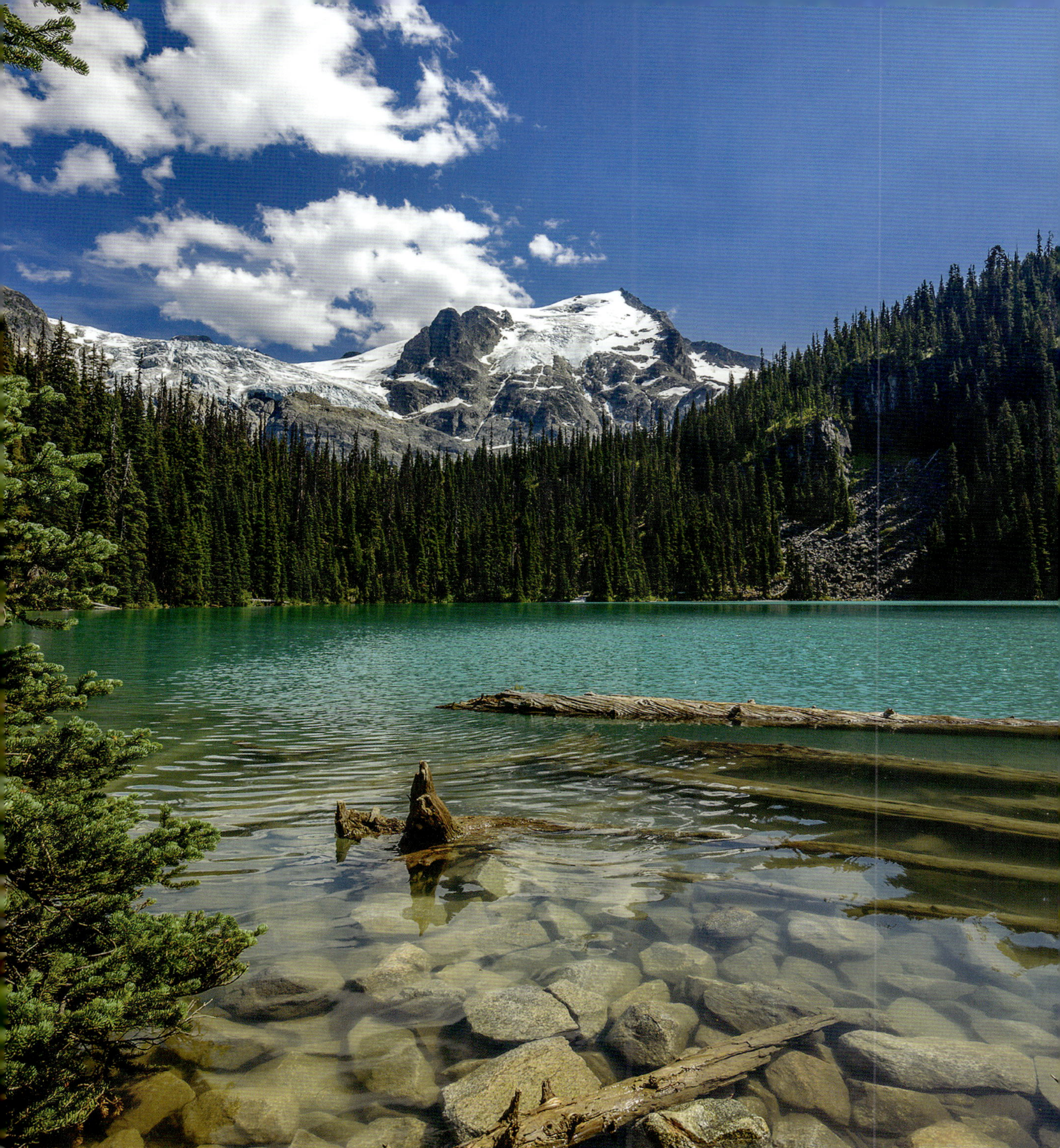

As Joffre Lakes has increased in popularity, a day pass system has been introduced to ensure the number of visitors does not damage this beautiful place. Ensure that you check online and book a day pass before departing.

↑ **Upper Joffre Lake has a spectacular view of the Matier Glacier, from which it gets its silt-laden water.**

Marble Canyon Provincial Park

Paddle over clear waters and view the largest freshwater stromatolites on Earth

What Makes This Hot Spot Hot?

- Pavilion Lake is a research site and its stromatolites have been studied by the Canadian Space Agency and NASA.
- The park is named for the towering limestone that forms steep cliffs up to 1 kilometre high.
- Lakes, marshy shores and rocky cliffs provide habitat for diverse species of birds.

Address: Smith Road off Hwy 99, Pavilion, BC
Tel.: (250) 320-9305
Website:

BC Parks

GPS Coordinates
Latitude: 50.87586
Longitude: –121.74947

Open year-round

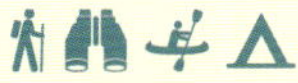

♿ **(Check ahead)**

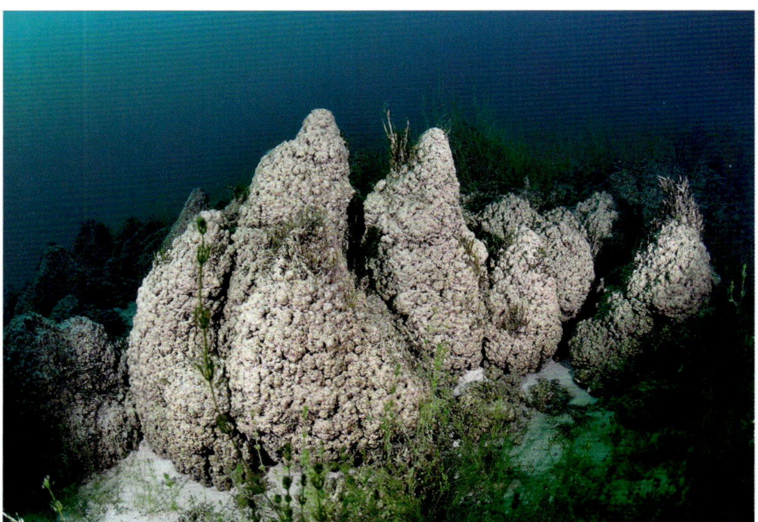

Three turquoise lakes sit in a valley between forested slopes and towering limestone cliffs jutting out of sparsely vegetated grassy hills. Marble Canyon Provincial Park hosts excellent birdwatching, is a popular fishing site and has attracted interest from scientists for its freshwater stromatolites.

On the bottom of Marble Canyon's Pavilion Lake sit bulbous formations with a layered appearance. They may look like interesting rocks, but they are actually alive — sort of. These formations are called stromatolites, a type of microbialite, which is simply any structure made of sediment and microorganisms. Stromatolites are the specific type of microbialite found here, composed of layers of cyanobacteria, calcium carbonate and sediment. The Pavilion Lake stromatolites range in shape and size, with some measuring up to 3 metres tall. These are the largest-known freshwater microbialites in the world.

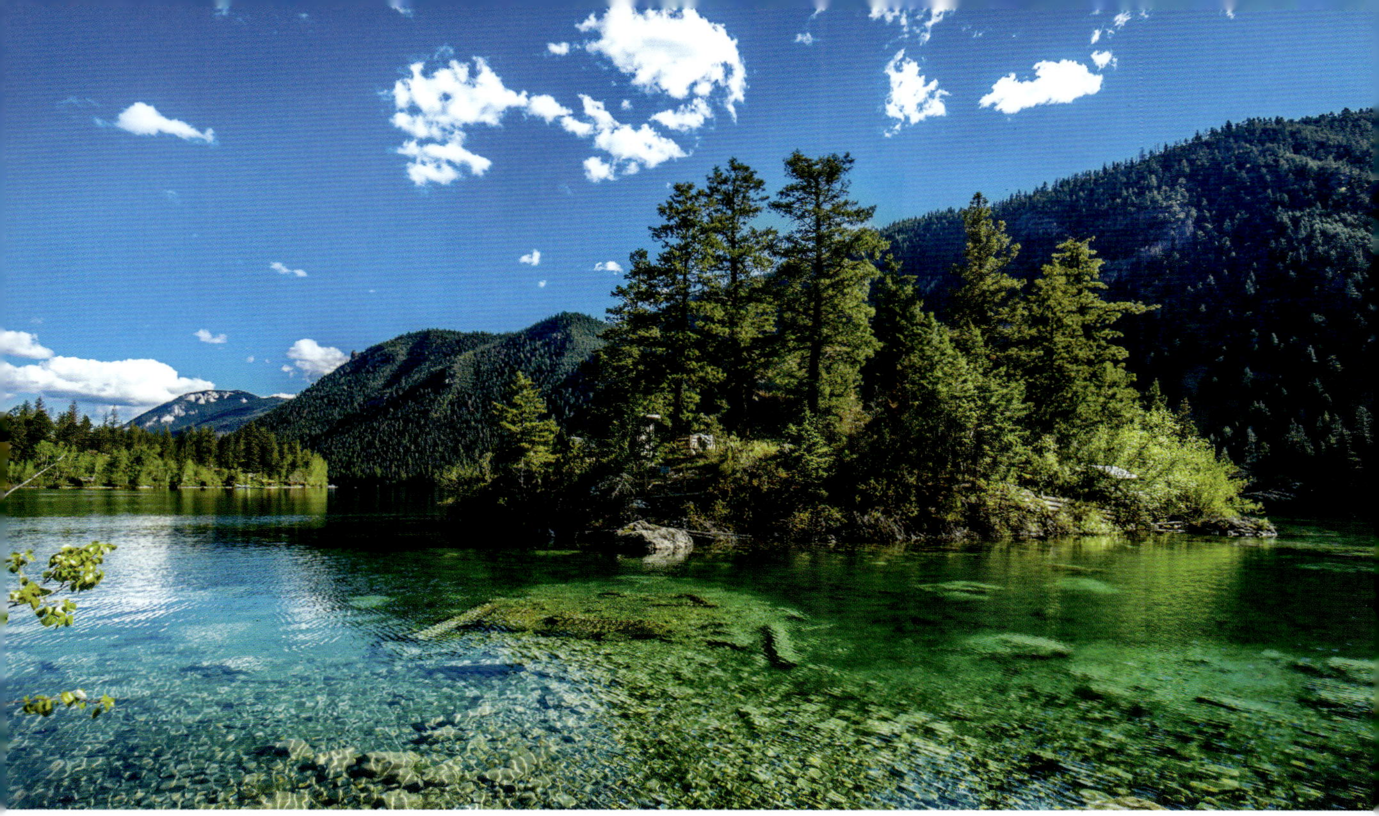

Fossil records indicate that microbialites are one of the oldest life forms on Earth, dating from 2.5 billion to 150 million years ago. Those in Pavilion Lake began to form about 11,000 years ago, and the outermost layer of cyanobacteria continues to expand them slowly. Scientists hope to learn more about the history of Earth, and potentially life on other planets, by studying them. Divers must obtain a special license due to the fragility and importance of these structures, but if you paddle on the clear water you can see the stromatolites below.

Pictographs found in the park indicate the importance of this area to the Ts'kw'aylaxw First Nation, on whose traditional territory the park sits. Both below and above the lake's surface the park has many features that make it special. The prominent white limestone cliffs are unique for the Squamish-Lillooet region. The cliffs, forests and lakes make this a diverse ecosystem and excellent birding spot. Loons and spotted sandpipers frequent the lakes and shores, while mountain chickadees and cedar waxwings prefer the dry coniferous forests.

This park is best explored with a kayak, canoe or paddleboard to both see the stromatolites and access a hiking trail to a waterfall on the east side of the lakes.

↑ When the waters are still, paddlers can catch a glimpse of the microbialites below the surface of Pavilion Lake.

← Pavilion Lake is home to the largest freshwater microbialites in the world.

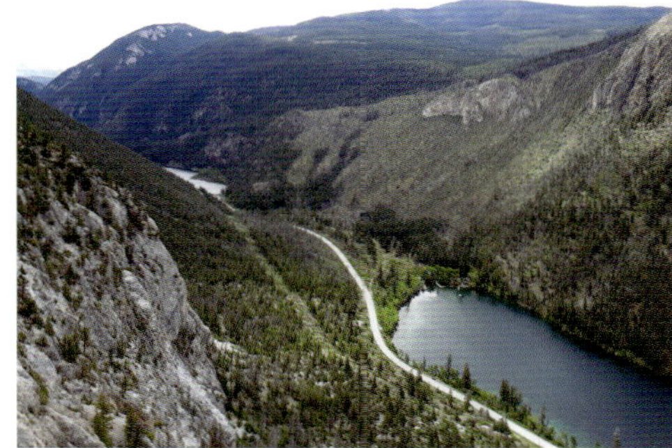

↑ Three beautiful lakes are surrounded by limestone cliffs and steep mountains.

Minnekhada Regional Park

A peaceful nature sanctuary nestled right in the city of Coquitlam

What Makes This Hot Spot Hot?

- Townsend's big-eared bats are found in the park.
- Visitors have easy access to marsh and woodland to explore.
- A hike to High Knoll provides viewpoints of the river and surrounding mountains.

Address: 4455 Oliver Road, Coquitlam, BC
Tel.: (604) 520-6442
Website:

Metro Vancouver

GPS Coordinates
Latitude: 49.299988
Longitude: −122.708405

Open May to September

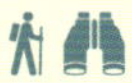

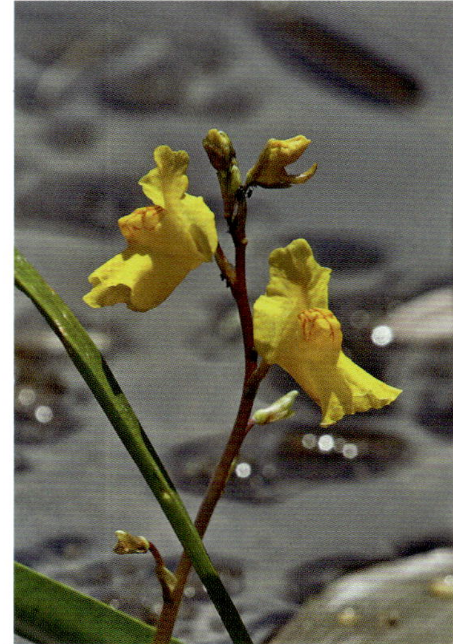

↗ **The carnivorous greater bladderwort traps unsuspecting prey in the wetlands.**

With opportunities to explore a variety of habitats while traversing just a few kilometres of walking trails, the easily accessed Minnekhada Regional Park is a great place to explore for the day with binoculars and bug net in hand. Hiking to the High Knoll viewpoint gives you great views over Pitt River and the surrounding area, with Mount Baker and the mountains of Golden Ears Provincial Park as the backdrop.

The park is home to many species of birds that reflect the diversity of habitats they can access within its boundaries. American bitterns, soras and Virginia rails lurk around the edges of the marshes, and there is a great deal of woodpeckers in the birch and alder stands, as well as among the evergreens in the older woodland. In the spring many types of swallows visit the marsh, including tree, violet-green and barn swallows. Even cliff and northern rough-winged swallows have been seen in the area. Waterfowl overwinter in the park, and it is one of the best places to spot ring-necked ducks in the area.

In the park's marsh, look for the yellow flowers of the greater bladderwort. These free-floating aquatic plants are carnivorous, using their tiny valve-lidded bladders not only for buoyancy but also to trap small crustaceans and other animals. The valves have stiff bristles that trigger the bladder to open and expand, and the resulting rush of water engulfs the unsuspecting animal inside the bladder.

Visit the park at dusk and you may be lucky enough to encounter one of its four species of bats, including the vulnerable Townsend's big-eared bat. Appropriately named, the bats have ears that measure nearly half the length of their body. These bats do not hide in crevices while they roost like many other bats, which, combined with their preference for lower elevation areas, makes them particularly vulnerable to human disturbance. If you can, join in one of the park's evening bat interpretive programs to learn more about this special animal.

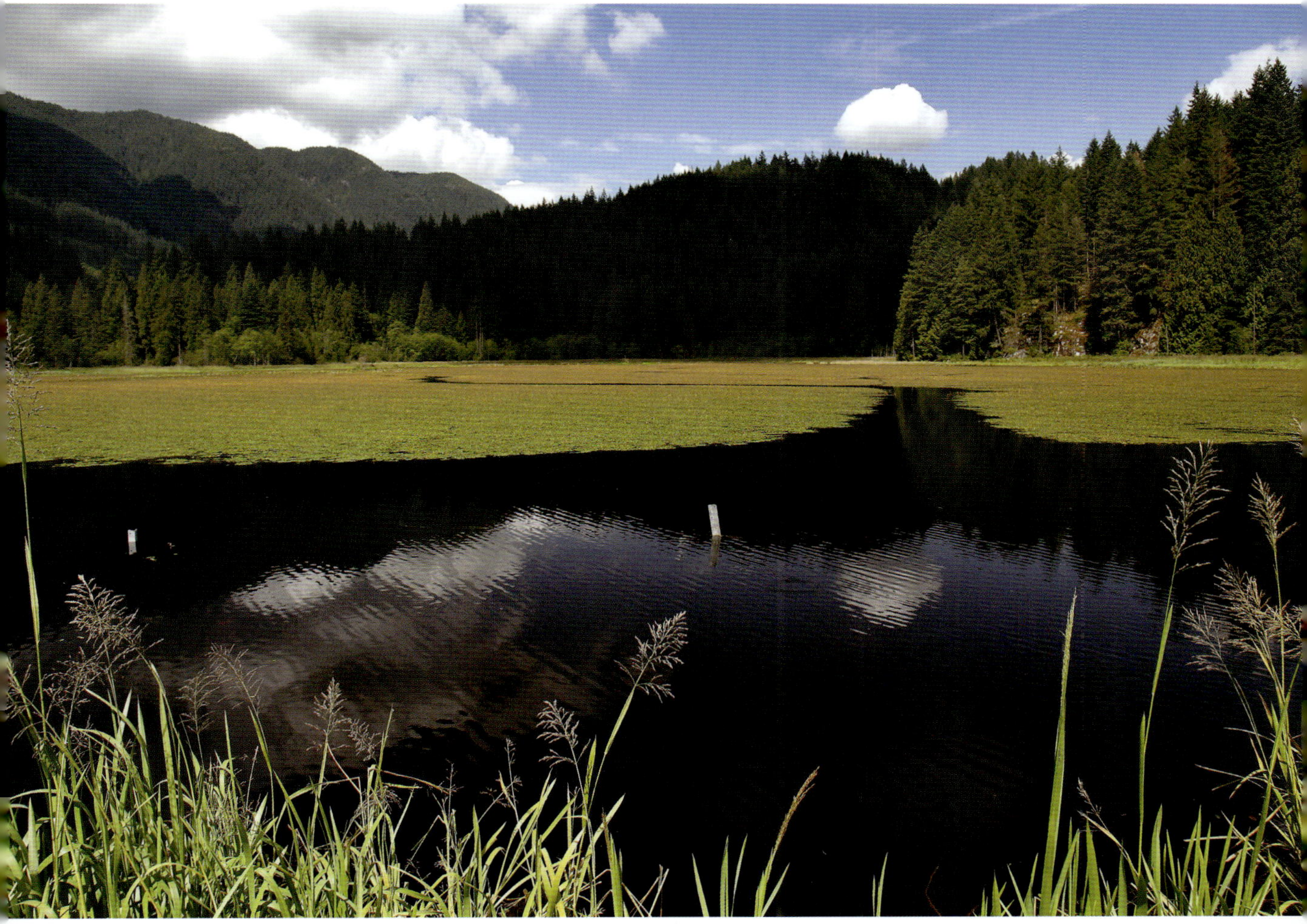

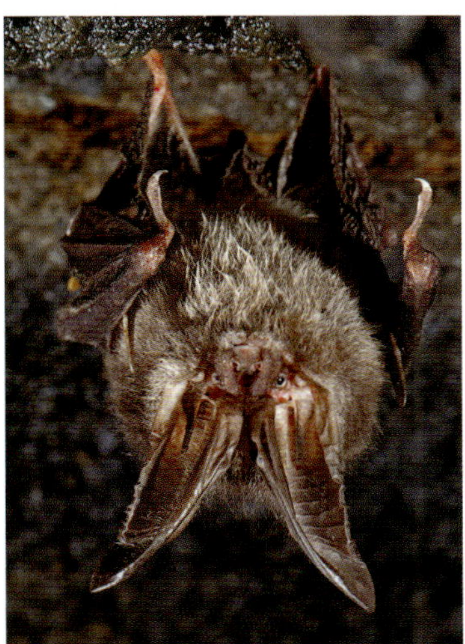

↑ The picturesque marshes of this regional park are a must-see.

← The Townsend's big-eared bat calls this park home.

Nairn Falls Provincial Park

Water cascades between water-carved potholes in the Green River

What Makes This Hot Spot Hot?

- British Columbia's provincial flower, the Pacific dogwood (a flowering tree), grows alongside a river coloured turquoise by glacial silt.
- Lucky hikers can catch a glimpse of the rubber boa, a well-camouflaged and harmless snake.
- Trails take hikers through tranquil coastal forests of cedar and hemlock.

Address: Sea-to-Sky Hwy (Hwy 99), 4 km south of Pemberton, BC
Tel.: (604) 986-9371
Website:

BC Parks

GPS Coordinates
Latitude: 50.29352
Longitude: −122.82507

Open year-round; campground open May 12 to October 1

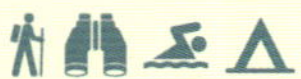

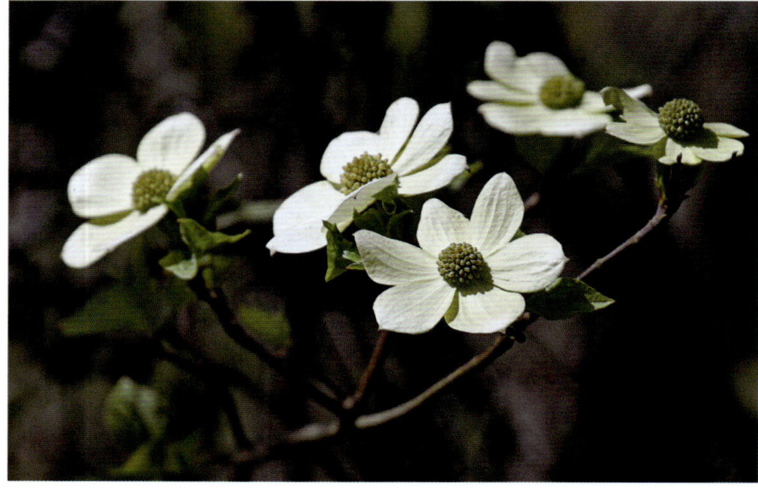

The Green River flows through the centre of Nairn Falls Provincial Park, which sits between Whistler and Pemberton. The rushing river is named for its turquoise colour resulting from sunlight reflecting off glacial silt. The beauty and location of the park make it a perfect place to set up camp while exploring this and other nature hot spots of the Sea-to-Sky Corridor. Although there are a few trails to hike within the park, the Nairn Falls Trail, which leads to the namesake waterfalls, is a must. The trail follows the Green River through coastal forests of cedar and hemlock for about half an hour before coming to upper and lower Nairn Falls.

The power of the water is evident by the smoothed granite through which the water has carved its path. The falls cascade over the rock and have created potholes where the water pools and churns, sending mist into the air, before falling farther. Rocky outcrops along the trail provide spectacular viewpoints of the falls. This trail was historically used by the Lil'wat Nation to gain access to Nairn Falls as well as to Mount Currie, the massive picturesque peak towering over the valley. The trail is

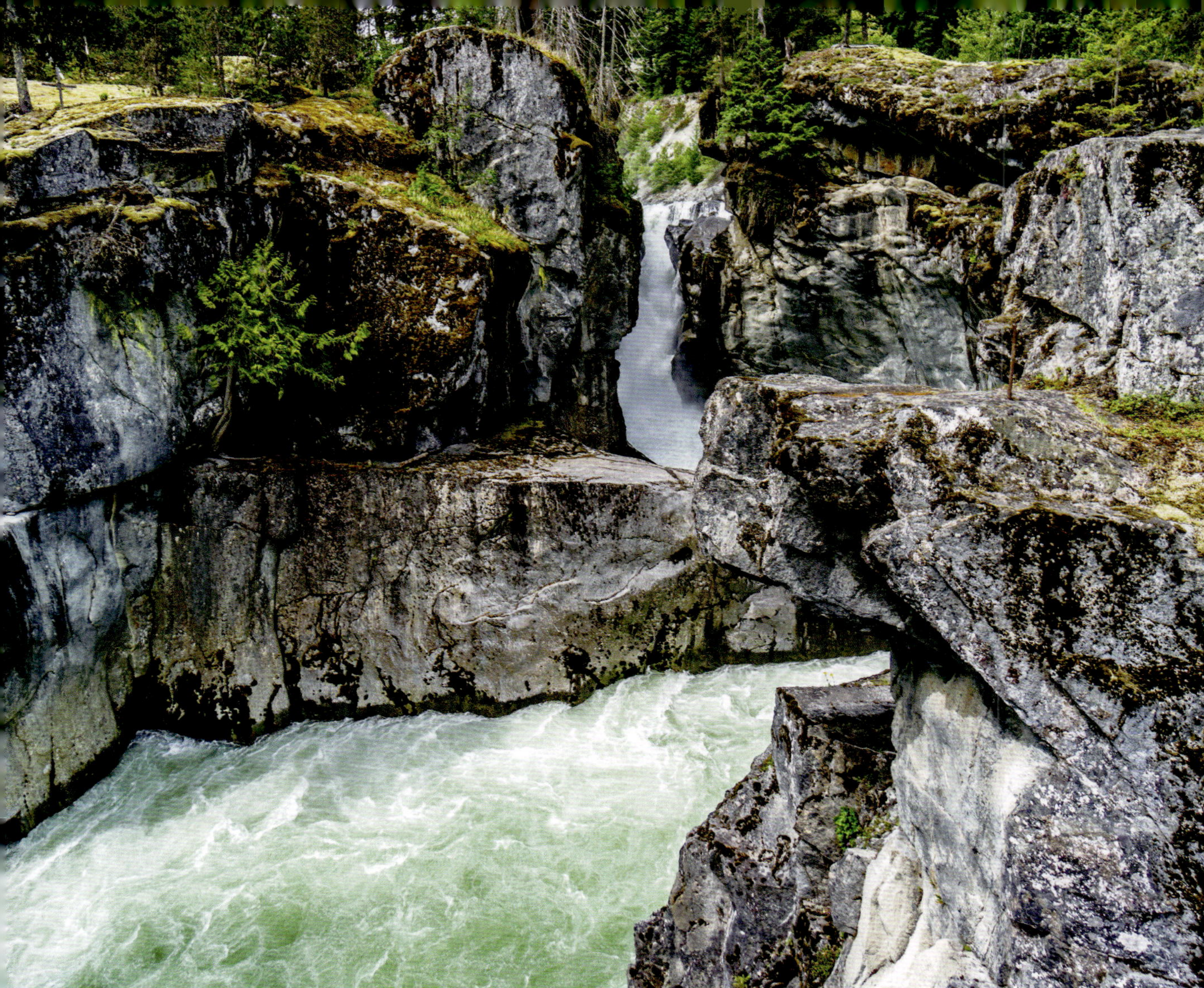

fairly easy but does have a couple steep drop-offs down to the river valley, so ensure you wear sturdy footwear.

Another notable hike in the park is the Coudre Point Trail, which meanders in and out of the forest along the river. In the park expect to see the Pacific dogwood, a flowering tree and British Columbia's provincial flower, along with deer and other wildlife. Also keep an eye out for the elusive rubber boa, which is the smallest member of the boa constrictor family. Completely harmless, these boas are greenish-brown and camouflage well on the forest floor. If one feels threatened it will curl into a small ball and poke its tail out. Their tail acts as a decoy to predators because it looks very similar to its head.

On hot summer days One Mile Lake, just north of the park closer to Pemberton, is an excellent place for a swim.

⬆ **The stunning waters of the Green River have carved beautiful features in the rock over which it tumbles and flows.**

⬊ **The Pacific dogwood blossoms alongside the trail.**

LYNN HEADWATERS REGIONAL PARK

Norvan Falls

Impressive falls are the highlight of a fungi-packed walk through North Vancouver wilderness

What Makes This Hot Spot Hot?

- Fall is a great time for a visit to experience the seasonal outburst of mushroom growth in the area.
- Accessible by public transit, this park is one of the most reachable hiking destinations in the region.
- Norvan Falls is a beautiful reward at the end of a hike that weaves along the water's edge through temperate forest.

Address: 4900 Lynn Valley Road, North Vancouver, BC
Tel.: (604) 224-5739
Website:

Metro Vancouver

GPS Coordinates
Latitude: 49.36157
Longitude: −123.0281

Open year-round

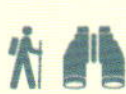

 **(Check ahead)**

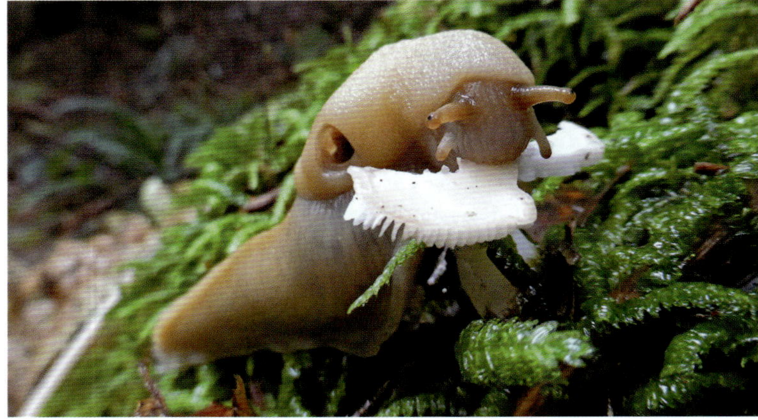

Lynn Headwaters Regional Park is criss-crossed with trails of varying difficulty and elevation, but one of the easiest hikes in this substantial protected land is to Norvan Falls, which can be accessed year-round if the weather co-operates.

The first section of the trail is a wide path that largely hugs the edge of Lynn Creek, with many access points to pop in and explore the clear waters and large stones of the river's edge. Look out for remnants of early logging activity in the area, where tools long forgotten still lie, idle and rusted.

After veering off Lynn Loop Trail onto Headwaters Trail and continuing along for a few more kilometres, you will hear the unmistakable sound of Norvan Creek rushing over the falls, signalling that you have nearly reached your destination, although there are opportunities to continue farther into the park. A steep path allows you to make your way down towards the edge of the creek below the falls, providing impressive views and a great afternoon picnic location.

This hike through second-growth temperate forest drenched in moisture and moss is perfect for mycology enthusiasts to explore in the fall. Most of this diverse set of fungal species becomes more noticeable when fruiting bodies spring forth from decaying organic matter in the autumn, especially along fallen logs and up the trunks of dead or dying trees. The visible part of each mushroom is only a small portion of the entire organism. Most of the year, fungi stay hidden from view, made up of hyphae, hair-like filaments that spread out and penetrate the decaying host. This network of hyphae, called the mycelium, forms a fruiting structure when it is ready to spread its spores.

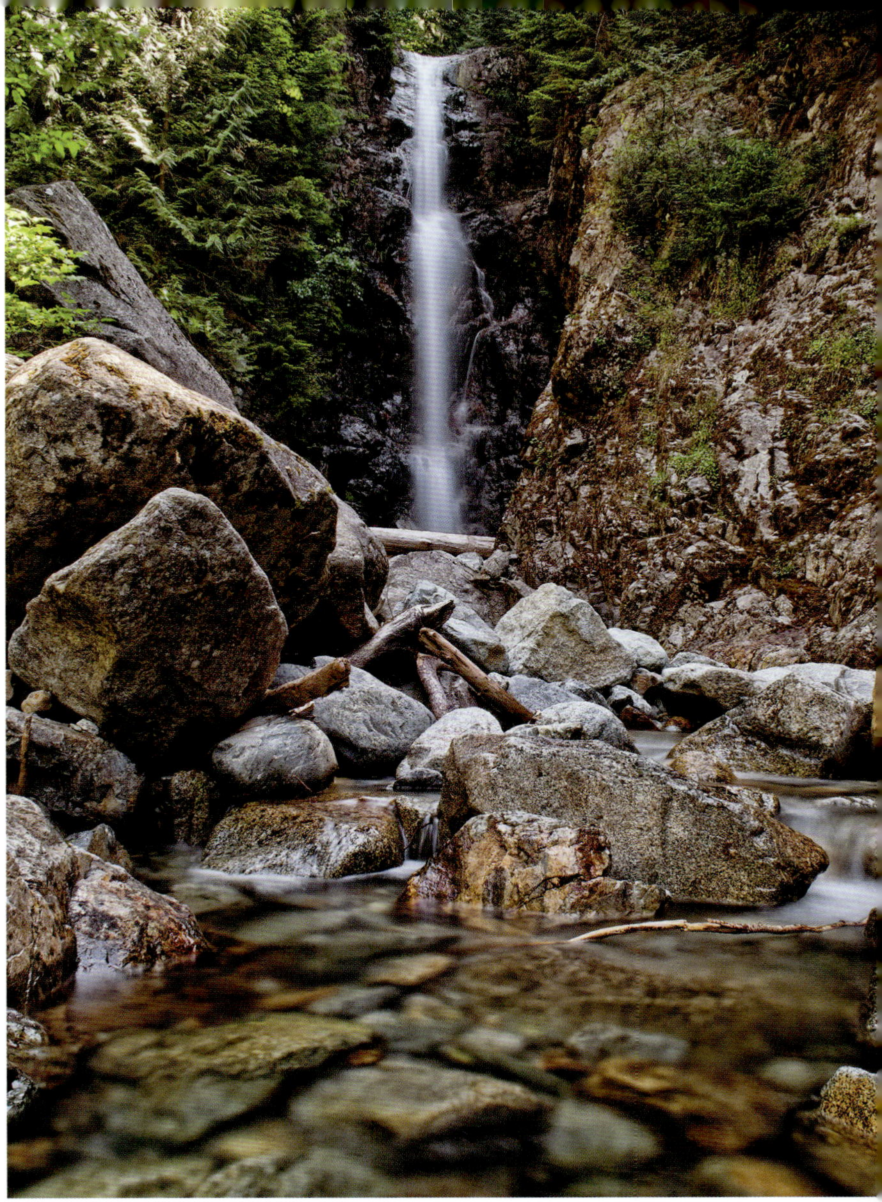

One favourite mushroom to look out for is the wonderfully named shaggy scalycap, typically found near the base of trees and stumps. It brings to mind a vision of toasted marshmallows around the campfire. This charming inhabitant is just one of innumerable species of fungi worth searching for in the park — the shapes, sizes, colours and textures of the fungi here are well worth a journey into the forest during the fall rains.

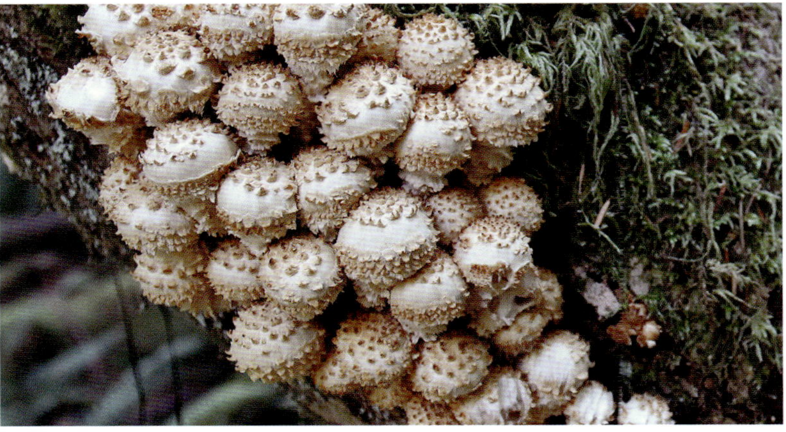

Pacific Spirit Regional Park

A stunning natural space teeming with life right in the city of Vancouver

What Makes This Hot Spot Hot?

- A variety of ecosystems and easy access by public transit make this park a wilderness wonderland.
- Marsh, old-growth cedars, rocky intertidal zone and an abundance of wildlife are all within 20 minutes of hiking.
- Birds, squirrels and many other forest residents give the space a tranquil, wild feeling within the city.

Address: 5495 Chancellor Boulevard, Vancouver, BC (For more information about access points, see the park map on the website below.)
Tel.: (604) 224-5739
Website:

Metro Vancouver

GPS Coordinates
Latitude: 49.25307
Longitude: −123.21639

Open year-round

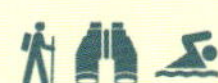

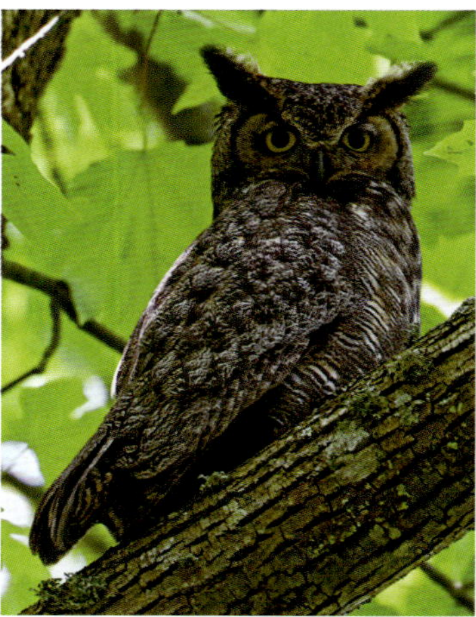

Great horned owls and other birds are heard in the forest.

Passing through a forest is part of the daily commute for many lucky university students. Pacific Spirit Regional Park, composed of rainforests, beaches, bogs and estuaries, covers 308 hectares with over 70 kilometres of trails. This green space sits between the University of British Columbia and the city of Vancouver. In the heart of an old-growth forest, standing beneath towering cedars and Douglas-fir, visitors feel surrounded by rugged wilderness — a true escape from the hustle and bustle of the city.

Native plants are abundant and diverse. Near the cedars are alders and vine maples looming over salmonberry bushes, as the waxy leaves of salal shine in among ferns and flowers. In an effort to protect this diverse area, which was originally part of the UBC's endowment land, the site was established as a regional park in 1989. It is now maintained by the dedicated volunteers of the Pacific Spirit Park Society and Metro Vancouver.

Different ecosystems are accessible from the park's many entrances. Crabs scurry through the intertidal zone at Acadia Beach, while sword ferns line a shaded path through the forest just a stone's throw away. Following a short loop from Acadia Beach along the Salish Trail, connecting to the Spanish Trail and ending at Spanish Banks Beach (all of which is just a small percentage of the park's trails), a hiker will encounter sandy and rocky beaches, go on a beautiful canyon-side stroll and explore wetlands next to an old-growth forest. Bird, amphibian and small mammal sightings are common. Pacific wrens and small songbirds sing along the trails, great horned owls are

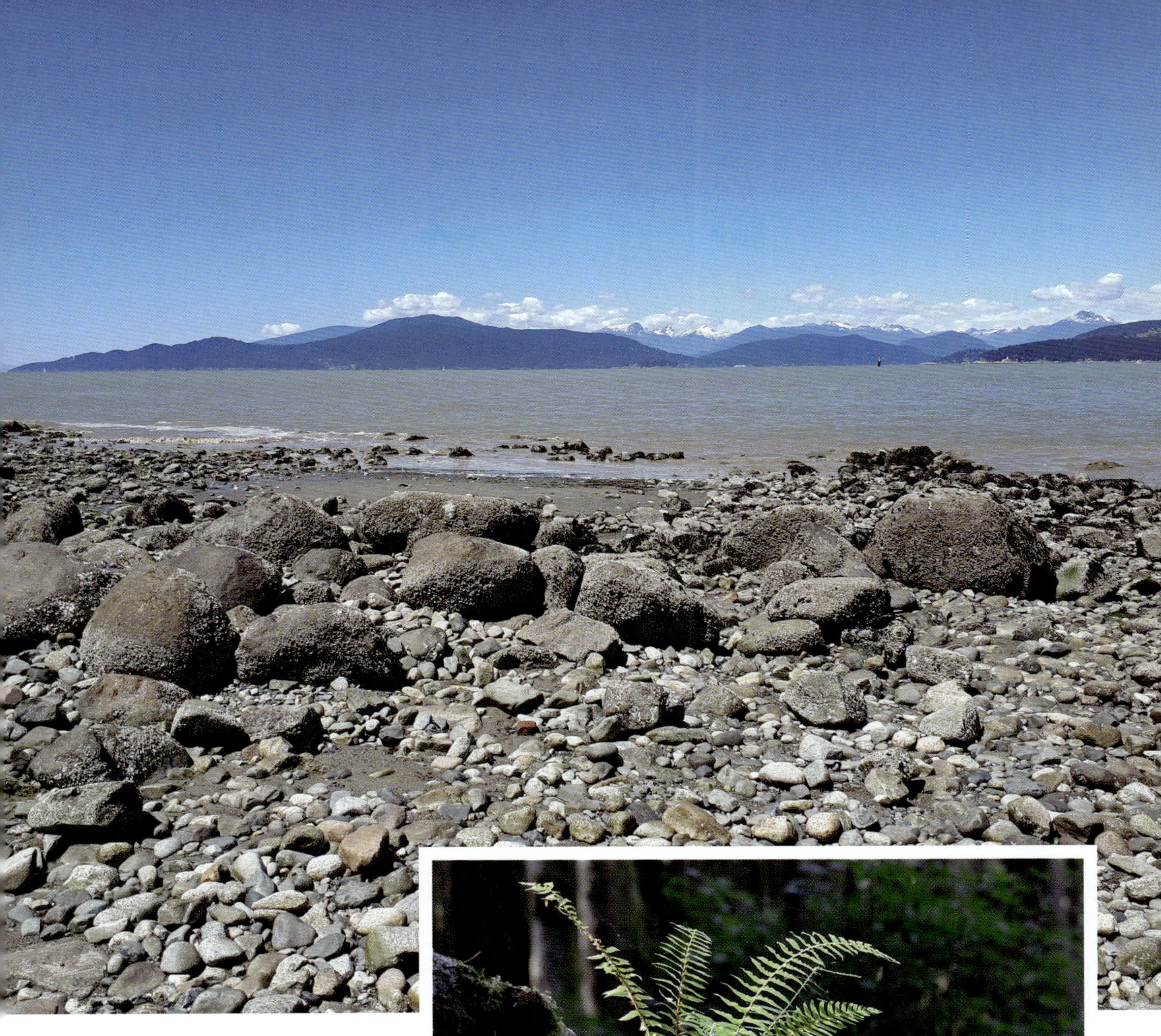

often heard in the evenings
hooting from tree branches
above and bald eagles are a
regular sight as they swoop
down from trees to catch fish.
Occasionally larger mammals,
such as coyotes, are sighted.
With all this plant and animal
life, this park is truly one
of the most accessible and
diverse natural spaces in
the province, and it is right
in the heart of Vancouver.

↑ **Ferns and moss cover the understory
of the park's lush treed areas.**

↖ **The rocky intertidal zone hosts
many marine invertebrates, such
as barnacles, mussels and crabs.**

Pitt-Addington Marsh Wildlife Management Area

Forty kilometres east of Vancouver, this wetland habitat is an important area for birds in the Lower Mainland

What Makes This Hot Spot Hot?

- The habitat is one of the only coastal breeding grounds of the grey catbird.
- Ninety species of songbirds have been recorded in the area.
- There are over 50 kilometres of raised dykes to explore between tracts of marshland.

Address: Rannie Road, Pitt Meadows, BC
Tel.: N/A
Website:

Government of BC

GPS Coordinates
Latitude: 49.32992
Longitude: −122.63762

Open year-round

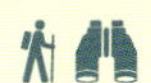

The many kilometres of dykes and trails that traverse the Pitt-Addington Marsh Wildlife Management Area allow for countless hours of birding year-round. Over 50 kilometres of accessible dykes can be explored, and five covered viewing towers and three viewing platforms spread throughout the area provide great lookouts. The dykes define four large, separated marshes, all ripe with life.

One of the best trails for bird activities is along the Nature Dyke Trail, where salmonberry, blackberry and other shrubs encroach onto the path, attracting many songbirds into the dense brush. More than 90 songbird species have been recorded in the area, including orange-crowned, Townsend's, black-throated grey and yellow warblers. Wood ducks and hooded mergansers use the nest boxes installed along this dyke. In the winter many more waterfowl descend onto the wetlands of the management area, as do mute, tundra and trumpeter swans.

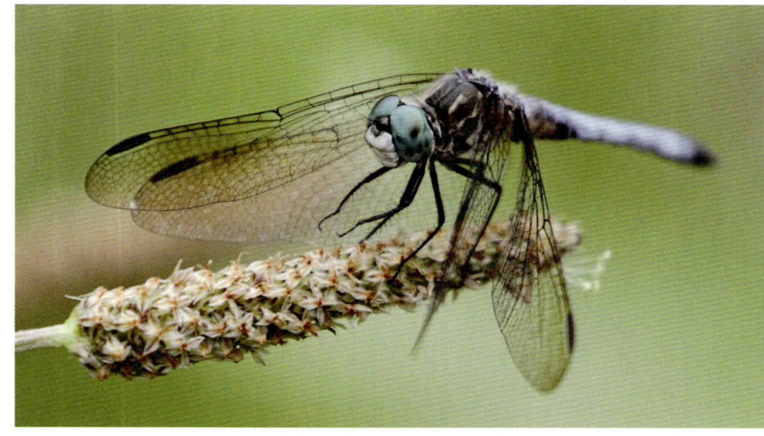

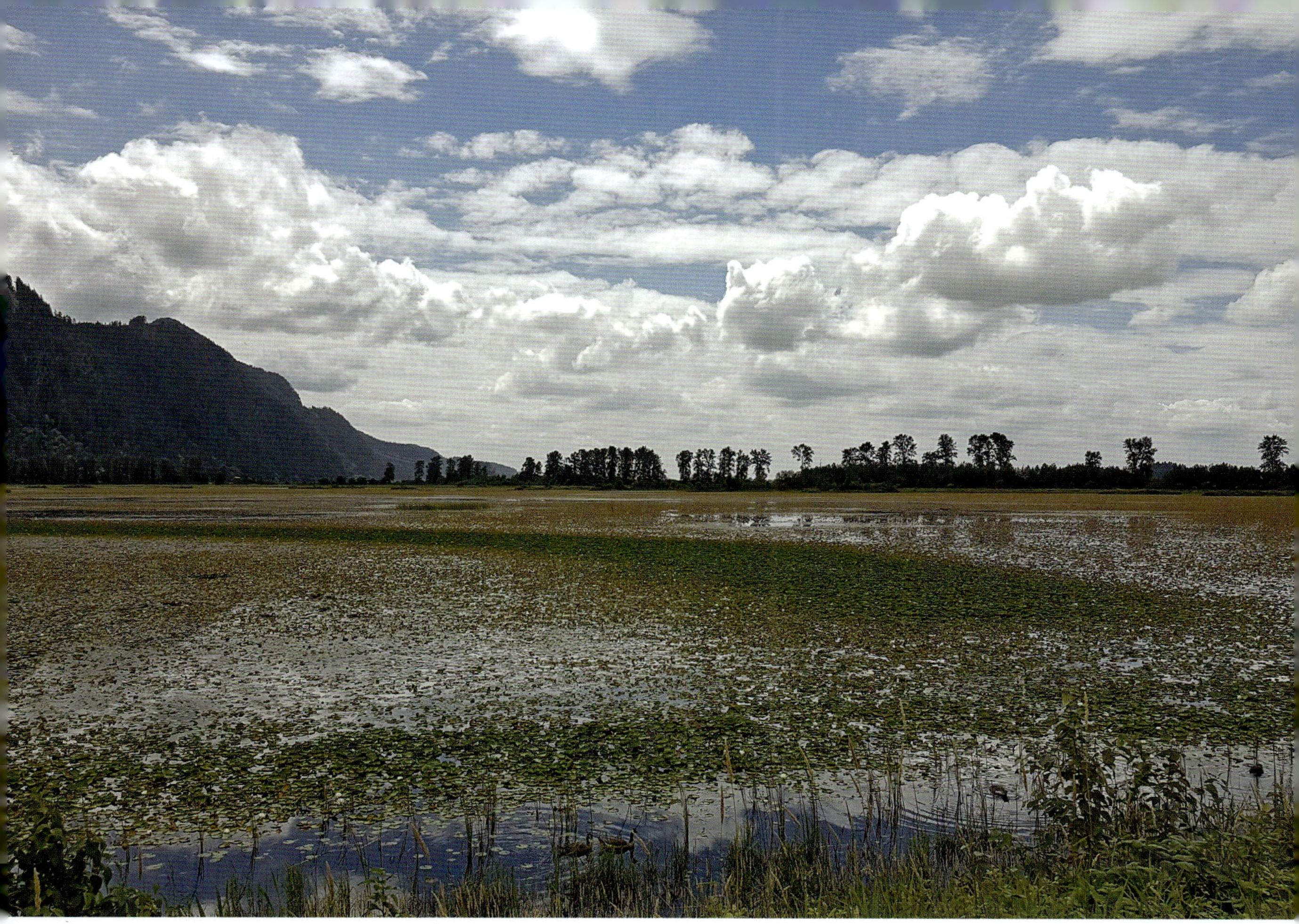

Although generally rare in the Lower Mainland, the grey catbird is commonly seen throughout the Pitt-Addington Marsh Wildlife Management Area, which is one of the only known breeding locations of this species along coastal British Columbia. The area also supports the largest concentration of osprey in the Lower Mainland. You can find them nesting on the pilings that line the Pitt River.

Dragonflies zip across the dykes catching insects on the wing. Look out for the western pondhawk, dot-tailed white-face and blue dasher along the far dyke of the Katzie Marsh. About 250 species of plant have been identified in the Pitt-Addington Marsh, including Labrador tea, bog-laurel, hardhack, bur-reed and bladderwort.

Within the park is the specially designated Pitt Polder Ecological Reserve, which protects 88 hectares of the rapidly disappearing Fraser Valley boglands. This designation is crucial, because it allows the highest level of protection for important habitat in the province.

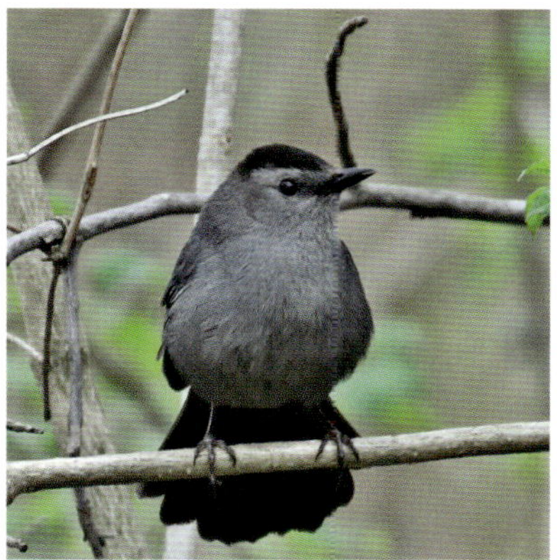

↑ **Grey catbirds are locally rare along coastal British Columbia but are found nesting in this hot spot.**

↖ **Many kilometres of raised dykes through wetland habitat make for a birding paradise.**

← **A perched blue dasher watches over his territory.**

Shannon Falls Provincial Park

Melted glacial water carved through granite has created a majestic waterfall

What Makes This Hot Spot Hot?

- The cascading Shannon Falls is the third-highest waterfall in British Columbia.
- A hike or gondola ride takes visitors to the mountain vista, from which the source of the falls can be seen.
- Hiking in the park's subalpine environment can be a magical chance for wildlife viewing.

Address: Sea-to-Sky Hwy (Hwy 99), 3 km south of Squamish, BC
Tel.: (1-800) 689-9025
Website:

BC Parks

GPS Coordinates
Latitude: 49.66997
Longitude: –123.15644

Open year-round

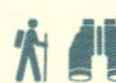

♿ (Check ahead)

→ **The falls are visible from the highway, but the quick hike in to get a closer look is well worth it.**

Just south of Stawamus Chief Provincial Park, Shannon Falls plummets a spectacular 335 metres, making it the third-highest waterfall in British Columbia. This breathtaking waterfall is accessed by a leisurely 5-minute walk from the parking lot. This short stroll through coastal forest leads to the base of the falls where cascading water churns in the rocky riverbed and eventually flows into the ocean. The waterfall is fed by melting snow and glaciers from the surrounding mountains and, as such, is at its most powerful on warm spring days. Many visitors choose to walk to the base and then spend a relaxed afternoon in the picnic area.

Shannon Falls is an important place to the Skwxwú7mesh First Nation. There are tales of a two-headed serpent named *Say-noth-ka* carving a path through the granite and creating the falls by repeatedly travelling up and down the mountain. The name of the park and falls come from William Shannon, who sourced clay from the

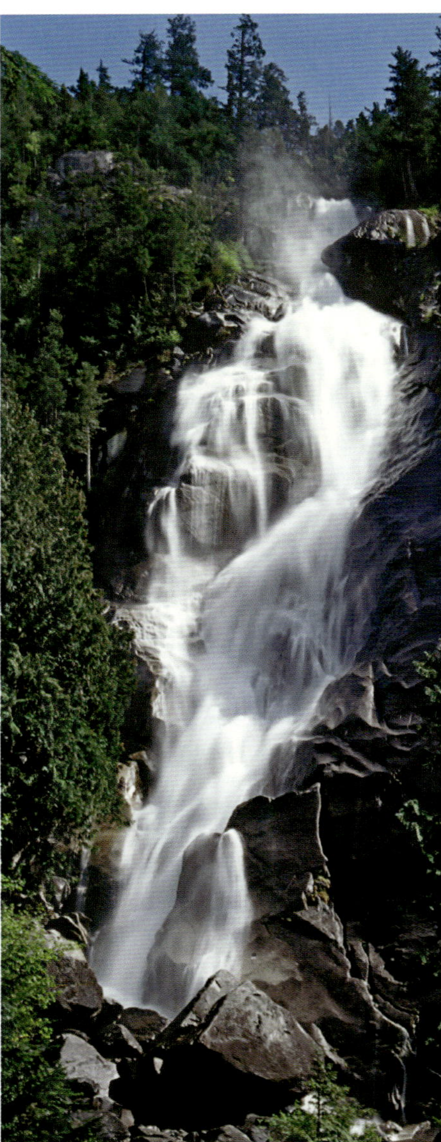

land to make bricks. The area was later used for logging, which is evidenced by the notches you can see in the large stumps on which loggers placed platforms to stand on while felling towering cedar and fir trees. Following the period of logging, the land was donated to BC Parks in 1982.

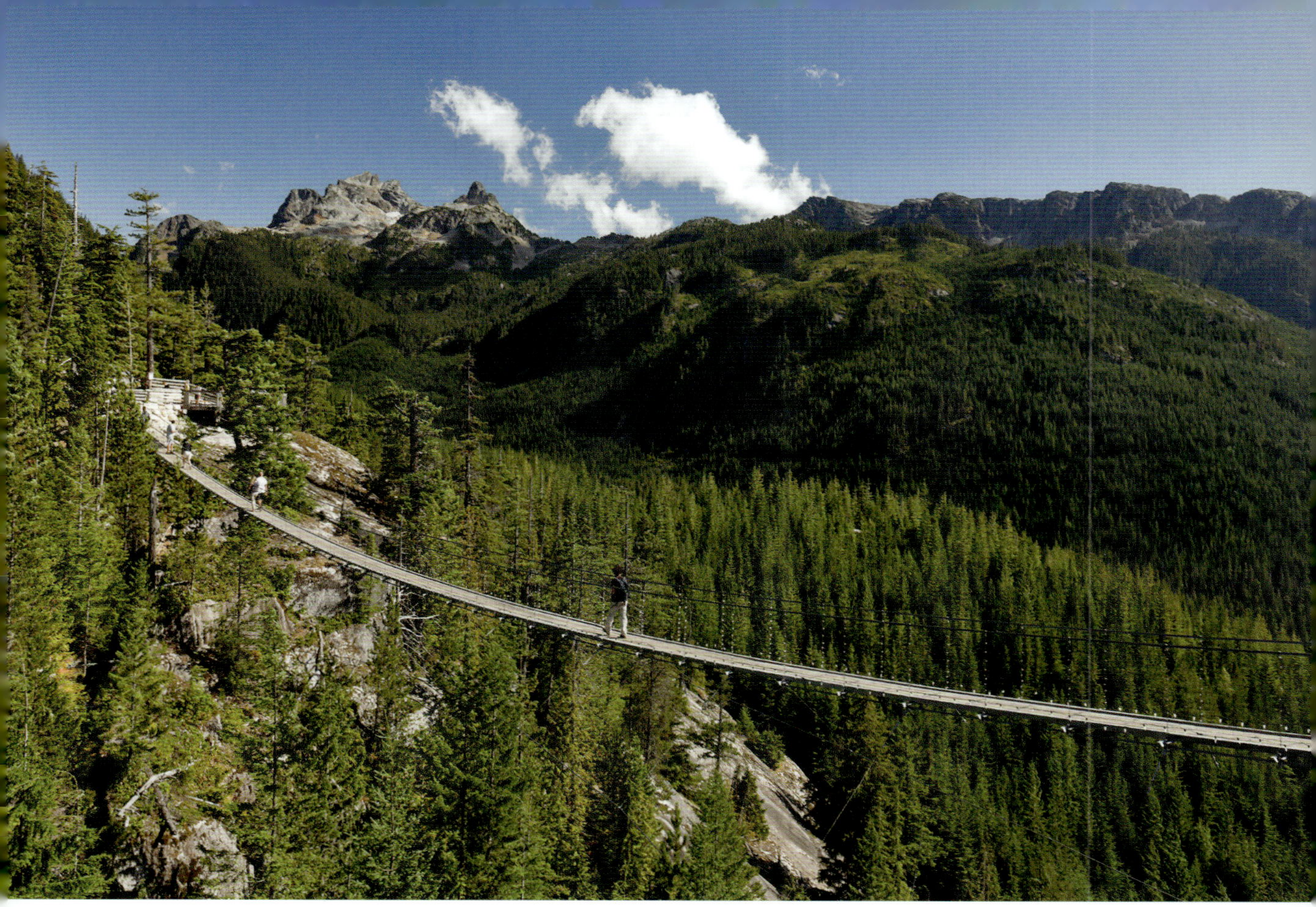

For a bird's-eye view, hike or take the Sea to Sky Gondola to the alpine environment above the falls. From this vantage point, the picturesque mountains that feed the falls become visible. There are a number of hiking trails and a suspension bridge with view-points of Howe Sound and Squamish. The Wonderland Lake Loop, in particular, is a spectacular hike. On the trail you will see blueberry bushes and alpine flowers and visit a small alpine lake. Keep an eye and an ear out for the sooty grouse, a well-camouflaged ground bird. These birds have unique-sounding calls — the male with his low-pitched hoot and the female with her cackle.

↑ After a quick gondola ride or steep hike, the suspension bridge offers visitors panoramic views of the surrounding mountains, including Sky Pilot and Copilot, both of which feed Shannon Falls with their snow melt.

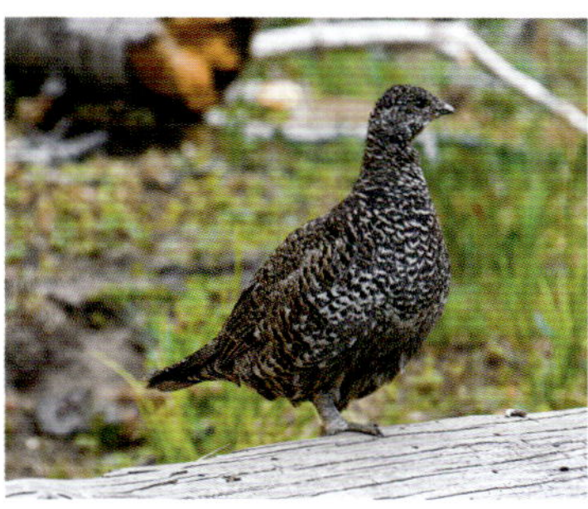

← Sooty grouse are often heard on the trails.

Skwelwil'em Squamish Estuary

A combined effort by the S<u>k</u>wx<u>w</u>ú7mesh Nation and the Ministry of the Environment keeps this area a wild sanctuary

What Makes This Hot Spot Hot?

- Glacial water from the Squamish River meets the ocean in Howe Sound in this estuarine environment.
- The diverse marine and forest habitats in this small area support a variety of life.
- Many species of fish, including the historically important eulachon, use the estuary and Squamish River for spawning.

Address: Spit Road, Squamish, BC
Tel.: (604) 815-4994
Website:

District of Squamish

GPS Coordinates
Latitude: 49.70472
Longitude: −123.17351

Open year-round

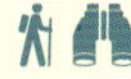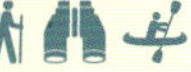

Visitors walking the trails or paddleboarding the channels of the Skwelwil'em Squamish Estuary will quickly notice a diverse habitat of grassy marshes, open mudflats and hemlock forests. This area is a sanctuary that supports an abundance of wildlife, including over 200 species of birds alone. Kingfishers, shorebirds like spotted sandpipers and songbirds like the marsh wren can all be found here. Both land and marine mammals frequent the estuary, including black bears, river otters and seals. Keen's myotis, a red-listed species that is one of 16 bat species in British Columbia, roosts in the forests.

Opening into the ocean alongside the estuary is the Squamish River. The river and its tributaries are important spawning grounds for salmon and trout. Coho, pink, chum and chinook salmon — as well as steelhead, cutthroat and bull trout — all make their way from the river to the open ocean where they spend the majority of their adult lives. Although some species, such as pink salmon, head straight to the open ocean, many others make a pit stop in the protected brackish waters of the estuary. This "nursery of the sea" is particularly important for chinook salmon. Chinook enter the estuary as juveniles only 15 millimetres in length and grow up to 120 millimetres before entering the ocean as smolts.

Between the Squamish River and the estuary, a strip

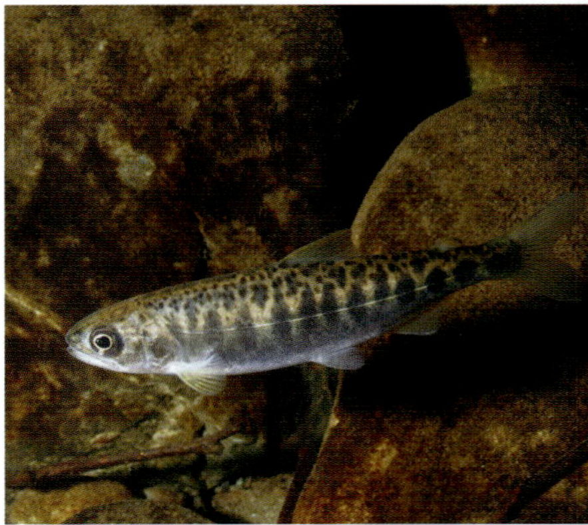

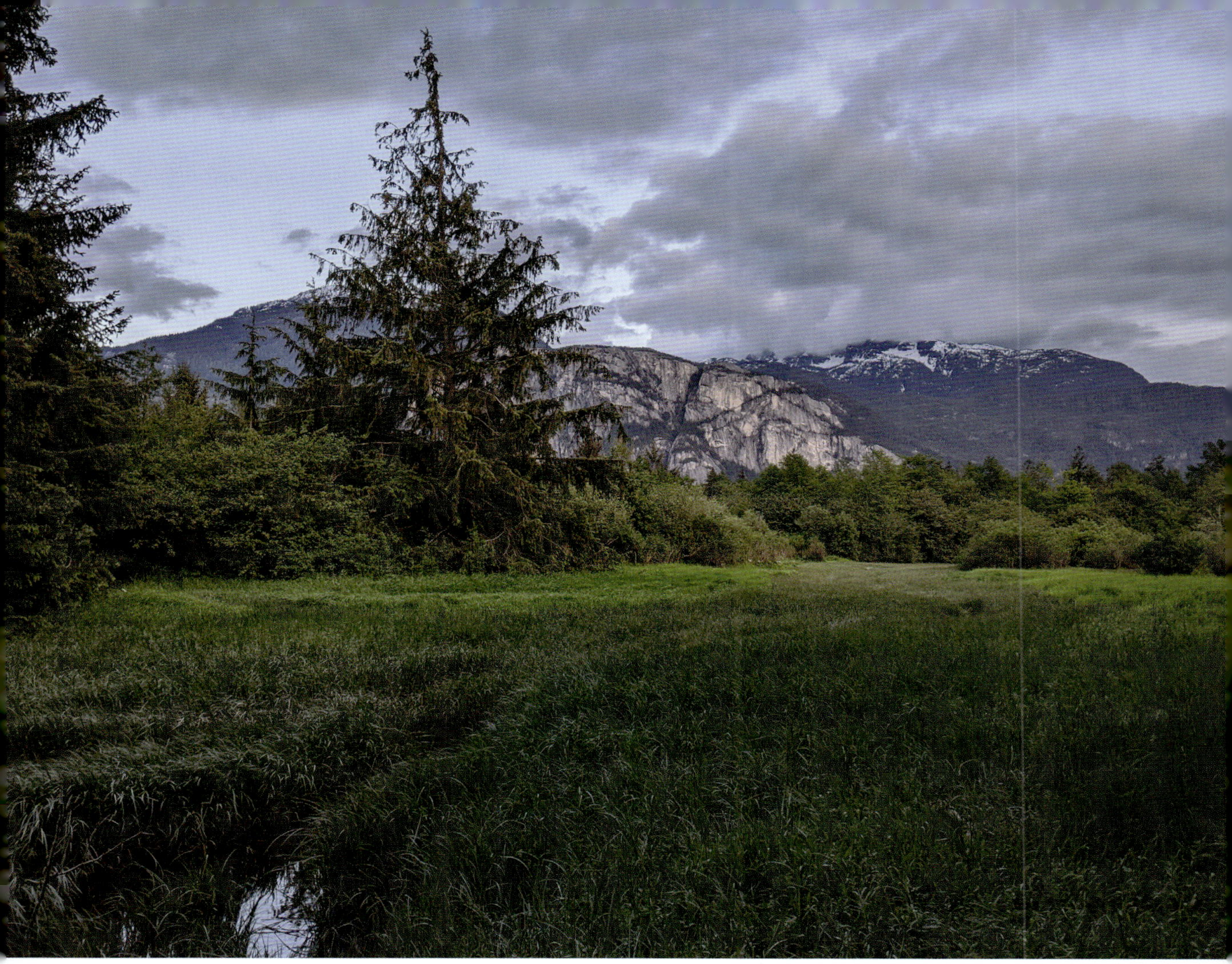

of land called the Spit was built in the 1970s. Initially intended to be a coal port, the Spit ended up providing windsport enthusiasts access to the waters of Howe Sound. Unfortunately the Spit had unintended environmental consequences; it funnelled juvenile salmon and trout directly into the open ocean, resulting in a drastic decline in chinook salmon stocks. In 2022 conservation efforts came to fruition and a large portion of the Spit was modified, allowing juvenile salmon and trout proper access to the estuary for the first time in 52 years.

The estuary acts as a sponge for both nutrients and pollutants, which makes it a sensitive environment. By continuing conservation efforts to protect our watersheds, we can ensure that this estuary, as well as others, remains safe for the many species that call this unique ecosystem home.

→ **Black bears frequent the estuary and surrounding forest.**

← **This juvenile chinook salmon is about 6 months old.**

↑ **Estuary visitors will find stunning views of the surrounding mountains at any time of the year.**

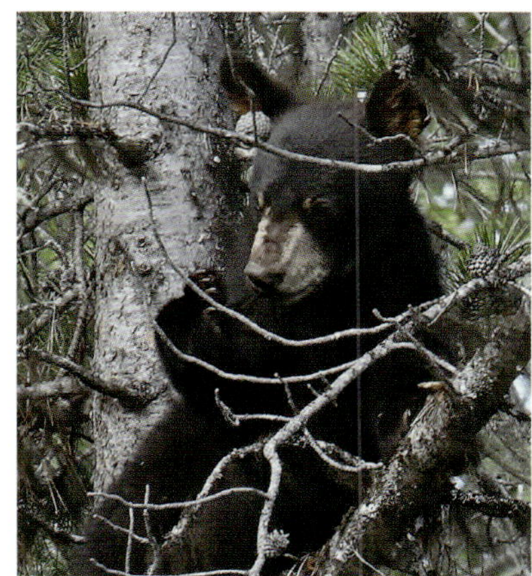

Stanley Park

One of the world's most famous urban parks, Stanley Park has much nature to explore just a stone's throw from downtown Vancouver

What Makes This Hot Spot Hot?

- The park has been deemed an Important Bird Area for the conservation of birds and biodiversity.
- It hosts one of the largest great blue heron nesting colonies in all of North America.
- The Stanley Park Ecological Society offers programs for all ages to enhance your nature experience.

Address: 2099 Beach Avenue, Vancouver, BC
Tel.: (604) 873-7000
Website:

City of Vancouver

GPS Coordinates
Latitude: 49.29232
Longitude: −123.14586

Open year-round

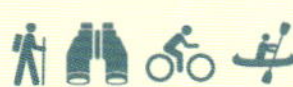

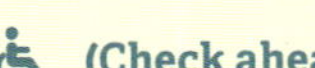

♿ **(Check ahead)**

→ **The herons' beach ball-sized nests fill the trees near the Vancouver Board of Parks and Recreation offices.**

Stanley Park is recognized as one of the world's best urban parks — its 400 hectares of diverse land is a natural oasis close to downtown Vancouver. Half a million trees, beautiful beaches and easily accessed intertidal life make this an urban park worth exploring with binoculars and pocket ID books.

The famous seawall is the world's longest uninterrupted waterfront path, allowing for perfect views of Burrard Inlet and English Bay. Stanley Park was established as a city park in 1888, and some things have never changed: biking in the park has been popular since the early 1900s.

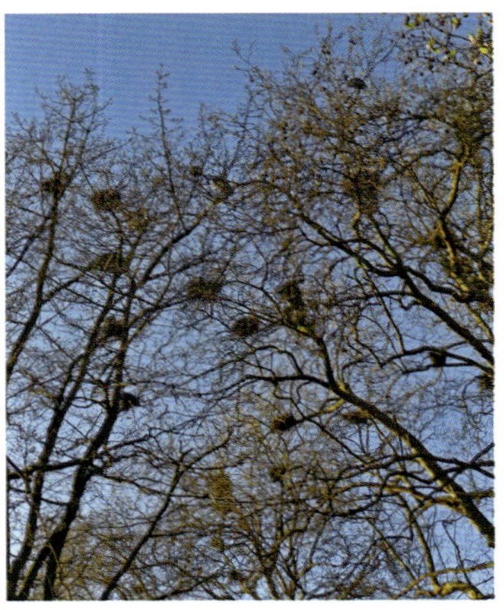

The Stanley Park Ecological Society provides many wonderful nature programs that add even more opportunity for nature-based family fun.

As an internationally recognized Important Bird Area, Stanley Park is a birder's paradise. A part of the Pacific Flyway, spring migration brings waves of diverse avian life. In the fall and winter large rafts of overwintering Barrow's goldeneye come to the protected waters in and around Stanley Park. British Columbia is home to 60 per cent of the world's population of this duck species, and their large wintering colonies are worth a wet winter stroll through the park.

Another must-see birding spectacle takes place just outside the Vancouver Board of Parks and Recreation offices. Stanley Park's coastal great blue heron colony is one of the largest nesting colonies of this species in all of North America. This colony is of special importance because, although great blue herons are widespread across the globe, this particular subspecies is non-migratory and depends on local sites for safe nesting and feeding. As a result of disturbance and habitat loss, the coastal great blue heron is blue-listed and likely close to endangered.

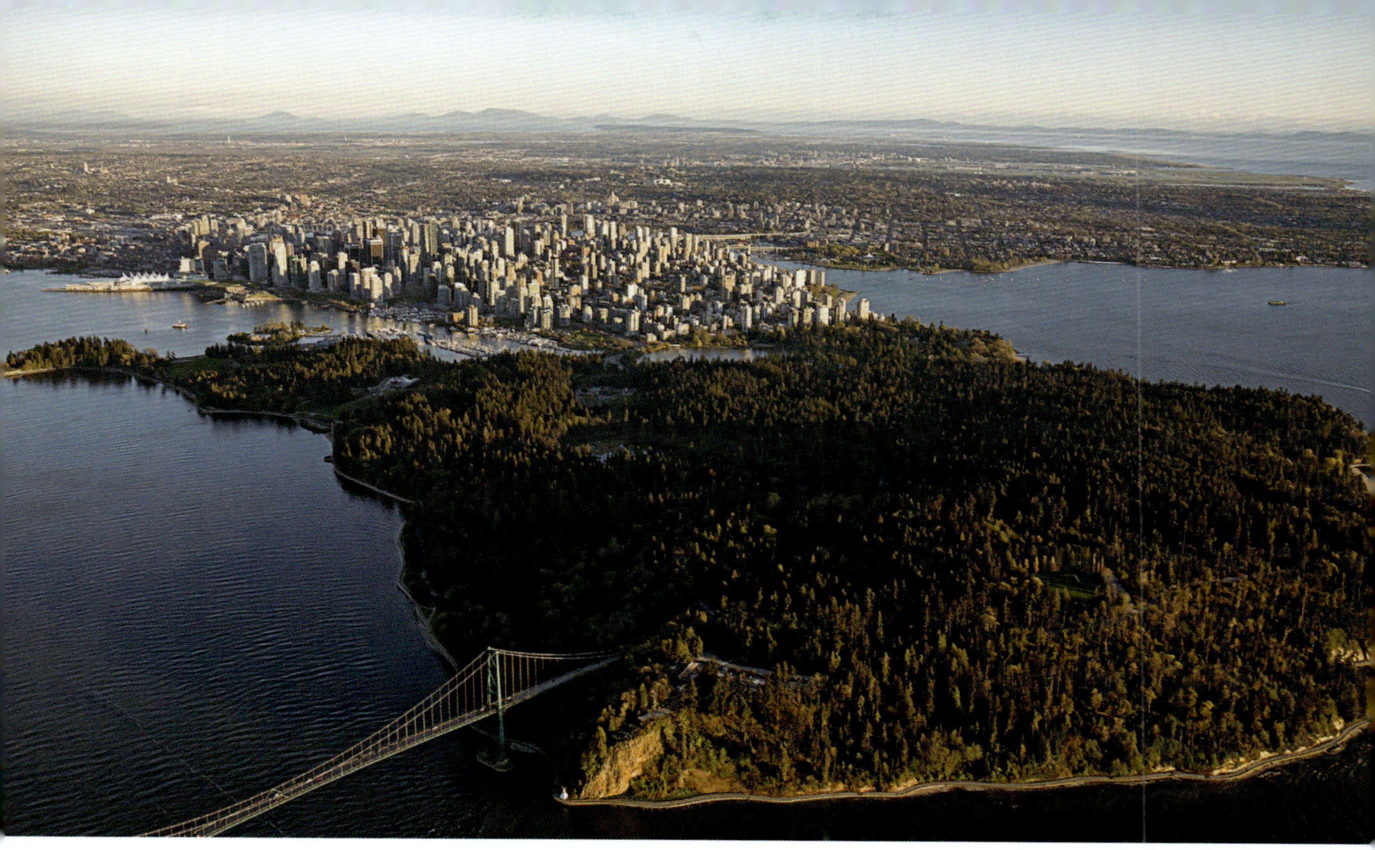

Great blue heron colonies have been recorded in the park since 1921, and today the colony is composed of 80 to 100 pairs. Although the heron nests are high up in the canopy, you can still get a glimpse into the private lives of these prehistoric-looking nestlings by tuning into the park's heron cam on the city's website.

The chicks are fed for about 60 days at the nest with hatching spread out over the early spring, so there are ample opportunities throughout the spring to witness this urban birding extravaganza. Once the chicks have grown a little more they may be seen feeding with adults outside the nest as early as June, with all young leaving the nest before August's end.

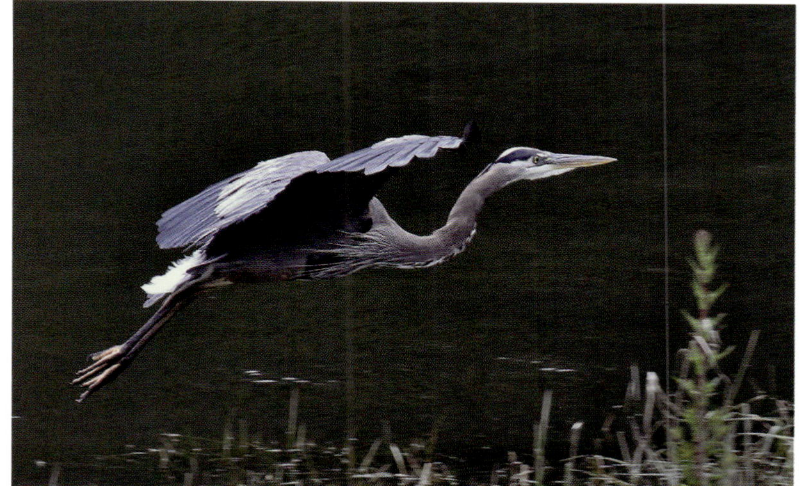

↑ An adult great blue heron flies down to the water in search of a meal to bring home to its hungry chicks.

↖ An aerial view of Stanley Park reveals its truly impressive size.

Stawamus Chief Provincial Park

BC Parks and the province's rock climbers merge the sport of rock climbing with environmental preservation

What Makes This Hot Spot Hot?

- The Stawamus Chief stands over the town of Squamish and can be seen from nearly everywhere in the valley.
- Peregrine falcons nest on rocky ledges and outcrops in March and April.
- The top of the Stawamus Chief affords magnificent views of the surrounding mountains and the ocean.

Address: Sea-to-Sky Hwy (Hwy 99), Squamish, BC
Tel.: (604) 986-9371
Website:

BC Parks

GPS Coordinates
Latitude: 49.67865
Longitude: −123.15457

Open year-round

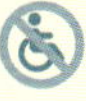

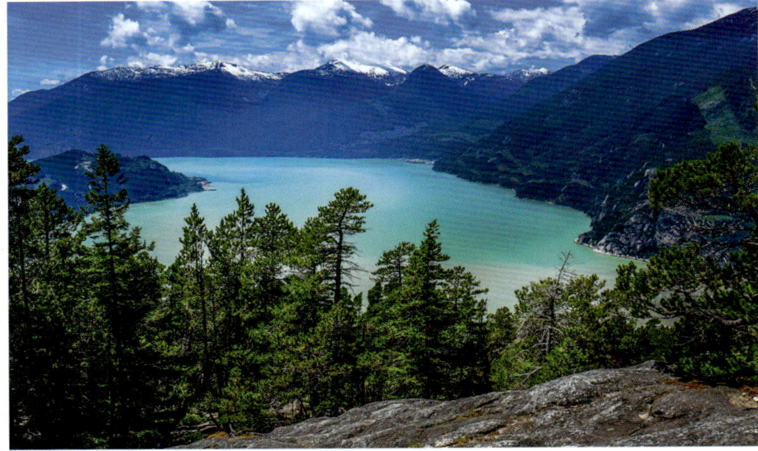

Towering over the Squamish Valley, the Stawamus Chief is an abruptly vertical 700-metre high granite dome. The face of this volcanic rock was slowly carved and polished by glaciers, which has made the park's impressive namesake a popular destination for rock climbers from around the world.

The hiking trails to its three peaks are clearly marked from the main parking lot. Fairly steep but well maintained with stairs, the first peak is generally hiked as a round trip in two to three hours. The trail will guide you through fir and cedar forests alongside a small creek. There are no open areas along the way, which makes the vista all the more breathtaking upon reaching the top. From the first peak, hikers are rewarded for their hard work with a magnificent view of Howe Sound and the nearby mountains. While many visitors conquer just the first peak, trails at the top lead to the other two peaks. In the summer months the ocean reflects a turquoise blue as a result of the silty glacial water flowing in from the Squamish River. At the mouth of the river, which enters the ocean from the north, you will see a large, open area. This is the Skwelwil'em Squamish Estuary — worth a visit once you return to sea level for its spectacular birding opportunities and scenery, which includes a stunning view of the Chief itself.

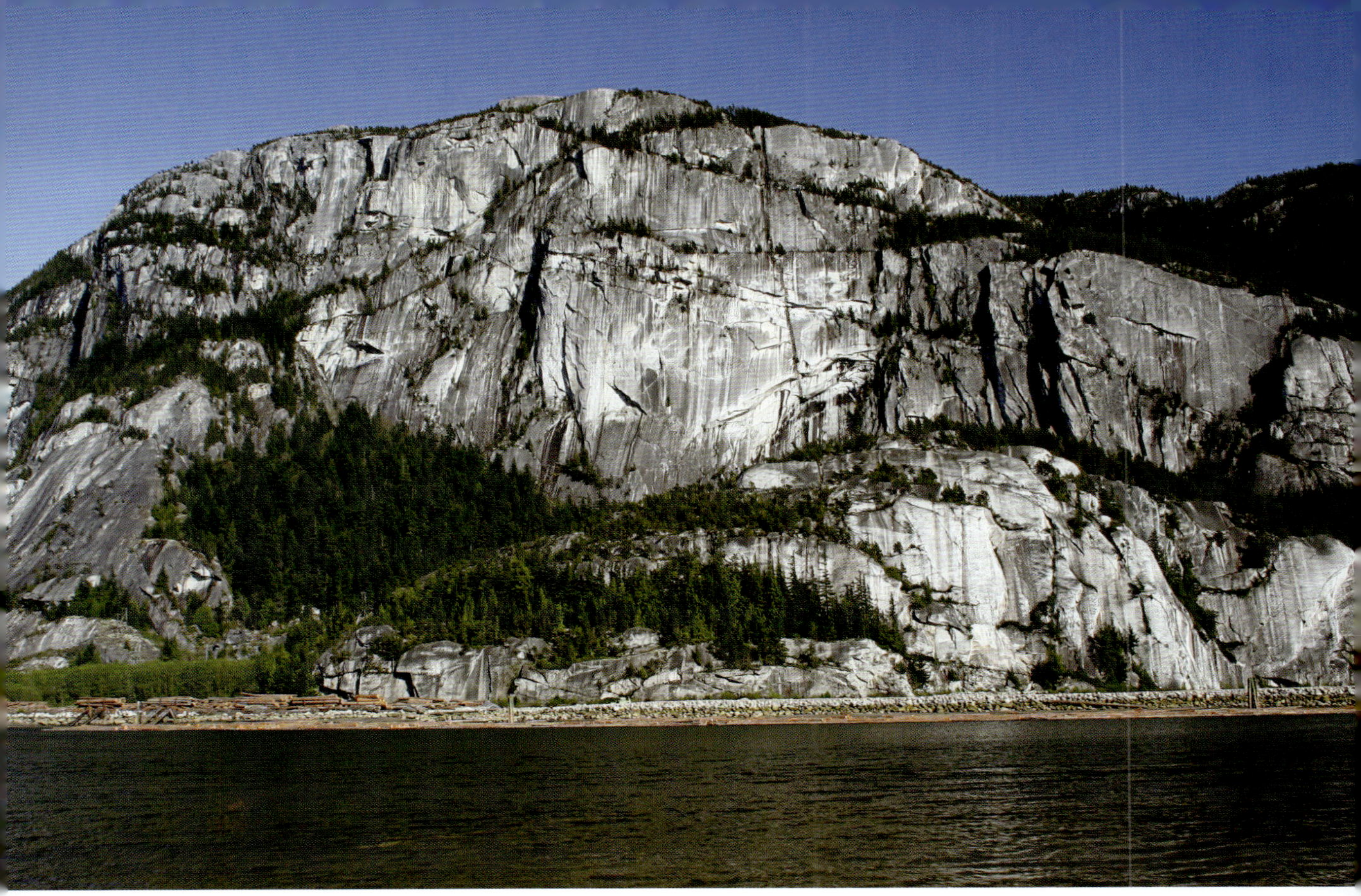

Peregrine falcons have chosen the Stawamus Chief as a nesting site, and measures are taken to protect the endangered bird during this sensitive time. Certain climbing routes are closed during nesting season in March and April. This is a good time to bring your binoculars to the open grassy area near the main parking lot and look for falcons on the rock face. Also keep your eyes skywards: the peregrine falcon is the fastest animal in the world, flying at speeds of up to 300 kilometres per hour, and it mainly preys on other birds.

Rapid temperature changes due to our changing climate have resulted in a number of rockfall events on the Stawamus Chief. Ensure that you are obeying any closure signs along the base of the Chief.

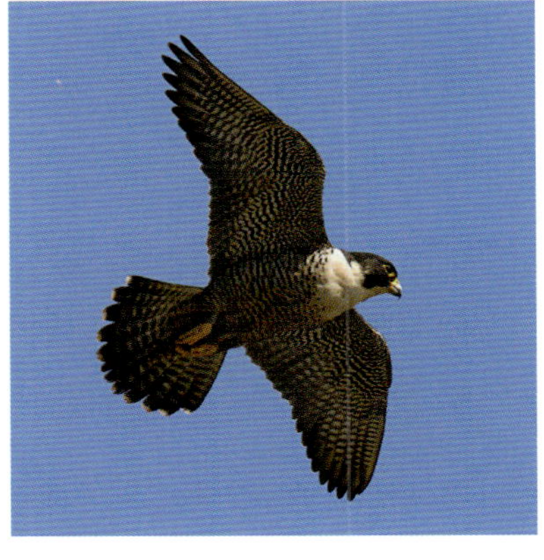

↑ The peregrine falcon, which is found nesting here in March and April, is the fastest animal in the world.

↖ Stawamus Chief towers over the town of Squamish.

← The view from the top of the hiking trail, looking over the beautiful turquoise waters of Howe Sound.

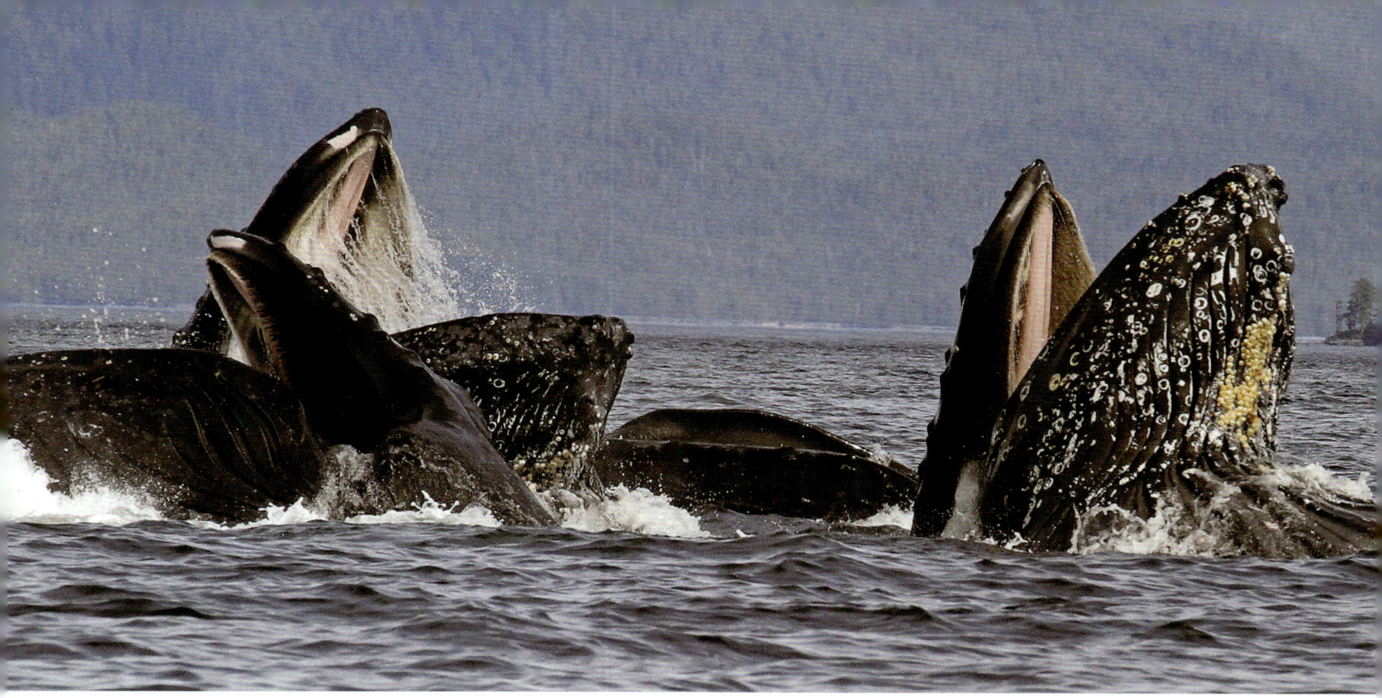

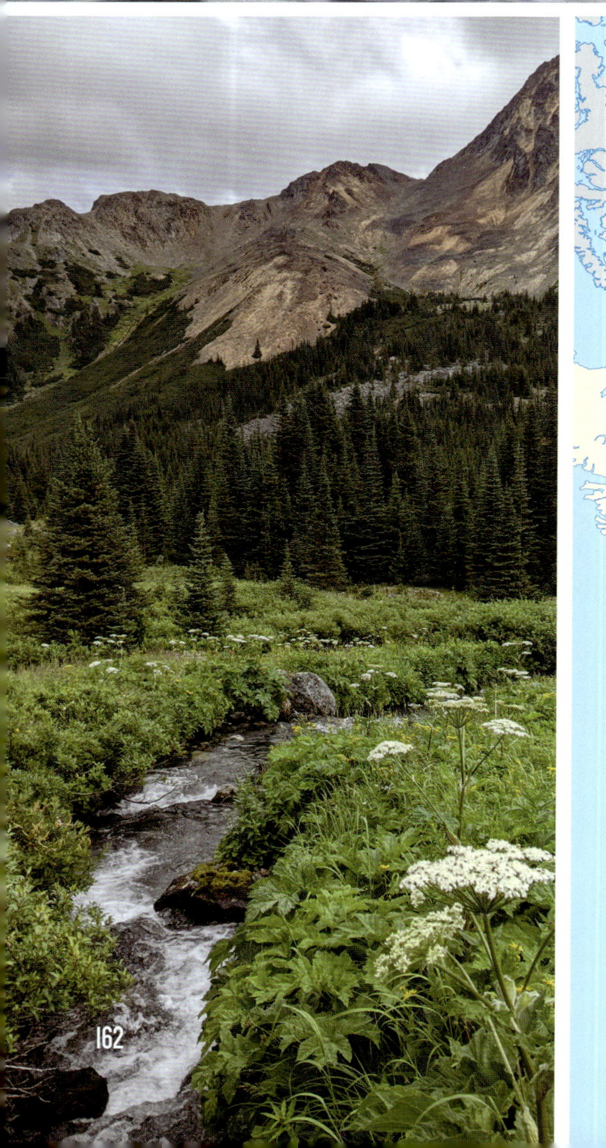

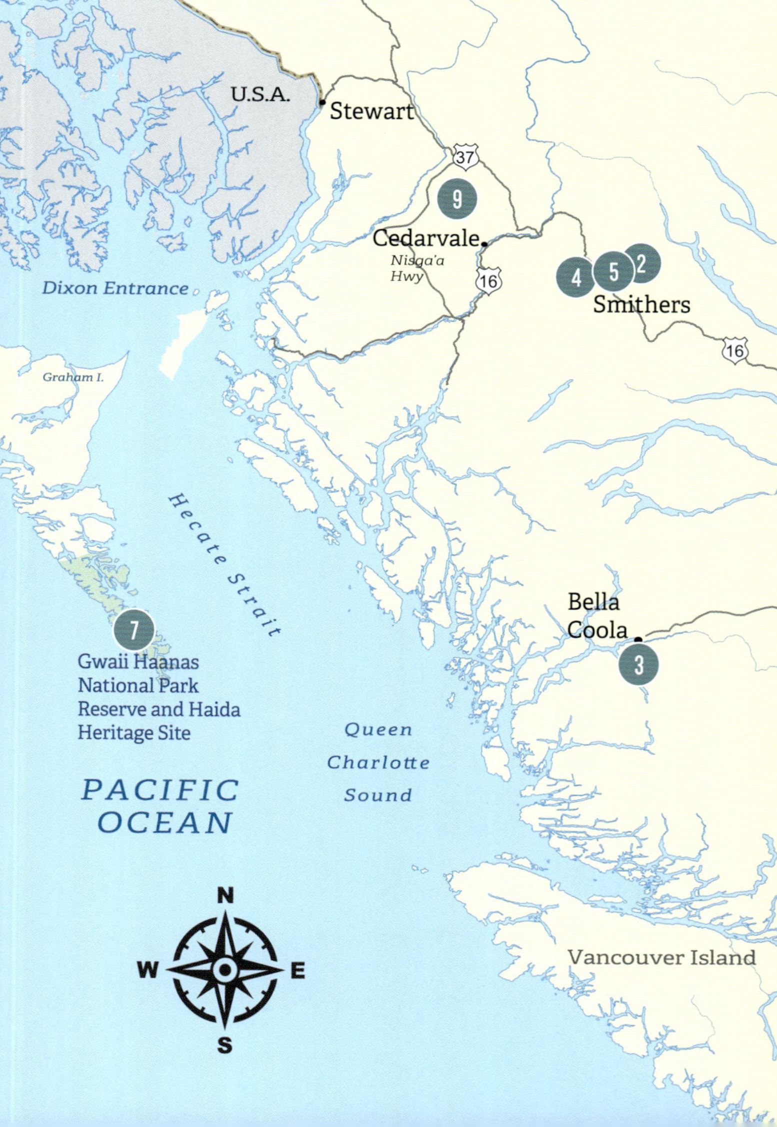
U.S.A.
Stewart
37
9
Cedarvale
Nisga'a Hwy
16
4 5 2
Smithers
16
Dixon Entrance
Graham I.
Hecate Strait
7
Gwaii Haanas National Park Reserve and Haida Heritage Site
PACIFIC OCEAN
Bella Coola
3
Queen Charlotte Sound
Vancouver Island
N
W E
S

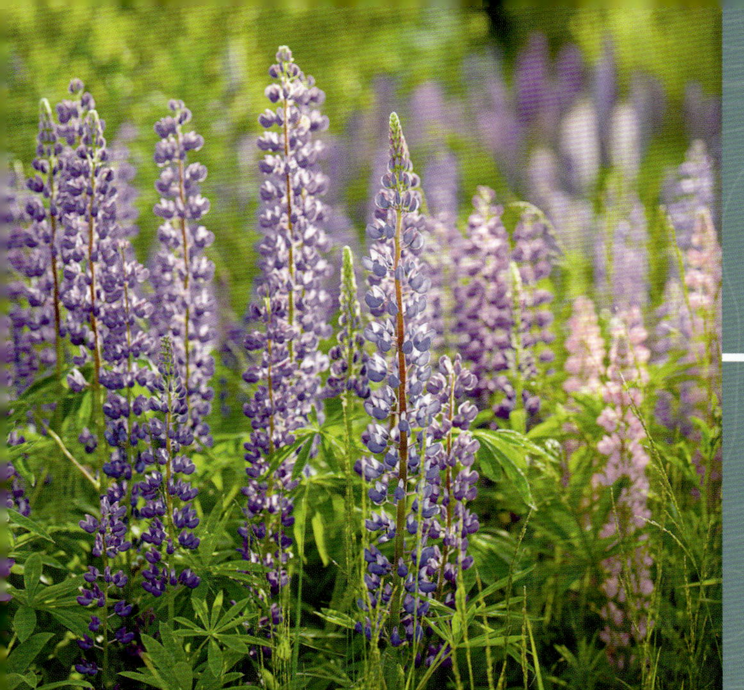

Central British Columbia

Ancient Forest/Chun T'oh Whudujut Provincial Park

A northern stand of inland old-growth temperate rainforest that is home to 1,000-year-old trees

What Makes This Hot Spot Hot?

- Part of the Interior Wet Belt, this is the farthest known inland temperate rainforest in the world.
- Some of the massive western redcedars are thought to be 2,000 years old.
- Around 900 plant species have been identified in the park, including a rare bog orchid.

Address: Yellowhead Hwy (Hwy 16) East, 115 km east of Prince George and 103 km west of McBride, BC
Tel.: N/A
Website:

BC Parks

GPS Coordinates
Latitude: 53.76322
Longitude: −121.21870

Open year-round

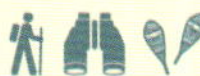

 **(Check ahead)**

Within the traditional territory of the Lheidli T'enneh, this stand of trees protected within the boundary of Ancient Forest/Chun T'oh Whudujut Provincial Park is part of the farthest inland old-growth temperate rainforest known to date. Located some 800 kilometres from the ocean, these massive redcedars can thrive so far from the coast thanks to the heavy snowfall that descends on the forest in the winter. The deep snowpack melts in the spring, restoring water supplies in the groundwater and springs and flooding areas of the forest floor.

Aging the trees becomes quite difficult after they have achieved their great size. Although the trees remain alive, giant redcedars often become hollow with age. The heartwood of a tree provides structural support but is composed of dead cells, so living tissue can still thrive around a hollow core, leaving in tact the vital conduit between roots and canopy. Some of the trees in the area are upwards of 1,000 years old, and some time-worn giants may be closer to 2,000 years old, their age an unsolvable mystery. This truly is an ancient forest.

Trees of this great maturity attract a special array of flora and fauna. The park is home to over 200 species of lichen alone! A notable favourite is gold dust lichen, which encrusts the weathered and paled cedar trunks and gilds the forest with an extra layer of life. Devil's club inhabits much of the undergrowth. The stems and leaves of this plant are covered with a dense armour of needle-like spines that are extremely irritating if touched. This gives visitors one more reason to stay on the trails, though protecting this rare ecosystem is surely reason enough. During a biological assessment of the park's plant life, bog adder's-mouth orchids were discovered in the area — the first time this rare species had been documented in the Interior since 1932. The red-listed joe-pye-weed is also found within the boundaries of the park.

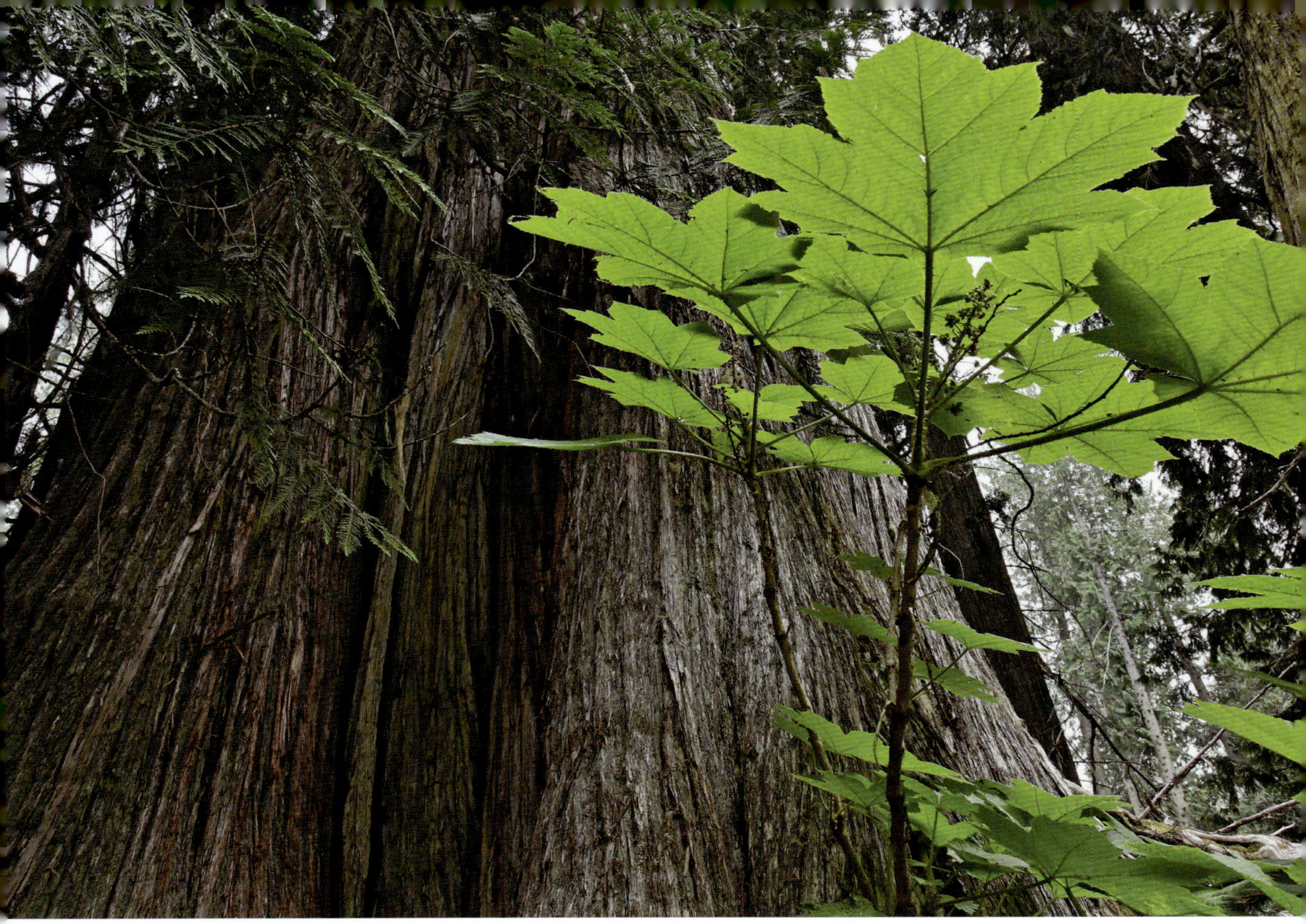

This magnificent forest was very close to certain destruction, and it exists today thanks to many passionate individuals working together to ensure the giant trees remained. In 2005 Dave Radies, a graduate student studying old-growth forests of the Interior Cedar-Hemlock Zone, stumbled across this stand and saw telltale forester's red spray-painted on numerous trunks, which meant some of these ancient trees were tagged for removal. After he alerted the public of this special area and its solemn fate, the community rallied together. The following year, the Ancient Forest Trail was built by devoted volunteers, and two years after that the harvesting plans were cancelled. The area was officially designated a provincial park in 2016. The 450-metre boardwalk of the Universal Access Trail ensures that everyone gets to enjoy this unique forest nestled between mountain ranges along the Rocky Mountain Trench.

↑ Devil's club creates dense, and uninviting, undergrowth.

↓ Gold dust lichen covers the trunk of many of the old-growth cedars of this forest.

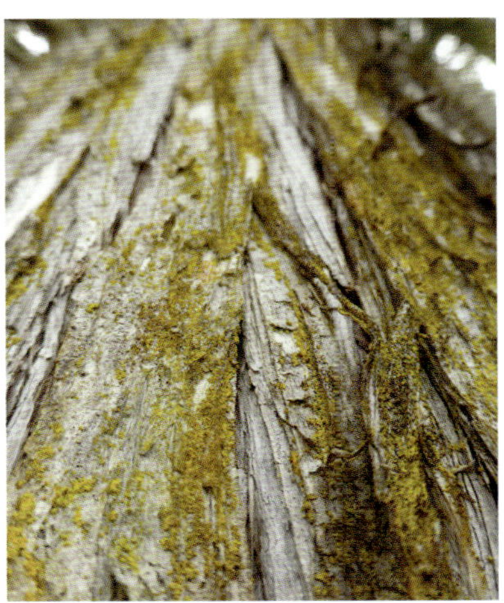

Babine Mountains Provincial Park

A conservation success story: old mining sites that have been reclaimed by wildflowers and trees amid towering rocky peaks

The colourful rocky peaks and treed valleys of the Babine Mountains jut into the skyline on the western side of Bulkley Valley. The mountains are a place of importance for the Wet'suwet'en and Ned'u'ten Nations, whose hunting, trapping and trading trails weave through the landscape. Once threatened by mining, this park was established to protect the alpine tundra and subboreal spruce ecosystems, allowing wildlife to flourish.

Hiking the Silver King Basin to Hyland Pass is one way to experience the varied ecology of the Babines and get a glimpse into its mining history. The now-abandoned Silver King Mine once extracted silver, copper, lead and zinc from the mountainside. Although it was only mined from 1913 to 1937, a road into the basin, now a hiker's trail, was constructed in 1946 to access the nearby Cronin Mine, which was

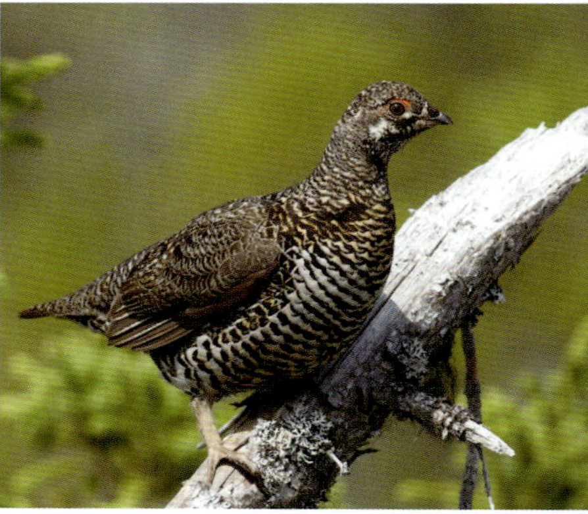

more productive. There was renewed interest in the Silver King Mine in 1980, but by then protection of the area was well underway. Old mining carts and tracks grown over by paintbrush and fireweed are all that remain of the mine after the Babine Mountains were designated a provincial park in 1984. This designation was largely due to the efforts of Joe L'Orsa, an environmentalist for whom an overnight cabin in the park is named.

In the valleys are meadows of wildflowers and forests of subalpine fir and lodgepole

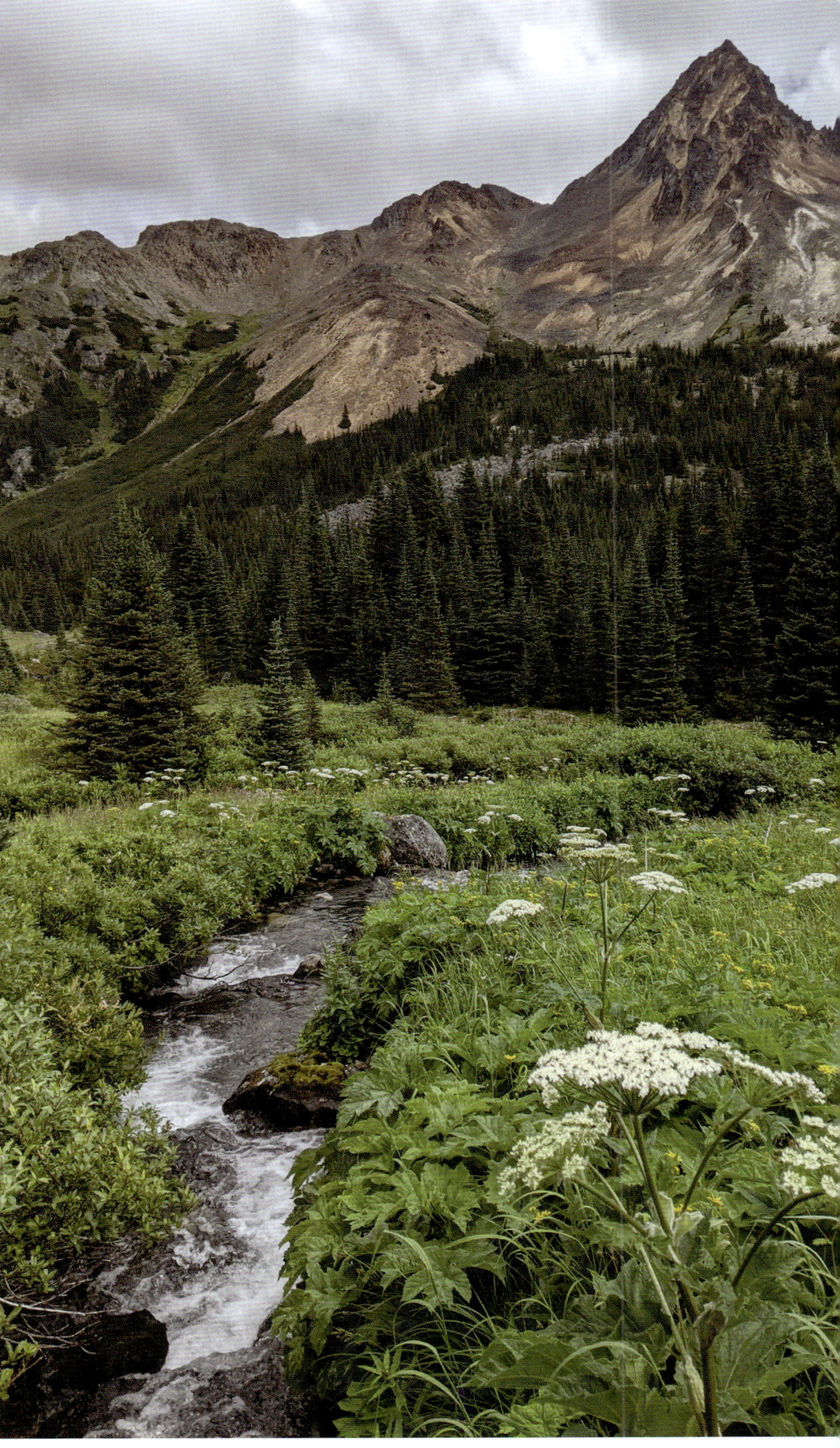

→ **Wildflowers blanket the valleys below the colourful peaks of the Babine Mountains in the Silver King Basin.**

← **Spruce grouse and other wildlife are able to flourish in the park due to successful efforts to stop mining in the park in the 1980s.**

pine. The most northern stands of whitebark pine can be found within the park's boundaries. Venturing above the trees, past the screeches of marmots in talus slopes, the alpine landscape offers beautiful views of the surrounding mountains. In this harsh, windswept ecosystem, short grasses and patches of stonecrop peek out from shallow soil between lichen-covered rocks. This is a drastic contrast to the forests below. Together these ecosystems are home to many species of plants, birds and mammals. The successful conservation efforts in the Babines have allowed the mountain goats who live there year-round to thrive and have created protected seasonal habitat for black bears, lynx and wolves.

GREAT BEAR RAINFOREST

Bella Coola Valley

The Great Bear Rainforest is famous for the elusive Kermode bear

What Makes This Hot Spot Hot?

- The Great Bear Rainforest is one of the world's largest remaining coastal temperate rainforests.
- The rainforest is home to the greatest density of grizzly bears in Canada, as well as the rare Kermode bear, a white black bear.
- Nuxalk guided tours allow visitors to learn about their incredible history and culture as well as visit sacred places in their territory.

Address: Chilcotin-Bella Coola Hwy (Hwy 20), Bella Coola Valley, BC
Tel.: (250) 799-5202
Website:

Bella Coola

GPS Coordinates
Latitude: 52.37928
Longitude: –126.76396

Open year-round

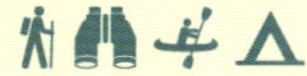

The Bella Coola Valley acts as a gateway into the Great Bear Rainforest, an awe-inspiring destination for not only bear-watching, but to experience the culture, stories, language and land of the Nuxalk Nation. With the valley stretching 80 kilometres along the Bella Coola River, the small community here and the surrounding area can be reached by land, air and sea, including ferry services.

Grizzly bears and black bears are found throughout the Bella Coola Valley and adjoining Tweedsmuir Park. The Great Bear Rainforest, one of the world's largest intact coastal temperate rainforests, is home to a special population of black bears. One in every 10 black bears here has a cream-coloured coat, thanks to a recessive gene found in this particular population. These dramatic white bears are not albino, and both parents have to carry and pass on the gene for the offspring to be white. Catching a glimpse of a Kermode bear is one of British Columbia's most sought-after and unique nature-viewing experiences, and although uncommon, there is always a chance one will reveal itself along the river's edge as it hunts for fish.

The Great Bear Rainforest supports Canada's largest and densest population of grizzly bears, who depend on the large intact forest since much of their historic range has dramatically shrunk. The grizzlies of the coast are much larger than their Interior relatives, thanks to the easy access of spawning salmon each fall. The largest males have been recorded to weigh over 500 kilograms after their fishy autumn feast! In the spring, watch for bears feeding on new plant roots and shoots, or plan your trip around the salmon spawn between late July and early October to see grizzlies and black bears feasting on salmon in the rivers and streams. Mid-August to late September will likely provide the best viewing opportunities. To avoid conflict with the larger, more aggressive grizzlies, black bears tend to drag their fish farther into the forest, which in turn provides important

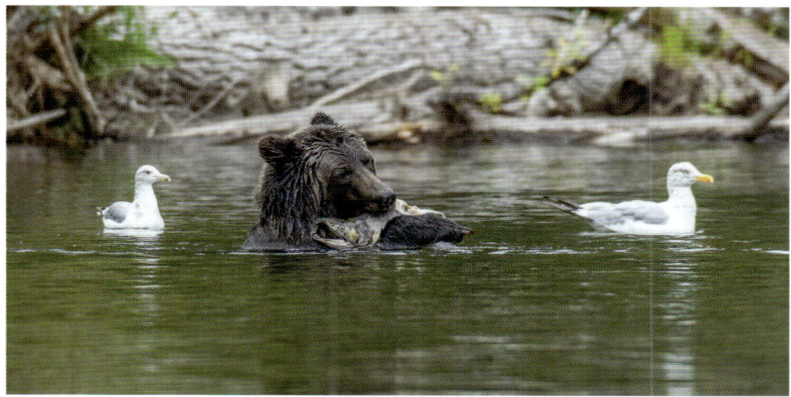

nutrients to this habitat.

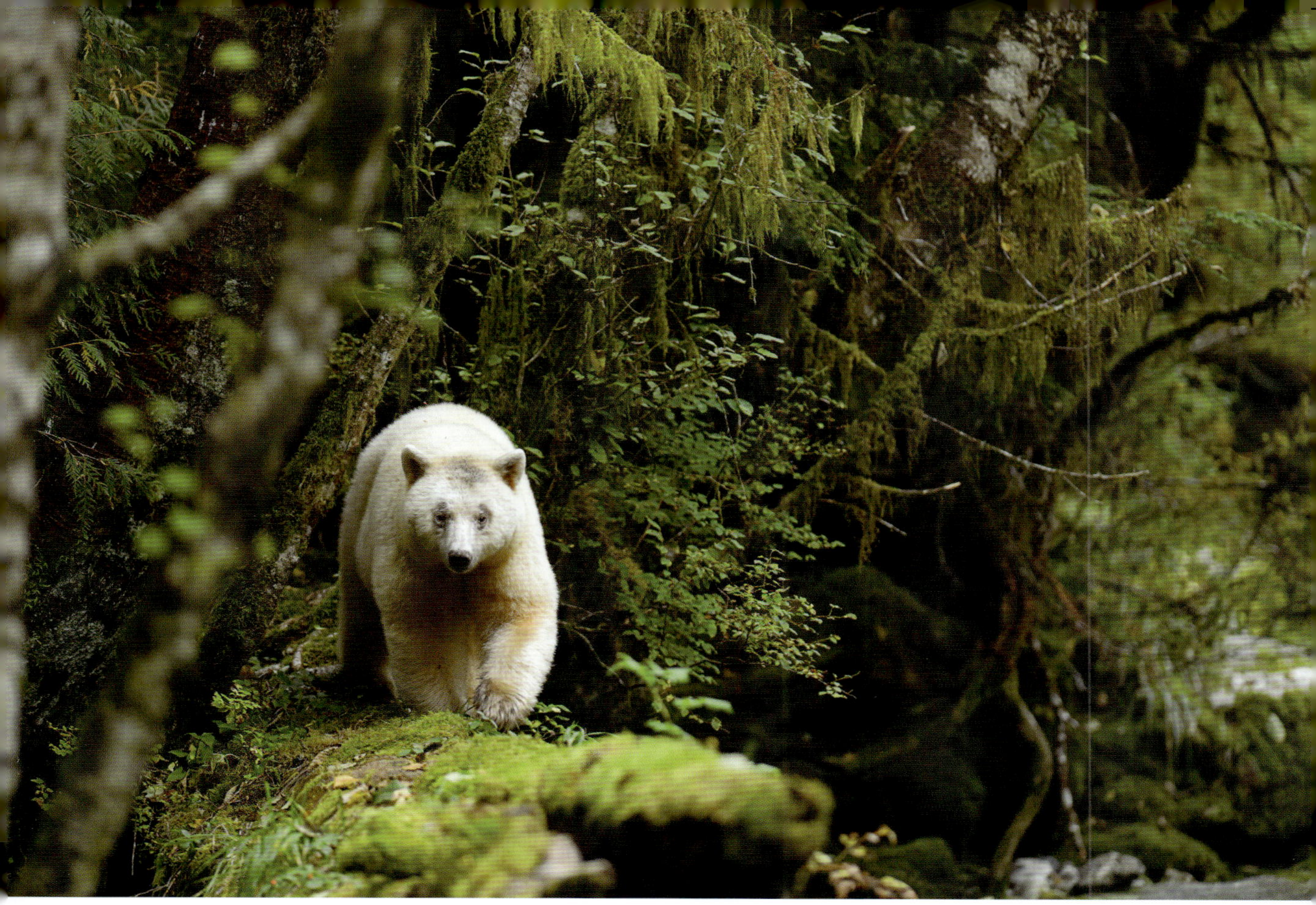

While you have a good chance of spotting bears while driving and occasionally while hiking, the best way to guarantee safe, successful and low-impact viewing is to book a bear-watching tour, either by boat or from the land.

This valley has been home to the Nuxalk Nation since time immemorial, and as guests in their territory, they ask that you follow their four protocols during your visit: respect all beings, ask permission first, take care of the land and each other, and be happy! There are multiple sacred sites within their territory, including the Squmalh Petroglyphs, incredible rock carvings that are thousands of years old, as well as several hot springs. Visiting these places should only be done with an accredited Nuxalk guide to ensure the sites remain protected and respected.

↑ **The Kermode bear is a rare and thrilling sight in the Bella Coola Valley.**

↓ **A grizzly bear catches a spawning salmon.**

Crater Lake Trail

A short hike takes you up into the alpine and right into mountain goat territory

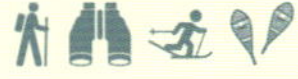

A mountain goat and her kid lounge on a rocky slope.

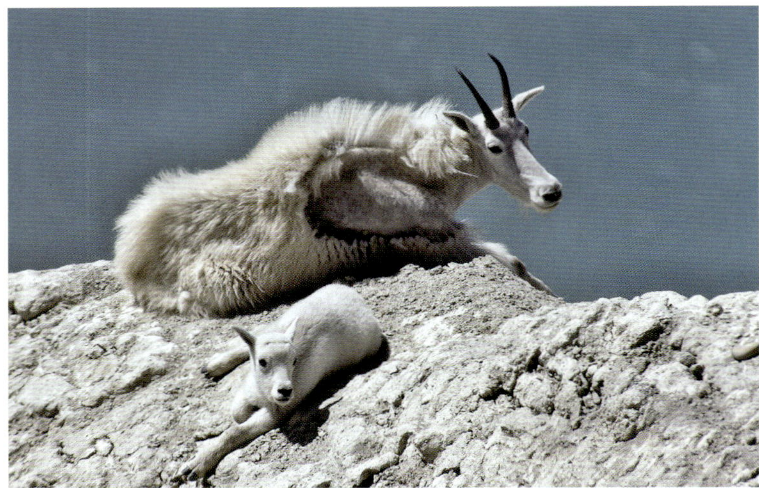

Although Hudson Bay Mountain attracts most of its visitors in the form of sports enthusiasts exploring its snow-covered mountainside, this area is also a summer destination for nature lovers. As the drive to the ski hill already brings you to a high elevation, it is not too long before you are nestled in delightful alpine meadows after a short, but mosquito-dense, hike through the last stretch of the treeline. A small reflective tarn called Crater Lake is your destination: a charming little lake nestled in the amphitheatre-like cirque that was carved by a glacier long since melted. Watch for hoary marmots, which will surely be watching as you cross through exposed meadows.

Plan your trip with the bloom times for alpine wildflowers in mind, and you will be rewarded with blankets of blue, pink, yellow and white flowers. Pink and white mountain-heathers carpet the area, each colour seemingly claiming separate parcels of land as its own. Look out for green false hellebore, forget-me-nots and Alaska violets along the trail. Sedums, like the western roseroot, can be found flowering well above the treeline, where moss campion also clings to the barren landscape.

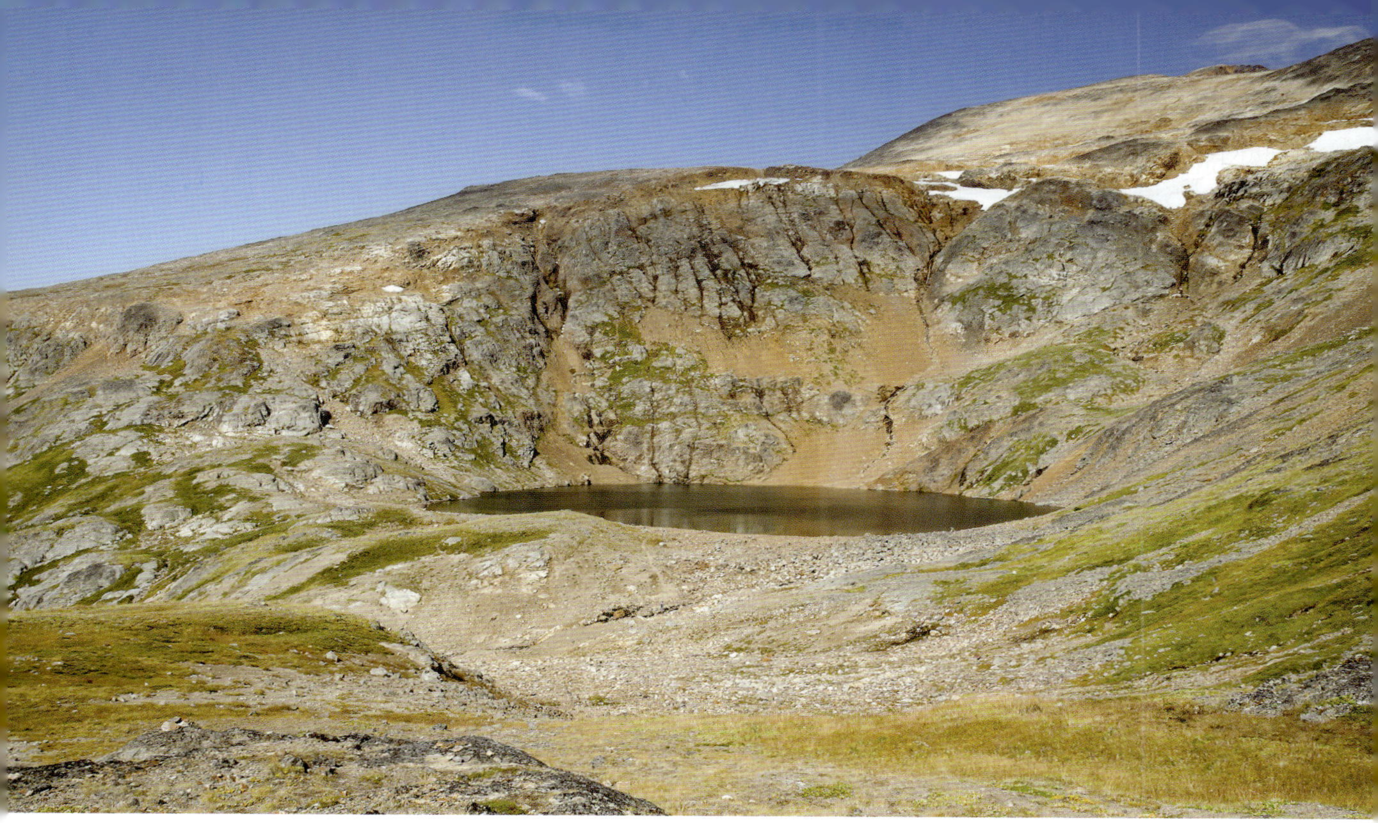

Of course, these plants are displaying showy flowers for a reason, and the harsh, exposed environment does not deter robust bumble bees. The large size and fuzzy bodies of bumbles help them retain heat as they travel from flower to flower collecting pollen in their baskets. Their meticulous work helps to ensure that wildflowers will bloom in the meadows for years to come.

Horned larks are a highlight of this alpine adventure as their musical song can be heard ringing out across the meadow. In the summer keep an eye out for fledgling larks nestled low to the ground while they wait for an adult to return with food. Horned larks begin nesting as soon as snow-free patches appear in the meadows, constructing fine woven baskets to house their families. Sometimes females will create "pavings" beside their nests, a small collection of pebbles, clods of soil and other materials that resembles a walkway.

This region is home to a healthy population of mountain goats that frequents the slopes of Hudson Bay Mountain between June and October, although the best time to spot them is August and September. Among the world's most skilled mountaineers, these agile ungulates usually stay close to cliffs so that they can make a quick escape up often near-vertical slopes to safety.

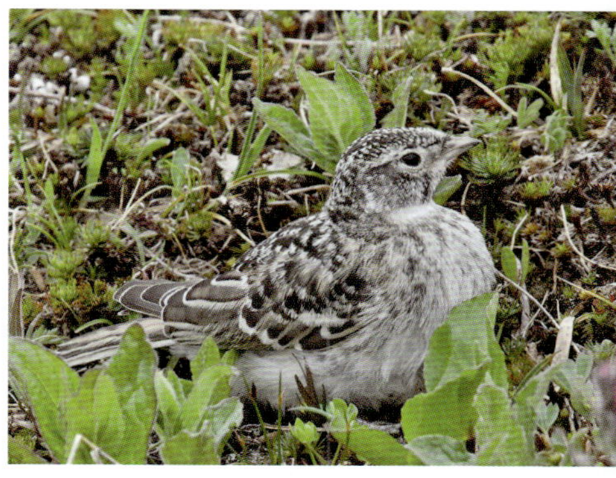

↑ **A fledgling horned lark blends into the alpine groundcover.**

↖ **Crater Lake, your rewarding destination after a hike.**

Driftwood Canyon Provincial Park

Fossils found here dating back 51.7 million years ago have given scientists insight into the history and evolution of salmon, insects and plant life

What Makes This Hot Spot Hot?

- A beautiful forest surrounds an Eocene fossil site that's 51.7 million years old.
- Important fossils have been found here, including the oldest-known salmon species *Eosalmo driftwoodensis*.
- Ferns and trees typical of northern BC can be found both living and preserved as fossils at this site.

Address: Driftwood Road, 16 km west of Smithers, BC
Tel.: (250) 877-1782 (Bulkley Valley Museum)
Website:

BC Parks

GPS Coordinates
Latitude: 54.82644
Longitude: −127.02129

Open mid-May to September

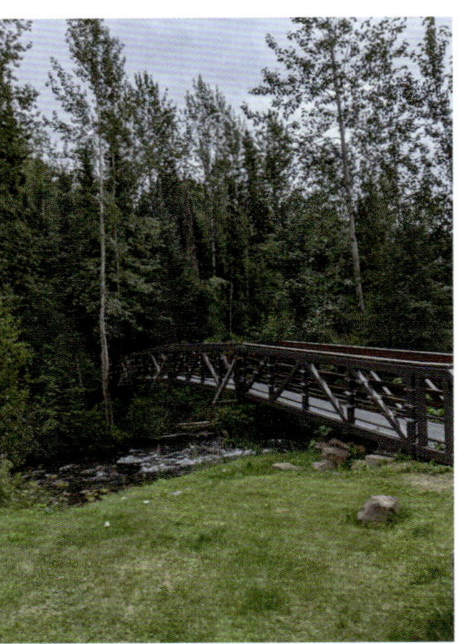

Around 51.7 million years ago, during the Eocene era, a freshwater lake in a tropical forest flourished with salmon and insects. Now known as Driftwood Canyon, this northern forest is very different and only fossils remain to tell the story of this once tropical oasis.

Bulkley Valley Museum in Smithers has a permanent display of Driftwood Canyon fossils, including the famous *Eosalmo driftwoodensis*, the oldest-known member of the salmon family. This fossil tells an important story about the history of salmon, who once spent their entire life cycle in freshwater. Nearby in Witset Canyon the Wet'suwet'en people can be seen using traditional fishing methods to catch modern-day salmon as they journey from salt to freshwater to spawn.

Along the trail through Driftwood Canyon, bumble bees and flies pollinate flowers, ants burrow and aerate soil, and beetles break down detritus in the forest. An incredibly diverse class, insects make up over half of all known animal species, each playing an important role in the ecosystem. Fossils of many ancestors of modern insects can be found in the shale bed at the trail's terminus. Lacewings, wasps and water striders are among the 20 families of insects preserved in amazing detail. Driftwood Canyon is the northernmost

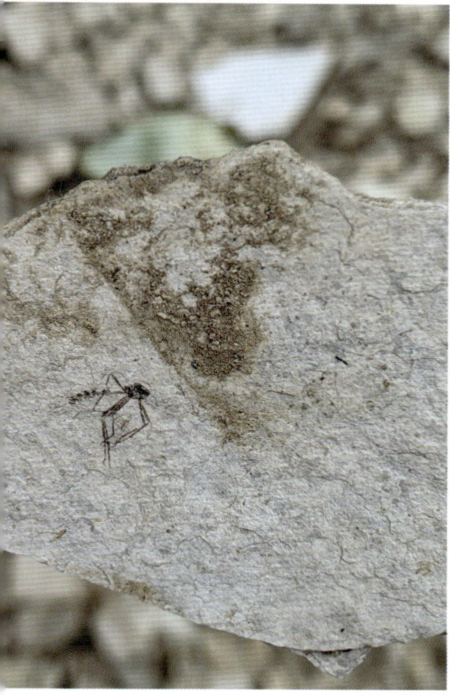

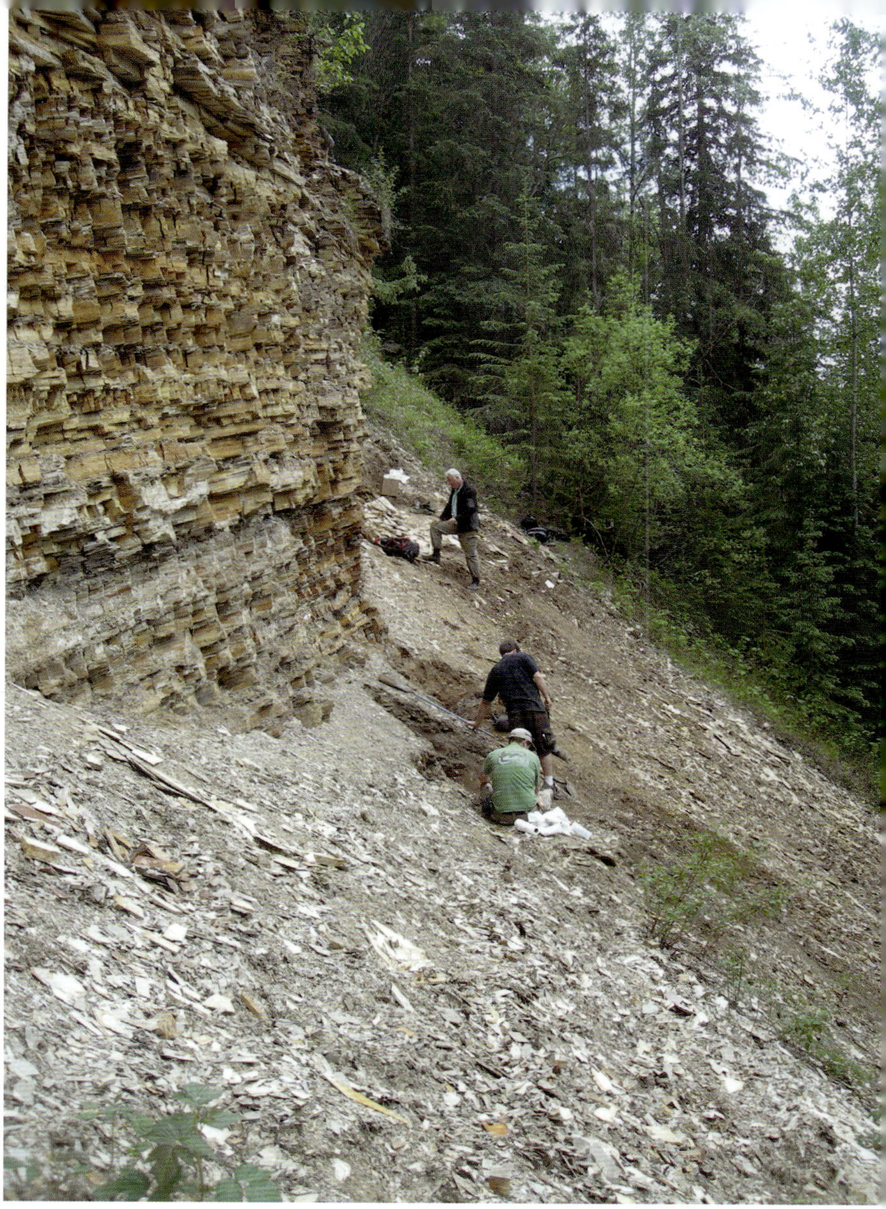

↑ Many important fossils have been excavated from this shale cliff, including mammals, insects, plants and fish. This site is not accessible to the public.

Eocene insect fossil bed and has been declared one of the most important in the world.

Important mammal fossils have been found here as well. A hedgehog the size of a thumbnail and small tapirs roamed the forests of ferns, alder and spruce — all plants that can be found in Driftwood Canyon both alive along the trail and in the fossil record. Other plant fossils are abundant, including ginkgo and dawn redwood, which today are not found in this northern ecosystem.

Both a museum visit and walk to the fossil bed at Driftwood Canyon are recommended. The viewing site for the fossil bed often has some fossils next to the interpretive sign, but fossil hunting and entering the fossil site itself is not allowed.

Flatbed Cabin Pools Trail

Dinosaur trackways are visible right along the trail by Flatbed Creek

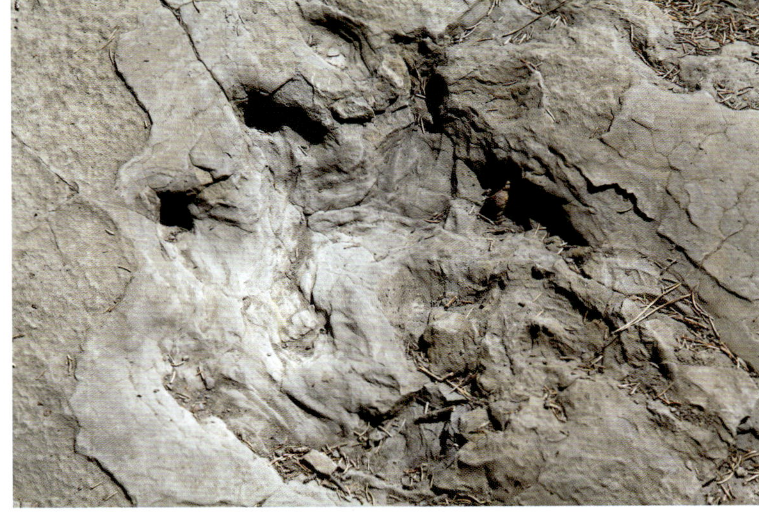

What Makes This Hot Spot Hot?

- Visitors can follow theropod, ornithopod and ankylosaur trackways on this 3-kilometre return hike.
- A nearby bone bed is Western Canada's oldest-known dinosaur material.
- Many other special fossils have been found in the geopark, from Precambrian to Cretaceous.

Address: 1 km southeast of Tumbler Ridge, Don Phillips Way (Hwy 29), Tumbler Ridge, BC
Tel.: (250) 242-3123
Website:

Tumbler Ridge Global Geopark

GPS Coordinates
Latitude: 55.11436
Longitude: –120.98325

Open year-round

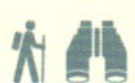

Along the eastern slopes of the Rocky Mountains, you will find Tumbler Ridge Global Geopark, the first park with this designation in western North America. Although the geopark title holds no protection for the land within its boundaries, Gwillim Lake, Bearhole Lake, Wapiti Lake and Monkman provincial parks all fall at least partially within the geopark.

The geological formations here range from the Precambrian to Cretaceous periods and include much more recent Pleistocene deposits. Many fossils can be found within the park boundaries, from Cretaceous dinosaur trackways and bone beds to Triassic fishes and marine reptiles. Dinosaur bones in the area span nearly 60 million years. The local Dinosaur Discovery Gallery has many fossils, imprints and casts on display, but visitors are able to check out some of the fossil sites to get a first-hand experience of these prehistoric remains.

In 2000, two local boys discovered a dinosaur trackway while water tubing along Flatbed Creek. This led to an explosion of additional finds in the surrounding area. In fact,

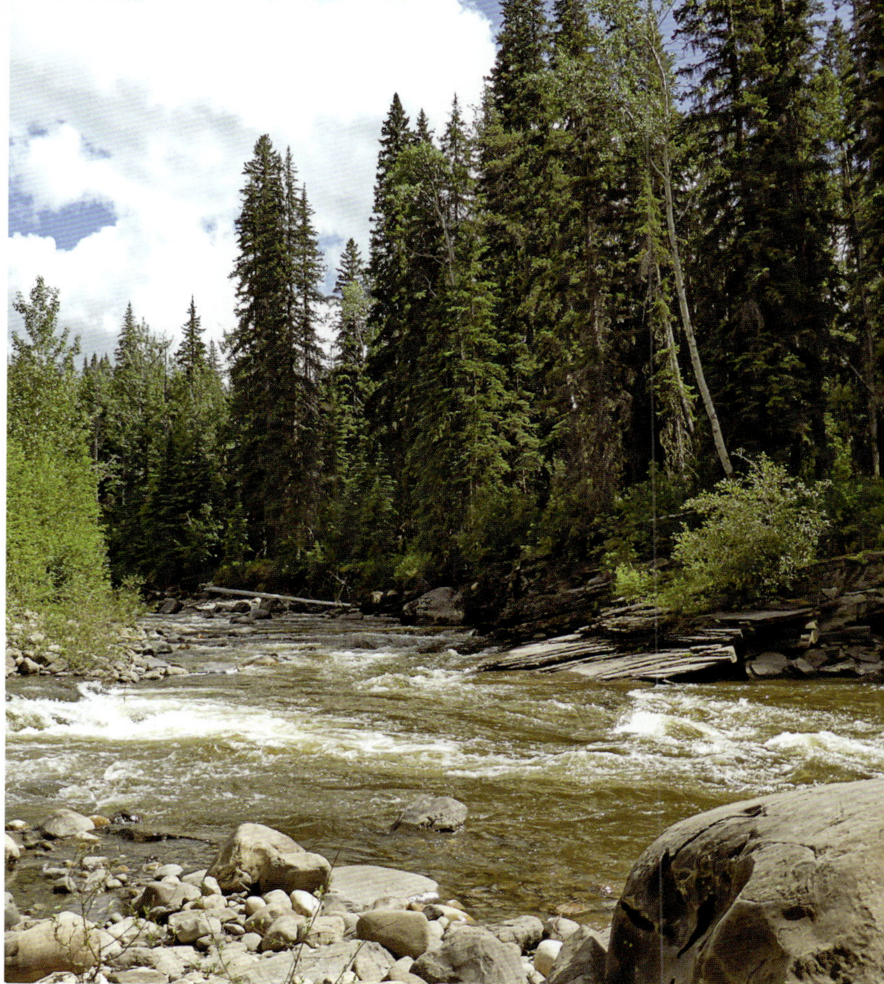

many fossils were discovered by amateur fossil enthusiasts! Fossils are still being found, so if you think you may have discovered a new dinosaur footprint or bone, leave it be and contact Peace River Region Palaeontology Research Centre at (250) 242-DINO or email prprc@pris.ca.

Tracks of three kinds of dinosaurs have been found in Tumbler Ridge: ankylosaurs, known for sometimes having large clubbed tails; theropods, bipedal dinosaurs built for speed; and ornithopods, grazers that used their stiff tails for balance. Be careful not to walk directly on any of the footprints so that you do not speed up their erosion.

The original 26 ankylosaur prints of Flatbed Creek are only accessible when the creek water level is low, and they are now very faint as they continue to be weathered by natural water flows. In addition to the Flatbed Cabin Pools Trail, dinosaur tracks can be seen on the Wolverine Dinosaur Trail, although unguided exploration is discouraged. Tours can be booked for both sites through the Tumbler Ridge Museum Foundation by calling the Dinosaur Discovery Gallery. A special evening lantern-lit tour is offered for the Wolverine Trail, where tracks barely visible by day are revealed in low light.

Although fossils are the main attraction of the Flatbed Cabin Pools Trail, scan the surrounding understory for wildflowers blooming in the early summer, and peek through the trees near the start of the trail to catch a glimpse of a massive bog. Watch for black bears throughout the geopark as they feed on vegetation along the roadside.

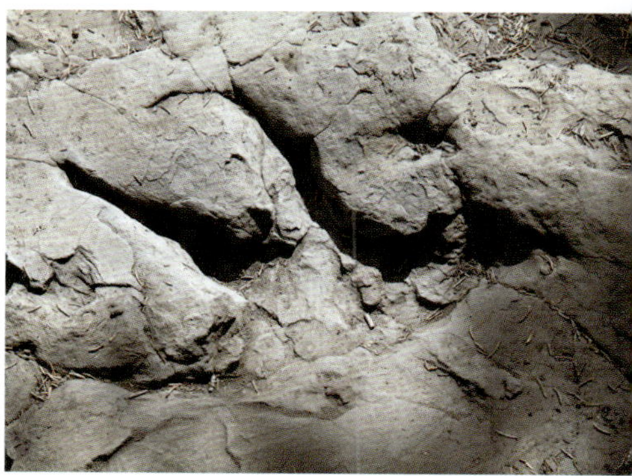

GWAII HAANAS NATIONAL PARK RESERVE, NATIONAL MARINE CONSERVATION AREA RESERVE AND HAIDA HERITAGE SITE

Gwaii Haanas

Protected from sea floor to mountaintop — with mossy rainforests, lively intertidal zones and many of its own subspecies — this park reserve is a treasure

What Makes This Hot Spot Hot?

- The lush, ancient rainforest filled with towering cedars inspired Haida activists to lobby to get the southern third of the Haida Gwaii archipelago protected.
- Many distinct and endemic subspecies call these isolated islands home.
- Heritage sites are found throughout the protected area, containing art and architecture that highlights the rich history of the Haida Nation.

Address: Haida Gwaii, BC
Tel.: (1-877) 559-8818
Website:

Parks Canada

GPS Coordinates
Latitude: 52.46827
Longitude: −131.5596

Open year-round

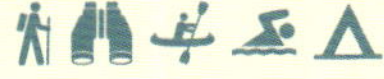

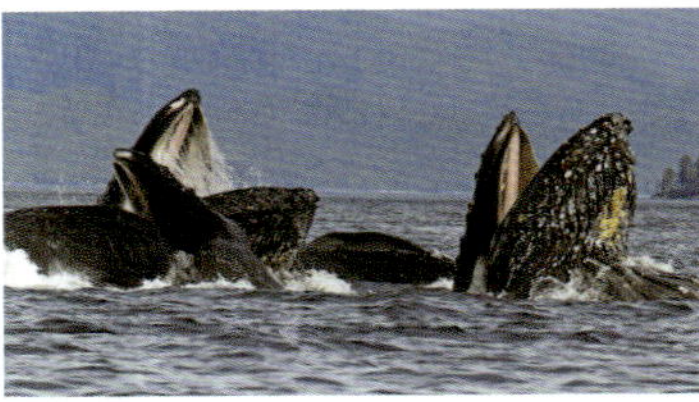

Haida Gwaii is a large archipelago separated from British Columbia's west coast. Hecate Strait, which runs up to 140 kilometres across, isolates Haida Gwaii from the Mainland, creating a barrier that has segregated wildlife to the islands. Evolving in isolation, 39 subspecies of plants and animals found nowhere else in the world thrive here. This includes the Haida Gwaii black bear, which has superior jaw strength to its Mainland counterpart — better for crushing hard-shelled critters in the intertidal zone.

Birders, botanizers and marine enthusiasts will all find something to delight them on these islands. Although the number of bird species, approximately 300, is lower than the adjacent Mainland's, there are more unique types to spot, such as the yellow-billed loon and the short-tailed albatross. During the last ice age, British Columbia was blanketed in glaciers; however, back then, parts of Haida Gwaii remained uncovered or were only coated in a thin layer of ice and snow. As a result, some plants here were unaffected by glaciation and quickly repopulated the islands, making this environment particularly special.

Gwaii Haanas National Park Reserve, National Marine Conservation Area Reserve and Haida Heritage Site is the perfect place to experience the wonders of this archipelago. This vast park reserve offers kayaking opportunities to explore the area by water as well as hiking trails, campsites and cultural heritage sites, including those of the Haida Nation that date back some 14,000 years. Visit Hlk'yah GaawGa, where in 2013 a monumental pole was erected to acknowledge the 20th anniversary of the Gwaii Haanas Agreement and the continued cooperative work between the Council of the Haida Nation and Parks Canada. After resident Haida blocked roads to protest the logging of the archipelago's ancient rainforests, the Gwaii Haanas Agreement was established by the Government of Canada and the Council of the Haida Nation to cooperatively manage and protect the cultural and natural treasures of this area.

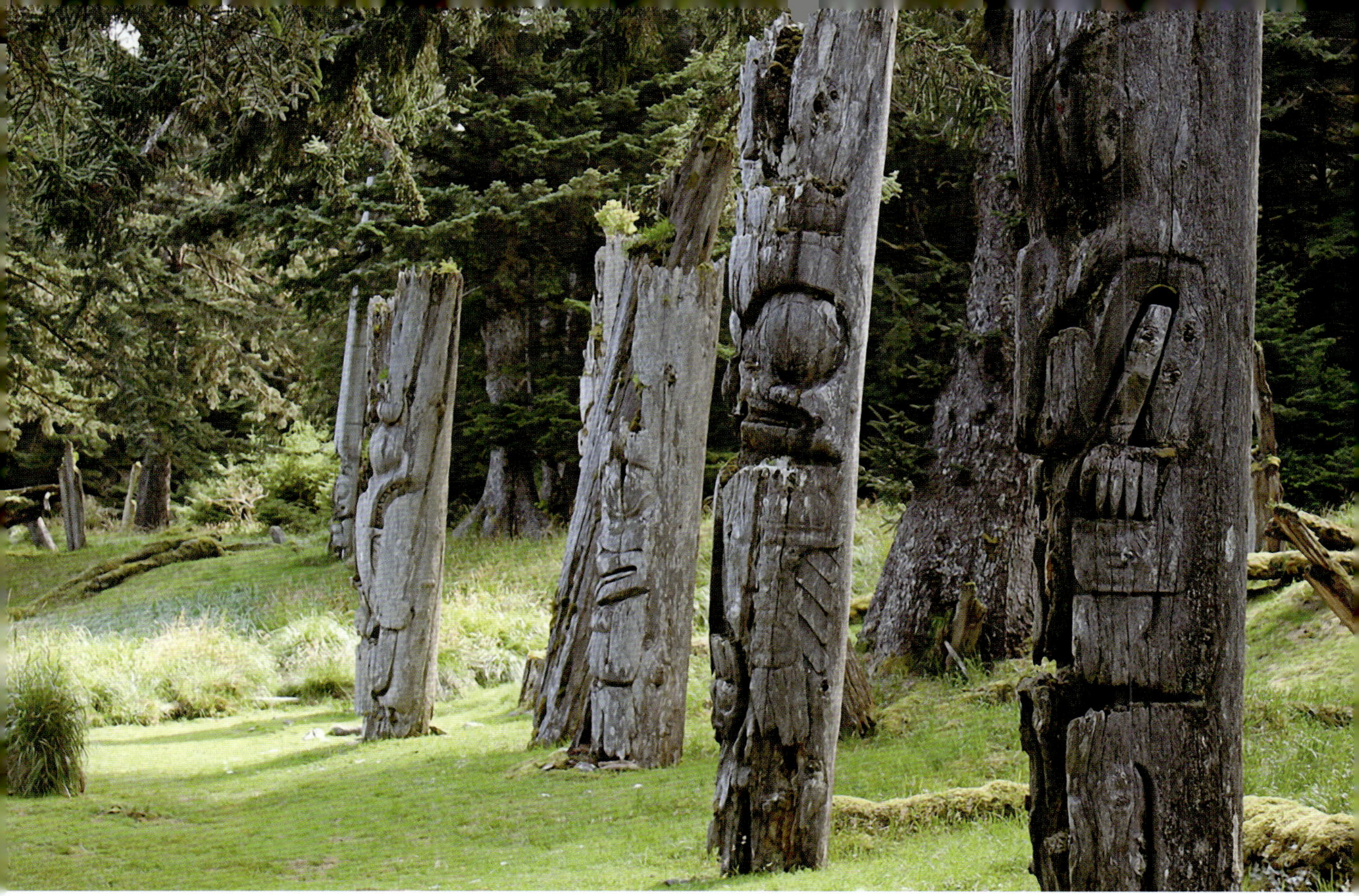

Haida Gwaii can be accessed only by boat or seaplane. Your visit to Gwaii Haanas will not be interrupted by the sounds of cars, since there are no roads in the park reserve. To enter, you must reserve a spot, attend a mandatory orientation about travel, safety and the natural and cultural history of the region and then receive a trip permit.

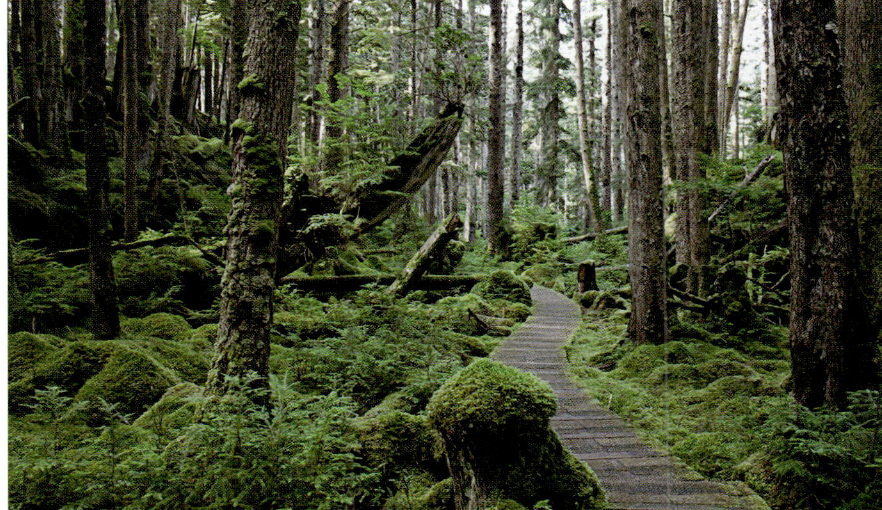

↑ Lush rainforests of towering cedar surround boardwalks and trails.

Poles found on SGang Gwaay mark what was once a community of 300 Haida people.

Mount Robson Provincial Park

This park is named for a breathtaking peak that towers over meadows, forests and clear alpine streams

What Makes This Hot Spot Hot?

- The park protects the headwaters of the Fraser River.
- Drastic changes in elevation encourage diverse ecosystems, flora and fauna.
- Mount Robson has a rich history among the Indigenous Peoples in the area.

Address: Off Yellowhead Hwy (Hwy 16), 33 km northeast of Valemont, Fraser-Fort George, BC
Tel.: (250) 566-4038
Website:

BC Parks

GPS Coordinates
Latitude: 53.03385
Longitude: –119.23158

Open year-round

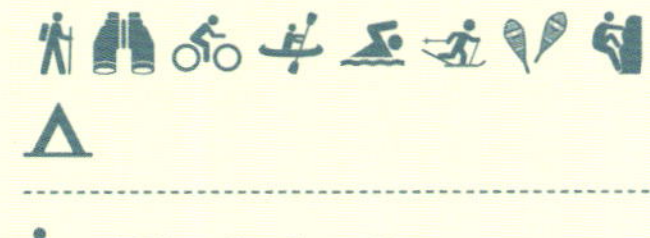

♿ (Check ahead)

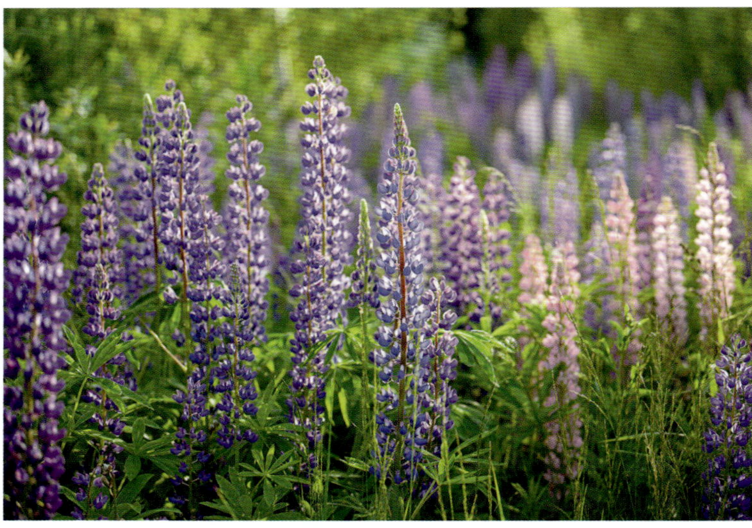

↗ **Fields of lupine and other wildflowers paint the alpine meadows.**

T his UNESCO World Heritage Site is home to the highest mountain in the Canadian Rockies, which is also the second-highest in British Columbia. At 2,975 metres, Mount Robson, the park's namesake, is a spectacular rock face. Because of the horizontal strips of coloured rock — limestone, dolomite and quartzite — the people of the Texqakallt Nation refer to the peak as *Yuh-hai-has-kun*, or "the Mountain of the Spiral Road."

Established in 1913 and charged with the important task of protecting the headwaters of the mighty Fraser River, this park is the second-oldest in British Columbia. Downstream, the Fraser River flows through many other nature hot spots before entering the ocean in Vancouver. The river provides life to a large portion of British Columbia in the form of nutrients, a spawning ground, food and water. It is amazing to think that it all begins in this park. Hikers can explore the river's origins on the gentle Fraser River Nature Walk.

There is a wide variety of

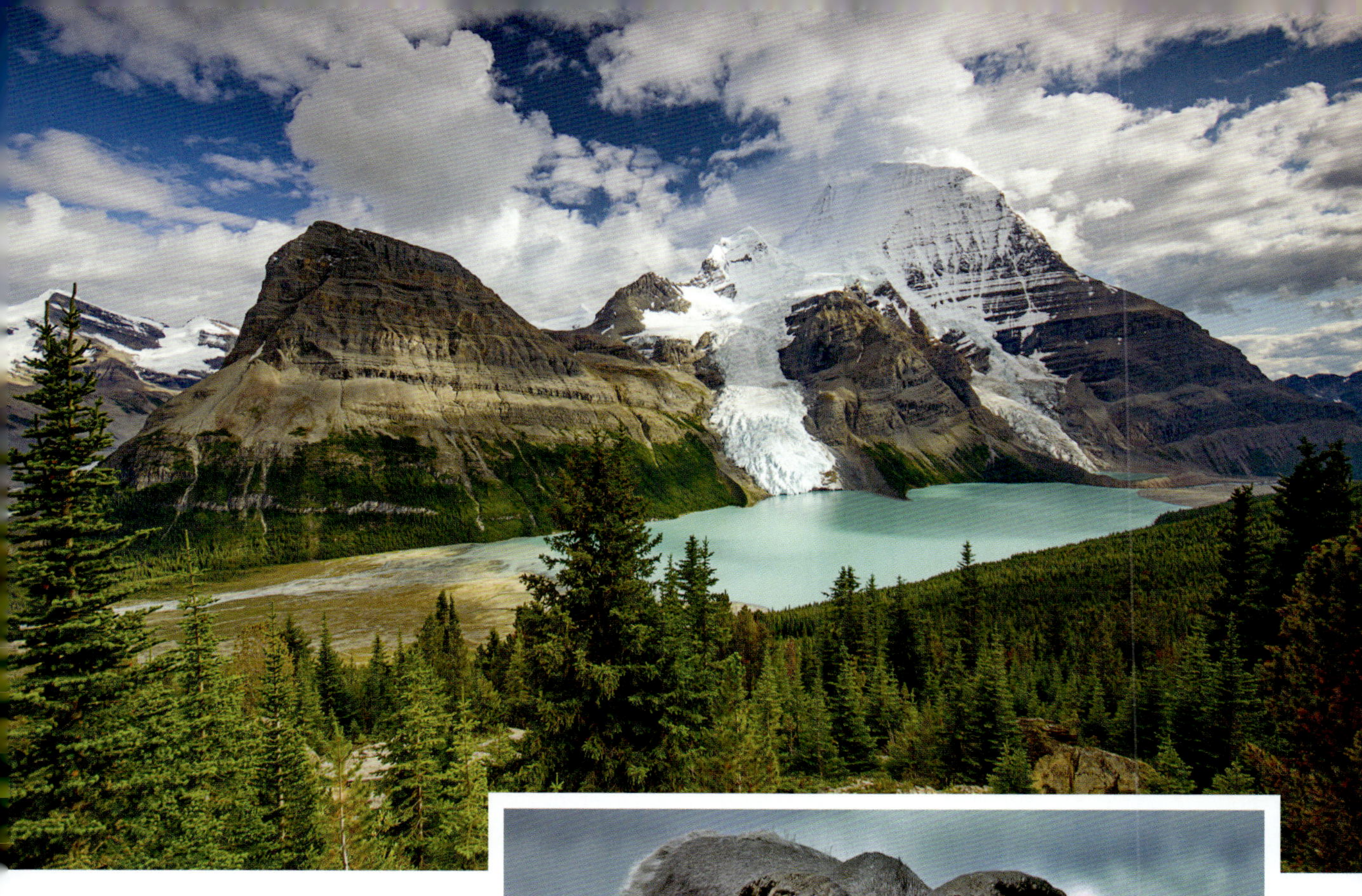

ecosystems within the park and an abundance of splendid views and wildlife to discover. Every other June the park hosts its Bird Blitz, when birders come together to count the species of birds in the park. There is no shortage, with over 180 recorded species found — including golden eagles in the alpine tundra environment. Elk, bears, Rocky Mountain bighorn sheep and moose live here, among other animals. Bring binoculars if you have them, not just for the birds but also to watch for mountain goats on the surrounding cliffs. The plant life here is not inconspicuous either. Lupine, thimbleberry, redcedar, lodgepole pine and spruce are all found at varying elevations.

Mount Robson Provincial Park deserves a few days, and the Robson Meadows Campground is a fantastic place to make base camp. From there you can explore the wetlands, meadows, forests and alpine environments on the park's many trails.

↑ **Lucky hikers may catch a glimpse of a Rocky Mountain bighorn sheep.**

↖ **Mount Robson towers over the surrounding forest.**

Nisga'a Memorial Lava Bed Provincial Park

The dramatic landscape resulting from one of Canada's most recent volcanic eruptions is rich in both history and species diversity

What Makes This Hot Spot Hot?

- Explore a landscape that was the site of a devastating volcanic eruption that changed the area forever.
- Unique log moulds were created when molten rock cooled around the trunks of trees.
- This truly unique park elegantly weaves the natural and cultural histories of the Nisga'a Nation's amazing land.

Address: Aiyansh, Nisga'a Hwy (Hwy 113), BC
Tel.: (250) 638-8490
Website:

BC Parks

GPS Coordinates
Latitude: 55.095140
Longitude: –128.970552

Open year-round

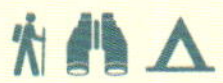

♿ **(Check ahead)**

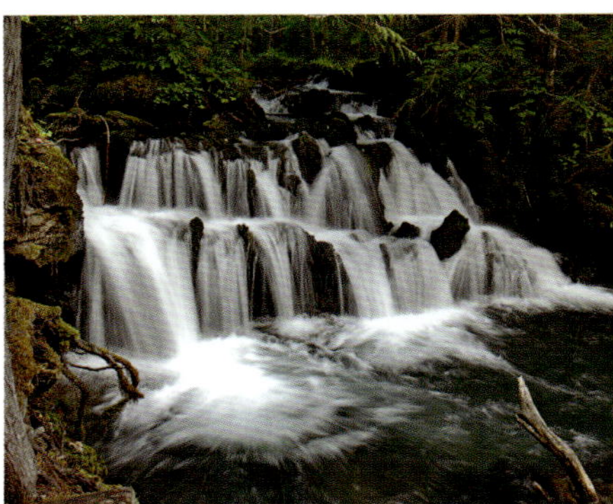

Almost 300 years ago, a volcanic eruption burst forth from the Tseax Cone. As molten rock spilled from the crater, it covered everything in its path, including two Nisga'a villages, and tragically killed more than 2,000 people. Nisga'a Memorial Lava Bed Provincial Park (also known as Anhluut'ukwsim Laxmihl Angwinga'asanskwhl Nisga'a), which is co-managed by the Nisga'a people and BC Parks, remains a memorial site for those lost, an amazing opportunity to learn about the Nisga'a Nation and their history, and a chance to experience a unique nature hot spot.

The expansive lava beds still dominate the landscape, providing an opportunity to investigate the slow and dramatic return of life to this harsh, barren landscape. Lichens were the first species to establish on the lava rock, encrusting the rough rubble. Over time the lichen growth thickened, and trapped leaves, dirt and debris built up in the crevices, allowing other species to move in. Although vast portions of the lava fields still only support lichens and a few tough, low-lying plants, areas near water sustain the growth of large trees and a healthy forest community. In some areas, the lava rock is 12 metres deep and buries the rushing waters of Lax Mihl (Crater Creek), which still flows through underground passageways.

Beautiful falls found within the park are easily accessed through short, flat, well-maintained trails. Do not miss the opportunity

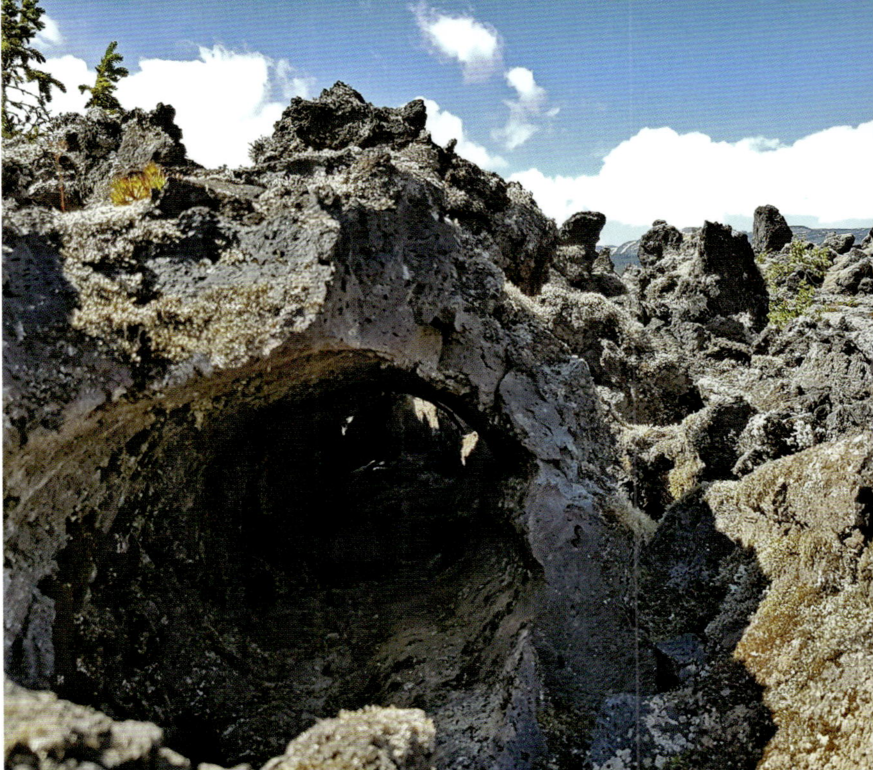

→ **Visitors will find unique log moulds, which were created when lava quickly cooled around engulfed trees.**

← **Ksiluuyim Agiiy (Vetter Falls) cascades artfully into turquoise waters.**

to take in the breathtaking sight of white, rushing water hitting the calmer flow of a turquoise stream, surrounded by dense conifers and a moss-covered forest floor. Ksiluuyim Agiiy (Vetter Falls) is a stunning set of waterfalls where glacier-fed waters spill over a short ledge before continuing downstream.

Among the most fascinating lava formations found in the park are log moulds. As the lava flowed across the landscape and destroyed everything in its path, it surrounded, toppled and burned large trees. In some cases, when the lava cooled quickly enough around a tree, it formed a mould of the tree. The trees burned or eventually rotted away, leaving dramatic hollow tubes on the landscape. This area is also a great place to examine some small but tough inhabitants of the lava beds. Three-toothed and spotted saxifrage root in the cracks, and the bubbly green and bright red leaves of spreading stonecrop form small mats on even lava. The Nisga'a call them lava berries for this reason.

The only way to access the Tseax Cone is through a guided hiking tour, allowing for the protection of this important and sensitive area. Tours begin from the visitor centre, which is built in the style of a traditional longhouse with many interpretive displays on the history and culture of the Nisga'a. Make sure you also visit the impressive Nisga'a Museum, Hli Goothl Wilp Adokshl Nisga'a ("the Heart of Nisga'a House Crests"). Here you become immersed in the deep roots and culture of the people, including the long, painful battle for a treaty that acknowledged their claim to this beautiful land they have always called home.

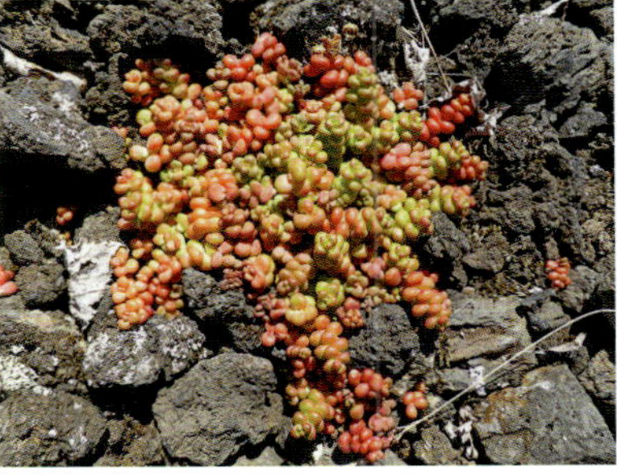

↑ **Vibrant spreading stonecrop creeps across the harsh lava landscape.**

TUMBLER RIDGE GLOBAL GEOPARK

Quality Falls

A beautiful trail to a waterfall is also the site of an important bird discovery

What Makes This Hot Spot Hot?

- Rock formations nearly 100 million years old have resulted in a cascading waterfall.
- This area is an important contact zone between eastern and western bird species.
- Wildflowers can be found all along the trail to the falls.

Address: Heritage Hwy (Hwy 52), Tumbler Ridge, BC
Tel.: (250) 242-3123
Website:

Tumbler Ridge Global Geopark

GPS Coordinates
Latitude: 55.15596
Longitude: −120.93969

Open year-round

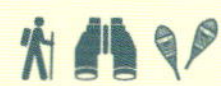

↗ **Bunchberries have an explosive pollination strategy. Once triggered, mature, unopened flowers burst open in 0.4 milliseconds and catapult pollen into the air.**

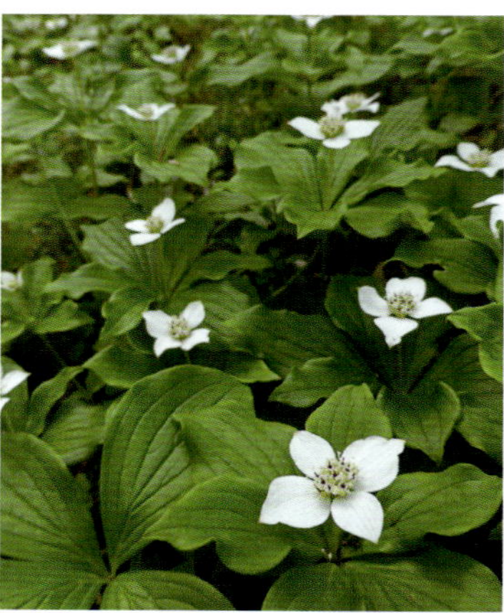

There is much to explore within Tumbler Ridge Global Geopark, as the boundaries incorporate 43 geosites of geological and aesthetic interest. These sites include unique rock formations, canyons, mountain summits, caves and many breathtaking waterfalls. Monkman Provincial Park falls within the boundary of the geopark and has some of the most magnificent waterfalls in northern BC, including the Monkman Cascades — a series of 10 waterfalls within the span of a few kilometres.

However, access to many of these falls are limited to those with extensive backcountry experience, and some require rugged multiday hikes to reach. Although there are many hiking trails that lead to waterfall views within the geopark boundary, Quality Falls is one of the best options for an easy day-hike that does not require extensive travel down long gravel service roads. The layering of sandstone and shale has created a beautiful formation for the waters of Quality Falls to cascade over, as the shale erodes more easily than the sandstone, creating distinct lips and layers in the rock.

Tumbler Ridge Geopark is impressive not only for its geology but for its ecology as well, as eastern and western bird species overlap on this eastern edge of the Rocky Mountains. Bird enthusiasts may encounter Townsend's, MacGillvray's and Audubon's warblers, as well as their eastern relatives the black-throated green, mourning and myrtle warblers.

Although this contact zone has resulted in a lot of hybridization between closely related species, a special discovery at

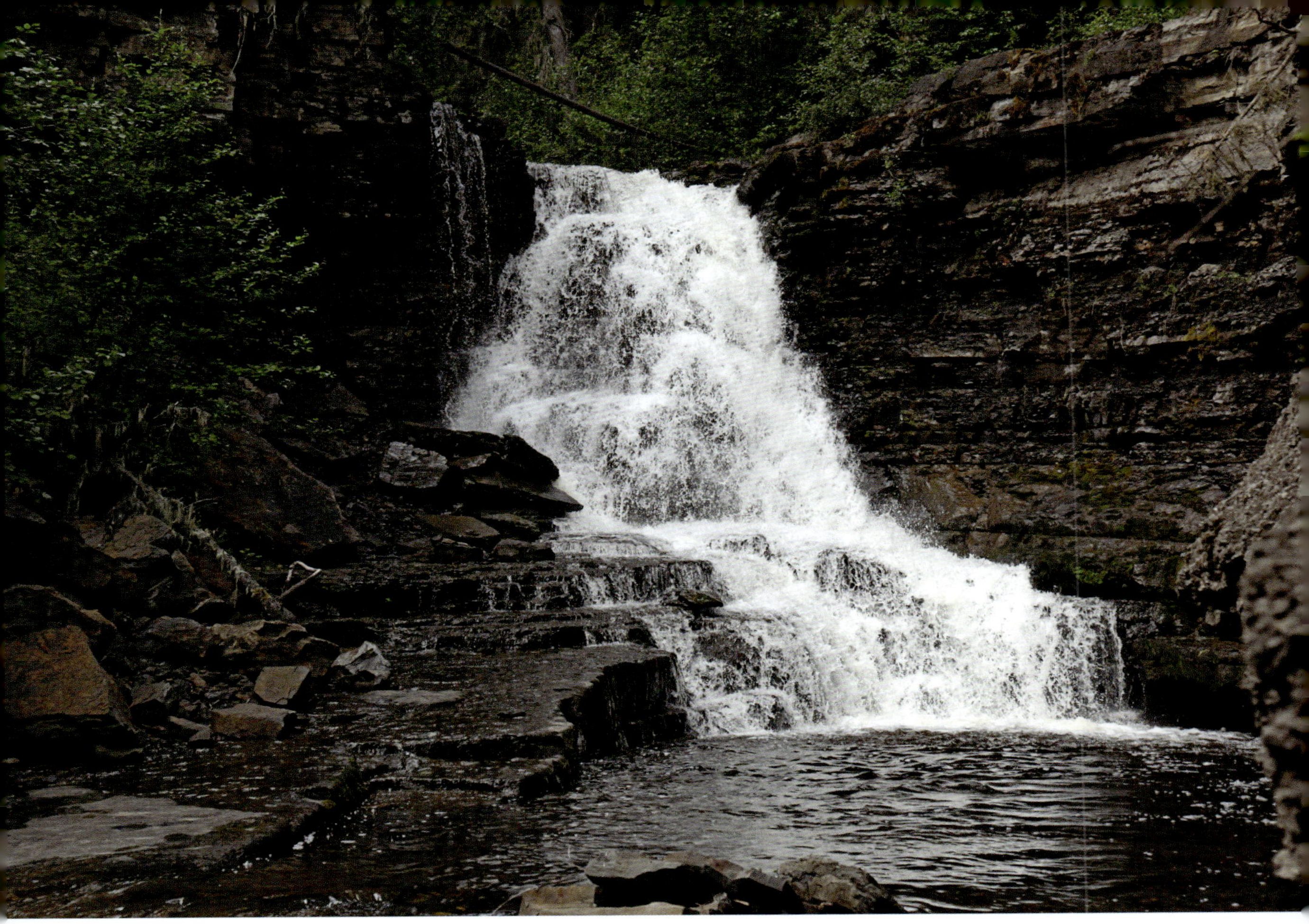

Quality Falls actually led to the classification of a distinct species. At the time of this discovery, the winter wrens in British Columbia were considered the same species as those occurring in the rest of Canada. The species was assumed to be geographically separated into eastern and western populations. At the trailhead of this hike, researchers discovered both populations singing their distinct songs within 100 metres of each other. After netting birds of both populations and obtaining blood samples, DNA analysis showed that these two forms did not interbreed and were in fact distinct. As a result, the western population was declared its own species — the Pacific wren.

Tumbler Ridge is also a great place to encounter a mix of western and eastern plant species. In the early summer the trail down to the falls is surrounded with flowering bunchberry, pink wintergreen, tall bluebell and twinflower, the latter a supposed favourite of the 18th century botanist Carl Linnaeus.

↑ The rock formation of Quality Falls is composed of weathered shale and sandstone.

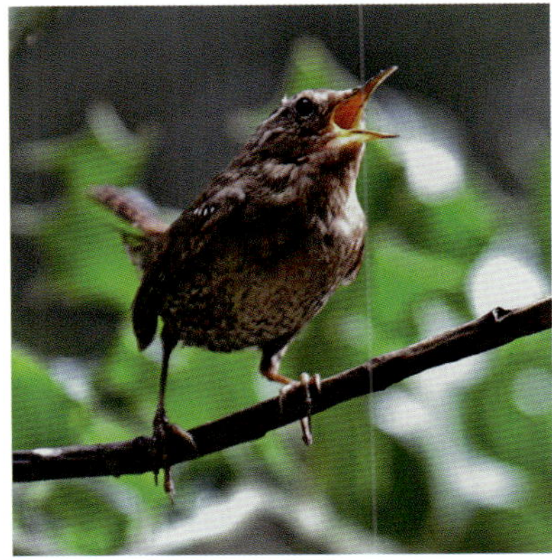

→ The Pacific wren is now its own species after it was encountered singing its distinct song alongside that of its eastern relatives.

Scout Island Nature Centre

In the heart of Williams Lake, a birding paradise awaits

- The area is frequently visited by American white pelicans.
- A short trail weaves through wetland, shoreline, forest and field.
- A great diversity of nesting birds is found here, from raptors to waterfowl to warblers.

Address: 1305 A Borland Road, Williams Lake, BC
Tel.: (250) 398-8532
Website:

Scout Island Nature Centre

GPS Coordinates
Latitude: 52.12024
Longitude: –122.12043

Open year-round

↗ **During the breeding season, American white pelicans sport a bill horn on their upper bill.**

→ **A curious common yellowthroat makes its presence known along the trail.**

Visitors to Scout Island Nature Centre in the city of Williams Lake will find a wildlife sanctuary and birder's paradise bursting with avian activity year-round. The centre includes wetland, lake, grassland and woodland habitats.

Operated by the Williams Lake Field Naturalists, this is a wonderful destination for not just nature viewing but also nature education, as the centre offers activities and programs for all ages. Two and a half kilometres of trail will take you through the varied habitats over the 9.69 hectares of protected land. Nest boxes are installed throughout the park to support breeding bird populations, from tree swallows to wood ducks. An osprey pair takes full advantage of the platform installed for them. Bat boxes provide roosting shelter for little brown bats after a busy night catching mosquitoes on the wing.

The early summer provides ample opportunity to watch bird families feeding together. Wood ducks, cinnamon and green-winged teals, and red-necked grebes are just some of the summer residents that breed in the wetland habitat found in the park. Yellow-headed blackbirds are abundant, and the striking plumage of the males makes them easy to spot as they sing while perched on cattails and bulrushes. Bullock's orioles, yellow warblers, common yellowthroats and many other songbirds breed within the wild spaces of Scout Island.

The Cariboo Chilcotin area is home to the only nesting colony of American white pelicans in British Columbia, found within the provincial park protecting Strum Lake, 70 kilometres northwest of Scout Island. Although they do not nest in Williams Lake, they are frequent visitors. There are few fish in Strum Lake, so these giant birds make regular flights to feed at lakes up to 164 kilometres away from their nesting sites. There is a good chance to see these provincially rare birds at Scout Island, and if they are present, they are hard to miss. Their bright white plumage is contrasted with jet-black primary wing feathers. Pelicans are most famous for

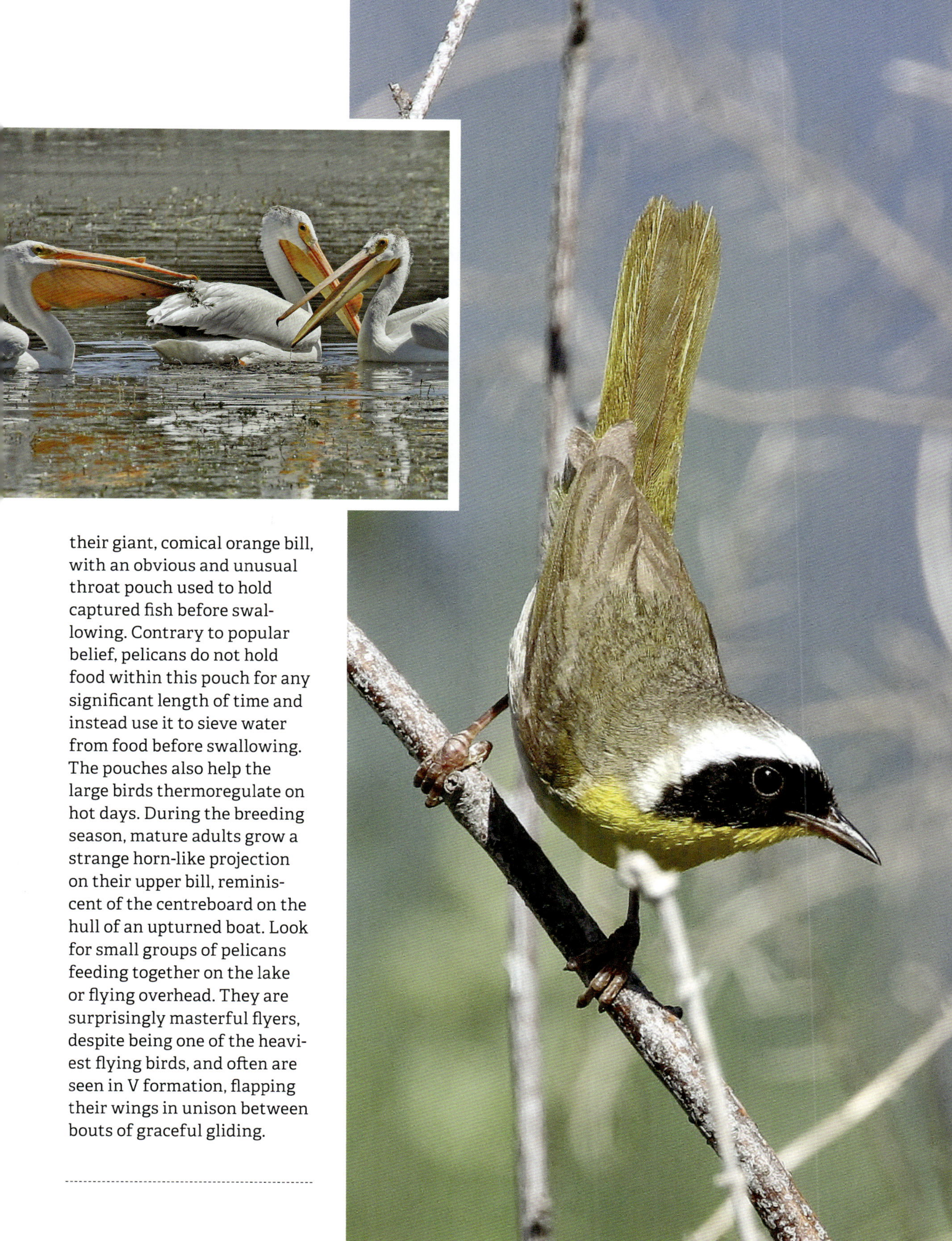

their giant, comical orange bill, with an obvious and unusual throat pouch used to hold captured fish before swallowing. Contrary to popular belief, pelicans do not hold food within this pouch for any significant length of time and instead use it to sieve water from food before swallowing. The pouches also help the large birds thermoregulate on hot days. During the breeding season, mature adults grow a strange horn-like projection on their upper bill, reminiscent of the centreboard on the hull of an upturned boat. Look for small groups of pelicans feeding together on the lake or flying overhead. They are surprisingly masterful flyers, despite being one of the heaviest flying birds, and often are seen in V formation, flapping their wings in unison between bouts of graceful gliding.

Wells Gray Provincial Park

Where viewing iconic waterfalls and spotting bears snatching salmon from the river can be combined into a day trip

What Makes This Hot Spot Hot?

- Salmon make an epic journey from the Pacific Ocean to the BC Interior, where bears feed upon them in the river during spawning.
- A number of scenic waterfalls are found in this landscape, which was sculpted by volcanic action and glaciers.
- As an important wildlife corridor, Wells Gray has many opportunities to see wildlife while hiking or canoeing.

Address: Clearwater Valley Road, 10 km north of Clearwater, BC
Tel.: (250) 674-3334
Website:

BC Parks

GPS Coordinates
Latitude: 51.92815
Longitude: −120.13195

Open year-round

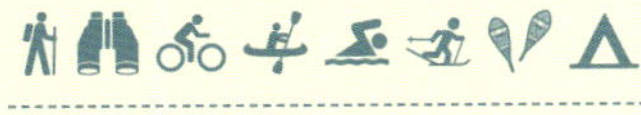

♿ **(Check ahead)**

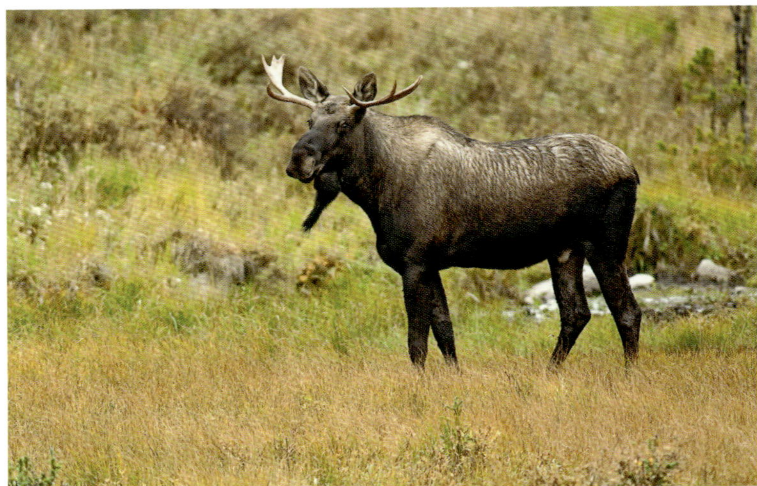

Wells Gray Provincial Park protects some of British Columbia's most scenic treasures. Sculpted by glaciers and riddled with volcanic features, this large park in the Interior has expansive stretches of remote wilderness that complement its easily reachable southern section. This combination of accessibility and high-level protection allows the park to thrive, which in turn makes the plants, animals and sights all the more beautiful to behold.

Clearwater Lake, which is surrounded by mountains, is a perfect home base and stunning from both shore and canoe. It was once a large glacier-carved basin that was later dammed by lava and filled with water to create the lake we see today. The outflow of the lake pours over the lava dam, creating Osprey Falls.

Stepping onto one of the park's many trails just off the road, visitors will feel fully immersed in nature, despite being in a popular recreational area. Bears are often sighted alongside creeks hunting for fish. The best time to see them is from August to October, when sockeye

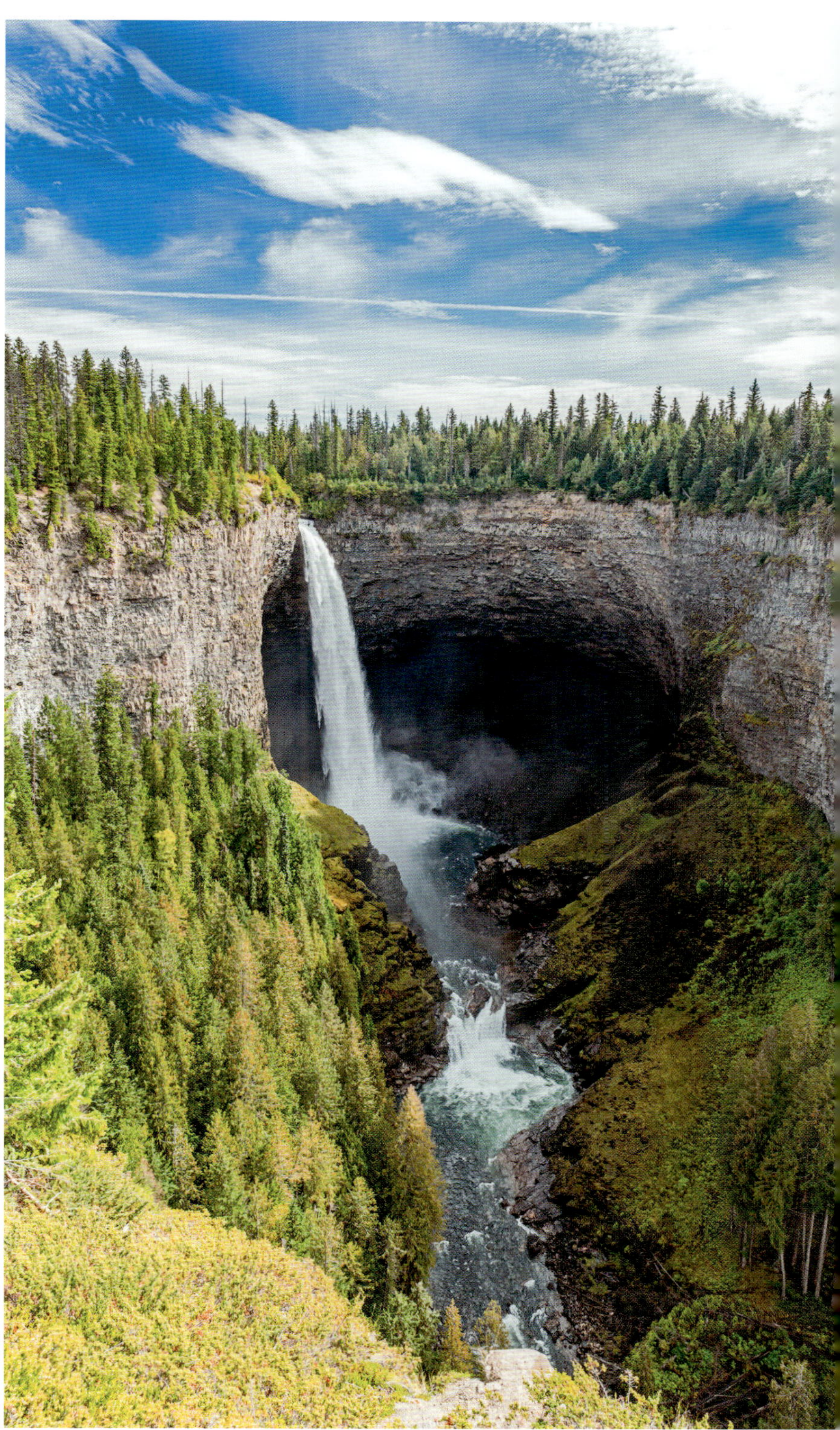

→ **Helmcken Falls is arguably the most majestic waterfall in British Columbia and is easily reachable on foot.**

☙ **Moose and other wildlife roam the park.**

salmon are spawning and the bears emerge from the forest to feed at the river's edge. One of the most impressive places to view this is Bailey's Chute, where the rivers teem with salmon struggling up the fast-flowing water.

Well-known for its waterfalls, the park hosts the iconic Helmcken Falls, an uninterrupted tower of free-falling water along the Murtle River. Easily one of the most visited sites in the park, this spectacular waterfall is the fourth-highest in Canada and continues to have an amazing impact on the landscape. The rock in the basin, where the water falls, continues to be carved by the falling water.

For the inquisitive mind, there are guided hikes and horseback tours throughout the park, and for the adventurer there are many backcountry trails. The alpine meadows and dense forests are home to many animals. Moose utilize Wells Gray as a winter habitat, roaming through snow-covered forests and across fields. The park also hosts many deer and coyotes.

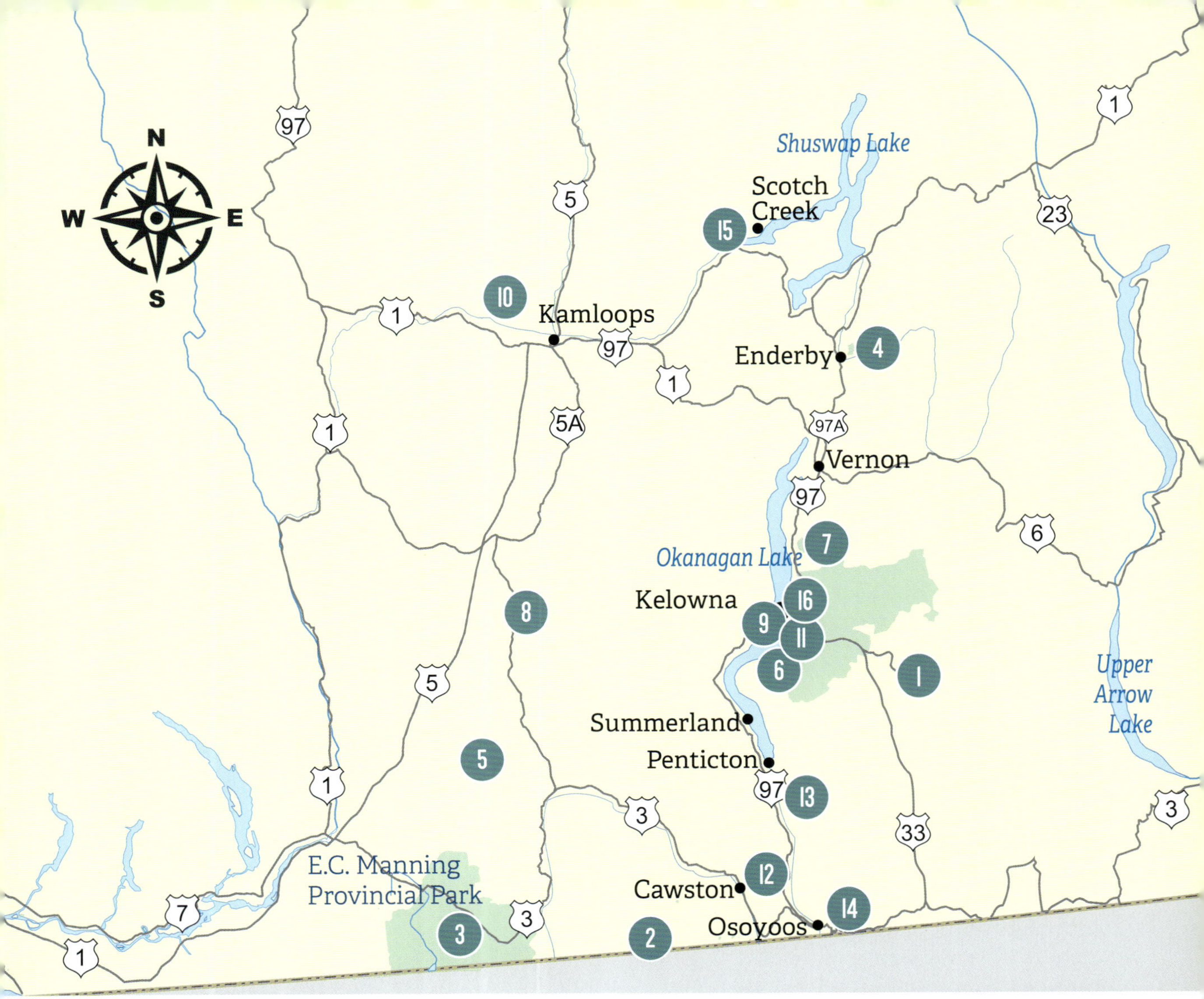

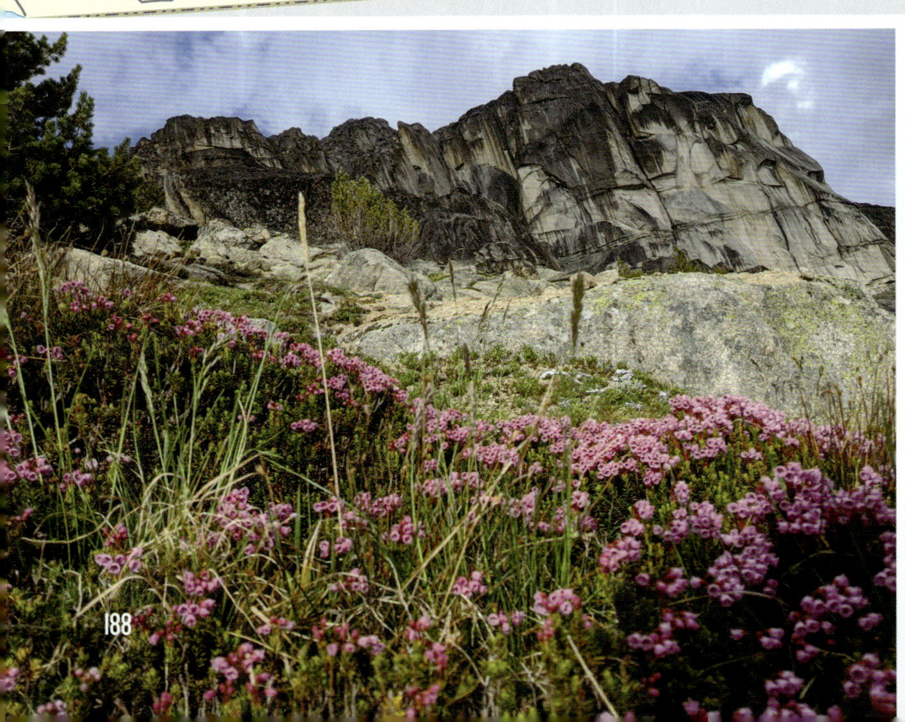

Shuswap Lake
Scotch Creek
15
10
Kamloops
Enderby
4
Vernon
97A
97
7
Okanagan Lake
Kelowna
16
9
11
6
1
Summerland
Penticton
13
97
33
E.C. Manning Provincial Park
3
3
Cawston
12
2
14
Osoyoos
Upper Arrow Lake
97
5A
5
1
7
23
6
3
N
W   E
S

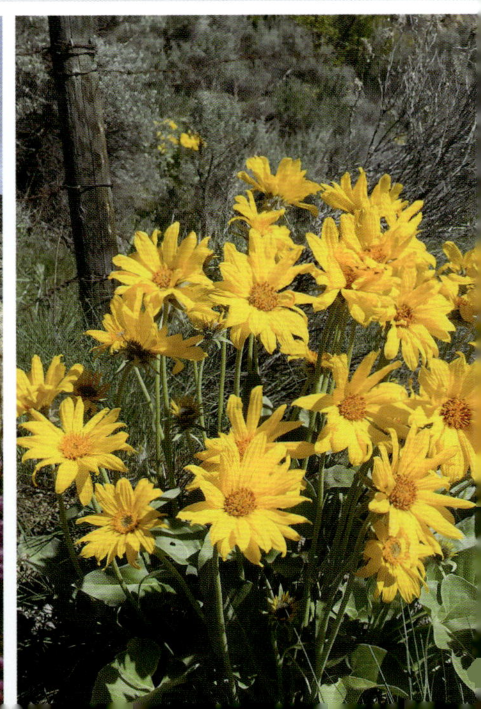

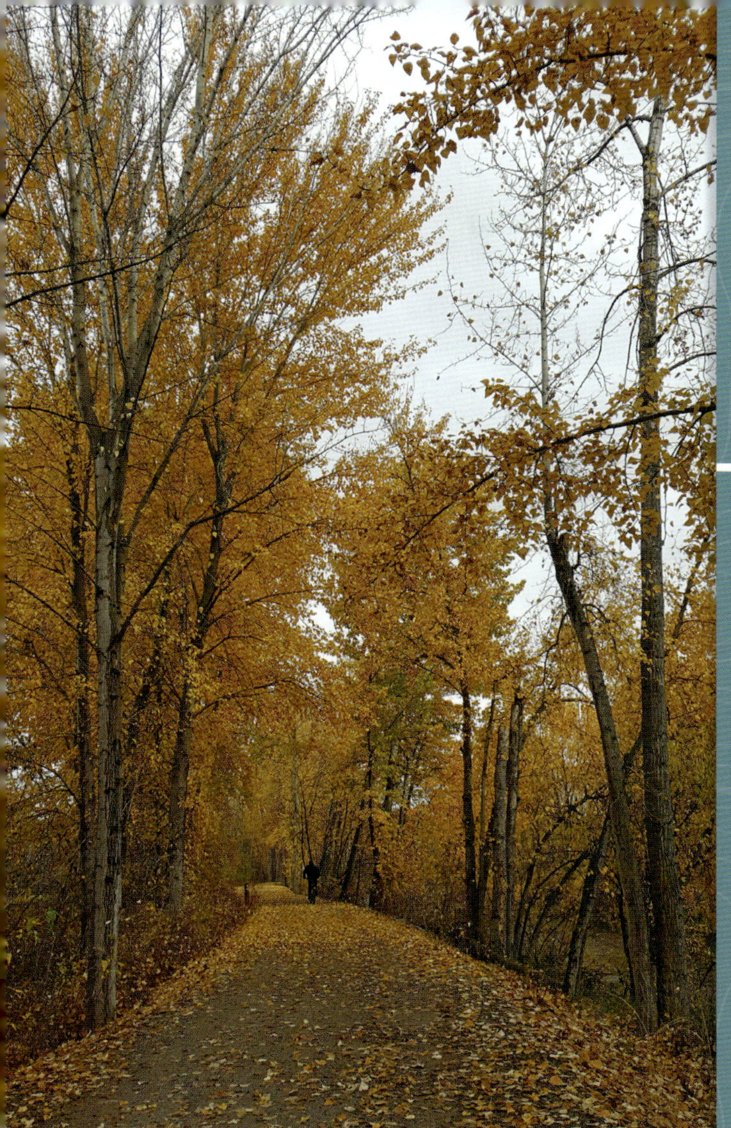

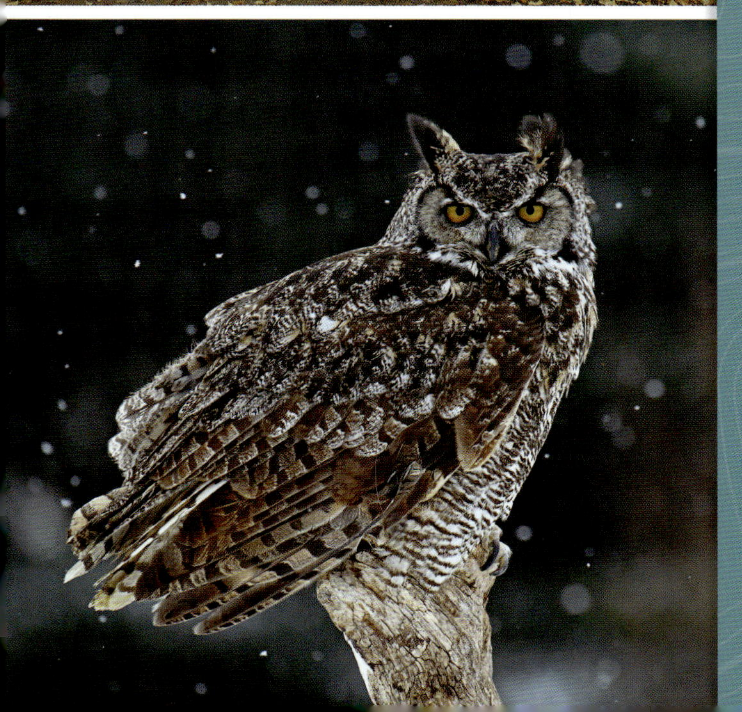

Okanagan, Similkameen and Area

Big White Mountain

Whether summer or winter, the natural beauty of the alpine is always on display in this Okanagan gem

What Makes This Hot Spot Hot?

- The alpine tundra gives visitors spectacular hiking opportunities.
- This area is bordered by an ecological reserve, providing sanctuary for the plants and wildlife.
- One of British Columbia's treasured winter wonderlands, Big White Ski Resort offers skiing, snowboarding and snowshoeing.

Address: 5315 Big White Road, Kelowna, BC
Tel.: (250) 765-3101
Website:

Big White Ski Resort

GPS Coordinates
Latitude: 49.72161
Longitude: −118.92659

Open for winter activities from late November to early April; open for summer hiking from mid-June to early September; visit the website for specific dates

Big White Mountain is well known as a ski resort by locals in the Okanagan. What many people do not know about are the spectacular winter snowshoeing and summer hiking opportunities for the nature enthusiast. In the summer, alpine flowers, such as mountain arnica and purple lupin, flourish in the grassy meadows, hardy trees surround the trails and the alpine tundra offers delightful views and chances to bird watch. Wildlife thrives here, in large part thanks to Big White Mountain Ecological Reserve just northeast of the resort. The reserve itself does not have any developed trails and serves as an important area for its ecosystems and unique high-elevation wetlands. Stay on the designated hiking trails to help protect this important space.

Hike to the top of the mountain on the Falcon Ridge Trail or to Rhonda Lake on a trail that meanders in and out of the forest. Old-growth stands of spruce trees interspersed with open meadows provide habitat to many unique species of animals, including moose, porcupines, pine martens and bears.

Rhonda Lake is well worth the hike. This beautiful alpine lake makes for a fantastic lunch spot and gives hikers entry to the upper trails, which can be accessed more easily on weekends when the Bullet Chair lift is open. These trails are in the alpine tundra and are too windswept to support the tree growth found at lower elevations. Small, hardy alpine plants dominate and lovely lichens paint the rocks.

Once the area is buried deep in snow, delight in the bluebird days Big White Mountain Ski Resort offers above the layer of wintry clouds that cover the valley. Discover the same spaces in a whole new way. Snowshoeing trails weave through the forest around the mountain's base, and skiers and snowboarders enjoy the alpine.

→ **Meadows of alpine flowers replace blankets of snow in the spring and summer.**

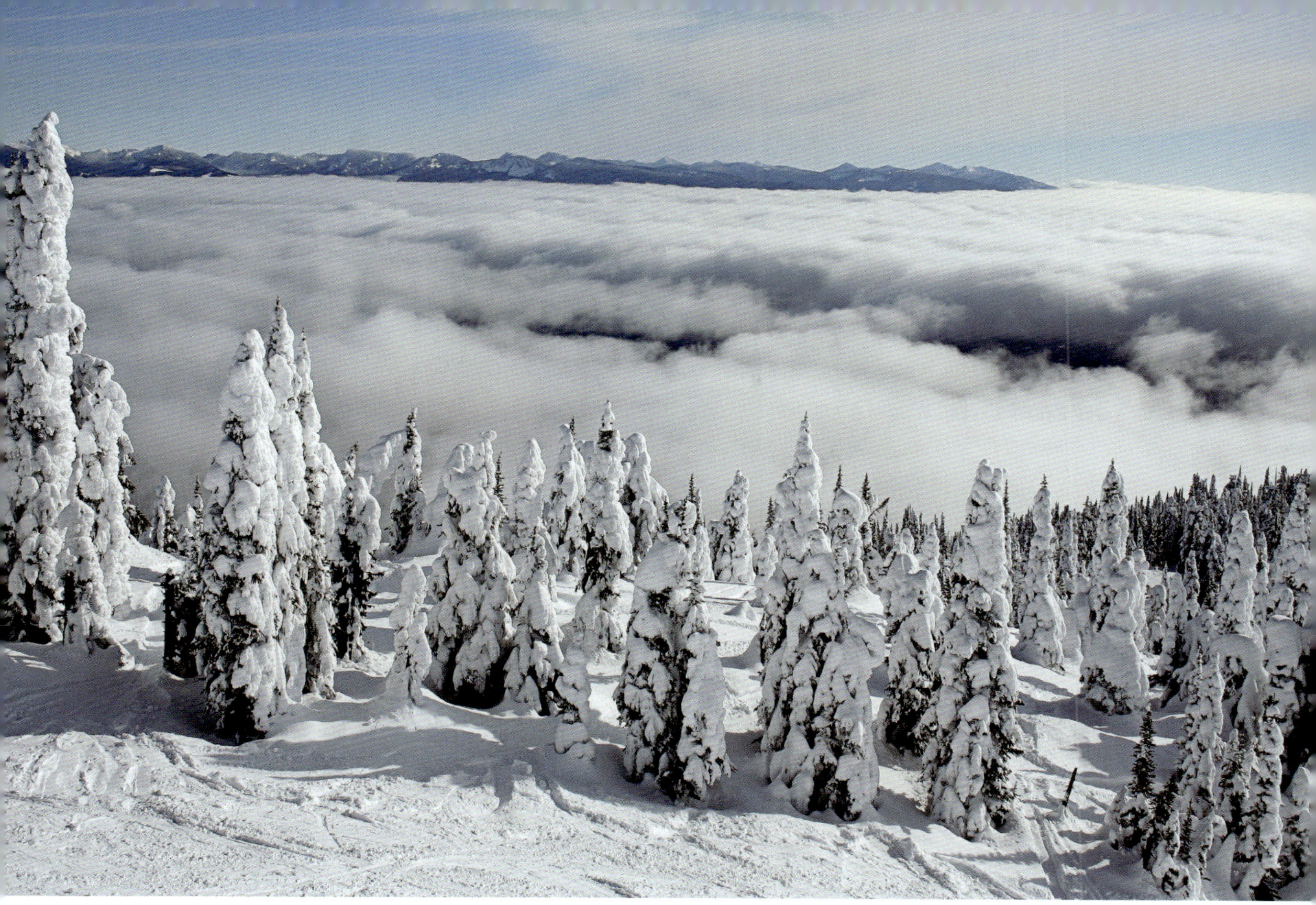

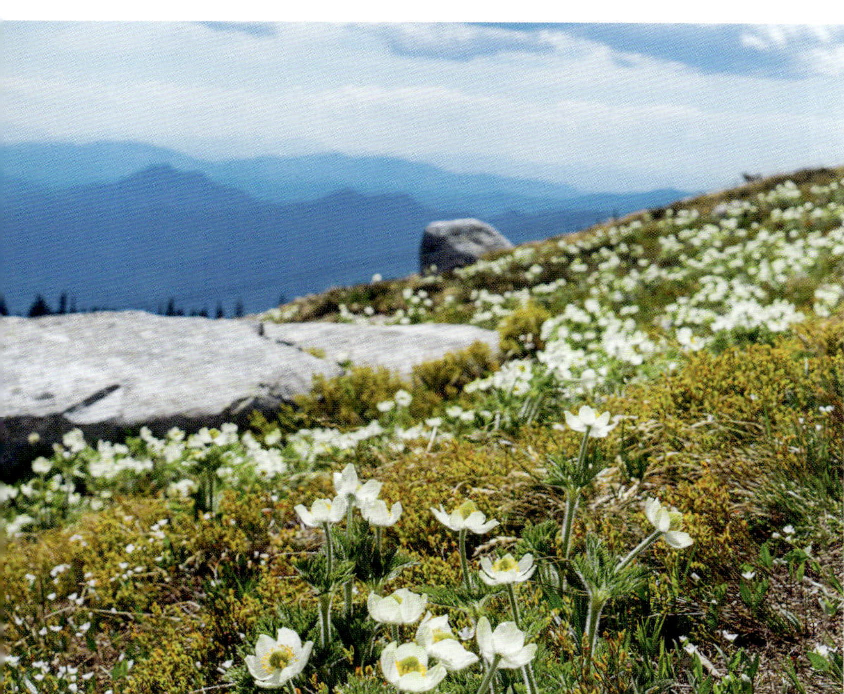

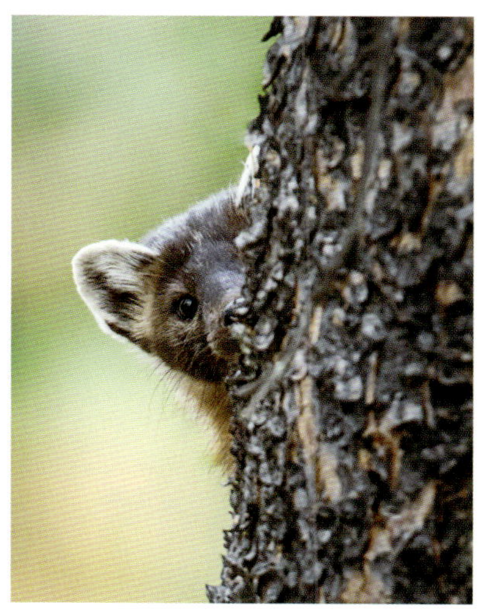

↑ In the winter months Big White is worth a trip just to get above the clouds and into the sunshine.

↓ A pine marten peeks out from behind a tree.

Cathedral Provincial Park

Brilliant blue lakes sit in an alpine oasis for mountain goats, above the desert of the Okanagan-Similkameen

What Makes This Hot Spot Hot?

- The park encompasses a transition zone between the wet Cascade Mountains and the dry desert of the Okanagan.
- Stunning blue lakes are surrounded by forests and open meadows.
- Mountain goats frequent this park, roaming the rocky cliffs and grazing on wildflowers.

Address: Ashnola River Road, south of Keremeos, BC
Tel.: (250) 766-7972
Website:

BC Parks

GPS Coordinates
Latitude: 49.06454
Longitude: –120.33277

Core area open June to September; backcountry open year-round

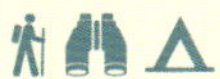

♿ **(Check ahead with Cathedral Lake Lodge)**

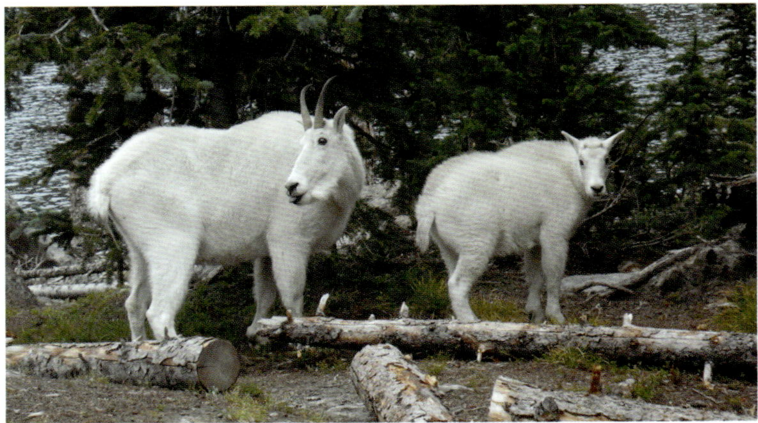

Granite peaks and ridges tower over jewel-blue lakes nestled in subalpine forests and meadows of wildflowers. A variety of birds and other wildlife, including a healthy population of mountain goats, call this space home. Cathedral Provincial Park has aspects of both the dry desert of the Okanagan and the lush forests of the nearby Cascade Mountains. Whether you are craving an adventurous hike with panoramic views or a more relaxed wildlife-watching experience, Cathedral Provincial Park has a lot to offer.

Flora and fauna throughout the park is as varied as the landscape itself. Subalpine forests of pine and fir surround the lower lakes. There are many trails that take hikers around these lakes, or up into the alpine. Above the trees, open grassy meadows and fields of wildflowers frame the towering granite peaks and ridges with red paintbrush, lupin and heather. On a clear day, hikes along these ridges offer spectacular views of the surrounding mountains and lakes. For a panoramic view of the park, the Lakeview Mountain Trail takes hikers to Lakeview Mountain, which is the tallest point in the park.

Mountain goats are a common sight in the park.

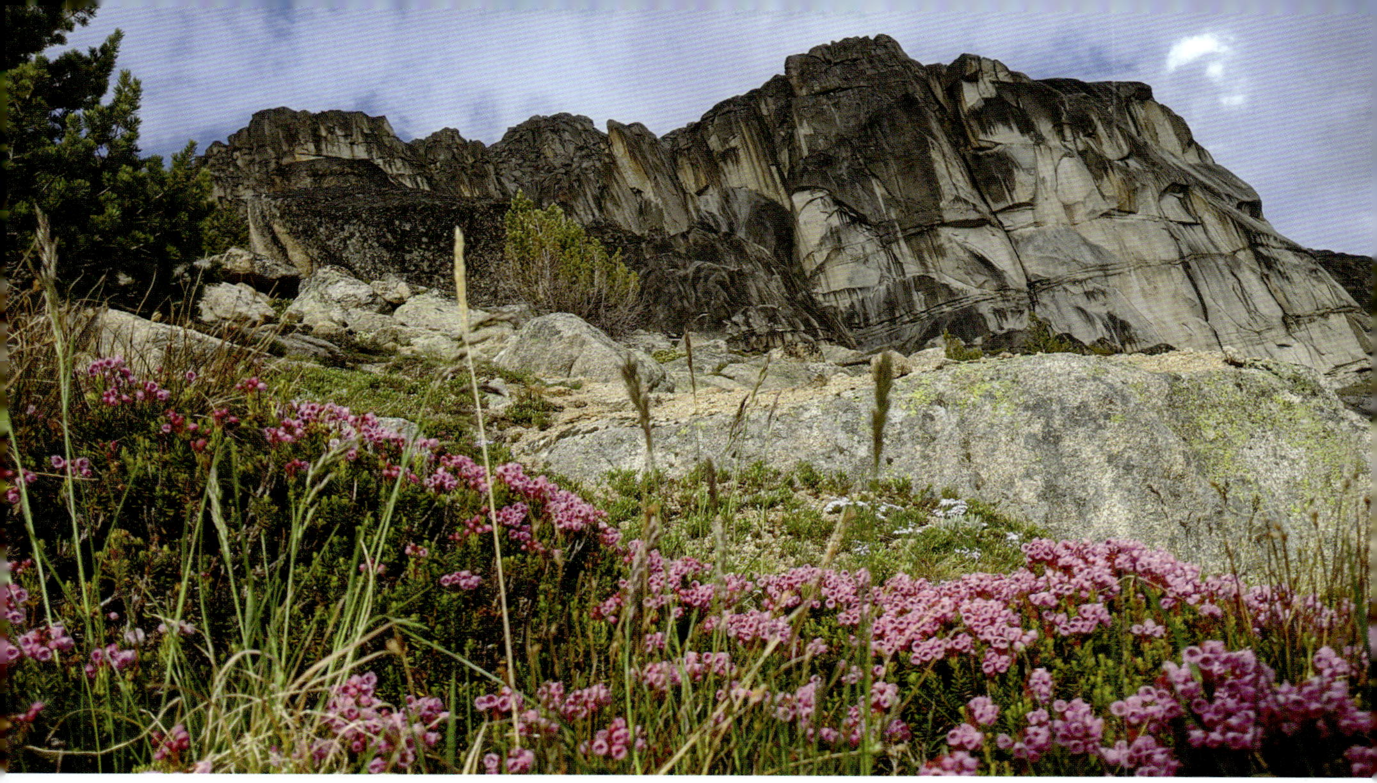

They thrive in the alpine landscape, climbing the sheer rock faces and sometimes jumping between ledges only a few centimetres in width. Their two-toed hooves have grippy pads and hard edges, both of which give the goats amazing climbing abilities. When not scaling rocky cliffs, they may be found in meadows and near campsites grazing on wildflowers, grasses and sometimes lichens. Other mammals that call this park home include bighorn sheep, moose, marmots and the red-listed badger. The landscape is also home to a variety of birds, including commonly sighted mountain chickadees and pine siskins, as well as mountain bluebirds, spruce grouse and prairie falcons — the latter can be spotted nesting in cliffs and open grasslands. The Rim Trail gives hikers an opportunity to explore the varied terrain featured throughout the park.

The park lies within the traditional territory of the Syilx and Nlaka'pamux Nation and was used for hunting, fishing and gathering plants. Over 800 lithic artifacts have been found here, including basalt flakes and objects made of white siltstone and chert. Today, visitors may choose to hike in or utilize the shuttle service offered by Cathedral Lakes Lodge. The service allows explorers of varied fitness and abilities to experience the alpine. Camping is available at designated sites near one of three lakes: Lake of the Woods, Pyramid Lake and Quiniscoe Lake. Check ahead as facilities and campfire regulations vary between the sites.

↑ Pink heather blooms in an open meadow below Grimface Mountain.

← Mountain goats graze in the meadows, scale rocky cliff faces and wander the lakes and valleys.

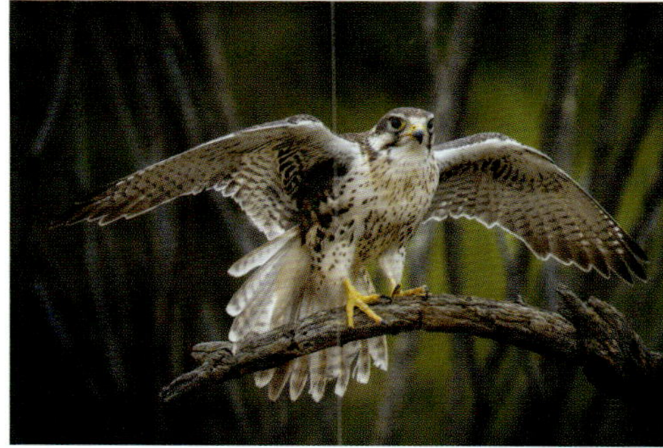

↑ Prairie falcons can be spotted on the rocky cliffs and over open meadows of the park.

E.C. Manning Provincial Park

Year-round recreational activities encourage visitors to explore the park on foot or by skis and snowshoes

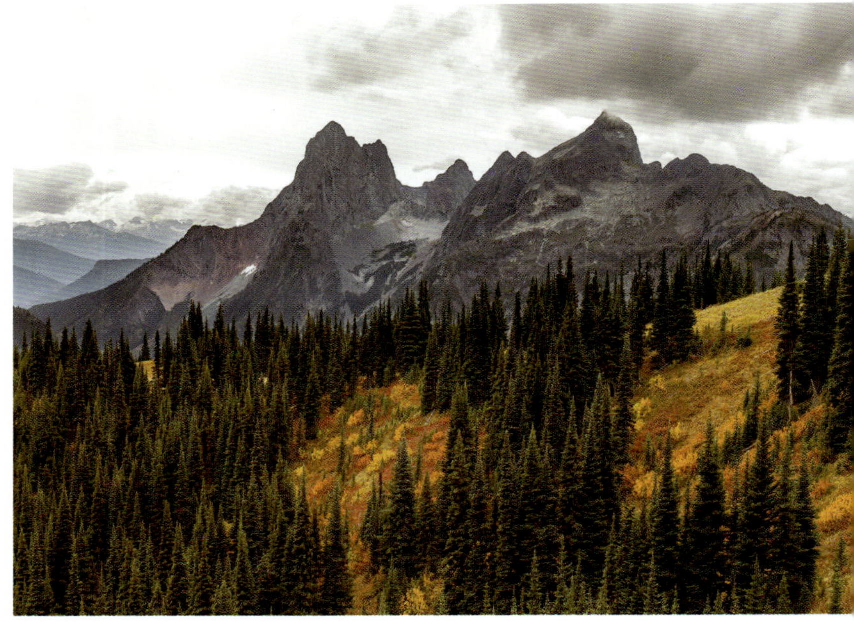

What Makes This Hot Spot Hot?

- Every June, a two-day Bird Blitz is hosted in the park, during which birders identify the various birds living in the area.
- The park sits on the northernmost section of the famous Pacific Crest Trail.
- People of all hiking abilities can enjoy the mid-summer bloom of alpine flowers and river otters playing in nearby bodies of fresh water.

Address: 7500 Crowsnest Hwy (Hwy 3), Manning Park, BC
Tel.: (604) 668-5953
Website:

BC Parks

GPS Coordinates
Latitude: 49.08333
Longitude: −120.83333

Open year-round

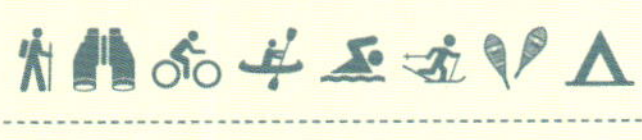

♿ **(Check ahead)**

Lying on the northernmost tip of the Cascade mountain range, E.C. Manning Provincial Park is known as the end of the 4,265-kilometre Pacific Crest Trail, which connects Mexico and Canada. The park's location makes it an ideal spot to get out and stretch your legs when travelling between inland British Columbia and the coast, though it is also a destination for campers and hikers from around the province.

Rhododendron Flats, an easy loop right off the Crowsnest Highway (Highway 3), makes for a spectacular stroll in mid-June. The forest canopy shades areas of beautiful red rhododendrons, which bloom alongside the trail. Although more challenging, the Skyline Trail affords spectacular views of the surrounding mountains. Lightning Lake, a popular campsite, gives visitors access to many hiking trails and the chance to canoe. All of the trails in the park offer abundant wildlife viewing opportunities, with mammals such as deer, moose, bears, hoary marmots and coyotes roaming the park. On the lake and riverside trails, look for sleek river otters in the water or sunning themselves on the banks.

Strawberry Flats is a marvellous place to stop and birdwatch. The rufous hummingbird and Canada's tiny calliope hummingbird are often spotted in these open meadows. Other popular birding locations include Beaver Pond, where you may see water-loving birds such as sandpipers. White-tailed ptarmigan and grey-crowned rosy-finch can be found in the alpine areas of the park. A series of trails, including the Paintbrush Nature Trail and Heather Trail, provide access to the alpine. Alpine flowers are generally in full bloom by mid-summer, so whatever trail you choose to travel, the flowers provide bursts of colour along your journey. Splashes of brilliant purple from the lupines amid red paintbrushes and an array of pinks and yellows are truly a magical sight.

Winter recreation is a large part of Manning Park. Groomed nordic ski trails and a downhill skiing provide access to views of snow-covered peaks, and winter campsites immerse travellers in the grandeur of an alpine environment blanketed in snow. Whatever the season, prepare to be impressed by the natural beauty of this park.

↑ **Visitors tour Lightning Lake by canoe.**

Enderby Cliffs Provincial Park

Dramatic cliffs of volcanic rock provide a unique habitat for wildlife and a viewing platform for hikers

What Makes This Hot Spot Hot?

- Turkey vultures, red-tailed hawks and eagles soar in updrafts created by the cliff faces.
- Standing atop sheer rock cliffs offers outstanding views of the North Okanagan and Shuswap region.
- The cliffs are tertiary rock formations of lava carved by receding glaciers.

Address: Grindrod, BC
Tel.: (250) 260-3041
Website:

BC Parks

GPS Coordinates
Latitude: 50.57597
Longitude: −119.10456

Open year-round

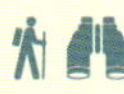

Escape civilization on the Tplaqin Trail as it weaves its way to the top of Enderby Cliffs. This often-quiet trail is a delight for hikers, naturalists and geology enthusiasts. The picturesque cliffs were formed by glaciers gradually eroding the hardened lava of which the cliffs are composed. The cliffs are topped with tranquil, grassy plateaus that contrast the bare, rocky face. From the top there is a stunning view of the Shuswap and Okanagan valleys.

The rugged but well-marked trail ascends 670 metres through old-growth stands of Douglas-fir, hemlock and larch trees. The forests are occasionally interrupted with grassy fields dotted with ladyslippers and glacier lilies, among other flowers. Nearing the summit the trail leaves the coniferous forest behind, and stands of deciduous trees and small shrubs dominate the open plateaus. Songbirds sing, while golden eagles and red-tailed hawks soar on updrafts. If you have binoculars bring them, but even with the naked eye you cannot miss these magnificent birds. Along with views of birds hikers have a spectacular view of the valley below. The Shuswap River weaves through farmland where the Okanagan and Shuswap valleys meet. From this vantage point the fields appear to be a patchwork quilt of green and yellow squares.

The cliffs are a protected area and host a wide variety of wildlife. The sheer rock faces make them an ideal habitat for bats, swallows and other cliff-dwelling birds. The park extends beyond the trail system, and the vegetation in these isolated sections provides habitat for mule deer, lynx, moose and black and grizzly bears. Keep an eye out in muddy areas along the hike for the tracks of some of these larger mammals. Remember to be respectful of the slow-growing plants in the windswept environment by staying on the trail, and be careful of the steep cliff drop-offs.

→ **The vertical cliff faces make a perfect habitat for cliff-dwelling birds and bats.**

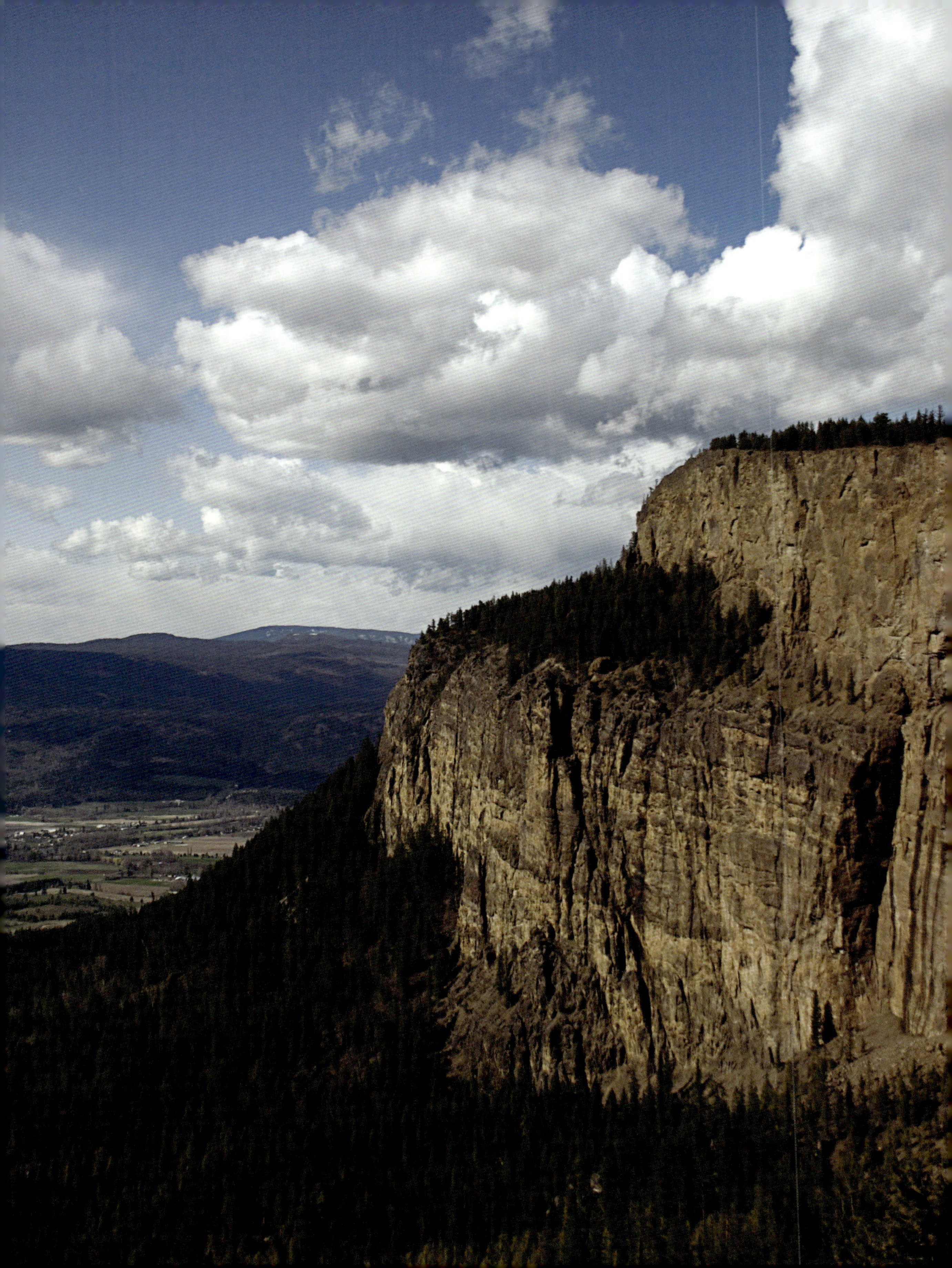

Hudson's Bay Company Heritage Trail

Transition between two distinct ecosystems

What Makes This Hot Spot Hot?

- Hikers can walk the transition between lush coastal forests and fir and pine forests.
- Beautiful creeks and ponds along the route provide water for a host of wildlife.
- This hot spot is also an opportunity to hike in the footsteps of First Nations and fur traders.

Address: A number of access points exist between Hope and Tulameen, BC
Tel.: (604) 869-1274
Website:

Hope Mountain Centre

GPS Coordinates (western trailhead):
Latitude: 49.37173
Longitude: –121.25578

Open year-round, generally hiked July to September

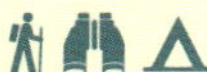

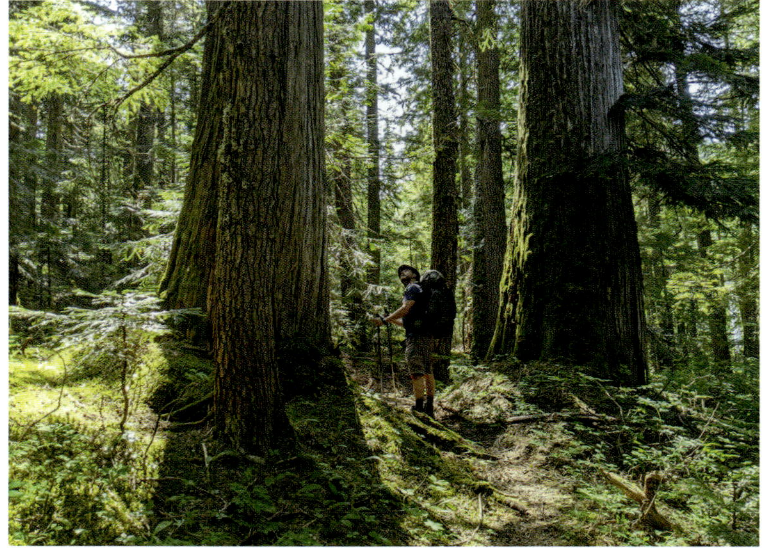

The Hudson's Bay Heritage Trail connects Tulameen and Hope like it initially connected three nations — the Stól:lo, Nlaka'pamux and Similkameen — for trading and hunting. It later became part of a European fur trading route. The trail spans 74 kilometres and transitions from coastal forest on the west end of the trail to dry Interior conditions on the east end.

From plants and fungi to mammals and birds, there is something new at every turn. The forests on the west end are typical of a coastal environment; fir, cedar and hemlock tower above ferns, columbine and buttercups. The lush, wet forests come with cascading creeks and muddy bogs. Skunk cabbage, one of the first signs of spring, pops its pungent yellow blooms out of the muddy wetlands.

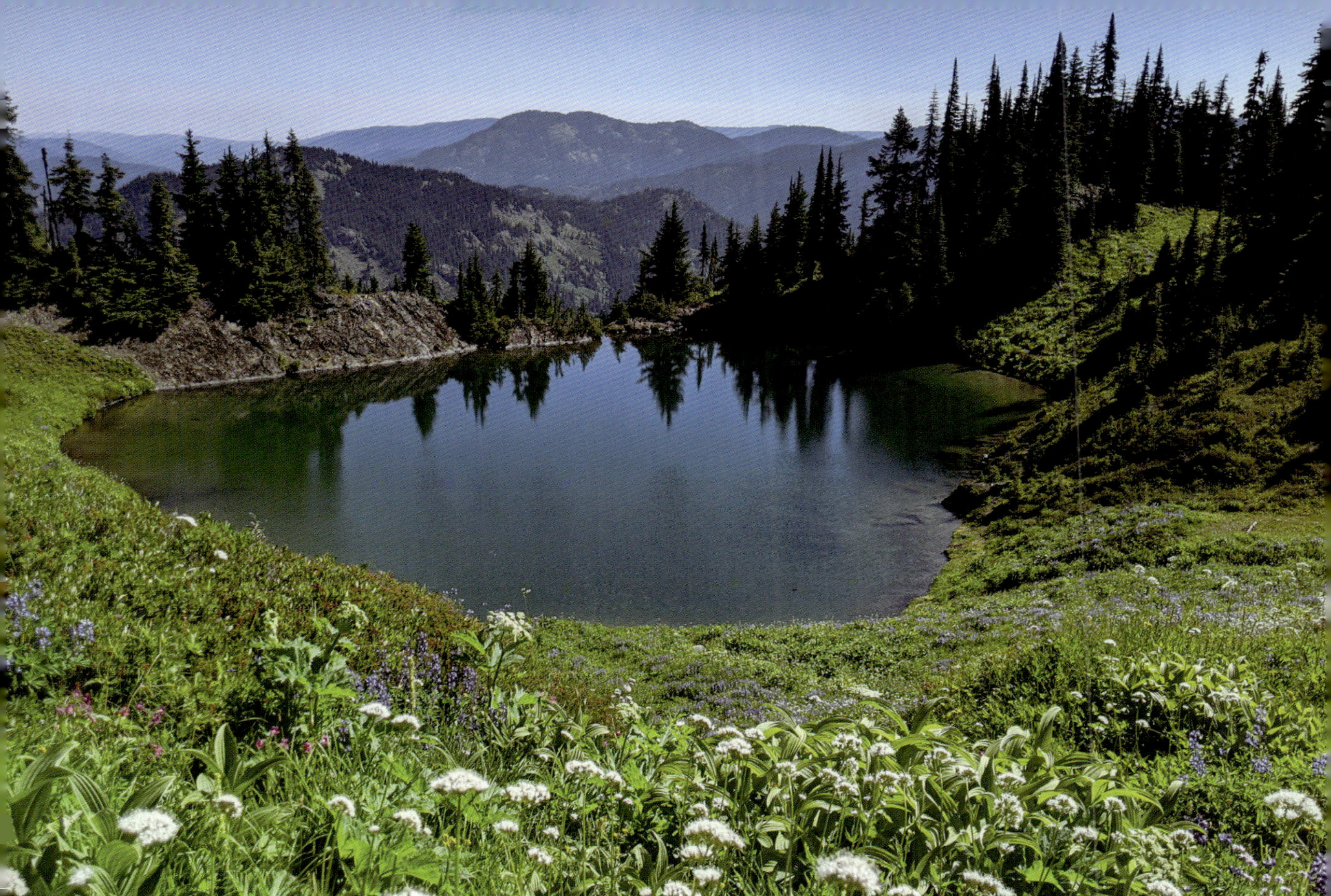

Bears eat skunk cabbage in the spring as a diuretic to jump start their digestive systems after hibernation.

The wet west turns to open alpine meadows containing red paintbrush and aster, and gradually transitions into the dry eastern forests of fir and pine. The heritage status of the trail protects the forests and wildlife along it from logging. Moose, bears, pikas, deer and bats all rely on the varied ecosystem in this corridor. Open meadows at higher elevations make for beautiful views of the surrounding topography, including Tulameen Mountain and the Cascades. A number of lakes and ponds can be found, including the shimmering blue Palmer's Pond, which is situated in an open meadow and surrounded by small groves of stunted fir trees.

Hikers can choose to through-hike this trail or utilize logging roads to access shorter sections and day hikes. One should ensure they have thoroughly researched their route and are fully prepared. Unfortunately flooding in 2021 has impacted access. The best way to get up-to-date conditions and access information is the Facebook group "Hudson's Bay Company (HBC) Heritage Brigade Trail info" (facebook.com/groups/3509645879359951).

↑ **Palmers Pond is an HBC Trail favourite, with stunning views and beautiful blue water.**

← **The Sowaqua Valley has towering cedars typical of coastal forests.**

Johns Family Nature Conservancy Regional Park

Watch the story of forest succession following a wildfire unfold

What Makes This Hot Spot Hot?

- The Okanagan Mountain Park wildfire burned this park to the ground in 2003, beginning a cycle of forest succession.
- A hike to the top of the rocky bluffs rewards visitors with a panoramic view of Okanagan Lake and the city of Kelowna.
- The rubber boa is frequently seen moving between the rocks beneath the bluffs.

Address: 6970 Chute Lake Road, Kelowna, BC
Tel.: (250) 469-6232
Website:

Regional District of Central Okanagan

GPS Coordinates
Latitude: 49.77392
Longitude: −119.52135

Open year-round

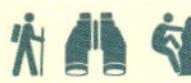

This changing landscape tells the story of forest succession following the Okanagan Mountain Park wildfire. In the 2003 fire Cedar Mountain Regional Park, as it was then known, burned to the ground, including all of the western redcedars for which the park was originally named. In 2013 the Johns family, who owned land near Cedar Mountain, generously donated 323 hectares to the Central Okanagan Land Trust for expanding and preserving the park. To honour this donation the name was changed from Cedar Mountain Regional Park to the Johns Family Nature Conservancy Regional Park.

Although regrowth has been in action for years, the effects of the wildfire remain obvious. Charred standing and fallen trees still cover the park. Immediately following the fire the park was devoid of life and the soil was inhospitable for plant growth. Nitrogen-fixing plants such as fireweed, clover and alder quickly took root, beginning the succession of the forest. These plants have root-dwelling micro-organisms that move much needed nitrogen into the ground. A decade and a half after the fire, grasses and flowers, along with mushrooms, pine and alder, now shape the landscape. Chocolate lilies have bloomed and the aspen, currently covering much of the treed areas, will eventually give way to cedar, fir and pine, continuing the succession.

As you enter the park follow an established trail and look for a smaller one to the right that leads to the base of the large rock face frequented by Kelowna rock climbers. Here you can choose to hike to the lookout by following the steep trail to the right, or you can explore beneath the rock face.

Alongside plants, animals, too, are reclaiming this area as home. From the littlest crab spider on a tree to a deer munching on leaves, it is not uncommon to see wildlife in this park. You may even

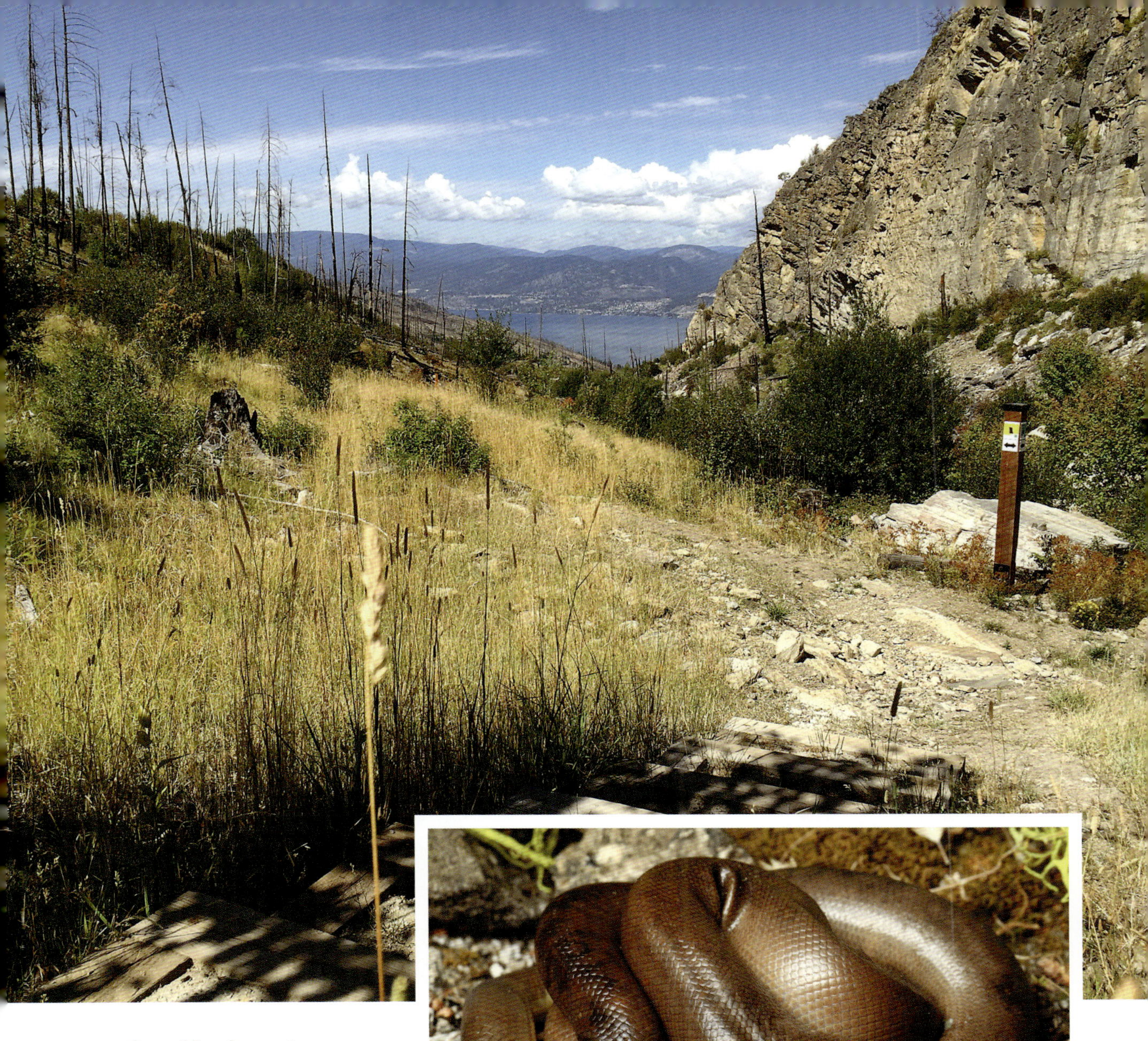

see the rubber boa, a true constrictor, in among the rocks. Rubber boas are a harmless, greenish-brown snake and do not bite. When threatened they will curl into a ball, hiding their heads and poking out their tail as a decoy, quick to surrender under any real threat. Due to human encroachment on their habitat, combined with a low reproductive rate, rubber boas are deemed a species at risk. Consider yourself lucky if you see one, and observe from a distance.

↑ The rubber boa curls up in a ball when feeling threatened.

↖ The park has changed and grown since the 2003 wildfire.

Kalamalka Lake Provincial Park

This marl lake shines a brilliant blue-green in a dry grassland that showcases plenty of unique wildlife

What Makes This Hot Spot Hot?

- This park boasts a particularly large number of plant species, as well as a rare butterfly.
- Rattlesnakes may be seen during the warmer months.
- Stone artifacts remain in old village sites that were traditionally used by the Okanagan First Nations.

Address: North Okanagan, BC (Parking is 10 km south of Vernon's city centre on Kidston Road)
Tel.: (250) 548-0076
Website:

BC Parks

GPS Coordinates
Latitude: 50.1858
Longitude: −119.24878

Open year-round

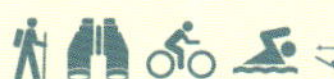

During the hot summer months Kalamalka Lake becomes a brilliant blue-green. Glaciers left behind deposits of limestone-rich mud, referred to as marlstone, and as the water warms during the summer the limestone crystals dissolve and reflect sunlight, giving the lake its turquoise colour.

The marl lake is surrounded by dry grasslands and stands of Douglas-fir and ponderosa pine. These trees have thick, fire resistant bark that allows them to stay alive in some forest fires. The dry grassland ecosystem is a haven for a number of rare and unique species, featuring many birds and over 400 plants. A unique insect to watch for is the immaculate green hairstreak — a small butterfly characterized by emerald-green wings dotted with a line of white spots. Look for its fuzzy, green caterpillar feeding on the yellow flowers of wild buckwheat.

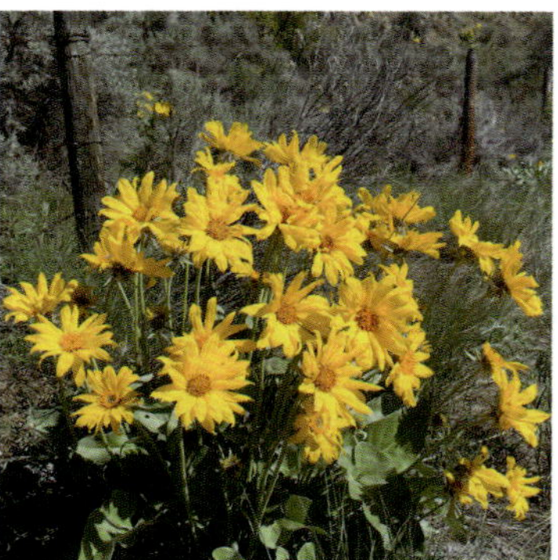

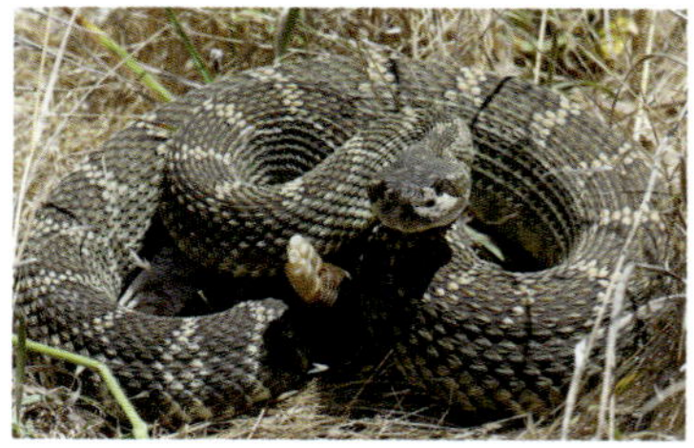

The park is well known for its rattlesnake population. Although they are venomous, rattlesnakes will not bite unless they feel threatened. If you do happen to cross paths with one and can stay a couple metres away, have a look at its rattle. Snakes must shed their skin when they grow, and each time they

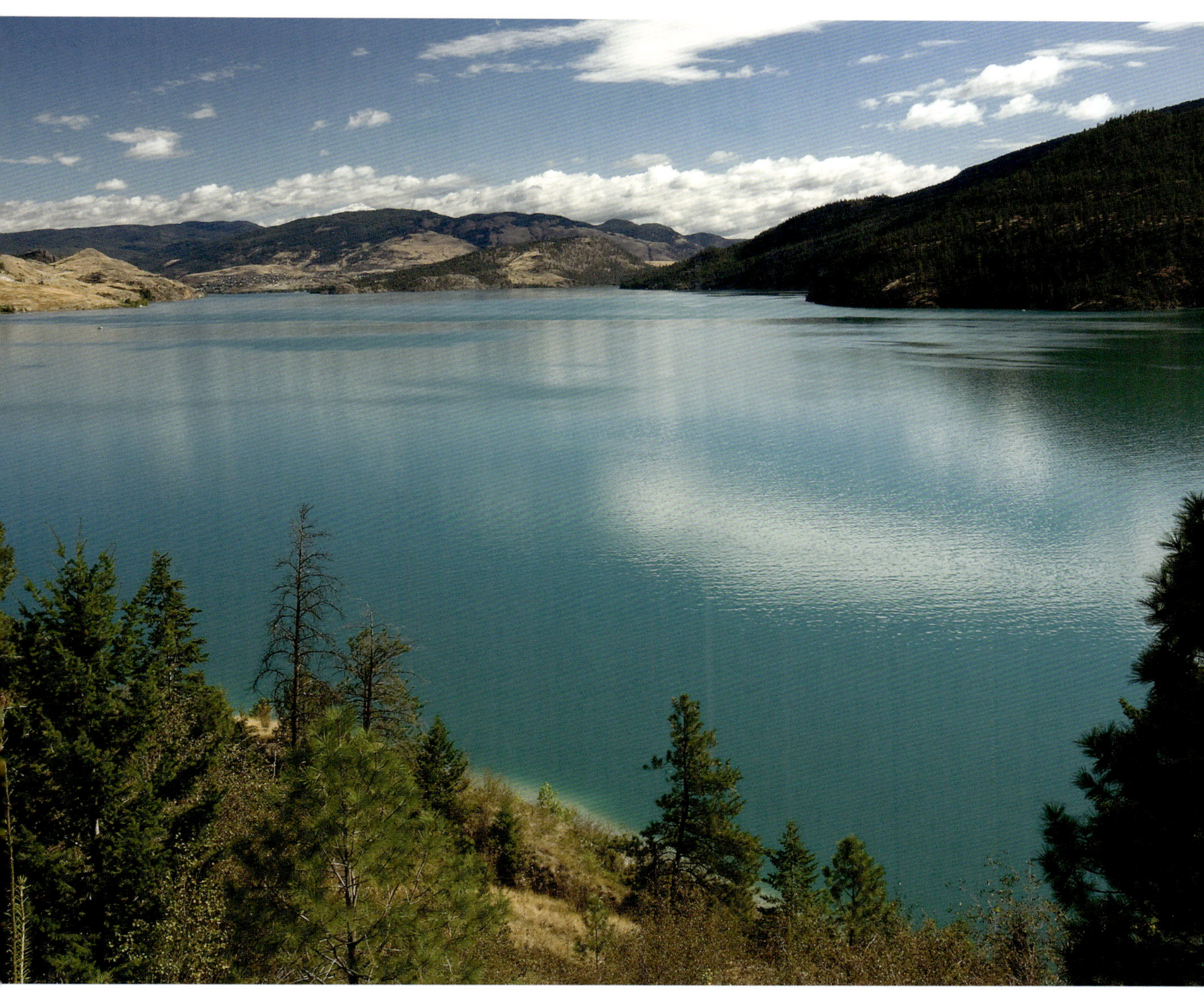

do so the snakes develop a new rattle segment, which they shake to warn people and other animals when they are too close. Detour around the snake, giving it a wide berth, and remember you are a visitor in its habitat. Proper footwear, such as boots that cover your ankles, is a good precaution to take while hiking in this area. Kalamalka Lake is a beautiful and welcoming place for a swim on a hot summer's day at one of the designated swimming sites. In the winter cross-country skiers may enjoy the trails around the park. Although the paths are not groomed, they can make for a lovely day of skiing in the right conditions.

↑ This marl lake turns a beautiful shade of blue during the summer months.

↖ Visitors may see arrowleaf balsamroot blooming alongside the trails.

← If you are approaching a rattlesnake you will soon know it by the warning sound it makes with its rattle.

Kentucky-Alleyne Provincial Park

An oasis of clear blue lakes amid cattle land provides habitat for birds, western toads and a variety of plants

What Makes This Hot Spot Hot?

- Open pine forests of the Okanagan-Similkameen surround two shimmering turquoise lakes.
- Conservation efforts have helped western toads flourish as they develop from tadpoles to toadlets in a small pond.
- Wildflowers, lichens and fungi are abundant throughout the forests.

Address: 6 km west of Hwy 5A on Bates Road, Aspen Grove, BC
Tel.: (250) 320-9305
Website:

BC Parks

GPS coordinates
Latitude: 49.90910
Longitude: –120.56552

Open year-round, but phone to ask about winter road conditions

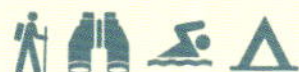

♿ **Check ahead**

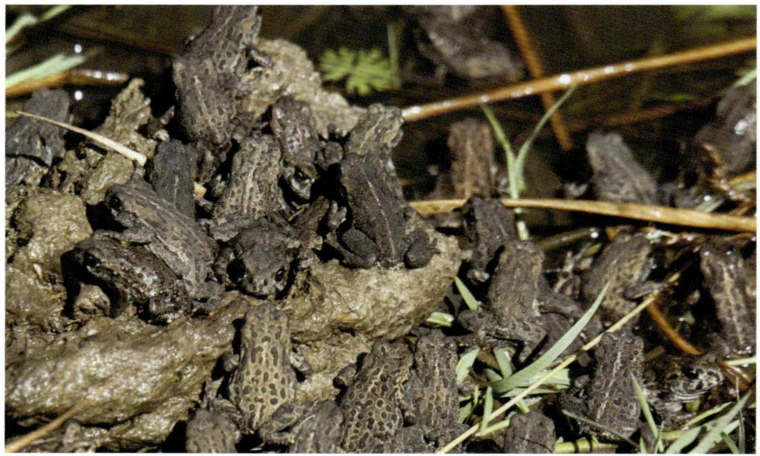

Alluring turquoise lakes and small marshy ponds provide important habitat for western toads and other species in dry Interior grasslands and forest. Surrounded by cattle country, Kentucky-Alleyne Provincial Park was established in 1981 to protect a truly remarkable ecosystem, which is home to waterfowl, western toads, flowers and fungi.

In forests of Douglas-fir and ponderosa pine, flowers bloom and fungi flourish. Bright yellow arnica lights up the forest floor. Wild roses bloom pink alongside wild strawberries, and fairyslippers. The trees are covered in a variety of lichens — an indicator of good air quality. For the fungi enthusiast, the forest is abundant in mushrooms. Polypores form shelves and bulbs on the trunks of coniferous trees, orange jelly spot fungi decorate logs, and the fruiting bodies of slippery jacks and other species pop up from the forest floor.

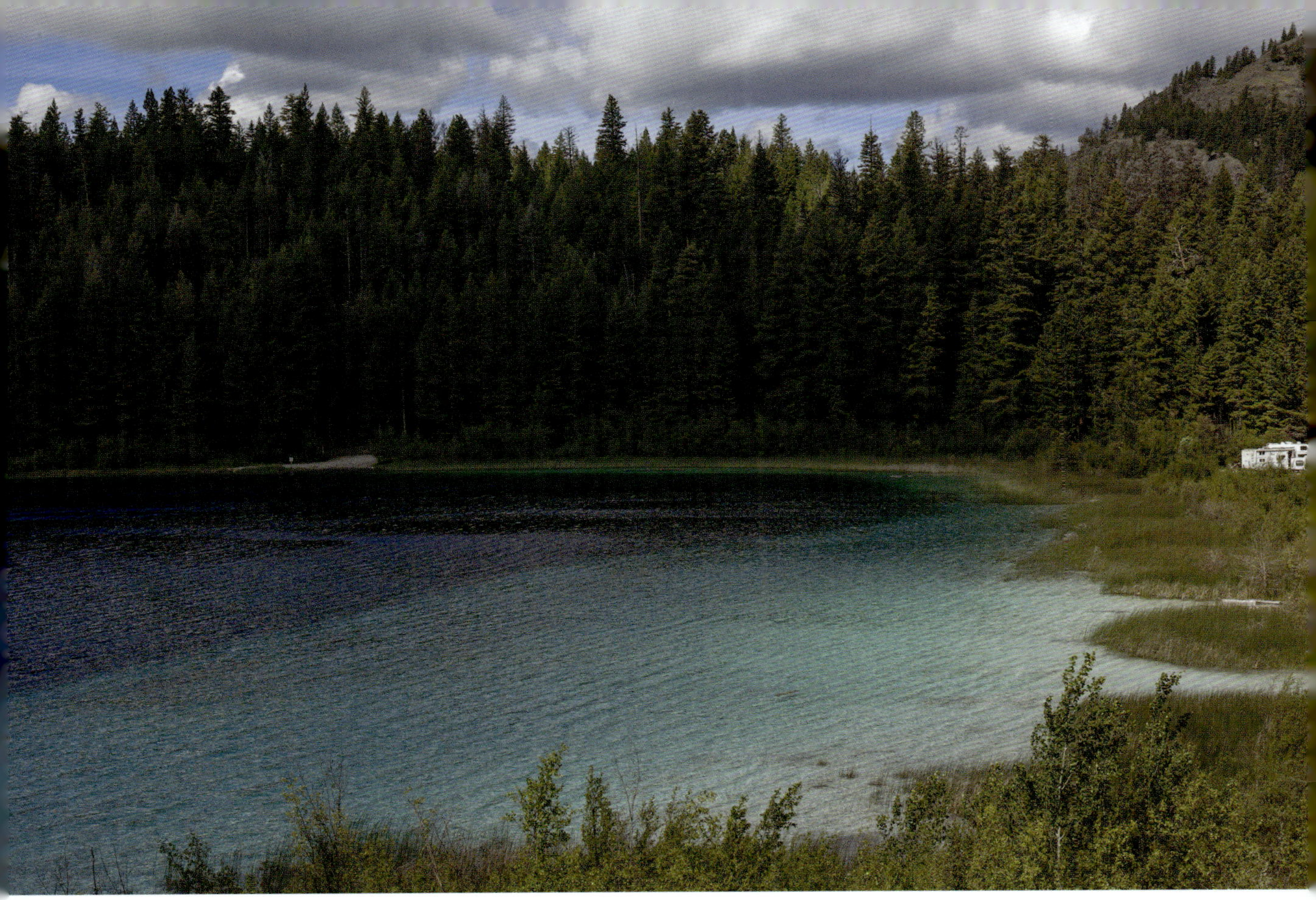

The western toad, a species of special concern, calls this forest home. The toads are an important part of the ecosystem, consuming insects and serving as a food source for snakes, coyotes and some birds. In early spring adult toads move from the forest to the warm shallow waters of the West Pond to breed and lay their eggs. By June tadpoles line the shallows, developing into toadlets by mid-July and August, when they are ready to make their way into the forest. In 2013 volunteers from the Nicola Naturalist Society installed a culvert to guide the toadlets under the road that separates the pond and forest, greatly increasing their chances of survival.

This diverse habitat makes for excellent birdwatching. Loons and other waterfowl are common sights on the lakes and ponds; yellow and MacGillivray's warblers have been seen in the grasses and bushes along the lakeshores; and hairy woodpeckers and great horned owls enjoy the coniferous forest. Between swimming, meandering the forest trails, birdwatching and perhaps sighting toads or tadpoles, this park is worth staying in for a couple of days. The campground does get busy in the summer, and it is worth booking ahead to ensure a site.

↑ The beautiful blue waters of Kentucky Lake are inviting for swimmers, boaters and birds.

← Western toadlets emerge from the west pond and make their way to the forest in the summer.

↓ A western toad in Kentucky-Alleyne Provincial Park.

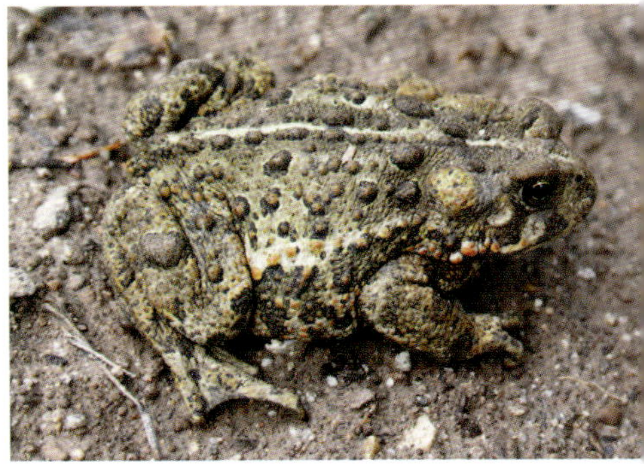

Knox Mountain

Friends of Knox Mountain advocate and practice stewardship, keeping the largest natural space in Kelowna visitor and wildlife friendly

What Makes This Hot Spot Hot?

- A spectacular array of flowers bloom in the spring and early summer.
- Visitors can drive, bike or hike to the top of Knox Mountain for beautiful views of the Okanagan Valley and the city of Kelowna.
- A variety of ecosystems within the park supports diverse wildlife close to Kelowna's downtown core.

Address: 450 Knox Mountain Drive, Kelowna, BC
Tel.: (250) 469-8800
Website:

City of Kelowna

GPS Coordinates
Latitude: 49.9087
Longitude: −119.49159

Open year-round

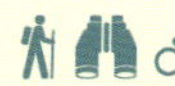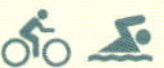

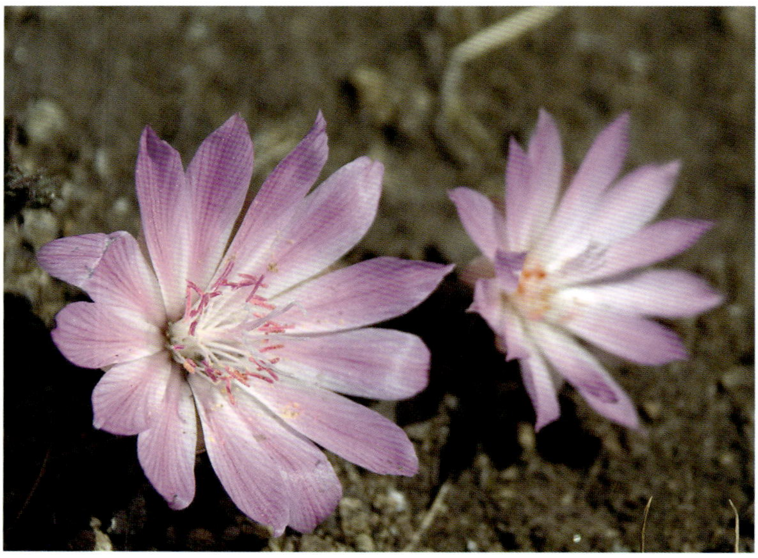

⌃ **The bitterroot flower blooms close to the ground.**

British Columbia usually evokes images of snow-peaked mountains and dense rainforests. However, the Okanagan and Similkameen valleys have something quite different to offer. At Knox Mountain, the largest natural space in Kelowna, an extensive trail system winds through a dry and delicate ecosystem composed of grasslands and pine and Douglas-fir trees. Just 3 kilometres north of downtown Kelowna, this park is an easily accessible natural oasis. For a space with so many visitors Knox Mountain is well preserved thanks to the Friends of Knox Mountain, who are in charge of the stewardship in the park.

During the spring and early summer months flowers bloom in the open, grassy fields. Dominated by arrowleaf balsamroot, arnica and brown-eyed Susan, the meadows are a charming display of green interlaced with striking yellow. Other flowers to look for include the purple sagebrush mariposa lily and the pink bitterroot, which

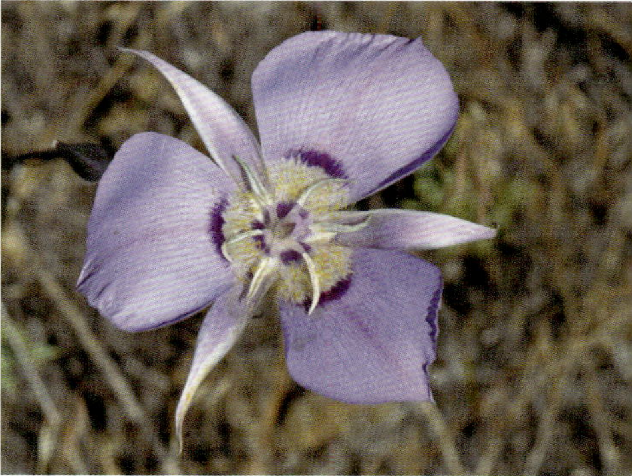

flowers low to the ground. Pricklypear cacti thrive in this environment and are well camouflaged on the dry ground.

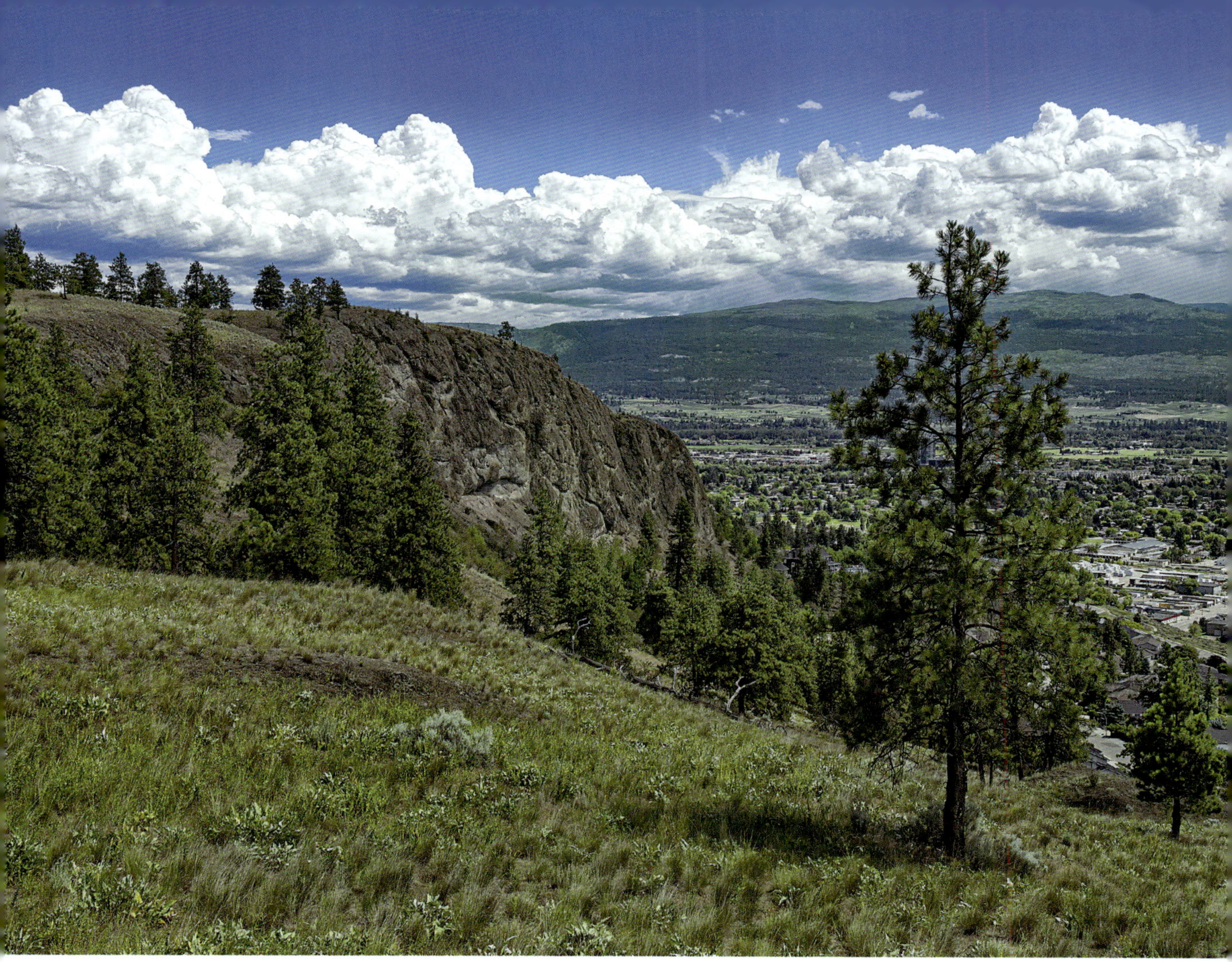

Beginning on the shores of the Lake Okanagan, the park rises 300 metres to the top of Knox Mountain. On the trail to Paul's Tomb, which is a rocky beach, hikers will stay on a relatively flat trail that passes through grassy fields into a cooler pine and fir forest. The beach itself is a flat rocky bay, a lovely place for an afternoon swim. Alternatively, other trails or the paved road that takes you farther into the park bring you to the top of the mountain, where there is a mixture of grasslands, trees and marshes. There are multiple lookout points over Kelowna and the Okanagan Valley as you ascend. The park is frequented by local birders in search of songbirds, like the western bluebird, the chestnut-backed chickadee and the western meadowlark. You may also encounter a yellow-bellied marmot or mule deer grazing in the meadows.

↑ **The view from Knox Mountain overlooking Kelowna.**

↓ **The sagebrush mariposa lily blooms early in the summer, adding a splash of purple to the grasslands.**

LAC DU BOIS GRASSLANDS PROTECTED AREA

Mara Hill

Uniquely adapted flora and fauna call these dry grasslands home

↗ **The brittle pricklypear cactus can be found in the middle grasslands of Lac du Bois.**

→ **An artistic composition of lichens paints the landscape of Mara Hill.**

On the south end of the 15,712-hectare Lac du Bois Grasslands Protected Area, the picturesque Mara Hill stands out with striking geological formations. Exposed basalt has created spectacular cliffs, and sediments that were deposited by ancient lakes are now visible in the form of hoodoos along the lower slopes of Mara Hill. These pillars of weathered volcanic rock create a stunning backdrop for this ecologically diverse habitat.

Although the canyons, cliffs and open vistas of this area may seem void of life at first glance, there is much to be discovered. Grasslands provide habitat for 30 per cent of British Columbia's at-risk species, while making up only 1 per cent of the land base. These important areas support an abundance of wildlife and have been a key focus of conservation efforts for rare species, like the sharp-tailed grouse.

Just north of the railway tracks on Tranquille Road, Cinnamon Ridge Trail and Mara Trail are two of the most easily accessible hikes in the park. The trails provide excellent opportunities for viewing wildlife while admiring the unique geology of the area and the beautiful views of the surrounding grasslands. The trails in this area become more challenging as the elevation increases, so steady feet and good hiking shoes are required. In the hot summer months keep your eyes peeled

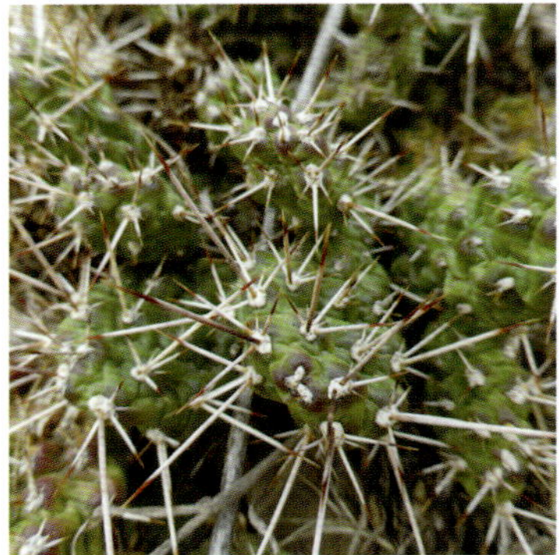

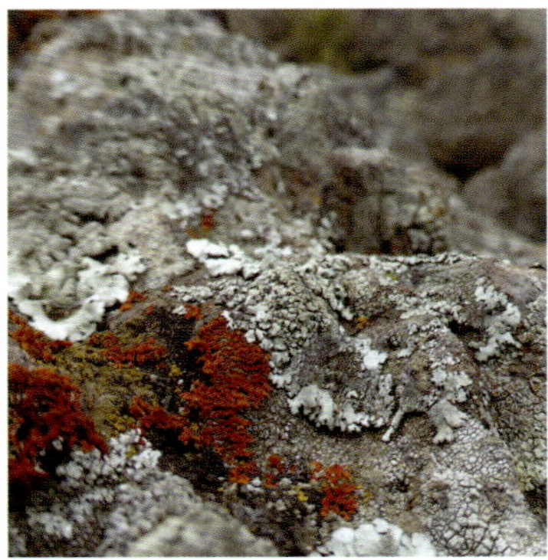

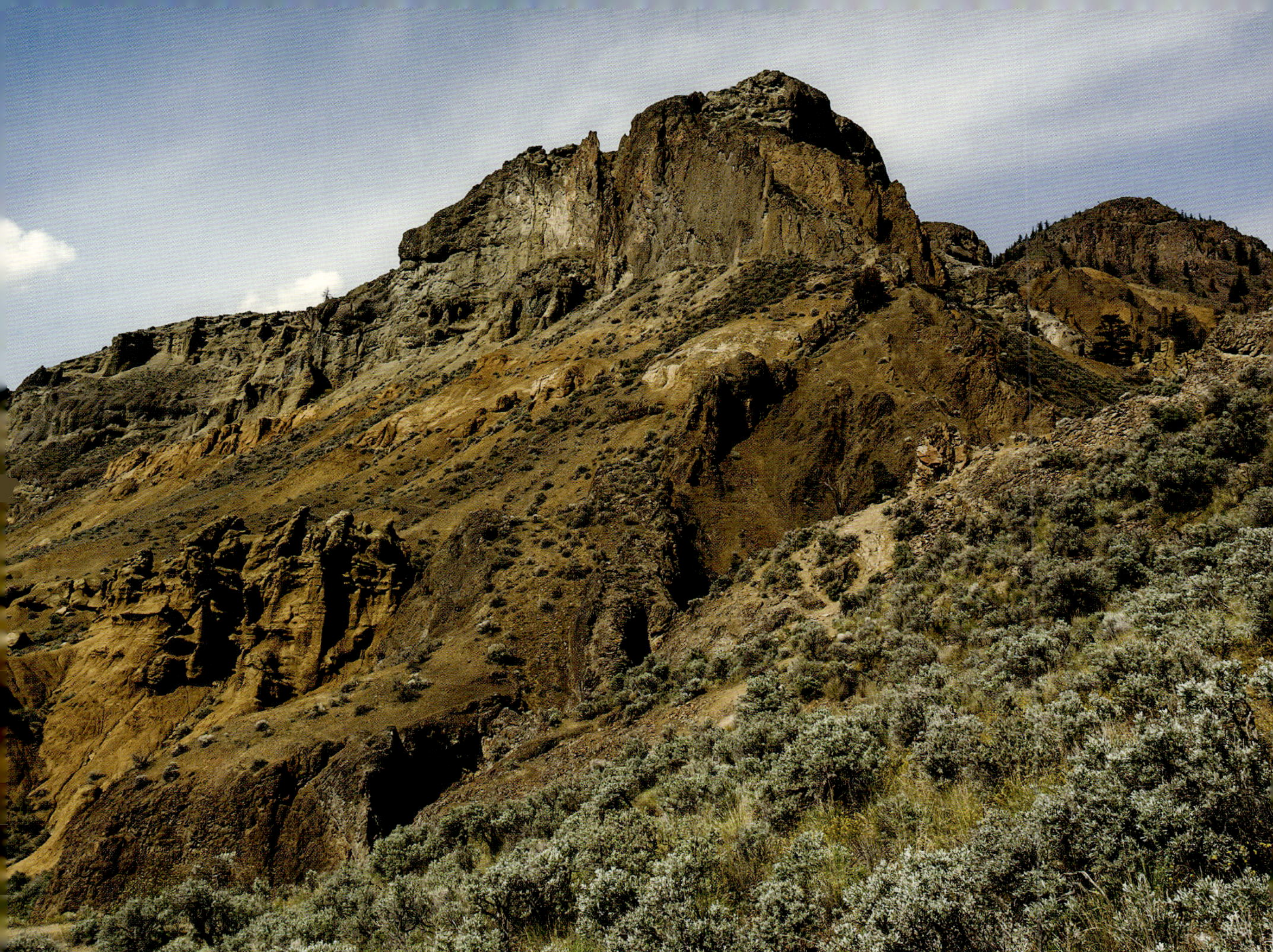

for the shy western rattle-snake, waiting out the sun to hunt in the cooler night.

The hot, dry climate leaves a harsh and delicate ecosystem with poor soil development, which makes for some unique local organisms. The bunchgrasses that cover the landscape are supported by a fragile layer of lichens, mosses and cyanobacteria. This cryptogamic crust helps retain moisture while stabilizing and fertilizing the soil. For this reason, it is critical that visitors stay on the trail.

Many plants here, like the big sagebrush, common rabbitbrush and prairie sagewort, have a distinct silvery look to them. This is due to tiny hairs covering their leaves, a trait that reduces water loss in this harsh climate. California bighorn sheep can often be seen on the slopes of Mara Hill or at nearby Dewdrop Cliffs. If you are lucky, you might be able to catch a glimpse of the blue-listed Lewis's woodpecker. This salmon-bellied bird may be seen behaving more like a flycatcher than a woodpecker as it captures meals on the wing.

↑ The release of iron from the volcanic rock gives Cinnamon Ridge its name, one of the amazing geological features of the beautiful and barren-looking grassland.

Mission Creek Greenway

A river runs through a variety of ecosystems that have many wildlife-viewing opportunities

Gaining momentum from a large watershed, Mission Creek moves through 43 kilometres of diverse ecosystems until it empties into Okanagan Lake. The Mission Creek Greenway is a trail system that runs alongside just over 15 kilometres of this waterway. This creek is an important breeding ground for the kokanee salmon, a landlocked species of sockeye salmon that spends its life in freshwater lakes. These fish were of great importance to the Okanagan First Nations, who would use the spawning season as an opportunity to harvest the fish, preserving them for the winter. In the 1950s the city dyked and altered the river in an attempt to reduce seasonal flooding. This caused the kokanee salmon population to plummet, which makes it all the more important for us to protect our watersheds from pollution.

The gravel walkway is largely shaded by deciduous trees that showcase their shades of orange, yellow and red leaves in the fall. The sight is so stunning that many Okanagan photographers choose this area as a location for engagement and other professional photo shoots.

As the greenway encompasses such a large area and so many habitats, it is an excellent place to spot a large variety of birds, particularly owls. Well hidden during the day five owl species, including the great horned owl, western screech owl and long-eared owl can all be found calling and hunting after dark.

At first glance the ground beneath the trees appears to be made up of only grass,

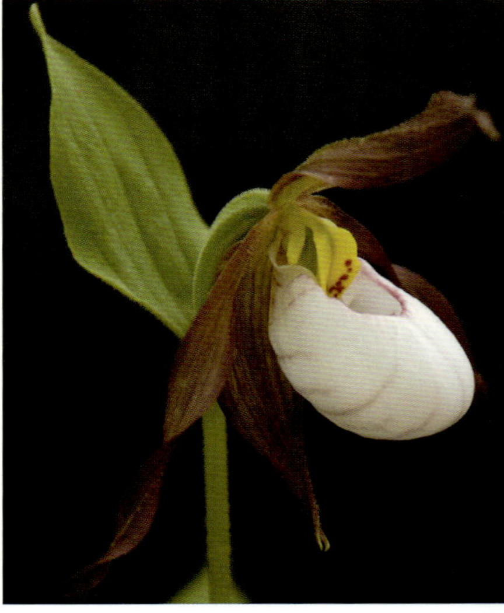

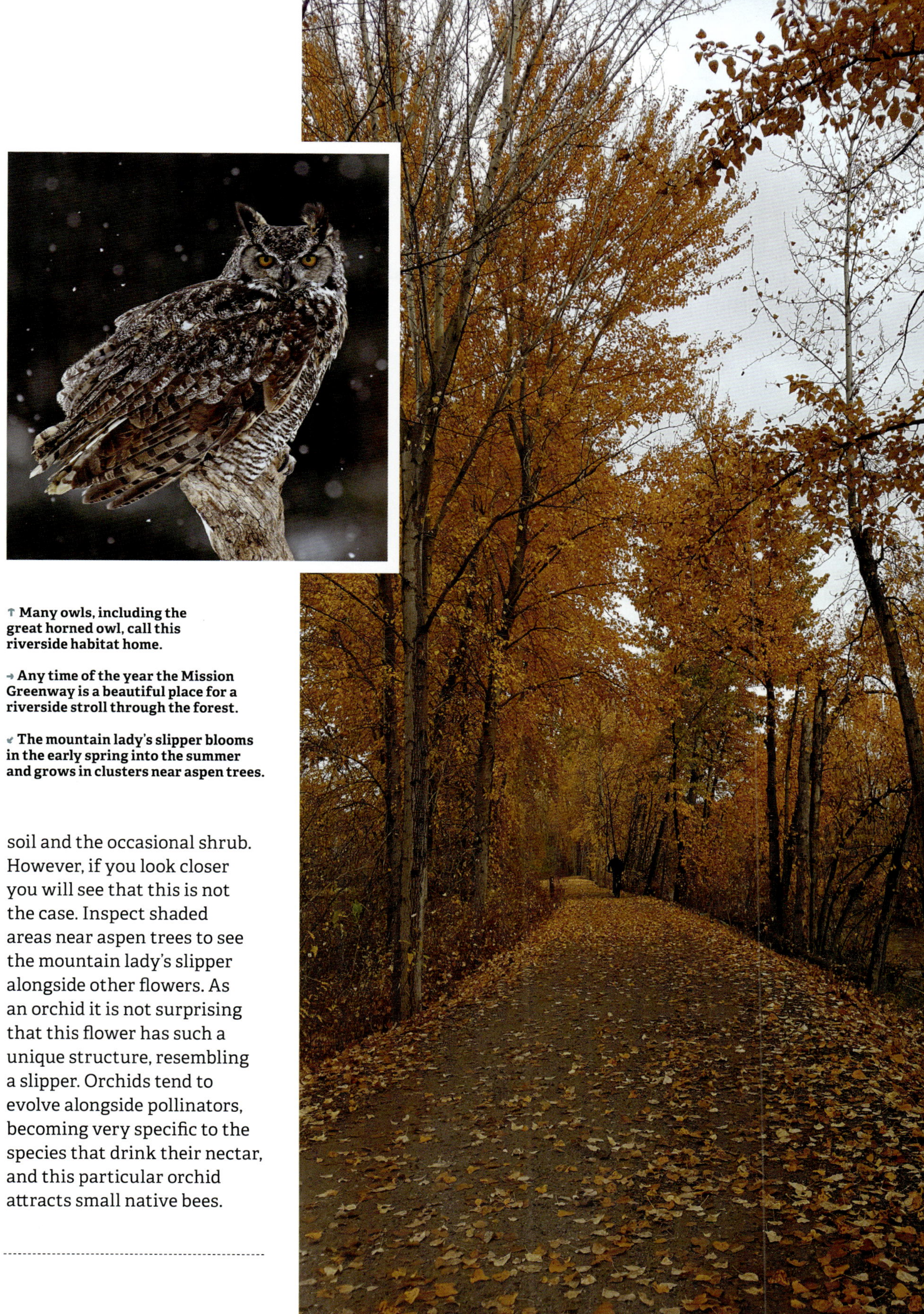

soil and the occasional shrub. However, if you look closer you will see that this is not the case. Inspect shaded areas near aspen trees to see the mountain lady's slipper alongside other flowers. As an orchid it is not surprising that this flower has such a unique structure, resembling a slipper. Orchids tend to evolve alongside pollinators, becoming very specific to the species that drink their nectar, and this particular orchid attracts small native bees.

SOUTH OKANAGAN GRASSLANDS AND PROTECTED AREA

Mount Kobau

At the top of a mountain in a desert lies a secluded haven for stargazers

What Makes This Hot Spot Hot?

- Stargazers can search the night sky for constellations from the top of a mountain at one of the premier stargazing spots in Canada.
- From a viewpoint small, coloured pools give Kliluk Lake a spotted appearance during the summer.
- Visitors can hike through a protected ecosystem inhabited by rare desert plants.

Address: South Okanagan Grasslands and Protected Area, Cawston, BC
Tel.: (1-800) 689-9025
Website:

BC Parks

GPS Coordinates
Latitude: 49.11105
Longitude: −119.66694

Open year-round

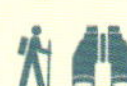

↗ **The Brewer's sparrow is very well adapted to, and even dependant on, this ecosystem.**

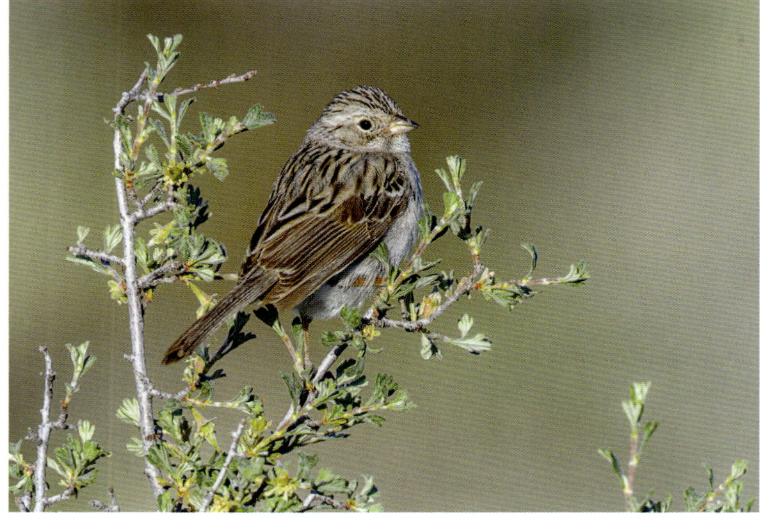

One of four sites that compose the South Okanagan Grasslands Protected Area, Mount Kobau is well known as a stargazing destination. A drive or hike up the mountain gives visitors access to a panoramic view of the Okanagan Valley, which is beautiful both day and night. To protect the endangered ecosystem of dry grasslands this provincial park was established as a conservation area in 2001.

At night the vast sky is painted with stars, making Mount Kobau one of the best stargazing sites in Canada.

At the summit the sky is an uninterrupted canvas for starry nights. An annual stargazing event is held on the mountain summit every summer. There is a rough road through open pine forests and fields of desert flowers that ends in a parking lot close to the summit. From the parking lot walking trails meander around the mountain; an additional kilometre of established trail leads to the summit.

Bighorn sheep and sagebrush find protection here, but the park is also home to some of Canada's smaller treasures. Look closely at the

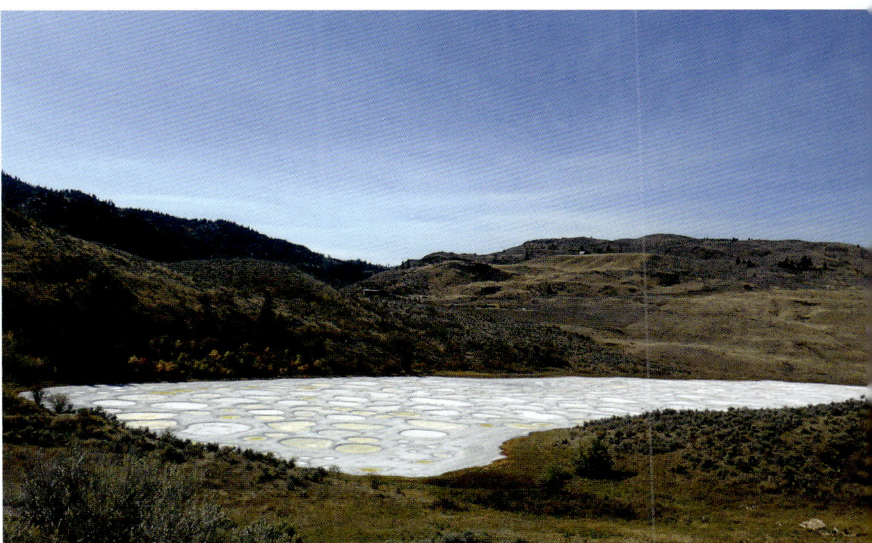

lichen coating trees and rocks and you may spot species that are new to scientists. One of the most impressive animals of the area is the Brewer's sparrow, a desert-adapted bird that can live for a week or more without a drink of water. These birds are dependant on the sagebrush for nesting habitat and materials, as well as a place to eat and sleep.

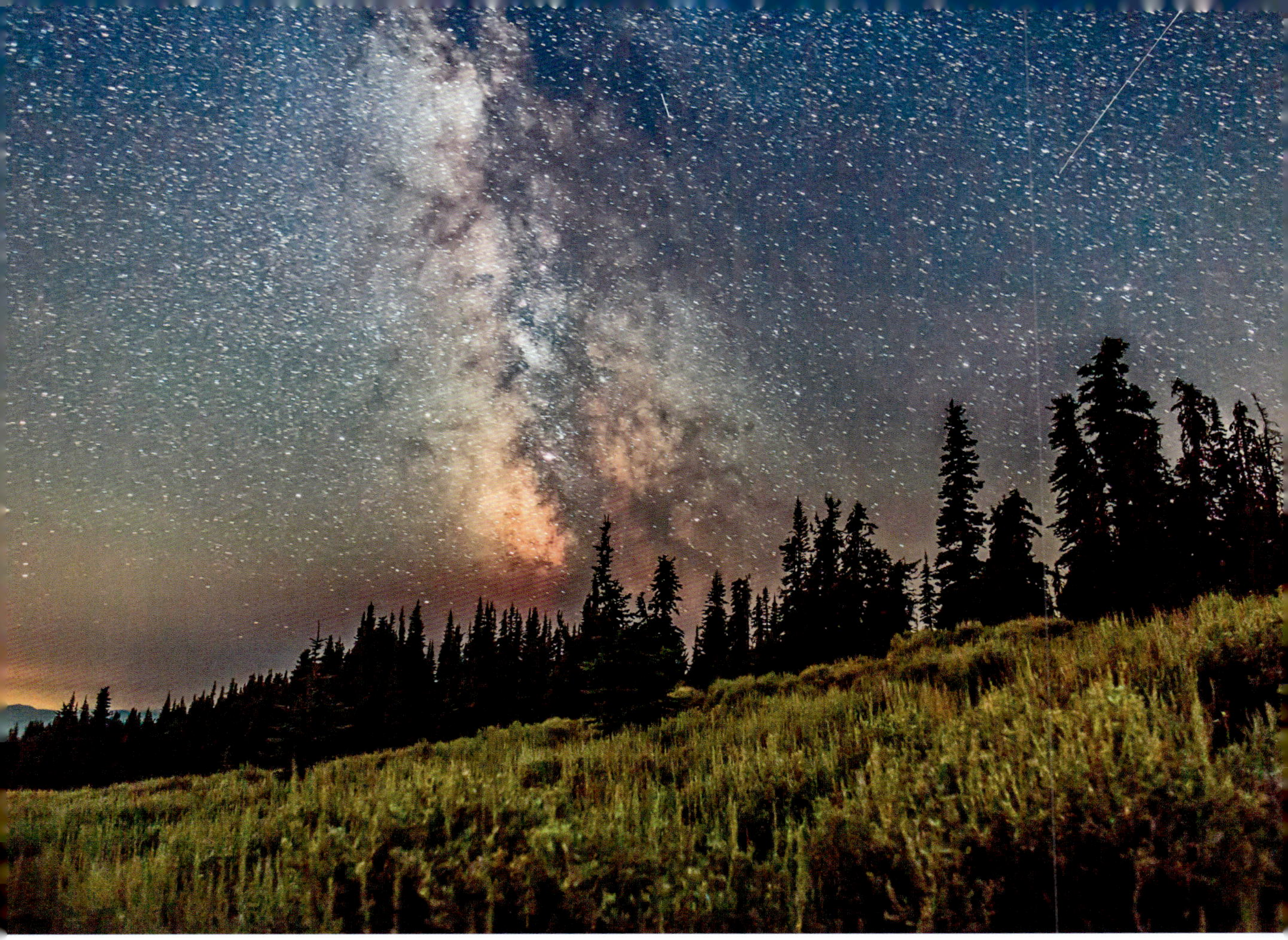

Although not technically in the protected area, Kliluk Lake, sometimes referred to as Spotted Lake, can be seen from the summit and is worth a closer look. During the summer much of the water in the lake evaporates. The mineral-rich lakebed is left with different coloured pools, which give the lake a unique spotted pattern. The lake was an important place of healing to the Okanagan First Nations.

Skaha Bluffs Provincial Park

Towering cliffs and shaded valleys provide important habitat for animals big and small

What Makes This Hot Spot Hot?

- The park is a protected area and important migration corridor for bighorn sheep.
- Visitors can take in panoramic views of Skaha Lake and the city of Penticton atop rocky bluffs.
- This is a geological paradise that is ideal for cliff-dwelling birds and bats.

Address: Smythe Drive, Penticton, BC
Tel.: (250) 548-0076
Website:

BC Parks

GPS Coordinates
Latitude: 49.4307
Longitude: −119.56393

Open March 1 to November 15

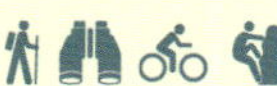

→ **Forests and grasslands surrounded by rocky cliffs are characteristic of Skaha.**

Named for the rocky bluffs that define the surrounding landscape, Skaha Bluffs Provincial Park is a place of geological interest to naturalists and rock climbers from around the world. Visitors can walk on a trail system that passes through valleys carved by the ebb and flow of glaciers and gaze upon rocky outcrops that provide habitat to a variety of birds as well as four bat species. White-throated swifts dart in and out of rock cavities, and the call of the western screech owl echoes through the canyons. Particularly well adapted to this environment is the canyon wren. With a low centre of gravity and large feet, this songbird scales rock faces with ease, thrusting its narrow head into rock holes as it forages for insects.

From the parking lot, the park's trails move through dry grasslands with shallow, rocky soil and pine forests. If you are lucky you may see bighorn sheep grazing in the grasslands. This is an important protected habitat for these aptly named sheep — their horns can weigh up to 14 kilograms. Also keep an eye out for western rattlesnakes basking on sun-heated rocks. A blotchy, brown snake with a large triangular head, this species is easily recognizable by the rattle on its tail. Each time a rattlesnake sheds its skin a new segment of its rattle is produced. Rattlesnakes are not aggressive and will only bite in defense. If you do see one remember you are in its home. Give it space and either backtrack

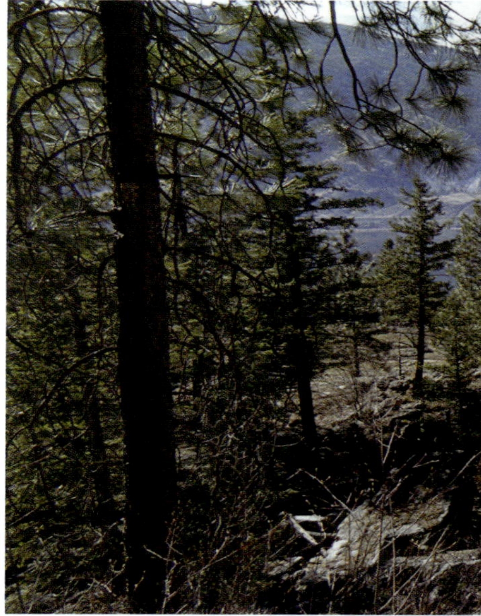

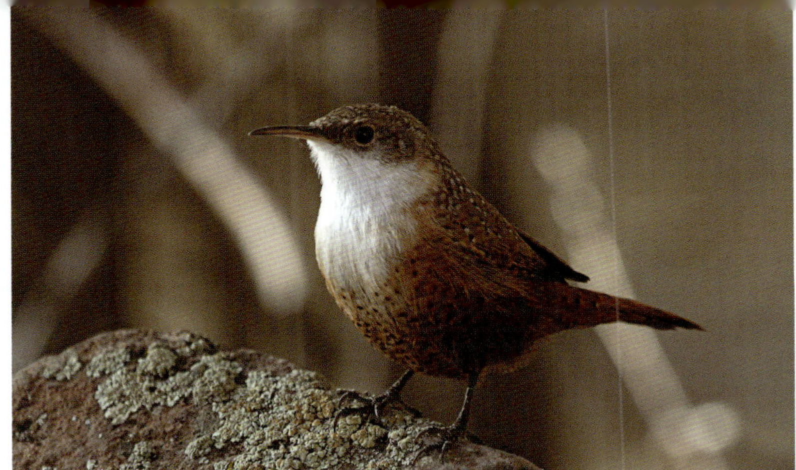

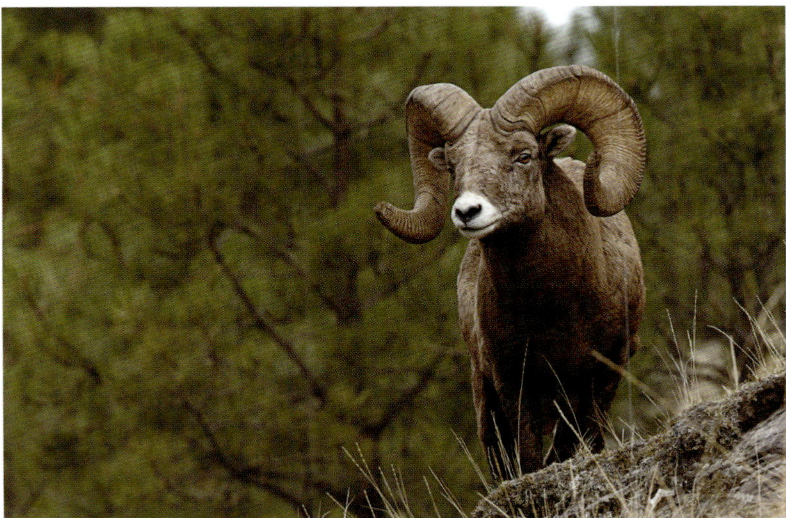

or go around it if possible.

As the trails make their way into the park's shaded valleys, the vegetation changes dramatically. An abundance of greenery surrounds the low points of the valley where water gathers. This habitat is ideal for the Pacific chorus frog. Although it can be found quite far from water, it relies on small pools for breeding. Look for this small, bright-green frog on the ground or climbing up short plants.

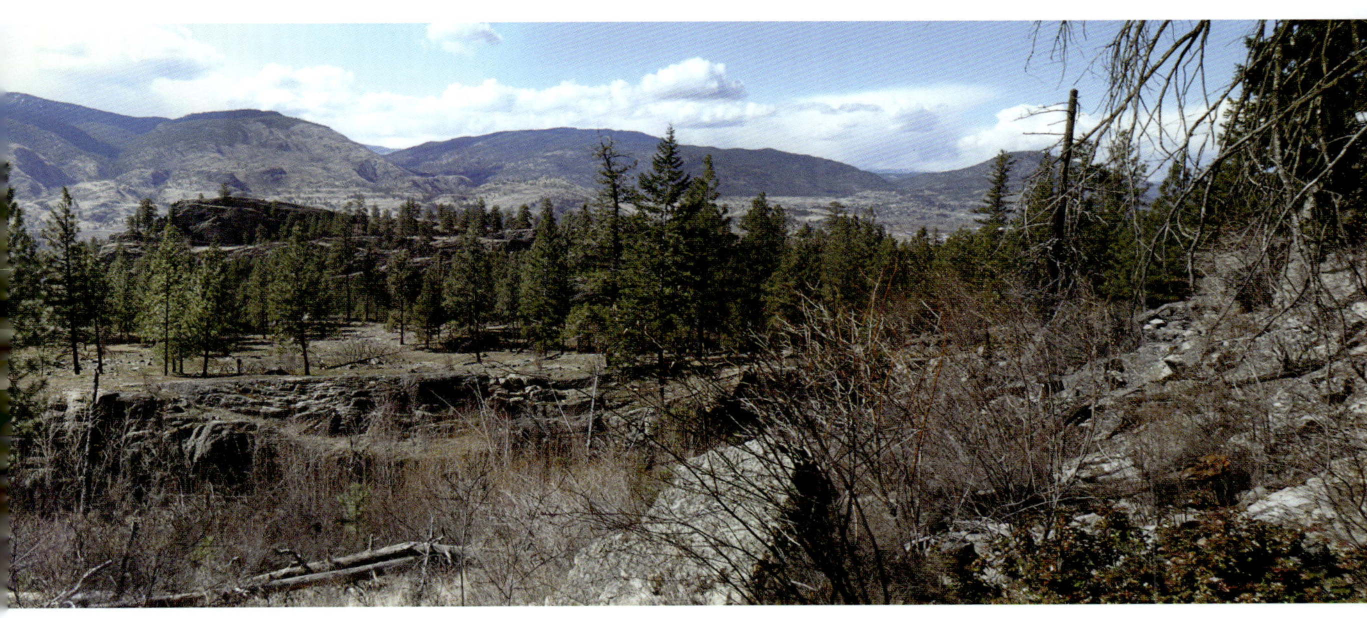

sẁiẁs Provincial Park

Previously known as Haynes Point, this park protects many rare amphibian, plant and bird species

What Makes This Hot Spot Hot?

- The park is located on a peninsula that connects to a sandbar, which creates a land bridge and makes the lake crossable by foot.
- The calliope hummingbird, Canada's smallest hummingbird, calls this park home.
- Unique hardy plants thrive in the dry, desert-like conditions of this park.

Address: 32nd Avenue, Osoyoos, BC
Tel.: (778) 437-2295
Website:

BC Parks

GPS Coordinates
Latitude: 49.01483
Longitude: −119.45769

Open year-round

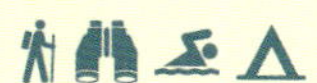

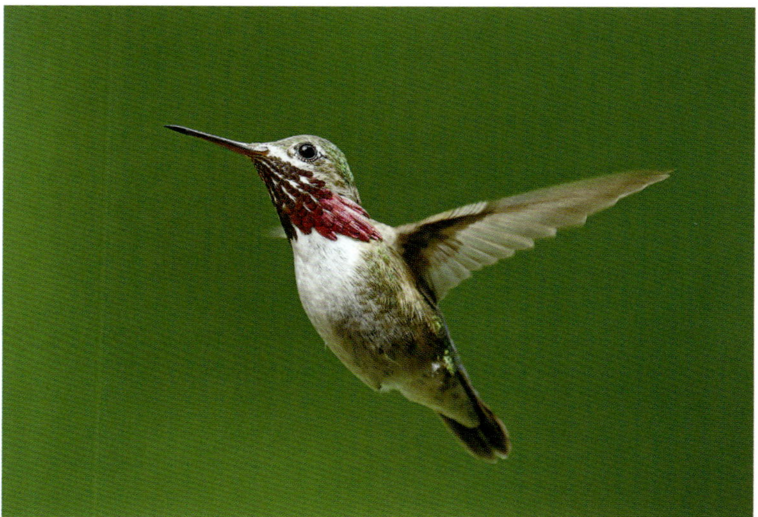

↗ **The calliope hummingbird is the smallest hummingbird in Canada.**

Upon the discovery of an important archaeological site containing the remains of the Osoyoos Indian Band's Okanagan ancestors, management of this provincial park was handed from BC Parks to the Osoyoos Indian Band. The name was changed from Haynes Point to sẁiẁs Provincial Park, the Okanagan First Peoples' name for the area. sẁiẁs, meaning "a shallow or narrow place in the middle of a lake," refers to the traditional crossing point of Osoyoos Lake by foot or on horseback. The park is situated on a peninsula that extends almost completely across the lake. The tip of the peninsula meets a shallow sandbar that continues to the other side.

sẁiẁs Park is a popular site for birders, plant enthusiasts and those interested in herpetology, the study of amphibians and reptiles. Containing dry grasslands, this small desert park attracts flocks of lakeshore and marshland birds. Alongside marsh wrens, yellow-headed blackbirds and families of quails, Canada's smallest hummingbird, the calliope hummingbird, calls this park home. They may be small, but the bright purple throat is difficult to miss. Lookout towers and benches along the 2-kilometre trail ensure many opportunities to view wildlife.

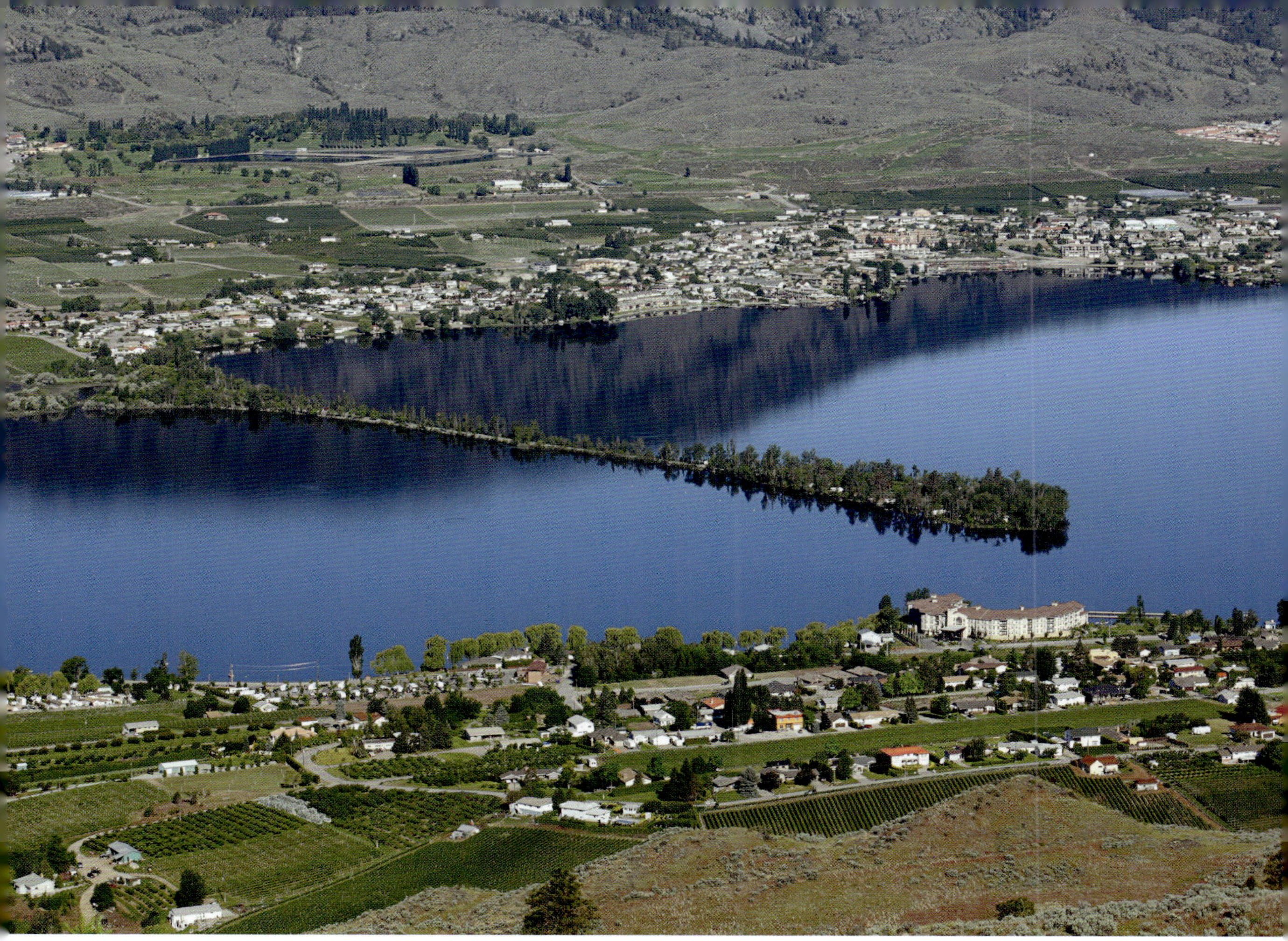

A marshy haven within the dry desert, this park was initially established in an effort to protect its desert plants. Species such as bushy cinquefoil, awned cyperus and peach leaf willow flourish in this environment. Alongside these plants, the park also provides refuge to a number of endangered animals, such as the blotched tiger salamander.

Although this red-listed amphibian spends much of its life seeking shade in underground burrows or beneath stumps, it is sometimes seen by lucky visitors. Painted turtles are much less elusive, openly sunbathing on logs in the marsh. As you walk the trails, tread lightly and look for the spadefoot toad before it burrows into the mud with its spade-shaped hind legs. The amount of amphibian and aquatic reptile species supported by this otherwise dry environment speaks to the park's continued importance as a protected area.

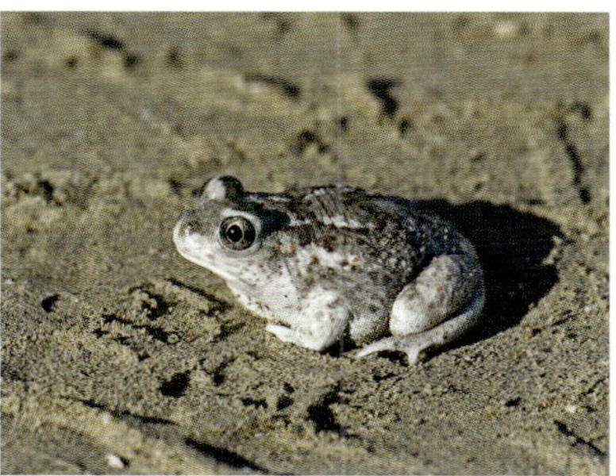

↑ The spadefoot toad is one of the amphibians found in the wetlands of the park.

↖ The peninsula on which the park sits spans nearly the entire width of Osoyoos Lake.

Tsútswecw Provincial Park

Millions of sockeye salmon migrate back to the waters where they were born to start the life cycle once more

What Makes This Hot Spot Hot?

- The park is home to one of the largest sockeye salmon runs in North America.
- Every fourth year is a dominant run, when millions of salmon return to spawn.
- Important riparian habitat supports many species on land and in the water.

Address: 5 km north of Squilax on Squilax-Anglemont Road, BC
Tel.: (250) 955-0861
Website:

BC Parks

GPS Coordinates
Latitude: 50.91783
Longitude: −119.62511

Open year-round

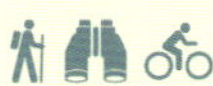

(Check ahead)

→ Sockeye salmon travel the river to find an area with the right conditions, where each female lays thousands of eggs.

There are many notable rivers to view the spectacular salmon runs that occur throughout British Columbia, but the Adams River hosts one of the most impressive. A trip to Tsútswecw Provincial Park in the fall provides opportunities to see multiple species of salmon travelling up the river to spawn, including coho, pink and chinook varieties. The truly astounding event, however, is the sockeye run.

The most famous and brilliantly coloured salmon species in BC, sockeye return to the Adams River to spawn in the same fresh waters they were born. Retracing the path they navigated to reach the ocean years earlier, these salmon travel thousands of kilometres to the alluvial gravel riverbeds of this area, which creates an ideal habitat for developing salmon.

Although some sockeye return to the river each year, every fourth year is a dominant year, and the number of returning salmon is staggering. This four-year pattern is thanks to a phenomenon called cyclic dominance,

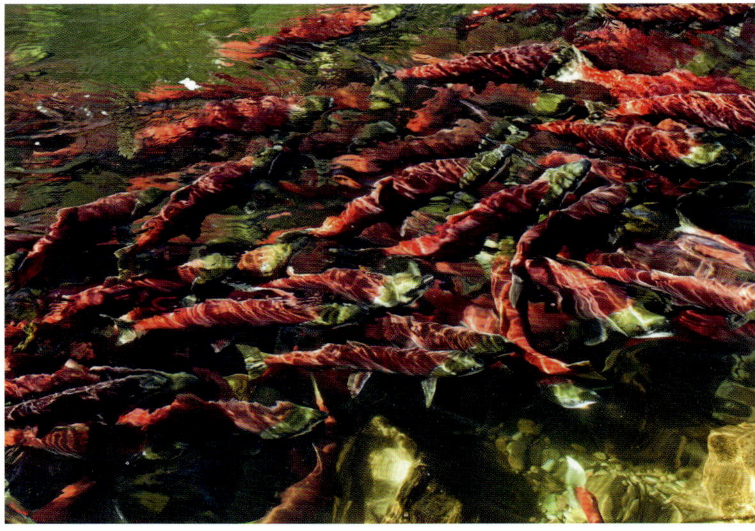

where most offspring produced in any one brood return to spawn four years later, although they may be mature anywhere between the ages of 2 and 6 years old. The next major spawning run is anticipated for 2026, but the subdominant run the year following each dominant run is still exciting, with hundreds of thousands of salmon returning to these waters.

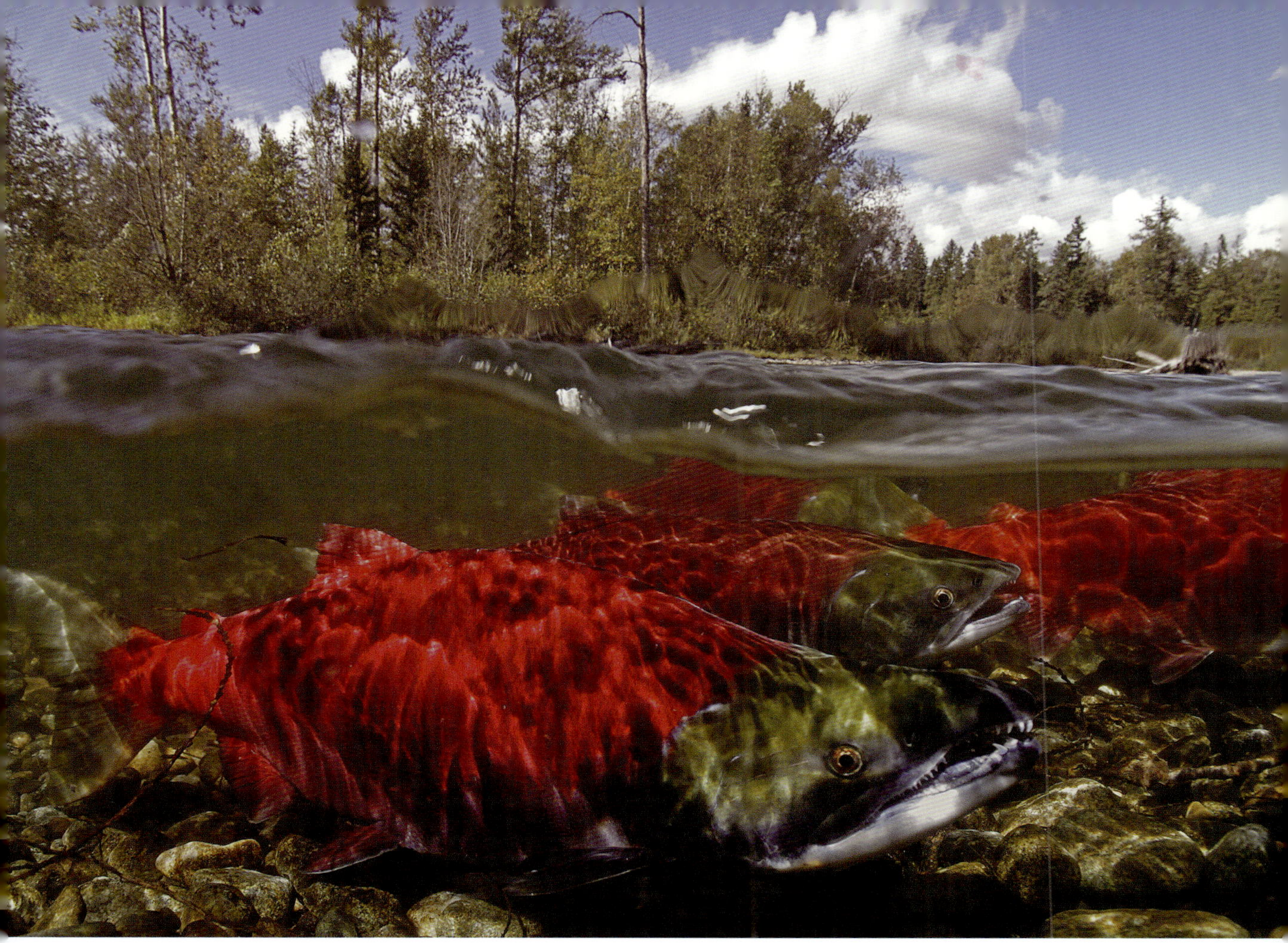

While the salmon spectacle is definitely a must-see, Tsútswecw Provincial Park is an excellent place to visit any time of year, with 26 kilometres of trails to explore. The park protects 11 kilometres of critically important habitat along the riverbank, and the dying bodies of the mated salmon replenish the system and provide vital nutrients to support the surrounding terrestrial ecosystem. During dominant years, visit the park in the first three weeks of October to witness the sockeye spawning; other species of salmon can be seen spawning slightly earlier in the season. A large viewing platform offers a prime spot to watch, as the salmon search for the perfect place to lay their eggs.

↑ **Spawning male sockeye salmon develop a brilliant red body, humped back, green head and hooked beak.**

↓ **Bald eagles visit the river during the spawning season for a fishy feast.**

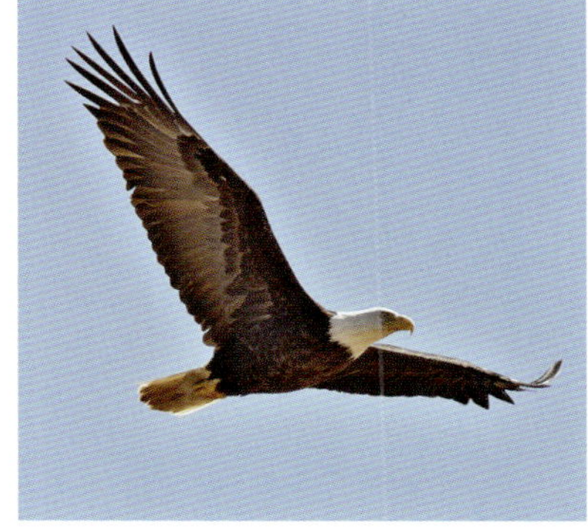

UBC Okanagan Trails

This trail system is an excellent example of how a university can incorporate green spaces

What Makes This Hot Spot Hot?

- From early morning bird walks to a stroll through the forest or alongside a pond, these trails have plenty to enjoy.
- The trails offer an immersive natural experience on a university campus and close to the city of Kelowna.
- Approximately 170 species of plants and animals exist on and around the trails.

Address: 3333 University Way, Kelowna, BC
Tel.: (250) 807-8000
Website:

UBC Okanagan Campus

GPS Coordinates
Latitude: 49.93986
Longitude: –119.39671

Open year-round

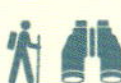

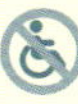

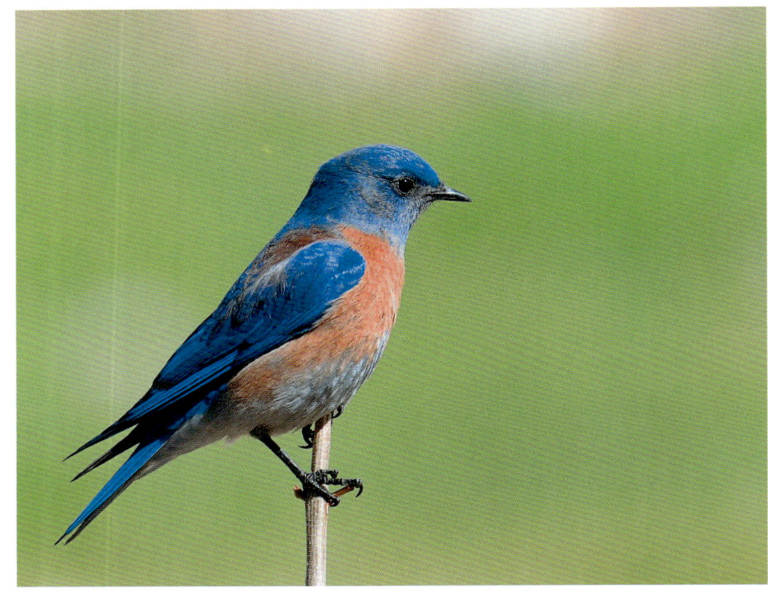

↗ **Western bluebirds enjoy the open spaces in nearby fields.**

Their ease of access and wild biodiversity make the UBC Okanagan Trails a joy for Kelowna locals. The trails may be on the University of British Columbia's Okanagan campus, but the university welcomes the sensitive use and enjoyment of its campus trail system by Okanagan residents as well as visitors. Although the trails are less than 2 kilometres long, they meander through a wide variety of habitats.

The Old Pond Trail, which loops around a gorgeous little pond teeming with life, is just steps off a paved road. Once you hear the red-winged blackbirds start calling through the reeds that line the pond's edge, it is easy to feel immersed in nature. In the evening great horned owls can be heard from the trees, and bats swoop down to drink from the pond before their nightly hunt for insects.

North of the campus the Pine Trail loop takes off into the forest and is connected

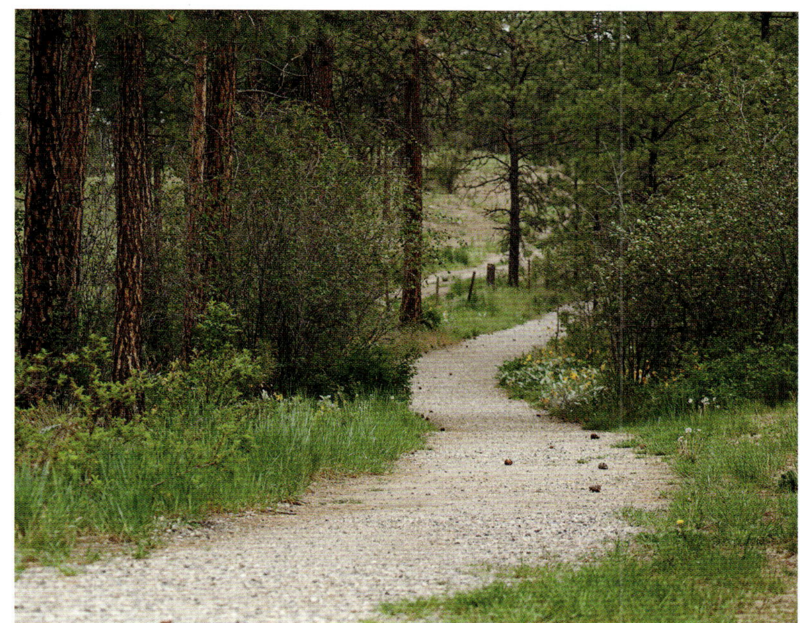

to the Old Pond Trail by the Juniper Trail. The Pine Trail borders green spaces and connects to trails around Robert Lake. The trail is also a sanctuary for early morning birding and afternoon strolls. Pine siskins and downy woodpeckers, among other birds, can be heard calling in the forest. Bring binoculars to gaze at the bordering fields where western bluebirds are often perched along fences.

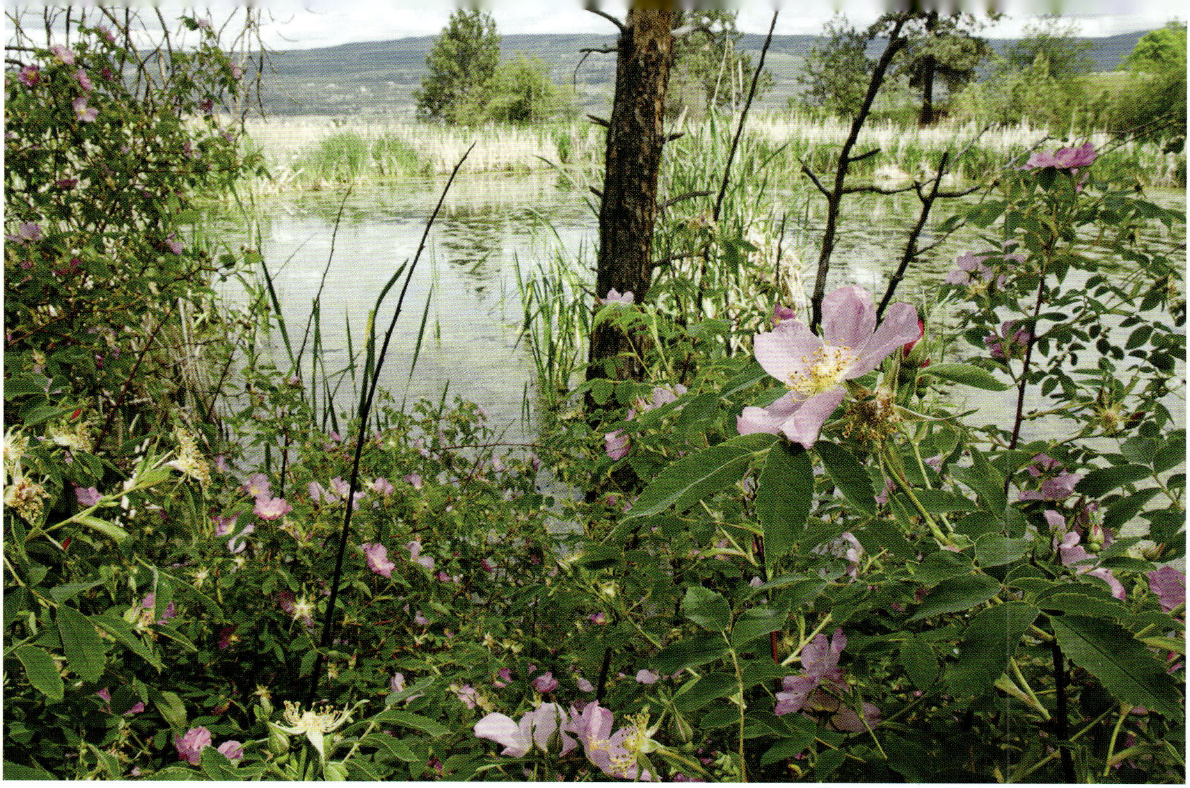

Insects are found during the warmer months on any of the trails. Mourning cloak butterflies, with their brown wings with white and blue markings, and cabbage white butterflies may be seen fluttering about. Look closely at the trees and ground and you will see many species of lichen, fungi and moss in this pine forest. In a 2015 survey of the area, 170 species were found on and around these trails. The campus is easily accessible by bus, but if you are driving, note that paid parking is in effect 24 hours.

↑ **Listen for the call of birds in the dry pine forests.**

↖ **The Old Pond Trail, a short walk from the bustling campus, feels secluded and hosts many plants and animals.**

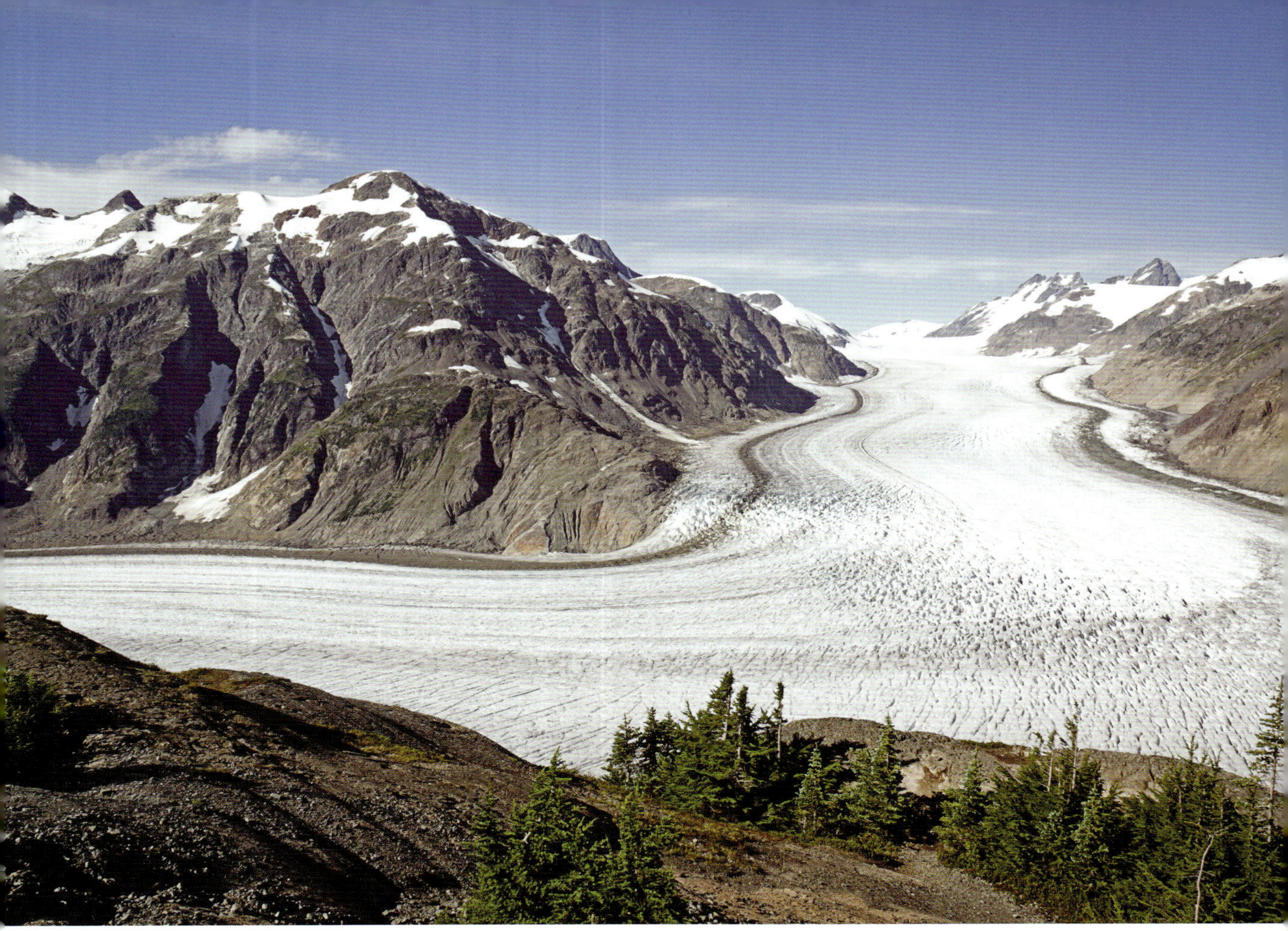

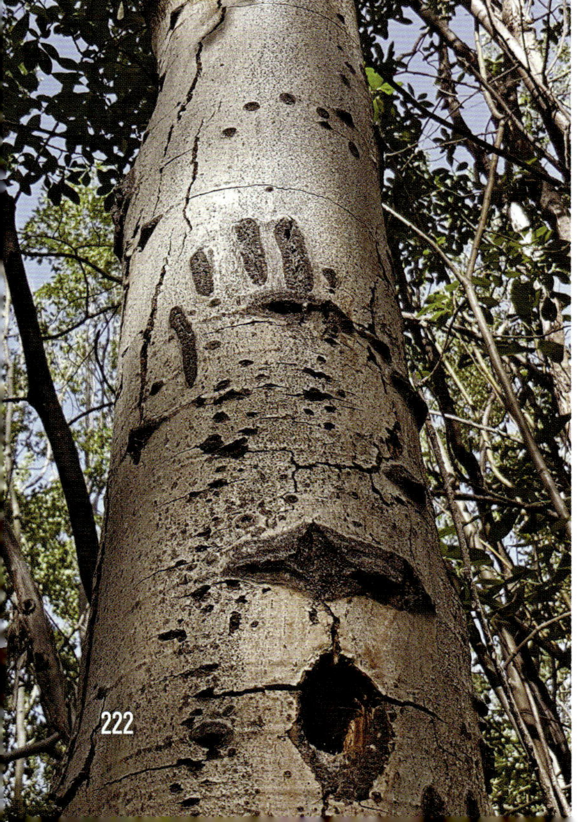
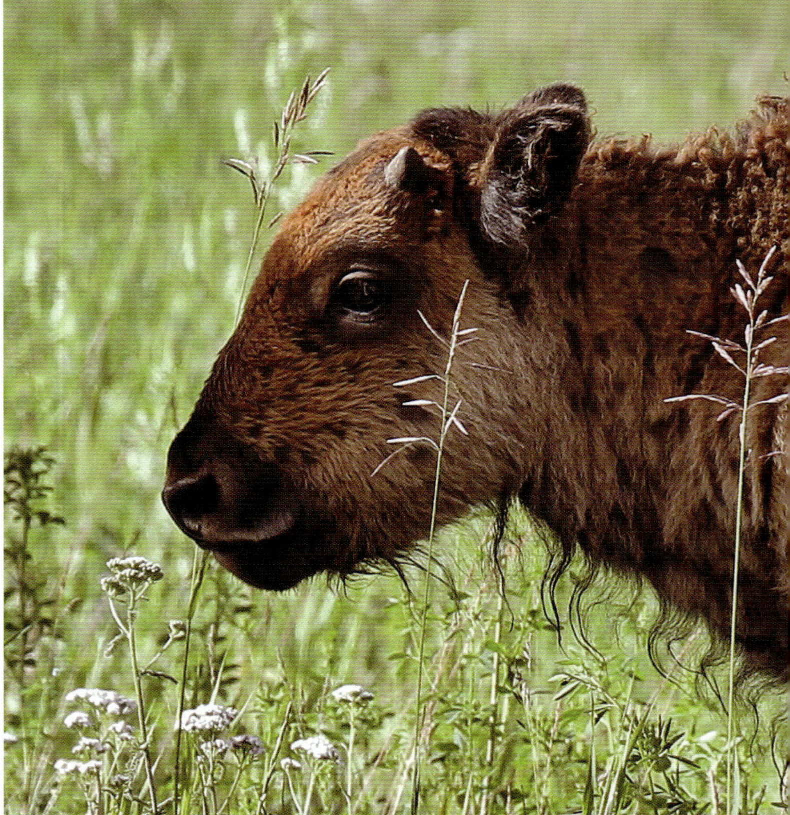

Northern British Columbia

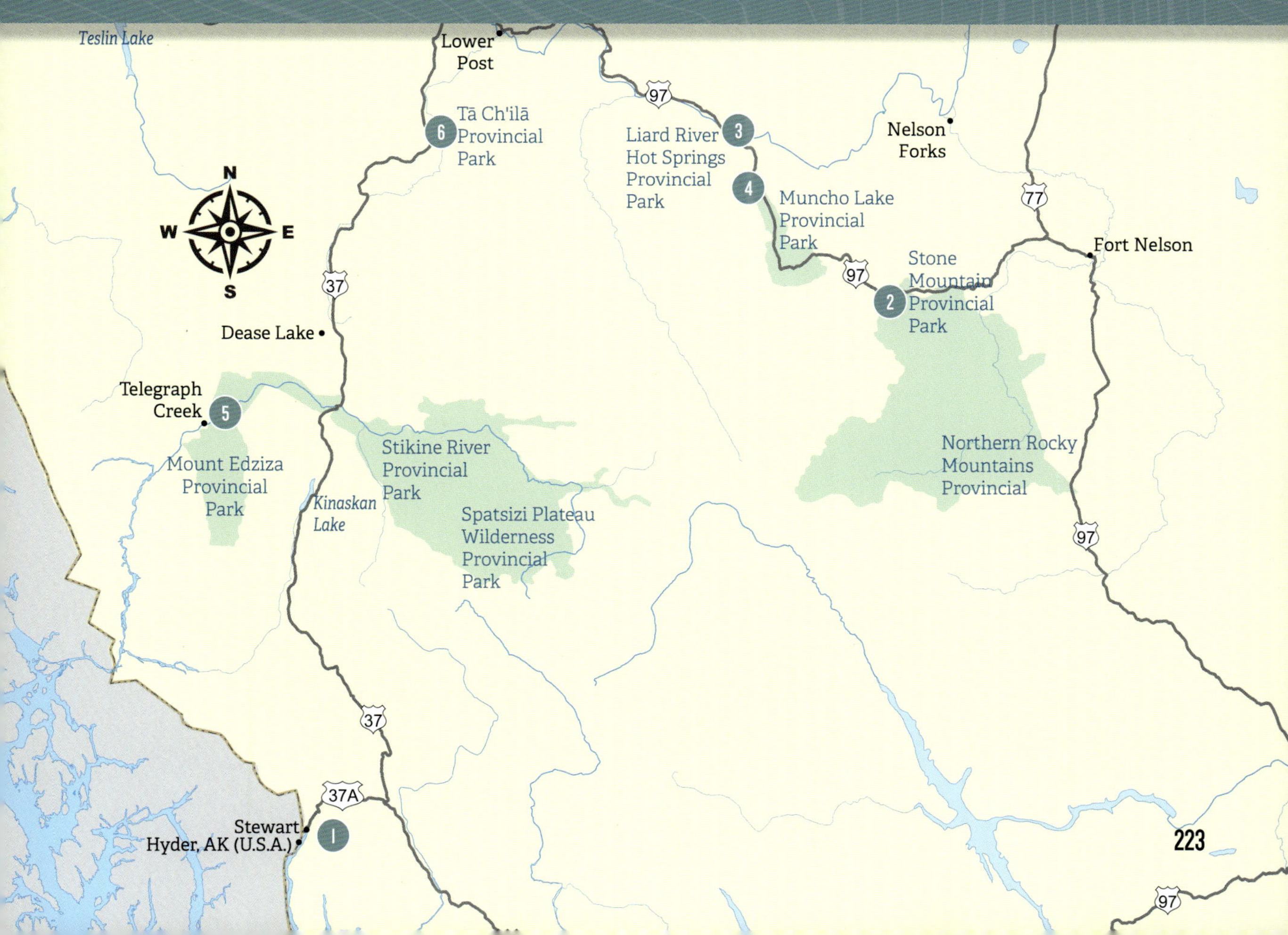

Bear and Salmon Glaciers

The glaciers are all on BC soil, but you will need your passport to make the most of these breathtaking views

What Makes This Hot Spot Hot?

- Views of beautiful glaciers and waterfalls are all along the drive into Stewart.
- Salmon Glacier is the fifth largest glacier in Canada.
- Marmots and other wildlife can be seen from the road and lookouts.

Address: Glacier Hwy (Stewart Hwy or Hwy 37A), Stewart, BC
Tel.: N/A
Websites:

BC Parks

Stewart Tourism

GPS Coordinates
Latitude: 56.09745
Longitude: −129.66740

Open year-round, conditions permitting

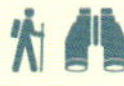

 (Check ahead)

The drive along the appropriately named Glacier Highway (also known as Stewart Highway or Highway 37A) into the small town of Stewart is one of the most picturesque drives in the province, with spectacular views around every corner. There are many pull-offs along the road to support the nature lover's desire to stop and admire the dramatic surroundings as the drive takes you past many glaciers, mountain waterfalls, rushing rivers, rolling streams and steep rock walls. Watch for wildlife on the road, as black bears and grizzlies are found in the area, and there is opportunity for roadside birding. Listen for the short, burry calls of the western tanager for a chance to catch a glimpse of this shy yet lavishly coloured bird.

Glaciers often appear blue, simply because, just as in large bodies of water, the molecules in these massive pieces of compressed ice absorb other colours of light more efficiently than blue. The pressure that creates such a dense piece of ice also squeezes out air bubbles that would otherwise make the ice appear white.

The most famous ice formation along this stretch of highway is the Bear Glacier, protected within provincial parkland. Although it once completely filled the Bear River Pass, the glacier began to retreat in the 1940s, and where once was ice, now a lake has formed. Although the beautiful glacial tongue is still an awe-inspiring roadside stop, it is worth looking for evidence in the rocks and slopes of its once grander size. This rapidly shrinking glacier is a startling reminder that glacial retreats are among the most dramatic indicators of climate change.

Bring your passport with you on this trip, because once in Stewart, a worthwhile crossing through American soil will bring you back across the border into BC to admire the magnificent Salmon Glacier. The drive takes you through the Alaskan ghost town of Hyder, where the only customs you will encounter is when you re-enter Canada. The 37-kilometre drive to the lookout over the glacier provides additional wildlife viewing opportunities. You will have a good chance of seeing hoary marmots along the way between May and August, the only months of the year they are not hibernating. Marmots thrive in rocky alpine terrain, hiding from predators in burrows. In the summer you may see moms feeding and sunbathing with their babies, who stay with them for two years before venturing off on their own.

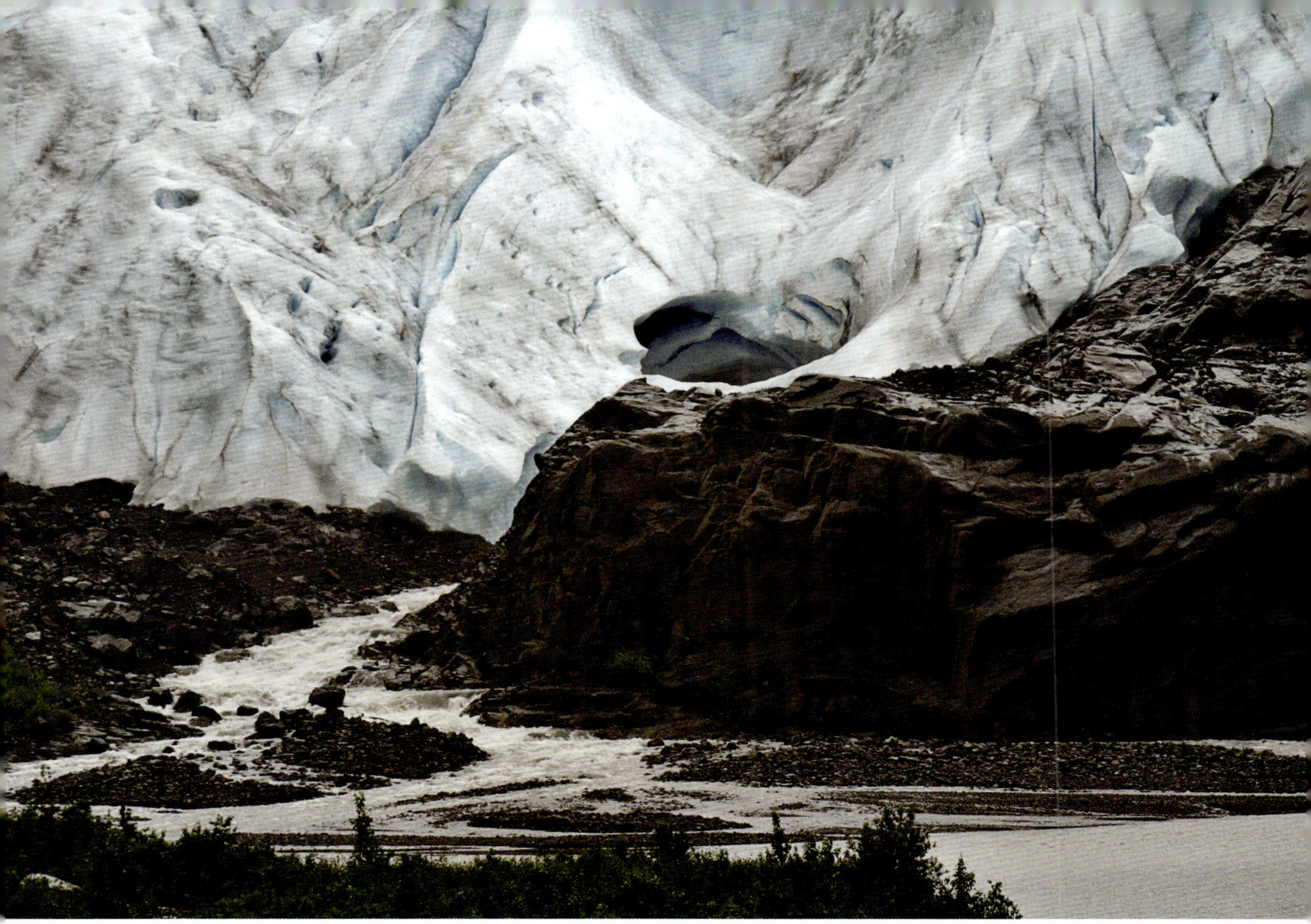

Salmon Glacier, found just on the Canadian side of the border, is the fifth largest glacier in the country. From the viewpoint you can see where the enormous ice field splits into two tongues. Look for terminal moraines near the glacial toe, where sediments scraped and carried by the river of ice are deposited.

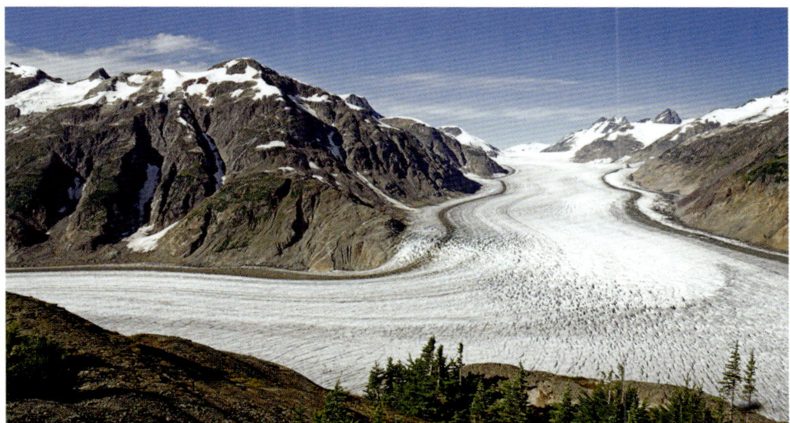

⬆ **Views of the massive Salmon Glacier are worth the trek through American soil.**

⬉ **Meltwater rushes down from the toe of Bear Glacier.**

STONE MOUNTAIN PROVINCIAL PARK

Flower Springs Lake Trail

Alpine meadows contrasted with stark mountain views

What Makes This Hot Spot Hot?

- This area provides habitat for woodland caribou and other large mammals.
- Diverse wildflowers blanket the alpine meadows.
- The end of the trail is marked by a large glacial lake nestled at the bottom of Mount Saint George.

Address: Summit Lake Campground, Stone Mountain Provincial Park, Alaska Hwy (Hwy 97), Northern Rockies B, BC
Tel.: (250) 776-7000
Website:

BC Parks

GPS Coordinates
Latitude: 58.651457
Longitude: –124.648311

Open May to mid-September (the park closes when snow falls)

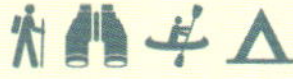

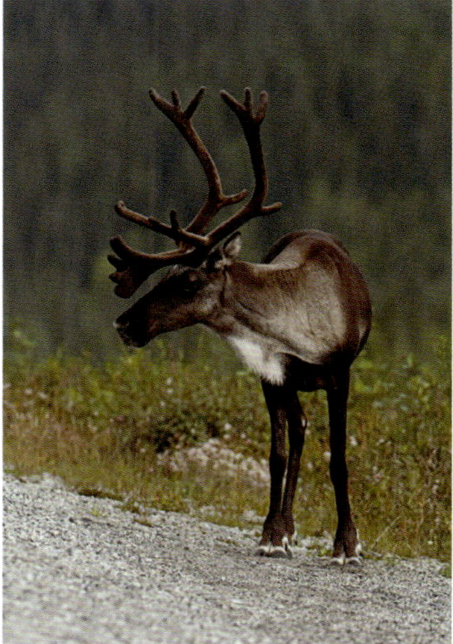

▸ **A male woodland caribou with his velvety antlers.**

Giant masses of exposed stone mountains rise from green valleys, making Stone Mountain Provincial Park a must-see destination in northeastern British Columbia. The park lies largely within the alpine tundra geoclimatic zone, so trees are already sparse even before you begin hiking farther up into the alpine meadows. Summit Lake Campground in the park is one of the most exposed campgrounds in the entire province, sitting about 1,270 metres above sea level, so if you are planning on camping, be prepared for a windy night.

For experienced backpackers, there are plenty of opportunities for backcountry exploration, but the park also offers several day-hikes to fantastic views of alpine meadows and glacial lakes. The Flower Springs Lake Trail comprises two routes: the lake edge route is a 13.6-kilometre return hike to a lovely lake at the base of Mount Saint George, and the radio tower route is a 10.2-kilometre return hike that follows a radio tower road. The second route is shorter and provides a more gradual ascent for the first half of the hike. The trail traverses through moist, flooded land as it traces the North Tetsa River but quickly climbs into more exposed meadow.

As you gain elevation throughout the hike, trees become more and more sparse, but the early summer wildflowers continue to impress, adding splashes of colour to the green meadows. Mountain lupines, white mountain-heather, field locoweed, mountain monkshood, shooting star, narcissus anemone and moss campion are highlights along the trail.

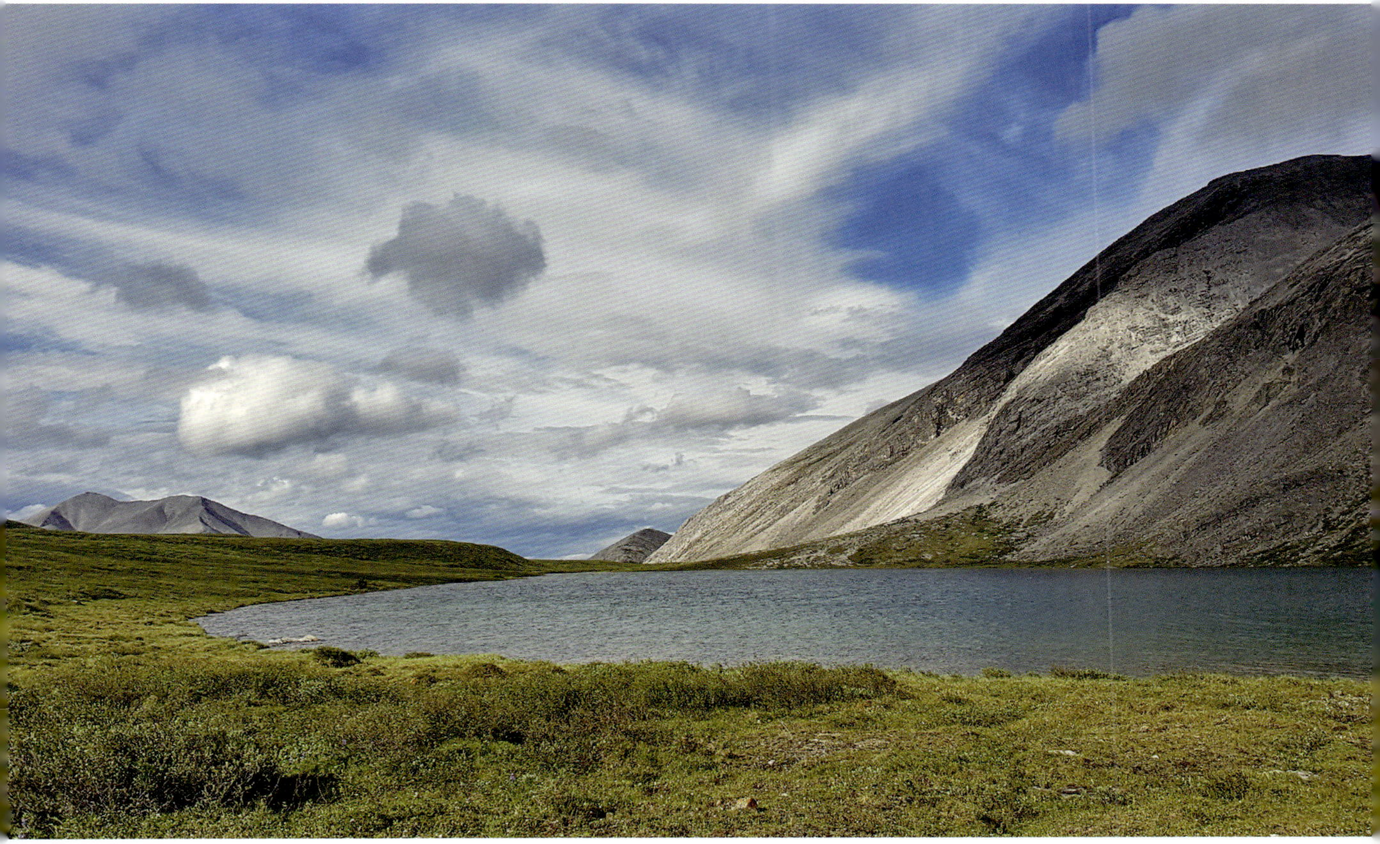

During dawn and dusk, woodland caribou are known to visit Flower Springs Lake. Unique to the deer family, both male and female caribou grow antlers, although some females only grow one, and others none at all. Caribou are also special in that their winter diet is almost exclusively lichens, which is the reason for their winter migration into coniferous forests. Their wide hooves act as snowshoes in deep snow and also help them dig out lichens. In the summer they spend most of their time in the alpine regions, where snow patches provide refuge from the heat and biting insects.

The park is home to other large mammals, so look out for mountain goats, moose, black bears and grizzly bears. Smaller mammal species live in the park as well, including dusky shrews, porcupines, least chipmunks and several species of vole. Pack your binoculars and be on the lookout for boreal chickadees, American tree sparrows and American pipits, which can be spotted bobbing their tails in the open meadows near the glacial lake.

↑ **The bright blue water, bright green meadow and light-grey mountains provide a picture-perfect backdrop to this hike.**

↓ **White mountain-heather form dense mats along the trail.**

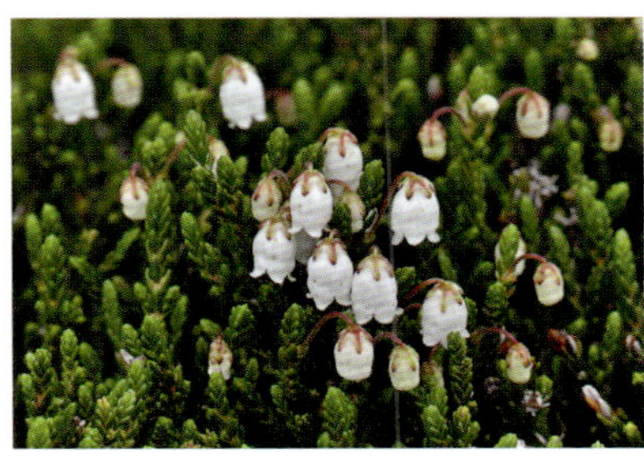

Liard River Hot Springs Provincial Park

Exceptional and provincially unique organisms call these hot waters home

What Makes This Hot Spot Hot?

- This is the only place in the world where you can find hotwater physa snails.
- Species found way outside their normal range thrive in the warm waters here.
- Wood bison are locally abundant within the park and easy to spot from the road.

Address: 497 Alaska Hwy (Hwy 97), Muncho Lake, BC
Tel.: (250) 776-7000
Website:

BC Parks

GPS Coordinates
Latitude: 59.41987
Longitude: −126.08982

Open year-round

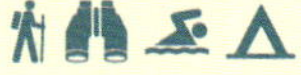

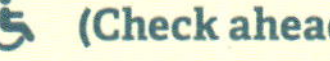 (Check ahead)

Like many hot springs scattered across the province, Liard River Hot Springs Provincial Park is a popular destination for those looking for a tranquil and steaming dip in natural waters. However, these springs are unlike any other in the province and are home to species found nowhere else in the world. As a general rule, hot springs are brimming with specialized organisms that are able to make a living in these unusual and harsh conditions. These hot springs take it one step further, providing refuge to some rare species, even by hot spring standards.

The Liard River system has at least six hot springs feeding into pools and streams that eventually drain into a marsh. As hot water flows into shallower areas farther from the source, it cools off, depositing calcium carbonate that was picked up as the water moved through underground limestone deposits. The carbonate minerals from the water harden to form deposits of tufa, a type of limestone. Chara, thought to be a late common ancestor of algae and land plants, becomes encrusted in the calcium carbonate and provides a habitat for Liard River's rarest animals.

The hotwater physa is a tiny freshwater snail found here and nowhere else in the world. The snails thrive in waters between 23 and 40 degrees Celsius, feeding on organisms that live on the chara's crusty surface. Between 3 and 9 millimetres in length, this tiny mollusc needs the support of the park's visitors to ensure its survival, or else it faces global extinction. Do not disturb the sensitive habitat in the marsh, as the wide boardwalk provides fabulous viewing opportunities in this unique environment without having to touch anything. The use of all soaps, oils, sunscreens and other skin products by bathers is prohibited in the springs upstream to protect this spectacular nature hot spot.

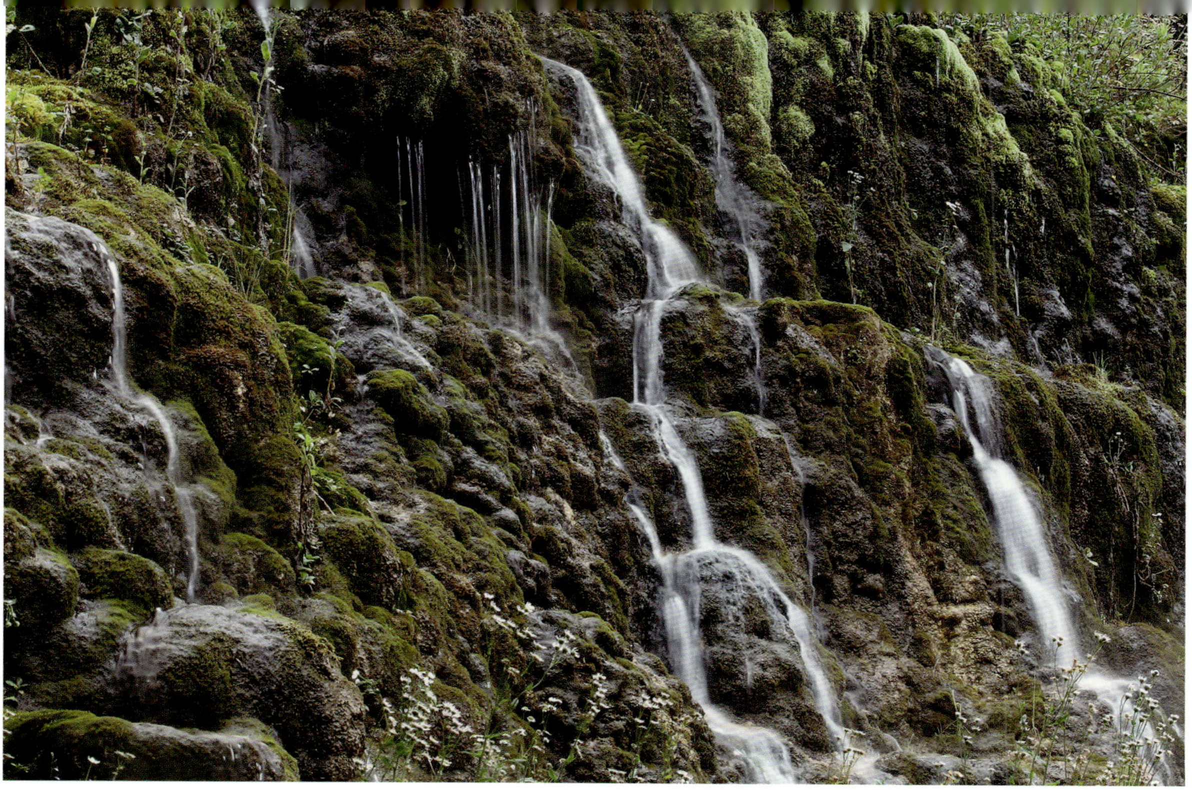

Other provincially rare natives to the marsh are thankfully much easier to spot than the miniscule physas. A population of lake chub is found here, able to tolerate the high temperatures. Look for this small, well-camouflaged fish darting around in small clearings in the marshy water surrounding the boardwalk. The plains forktail, a dainty damselfly typically found in the most southern reaches of Canada's prairies, can be spotted along the boardwalk. Unique populations like these are probably relicts of warmer days: during a warming after the retreat of the glaciers that once covered the province, these species were likely more widespread, but their range is now constrained to the hot springs.

Liard River Hot Springs Provincial Park is also home to some impressive large mammals, including moose, which are sometimes seen visiting the warm marsh waters. In the forests surrounding the hot springs, the Nahanni population of wood bison is locally abundant. Watch for the hefty solitary males, who may weigh up to 900 kilograms, feeding or resting in clearings beside the highway, as well as large herds of females and their calves, often accompanied by yearlings and a few bulls. As North America's largest land mammals, wood bison are hard to miss, and these imposing giants are certainly not shy, requiring traffic to yield to them, and not vice versa.

↑ A raised boardwalk takes you up to the Hanging Garden, where tufa creates a terraced base for plants to grow.

↓ A wood bison calf makes for a memorable wildlife sighting in this provincial park.

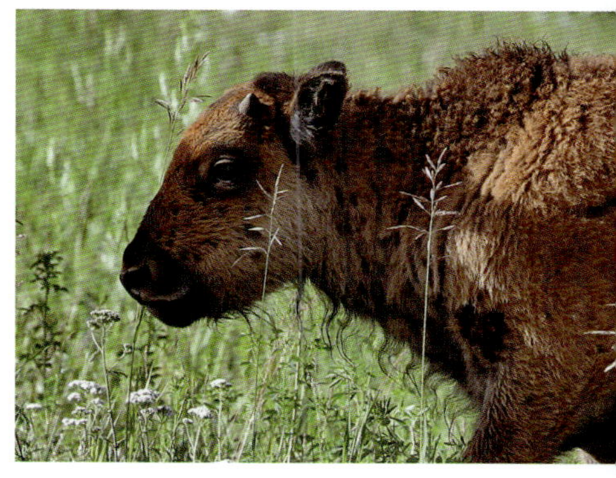

Muncho Lake Provincial Park

Abundant spring wildflowers, a beautiful jade-green lake and fantastic wildlife-viewing opportunities

↗ **The delicate flower of the unassuming common butterwort reveals nothing of its carnivorous tendencies.**

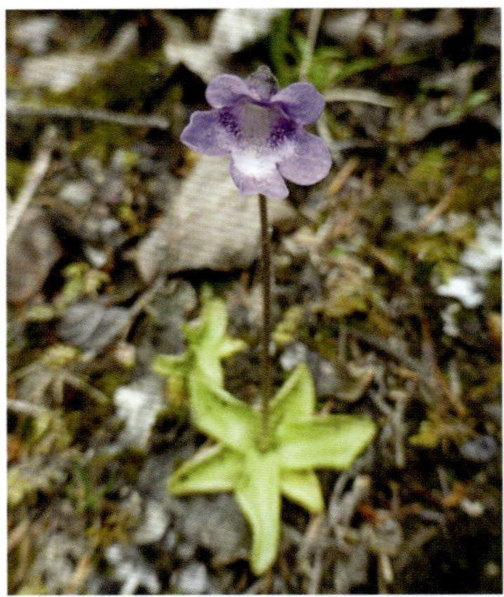

Muncho Lake Provincial Park offers great opportunities for camping on the water, where you will fall asleep to the enchanting tremolo call of the common loon echoing across the jade-green lake. The park has much to offer outside of lake views, however, with something for everyone — especially botany, zoology and geology enthusiasts.

Visible from the Alaska Highway (Highway 97), which cuts through the park, Folded Mountain provides a picture-perfect snapshot into how these mountains came to be. For over a billion years, the land that now makes up the mountains of the region was a shallow seabed that, accumulating layer after layer, ultimately formed sedimentary rock. Since then the land has been transformed as tectonic plates shifted and collided, forcing the once-horizontal rock layers to buckle and fold, now clearly revealed in the patterns of Folded Mountain.

Limestone, dolomite and shale were carved from the mountains by ancient glaciers, creating a fine rock flour. These mineral deposits are important for hoofed mammals that require the elements present in the rock flour for their tooth, hair and bone growth. As a result, these animals travel many kilometres to access these mineral licks. Stone's sheep, a subspecies of the thinhorn sheep, visit the licks often in the spring and early summer, but you may also spot this agile mammal along the roadside and hiking trails in the area.

The trail at the Mineral Licks Viewing Area, marked from the highway, is a 1.5-kilometre loop that provides a good chance to see Stone's sheep and other ungulates, as well as offers fabulous wildflower viewing along the trail. In the spring and early summer be on the lookout for common butterwort. This small, unassuming herb, with its single violet, funnel-shaped flower, is surprisingly a carnivorous plant. Look closely at the chartreuse basal leaves, and you may notice insects that have fallen victim to this plant's unique adaptation. The upper surface of the leaves creates a greasy secretion to trap its food, and the rolled edges prevent prey from escaping along the leaf perimeter. Trapped insects, which are slowly digested by enzymes secreted by the plant, help it survive in nutrient-poor soils.

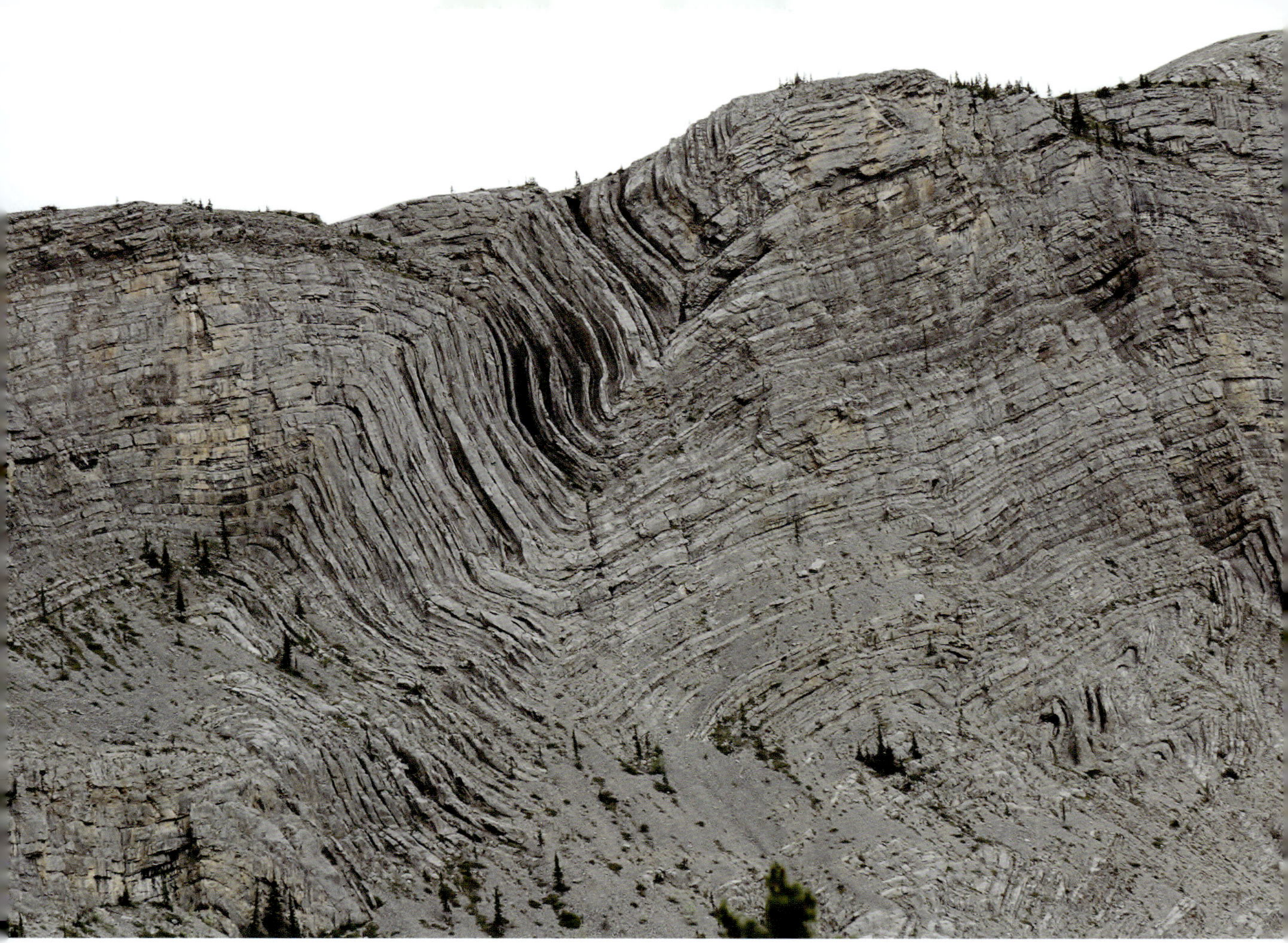

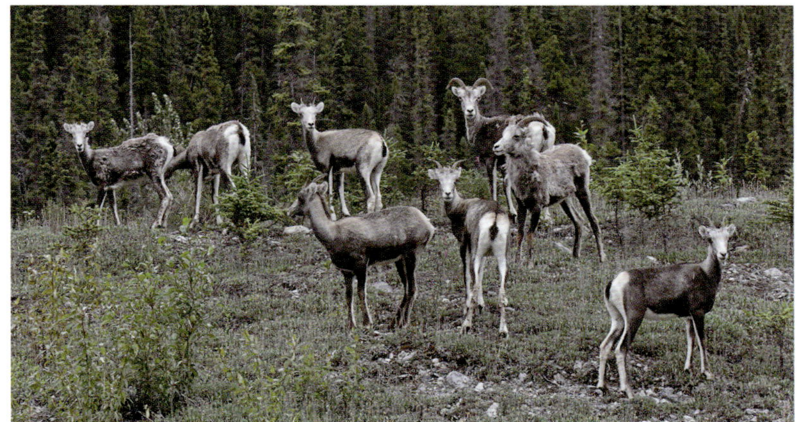

↑ **Small groups of Stone's sheep may be spotted along open slopes throughout the park.**

↖ **Folded Mountain reveals its geological history in waved layers of sedimentary rock.**

Stikine River Canyon

Eighty kilometres of steep-walled canyon are unlike anything else in Canada

What Makes This Hot Spot Hot?

- Sometimes referred to as the Grand Canyon of the Stikine, the canyon has walls that rise 300 metres from the raging river below.
- The chasm ranges from 200 metres to as little as 2 metres wide.
- Bank swallows nest along the sandy banks of the roadside en route to canyon views.

Address: Telegraph Creek Road, Telegraph Creek, BC
Tel.: N/A
Website:

BC Parks

GPS Coordinates
Latitude: 58.01325
Longitude: −130.97709

Open year-round, conditions permitting

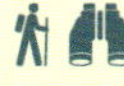 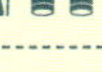

♿ (Check ahead)

↗ You can find large numbers of bank swallows nesting in the soft, sandy substrate along the road.

Eighty kilometres of steep-walled canyons rise up from the raging waters of the Stikine River, which carved away at the basalt and sedimentary rock over great expanses of time to create the dramatic vista you see now. This impressive river, which passes through Stikine River Provincial Park and traces the northern edge of Mount Edziza Provincial Park, becomes impassable as it flows through the canyon, making exploration on water only possible in the Upper Stikine.

The drive to the canyon is not for the faint of heart — much of Telegraph Creek Road on this 110-kilometre journey from Dease Lake is narrow, winding and steep, including grades up to 20 per cent as the road crosses water where the Tuya River meets the Stikine. There are no shoulders, few signs and no facilities along the way, so plan ahead and know what you are getting into before committing to the journey. That said, for those willing to make the drive, the views are fabulous. There is a pull-off with a great view of the Stikine Canyon without

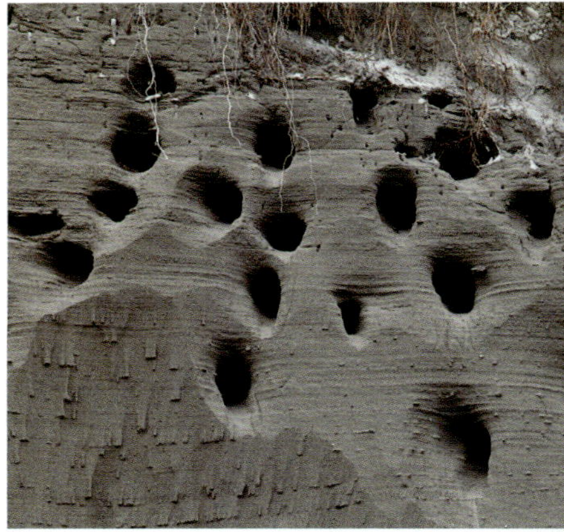

having to go all the way into the town of Telegraph Creek. You can also look out over the Tuya River earlier on the drive near the northern edge of the park border. Although expensive, plane and helicopter flights over the canyon are available and would make for a once-in-a-lifetime experience. If you visit in the autumn, the fall colours alongside the steep canyons look incredible.

More than 300 mountain goats call this canyon home, using the steep cliffsides as an escape route from their predators, so look for white dots perched on distant cliffs when you stop to admire the canyon. You will pass a large colony of bank swallows on

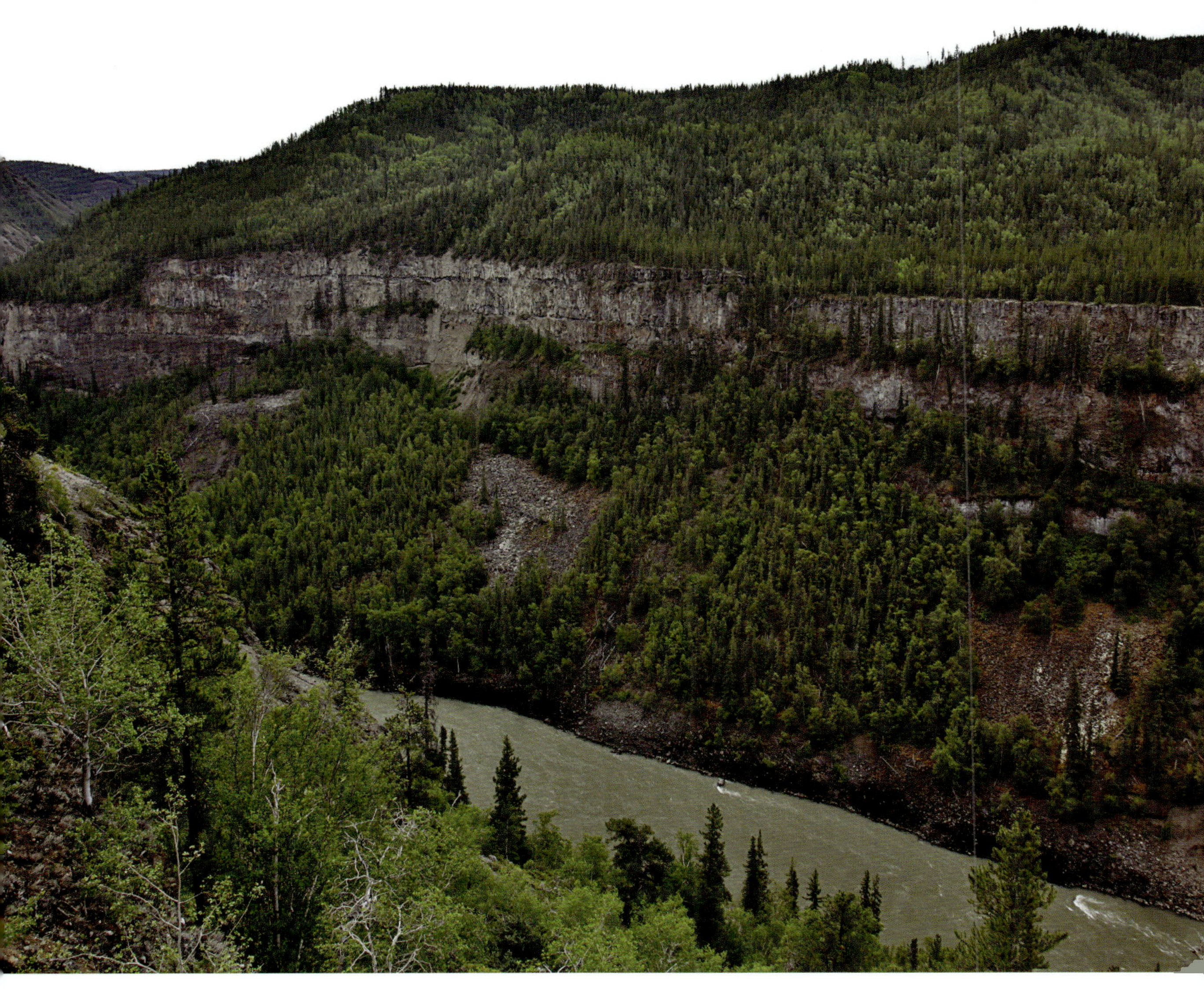

A lookout reveals the near vertical drop from the top of the canyon to the rushing river below.

your drive through the park, thankfully along a stretch with enough space to pull over and admire these acrobatic birds. The quick, fluttering movements of these small swallows are a sight to see, as they swoop around each other in the air, catching insects on the wing. Right next to the road, in the high vertical sandy banks, are a large group of nesting holes. These nest chambers are dug out by the male bank swallows using their feet, wings and conical bills. They burrow about a metre straight into the bank!

Tā Ch'ilā Provincial Park

A paradise lake nestled in the boreal forest that feigns a tropical destination

What Makes This Hot Spot Hot?

- Boya Lake's marl bottom results in brilliant turquoise hues.
- The complex lake system is a perfect opportunity for exploration by canoe or kayak.
- A beautiful trail leads to an active beaver lodge.

Address: Liard Plain, Stikine Region, BC
Tel.: (250) 638-8490
Website:

BC Parks

GPS Coordinates
Latitude: 59.36849
Longitude: −129.10868

Open May to September

(Check ahead)

↗ **A beaver heads back to the shore in search of suitable branches.**

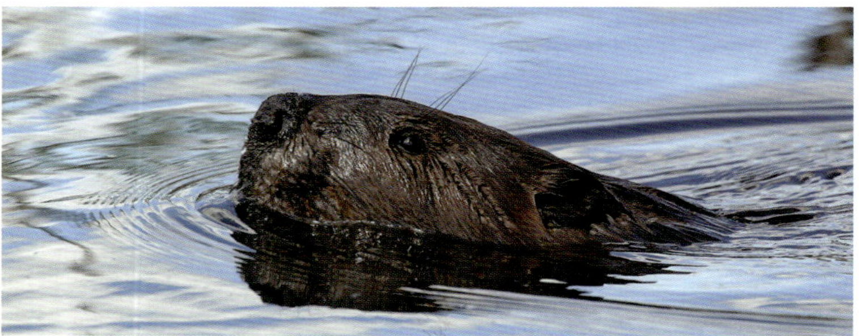

When you first arrive at the water's edge of Boya Lake in Tā Ch'ilā Provincial Park, you might need to pinch yourself to be sure you have not been transported to the Caribbean. This lake's stunning aquamarine colour is thanks to its marl bottom, consisting of a mixture of silt and shell fragments. The colour reflecting from the bottom through crystal-clear waters makes for a striking, almost tropical scene, although a scan of the trees, wildflowers and snow-capped peaks will bring you back to northern British Columbia's beautiful Liard Plain landscape.

The body of water you see from the campground and day-use area comprises only a small portion of the total area of the lake. Made up of many islands, complex winding inlets and channels, and other smaller bodies of water cut off from the main lake, the lake's convoluted characteristics make it the perfect park for exploring by canoe or kayak. If you do not have your own, it is possible to rent one from the BC Parks Area Supervisor on site. As this is one of the few lakes in this area of the province that is warm enough to swim in, be sure to come prepared for some water exploration.

Tā Ch'ilā Provincial Park has two short hiking trails that are each worth exploring. The Lakeshore Trail loop, accessed from the north end of the campground, provides additional views of winding shoreline and radiant water.

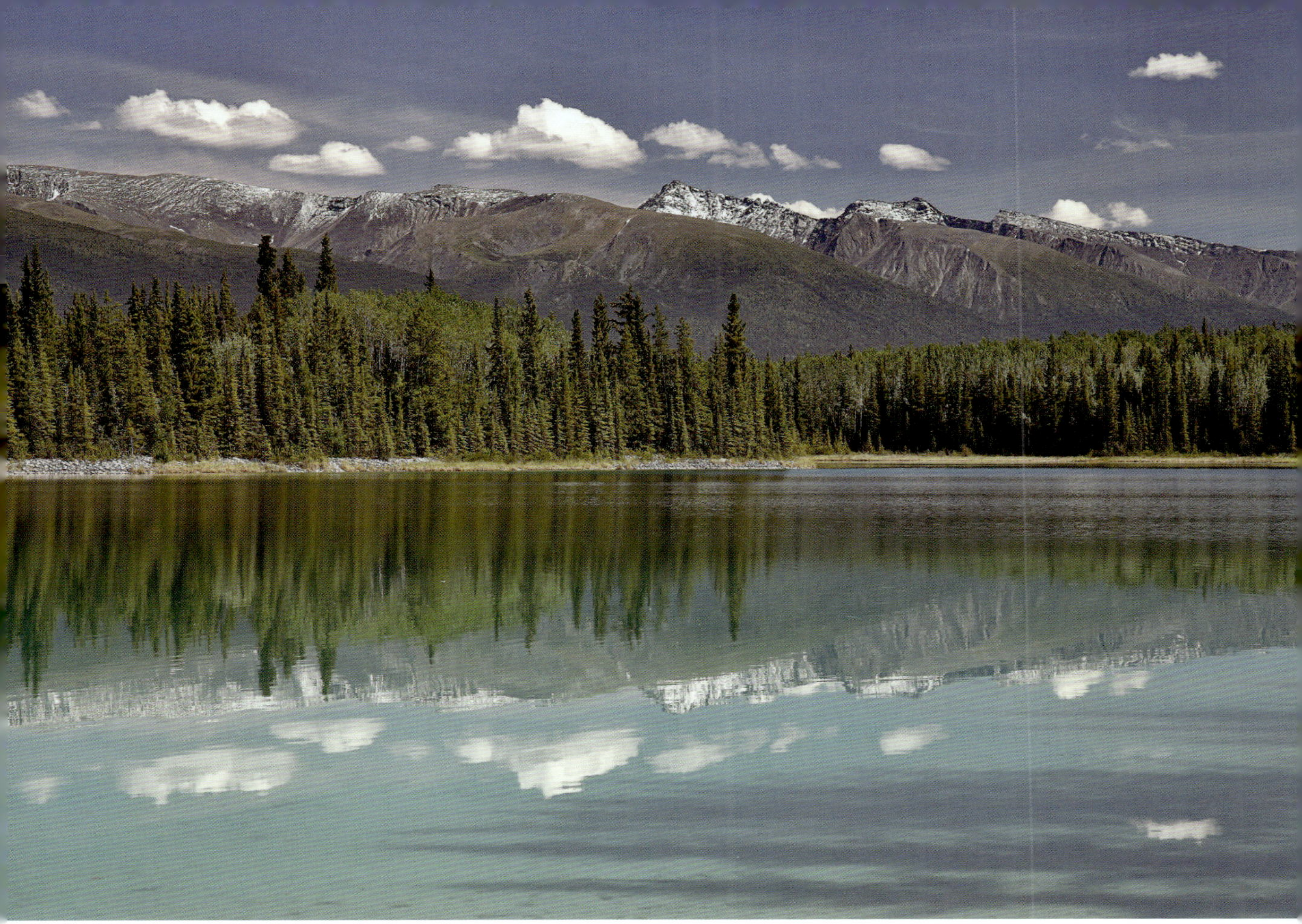

work of Canada's hardworking celebrity species, the North American beaver. As beavers drag branches and logs from the shoreline to their dams or lodges, dirt and debris mix in with the marl bottom. A viewing platform is set up for watching these beavers at work. Keep an eye out for them as they travel back and forth to pick up branches either for immediate consumption or to store for the winter ahead. If they notice you watching they may perform one of their signature behaviours — giving each other warnings by slapping their fat, leathery tails on the surface of the water.

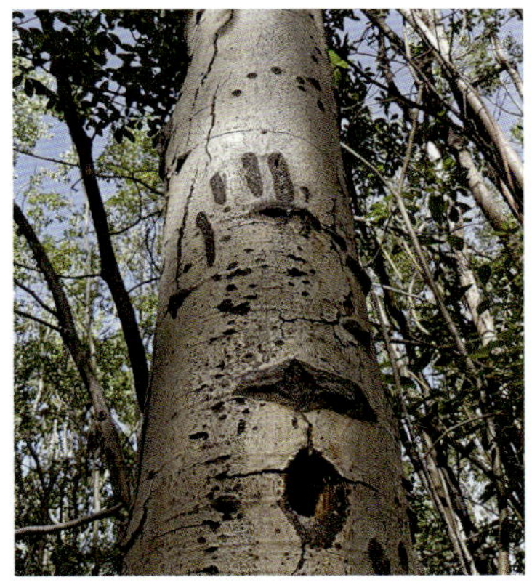

From the south end of the day-use area a trail leads along an esker before retreating back down to the water. You may notice the water is less clear and blue in this area of the park, thanks to the tireless

↑ On a sunny day Boya Lake gives the impression of a more tropical paradise.

← A woodpecker cavity and bear-claw scars show that beavers are not the only animals making use of the nearby trees.

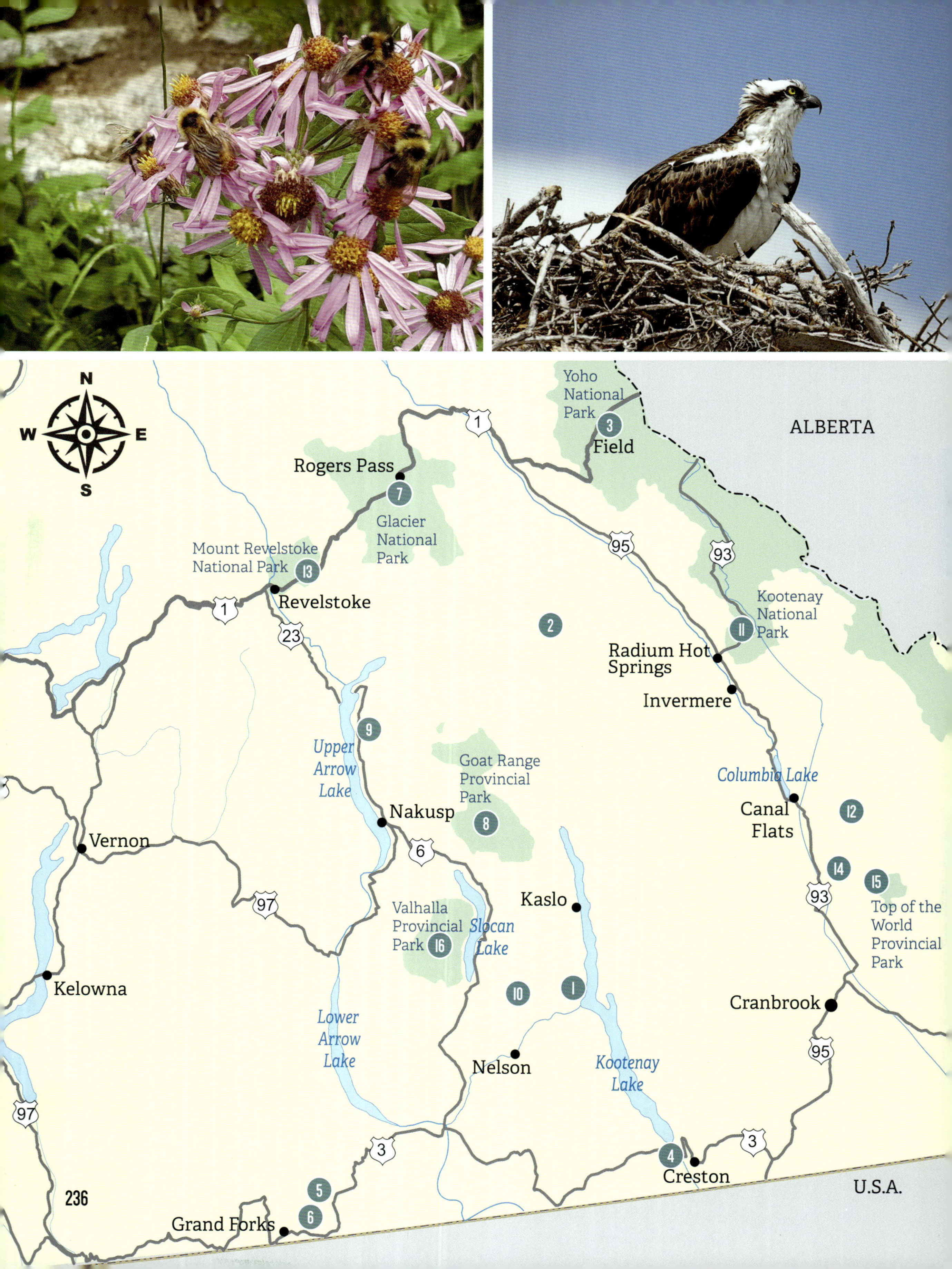

ALBERTA
Yoho National Park
Field
Rogers Pass
Glacier National Park
Mount Revelstoke National Park
Revelstoke
Radium Hot Springs
Invermere
Kootenay National Park
Upper Arrow Lake
Goat Range Provincial Park
Nakusp
Columbia Lake
Canal Flats
Vernon
Kaslo
Valhalla Provincial Park
Slocan Lake
Kelowna
Lower Arrow Lake
Nelson
Kootenay Lake
Cranbrook
Top of the World Provincial Park
Creston
Grand Forks
U.S.A.
N W E S
1
3
7
13
2
11
9
8
6
16
10
1
12
14
15
4
5
6
95
93
23
97
97
95
93
3
3

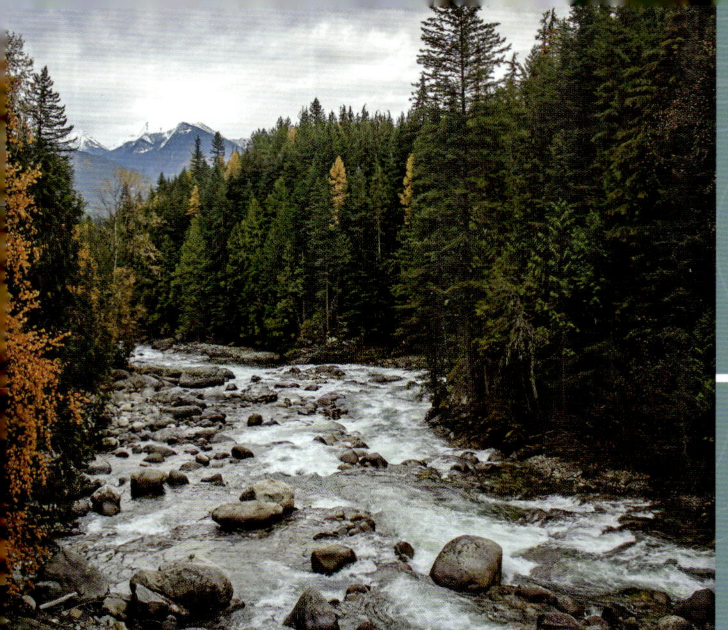

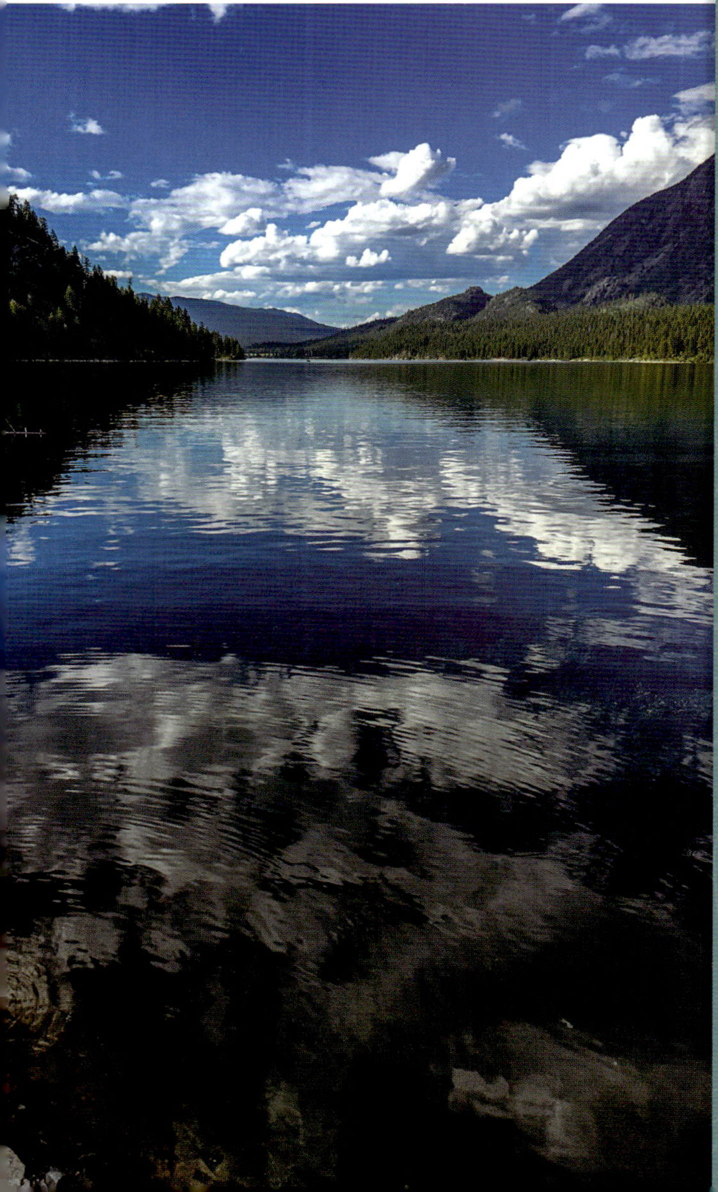

The Kootenay Region

Ainsworth Hot Springs

A must-do hot spring in the Kootenays and a swim through a uniquely shaped limestone cave

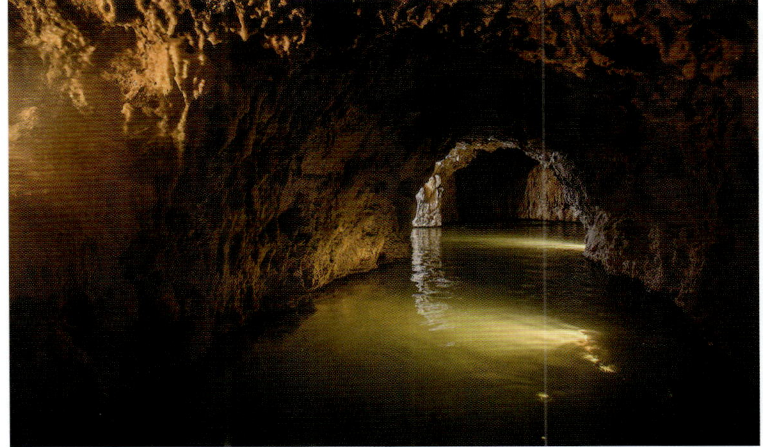

What Makes This Hot Spot Hot?

- Visitors can relax in two developed mineral hot springs and take a quick dip in a cold pool.
- Steaming water seeps out of the rock, flowing into a horseshoe-shaped cave where it creates a natural sauna.
- The nearby Cody Caves, carved out of limestone and filled with magnificent cave features, are the origins of the hot spring's waters.

Address: 3609 Balfour-Kaslo-Galena Bay Hwy (Hwy 31), BC
Tel.: (1-800) 668-1171
Website:

Ainsworth Hot Springs

GPS Coordinates
Latitude: 49.73574
Longitude: –116.91131

Open year-round, entry to pool by reservation only

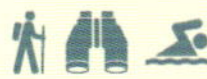

With hot springs and scenic views, this hot spot is well known as a place to relax. The Ainsworth Hot Springs were used by the Ktunaxa First Nation as a place of healing and are traditionally called *nupika wu'u*, which translates to "spirit water." The developed hot springs are famous for their cave-swimming feature. In its natural state the cave was over 2 metres long but has since been carved into a 46-metre horseshoe in which visitors can float and wade.

Near the back of the cave hot water flows out of the rock and into the pool. The water goes on quite the underground journey before ending up in these springs. Starting in the nearby Cody Caves, the water flows underground through cracks in the bedrock, gradually increasing in temperature. When it eventually reaches Kootenay Lake it is forced upwards and flows out of the rock, filling the pools with steaming water.

To see the origins of these waters as well as stunning limestone cave formations, book a tour of the Cody Caves through Cody Cave Tours. From the caves the water is pulled underground and completely refills the hot springs

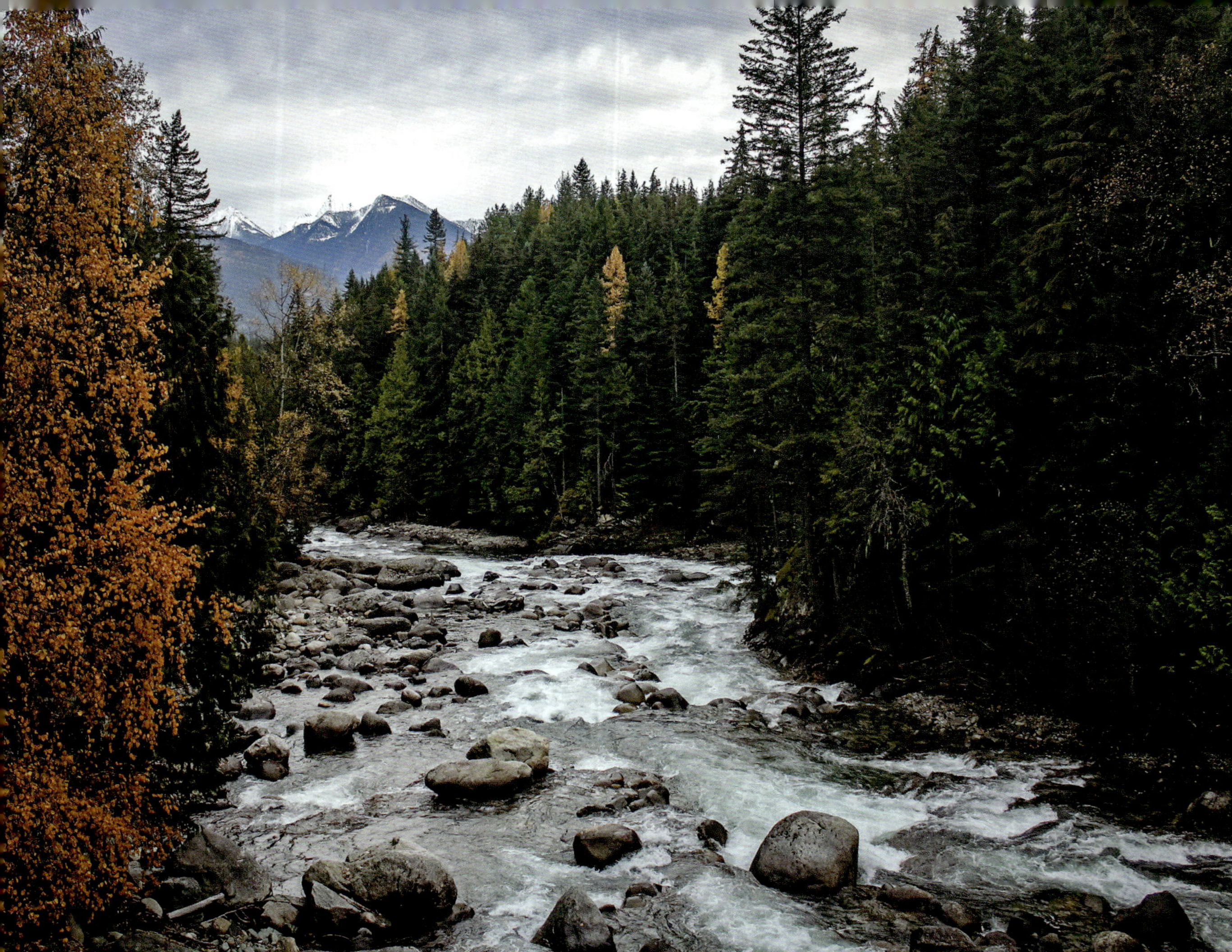

up to six times each day! To experience the surrounding wildlife and landscapes, enjoy a day of hiking in the nearby town of Kaslo, which has a number of hikes, including to Mount Buchanan, a lovely trail through mountain meadows leading to a lookout over Kootenay Lake. The Wagon Road Trail is great for a stroll through the forest to Fish Lake, where hikers will see swallowtail butterflies fluttering alongside other insects, all of which attract a wide variety of insect-eating birds. Look for the brightly coloured yellow warbler chirping as it darts between the trees. On the lakes a variety of ducks, including the goldeneye, is a common sight. A soak in the hot springs with a beautiful view over Kootenay Lake will be particularly relaxing after a day of hiking and wildlife watching.

As Ainsworth Hot Springs is a developed resort there is an entry fee to access them. As well, Cody Caves have only guided tours to protect the caves' delicate features.

↑ **Hike the trails of the nearby community of Kaslo for wildlife watching opportunities.**

← **Steaming water seeps out of the rock into a horseshoe-shaped cave.**

Bugaboo Provincial Park

A rare opportunity to stand amongst glaciers as they carve rugged peaks and shape an alpine landscape

What Makes This Hot Spot Hot?

- Visitors can get up close to glaciers in a magnificent alpine landscape surrounded by granite spires.
- Hummingbirds and insects dart between alpine flowers blooming in meadows.
- Stargazers can look to the sky high in the mountains far from any light pollution.

Address: Bugaboo Creek Forest Service Road, 50 km west of Spillimacheen, BC
Tel.: (403) 678-3200 (Alpine Club of Canada for hut reservations)
Website:

BC Parks

GPS Coordinates
Latitude: 50.74572
Longitude: –116.72693

Open year-round

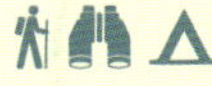

Bugaboo Provincial Park sits in the traditional territory of the Ktunaxa/Kinbasket and Shuswap Nations. The drainage that the glacier melt flows through provides water for beautiful forests and flowers and was used as a hunting ground. This drainage is now the main hiker access into the park via the Kain Hut Trail. In the mid-1890s miners, in their quest for gold, stumbled upon this landscape of granite spires towering over glaciers. When they found not much other than pyrite and galena they gave this area the name Bugaboo, thought to be old mining slang for a "worthless prospect." As it turns out precious metals weren't the treasure that would draw people to Bugaboo Provincial Park, it was the glaciers and granite spires. The park has a rich history of skiing and mountaineering, beginning in 1910 when Austrian mountaineer Conrad Kain climbed the prominent Bugaboo Spire. It wasn't until 1995 that the now-popular area officially became a provincial park.

The steep Kain Hut Trail connects the otherworldly expanse of granite and glaciers to the forest below. Between the forest and alpine, rufous and calliope hummingbirds dart between flowers, drinking nectar and feeding upon small insects. As elevation increases the soil becomes thinner, fireweed is replaced by shorter shrubby plants, such as heather, and clear streams formed beneath the glaciers pour over bare granite.

In the true alpine, the landscape of granite peaks and ice-blue glaciers is truly awe-inspiring. The slow-moving rivers of compact ice pour over the landscape, and as they shift the ice cracks, forming deep crevasses. This open landscape feels magical during the day, but truly shines at night where, far from any city lights, it provides beautiful stargazing and an occasional view of the aurora borealis. Overnight visitors to the park can camp in the alpine, or the Conrad Kain Hut can be booked for overnight stays in advance.

Glaciers are an important part of BC's past, present and

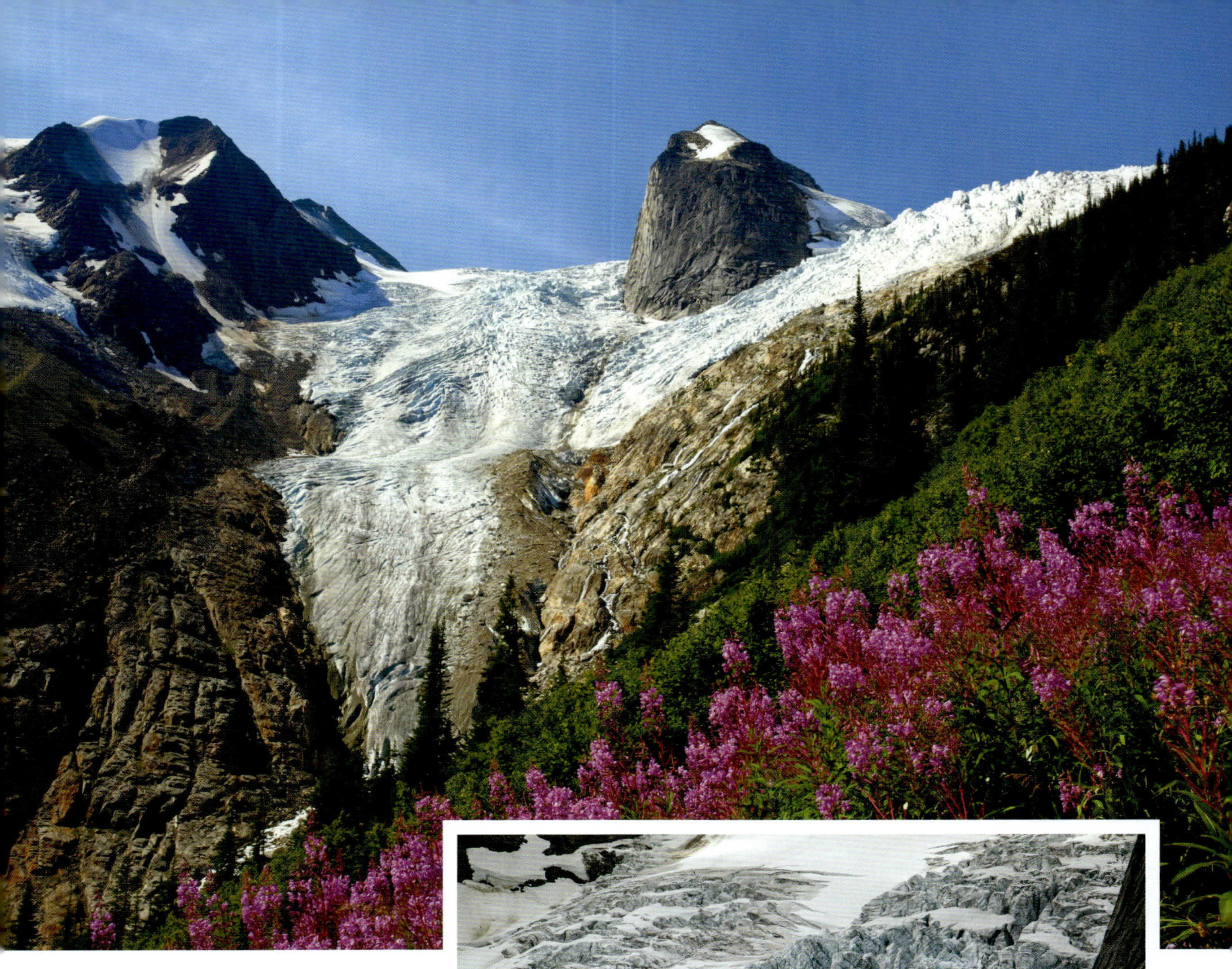

future. They have carved valleys and mountains, created lakes and rivers, and on a large scale separated animal populations, leading to new species. Just 10,000 to 25,000 years ago the province was under ice. Visiting Bugaboo Provincial Park provides a glimpse into how glaciers have shaped the province and their importance in the present as they currently hold about 69 per cent of the world's freshwater. It is hard to imagine the Bugaboo landscape without these vast expanses of ice, but in the last 100 years the Bugaboo Glacier has receded over 2 kilometres. It is so important that we work to protect ecosystems such as these in our changing world.

↑ Crevasses form as deep cracks through the glacier's compact ice as it slowly moves over the granite below.

↖ The hike in boasts views of the glaciated landscape through meadows of fireweed.

YOHO NATIONAL PARK

Burgess Shale

These rocky slopes protect some of the world's most important fossils

What Makes This Hot Spot Hot?

- There are opportunities to learn about the origins of modern plant and animal life while looking at fossils.
- Amazingly detailed fossils give a glimpse into life over 500 million years ago.
- Visitors can enjoy interpretive tours of two important fossil sites while hiking in the Rocky Mountains.

Address: Field, BC
Tel.: (1-800) 343-3006 (Burgess Shale Geoscience Foundation)
Websites:

Burgess Shale Geoscience Foundation

GPS Coordinates
Latitude: 51.39686
Longitude: –116.48698

Open mid-June through mid-September when guided hikes are available, conditions permitting

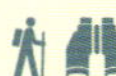

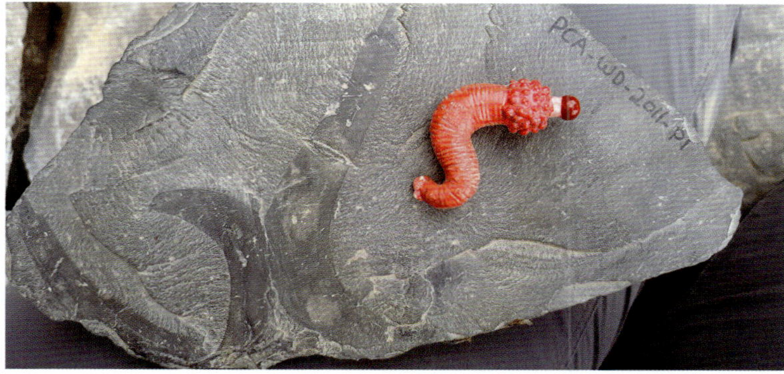

↑ **Scientists were able to create a model of animals such as *Ottoia*, a completely soft-bodied creature, from these well-preserved fossils.**

In Yoho National Park, visitors can see some of the most important fossil beds in the world. The remnants of marine life from 505 million years ago are preserved in the alpine of the Rocky Mountains.

There are two sites to visit in the park, each a rewarding hike with views of the Rockies. The fossilized creatures at these sites give us a glimpse into the Cambrian period, when the first complex animals and ecosystems appeared in the fossil record. Truly representing an explosion of life, some 120 animal fossils found in the Burgess Shale fit into phyla (a classification of living things) that we did not know existed.

Mount Stephen was the first site to be discovered, in 1886, following reports of "stone bugs" being found by railway workers. The tour to the site is a steep but manageable 8-kilometre hike to an abundance of fossils, including many trilobites, which are ancient and extinct arthropods.

In 1909 Charles Walcott, a paleontologist and the leading expert on Cambrian fossils at the time, happened upon a fossil of *Marrella splendens* alongside a trail. With its long head spikes, *M. splendens* is thought to be an ancestor of many modern arthropods, such as crustaceans and

arachnids. After following a path of shale debris up the rocky slope, Walcott discovered what would later be called the Walcott Quarry. The renowned Walcott Quarry tour is a 22-kilometre round trip. The fossils at this quarry are so well preserved that soft body parts are identifiable and can even show who ate who in this ancient ecosystem. A once-bustling ocean saw a sudden landslide of sediment, which created an environment low in oxygen that turned out to be perfect for preserving creatures with mostly or entirely soft bodies, including ancient sponges and worms.

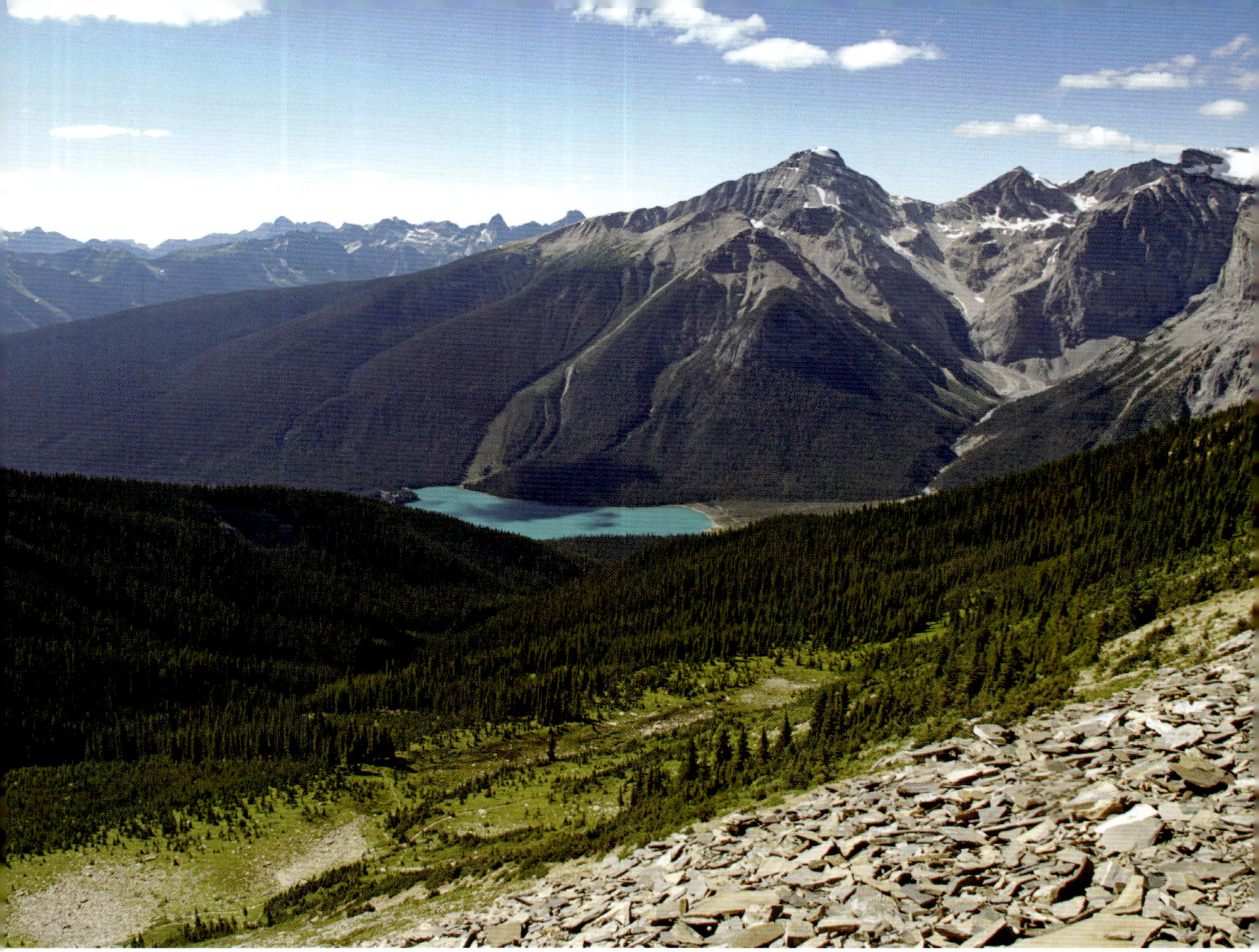

To protect the delicate nature of the sites, visitors require guides. Both the Burgess Shale Geoscience Foundation and Parks Canada offer excellent interpretive tours in which you are able to get up close and learn about many of the fossils. At the quarries, guides talk about the fossils and pass around spectacular examples of each, and then visitors are allowed time to explore the shale on their own. Nearly every overturned rock reveals another fossil.

↑ A charming view of Emerald Lake from the Walcott Quarry.

↓ The hike to the Walcott Quarry includes trails through alpine meadows.

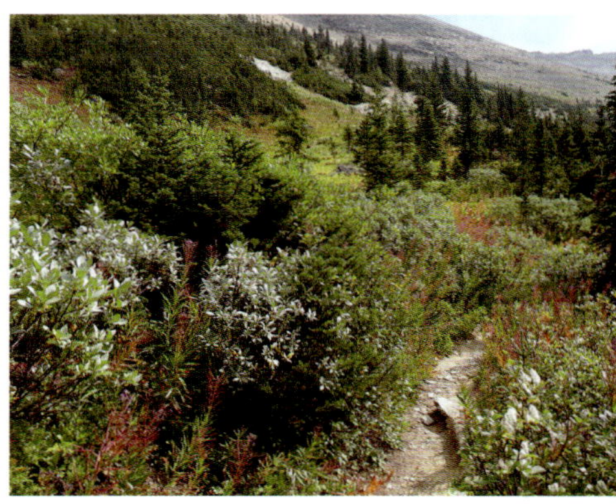

Creston Valley Wildlife Management Area

These wetlands are British Columbia's most important inland habitat for migratory birds

What Makes This Hot Spot Hot?

- Nearly 400 species of birds, mammals and amphibians use these wetlands as a home or stopover during migration.
- Ongoing research and active wetland management ensure the continued health of the wetlands and the species that call them home.
- These wetlands provide flood control for the surrounding area.

Address: 1760 West Creston Road, Creston, BC
Tel.: (250) 402-6900
Website:

Creston Valley Wildlife Management Area

GPS Coordinates
Latitude: 49.12105
Longitude: −116.63496

Open year-round

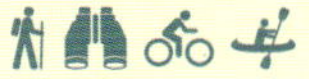

Water spills from the nearby Kootenay River into Duck Lake and its surrounding wetlands, creating a paradise for wildlife. Recognized as a Ramsar Wetland of International Importance and an Important Bird Area, these lakes and marshes are protected and thriving.

The year-round biodiversity supported by these wetlands is impressive. Many species of amphibians, mammals and birds frequent the area. Moose and species at risk such as the western painted turtle are not uncommon sights. Both the northern leopard frog and Forster's tern have chosen this site to host their only breeding populations in British Columbia.

These wetlands are considered the most important inland area for migrating birds, allowing them to rest, feed and nest. The area supports many plants used by birds as materials for making nests, which are

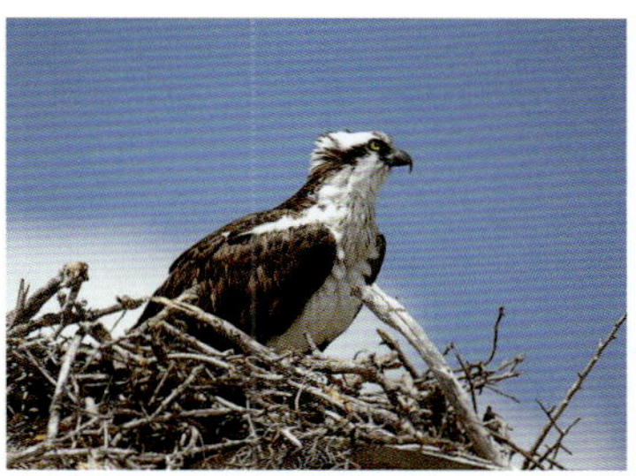

↑ **Osprey use large sticks to build their nests high up in trees or atop human-made structures.**

↓ **The northern leopard frog calls these wetlands home.**

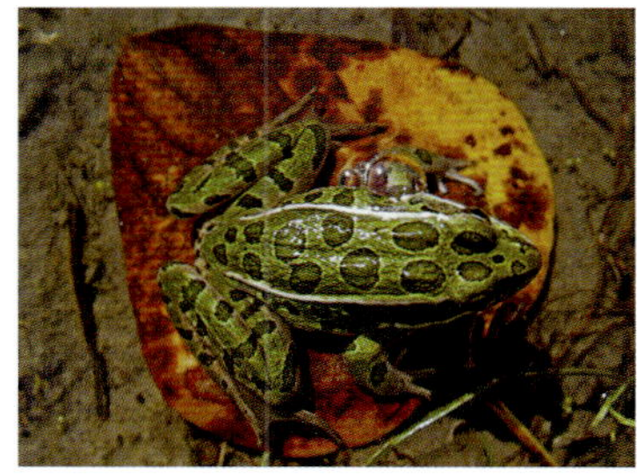

very diverse among species. Songbirds will often weave delicate nests out of grasses, sometimes incorporating snakeskins. Tundra swans pile a variety of grasses and twigs over natural features

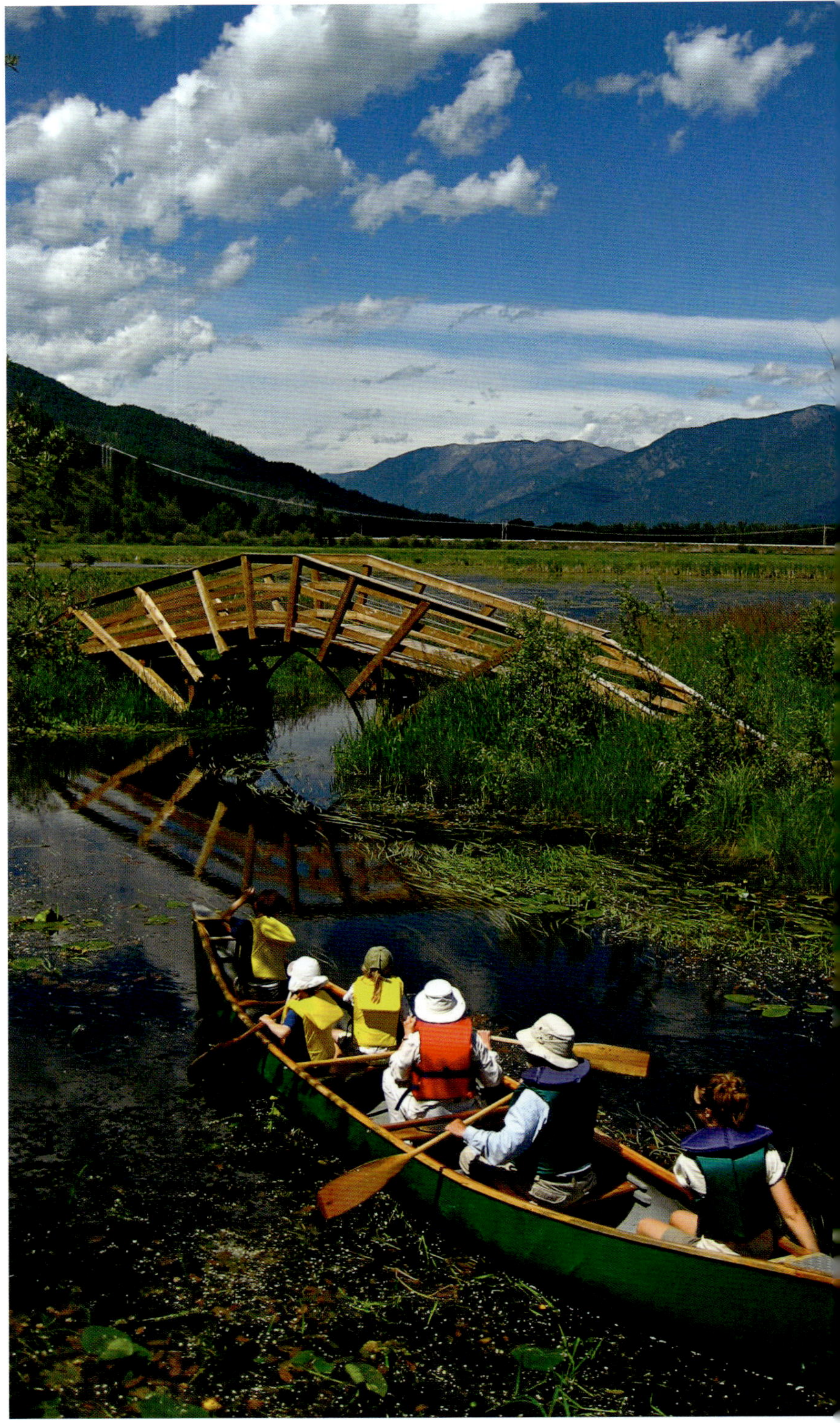

→ **A paddle through the wetlands reveals a unique perspective.**

on the ground. Nuthatches will nest in hollows in trees, and some birds, such as the osprey, make messy-looking nests by piling large sticks high up in tall trees. Plastics and other garbage can sometimes be mistaken by birds as nest-building material. That is why the conservation and protection of this area during nesting season are of particular importance.

Healthy wetlands are vital not only to the plants and animals that call them home but also to human populations. Running parallel to the Kootenay River, these wetlands act as storage tanks when water levels are high, providing flood control for the nearby city of Creston. Wetlands also purify and feed groundwater sources. The conservation effort involved in protecting this wildlife management area is no small feat. Active wetland management, continuous research and hard work keep these wetlands healthy.

GLADSTONE PROVINCIAL PARK

Deer Point Trail

Hike along a forested ridge above BC's warmest tree-lined lake

What Makes This Hot Spot Hot?

- This great hike takes you high above the expansive Christina Lake.
- Spring wildflowers line the trail and chipmunks carefully watch from the undergrowth.
- Columbian ground squirrels are present around the campsites at the base of this hike.

Address: 3535 East Lake Drive, Christina Lake, BC
Tel.: (250) 584-9025
Website:

BC Parks

GPS Coordinates
Latitude: 49.12871
Longitude: –118.24689

Open year-round

♿ **Check ahead**

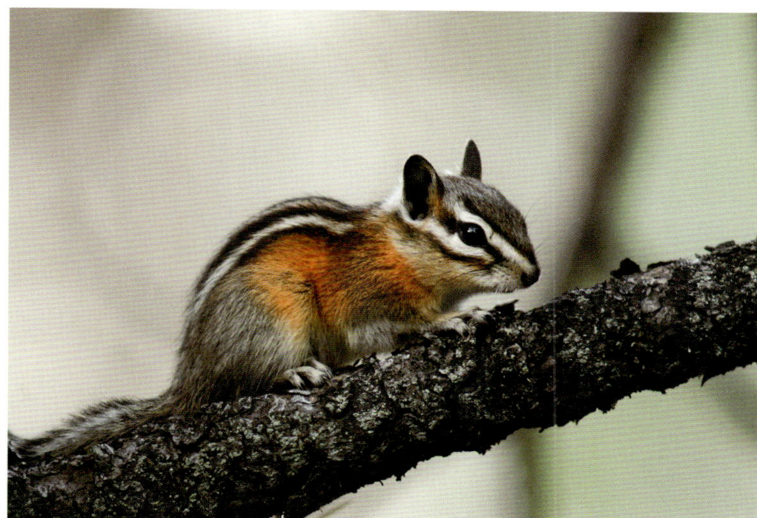

↗ **Yellow-pine chipmunks will let you know your presence doesn't go unnoticed.**

Just east of Grand Forks you'll find Christina Lake, the warmest tree-lined lake in the province and a perfect destination for canoeing, kayaking and swimming. Gladstone Provincial Park envelopes its northern half, protecting diverse habitats — from the shoreline up into alpine meadows. Wintering deer and elk seek refuge in the park, as do blue-listed species like grizzly bears and California bighorn sheep.

While most people visit for the easy lake access, exploring by foot is also a rewarding nature experience. Deer Point Trail is a beautiful hike that takes you high above Christina Lake. This hike can be started off Biner Road or from the popular Texas Creek Campground. Look for Columbian ground squirrels around the campsites before starting your hike, which starts off steep but flattens out once you reach a ridge well above the lake.

Early on you'll walk through a tall thicket of thimbleberry, which should serve as a reminder that black bears are also active within the park. Douglas-fir and ponderosa pine dominate the forest, while paper birch and Rocky

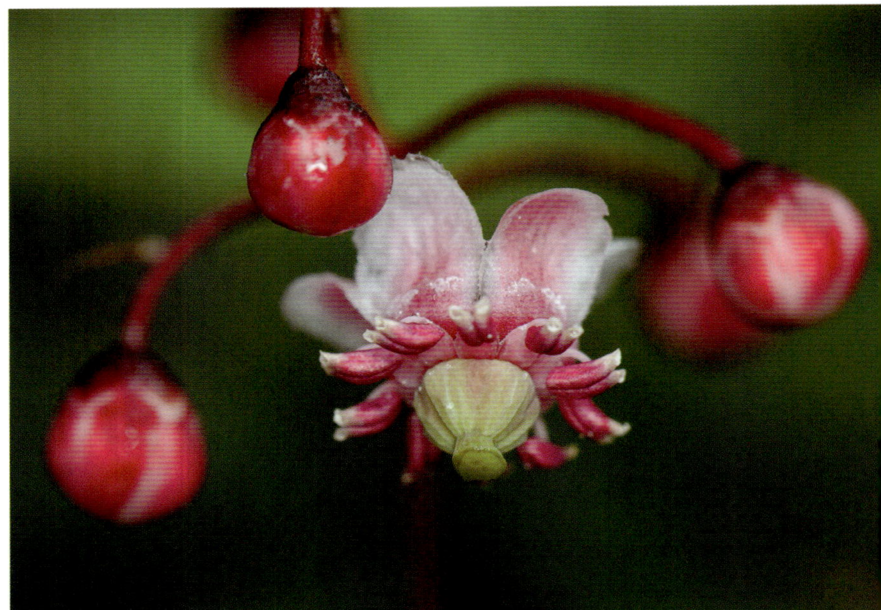

→ **Though easy to miss, the tiny pipsissewa flower is an intricate beauty when examined up close.**

Mountain maple represent some of the beautiful deciduous trees here. You'll likely encounter yellow-pine chipmunks scolding as you pass by. Seemingly never relaxed, these adorable seed-storing machines spend much of their time gathering and caching food during the warm season — forever in preparation for the next winter.

Be on the lookout for pale swallowtail and Lorquin's admiral butterflies drifting through sunny patches in the forest. Visit this park in the spring and early summer for the best birding and flower-finding opportunities. Twinflower, harsh paintbrush, broadleaf lupines and pipsissewa can all be seen along this trail.

There are over 48 kilometres of trails within Gladstone, two of which begin at the terminus of Deer Point Trail (if you are looking for an even longer adventure). However, be aware that these backcountry trails are no longer regularly maintained by BC Parks, so plan carefully and know your abilities. The first half of Deer Point Trail, up until Trapper Creek Campground, typically remains clear, but beyond that point optimal trail conditions are not guaranteed.

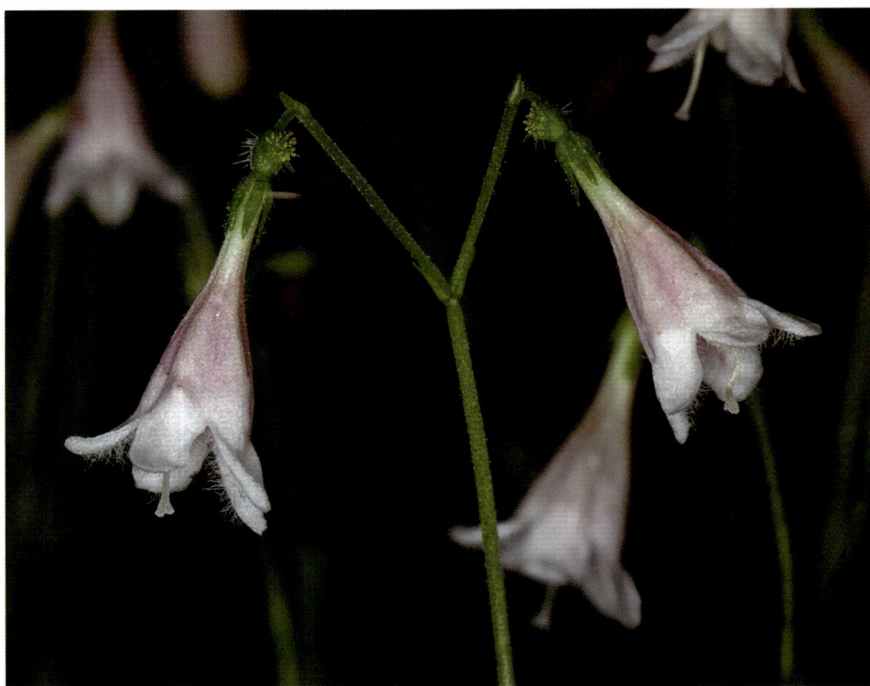

↑ **Delicate and diminutive twinflowers bloom along Deer Point Trail, always found in pink nodding pairs.**

Gilpin Grasslands Provincial Park

This park protects an exceedingly rare example of grassland ecosystem, creating a bird haven just off Crowsnest Highway

Once a cattle ranch, Gilpin Grasslands Provincial Park was purchased by BC Parks to protect a remnant grassland ecosystem. Now it's undergoing regeneration to a more natural state and attracting a great diversity of wildlife at the same time.

There's no formal entrance to this park, but parking is available at an ATV club staging site along Gilpin Forest Service Road. Nearby you'll find the trailhead, sometimes marked as Larry's Trail, Bundschu Trail or both. This access point actually begins outside the park boundaries but weaves you through the heart of the grasslands.

Keep an eye out for blue-listed California bighorn sheep seeking shade under some of the larger trees on hot days. In the spring you'll find Lewis's mock orange in bloom, its beautiful fragrance following you along the trail. This shrub, BC's only native hydrangea, got its name from its sweet scent and white flowers, which are reminiscent of citrus blossoms.

The open grasslands are the perfect setting for birding, so binoculars are a must. Listen for the whistling and gurgling song of western meadowlarks as well the sweet, descending notes of the blue-listed canyon wren, sung by both the males and females. Male lazuli buntings are easy to spot despite travelling low through the pines and shrubs, their brilliant blue feathers contrasted against a pumpkin-hued breast.

Ponderosa pines grow solo and in clusters throughout the grasslands, and many standing dead trees, called snags, pepper the meadows. These trees create the preferred habitat for the red-listed Lewis's woodpecker, which nests in the snags, as well as American kestrels, North America's smallest and most colourful falcon. Eastern and western

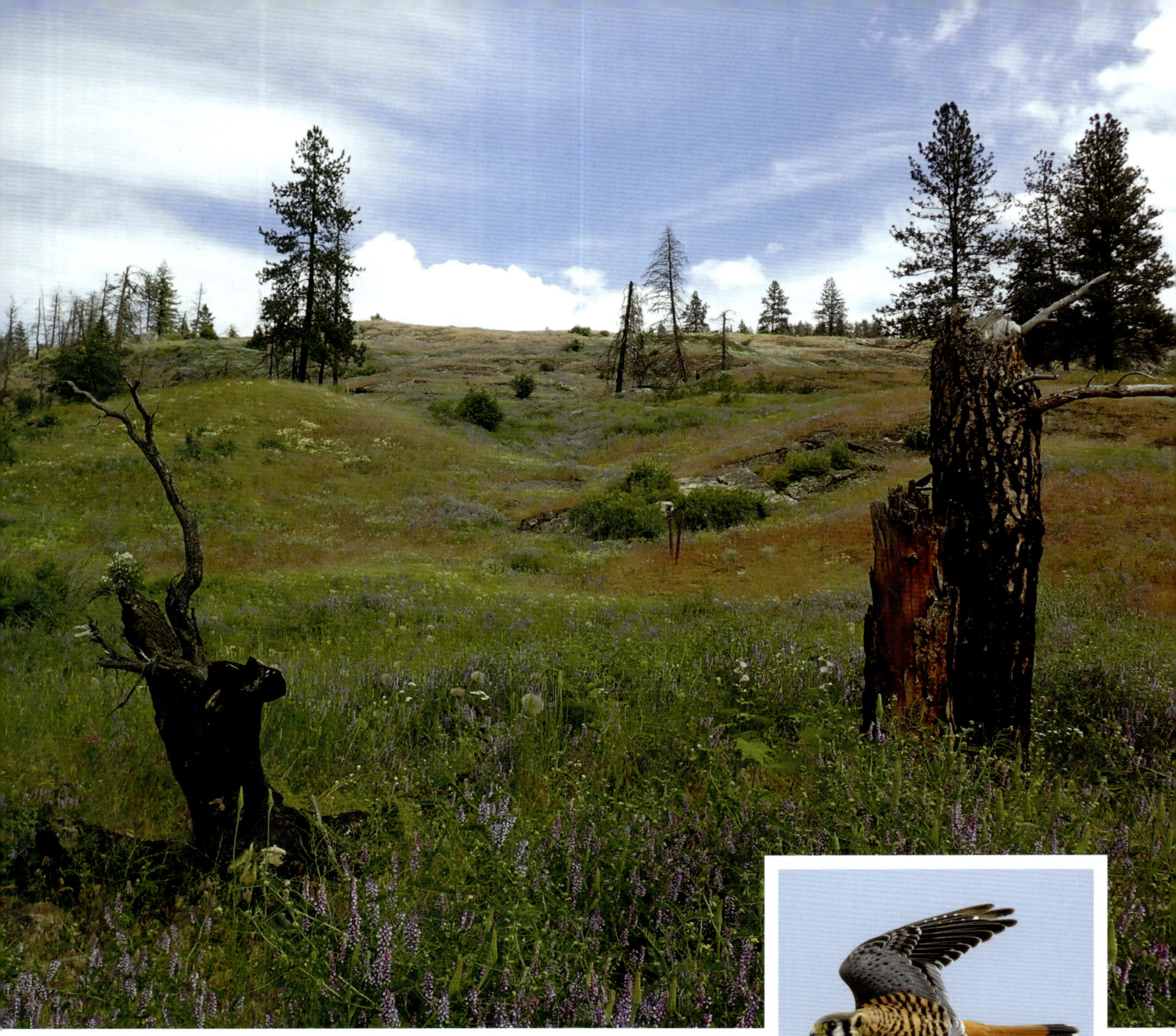

kingbirds cross over here and both may be seen harassing kestrels from tree to tree.

As this is former ranchland, the park is home to many introduced species of plants, including an abundance of hairy vetch and hoary alyssum, which covers the hillsides. That said, it's still an incredible location for botanizing. Be on the lookout for common blanketflower, arrowleaf balsamroot, linear-leaf phacelia, showy milkweed, and brittle pricklypear cactus.

Beware of poison ivy that may be growing right along the path, and you're likely to come out with a tick or two on your clothing as you exit the grasslands. Tuck your pants into your socks before the hike and give everyone a good check before getting into your car afterwards.

↑ **Diminutive American kestrels hunt in the open grasslands, snatching up everything from grasshoppers to songbirds.**

↖ **Gilpin Grasslands is a stunning setting for a day of birding and botanizing.**

Glacier National Park

Rugged mountains surrounded by cedar rainforest demonstrate the important role glaciers play in shaping landscapes

What Makes This Hot Spot Hot?

- Views of glacial recession shaping the landscape are available on many of the park's scenic hikes.
- Rogers Pass, where the Canadian Pacific Railway found its way through the towering Selkirk Mountains, is a National Historic Site.
- The park encompasses part of the oldest inland old-growth cedar rainforest in the world.

Address: 9520 Trans-Canada Hwy (Hwy 1), Rogers Pass, BC
Tel.: (250) 837-7500
Website:

Parks Canada

GPS Coordinates
Latitude: 51.30403
Longitude: −117.52388

Open year-round, though trails may be inaccessible for hiking during the winter

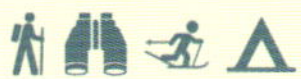

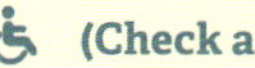

(Check ahead)

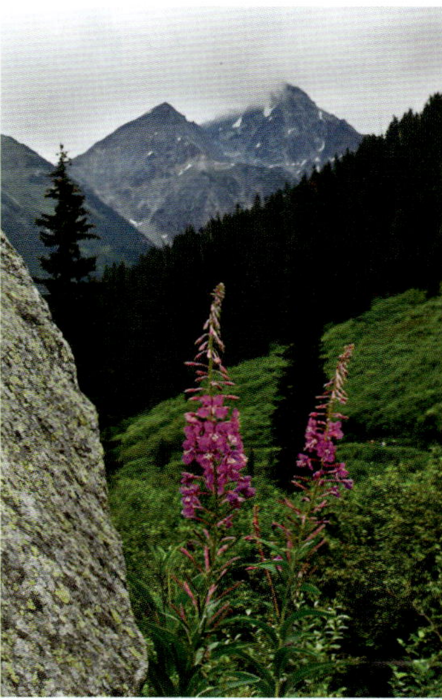

This park holds a special place in Canadian history as British Columbia's first national park. Rogers Pass runs through the centre of Glacier National Park. A natural low point between the highest peaks of the Columbia mountain range, it was the last puzzle piece in the Canadian Pacific Railway. The Abandoned Rails Trail features artifacts and interpretive historical signs from the site's earliest days. The Rogers Pass Discovery Centre is a valuable stop for information about the park's ecosystems and history, including the important role the park played in mountaineering.

Glacier National Park shares the world's oldest inland old-growth cedar rainforest with Mount Revelstoke National Park. The Hemlock Grove Boardwalk makes for a lovely stroll through this unique environment, with massive hemlock and cedar trees towering over the path.

A more difficult hike, the Great Glacier Trail is a must-do for the avid hiker. People often speak of ancient glacial events creating the land we see today. This 6.5-kilometre round trip allows visitors to see the erosion process in action. Although the Great Glacier is no longer visible from the trail, its impact does not go unseen. In fact, as the glacier recedes it continues to shape the landscape.

Fireweed is a common and beautiful sight at higher elevations, particularly in areas just beginning to support plant life. The plant has beautiful pink flowers and is responsible

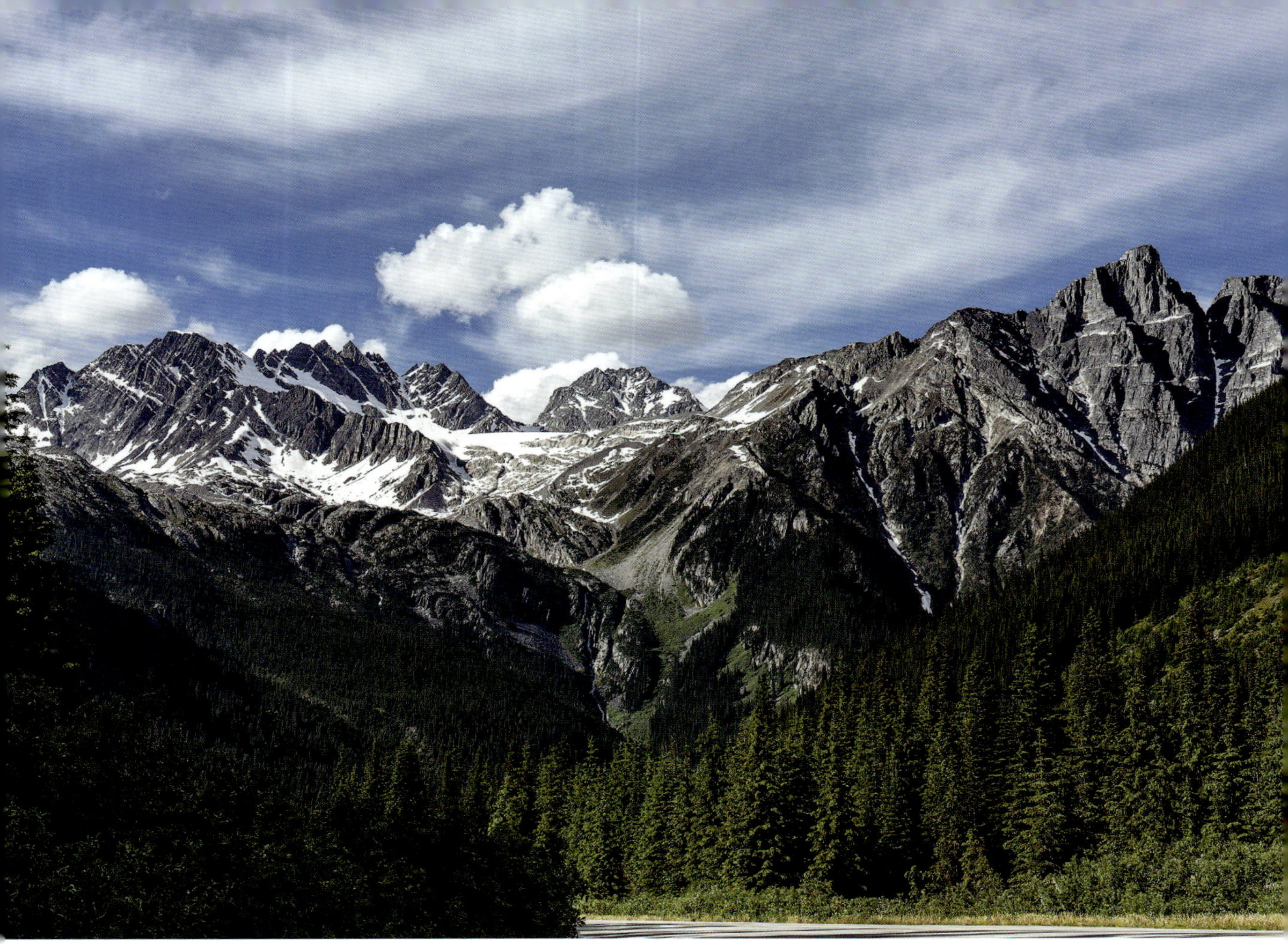

for fixing nitrogen in the soil, encouraging further plant growth. Western anemone is another magical sight in the alpine areas. It blooms as a small white flower in the spring, but by mid-summer it looks like a hairy puffball towering over other alpine flowers, such as the spotted saxifrage and bright monkeyflower.

At lower elevations, near the beginning of the trail, lush forests thrive on glacial runoff. As the trail gains elevation and nears the glacier, the landscape changes dramatically — a forest replete with rich vegetation becomes a rocky valley with talus slopes and patches of new vegetation. As of 2017 this glacier has receded over a kilometre since the late 1800s. More alpine and glacier viewing opportunities require trekking farther into the backcountry on trails, such as the steep but worthwhile Hermit Trail.

↑ It is easy to see the recent effects of glaciers in this rugged and mountainous landscape.

← Fireweed is a nitrogen-fixing plant often found in recently disturbed areas, making soil habitable for new plant life.

↙ Cinnamon black bears are sometimes seen roaming the wilderness.

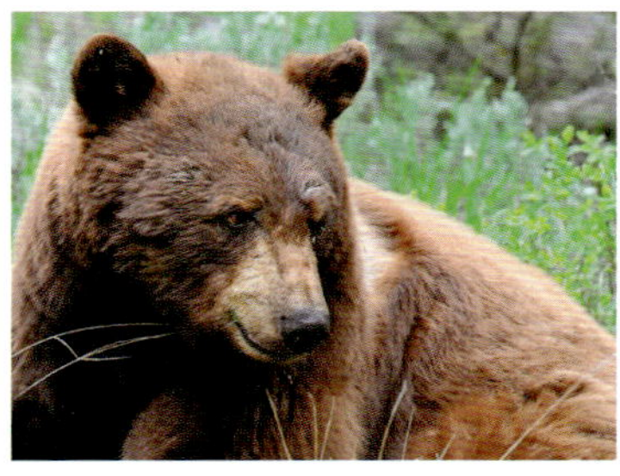

Goat Range Provincial Park

Special grizzly bears saunter alongside clear alpine streams in this rugged wilderness

What Makes This Hot Spot Hot?

- The rare white-hued grizzly bear lives in this protected area, alongside mountain goats and other delightful forms of wildlife.
- The giant Gerrard trout spawns exclusively in this park, which makes this an important area for its survival.
- The park's rugged scree slopes and alpine meadows make it appealing to the backcountry naturalist.

Address: Accessible via forestry roads from Hwy 6 or Hwy 31, north of Kaslo, BC
Tel.: N/A
Website:

BC Parks

GPS Coordinates
Latitude: 50.23666
Longitude: –117.24643

Open year-round

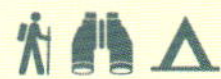

As its name indicates, this park is a protective habitat for mountain goats, but it also holds many other gems. The rare white-hued grizzly bear can be found here and is recognizable by its blond coat, if a hiker is lucky enough to spot one from a distance. Woodland caribou, elk and small mammals, such as fishers, also wander this wild space. One may even hear the hoot of a short-eared owl in the winter and spring.

Below the surface of the Lardeau River is a highly important species for this area: the Gerrard rainbow trout. Goat Range Provincial Park contains the only waterways in which this trout spawns. It is an interesting species of fish because the males are particularly aggressive during spawning, meaning only the stronger and larger trout breed. As a result, the Gerrard trout has evolved to be very large. On average a spawning fish will be around 80 centimetres long.

From low to high elevations, old-growth stands of trees turn into alpine meadows with clear streams and scree slopes — all in one hike. The park is rugged and remote, greatly contributing to its beauty as a natural space. Within the park and immediate area are some amazing hikes. Hikers should be experienced, prepared and bear aware in this area. The only truly maintained hike within the park is the Wilson Falls Loop on the southern side. It is accessible by East Wilson Creek Forestry Service Road off of Highway 6 and leads to a spectacular waterfall through large cedar trees up to 1.5 metres in diameter. From the same road, the Alps Alturas Trail is a beautiful hike into exemplary alpine environs that feature scree slopes, white heather and alpine lakes. There are a number of other hikes in and around the park, including the spectacular Meadow Mountain. All the trails afford sensational wilderness-viewing opportunities.

→ **The Alps Alturas Trail is a wonderful way to experience the alpine.**

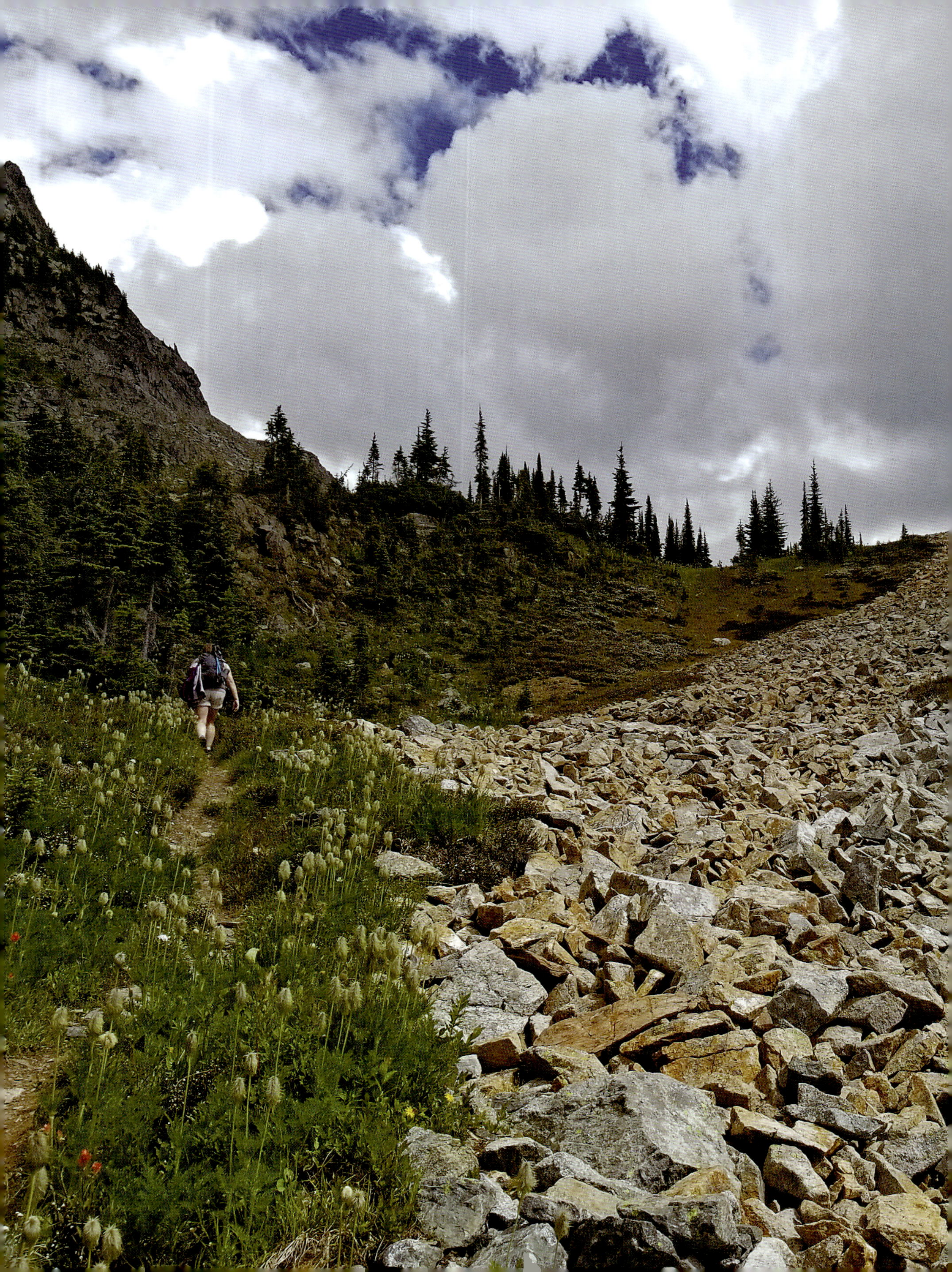

Halfway Hot Springs

A well-maintained campground with a natural hot spring that is close to recreational opportunities

What Makes This Hot Spot Hot?

- This spot boasts a true, natural hot spring experience in an area where you can find many developed hot springs.
- Many nearby hikes and birding opportunities make this campground a good home base after a day of adventures.
- A winter snowshoe followed by a dip in the hot pools is an experience not easily forgotten.

Address: The turnoff from Hwy 23 is 26 km north of Nakusp, BC. See the website below for specific details.
Tel.: N/A
Website:

Recreation Sites and Trails BC

GPS Coordinates
Latitude: 50.50358
Longitude: –117.78373

Open year-round

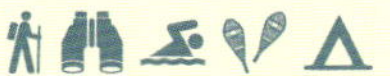

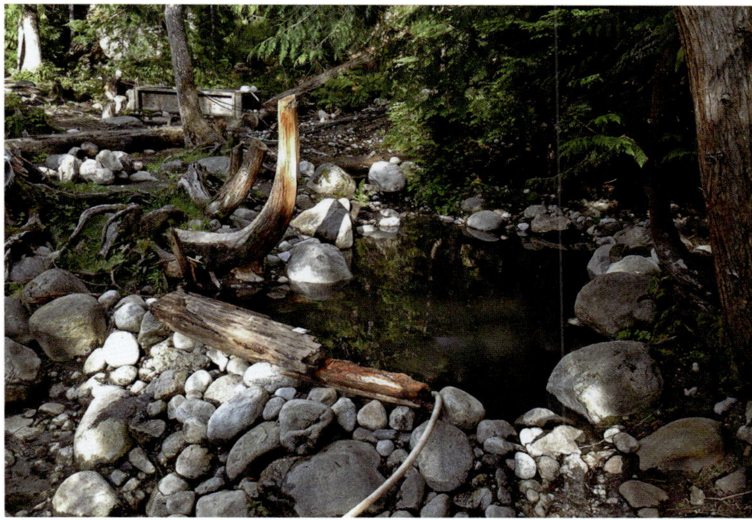

A must-do on a tour of British Columbia hot springs, the Halfway Hot Springs are almost exactly halfway between Revelstoke and Nakusp. Surrounded by the beautiful trees and moss-covered roots of a riverside forest, this site is a perfect place for a relaxing camping trip. As the springs have become more popular, what used to be a rugged and difficult hike has become easier thanks to Recreation Sites and Trails BC. The hot springs are now a relatively established camping site with well-maintained trails and stairs. However, despite the site being well maintained, the road to the springs is still bumpy so a four-wheel drive vehicle is highly recommended.

For winter hot spring enthusiasts, snowshoeing is still necessary to reach the pools, but the winter trek there is well worth the effort as these geothermal springs are quite hot all year. Depending on the season hot spring users can adjust the temperature of the springs by tweaking how much hot spring water and cold water from the

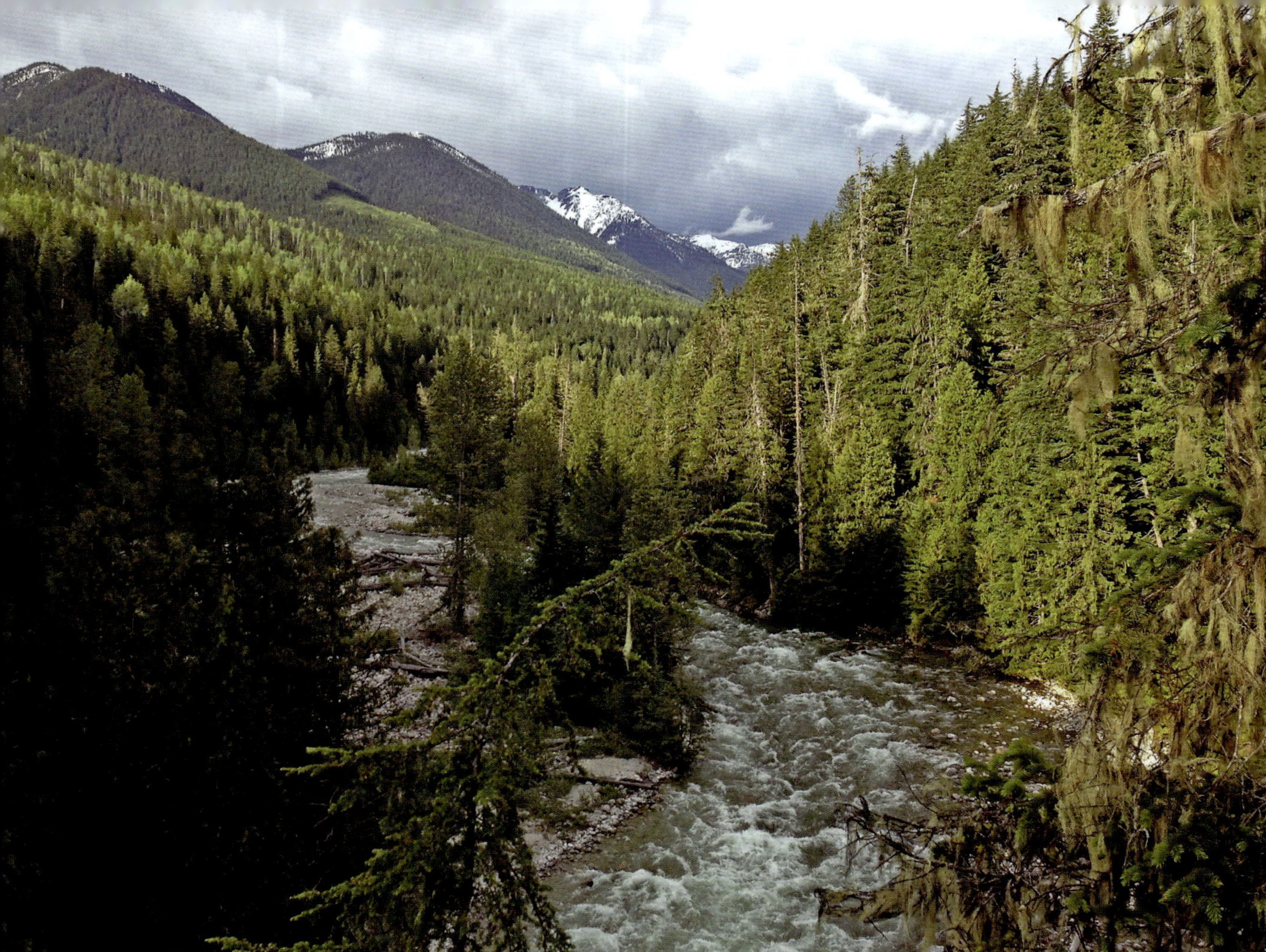

Halfway River flow into the rocky pools. For instance, you may choose to add more hot water from a hose connected to the springs or more cold river water from another hose. When you are not relaxing in the pools, check out the forest trails around the springs or soak in the natural beauty along the riverside.

The surrounding area has been referred to as the Valley of Hot Springs, and it does live up to its name. Although the Halfway Hot Springs are the only accessible undeveloped springs, there are two well-known commercial hot springs nearby: Halcyon and Nakusp. The waters of all the springs eventually drain into the Arrow Lakes. What was once two widened areas in the Columbia River has essentially become one large lake following the building of a dam. The lakes are surrounded by wetlands and marshes as well as beautiful mountains and forests. If you feel the need to move out of relaxation mode there are many fantastic recreational opportunities nearby in the form of hiking, paddling and bird and wildlife watching.

The river drains into the Arrow Lakes.

Rocky pools hold spring water that has been heated far underground.

Kokanee Glacier Provincial Park

A mining mecca turned conservation hub and hiking paradise

What Makes This Hot Spot Hot?

- Pollinators, including butterflies and bumble bees, flourish in meadows of wildflowers.
- Hikers can access alpine lakes surrounded by steep terrain and glaciers.
- The park provides habitat for grizzly bears, marmots and grouse.

Address: 15 km north of Hwy 3A
Tel.: (250) 352-3433 (Nelson visitor centre)
Website:

BC Parks

GPS Coordinates
Latitude: 49.72669
Longitude: –117.15648

Open year-round

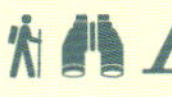

As with a number of the more remote parks of British Columbia, this landscape was initially known for its mining. Veins of silver and gold ore cut through the granite bedrock of the park. Miners pushed the limits of their trade on the steep cliffs throughout the park. Today many old mining trails are used for hiking and weave through the park. The trails in the park take hikers to stunning lakes, around magnificent glaciated peaks and through forests and alpine meadows.

The largest glacier in the park, the Kokanee Glacier — the park's namesake — is visible from the Kokanee Glacier Cabin. For visitors wanting to have a base camp from which to explore, the cabin is luxurious for the backcountry and can be booked for a night. This cabin was built in honour of Michel Trudeau, who died tragically in an avalanche at Kokanee Lake.

The shallow soil on the granite bedrock doesn't support large trees, but stands of Engelmann spruce and whitebark pine can be found around the beautiful blue lakes and open meadows, which, when in bloom, are their own little ecosystems abuzz with insects.

An abundance of life, including plants, insects and birds, exist in these meadows. Each species has a unique relationship with the other species found here. White pasqueflower is one of the first wildflowers to bloom as the snow melts and provides much needed pollen to some solitary bees as they build nests. Clumps of purple aster dot the alpine meadows and are often covered in bumble bees, flies and butterflies — all of whom carry pollen between the flowers. The leaves of the beautiful hookedspur violet host the caterpillars of zerene fritillary butterflies before they metamorphose into pollinators themselves. The brilliant yellow of glacier lilies attracts bumble bees, and rhododendrons are frequented by

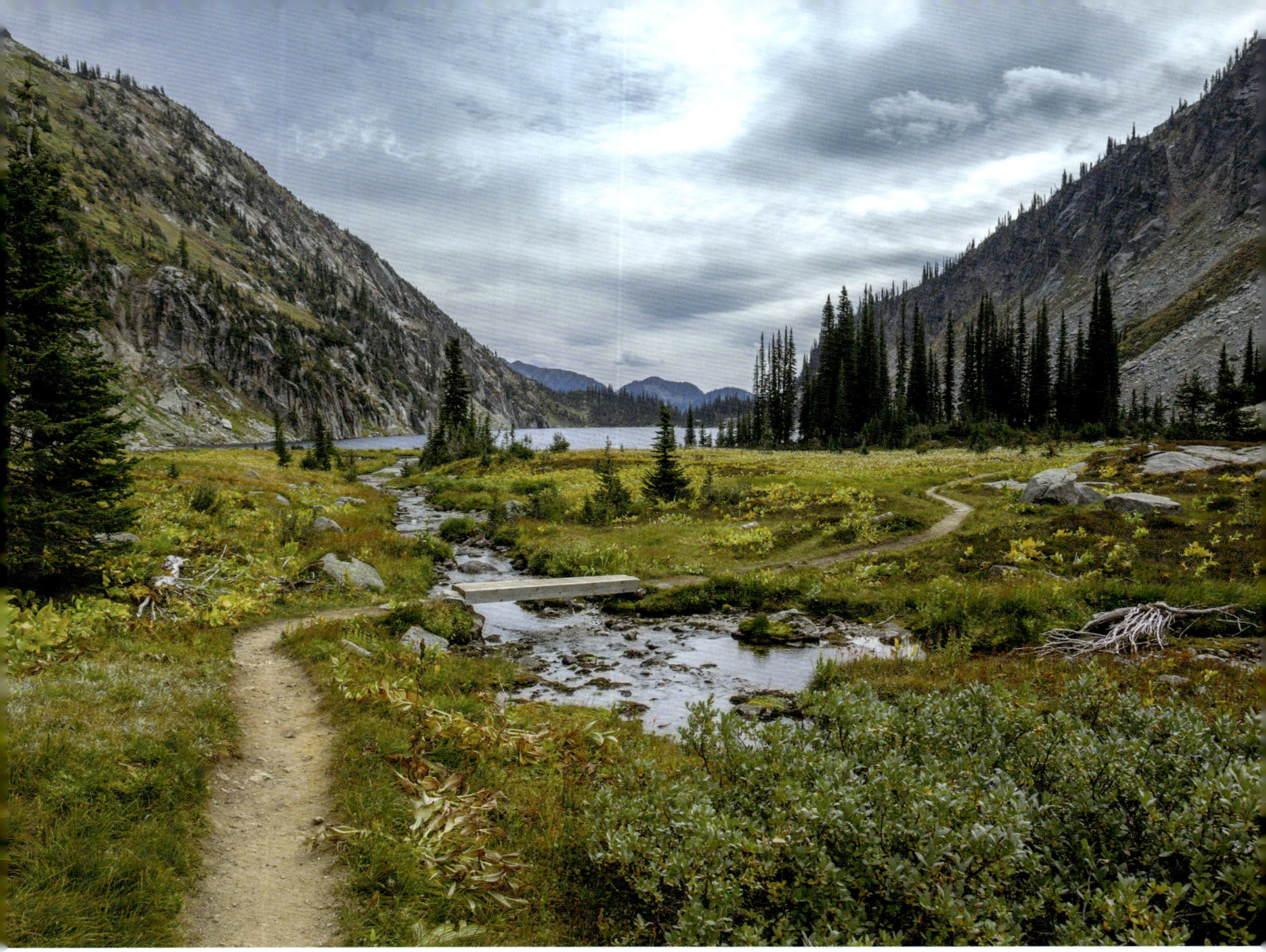

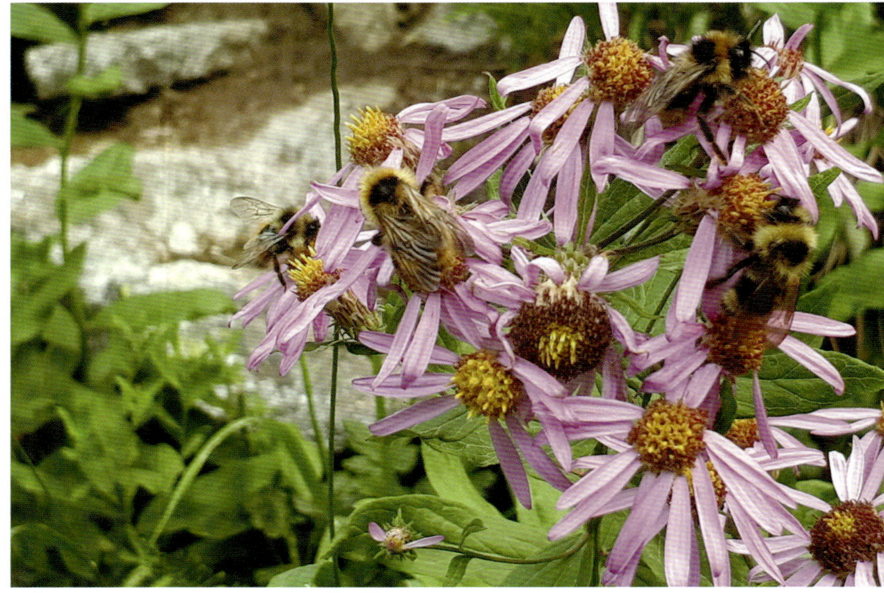

hummingbirds for nectar and to build their delicate nests.

The park is a particularly important habitat for grizzly bears as well as several other mammals, including pikas, hoary marmots, martens and a small population of mountain goats. With a number of different entrances and trails, there is no wrong way to explore this park.

Kootenay National Park

Check out the park's unique Paint Pots before taking off on a scenic hike into the forest

What Makes This Hot Spot Hot?

- Forest succession following fires in 2003 offers visitors a different visual experience every year.
- The Paint Pots, pools of spring water in ochre beds, are a geological beauty and important to many local Indigenous Peoples.
- Abundant in birds, mountain goats and even grizzly bears, this park is an ever-changing wildlife haven.

Address: Banff-Windermere Hwy (Hwy 93), north of Invermere, BC
Tel.: (250) 347-9505
Website:

Parks Canada

GPS Coordinates
Latitude: 50.97468
Longitude: −115.94727

Open year-round

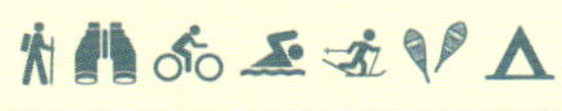

♿ (Check ahead)

Excellent for a wide variety of short excursions, Kootenay National Park has a lot to offer and is relatively easy to access. From glaciers to meadows and mineral baths, this park is an adventure waiting for you. A section of the Burgess Shale, which is an important fossil bed and another nature hot spot, lies in this park. Other main attractions are the Paint Pots, which are cold mineral spring pools sitting in beds of ochre. The shape and colour of the pools make one want to dip a large paintbrush in them! The Niitsitapi, Ktunaxa and Stoney Nations all collected ochre from this area to create paint for various purposes.

The park experienced five lightning wildfires in 2003, and the short Fireweed Loops take hikers on interpretive walks through a burned area. Fireweed and other plants moved in rapidly and are restoring nutrients to the soil. Hiking along these trails is a fantastic opportunity to see a recently burned forest growing and changing. The northern hawk owl, for which burned areas create new habitat, is nesting and living here. Other species that will thrive in the forest as succession continues are grizzly bears and moose. Grizzlies love huckleberries, which generally appear at their best 25 years after a fire.

For something completely different, Marble Canyon Trail leads hikers to a river that cuts through a steep limestone and dolomite gorge, with spectacular mountain views en route. Keep an eye out and you may be lucky enough to spot a bighorn sheep.

With over 200 kilometres of trails, some just off the road and others deep into the backcountry along glaciers and up mountains, this park has something for everybody. And all visitors can agree that an ideal day of fun exploring the park finishes with a soak in the warm waters of Radium Hot Springs.

➚ **Fireweed is a common feature of the alpine as well as one of the first plants to regrow in areas affected by forest fires.**

➚ **The northern hawk owl enjoys the habitat created by the park's 2003 fire.**

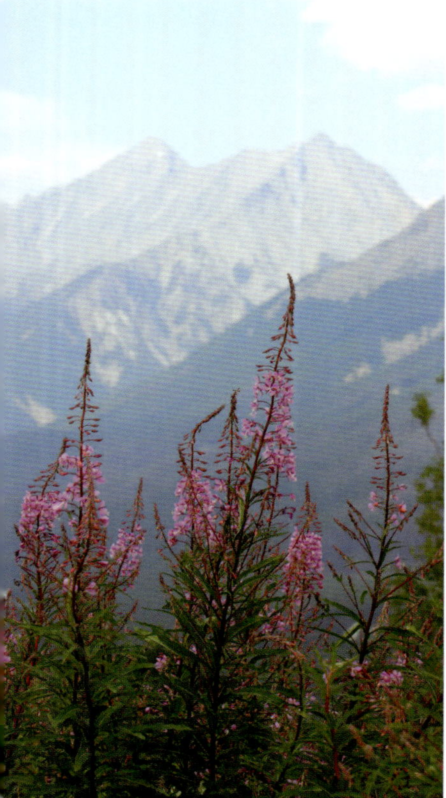

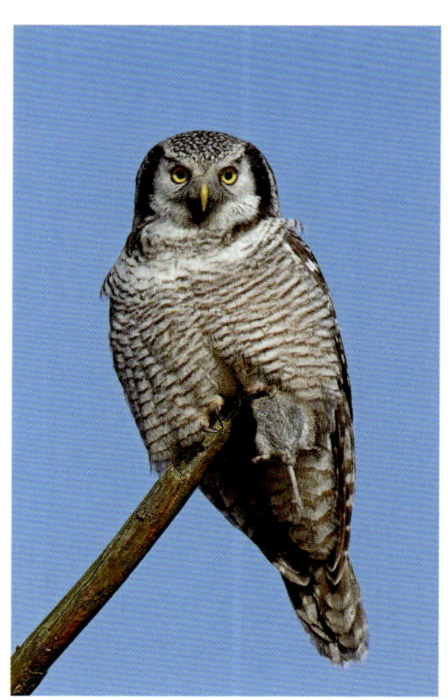

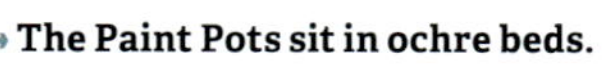
→ **The Paint Pots sit in ochre beds.**

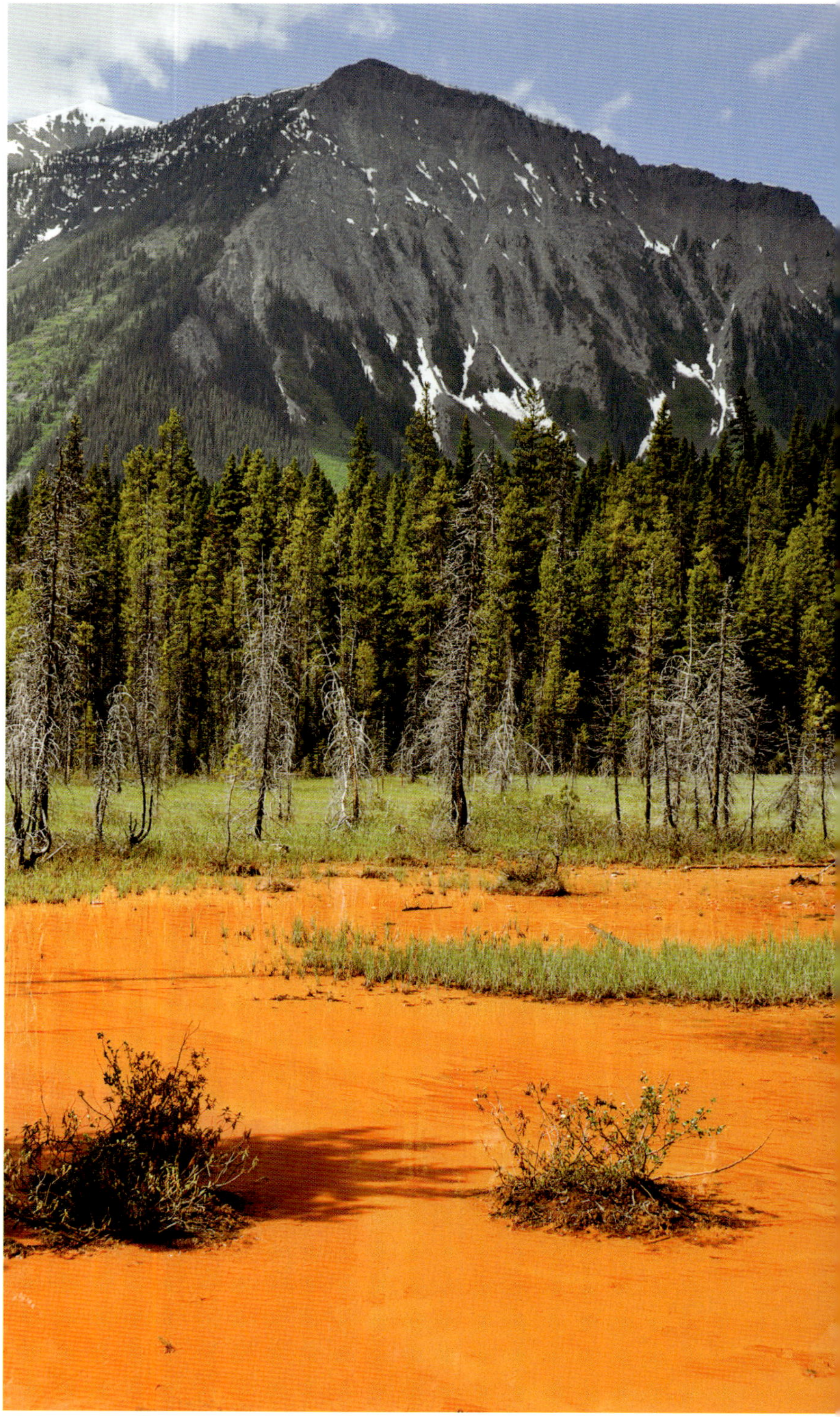

WHITESWAN LAKE PROVINCIAL PARK

Lussier Hot Springs

These hot springs offer chances to watch wildlife right from the rocky pools

What Makes This Hot Spot Hot?

- Mineral-rich heated water seeps out of the earth and flows between rocky pools into a frigid river.
- Belted kingfishers are one of many birds that call this forest home.
- Wildlife watching opportunities abound, and camping is available on nearby lakes.

Address: Whiteswan Lake Provincial Park, 17 km east on Whiteswan Lake Forest Service Road off Hwy 95, East Kootenay, BC
Tel.: (250) 422-3003
Website:

BC Parks

GPS Coordinates
Latitude: 50.13515
Longitude: −115.5768

Open year-round

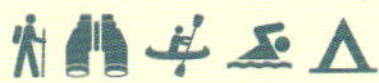

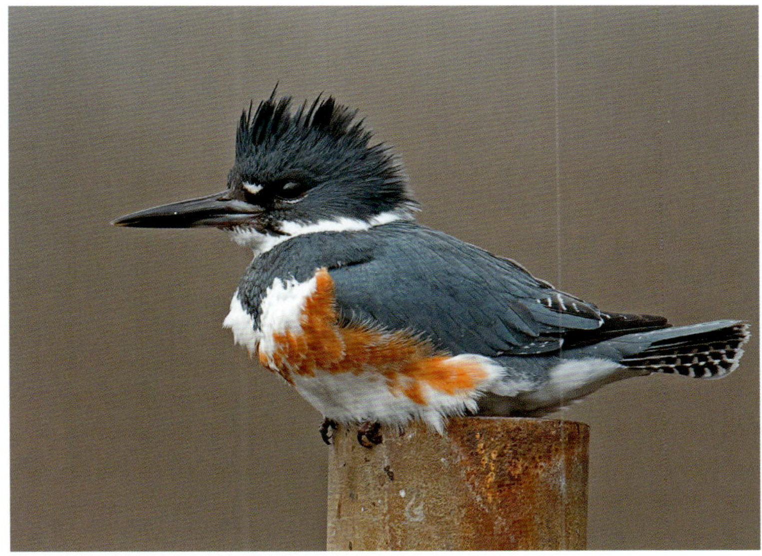

Natural, undeveloped hot springs alongside a river make for a relaxing experience. The hot springs are situated in Whiteswan Lake Provincial Park, where there is no shortage of wildlife. A quick hike off of the forestry service road leads to a little paradise. The benefits of these serene springs have been known to the Ktunaxa Nation for at least 5,000 years. They used the surrounding area as a seasonal hunting ground. When trappers, prospectors and guides arrived they began soaking in the waters after long days of hard work. The water can be as hot as 43 degrees Celsius, but cools as it flows between pools. And if you do overheat there is a frigid river right next to the springs that will cool you down.

Dense forest surrounds the river and protects moose, mountain goats and bears, both black and grizzly varieties. Keep an eye out for the belted kingfisher, one of a few bird species in which the females are more colourful

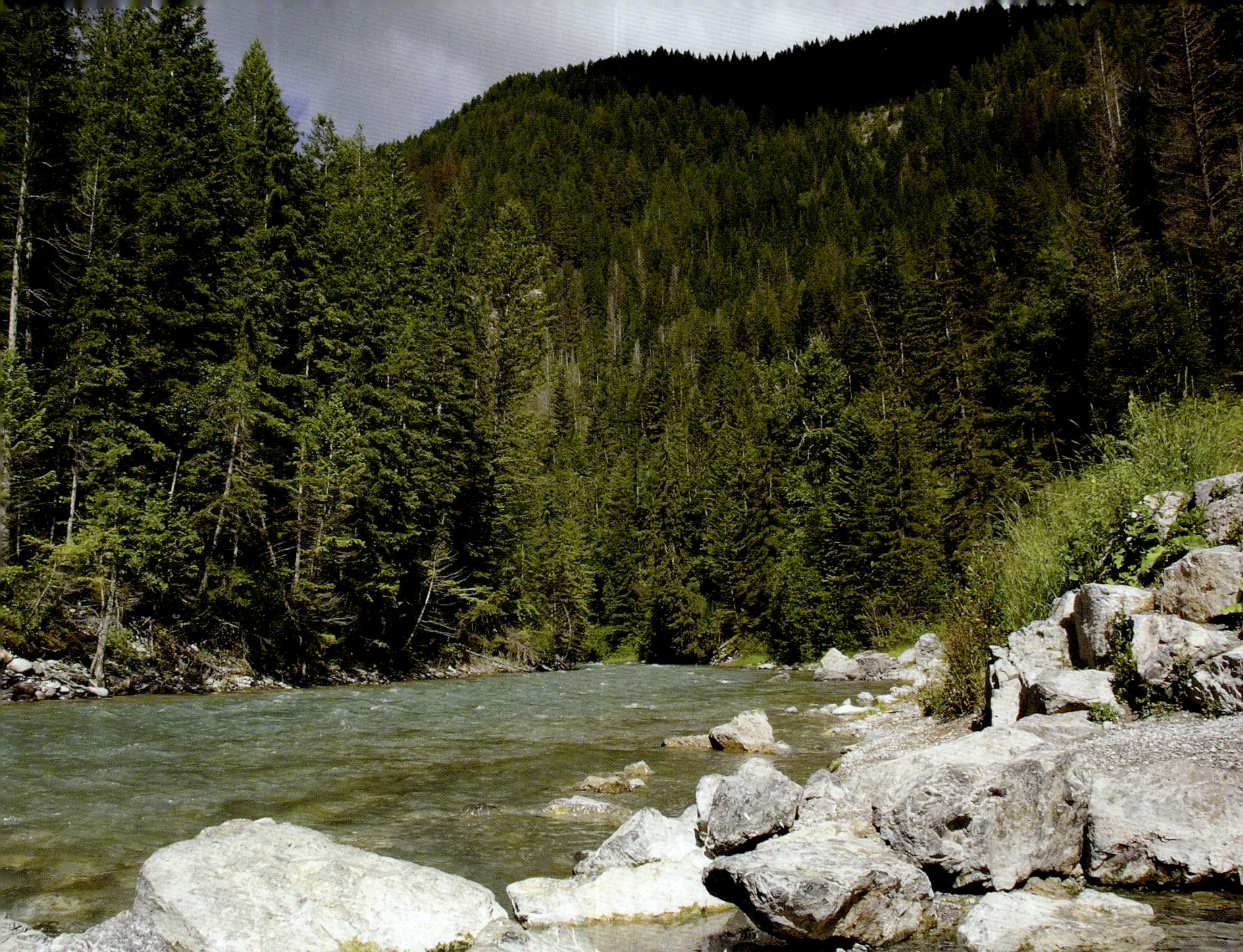

than the males, as well as other birds around the river or in the nearby lakes and forests. As you relax, look up and you may just spot a bald eagle soaring overhead.

A hot spring enthusiast with a sharp nose may notice a slight egg odour. As the water flows and is heated underground it becomes rich in minerals, such as sulphur. The smell is not the sulphur itself, but a gas produced by sulphur-eating bacteria deep underground. The water is harmless to bathe in so go ahead and relax in the serene pools while soaking in the surrounding wilderness. In the winter, enclosed by snow-covered trees that muffle the sounds of the forest, the steaming baths provide a completely different experience.

Basic toilets and changing rooms are available at the parking area. Just past the springs, Alces Lake offers camping facilities, and both Alces and Whiteswan lakes provide canoeing, swimming and more wildlife watching opportunities.

↑ **The Lussier River, as seen from the hot springs.**

↖ **The female belted kingfisher is a rarity among birds as she is more colourful than her male counterpart.**

Mount Revelstoke National Park

Alpine flowers bloom in open meadows that showcase the serenity of mountain life

What Makes This Hot Spot Hot?

- Visitors can travel from an inland cedar rainforest to a mountain summit within an hour.
- The alpine tundra supports a wide variety of wildflowers in the late summer.
- Birders have an opportunity to see three true alpine birds: the golden eagle, rosy finch and American pipit.

Address: Revelstoke, BC
Tel.: (250) 837-7500
Website:

Parks Canada

GPS Coordinates
Latitude: 51.06815
Longitude: −117.97119

Open year-round with some road restrictions

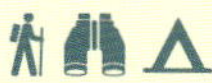

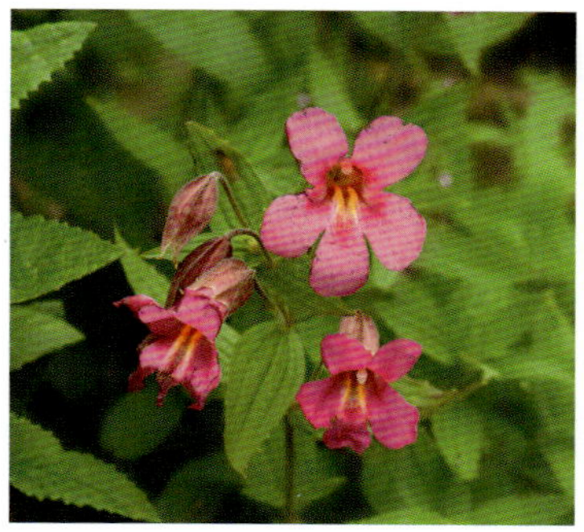

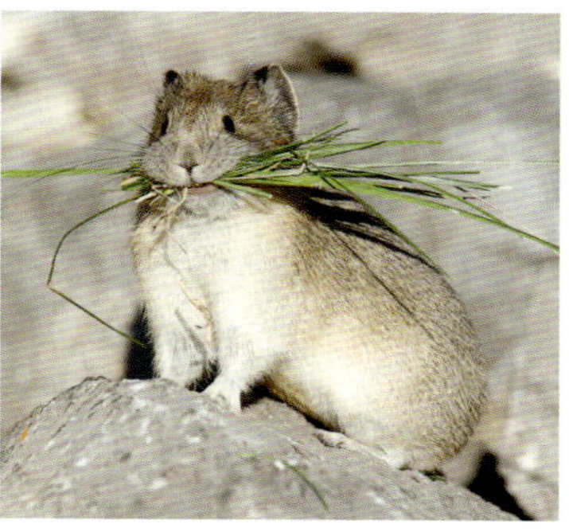

↑ **A pika feeds on the alpine vegetation.**

↖ **Delicate pink monkeyflower flourishes in the alpine tundra.**

Move from the farthest inland cedar rainforest in the world to alpine tundra in a short, scenic drive to the Meadows in the Sky Parkway. Breathtaking viewpoints and short interpretive walks along the way make the drive alone worth the trip. Once at the parking lot you will notice a stunning display of alpine wildflowers. With the height of the bloom taking place in early August, look for the delicate white mountain-heather — with its small, white bell-shaped flowers — amid red paintbrush, pink monkeyflower, mountain arnica and spotted saxifrage, which is characterized by small yellow, orange and pink dots arranged on white petals.

Take a short stroll on a hemlock-shaded loop trail leading to Balsam Lake, or enjoy the informative First Footsteps Trail, which loops through hemlock groves and subalpine meadows with unforgettable views of the surrounding Monashee and Selkirk mountains. The trail features sculptures, artwork and interpretive signs

from the Secwepemc and Okanagan First Nations.

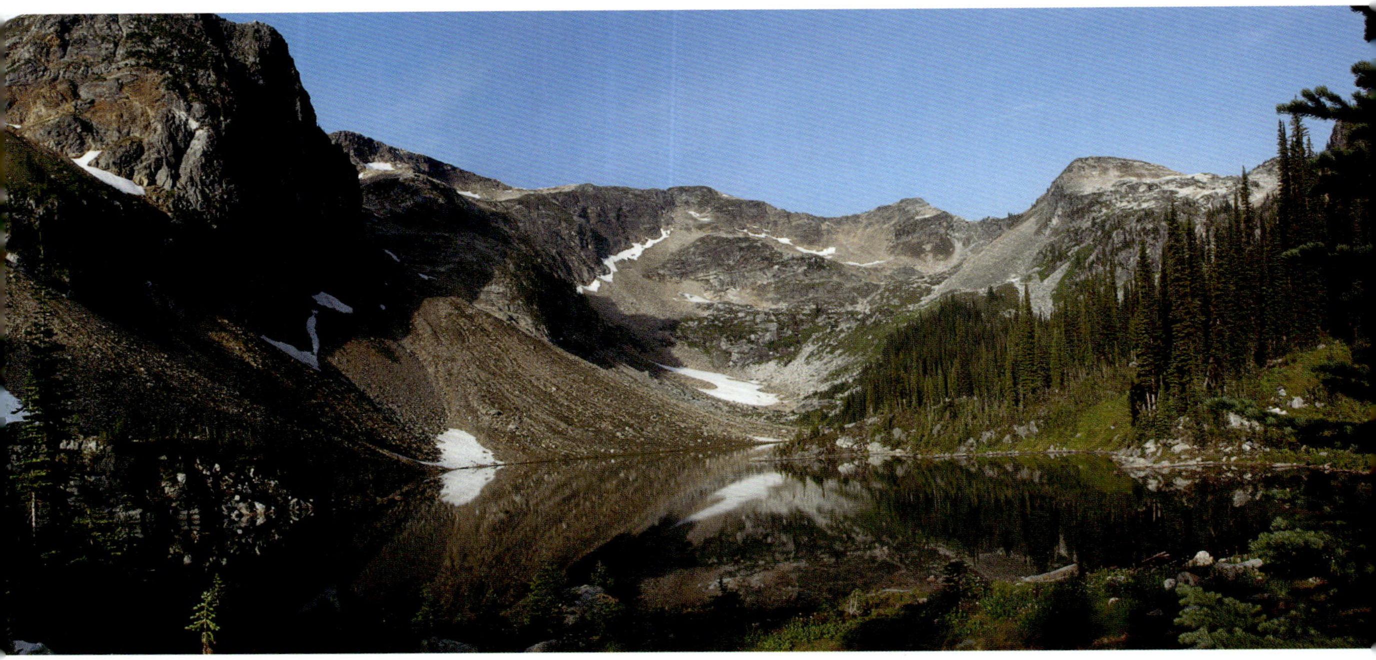

To experience true alpine tundra, a short uphill hike on the Upper Summit Trail will take you to the top of Mount Revelstoke. The golden eagle, rosy finch and American pipit are three true alpine birds found in this park, making this trek potentially very rewarding.

Hikes to Eva and Jade lakes can be done as long days — 6- and 13-kilometre round trips, respectively — or overnight camping trips. These less-travelled trails meander through hemlock forests, meadows blanketed in alpine flowers and scree fields. Watch for the pika, a small mammal inhabiting the rocky slopes of the alpine. A cousin of the rabbit with small, round ears, the pika is very sensitive to climate change. As temperatures increase they flee to higher altitudes. Stay on the trail and respect the park's rules so as to preserve the food sources and remaining habitat of this high-altitude critter.

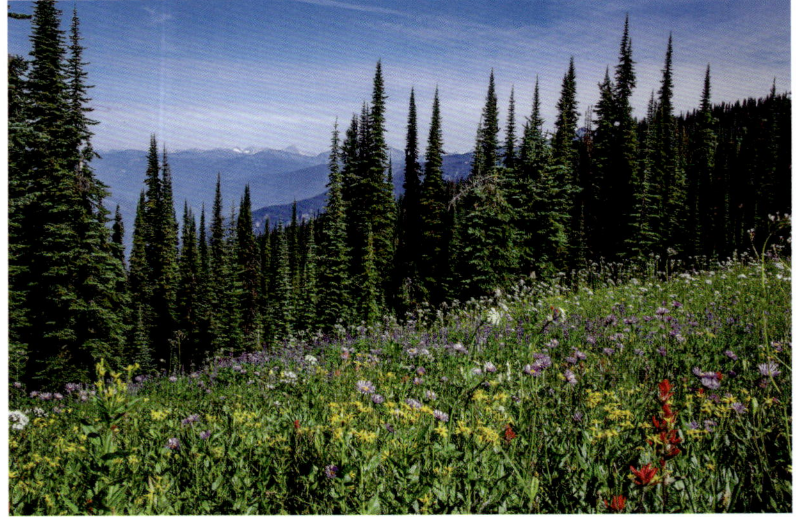

↑ **Wildflowers bloom in abundance in tranquil meadows.**

↖ **Jade Lake is a popular campsite for backcountry campers.**

Premier Lake Provincial Park

A popular and easily accessed fishing hole in a gorgeous landscape

What Makes This Hot Spot Hot?

- A number of clear, emerald lakes are surrounded by trails and beautiful scenery.
- Well known for its fishing, this park has plenty of life in the water, including rainbow trout and western painted turtles.
- In the fall, larch trees turn yellow and shed their needles in green forests of Douglas-fir.

Address: Skookumchuck, BC
Tel.: (250) 422-3003
Website:

BC Parks

GPS Coordinates
Latitude: 49.90983
Longitude: –115.64895

Open year-round

(Check ahead)

Known for its fishing opportunities, Premier Lake Provincial Park is settled in the Rocky Mountains and named for the large body of water in its north end. First used as a fishing site by the Ktunaxa Nation, Premier Lake is still one of the most popular fishing lakes in the Kootenays. For those wanting to learn more about the fish in the lake, there is a fish ladder with interpretive signs about the life cycles of the resident rainbow trout close to the southern end of the lake.

The park has four other lakes close by, meaning there is no lack of places to explore. Douglas-fir and western larch trees line the banks of the park's emerald-coloured lakes. In the fall the needles of the larch turn yellow, a stunning contrast to the water and surrounding forests. We tend to associate falling leaves with deciduous trees, and although larch trees have needles they are in fact deciduous and drop their yellowing needles in time for the winter.

The Premier Lake Trail is a must-do loop that guides visitors through meadows and

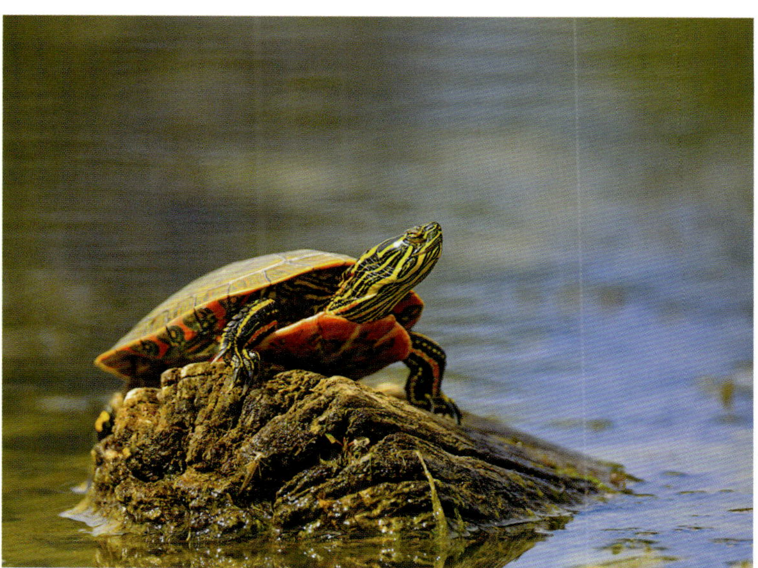

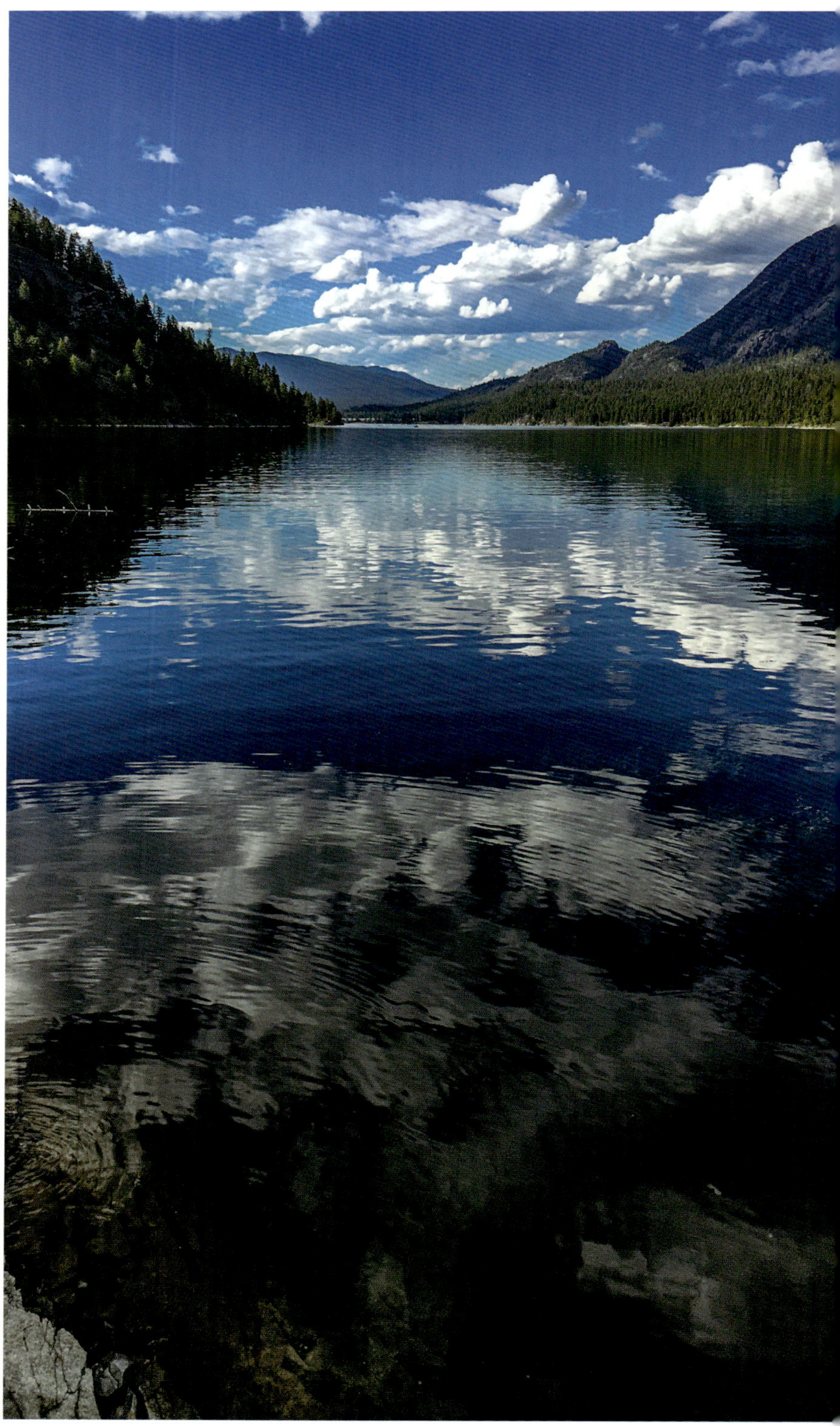

forests and connects Premier Lake to three other lakes. At Turtle Lake the western painted turtle is often seen sunning itself on logs just out of the water. If you visit in the late spring watch your step, as the female turtles journey out of the water to find a nice spot to lay their eggs. Some of these turtles have been known to go over 100 metres away from water to lay their eggs! In the winter the turtles burrow into the soft sediment on the lake bottom and hibernate until warmer weather. The trail continues through more beautiful landscapes with stops at Yankee and Canuck lakes. A separate trail leads visitors to Quartz Lake, a favourite local swimming spot. Always watch for birds and other wildlife on your hike. The nearby Premier Ridge is an important space for wintering herds of elk, deer and bighorn sheep.

➜ The waters of Premier Lake Provincial Park are surrounded by a breathtaking mountainscape.

⬅ Western painted turtles sunbathe on logs around Turtle Lake.

Top of the World Provincial Park

The lakes and meadows of this alpine plateau are not to be missed

What Makes This Hot Spot Hot?

- An easy hike in affords days of exploration through meadows, forests and true alpine landscapes.
- The spectacular base camp at Fish Lake hosts many birds, including osprey.
- Alpine flowers blanket fields in shades of purple, red and yellow.

Address: To access the trailhead turn east 4.5 km south of Canal Flats and follow about 50 km of forest service roads
Tel.: (250) 489-8540
Website:

BC Parks

GPS Coordinates
Latitude: 49.88528
Longitude: −115.46989

Open year-round

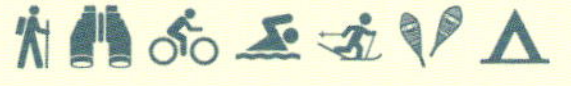

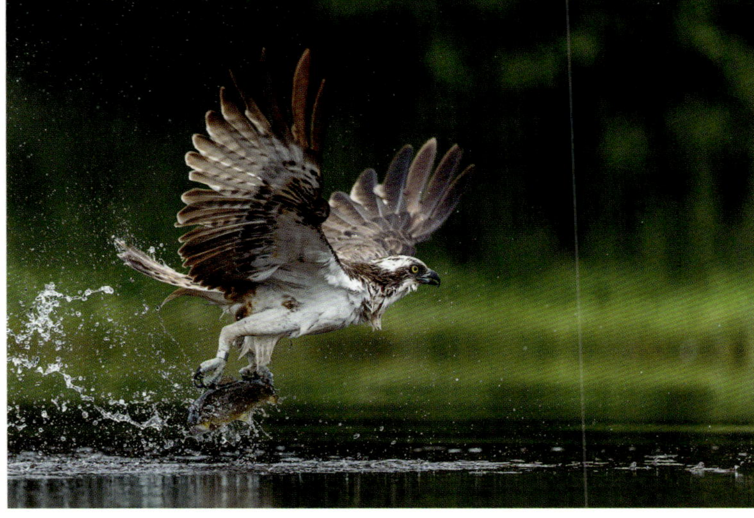

The hike in to Fish Lake, Top of the World Provincial Park's main access point and hub of activity, is a fairly flat meander through beautiful forests along a river. The nature of the main access trail makes this a family-friendly outdoor expedition. Spectacular hike-in campsites and a shared backcountry cabin are a great home base from which to explore the landscapes surrounding the lake.

With forests, meadows and mountain peaks close by one could stay at this campsite and hike for days! From Fish Lake, many trails afford opportunities to explore surrounding lakes, ridges and viewpoints.

Fish Lake supports a large bird population. Pine grosbeaks and boreal chickadees sing in the forest, while the distinct call of the common loon echoes over the lake. When trout are spawning in the lake a bald eagle or

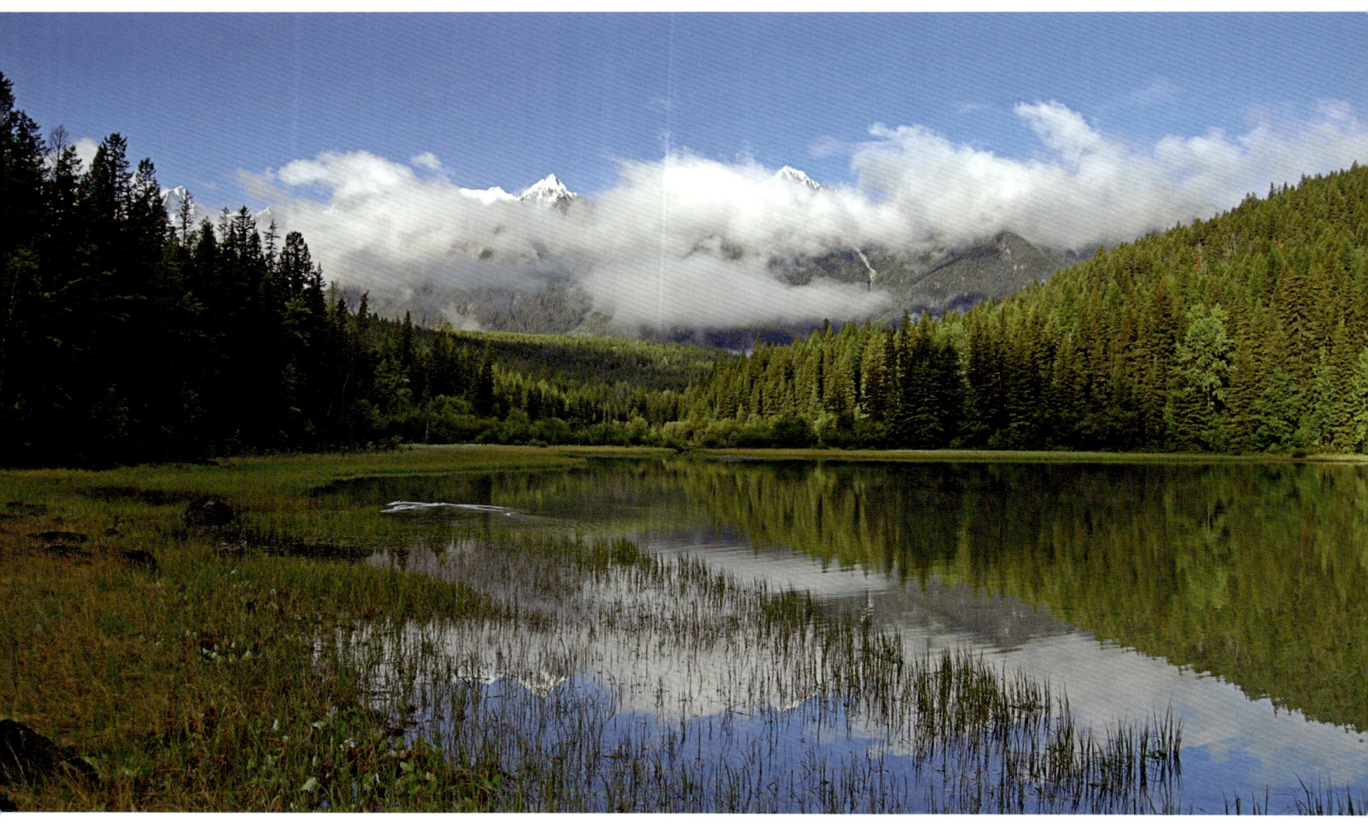

osprey may swoop down from the trees to grab a meal just beneath the water's surface. As you venture away from the lake, alpine wildflowers bloom in meadows. Mule deer are common sights in the alpine meadows, where flowers, such as the red paintbrush and broadleaf arnica, paint the grassy fields red and yellow. Since the majority of the park is at a high elevation the trees are typical of alpine and sub-alpine environments. As the elevation increases, the trees gradually disappear, leaving hikers with panoramic views of the surrounding mountains.

While hiking in or out of the park, take a detour and look for Crazy Creek and Crazy River, places where flowing water abruptly appears out of the rocks. Water has dissolved the limestone bedrock and created underground channels through which the creek and river flow before they suddenly appear. Another geological feature of importance in this park is chert, which the Ktunaxa Nation used to make tools and weapons. Chert is a tough sedimentary rock, which forms sharp edges when chipped. Chert from this plateau was highly valued and traded extensively.

↑ **A serene, lake-side morning in Top of the World Provincial Park.**

← **An osprey catches a trout just beneath the water's surface.**

Valhalla Provincial Park

Hikers must prepare to feel an overwhelming sense of awe at the outstanding scenery

What Makes This Hot Spot Hot?

- It takes multiple visits to explore this varied park.
- Mountain goats munch on grass in open fields near rocky slopes, while in the lower-elevation forests, grouse flutter between large trees.
- Pictographs from the Sinixt Nation and lakeshore campsites make canoeing an excellent way to explore.

Address: The park is accessible by a number of trailheads and forest service roads as well as by boat from Slocan, Silverton and New Denver, BC
Tel.: (1-800) 689-9025
Website:

BC Parks

GPS Coordinates
Latitude: 49.8787
Longitude: −117.57156

Open year-round

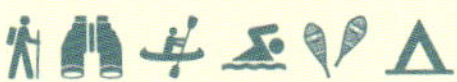

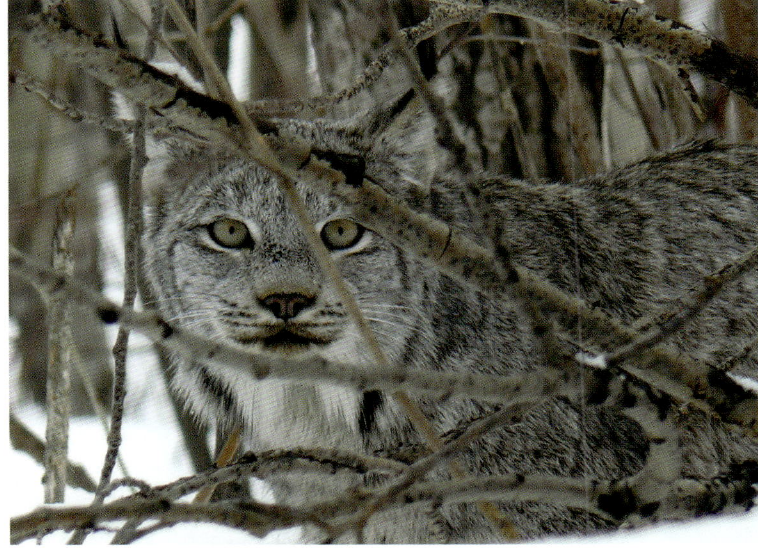

The Valhalla Range of the Selkirk Mountains is nestled between the Arrow and Slocan Lakes and protects an impressive array of wildlife and habitats. The elevation range enclosed in this protected area means wildlife can move through an entire watershed, from the slightest trickle of snow melting on a mountain to a rushing river or waterfall entering a lake.

The breathtaking scenery of the park is what draws many backcountry campers, hikers and canoeists. Spotting mountain goats as they make their way down steep rocky slopes on a misty morning is truly a magical sight. The park's landscape is characterized by jagged rocky spires, calm alpine lakes surrounded by serene meadows and dense forests of many tree species, including western redcedar and hemlock. Huckleberries grow close to the moss-covered forest floor at lower elevations. Higher up, blackberries, heather and grasses

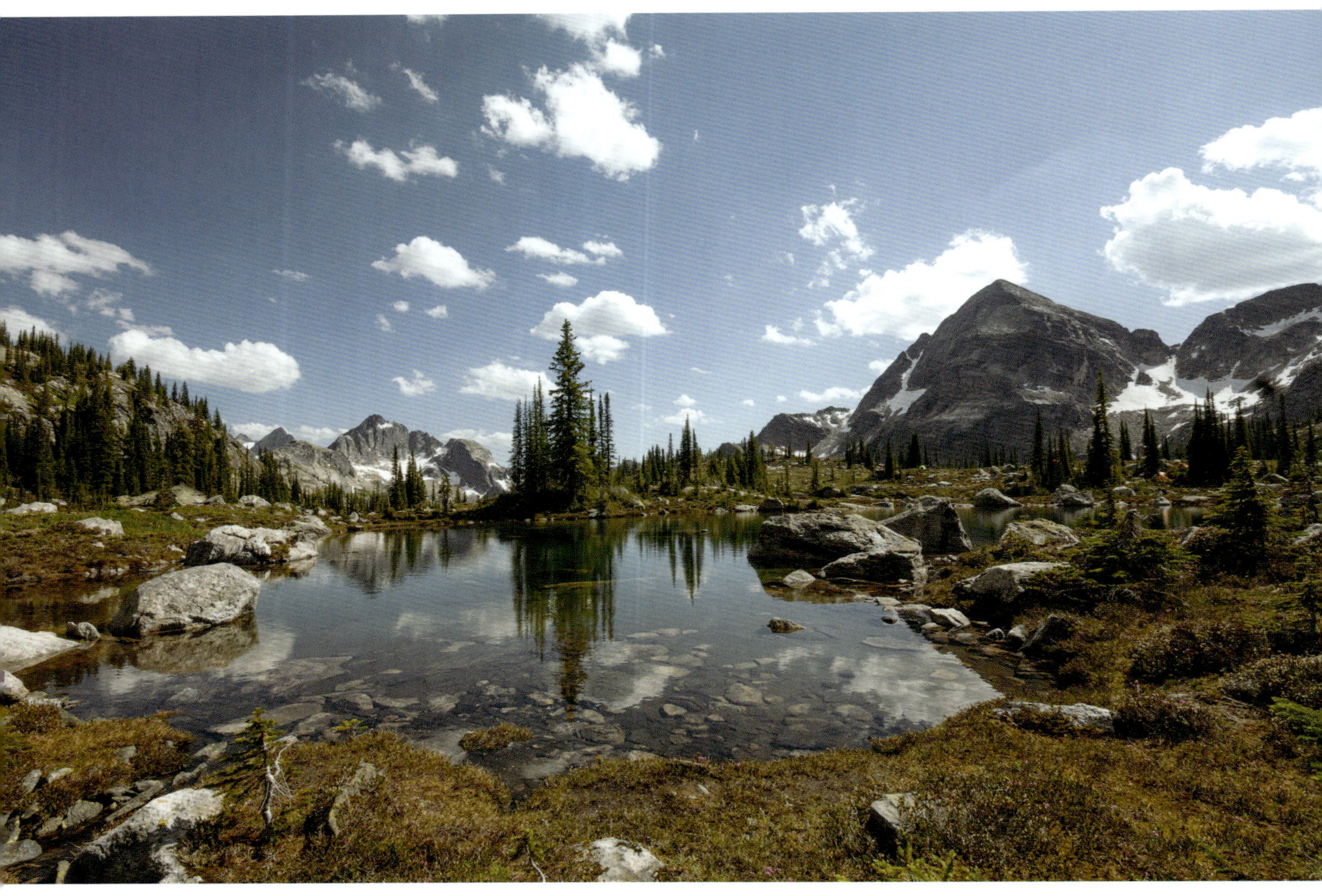

dominate the landscape between forested areas.

Each environment provides a niche for different animals. Grizzly and black bears, lynx, bobcats, otters and a wide variety of other mammals inhabit various regions of the park. For birders, golden eagles and white-tailed ptarmigans frequent the alpine areas, while grouse, songbirds and waterfowl are abundant throughout the park.

The Gwillim Lakes area is a recommended destination for backcountry hikers and campers. Found at the end of a beautiful trail through amazing alpine forests and along lakes, the Gwillim Lakes are absolutely stunning.

The park is well known by hikers, but canoeing along the lakeshore of Slocan Lake is another a pleasant way to experience the park. There are even marine campsites along the shoreline for those looking to do overnight kayak or canoe trips. Look for pictographs from the Sinixt Nation as you paddle the shoreline.

↑ **The Gwillim Lakes area is a gorgeous destination with a scenic trail.**

↖ **Lucky visitors may spot a lynx from the trails.**

Index

Photo Credits

Alan Burger: 204, 205 (bottom).

Alan Dyer/VWPics/Alamy Stock Photo: 213 (top).

Big White Ski Resort: 191 (bottom left).

Charles Seaborn: 68.

Chloe Johnson: 243 (top).

Christina Smyth: 10, 11 (bottom), 17 (bottom), 52, 53 (bottom), 61, 69, 70, 71 (top), 120, 125, 127 (top), 131 (bottom), 143 (bottom), 151 (top), 157 (top), 162 (bottom left), 167, 172, 173 (left), 188 (left), 193 (top), 197, 206, 207 (bottom), 210, 214–215 (bottom), 236 (left), 242, 243 (bottom), 257.

Claudio Contreras Koob/Nature Picture Library: 145 (bottom).

Creston Valley Wildlife Management Area: 244 (bottom), 245.

Dan Strickland: 34.

Darren Handschuh: 221 (top).

David Gluns: 238.

David Greenwood: 173 (right).

Doug Fraser: 8 (left and right), 12, 13 (bottom), 14, 15, 18, 19, 22, 24, 25, 26, 27, 31, 32, 33, 47, 51 (top), 54, 55, 58, 59, 62, 63 (top), 65 (bottom), 67 (bottom), 73, 74, 75 (bottom), 76, 77, 79 (bottom), 83, 85, 86, 90, 91 (top), 93, 94, 95 (bottom), 99 (bottom), 101, 102, 103, 105 (bottom), 106, 108, 109 (bottom), 110, 111, 122, 123 (bottom), 129 (bottom), 133 (middle and bottom), 144, 145 (top), 149 (bottom), 151 (bottom), 153 (bottom), 157 (bottom), 159 (bottom), 165 (top), 170, 171 (bottom), 174, 175 (bottom), 179 (bottom), 180, 183, 185, 219 (bottom), 222 (bottom right), 225 (top), 227, 229, 231, 232, 233, 234, 235 (top), 247, 268.

Eduardo Baena: 142.

Emmett Sparling: 117.

Fyre Mael: 45 (left).

Gemma Taylor, Off Track Travel: 198, 199.

Hell's Gate Airtram Inc.: 137.

Jake Orr: 263 (top).

Jennifer Dickie: 127 (bottom left).

John Avise: 140.

Josh Hoggan: 254, 255.

Kelly Balkom: 127 (bottom right).

Landon Sveinson: 43.

Lauren Bally: 250.

Leigh McAdam: 263 (bottom).

Lena Dietz Chiasson: 65 (top).

Lyndsay Fraser: 20, 28, 29, 30, 36, 37, 46, 57, 67 (top), 75 (top), 78, 79 (top), 80, 84, 87, 88, 89, 97 (bottom), 98, 109 (top), 123 (top), 148, 152, 153 (top), 158, 165 (bottom), 175 (top), 181, 182, 208, 213 (bottom), 222 (bottom left), 230, 235 (bottom), 249 (top).

Manning Park Resort: 195.

Margo Yacheshyn: 221 (bottom).

Meghan McElroy: 11 (top).

Meredith Wires: 53 (top).

Monnik Mediaworks: 42.

Norris Weimer: 192.

Ocean Outfitters Tofino: 45 (top right and bottom right).

Parks Canada: 21.

Parks Canada/Brady Yu: 177.

Parks Canada/Stef Olcen: 162 (top), 176.

R. Tabor, USFWS: 156.

Regional District of Central Okanagan: 201 (top).

Samantha Hanley: 189 (top), 211 (right).

Shannon Harrison: 237 (bottom), 265.

Shelley Besler: 253.

Shutterstock

2009fotofriends: 99 (top); Agami Photo Agency: 92, 249 (bottom); Alberto Loya: 259 (right); Alf Damp: 35; Alisa Khliestkova: 269; Alyssa Gunn: 237 (top), 239; Amanda Guercio: 166; Anatoliy Lukich: 51 (bottom); Anne08: 60, 257 (top); Beat J Korner: 219 (top); Bjoern Alberts: 187; Brandon Stoy: 267; Brian E Kushner: 260; Chris Hill: 189 (bottom); chris kolaczan: 226; Colin D. Young: 107 (bottom); Cory Stevens: 209; Cyrustr: 163, 178; Daniel Bruce Lacy: 39 (bottom); David P. Lewis: 259 (top left); Dennis Jacobsen: 259 (bottom left); EB Adventure Photography: 48, 139, 159 (top); ElenaGwynne: 81; feathercollector: 134; Feng Yu: 150, 218; Ferenc Cegledi: 251 (top); Galyna Andrushko: 49; Ghost Bear: 191 (bottom right); Greg Amptman: 40; Hans Debruyne: 95 (top), 171 (top), 222 (top), 225 (bottom); Harry Beugelink: 113 (top), 135 (top), 143 (top), 147; Hide Matsui: 205 (top); Iryna Kvarts: 107 (top); J Macrae: 138; JamesChen: 16; James Wheeler: 149 (top); JayPierstorff: 193 (bottom); JeniFoto: 38; Jeremy Eade: 41; JmjCarter2: 17 (top); Jukka Jantunen: 246; Justin Atkins: 191 (top); Kane513: 251 (bottom); karamysh: 135 (bottom), 141; Kevin Oke Photo: 64; Klara_Steffkova: 97 (top); klarka0608: 129 (top); Leksele: 154; Lisa Pedscalny: 116; LMIMAGES: 266; Ludmila Ruzickova: 241 (bottom); Lukas Uher: 179 (top); Marina Poushkina: 128; mark_whale: 131 (top); Max Lindenthaler: 217 (top); Michael Schrober: 264; Monika Gregussova: 13 (top); mooseh-enderson: 262 (right); Nature's Charm: 39 (top); NaturesMomentsuk: 169 (top); Neil Podoll: 104, 105 (top); Nikki Gensert: 63 (bottom); P Sahota: 169 (bottom); Patagonian Stock AE: 186; Pierre Leclerc: 119 (top); 121 (bottom); Randimal: 146, 217 (bottom); ribekak: 113 (bottom), 130 (bottom); riekephotos: 261; robcocquyt: 161 (top); Roshan_NG: 155, 203; Russ Heinl: 23 (bottom); Ryan M. Bolton: 202 (bottom); Ryan S Rubino: 161 (bottom); Ryzhkov Sergey: 71 (bottom); Sara Hysong-Shimazu: 91 (bottom); Shawna and Damien Richard: 4; Shpatak: 72; SimonaKoz: 160; SM Jones: 207 (top); Stephen Viszlai: 188 (right), 202 (top); Steve Byland: 236 (right), 244 (top); Steve Smith: 115; Svetlana Foote: 113 (middle), 119 (bottom); Takahashi Photography: 220; Thitsanu Angkapunyadech: 155 (bottom); Tim Zurowski: 133 (top), 212; Tomas Nevesely: 241 (top); Tom Reichner: 215 (middle); vagabond54: 215 (top), 262 (left); William Drumm: 8 (middle), 23 (top); yhelfman: 124.

Tim Barker: 194.

Todd Battey: 201 (bottom).

Trevor Churchill: 216.

Veronica Norbury: 121 (top).